Christopher Turner

Box 837

INTERNATIONAL MARKETING

The Irwin Series in Marketing

Consulting Editor:
Gilbert A. Churchill   *University of Wisconsin, Madison*

Fifth Edition

INTERNATIONAL MARKETING

Philip R. Cateora

Professor of Marketing and
International Business
University of Colorado

1983

RICHARD D. IRWIN, INC.
Homewood, Illinois 60430

To Nancy
and
Deborah, Phyllis, and Hank

ISBN 0-256-02844-3

Library of Congress Catalog Card No. 82–82526

Printed in the United States of America

1 2 3 4 5 6 7 8 9 0 K 0 9 8 7 6 5 4 3

PREFACE

Never in modern history have United States businesses been so deeply involved in international trade. An increasingly larger number of businesses are exporting, importing, and/or manufacturing abroad. Others, though not directly engaged in foreign business, do not escape the effects of their customers and competitors doing business overseas. The world is moving closer to being a one-world economic market system and whether or not a company wants to participate, it is becoming less and less feasible to escape its influence. For the business student today not to have an understanding of international business is to have an incomplete business education.

This Fifth Edition of *International Marketing* focuses on marketing management problems, techniques, and strategies necessary to incorporate the marketing concept into the framework of the world marketplace. The necessity of understanding the impact of a country's culture and environment on a marketing program is emphasized as well as the problems of competing in markets of different cultures. Also, this edition reflects an increasing awareness of many U.S. firms, especially the smaller firm, to international marketing. Thus, the problems and techniques of export marketing are highlighted. Underlying the strategic approach of this edition is an awareness of and concern with the continually expanding social consciousness of business. Worldwide consumerism, business ethics, economic and social development of countries, and the fundamental questions which arise when a multinational corporation intrudes on the fabric of a country's culture are examined.

It is assumed the reader understands fundamental marketing concepts, so no attempt is made to cover all areas of basic marketing or to explain commonly used marketing terms. Rather than present principles of marketing using international examples, the book explores those aspects of marketing unique to international business. The differences in marketing from country to country are less conceptual than environmental; thus, consistent focus is on the environment and on the modifications of marketing thought and practices occasioned by environmental differences.

The environmental approach to international marketing permits a truly worldwide orientation. The reader's horizons are not limited to any specific nation or to the particular ways of doing business in a single nation. Instead, the book provides readers with an approach and framework to identify and analyze the important environmental uniqueness of each nation or region. In the author's opinion, the key to successful international marketing is adaptation—adapting to an ever-changing, mostly uncontrollable, and to the inexperienced, frequently incomprehensible environment. A primary objective of the text is to raise the student's consciousness of the importance of culture in marketing so when confronted with the task of marketing in a foreign milieu, the impact of crucial cultural issues will not be overlooked.

The text portion of the book provides a thorough coverage of the subject with specific emphasis on the planning and strategic problems confronting companies that market into and from all foreign countries. Throughout the text cultural differences are stressed, and "How are cultures different?" is frequently asked. The "boxes" are designed to provide the reader with interesting and sometimes humorous examples of these differences while illustrating points made in the text. The case mix includes short cases reflecting a single, specific problem, and longer, more integrated cases applicable to the general subject of the section. The cases can be analyzed using the information provided in the case, or they lend themselves to more in-depth analysis with the student engaging in additional research and data collection.

Many individuals have contributed to the completion of this book. I especially want to acknowledge the support and creative assistance of Nancy Cateora without whose help this edition would never have been completed on schedule. In addition, I wish to acknowledge the helpful assistance of Myra Ramos, Cathy Morris, and Tammy Priday who provided the author with valuable research assistance and manuscript preparation, and the many students who read and criticized this and earlier editions. To the publishers and authors who permitted the reproduction of articles, cases, and other materials, I am also indebted.

Philip R. Cateora

CONTENTS

ix

PART THREE

WORLD MARKET PATTERNS

Breadth and scope of international marketing research. The research process. Defining the problem and establishing research objectives. Problems of the availability and use of secondary data. Sources of secondary data: *U.S. government. International organizations. Governments of foreign countries. Chambers of commerce. Trade, business, and service organizations.* Problems of gathering primary data: *Unwillingness to respond. Sampling in field surveys. Language and comprehension.* Problems in analyzing and interpreting research information. Estimating market demand. Responsibility for conducting marketing research. Multinational marketing information systems.

Strategic implications for marketing. Opportunities: *Competition. Market complexity. Market barriers. Regulation. Profit.* History of multinational economic organizations: *European Community: A long time coming. European cooperation after World War* II. *The European Community today.* La raison d'etre: *Economic factors. Political factors. Geographic proximity. Social factors.* Patterns of multinational cooperation: *Regional cooperation groups. Free-trade area. Full customs union. Common Market. Political union.* Multinational markets today: *Europe. Africa. The Americas. Middle East. Asia.*

Marketing and economic development: *Stages of economic development. Infrastructure and development. Objectives of developing countries. Marketing's contribution neglected.* Marketing in a developing country: *Level of marketing development. Influence of import orientation. Demand in a less developed country. Less developed countries and long-range potential.* Socialist countries—a special case: *Estimating demand. Communications process. Negotiating a trade. Changing market behavior and potential.* Trends in world consumer markets.

CASES—PART THREE

PART FOUR

INTERNATIONAL MARKETING MANAGEMENT I

Strategic planning: *Company objectives and resources. International commitment and philosophical orientation. The planning process. Product portfolio analysis.* Organizational strategy: *Basis for organization. Structural basis.*

Locus of decision. Maintaining flexibility. Headquarters organizational alternatives: *Centralization, regionalization, and decentralization. Patterns of responsibility.* Owned international affiliates: *Branches and subsidiaries. Joint ventures. Consortia.* External arrangements: *International licensing. Franchising. Management contract. Open distribution.*

Reading: Multinational strategic market portfolios (Ford Tractor has developed an analytical approach to planning designed for use in environments outside the United States), 397

PART FIVE

INTERNATIONAL MARKETING MANAGEMENT II

17. Pricing in international markets **553**

Pricing policy: *Pricing objectives. Approaches to international pricing.* Cost factors: *Taxes and tariffs. Inflation. Exchange-rate fluctuations. Middleman and transportation costs.* Price escalation: *Sample effects of price escalation. Strategic approaches to price escalation.* Market pricing: *Demand. Competition. Dumping.* Administered pricing: *Countertrades. Price setting by business groups. Government-influenced pricing. International agreements.* Intracompany pricing strategy. Price quotations.

18. The international distribution system **579**

Structural analysis. Domestic middlemen: *Domestic agent middlemen. Domestic merchant middlemen.* Middlemen in foreign markets: *Agents in customer countries. Foreign merchant middlemen.* Company distribution abroad. Government affiliated middlemen. Facilitating agencies.

Reading: Demystifying Japanese distribution, 603

19. Developing and managing distribution channels **614**

Channel strategies and policies. Adapting to distribution patterns: *General patterns. Wholesale patterns. Retail patterns.* Factors affecting choice of channels: *Cost. Capital requirement. Control. Coverage. Character. Continuity.* Locating, selecting, and motivating channel members: *Locating middlemen. Selecting middlemen. Motivating middlemen. Terminating middlemen.* Channel control.

20. Export trade mechanics and logistics **644**

Regulations and restrictions of exporting: *U.S. export restrictions. Import restrictions.* Foreign-trade zones. Export documents. Packing and marking. The foreign freight forwarder. Foreign commercial payments: *Letters of credit. Bills of exchange. Cash in advance. Open accounts.* Export shipping. Logistics: *Interdependence of physical distribution activities. Effect of environment on physical distribution costs. Benefits of physical distribution systems.*

PART SIX

CORPORATE CONTEXT OF MARKETING

21. Financial requirements for international marketing 691

Capital needs for international marketing: *Working capital requirements. Capital investment.* Sources of funds for international marketing operations: *Private sources. Government sources. Eurodollar market.* Financial risks: *Commercial risk. Political risk. Foreign exchange risk.* Financial risk management. Payout planning and strategy.

22. Coordinating and controlling world market operations.......... 714

Control as a management tool. Developing an international control system: *Unique factors in international control. Control sequence. Analytical problems of control.* Areas of control: *Volume control. Price control. Product control. Promotional control. Channel control. Marketing personnel control. Profit control.* Home-office responsibility.

PART ONE

AN OVERVIEW

CHAPTERS:

1. Scope and challenge of international marketing
2. Marketing and world business: Past and present
3. International trade concepts and theory

CASES:

I-1. When is a company multinational?

I-2. Computers U.S.A., Inc.

I-3. Fasteners, Inc.—Equal opportunity for women in the international business division

Chapter 1

Scope and challenge of international marketing

A small fishing-tackle company in Boulder, Colorado, annually sells about $6,000 worth of hand-tied fishing flies to the Japanese; the H. J. Heinz Company sells 1,400 different products to consumers in the United States and 150 foreign markets for a total sales volume in excess of $2 billion. Neither company is the smallest nor the largest U.S. firm engaged in international business, but they epitomize the trend in the internationalization of U.S. business and company attitudes about foreign marketing. The attitude was best expressed by the Colgate-Palmolive Company official who said, "The thinking no longer is U.S. market versus international market; now we consider the United States just one of all our markets."

For many businesses today, foreign involvement demands increasingly more effort and resources than domestic interests. Export trade, which once played only a minor part in the country's economic picture, now occupies a huge, rapidly expanding role. Exports from the United States totaled approximately $245 billion in 1981. In terms of jobs, this means over 4.6 million persons now have export-related jobs; i.e., about 1 million more than in 1973 and twice the total of the early 1960s. One manufacturing job in six involved an export product in 1982, whereas in the mid-1960s, the comparable ratio was 1 in 14.

A recent study reported that 3,540 U.S. companies had over $200 billion invested in 24,666 foreign affiliates, up considerably from the mid-1950s when 2,842 U.S. companies had about $25 billion invested abroad. In 1981, U.S. foreign investments generated an estimated $40 billion of profit for an approximate 20 percent return on investment.[1]

World business, multinational company, transnational and *world enterprise* are all terms being used with greater frequency as a significantly larger number of businesses become international both in philosophy and in scope of operations. For a continually growing number of firms, the entire world is considered a marketplace for their products. Rather than ask: "Where in our country should a new plant be built or a new market be developed?" more firms are asking: "Where in the *world* should a new

---

[1] "Companies Profit From Investments They Made Years Ago in Plants Overseas," *The Wall Street Journal,* March 11, 1981, p. 48.

product be made or sold?" No longer is foreign business an afterthought as was often the case among U.S. companies prior to World War II. Businesses are taking a more interested look at the potential profits that result from active participation in markets outside the political boundaries of the United States. A few U.S. companies are going so far as to think of themselves as international concerns with large U.S. operations instead of American companies with foreign plants. General Motors, for example, talks about manufacturing "world cars" that can be assembled from parts made wherever production would be most efficient; in fact, the J car is just such a car. It is theoretically possible for GM to build a J car with a West German front end, an Australian rear, an American suspension, a Japanese transmission, and a Brazilian engine. In reality, the company's manufacturing units in each country produce most of the parts needed for domestic assemblage; but certain key components, including engines and transmissions, are produced in specialized locations and used around the world.[2] (See Box 1–5.) With the increased activity in international business has come a corresponding emphasis on international marketing.

INTERNATIONAL MARKETING DEFINED

International marketing is the performance of business activities that direct the flow of a company's goods and services to consumers or users in more than one nation. The striking similarity of this definition of foreign marketing and that of domestic marketing is intended. The difference between domestic marketing and international marketing is that the activities that take place are in more than one country. While this may appear a minor difference, it accounts for the complexity and diversity found in international marketing operations. The definition above is operational because marketing principles are universally applicable, and the marketer's task is the same whether applied in Dimebox, Texas, or Dar es Salaam, Tanzania. If this is the case, why the study of international marketing? The answer lies not with the mechanics of marketing but with the environment within which the marketing plan must be implemented. The uniqueness of foreign marketing is found in the diversity of unfamiliar problems and the variety of strategies necessary to cope with the different levels of uncertainty encountered in foreign markets. Further, by studying the familiar, *marketing,* in a new setting, *a different environment and culture,* we can better understand the familiar much in the same way that studying a foreign language helps us to understand the structure of our own language. Finally, not to be conversant with the international dimension of business is to be partially prepared for the responsibilities of today's business world.

---

[2] "GM Unveils Its 'J Car' in Europe," *World Business Weekly,* September 14, 1981, pp. 22–23.

INCREASED INTEREST IN FOREIGN MARKETS

Current interest in international marketing can be explained in terms of changing competitive structures coupled with shifts in demand characteristics in markets throughout the world. Many U.S. firms are meeting competition on all fronts (i.e., not only from other domestic firms but from foreign firms as well). As one source reports: the pianos at the Hilton and the Americana are not Steinways but Yamahas. So are the NBC organs that play background music for the "Tonight Show." Japanese products have assumed the proportions of a *tsunami*—tidal wave—that has swept the United States. Eighty-five percent of the binoculars, 70 percent of the calculators, 50 percent of the radios and motorcycles, and 30 percent of the television sets sold in this country are Japanese. The increased competition, however, comes from both East and West. Norelco (Holland), Libby (Swiss), Volkswagen (Germany), Honda (Japan), Necchi (Italy) are familiar brands in the United States, and for U.S. industry, they are formidable opponents in a competitive struggle for U.S. and world markets. Many familiar U.S. companies are now foreign controlled: Baskin Robbins and Good Humor Ice Cream (English), Motorola's Quasar (Japanese), Paul Masson Wines (Canadian), as well as Travelodge, Gimbles, Grand Union Department Stores, Keebler Cookies, and many others are all owned or controlled by foreign multinational businesses.

The vast domestic market that was once the private domain of U.S. businesses and provided them with an opportunity for continued growth has finally reached a point where the opportunity for limitless expansion is leveling off. For many businesses new market opportunities must be sought if profit margins are to be maintained. Companies with just domestic markets have found it increasingly difficult to sustain customary rates of growth, and many are seeking foreign markets to absorb accumulating surplus productive capacity. Companies with foreign operations have found earnings soaring from previously neglected overseas operations; the return on foreign investments is frequently higher than on investments in the United States. Reviewing the figures in Exhibit 1–1, it becomes obvious that for some companies the profit generated on investment abroad as well as the profit from foreign sales is better than in the United States. Understandably, the opportunity for high profit margins is a very important impetus for "going international."[3]

What occurred almost simultaneously with the economic changes in the United States was an appreciable increase in the economic well-being of other countries creating a ready-made market for U.S.-made products. The European Community [4] is a market comparable in size and potential to that

---

[3] Walter Kiechel III, "Playing The Global Game," *Fortune,* November 16, 1981, pp. 111–26.

[4] Formerly known as European Common Market or European Economic Community (EEC) but as of 1976 officially known as the European Community.

EXHIBIT 1–1: Some big players in the global game

Company	1980 Foreign earnings as percent of total	1980 Foreign assets as percent of total
Black and Decker	70.5	51.9
Boise Cascade	31.6	12.3
Carnation	25.4	23.6
Coca-Cola	65.5	41.4
F. W. Woolworth	56.0	38.3
Gillette	50.6	67.0
H. J. Heinz	37.5	41.9
IBM	52.4	45.9
Johnson & Johnson	53.9	35.8
NCR	59.9	45.2
Pfizer	62.8	57.2
Polaroid	62.9	30.5
Tonka	35.0	18.6
Xerox	44.9	42.8

Source: "Foreign Profit Performance," *Business International*, August 14, 1981, p. 263; August 21, 1981, p. 268; September 4, 1981, p. 287; and September 11, 1981, p. 293.

of the United States. Japan and other Far-Eastern countries, the Mid East, Latin America, and Africa have all become important markets for multinational companies. For those willing to leave the confines of their home territory, a wide variety of opportunities is available. Many U.S. companies that never ventured abroad until recently are now seeking new foreign markets. Companies which have foreign operations realize that they must cease running them with their left hand if they are to continue to grow. They have found it necessary to spend more money and time improving their marketing positions abroad since the competition for these growing markets from companies around the world is becoming more intense. For the firm venturing into international marketing for the first time, and for those already experienced, the requirement is generally the same—a thorough and complete commitment to foreign markets.

THE INTERNATIONAL MARKETING TASK

The task of marketing managers is to mold the controllable elements of their decisions in light of the uncontrollable elements of the environment in such a manner that marketing objectives are achieved. In general, the elements comprising the marketing environment with which the marketer must contend can be examined in terms of the degree to which their effect on marketing activities can be controlled by the decision-maker. Some of the environmental considerations can be viewed as internal to the firm in that greater control can be exerted over their influence on marketing operations. Generally included are such controllable elements as product, price, promotion, and channels of distribution. Other points can be considered as external to the firm and represent influences beyond the decision-maker's control. Included among the external or uncontrollable elements of the marketing environment are such conditions as the structure of competition, political forces, and cultural forces.

The task is made more difficult in international marketing because the marketer must deal with at least two levels of uncontrollable uncertainty instead of one. Uncertainty is created by the uncontrollable elements of the business environment at home that are applicable to foreign operations plus the uncontrollable elements of business environments found in the foreign country or countries in which a company operates. An illustration of the total marketing environment is presented in Exhibit 1–2.

The inner circle depicts the controllable elements that constitute a marketer's decision area, the second circle encompasses those environmental elements found at home which might have some effect on foreign operation decisions, and the outer circles represent the elements of the foreign environment for each foreign market within which the marketer operates. As the outer circles illustrate, each foreign market in which the company does business can (and usually does) present separate problems involving some or all of the uncontrollable elements. Thus, the more foreign markets in

EXHIBIT 1–2: The international marketing task

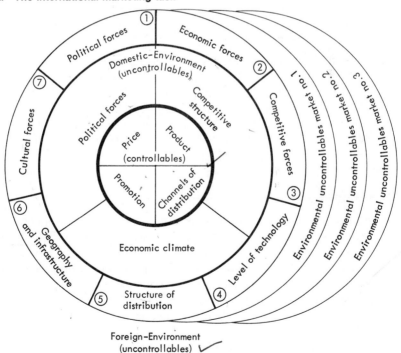

Foreign–Environment
(uncontrollables)

which a company operates, the greater the variety of foreign environmental uncontrollables there are to contend with. Frequently, a solution to a problem in country A is not applicable to a problem in country B.

Marketing controllables

The successful manager constructs a marketing program designed for optimal adjustment to the uncertainty of the business climate. The inner circle in Exhibit 1–2 represents the area under control of the marketing manager. Assuming the necessary overall corporate resources, the marketing manager blends price, product, promotion, and channels-of-distribution activities to capitalize on anticipated demand. These controllable elements can be altered in the long run and, usually, in the short run, to adjust to changing market conditions or corporate objectives.

Represented by the outer circles surrounding market controllables are the levels of uncertainty created by the domestic environment and the foreign environments. Although the marketer can blend a marketing mix from the controllable elements, the uncontrollables are just that and must be actively adapted to since their influence determines the ultimate outcome of the marketing effort.

Domestic uncontrollables

The domestic environment illustrated in Exhibit 1–2 by the second circle includes those elements which can have a direct effect on the success of a foreign venture, including political forces, competition, and economic climate in the home country. A political decision involving domestic foreign policy can have a direct effect on a firm's international marketing success. Such was the case when International Harvester's export license for the sale of a $300 million combine plant to Russia was revoked by the U.S. government. Restrictions on some types of trade with Russia were being used as a way for the United States to show its displeasure with Russia's political involvement in Poland.[5]

Competition from business firms located in the same base country provides another dimension of uncertainty in achieving the marketing objectives of the firm. The decision of General Electric to negotiate a cooperative agreement with France's Machines Bull and Italy's Olivetti computer manufacturers could have domestic and foreign impact on IBM's foreign market share.

The domestic economic climate is another important home-based uncontrollable variable which can have far reaching effects on a company's competitive position in foreign markets. The capacity to invest in plant and facilities either in domestic or foreign markets is, to a large extent, a function of

---

[5] "The Harvester Case," *The Wall Street Journal,* January 21, 1982, p. 22.

domestic economic vitality. It is generally true that capital will tend to flow toward optimum use; however, capital first must be generated before it can have mobility. Furthermore, if internal economic conditions deteriorate, restrictions against foreign investment and purchasing may be imposed to strengthen the domestic economy. Take for example the increased concern of the U.S. government over the American balance of payments and the resulting restrictions imposed or threatened to reduce the flow of U.S. dollars abroad. The foregoing illustrate the possible influence of the home environment on the marketer's task. Inextricably entwined with the effects of the domestic environment are the constraints imposed by the environment of each foreign country.

Foreign uncontrollables

Besides uncontrollable domestic elements, an even more significant source of uncertainty is the uncontrollable foreign business environments depicted in Exhibit 1–2 by the outer circles. A business operating in their home country undoubtedly feels comfortable in forecasting the business climate and adjusting business decisions to these elements. However, the process of evaluating the uncontrollable elements in an international marketing program often involves substantial doses of cultural, political, and economic shock.

BOX 1–1: How common is the Common Market?

Trying to develop one advertising campaign for several countries can be a real problem for the multinational firm. Consider, for example, that a Kellogg's Corn Flakes commercial aired in Britain would be banned in Holland because it boasts of "extra vitamins." It would be outlawed in Germany because "best to you" sounds like a "competitive claim." It would be off the air in France because children can't endorse products there. And it would be nixed in Austria because children in that country can't even appear in commercials; they have to be played by midgets.

Source: Adapted from Barry Newman, "Satellite Invasion: European States Face Problem of Controlling Their Neighbors' TV." *The Wall Street Journal*, March 22, 1982, p. 1.

A business operating in a number of foreign countries might find polar extremes in political stability, class structure, and economic climate as critical elements in business decisions. The dynamic upheavals in some developing countries further illustrate the problems of dynamic change in cultural, political, and economic climates over relatively short periods of time.

A listing of the more significant elements in the uncontrollable international environment is shown in the outer circles of Exhibit 1–2. These factors include (1) political forces, (2) economic forces, (3) competitive forces, (4) level of technology, (5) structure of distribution, (6) geography and infrastructure, and (7) cultural forces. They constitute the principal elements of uncertainty the international marketer must cope with in designing a marketing program. Each will be discussed in some detail in subsequent chapters.

The problem of foreign uncertainty is further complicated by a frequently imposed "alien status" that increases the difficulty of properly assessing and forecasting the dynamic international business climate. The alien status of a business results in greater emphasis being placed on many of the uncontrollable elements than would be found with relation to these same elements in the domestic market.

The political environment offers the best example of the alien status. Domestic marketers must consider the political ramifications of their decisions although the consequences of this environmental element are generally minor. Even a noticeable change in government attitudes toward domestic business when political parties change as a result of national elections is seldom very serious. This certainly is not the case in a foreign country. The political environment can be extremely critical, and shifts in governments often mean sudden changes in attitudes that can result in expropriation, expulsion, or major restrictions on operations. This area is covered in Chapter 6 which discusses the political considerations in assessing world markets. The fact is that the foreign company is *foreign* and thus always subject to the political whims of the government to a greater degree than a domestic firm.

Also a problem for some marketers attuned to *one* environment is the frequent inability to easily recognize the potential impact of certain uncontrollable elements within another environment to which they have not been culturally assimilated. Consequently, road signs of danger and indicators of potential in a foreign market may not always be read or interpreted correctly. The uncertainty of different foreign business environments creates the need for a close study of the operating environment within each new country. Different solutions to fundamentally identical marketing tasks are often in order and are generally the result of changes in the environment of the market. Thus, a strategy successful in one country can be rendered worthless in another by differences in political climate, stages of economic development, or other cultural variation.

BOX 1–2:   How you say it depends on the language

While waiting in a Swiss village to go by cable car to the top of a mountain, a visitor noticed a sign printed in three languages. In English it said: "Please do not pick the flowers." In German it said: "It is forbidden to pick the flowers." In French it said: "Those who love the mountains leave them their flowers."

Source: L. A. Richardson, "Notes From All Over," *Reader's Digest*, June 1980, p. 201.

ENVIRONMENTAL ADJUSTMENT

In order to adjust and adapt a marketing program to foreign markets, marketers must be able to effectively interpret the influence and impact of each of the uncontrollable environmental elements on the marketing plan for each foreign market in which they hope to do business. In a broad sense, the uncontrollable elements constitute the culture; the difficulty facing the marketer in adjusting to the culture (i.e., uncontrollable elements of the market place) lies in recognizing their impact. In a domestic market, the reaction to much of the uncontrollables' (cultural) impact on the marketer's activities is for the most part automatic. We are frequently unaware of the various cultural influences that fill our lives. We react in a manner acceptable to our society without thinking about it because we are culturally responsive to our environment. The experiences we have gained throughout life have become second nature and serve as the basis for our behavior. The task of cultural adjustment is perhaps the most challenging and important one confronting international marketers; they must adjust their marketing efforts to cultures to which they are not totally attuned. In dealing with unfamiliar markets, marketers must be aware of the frames of reference they are using in making their decisions or evaluating the potential of a market, since "judgments are derived from experience which is the result of the enculturative process." Once frames of reference are established in human beings, they become important factors that determine or modify our reactions to situations we will face later—social and even nonsocial—especially if the experience for which precedence in accustomed behavior is lacking.

BOX 1–3: Gift giving in China

Gift-giving is a much more important ritual in other parts of the world than in the United States. Since we do not give gift-giving as much emphasis as elsewhere, we sometimes make mistakes. Here are some things to be aware of when giving gifts in China.

An American businessman sent what he thought was an appropriate wedding present—a clock—to the daughter of a Chinese business associate. Soon after the wedding the gift was returned along with a curt note from the bride's parents. In China, the American learned, a clock is an inappropriate gift; the Chinese word for clock sounds like the word for funeral, and the gift of a clock signifies the relationship is dead.

When you give a gift is important also. Gifts should not be given in front of others for fear either giver or receiver will "lose face." If there is no good reason for a gift, the Chinese will reject it; and if this should happen in front of others, both parties would have lost face. A collective gift for a group at a banquet is acceptable and is part of the banquet ritual.

Source: Adapted from an excerpt titled "Time Runs Out on Yankee Giving Clock to Chinese," by Kathleen Reardon, published in *Business America—Colorado*, January 1982, p. 7.

Consequently, when a marketer operates in other cultures, marketing attempts may fail because of unconscious responses to frames of reference that would be acceptable in one's own culture but that are unacceptable in different surroundings. Unless special efforts are made to determine local cultural meanings for every market, the marketer is likely to overlook the significance of certain behaviors or activities and proceed with plans that result in a negative or unwanted response.

For example, a Westerner must learn that white is a symbol of mourning in parts of the Far East, quite different from Western culture's white bridal gowns. Also, time-conscious Americans are not culturally prepared to understand the meaning of time to the Latin Americans. These are cultural differences which must be purposely learned in order to avoid misunderstandings that can lead to marketing failures. Such failure actually occurred in the first situation when ignorance led to ineffective advertising on the part of an American firm; and the second misunderstanding resulted in lost sales when a "long waiting period" in the outer office of a Latin American customer was misinterpreted by an American sales executive. To avoid such errors, the foreign marketer should be aware of the principle of *marketing relativism, i.e., that marketing strategies and judgments are based on experience, and experience is interpreted by each marketer in terms of his or her own culture.* Thus, we take into the marketplace, whether at home or in a foreign country, frames of reference developed from past experiences which determine or modify our reactions to the situations we face.

BOX 1–4:   Did you say computer "softwear" or "underwear?"

Translations cause problems for the international marketer if they are not precise. Some recent mistakes include the Italian translation from English of an ad for a touch-toe drill for dentists; the translation came out "the dentist takes off his shoe and sock and presses the drill with his toe."

Sometimes the same English word has different meanings throughout the copy when translated. Such was the case when an Indonesian exchange student translated an instruction booklet accompanying a computer destined for Jakarta. The term *softwear* came out in various parts of the instructions as *underwear, tissue,* and *computer junk.*

Another example of poor translation happened to a U.S. business interested in selling heavy-duty wrapping paper to the Japanese. They hired a Japanese language "scholar" to do the translation, and he created a hitherto unknown Japanese character that meant "he who envelops himself in 10 tons of rice paper."

The lesson to learn from these mistakes is that not everyone who speaks a language can make precise, accurate translations.

Source: Adapted from: Sylvia Porter, "Poor Translations Cause More Than Embarrassment," Universal Press Syndicate, September 1981.

Cultural conditioning is like an iceberg—we are not aware of nine tenths of it. In any study of the market systems of different peoples, their political and economic structures, religions, and other elements of culture, foreign marketers must constantly guard against measuring and assessing the markets against the fixed values and assumptions of their own cultures. They must take specific steps to make themselves aware of the home-cultural reference in their analyses and decision making.

One authority suggests that "the unconscious reference to one's own

cultural values [is] the root cause of most international business problems overseas."[6] He refers to the unconscious reference as the natural "self-reference criterion" or SRC, i.e., it is automatic to refer to one's home-country frame of reference. In order to avoid errors in business decisions, the SRC must be isolated and recognized so that its biasing effect is minimized if not eliminated. To avoid the SRC it is necessary to make a cross-cultural analysis isolating the SRC influences. The following steps are suggested as a framework for such an analysis.

Step 1. Define the business problem or goal in terms of the home-country cultural traits, habits, or norms.

Step 2. Define the business problem or goal in terms of the foreign cultural traits, habits, or norms. Make no value judgments.

Step 3. Isolate the SRC influence in the problem and examine it carefully to see how it complicates the problem.

Step 4. Redefine the problem without the SRC influence and solve for the optimum business goal situation.

Obviously, this approach demands a knowledge of the culture of each foreign market as well as knowledge of one's own culture. Surprisingly, understanding one's own culture may also require additional study, since much of the cultural influence on market behavior remains at an unconscious level and is not clearly defined.

BECOMING INTERNATIONAL

Once a company has decided to "go international" it has to decide the way it will enter the foreign market and the degree of marketing involvement and commitment it is prepared to make. These decisions should reflect considerable study and analysis of market potential and company capabilities, a process not always followed. Many companies appear to evolve their international marketing through a series of phased developments with gradual changes in strategy and tactics as they become more involved.

Phases of international marketing involvement

Regardless of the means employed to gain entry into a foreign market, a company may, from a marketing viewpoint, make no market investment, i.e., its marketing involvement may be limited to selling a product with little or no thought given to development of market control. Or a company may become totally involved and invest large sums of money and effort to capture and maintain a permanent, specific share of the market. In general, a busi-

---

[6] James A. Lee, "Cultural Analysis in Overseas Operations," *Harvard Business Review,* March/April 1966, pp. 106, 111. Reprinted with permission.

Part 2 b) Exports as a form of Mkt Entry

ness can be placed in at least one of four distinct but overlapping phases of international marketing involvement.

No foreign marketing. In this phase, there is no active cultivation of customers outside national boundaries; however, sales may be made to foreign customers who come directly to the firm. Another way for a company's products to be sold in foreign markets would be via domestic wholesalers or distributors who sell abroad on their own without any explicit encouragement or knowledge of the producer.

Infrequent foreign marketing. Temporary surpluses caused by variations in production levels or demand may result in infrequent marketing overseas. The surpluses are characterized by their temporary nature; therefore, sales to foreign markets are made as goods are available with little or no intention of maintaining continuous market representation. As domestic demand increases and absorbs surpluses, foreign sales activity is withdrawn. In this phase, there is little or no change in company organization or product line.

Regular foreign marketing. In this phase the firm has permanent productive capacity devoted to the production of goods to be marketed on a continuing basis in foreign markets. At this stage, a firm may utilize foreign or domestic overseas middlemen or it may have its own sales force or sales subsidiaries in important foreign markets. The primary basis for production remains one of production for home markets. The foreign marketing portion is only an extension of the market for products presently being produced with, perhaps, some very minor modifications to meet foreign market needs. Substantial international investments of marketing funds and management skills are generally made in this phase of involvement. Further, products may become specialized to meet the needs of individual markets, pricing and profit policies tend to become equal with domestic business, and the company begins to become dependent on foreign profits.

World marketing operations. Companies in this phase are fully committed and involved in international marketing activities. Such companies treat the world as their market and the products they sell are not surpluses from a saturated home market, they are a result of planned production for world markets. This generally entails not only the marketing but the production of goods throughout the world. It is at this point that a company becomes an international or worldwide marketing firm dependent on foreign revenues.

Among U.S. firms there has been a very noticeable increase in activity in foreign marketing involvement at all levels, with an increasingly large number moving into phases three and four.

Changes in marketing orientation

Experience shows that when a company relies on foreign markets to absorb a permanent production surplus and depends on foreign profits, a significant change occurs in the marketing orientation of the firm. Businesses may move through the four phases of international marketing involvement one at a time, although it is not unusual for a company to skip one or more phases. As a firm moves from one phase of involvement to another, the complexity and sophistication of international marketing activity tends to increase. In the early phases of foreign marketing, a firm usually relies almost completely on an experienced export firm to handle its marketing tasks. As the firm gathers more experience and its involvement becomes increasingly more permanent, it may engage its own personnel in selling to specific foreign customers. In both cases, however, the marketing task is rather simple and uninvolved. Only after the firm reaches a point of dependence on the foreign market does it begin the total marketing task and cease to shift the responsibility of marketing to a third party. Although the firm may still utilize the services of many intermediate institutions in reaching an intended market, it is done within the framework of a total marketing plan designed to achieve specific objectives. Contrast this with the firm which sells to an intermediate middleman as a final customer with little or no concern about the product after the sale. In the latter case, the firm is involved in marketing but at a low level compared with the marketing-oriented firm which conducts marketing programs simultaneously in several national markets. As competition tightens in world marketing, more and more firms are finding it necessary to become marketing oriented in their international efforts regardless of their state of involvement.

Foreign market development

There are five basic alternatives for developing a foreign market. Each has particular advantages and shortcomings depending on company strengths and weaknesses, the degree of commitment the company is willing or able to make, and environmental characteristics of the foreign country.

Exporting. A company may decide to enter the international arena by exporting from the home country. This means of foreign market development is the easiest and most common approach employed by companies taking their first international step since the risks of financial loss can be minimized. Generally, early motives are either to skim the cream off the top of the market or gain a plus business that can absorb overhead. Although such motives are frequently the main reasons for exporting and might appear opportunistic, exporting can be a sound and permanent form of operating in international marketing.

Licensing. A means of establishing a foothold in foreign markets without large capital outlays is licensing. Patent rights, trademark rights, and the rights to use technological processes are granted in foreign licensing. It is a favorite strategy for small and medium-sized companies, although by no means limited to such companies, and not many confine their foreign operations to licensing alone. It is generally viewed as a supplement to exporting or manufacturing rather than as the only means of entry into foreign markets; nevertheless, the advantages of licensing are many. When capital is scarce, when import restrictions forbid other means of entry, when a country is sensitive to foreign ownership, or when it is necessary to protect patents and trademarks against cancellation for nonuse, licensing is a legitimate means of capitalizing on a foreign market. Although this may be the least profitable way of entering a market, the risks and headaches are less than for direct investments.

Joint ventures. For a variety of reasons a company may decide to share management with one or more collaborating foreign firms and enter into a joint venture. Joint ventures as a means of engaging in international business have accelerated sharply during the past 15 years. As in the case of licensing, one of the strongest reasons for entering joint ventures is that they substantially reduce political and economic risks by the amount of the partner's contributions to the venture. Further, many countries, especially less-developed ones, require joint ventures as a means of foreign investment. There are many reasons a joint venture would be attractive to an international marketer: (1) when it may enable a company to utilize the specialized skills of a local partner, (2) when it allows the marketer to gain access to a partner's local distribution system, (3) when a company seeks to enter a market where wholly-owned activities are prohibited, and (4) when the firm lacks the capital or personnel capabilities to expand its international activities otherwise.

There are a few objections to this means of developing a foreign market. The principal fear is loss of absolute control and perhaps loss of freedom of action in the production and marketing operations. Regardless of shortcomings, joint ventures are increasing, and in many countries, frequently are the only means of direct investment still open.

Manufacturing. A fourth and major means of foreign market development is manufacturing within the foreign country. This strategy is employed only when the demand justifies the investment involved. A company may manufacture locally to capitalize on low-cost labor, avoid high import taxes, reduce the high costs of transportation to market, gain access to raw materials, and/or as a means of gaining entry into other markets. For example, the only way to avoid the high tariffs imposed on an outsider by countries of the European Community may be to invest in one of the countries and thereby gain entry into the others. Generally, when a company makes production investments outside its home country, markets are serviced in the country where the manufacturing facilities are located as well as markets in other countries and, perhaps even exports back to the home country. For example, many U.S. manufacturing firms have found that lower labor and manufacturing costs and facilities outside the United States make possible exports to the United States at prices lower than if they manufacture there. In fact, most of the television sets sold in the United States by U.S. companies are not manufactured totally in America. Under these circumstances, domestic marketing considerations become a reason for investing in manufacturing facilities in foreign countries.

BOX 1–5: GM's J Car—where are you from?—all over the world!! The J car's global assembly and manufacturing lines

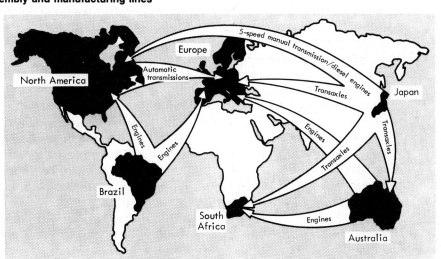

Source: "GM Unveils It's 'J Car' in Europe," *World Business Weekly*, September 14, 1981, p. 22. Reprinted by permission of the Financial Times, London.

Management contracts. A fifth and limited means of international market development may be through management contracts. This approach is generally employed not by choice but as the result of external pressures from the host government. After a government expropriates a foreign investment and finds a lack of national managerial capability and talent, it will sign a management contract with the deposed company. In return for a stated fee, the company continues to manage its former investment. Although not a desirable means of foreign market development, it can be better than nothing at all.

A frequent mistake is to look at these five ways of developing international markets as a sequence of steps to follow as a company becomes more involved instead of as strategic alternatives to foreign market development. Actually, it is possible for a single firm to be involved in all five at the same time in different countries throughout the world or to start at any stage.

ORIENTATION OF *INTERNATIONAL MARKETING*

Most problems encountered by the foreign marketer result from the strangeness of the environment within which marketing programs must be implemented. Success hinges, in part, on the ability to assess and adjust properly to the impact of a strange environment. The successful international marketer possesses the best qualities of the sociologist, psychologist, diplomat, lawyer, prophet, and business person.

In light of all the variables involved, with what should a text in foreign marketing be concerned? It is the opinion of the author that a study of foreign-marketing environments and their influences on the total marketing process is of primary concern and is the most effective approach to a meaningful presentation.

Consequently, the orientation of this text can best be described as an environmental approach to international marketing. By no means is it intended to present principles of marketing; rather it is intended to demonstrate some of the unique problems of international marketing. It attempts to relate the foreign environment to the marketing process and, thus, illustrate the many ways in which the environment can influence the marketing task. Although marketing principles are universally applicable, the environment within which the marketer must implement marketing plans changes drastically from country to country. It is with these difficulties created by different environments that this text is primarily concerned.

Furthermore, the text is concerned with any company marketing in or into any other country however slight the involvement or the method of involvement. Hence, such terms as *export trade, foreign trade,* and *international marketing* are used interchangeably; in strictly technical terms there may be definable differences, but for the purposes of this text no distinction is recognized since these activities describe in some measure marketing from one country to another.

The first section of *International Marketing* offers an overview of foreign marketing, including a brief discussion of the economic and historical implications. The next section deals exclusively with the uncontrollable elements of the environment and their assessment, followed by chapters dealing with world market patterns. Then, problems of international marketing management are discussed, with a final section on the corporate context of marketing in international business. In each chapter, an attempt is made to illustrate the impact of the environment on the marketing process. Space prohibits an encyclopedic approach to all the issues; nevertheless, the author has tried to present sufficient detail so readers will appreciate the real need to make a thorough analysis whenever the challenge arises. The text provides a framework for this task.

QUESTIONS

1. Define:

SRC	Marketing relativism
International marketing	Alien status
Foreign uncontrollables	Licensing
Domestic uncontrollables	Joint ventures
Controllable elements	Management contracts

2. "The marketer's task is the same whether applied in Dimebox, Texas, or Dar es Salaam, Tanzania." Discuss.

3. How can the increased interest in international marketing on the part of U.S. firms be explained?

4. Discuss the four phases of international marketing involvement.

5. Discuss the task of the marketer in the international marketplace.

6. Discuss the five alternatives for developing a foreign market.

7. Would there ever be a case when a firm might employ more than one of the five alternatives for developing a foreign market? Explain.

Chapter 2

Marketing and world business:
Past and present

Trading among nations has existed for thousands of years. History has identified the scope and importance of trade to the Egyptians, Assyrians, and Phoenicians. Archeological discovery of important artifacts suggests that trade was widely practiced prior to recorded history; and an international economy has existed since the time of Marco Polo and Christopher Columbus.

The multinational company, as we know it today, is not really new but dates back to the mid-1800s when Colt Industries, Inc., and Singer Company began operating much as multinationals do today. Ingersoll-Rand, International Harvester, General Electric, and H. J. Heinz are other examples of firms that have functioned as multinationals since the early 1900s. Even before the 1900s such organizations as the Hudson Bay Company, chartered in 1670, and the East India Company were operating on a worldwide basis, functioning much like a present-day Japanese trading company. They are frequently recognized as forerunners of the modern multinational firm.

Why do people trade? The answers are almost limitless. Certainly potential economic gain offers a strong motive; perhaps the desire for adventure or the desire to explore the unknown are equally strong motives. Surplus production, political motives, and humanitarian motives also provide incentives for trading activity.

The effects of trade are usually viewed in an economic context. Measurement of balance of payments, gross exports by product class, and debtor and creditor nation status are common. However, while the economies of world trade are important, the cultural and technolgical consequences of trade must be appreciated. At the same time the Phoenicians were trading their textiles in Mediterranean ports, they were also trading ideas, cultural patterns, and technological progress.

Historically, the role of the merchant trader has been held in low regard. The Islamic Arabs looked on foreign traders as intruders with contaminating religious and cultural ideas; the Catholic Church of the Middle Ages was skeptical of the pursuit of economic gains; and, even today the world trader continues to be feared whether U.S., Japanese, German, or any other economic power. This fear is being manifest in a significant move toward protectionism by a majority of countries, both developed and developing.[1] Regardless of the attitudes of society at any given time, international business has played and will continue to play a vital role in shaping the economic and social progress of the nations of the world. The purpose of this chapter is to review briefly the historical development of world trade and present an overview of the current position of international business in the world economy.

HISTORICAL OVERVIEW

As archeological discoveries advance our knowledge of the past, it becomes apparent there existed well-established trade patterns three or four thousand years before the birth of Christ. As the volume of trade grew in the pre-Roman era, great trading cities developed; the towns of Asia Minor—Miletus, Rhodes, Carthage, and Corinth—were developed primarily as trading centers. These trading cities made a wide range of contributions to the progress of civilizations. Businesses interested in the development of commerce took an active role in the development and administration of city affairs. The culture and administration of the trading towns produced some of today's important codes of commercial law and business practices. For example, the *disciplina etrusca* of the Etruscans (a people of ancient Italy) formed the basis of Roman law.

With the gradual decay of the Roman Empire, Europe degenerated into feudalism which discouraged trade in everything but the necessities of life that could not be locally produced.

During the 15th and 16th centuries two important movements influenced commercial reawakening in Europe: the Renaissance, or rebirth of learning, which dictated inquiry into one's environment, and the Reformation, which replaced the dominance of the Catholic Church with the political and economic power of local government. The breakdown of feudal power centers allowed for the emergence of stronger national power and corresponding increases in political and economic influence. Other important events during the period included the widespread use of the compass, which allowed more freedom in exploration, and the discovery of America in 1492.

Four important formative influences arose from the Age of Discovery. First, the participation of ruling powers in all foreign development evolved and was recognized as accepted procedure. Second (an out-growth of the terms of royal charters granted), political and economic power exercised in the colonies was coextensive. Third, powerful national states evolved, and, finally, facilitating agencies for world trade were developed.

From these converging forces of nationalism arose the economic and political philosophy of mercantilism.

---

[1] Art Pine, "Trade Representative Brock Battles Threat of Protectionism in U.S., Other Countries," *The Wall Street Journal*, March 23, 1982, p. 48.

MERCANTILISM

The philosophy of mercantilism was a key determinant of the nature and extent of political and economic legislation implemented until the late 18th century.[2] Although it defies accurate and detailed description, the basic doctrine of mercantilism was based on the idea that the only way for a nation to grow was to amass wealth at the expense of other countries or to exploit colonial interests. The philosophy implied a static approach to the resources of the world. It was assumed there was a limited amount of wealth in the world and that the country which amassed the greatest share would become most powerful. From this philosophy a number of logical developments followed: the expansion of national power as rapidly and forcefully as necessary to gain control over the sources of wealth, the development of powerful naval forces to protect a nation's distant wealth from encroachment, and the accumulation of a store of gold and silver. The

---

BOX 2–1: Early multinationals

The history of foreign influence in Venezuela dates back to the 16th century.

In 1528, Charles V repaid his debts to the Welsers, a German banking family, by granting them the Province of Venezuela through a "capitulación" (a contract awarded by the King to the head of an expedition, granting rights to discover, settle, and govern the new territory, while the Crown retained sovereignty over the land as well as property rights on certain minerals). The Germans formed expeditions to the interior of Venezuela and by 1535, reached as far as the Apure River in the south, and beyond Maracaibo in the west, to lands which are presently part of Colombia. However, in 1556 the King revoked the "capitulación."

In the 1600s, Venezuela was an agricultural community of little interest to Spain. However, the Spaniards enforced a commercial monopoly, including rules prohibiting trade with foreigners. The resultant stifling of economic growth spawned contraband trading with the Dutch, French, and British. Hides, cacao, and tobacco were exchanged for desirable consumer goods. Simultaneously, Venezuela paid tribute and taxes to the Spanish Crown. In the mid-1600s the economy expanded by means of a growing cacao trade with Mexico.

In 1728, the Basque Guipuzcoana Company—the earliest semblance of a multinational trading corporation in the Americas—was established. Years later it was granted a monopoly on all trade in the Province of Venezuela. The company eliminated smuggling as well as trade with foreign countries and provided Venezuela with all necessary merchandise. At the same time, it monopolized production and distribution of cacao.

It began exploiting the few agricultural products which brought high prices on foreign markets, thereby producing high profits. However, staples such as meat, corn, and sugar were neglected, and they had to be imported.

The company's actions created resentment among Venezuelan farmers who, in 1750, journeyed to Caracas to force the Governor to strip the Guipuzcoana Company of its powers. The Royal Grants were later revoked and the company dissolved in 1786.

Source: Nancy Smolens, "Way Back Then," "Business Venezuela," May/June 1977, p. 21.

---

[2] For a complete treatment of the theory and practice of mercantilism, see Eli Heckscher, *Mercantilism,* 2 vols. (London: George Allan and Unwin Ltd., 1936).

logic of bullion hoarding was based on the belief that supplies of gold and silver were limited and constituted real "wealth." Many of the trade barriers in existence today were first inaugurated during this period. Subsidy, tariff, control of production, and fixed pricing were all common methods of regulating trade during the Mercantilist Era.

With the dawning of the Industrial Revolution, new technology developed the industrial capacity of European industry to higher levels of achievement. The growth of industrialism saw the eventual disintegration of the mercantile doctrine which was replaced by a laissez-faire attitude on the part of government. The Industrial Revolution, in turn, led to a chain of innovations that caused social and economic change unparalleled in history, perhaps until the 20th century.

The new economic liberalism of the period aided the blossoming of world trade. Total world trade increased over threefold from 1850 to 1914. The nature of trade also changed to some degree. There was a shift in emphasis by the industrialized nations to exploiting raw material sources to meet the needs of an industrialized, urbanized society. Increased sources of agricultural products also were required, and from these needs came the development of world trade in the 20th century.

TWENTIETH CENTURY DEVELOPMENT

World War I and interwar period

Sweeping innovations in communication, petroleum, and other energy sources continued and accelerated during the 20th century, but, commercial competition shifted to military competition and, in 1914, Europe was plunged into a war which devastated the productive capacity of central Europe as well as causing almost 40 million human casualties. After the Armistice of 1918, a period of political and economic chaos settled over the European continent. Starvation, social disorginaization, and economic chaos plagued most of the countries of Europe until the mid-1920s.

The needs of postwar reconstruction and the availability of foreign loans, especially from the United States, allowed for a good measure of economic recovery by the late 1920s. World trade began to increase and reached a peak of almost $70 billion in 1929, up from $40 billion at the peak of the pre-World War I period. Then the Great Depression of 1929 spread worldwide; by 1938 world trade had decreased to approximately $27 billion. Unemployment, financial instability, and economic insecurity haunted most of the industrialized countries of the world.

During the interwar period there were two general trends which influenced the development of world commerce. The first trend was toward protectionism, the principal reaction to the Depression. The economic liberalism and laissez-faire tenets of the middle and late 19th century were ignored in the scramble to promote internal economic recovery. The second trend was toward negotiation and concession among countries of the world. In 1932 in the Ottawa Agreement, the countries affiliated with Great Britain negotiated an agreement whereby each would provide preferential treatment in exporting and importing within the British Commonwealth. It is interesting that this agreement was to become a major stumbling block to Great Britain's acceptance into the European Common Market in the 1960s, delaying her entry until 1971.

Post-World War II period

In 1939, the world was again plunged into tragic and destructive war. Most of the industrial nations of the world were involved, and again the destruction in terms of industrial capacity and human misery was unparalleled in history.

Several factors emerged from World War II which have profoundly influenced the development of world trade patterns since 1945. One major factor was the almost worldwide split of communist and noncommunist nations. The so-called iron curtain (around the USSR and eastern Europe) and bamboo curtain (around the People's Republic of China) provided as effective a barrier to international trade as they did to sound political cooperation. In post-World War II commerce, the types of trade, terms of trade, and volume of trade were influenced by the existence of the iron or bamboo curtains. As a result of this ideological split, traditional patterns of trade were disrupted. Other factors which had profound influences on the pattern of world commerce were the huge programs of economic assistance during the post-World War II period and the gradual dissolution of colonial powers that created scores of new countries in Asia and Africa. Economic assistance helped the war-ravaged world rebuild and new countries created new markets.

International cooperation is yet another factor which has characterized the development of international commerce since 1945. This cooperation is generally manifested in one of two forms. Countries have combined in different parts of the world to promote internal trade and mutual advantage in external trade, and voluntary associations for the exchange of ideas to facilitate the mechanics of world trade have developed. In 1947, The General Agreement on Tariffs and Trade (GATT) was negotiated in Geneva, Switzerland. By 1981, 85 countries had been granted full membership in the general agreement. GATT is a complex agreement (see Chapter 3 for a complete discussion of GATT), which provides a framework within which negotiations to encourage trade, and reduce tariffs and other restrictions to world trade take place among member nations.[3]

---

[3] Laura Wallace, "GATT's New Director, Arthur Dunkel, Brings Zest to World Trade Watchdog," *The Wall Street Journal,* March 3, 1981, p. 22.

WORLD TRADE AND THE UNITED STATES

In 1776 two major events occurred which were to shape evolving patterns of world trade far into the future. A Declaration of Independence was presented to England by her American colonies, and Adam Smith published his *Wealth of Nations*. Both these events presented demands for greater freedom to determine the destiny of commerce and socioeconomic affairs. The Declaration of Independence demanded that the colonies be free to determine their own destiny—a revolt against a basic tenet of mercantilism. The *Wealth of Nations* rejected protectionism and other forms of economic legislation and held out free trade as a positive alternative.

Under the terms of mercantilist philosophy, the colonies were expected to provide a source of raw materials and a market for manufactured products of the mother country. The results of these restrictions did not leave the American colonies with a large industrial base when the Revolutionary War was won in 1789. However, the years 1793 to 1808 were years of prosperity for the young republic. The export sector of the economy is estimated to have increased fivefold during this period. The combination of rich natural resources, an expanding frontier, a growing internal market, and favorable export conditions led to continued prosperity.

Great Britain remained predominant in world export trade from the early 18th century to the 1920s when the United States passed her. With the exception of one or two years, the United States has continued to be the world leader in export trade. Further, the United States has been the top world trader (exports and imports combined) since 1940. Beginning in the decade of the 1950s, however, some important changes began to occur in the pattern of world trade which were to have far-reaching effects on U.S. trade.

The rapid growth of war-torn economies and previously underdeveloped countries, coupled with large-scale economic cooperation and assistance, led to new world marketing opportunities. Rising standards of living and broad-based consumer and industrial markets abroad forced the American marketer to reappraise traditional approaches to foreign markets.

Competition for foreign markets increased steadily. Foreign markets were no longer as ready to absorb the surplus production of American industry. Emerging sentiments of nationalism, coupled with heightened world competition and rapidly developing industrial capacity, removed some of the magic from the "made-in-U.S.A." identification. In many cases, the export manager found that not only were traditional export markets declining or disappearing, but competition for remaining world markets had evolved. Lower labor costs, less-expensive raw materials, new plants and equipment, lower transportation costs, and trade barriers raised by dollar-short nations placed severe pressure on the ability of American business to compete in some important segments of the export market.

American business found it necessary to focus the same marketing skills used in domestic operations on foreign marketing opportunities. No longer was it sufficient to produce for export and rely on a gravity-flow channel to foreign markets. The total marketing program had to be designed to match company resources with potential foreign and domestic demand. During the 1950s, U.S. businesses relied heavily on foreign investment as a defense against the trade barriers and costs they began to face. The book value of U.S. foreign direct investment rose from about $12 billion in 1950, to more than $50 billion in 1966. By effectively linking their technological and managerial advantages with cheap overseas labor, the U.S. multinationals were able to increase their foreign earnings to a rate higher than they were able to achieve at home and certainly more than most native businesses could within the countries where the U.S. multinationals were operating. By the close of the 1960s, U.S. manufacturers were being challenged on two major fronts, in direct investment and in export markets. At the same time, they found that the overvaluation of the U.S. dollar made it profitable to import into the United States. Consequently, many companies that never considered going overseas went abroad to manufacture products which a few years earlier had been exported from American plants. These companies sought production facilities in developing nations to manufacture products for their European subsidiaries, and more importantly, for the U.S. market itself. The heavy increase in investments on the part of U.S. businesses heightened the concern of foreign countries so that by the middle of the 1970s, the continued exporting of capital for foreign investments raised deep concern both in the United States and abroad.

Direct investment challenged

In the 1960s, animosity toward foreign investment both in industrialized and in less developed countries was growing. Latin American countries were the most hazardous, with Chile, Peru, Bolivia, Mexico, and others expropriating direct U.S. investments or forcing investors to sell holdings to nationals. Just weeks before the then-president of Chile, Salvadore Allende, proposed the expropriation of most of the $965 million U.S. investment in that country, the Peruvian government announced a new industrial law which provided that the government buy control of all basic industries owned by foreigners and sell the equity to nationals.

Uncertainty about multinational investors, however, was by no means limited to Latin America or other underdeveloped countries. In Great Britain, one industrialist, apprehensive about increased foreign investment, warned that "Britain might become a satellite where there could be manufacturing but no determination of policy." While the British government generally viewed foreign investment favorably, guidelines were set for joint ventures between certain British and U.S. firms. In Canada, a similar concern about the size of foreign investment led the Royal Commission on Canadian Economic Prospects to recommend that foreign-owned subsidiaries be required to "Canadianize," that is, (1) appoint Canadians to companies' boards of directors, (2) staff key positions with Canadians, (3) ensure that a sizable minority of equity stock be sold to Canadians, (4) purchase supplies in Canada, and (5) aggressively seek export markets. And in the European Common Market, or EEC, U.S. multinationals were rebuffed in a variety of ways, ranging from tight control over proposed joint ventures to strong protectionist laws. Even Australia, one of the most open countries to foreign investment, questioned control of its basic industries by foreign investors.

The threat of economic domination by U.S. multinational firms felt by many nations was best stated in the popular book, *The American Challenge,* published in 1968, in which the author, J. J. Servan-Schreiber, wrote:

> Fifteen years from now it is quite possible that the world's third greatest indus-trial power, just after the United States and Russia, will not be Europe but *American Industry in Europe.* Already, in the ninth year of the Common Market, this European market is basically American in organization.[4]

Even though we will see in the next section that Schreiber's prophesy of U.S. MNCs' (multinational companies) domination of the world economy did not materialize, there was considerable alarm in the early 1970s about the size and strength of U.S. MNCs. The general reaction of many nations was to control MNC activity. Exhibit 2–1 shows the extent of U.S. investment abroad and a domination of markets by U.S. firms that existed in many countries during this period.

At the same time U.S. firms faced increased sensitivity to their investments, U.S. balance of trade continued to run at a deficit.

Balance of trade deficit

The beginning of the 1970s ushered in some firsts in U.S. world domi-nance of world trade. While still the largest world economic force, problems in the U.S. domestic economy began to show. A deficit in U.S. balance of trade occurred in 1971 for the first time since 1888. A deficit of $2 billion in 1971 grew to $26 billion in 1977 where it has remained through 1981. As Exhibit 2–2 illustrates, the United States when compared with Japan and Germany is in a considerably worse position. The U.S. government is taking several steps to decrease our imports and increase exports; how-ever, it appears that the economic conditions which permitted the United States to have a favorable balance of trade from 1888 to 1971 will not recur in the forseeable future. Other industrialized and industrializing coun-tries offer a level of competition for world markets that did not exist prior to the 1970s.

---

[4] J. J. Servan-Schreiber, *The American Challege* (New York: Atheneum Publishers, 1968), p. 3.

EXHIBIT 2–1:   Estimated U.S. share of certain industries in France, West Germany, and Italy, mid-1960s*

Percent-ages	Industries		
	France, 1963†	West Germany‡	Italy, 1965§
80 or more	Carbon black, razor blades and safety razors, synthetic rubber	Computers	Computers‖
60 to 79	Accounting machines, computers, electric razors, sewing machines		
50 to 59			Cosmetics
40 to 49	Electronic and statistical machinery, # telegraph and telephone equipment	Automobiles	
30 to 39	Elevators, tires, tractors, agricultural machinery	Petroleum	Pharmaceuticals
20 to 29	Machine tools, petroleum refining, refrigerators, washing machines		Soap, petroleum
5 to 19	Automobiles	Electrical-optics-toys,** food, machinery, vehicles-metal products††	Paper, tires

    * Other estimates vary.
    † Turnover figures.
    ‡ Percentage of capital of public companies.
    § Share in capital invested in industry (except where specified otherwise).
    ‖ Market share according to number of computers installed, 1969.
    # This includes computers, which were 75 percent.
    ** This includes computers, which were 84 percent.
    †† This includes automobiles, which were 40 percent.
    Source: Data on France and West Germany adapted from Christopher Layton, *Trans-Atlantic Investments* (Boulogne-sur-Seine, France: The Atlantic Institute, 1966), p. 19, with additions on France and all data on Italy from Robert Hellmann, *The Challenge to U.S. Dominance of the International Corporation* (New York: Dunellen, 1970), pp. 334, 100. Also see Mira Wilkins, *The Maturing of Multinational Enterprise: American Business Abroad from 1914 to 1970* (Cambridge, Mass.: Harvard University Press, 1974), p. 404.

Competition

What had happened to challenge the supremacy of American industry? Competition! Competition on all fronts—Japan, Germany, most of the industrialized world—but perhaps most disconcerting, many multinationals were beginning to experience competition from the developing world. Some companies were finding themselves in competition with their own foreign subsidiaries and companies in developing countries. Many of these countries became important enough economically to be reclassified from developing country to newly industrialized country or NIC. Brazil, Mexico, South Korea, Taiwan, Singapore, and Hong Kong all grew enough to be classified as NICs. What made these countries different from other developing countries was a relatively high per capita income, rapid industrialization in selected

EXHIBIT 2-2: **Merchandise exports, imports, and balance of trade**

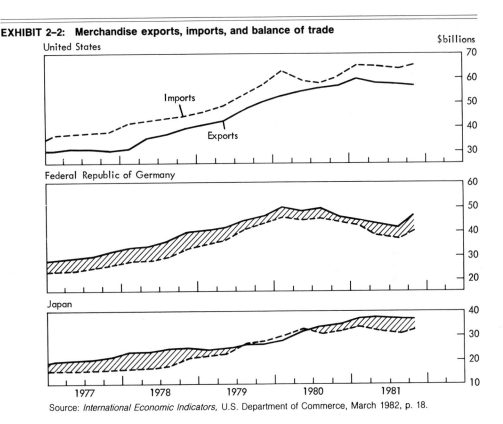

Source: *International Economic Indicators*, U.S. Department of Commerce, March 1982, p. 18.

industries which were locally owned or joint ventures with foreign MNCs, and aggressive competition in markets outside their home countries. Korea, for example, has become a major competitor in Asia for steel and shipbuilding. Partly because of growing Korean steel exports, Japanese steel exports to Asia declined in 1981.[5] Further, Korea's shipbuilding capacity has reached 4 million gross tons annually and is expected to exceed 6 million tons by the end of the decade; Japan's annual capacity is 10 million gross tons. In addition to NICs, developing countries like Venezuela have government-owned companies operating in neighboring countries. For example, one Venezuelan-owned company has a subsidiary in Puerto Rico producing canvas, cosmetics, chairs, and zippers; there are Chilean and Colombian companies in Puerto Rico, and in Georgia (U.S.A.) there is a Venezuelan company in agribusiness and a Bangladesh-owned company that makes mattresses.[6]

[5] John Marcom Jr., "Japanese Industry Watches Nervously as Korean Steel, Shipbuilding Develop," *The Wall Street Journal*, January 5, 1982, p. 26.

[6] For an informative account of third world MCNs see Kyung-Il Ghymn, "Multinational Enterprises From The Third World," *Journal of International Business Studies*, Fall 1980, pp. 118–22.

BOX 2–2: GNP of various countries compared with sales of selected corporations ($billions, 1980)

Netherlands	88.1
Mexico	76.2
Belgium	69.7
General Motors	63.2
Exxon	60.3
Switzerland	54.6
Argentina	49.7
Royal Dutch/Shell	44.0
Ford	42.8
Venezuela	41.2
Mobil	34.7
IBM	21.1
Thailand	20.6
Algeria	19.5
Chile	16.8
Peru	16.4

Source: Adapted from John Hein, "The Top 100 Economies," *Across the Board*, May 1980, pp. 9–10.

In short, "economic power and potential became more evenly distributed among the industrialized countries." The result was the United States lost some of its former competitive edge, especially in price management and technology. In fact, U.S. export prices, compared with those of Japan and western Europe, rose steadily from 1963, placing the United States at a trade disadvantage. Price, however, was not the only thing affecting the U.S. trade advantage. European and Japanese companies, which had traditionally lagged behind in engineering, manufacturing, marketing, and financial expertise, were rapidly catching up. In areas such as steel, television, and small commercial aircraft, there was a question whether the United States maintained any technological lead at all. The genius of American managers which had been feared by many, and considered as important competitively as capital and technology, was also being challenged. In the past 20 years, European managers learned well; as one U.S. executive pointed out, "there's a new generation of European managers . . . who can do things as well as we can."

In fact, the dominance of U.S. multinationals that Servan-Schreiber warned Europe about in 1968 did not develop. Instead, U.S. dominance declined while MNCs from other countries increased in size and influence.[7] By 1980, U.S. MNCs were losing position to multinationals of other countries. Exhibit 2–3 shows the dramatic change that occurred between 1963 and 1979. Of the world's 100 largest industrial corporations, 67 were U.S. owned in 1963 and by 1979, the number had dropped to 47.

---

[7] John Hein, "The World's Multinationals: A Global Challenge," The Conference Board, Report No. 84, 1981, p. 5.

EXHIBIT 2–3: The world's 100 largest industrial corporations, by country of origin

Country	1963	1979
United States	67	47
Germany	13	13
United Kingdom	7	7
France	4	11
Japan	3	7
Italy	2	3
Netherlands-United Kingdom	2	2
Netherlands	1	3
Switzerland	1	1
Canada	—	2
Belgium	—	1
Brazil	—	1
Mexico	—	1
Venezuela	—	1

Source: Adapted from John Hein, "The World's Multinationals: A Global Challenge," The Conference Board, Report No. 84, 1981, p. 5.

Although U.S. dominance of MNCs has declined, it does not mean the importance of the MNC on a world-wide basis has slipped. Quite the contrary, a Conference Board analysis found that if a corporation's sales were to be equated with a nation's output of goods and services, then 39 of the world's 100 largest money powers would be international corporations and 61 would be countries.[8] Instead of decreasing in importance, the MNC as a world economic force has increased in importance; and, with it's presence in most countries, it has become an increased concern of all nations to force the MNC into more "nationally responsible" economic units.

Business historians have described the 1960s and 1970s as the age of multinationals. As one scholar noted, "Larger corporations than the world had ever known leaped across national boundaries and seemed to challenge the power of governments to control them."[9] If the 1960s and 70s are to be known as the *age of the multinationals,* the decade of the 1980s will be known as the *era of adjustment* for both host countries and multinationals.

BOX 2–3: In just twenty-five years

News item February 1, 1957:

Japan may soon get its long-awaited "people's car." Keita Goto, Japanese industrial tycoon, currently is preparing to manufacture 120 small four-wheel trucks a month. Then he will swing into . . . passenger vehicles . . .

Source: From "Twenty-five Years Ago," *Forbes,* February 1, 1982, p. 155.

---

[8] Ibid.

[9] Allen R. Janger, "Organization of International Joint Ventures," The Conference Board, Report No. 787, 1980, p. 5.

Sovereign states will have to learn to live with, adjust to, and control the increasing world power of multinational firms. Multinational firms will have to learn to live with sovereign states that will become more sensitive to their investments and marketing activities. And finally, the world's economies will have to learn to adjust to the economic realities of slower growth, unemployment, resource shortages, and increased tension. In short, the multinational company will be confronted with manifestations of a whole host of challenges from the present well into the 1980s.

CHALLENGES IN THE 1980s

The decade of the 1980s promises to be one of adjustment—adjustment to a new world economic order. The post-World War II industrial and economic influence and the authority of the U.S. economy and U.S. multinationals is rapidly disappearing. There is no single reason the multinational tide is beginning to ebb, and there is no reason multinationals should not survive the challenges which confront them in the 1980s. Those that survive will be the ones which effectively confront and adjust to a changing world environment. In the opinion of the author, control of the MNC, worldwide economic conditions, a rise in protectionism, a changing complexion of competition, and an overall shift in attitudes toward multinational companies are the main challenges. All had their roots in the late 70s and they are the major obstacles facing multinationals in the 80s.

Control of multinationals

A key issue by the beginning of the 1980s was control of the multinational firm. Should control lie with the host country, with the country of origin, or—because of its size and power—should the multinational firm not be under any country's control? The charges leveled at multinational corporations were numerous: they meddled in the domestic affairs of the countries in which they did business; their operations were the main cause of the dollar crisis; they had an interest in perpetuating the oil crisis; they were creators of worldwide inflation; and "they act beyond the law."

These charges were, of course, greatly exaggerated, but the bases for them were understandable after a glance at a random selection of facts regarding the economic influence of multinationals during the 1970s. For example, of the 120 largest industrial corporations in Belgium, 48 were controlled partly or wholly by Americans. Ninety percent of Europe's production of microcircuits was controlled by American companies. But American multinationals were not alone; investment opportunities were open to other countries. For example, German corporations had more capital invested in South Carolina than anywhere else in the world except Germany.

Public attention continues to be focused on multinational corporations because of their growing power and the concern of many national governments over national sovereignty. Critics of U.S. multinationals charge that direct investment by U.S. corporations abroad creates unemployment at home and that multinational companies have given away technology resulting in products made by foreign labor competing with U.S. products at home. While many of these criticisms are easily refuted, they represent genuine fears held by many in the United States and throughout the world. Concern about the influence of MNCs leads to repeated cries from various groups for legislation to protect their economies. Appeals for protective legislation are heard by governments in Germany, France, Australia, Brazil, Japan, and the United States—in short, around the world. Germans are afraid of the Japanese, the Japanese are afraid of the Americans, and vice versa; and the Germans, Americans, and Japanese are afraid of the Third World. As global recession continues and world prices increase, the fear of MNCs intensifies and the cry for more control over their activities is heard from more and more countries. Certainly one of the major challenges facing MNCs is the issue of control. Aggravating this issue is the state of the world's economy.

Economic

The single most important event affecting world economies is the growing shortage of energy—principally, petroleum energy. Until the world, and the United States in particular, were jolted by the first Arab embargo of petroleum, the availability of energy was considered inexhaustible. Implications of a worldwide energy crisis for world trade are enormous. Continued growth of the industrialized world is dependent on energy, and, if the less developed world is to gain its industrialization goals, availability of economical supplies of energy is essential. Economical sources of power are necessary to fuel continued industrial growth and the individual growth of nations. Without economical power sources to provide energy, the industrialized world cannot supply the industrial material needed for development and expansion.

The economic inflation and negative balance of payments which resulted for most net importers of petroleum during the energy crisis created worldwide economic turmoil. Continued solidarity among OPEC nations further increased petroleum prices, intensifying the economic problems of the world. Prices for exported goods increased substantially, worsening the balance-of-payment problems for most importing countries. The less developed countries continue to be heavy borrowers of funds on worldwide markets to finance industrial growth.[10] The additional cost of inflation and the higher prices for goods aggravates their financial stability. Brazil, for example, had an outstanding debt of $61.2 billion in 1980. To make the interest payments

---

[10] For a comprehensive review of LDC debt see Bahram Nowzod, "Debt in Developing Countries: Some Issues for the 1980s," *Finance and Development,* March 1982, pp. 13–16.

BOX 2–4: Coping with an annual inflation rate of 100 percent in Argentina

Americans complain about double-digit inflation, but how about triple-digit inflation? For the fourth time since 1976, Argentina's annual inflation rate pushed above 100 percent. How do people cope when a short taxi ride costs nearly 20,000 pesos and 40,000 pesos (worth 1 million U.S. dollars in 1948) is not enough today to buy a simple restaurant meal with wine?

Survival takes skill and wit. With an inflation rate in excess of 8 percent per month, Argentines engage in short-term "high finance." When employees are paid at the end of the month, they rush to the banks and buy seven-day and 30-day certificates of deposit. The annual rate on 30-day CDs at one period after a devaluation was 155 percent. They frequently make enough in interest to cover inflation for the month.

Naturally, everyone must put off paying bills while paychecks are on deposit. This is one reason little neighborhood food stores in Argentina have withstood the advances of supermarkets that would have wiped them out in other countries. The neighborhood shopkeeper knows his customers and allows them to put their purchases on an informal account that is settled once a month. It might appear as if the merchant is giving his customers an interest-free loan; but that is not the case. The system works for the storekeeper too. He jots down purchases but *without the price*. When it comes time to pay, he totes up the bill at the *current price*, not the price at the time the goods were bought. This system is so vital for small merchants that it is practically impossible for regular customers to pay on the spot. You must charge it.

Source: Adapted from Everett G. Martin," Argentines Learn How to Endure Inflation, Frequent Devaluations," *The Wall Street Journal*, June 29, 1981, p. 1.

---

on this debt, Brazil uses 32 percent of all revenue generated from exports. While this is bad, it gets worse when the cost of oil imports are considered. Another 45 percent of their export revenues are needed to pay for oil; thus, Brazil has to spend 77 percent of all its export earnings just for debt-servicing and petroleum. The picture becomes gloomier when it is noted that Brazil imported other items beside oil and paid for them with new borrowed money. The world's international banks voice increasing concern over the substantial debts incurred by most of the world's developing countries who are also net importers of petroleum. Exhibit 2–4 shows just how desperate it is economically for some of the developing countries who are net importers of oil. It is estimated that external debt in developing countries has risen from $60 billion in 1970 to over $500 billion in 1981.[11] With such debt comes excessive inflation, further weakening their economies.[12]

One of the ramifications of higher oil prices and increased debt is inflation. Again, using Brazil as an example, inflation there has been increasing steadily from an annualized rate of 30 percent in 1977 to 120 percent in 1981. There were several factors that contributed to this inflationary increase, but surely, one of the more important was the rise in oil prices from $12 in 1979 to $32 a barrel in 1980. This price increase resulted in Brazil's oil

---

[11] Richard F. Janssen, "Third World's Debts, Totaling $500 Billion, May Pose Big Dangers," *The Wall Street Journal*, January 28, 1981, p. 1.

[12] Richard F. Janssen, "High Interest Rates Place Fresh Strain on Developing Nations, Banks Concede," *The Wall Street Journal*, February 10, 1981, p. 26.

EXHIBIT 2–4: External debt and percentage of export receipts necessary to pay for interest and oil for selected developing countries (1980)

Country	External debt ($ billions)	Interest payments as percentage of exports	Oil imports as percentage of exports
Brazil	61.2	32	45
South Korea	27.0	11	25
Argentina	21.4	29	7
Turkey	19.9	21	55
India	18.5	4	58
Philippines	12.1	12	36
Chile	10.6	18	36
Taiwan	7.5	4	20
Colombia	7.4	9	9
Thailand	7.0	6	27

Source: Richard F. Janssen, "High Interest Rates Place Fresh Strain On Developing Nations, Banks Concede," *The Wall Street Journal*, February 10, 1981.

bill rising to about $10 billion or approximately half the total of all the country's imports.[13]

Inflation and negative balances of trade are not solely the problems of developing countries. The rest of the industrialized world also has felt the pinch of high oil prices, inflation and—for several countries, including the United States—recession in 1982. This has had an impact on world trade, slowing it considerably to less than a 1 percent increase in 1981, after increasing by about 35 percent between 1975 and 1979.[14] Certainly world economic conditions will improve sometime during the 1980s; exactly when is a debatable question on which economists disagree. Until recovery begins, the trend toward countries being more protective of home-country industry will continue.[15] It is inconceivable to imagine the world reverting to the protectionism of the early 1900s, but it is possible that the freer trade of the 1950s, 60s, and 70s may be curtailed substantially in the 1980s. One of the greatest challenges facing multinationals during this decade will be the wave of protectionism which is beginning across the world.

Protectionism

The threatening economic conditions discussed above created a definite drift toward protectionism that probably will not abate until long after eco-

---

[13] "Brazil, a Burning Inflation Is Rekindling Recession," *Business Week*, May 11, 1981, p. 47.

[14] Alfred L. Malabre Jr., "Expansion of World Trade Slows Nearly To Halt, Reflecting Slumps Overseas, New Restrictions," *The Wall Street Journal*, May 28, 1981, p. 46.

[15] "France, Trying Protectionism to Curb Job Losses," *Business Week*, December 28, 1981, p. 69.

BOX 2–5: Nontariff barriers—bureaucrats at work or don't forget the apostrophe

Many of the most frustrating types of nontariff barriers are those imposed by bureaucrats at the local level. Many times their actions are not necessarily sanctioned by their government, other times they are; either way, the result is the same—restrictions on foreign trade. Here are two examples:

Nontariff barriers such as excessive inspection and complex technical standards used effectively to keep Japanese autos waiting on French docks are being used again on other goods. Importers of machine tools are required to obtain licensing visas in advance of delivery. It won't keep the product out but it does make the foreign a little less competitive. "It is more paperwork. It slows down delivery dates," says an international trade official.

The Japanese are a little more experienced than the French and they can do it with an apostrophe. Givenchy Japon complained recently that its application to import *l'Interdit* perfume was held up because the company left out an apostrophe between the *l* and *I*. Further, Korean electric fans that have passed rigorous U.S. tests cannot be sold in Japan until their cords are replaced with Japanese substitutes. Grain accepted in one Japanese port is rejected in another even though it is from the same shipload.

Source: Adapted from "France, Trying Protectionism to Curb Job Losses," *Business Week*, December 28, 1981, p. 69 and Art Pine, "At a Crossroads, Japan Nears a Choice of Easing Trade Curbs or Facing West's Ire," *The Wall Street Journal*, January 26, 1982, p. 1.

---

nomic conditions improve. The attitude that prevails among U.S. auto workers when they chant "every Japanese car an American buys puts four auto workers out of work," is echoed around the world and will ultimately harden public opinion toward more protection of local industry. It will take some time after the world's economies are again sound before freer trade returns. It is probably realistic for multinationals to plan to adjust to more, rather than less, local and national concern about foreign businesses.[16]

Import surcharges, quotas, trade-limiting pacts, and other nontariff barriers are indicative of the protective restrictions being used by many countries. Western Europe has imposed restrictions on textile imports from Japan; Mexico placed import restrictions on over 200 items previously unrestricted and it has increased import duties on over 300 others;[17] and the United States has engaged in several trade-limiting agreements that have caused Japan to "voluntarily" limit the quantity of color televisions, automobiles, and textiles exported to the United States. Japan volunteered to limit exports to the United States under the lightly veiled threat of stronger restrictions if the Japanese share of these markets continued to increase. The concern with protecting American markets has reached a point in some industries that some members of Congress want to retaliate against countries that restrict U.S. goods. In the communications and computer industries, U.S. markets

---

[16] "An Accelerating Drift toward Protectionism," *Business Week*, July 27, 1981, pp. 22–23.

[17] Lawrence Rout, "In Mexico Operations, Foreign Concerns Face Reams of Red Tape," *Wall Street Journal*, February 16, 1982, p. 1.

BOX 2–6: Is Japan's marketing success a better attitude?

Unfair business practices to low labor costs have been given as reasons for the success of the Japanese in world markets. But one experienced U.S. businessman suggests that it may also be a matter of attitude. To illustrate his point, he told the following story.

A U.S. businessman on a market-expansion trip lands on the shores of a developing country and is met by 1 million shoeless people. He cables headquarters: "No market here, people are so poor they don't even own shoes."

A Japanese businessman visiting the same country a week later and confronted with the same 1 million shoeless people cables his headquarters: "Tremendous market—send 1 million pairs of shoes."

Source: Frank B. Gibney, Vice Chairman, Board of Editors, Encyclopaedia Britannica Inc., Japan/U.S. Business Conference, St. Louis, September 25, 1980.

---

are open to foreign companies, but this is not the case in Japan and parts of Europe. There is serious discussion of passing legislation to impose the same restrictions on the importation of goods from a country to the United States as imposed on U.S. products in that same country. Two statements that best reflect the attitudes of a growing number of congressional leaders are: "the American Congress still believes in free trade, but after what's happened to consumer electronics and autos, reciprocity is becoming a motherhood issue" and "From now on, if you want to play in the U.S. market, it's going to be by the rules you wrote yourself." Retaliation in place of negotiation to fight protectionism would seem to only lead to more protectionism.[18]

In the United States, the strongest push for protectionism comes from trade unions which are calling for higher import taxes and quotas on everything from steel to textiles to shoes.[19] While it is doubtful that Congress would consider widespread protectionist legislation, some unions are suggesting laws be passed to require that imported goods sold in the United States have components that are produced in the United States. The President of the UAW is pushing for legislation that will specify North American content in all foreign cars sold in the U.S. The UAW has talked of content requirements as high as 75 percent. This proposal is not unlike the steps taken in Mexico in the 1960s when they too began requiring local content in all cars sold in Mexico. But they did have an infant industry to develop and/or protect.

Besides protecting U.S. markets, trade unions want to restrict U.S. direct investments. There have been strong lobbying efforts by U.S. unions for restriction of investment activity by U.S. MNCs. The MNCs argue that U.S. investment abroad creates jobs rather than decreasing jobs in the United States. The unions are unconvinced even though there is mounting evidence

---

[18] M. G. Warner, "Some Limits to Free Trade Gain Favor," *The Wall Street Journal,* January 14, 1982, p. 25.

[19] "Labor Takes a Turn Away From Free Trade," *Business Week,* July 27, 1981, p. 24.

that their job-exporting argument is mostly myth. A U.S. Department of Commerce study showed over 90 percent of U.S. imports came from affiliates in the industrialized/high-wage countries of the world rather than from U.S. subsidiaries in countries with cheap labor as alleged by U.S. unions.

The trade union movement toward protectionism is not confined to the United States; organized multinational unions are also directing efforts toward controlling the activities of MNCs. Further, in many European countries, trade unions have an important say in all acquisitions by foreign companies. In Sweden, for example, when U.S. E.S.B., Inc. (a U.S. battery maker) attempted to buy Tudor, a Swedish company, discussions included the unions as well as management. The unions demanded and got commitments on planned employment and capital investments before the merger took place. Although the Swedish unions do not have a legal right to approve acquisitions by a foreign company, the Swedish government does, and it will not approve mergers or sales without union agreement. Although there was never any hostility or animosity in the negotiations, it was clear that the unions were determined to preserve their jobs and create more jobs.

Potentially more restrictive and certainly more frightening to multinationals are some of the legislative plans under discussion in the European Community. Several proposals are under discussion, which, if turned into law, would affect MNCs regardless of which Common Market country they were operating in. One proposal is that workers sit on the boards of all companies. Another would force multinationals to disclose their global operations and strategic plans to European workers and to consult with those workers before taking any action that may have a substantial effect on their interests. The third, and most radical, would make corporate directors personally liable for damages should minority stockholders or creditors—or even employees—of a subsidiary suffer as a result of corporate-headquarter decisions favoring the interests of the parent company and its stockholders.

These issues are not new to Europe since some are already law in West Germany, Belgium, and the Netherlands. What is new is that, if passed by the European Community, they will become law throughout the Common Market. Whether or not such proposals will become law is heavily dependent on the prospect of increasing EC unemployment, already at a postwar high of 9.1 million of a 110 million work force.[20]

Just how protective nations become depends primarily on the health of the world's economies. If economies improve, unemployment decreases, and world currencies stabilize, then perhaps a global trade war can be avoided; otherwise, protectionism will grow and multinational companies will face one of their most serious challenges. Regardless of the direction of worldwide protectionism, competition continues to be a challenge in the 1980s.[21]

---

[20] Richard I. Kirkland Jr., "Bad News Brewing in Brussels," *Fortune,* December 14, 1981, p. 143.

[21] "Talking to Avert a Global Trade War," *Business Week,* December 21, 1981, p. 47.

Competition

Multinational firms will encounter considerable competition during this decade. Swiss, Canadian, German, Japanese, French, U.S., and many Third World countries—especially the NICs (Newly Industrialized Countries)—are now, and will continue to be, competing for all world markets. If protectionism increases as discussed, there will be greatly intensified competition for all unprotected markets.

In anticipation of higher tariffs, many MNCs have invested heavily in manufacturing facilities in their more lucrative foreign markets to protect themselves from the higher tariffs or from import restrictions. The United States particularly has been affected by this tactic with considerable investment in auto production by the Japanese and French. The Japanese have been among the heavier direct investors in the United States. By 1981, Japanese investors controlled 213 U.S. manufacturing firms and had minority ownership interest in 12 others. Investments have been in companies producing television sets, microwave ovens, metal bearings, electronic semiconductors, plastics, and lumber products.[22]

In addition, since U.S. markets are among the world's most lucrative, foreign companies have bought control or a major portion of many U.S. firms. Nestlé acquired Libby and Stauffer Foods; a French firm acquired a major position in A&P, the food retailer; and other U.S. firms such as Baskin-Robbins, Saks-Fifth Avenue, Kentucky Fried Chicken, and Capital Records are either owned outright or substantially owned by foreign companies. Among the largest exporters of grain, minerals, chemicals, and machinery from the United States are subsidiaries of Mitsui and Mitsubishi of Japan. If Fortune's 50 Top Exporters list included nonindustrial companies, Mitsui U.S.A. would have ranked fourth on the Fortune list just behind Boeing Company, General Motors, and General Electric. U.S. multinationals are no longer unchallenged at home or abroad.[23]

Regardless of where one goes, the Japanese are on the way or already there if there is market potential. Certainly the world's fiercest competitors, often accused of dumping and other unfair trade practices, the truth is Japan's success is more the result of good competitive business than unfair trade tactics. The Japanese plan their efforts carefully, and, once they decide there is a market, they pursue it effectively and efficiently. Frequently, the one difference between a successful Japanese business and an American business is the American attitude of looking at production and asking, "What have we got that we can sell abroad?" while the Japanese look and ask, "What will this country need? What will it buy that we can make?" They study a market they are not presently servicing and where there are signs

---

[22] John T. Norman, "Japanese Direct Investment in the U.S. Creating Jobs in 42 States, Study Says," *The Asian Wall Street Journal Weekly,* May 11, 1981, p. 2.

[23] "Japanese Trading Companies Joining Ranks of America's Biggest Exporters," *The Asian Wall Street Journal Weekly,* November 9, 1981, p. 4.

of rising incomes and concentrate on designing a product to meet specific needs. This direct effort has resulted in Japan exporting 42 percent of the world's ships, 72 percent of the motorcycles, 63 percent of the radios, and 49 percent of the world's cameras. Besides effective marketing and concentrated effort, the Japanese have a major advantage because their government plays an important role in aiding industries "targeted" for worldwide development. Industry plans are made to include the participation of government and the banks and it has been very effective. Every targeted industry, beginning with cameras and optics in the 1950s through automobiles in the 70s, has been successful. For the decade of the 1980s, Japan's Ministry of International Trade and Industry has made development of the computer by the early 1990s a national goal. It plans to spend $50 million in research with the computer industry in the first three years and as much as $450 million to $1 billion over a 10-year period to develop "fifth generation" computers and to establish Japan as a major computer technology leader.[24]

Besides competition from industrialized nations, MNCs are now facing competition from Third World countries: countries who have developed industries through investment by multinational companies and who now effectively can compete outside their own boundaries. "In Asia, the Middle East, Latin America, and parts of Africa, local subsidiaries whose parent companies are domiciled in other developing nations are beginning to successfully challenge established American affiliates."[25] Along with world economic conditions, the threat of increasing protectionism, and intensified competition, the MNCs also face negative world attitudes.

Attitudes toward MNCs

The challenges discussed are affected by and affect the attitudes held by people toward MNCs. The attitudes range from MNCs being thought of as the prime molders of world economic achievement and peace to charges that MNCs are rapacious, exploitative, immoral, and essentially malevolent institutions.[26] The truth perhaps lies closer to the positive attitude than to the negative one. Certainly not all MNCs are models of rectitude, but the majority are concerned with their impact, do make significant social and economic contributions, and have enriched the world in which we live in many ways. Regardless of the facts, however, what is believed is what most often matters because people, directly or indirectly, set or influence the policies which govern MNCs. The challenge in the 1980s is how MNCs should react to and adjust to the reality of the general hostility toward their existence.

---

[24] For an especially complete discussion of this topic, see "Japan's Strategy for the 80s," *Business Week*, December 14, 1981, pp. 39–120.

[25] "How the West Reacts to Export Challenges From the Third World," *World Business Weekly*, October 19, 1981, pp. 28–29.

[26] Joseph La Palombara, "Myths of the Multinationals," *Across the Board*, October 1976, p. 40.

BOX 2–7: The multinational—a love-hate relationship

It fiddles with its accounts. It avoids or evades its taxes. It rigs its intracompany transfer prices. It is run by foreigners, from decision centres thousands of miles away. It imports foreign labour practices. It overpays. It underpays. It competes unfairly with local firms. It is in cahoots with local firms. It exports jobs from rich countries. It is an instrument of rich countries' imperialism. The technologies it brings to the Third World are old-fashioned. No, they are too modern. It meddles. It bribes. Nobody can control it. It wrecks balances of payments. It overturns economic policies. It plays off governments against each other to get the biggest investment incentives. Won't it please come and invest? Let it bloody well go home.

Source: "Business Brief," *The Economist,* London, January 24, 1976, p. 68.

Attitudes appear to be consistent wherever you look. Even in the United States, where attitudes are more positive than elsewhere, one Opinion Research Corporation survey showed people believed by a margin of almost two to one that the government should discourage international expansion of U.S. enterprises and 66 percent believed that U.S. corporation operations abroad meant fewer jobs in the United States. Such attitudes prevail despite evidence that rather than decreasing jobs, MNCs make a positive contribution to home-country employment. The International Labor Office (ILO) in Geneva released a study that contradicted critics who accuse MNCs of exporting jobs to developing countries at the expense of industrialized countries' domestic employment. Rather than export jobs, the study found that MNCs are recession resistant and steady employers despite such corporations' increasing employment activity in developing countries.[27]

Other surveys support the view that MNCs are frequently thought of as a necessary means to economic achievement if they can be tightly controlled. The MNCs feel they are receiving a bum rap. They point proudly to their achievements in transferring technology to underdeveloped countries, of higher rates of employment, better working conditions, and other social contributions. But since what people believe is what matters, the attitudes toward MNCs will surely be an important challenge for the 1980s.

SUMMARY

U.S. foreign businesses will have their mettle tested on several fronts: *total competition* from German, Japanese, British, and other firms of revitalized economies; *political and economic concern* of developed and underdeveloped countries over foreign investment and trade which will be manifest in tighter restrictions; and *technology,* no longer the private domain of U.S. business. To meet these and other obstacles and be successful, perhaps even to survive, it will be necessary to make major adjustments in what may now be regarded as normal international corporate practices and be-

---

[27] "In Praise of the Multinational Company," *Business Europe,* August 21, 1981, pp. 265–66.

havior. Adjustments will have to be made in organizational structures to provide the control and flexibility necessary to meet new challenges. To be competitive there will be a need for greater investments in commitments to total marketing, along with a need to change attitudes vis-á-vis foreign partnerships and to heed the political and economic demands of hosts— in short, foreign investment must become multinational in orientation as well as in name.

The trading of goods and services between nations is a phenomenon which has endured for thousands of years. The factors that have assumed importance in the historical development of trade patterns have varied widely from the beginning of recorded history to the present. Wars, alliances, and technological improvements have constantly altered the differential advantages of trading nations.

The attitudes of nations toward world trade have historically vacillated between protectionism and liberalism. In the United States, an examination of historical tariff policy reflects the variation. Typically, waves of protectionism have swept around the world during periods of world economic recession; similarly, liberalism tends to be more prevalent during periods of worldwide economic progress.

The past decade has seen rapid development on all fronts with many previously underdeveloped countries making great strides in catching up with modern methods and technology. This rapid advancement was brought up short by a worldwide energy crisis that generated rapid inflation, heavy indebtedness, and recession. For the MNC, this portends a future of greater restrictions in addition to increased competition from around the world and at home. If U.S. foreign business is to continue to grow as it has through the decade of the 1970s, it must meet the challenges of the future with ingenuity.

QUESTIONS

1. Define:
   Mercantilism   NIC
   Industrial Revolution

2. How may a manager of international marketing benefit from knowledge of the history of world trade?

3. Identify the major factors underlying the historical success of trading centers. Explain the significance of each factor.

4. Differentiate between the composition of world trade before and after the Industrial Revolution. What additional modern-day differences might also be identified?

5. Set forth and explain the factors characterizing post-World War II trade development.

6. Explain the role of GATT in world trade.

7. Disclose the fallacies of mercantilist thinking.

8. The pattern of distribution of U.S. exports has shifted markedly over its history. What has caused these shifts, and what further shifting might one predict?

9. Select a single product or product group and trace the historical export patterns for this group from any given country. Consider both volume and destination in attempting to explain major changes.

10. "The Industrial Revolution in turn led to a chain of innovations that caused social and economic change unparalleled in history, perhaps until the 20th century." Comment on the international marketing significance of such change.

11. During the 1960s and 70s, U.S. direct investment has been challenged by host countries. What is the justification from the host countries' viewpoint?

12. Discuss one of the major challenges of the 1980s and show how it might affect international operations.

13. How can MNCs protect themselves against the rise in protectionism?

14. Should the United States begin to prevent foreign companies from acquiring U.S. firms? Why or why not?

15. Discuss why there are negative attitudes about MNCs from a U.S. perspective; from a European perspective; and from a less developed country perspective.

16. Why will the decade of the 80s be known as the *era of adjustment?*

Chapter 3

International trade concepts and theory

Trade is a small bag of gold coins offered for a share of the cargo of a clipper ship from China; a letter of credit to a bank in Zurich to permit wholesale purchase of watch movements; an oil pipeline across the Arabian desert to the sea; 29,000 Hungarian pigs for 20,000 wagonloads of Czechoslovakian firewood; the Brazilian government trading 1.3 million sacks of coffee for 25 million bushels of wheat owned by a U.S. company. Trade in every age and in every land is people exchanging something they have for something they want. The basis of all trade, domestic or international, is economic; and, unless purely politically inspired, nearly all the debates which for centuries have surrounded the topic of international trade have been argued in economic terms.[1]

The international executive needs to understand the underlying theoretical economic bases for international trade to fully appreciate the reasons for national economic policies whether of the home or host country. Certainly one of the more important uncontrollable environmental cultural constraints on companies' world trade efforts is national trade policies. To understand these trade policies and a company's position in the world economy, the international marketer must have a basic understanding of why nations trade.

Fundamental concepts and theories of international economics are essentially simple. The analysis derived from these simple concepts, however, is exceedingly complex; so complex, in fact, that no economist has been able to develop an analytical model which adequately takes all of the variables into consideration. The theory of international economics involves assumptions and accounts for only a few of the innumerable, unmeasurable, and sometimes unidentified variables. However, the theoretical economic constructs concerning international trade have sufficient accuracy and validity that anyone engaged in international marketing should have a basic familiarity with them. A noted international trade theorist asserts that "a good deal of misunderstanding and mismanagement on the part of our policymakers stems from this neglect of pure theory."

The discussion in this chapter provides a review of the basic ideas for individuals who have already studied this complex subject and it will introduce key theoretical concepts to those who have not had prior exposure.

---

[1] John C. Kimball, Ed., *The Trade Debate,* Department of State, Office of Public Communications, Bureau of Public Affairs (Washington D.C., 1978).

This chapter differs significantly from the typical treatise on international trade theory. While most books acknowledge that international trade theory is related to a market economy, they do not usually make this the primary focus of attention. In contrast, this discussion emphasizes the marketplace rather than production and makes direct comparison of the world marketplace and world market economics.

Three areas of theoretical analysis should be included in a complete work on international economic theory. The first (welfare economics) is the concept of comparative and absolute advantage; the gains which may be achieved by nations, groups, or individuals from international trade, and the underlying basis for these gains. The second area typically deals with monetary equilibrium and international balance of payments. The third area is closely related to the second, and analyzes the pricing mechanism through which prices of the factors of production are established in the international marketplace.

This chapter places special emphasis on the economic advantages to be derived from international trading. Monetary and pricing factors are considered at greater length in the pricing and financing chapters.

THE WORLD MARKETPLACE

Trading of goods has its roots in the earliest communal living experiences. Primitive people had a barter system, the early Greeks had their agoras, the Romans had their forums, and today we have our shopping centers. All these are marketplaces. It is not doing injustice to the term *market* to consider the entire world as a single marketplace today. A market is a place where buyers and sellers come together to exchange goods. Today, through intermediaries, the individual world citizen has access to the goods of the world in exchange for money.

If artificial barriers do not exist, the geographic size of the market for goods or services is most directly determined by the cost and speed of communications and the cost and speed of transporting goods or services. In recent years, each succeeding generation has found its marketplace grow larger until today we live in an era of a world marketplace. Not all goods or all marketplaces are involved in worldwide competition; however, the cost of transportation for many goods is prohibitive and there is insufficient differential production advantage to overcome these transportation costs. In theory, even high-bulk, low-value products may be placed in world competition; if the domestic price of portland cement, for example, is excessively high in one country or locality, the cement can conceivably be profitably shipped into that community. As a matter of fact, cement *is* regularly shipped from North to South America.

The emerging world economy in which we live not only brings us into world competition but brings significant advantages to both marketer and consumer. Marketers now find new markets open and small individual mar-

EXHIBIT 3–1: Dependence on world trade

	Value of manufactured exports, 1980 ($ billions)	Share of world exports, 1981	Exports as percent of GNP, —1980
United States	144	13.2	8.2
France	84	6.0	17.8
Germany	167	9.5	23.4
United Kingdom	86	6.0	22.3
Japan	124	8.0	12.5

Source: U.S. Department of Commerce, International Trade Administration, November 1981.

kets have grown and consolidated to the point that marketers can afford to produce or market in these countries. The consumer benefits through a wider range of goods offered and, unless there are artificial barriers such as tariffs, the opportunity to select the lowest-priced goods that can be produced anywhere in the world. Rapid growth of both imports and exports indicated that trading is beneficial, for no one buys or sells products unless they gain an advantage. Exhibit 3–1 shows just how important world trade is to many countries.

Marketing, including product differential advantage, consumer preference, advertising, and pricing, is assuming greater importance in the world scene. Emphasis on these factors is increasing for both consumer and industrial goods; at the same time, location and production economies have become less important. Whenever products leave the commodity category and become market differentiated, the advantage begins to accrue to the marketing-oriented company which can best fill customer needs and which offers the most benefits. No one knows this better than the U.S. automobile manufacturer competing with the Japanese.

Market-directed system

By purchasing goods and services in the marketplace and by placing one's own goods and services on the market, the citizen has, in essence, become subject to the market mechanism. The relevant market mechanism is that of the market in which the individual trades, so by trading in the world marketplace, one is subject to the world market mechanism. The purpose of this market mechanism is to regulate the flow and character of goods and services placed on the market and to establish a rate of return or price for those goods and services. Price serves as a primary variable in regulating supply and demand and aiding in resource allocation in a market system. If prices are too low, producers cannot afford to supply the market; if they are too high, consumers will not purchase the products.

Prices regulate local, domestic, and worldwide markets, and the free market inhibits those who provide unwanted goods or attempt to price goods above the market price. The worker who attempts to sell an obsolete skill or the manufacturer who cannot competitively produce a product must adjust price, product, or service to meet the needs of market conditions. Manufacturers who a few years ago were insulated from international competition and international markets now find the insulation of distance torn away. Open competition for markets, both domestic and international, is a major factor keeping industry "on its toes." One economist suggests that when industry is shielded from foreign competition in an attempt to protect a country's domestic producers, it only lessens the industry's future ability to compete. Such may be the case with steel and textiles in the United States.

Theoretically, the market is an automatic, competitive, self-regulating mechanism providing maximum consumer welfare and regulating the use of factors of production. The market metes out its rewards in proportion to productivity and demand for the products or services of the individual, firm, or nation. These two factors, market demand and productivity, are the crucial determinants of the standard of living differentials throughout the world.

Central planning system

There are essentially two methods of allocating goods and services and establishing prices. In their pure forms, one utilizes the market system and the other is guided by central planning.

In most modern economies, neither the market nor central planners are fully responsible for allocation and distribution of goods. The United States may be considered the champion of free enterprise and market system but each decade this country depends increasingly on central planning. At the other end of the spectrum are the Soviet Union and China with their differing philosophies of "pure" communism. With maturity, the Soviet economic system increasingly has taken market forces into account and continues to place greater emphasis on free market operations as it attempts to refine and improve its central planning systems. Market pricing, an anathema to Communist thinking, has become a major force in economic planning in the Soviet Union, and the market is increasingly being recognized in the People's Republic of China.

Central planning does offer certain economic benefits for a nation and facilitates allocation of scarce resources to meet governmental goals. Central planning may be used in an attempt to accomplish a variety of political objectives, such as emphasizing or deemphasizing certain sectors of the economy, maintaining full employment, or providing income redistribution. The United States is heavily involved in planning in agriculture but has proceeded cautiously in the consumer and industrial sectors.

Legislators in most free countries are reluctant to interfere with the market economy but have few compunctions about manipulating international trade. Most nations are willing to distort the world's free market system by establishing tariffs, nontariff barriers, and other methods of trade regulation and restriction. In these instances, political expediency or the judgment of governmental officials is being substituted for the impersonal, efficient selection process of the marketplace.

INTERNATIONAL TRADE AND ECONOMIC WELL-BEING

Gains from international trade are derived from variations in local production advantages; these, in turn, depend on differences in capital availability, specialization of labor, natural resource advantages, and labor or management skill advantages. The benefits of regional specialization on a national basis are so widely accepted that it is surprising that so many people debate the virtue of international regional specialization. No one would seriously question the logic of shipping rice from Louisiana, where water is plentiful, to arid Nebraska, but many individuals who do not understand the operation of the international marketplace would block equally logical transfers of goods from foreign countries. Such restrictions reduce the standard of living by attempting to refute the inherent logic of international trade.

World trading permits the fullest possible utilization of various regional advantages and, in turn, benefits both individuals and nations. The nation is benefited by using its skills and resources at the highest possible level of productivity. The individual benefits through the ability to purchase a higher standard of living. Profit for the manager provides the specific motivation for traders, but, ultimately, assortment of goods and price reduction to the consumer are the key forces underlying world trade. Price reduction is the benefit with which trade theories are primarily concerned. When two nations can produce a greater total amount of goods by specializing than the same two nations can produce individually, then there is a specific increase in productivity; and, with free trade, there is an increase in real income for the inhabitants of both nations. Besides the lower price on goods (which constitutes a greater real income if wages are constant), consumers benefit through having a broader selection of goods.

While lower price and wider variety are the benefits of international trade, the catalyst is profit. Middlemen who are actively engaged in the process of trading are most likely to be in trading for the profit they make. From the standpoint of the nation as a whole, the benefits of export marketing are increased foreign exchange and a satisfactory balance-of-payments position in the world economy. In recent years, the Soviet Union has aggressively sought joint ventures in many countries; the chief purpose is to build foreign markets for Soviet goods that will generate profits to help the nation's foreign exchange shortage. The CIA reports the number of such ventures has grown from 28 to 84 (including five in the United States). Lenin would be scandalized by such emphasis on profits.

World trade benefits to the consumer are clear: imports save money; maintain a competitive impact on domestic prices, production efficiency, innovation, and fashion; and supply merchandise not locally available, thus presenting a larger selection of styles and fashions. Yet trade barriers on some of the imports in greatest demand are costing the consumer up to 40 percent on price. In the short run, however, imports may cause severe unemployment, and this is one of the strongest political reasons why barriers to trade exist.

Like nearly all nations, U.S. policy on free trade has been one of ups and downs. In recent years, the economic benefits of free trade have been acknowledged by national leaders from both parties despite unrelenting pressures for increased trade protection. The U.S. always has been a strong proponent of free trade although politicians succumb to local industry pressures and resort to limited protectionism directly or indirectly. The most notable and recent involved the importation of automobiles. There have been some restrictions on imports but most pressure has been "arm-twisting" to get the Japanese to limit exports of autos to the United States under the thinly veiled threat that Congress may otherwise impose more severe restrictions. The Japanese complied by "voluntarily" limiting the number of automobiles shipped to the United States.

In both developed and developing countries, production capacity has increased rapidly. As labor becomes more skilled and greater capital becomes available for plant investment, world production capacity has outstripped market demand. Markets are glutted with goods; nations face low utilization of productive capacity; unemployment has risen; and these pressures inevitably lead to a growing emphasis on protectionism. Economic forces make it evident that the 1980s are becoming the decade of the "new protectionism"; a total reversal in the direction of 35 years of free trade and low tariffs started after World War II.[2]

Economic theories tend to assume goods are homogeneous, but in today's marketplace, quality, brand, and product differentials offer specific benefits to consumers. A further benefit of international trade is that it provides a substitute for factor mobility; goods rather than raw materials, laborers, or capital move from country to country or region to region. One measure of the extent of trade among nations is a country's balance of payments.

BALANCE OF PAYMENTS

When countries trade, a variety of financial transactions among businesses or consumers of different nations occur. Products and services are exported and imported, monetary gifts are exchanged, investments are made, cash payments are made and cash receipts are received, and vacation and foreign travel occurs. In short, over a period of time, there is a constant flow of money into and out of a country. The system of accounts that records a nation's international financial transactions is called its *balance of payments*.

The nation's balance-of-payments statement records all the financial trans-

---

[2] "The Erosion of Free Trade," *World Business Weekly,* June 8, 1981, p. 63.

actions between its residents and those of the rest of the world during a given period of time—usually one year. Because the balance-of-payments record is maintained on a double-entry bookkeeping system, it must always be in balance. As on an individual's financial statement, the assets and liabilities or the credits and debits must always offset each other. And like an individual's statement, the fact that they balance does not mean a nation is in particularly good or poor financial condition. A balance of payments is a record of condition, not a determinant of condition. Each of the nation's financial transactions with other countries is reflected in the balance of payments.

A nation's balance of payments presents an overall view of its international economic position and is an important economic measure used by governmental agencies such as treasuries, central banks, and other authorities whose responsibility is to maintain external and internal economic stability. The overall state of the balance of payments has an effect on a country's trade policies, its worldwide monetary value, and it may influence such domestic economic policies as wages, employment, and investment. The state of a country's balance of payments will affect the relative value of its currency and the ability of the country to acquire currencies of other nations. In international trade, countries continually assess the external positions and currency prospects of the countries with which they trade. As a consequence, a country's balance of payments also influences decisions of international businesses.

A balance of payments represents the difference between receipts from foreign countries on one side and payments to them on the other. On the plus side are export sales; money spent by foreign tourists; payments to the United States for insurance, transportation, and similar services; payments of dividends and interest on investments abroad; return of capital invested abroad; new foreign investments in the United States; and foreign government payments to the United States. On the minus side are costs of goods imported, spending by tourists overseas, new overseas investments, and the cost of foreign military and economic aid.

A balance-of-payments deficit occurs when international payments are greater than receipts. A deficit can be eliminated by: (1) increasing a country's international receipts, (for example, gain more exports or more tourists from abroad); or (2) reducing expenditures in other countries.

A balance-of-payments statement includes three major accounts: the *current account* which includes a record of all merchandise exports, imports, and services plus unilateral transfers of funds; the *capital account* which includes direct investment, portfolio investment, and short-term capital movements to and from countries; and the *official reserves account* which includes exports and imports of gold, increase or decrease in foreign exchange, and increases or decreases in liabilities to foreign central banks.

The current account is of primary interest to international businesses because it includes international trade and service accounts, that is, accounts of the value of all merchandise and services imported and exported by a country. The relationship between imports and exports is frequently referred to as the *balance of trade*. It is only one aspect of the balance of payments. If a country exports more goods than it imports, it is said to have a favorable balance of trade; if it imports more goods than it exports, it is said to have an unfavorable balance of trade. In only 3 years since 1970 has the United States had a favorable balance of trade. This means that for each year there was an unfavorable balance, the United States imported goods with a higher dollar value than the goods it exported. Causes of this imbalance were primarily the result of heavy U.S. demand for foreign petroleum, foreign cars, and industrial machinery.

The current account is generally the largest account in the balance-of-payments statement. Thus, in most situations where a country has a negative balance of trade it also has a negative balance of payments. However, both the balance of trade and the balance of payments do not necessarily have to be negative. At times, a country may have a favorable balance of trade and a negative balance of payments or vice versa. Such was the case in the United States during the Korean and Vietnam Wars when there was a favorable balance of trade but a negative balance of payments. This imbalance was caused by heavy foreign aid assistance by the United States to other countries and the high cost of conducting the Korean and Vietnam Wars.

Influences such as rapidly escalated international oil prices and national inflation have been major factors in the composition of imports and in the balance of payments for most nations, and have caused fluctuations of world monetary values. The Japanese import 90 percent of their oil and have seen their oil bill jump from 800 billion yen in 1970 to 5,509 billion yen in 1974 and 8 trillion yen in 1980. French oil imports grew seven times in franc value in the same period while French exports of the same period grew less than three times. The Brazilian situation was even more dramatic; the U.S. dollar value of Brazilian imports rose from $325 million to well over $4 billion in the same 10-year period. U.S. petroleum imports grew from $2.5 billion in 1970 to over $56 billion in 1979. Such imbalances have drastic effects on balance of trade, balance of payments, and, therefore, the value of local currency in the world market place.[3]

Factors such as these eventually require adjustments in the balance of payments through changes in exchange rates, prices, and/or incomes. In short, once the wealth of a country whose expenditures exceed its income has been exhausted, that country, like an individual, must reduce its standard of living. If its residents do not do so voluntarily, the rate of exchange of its money for foreign monies will decline; and through the medium of the

---

[3] "U.S. Balance of Payments is Looking Good with a Few Reservations," *Business International,* June 19, 1981, pp. 194–95.

foreign exchange market, purchasing power will be transferred from that country to another country.

In summary, the balance of payments, balance of trade, and exchange fluctuations all relate to the basic process of recording and adjusting international financial relationships and are important considerations in understanding how and why countries trade.

THEORY OF RELATIVE ADVANTAGE

Three theories of international trade have been developed in the past century and a half: classical, opportunity cost, and equilibrium theories. All three theories have at their core the concept of relative advantage. The following sections consider relative advantage from the viewpoints of absolute and comparative advantage. This presentation follows the classical analysis which simplifies the problem by studying only two products and two nations at one time. The opportunity and equilibrium models are not considered here; they add refinement, but, in so doing, add complications which need not concern the nonprofessional economist.[4]

Absolute cost advantage

When a good can be produced more cheaply in one country than in another, the first is said to have an absolute cost advantage. The situation in which one country has an absolute advantage over another country provides a basis for easy analysis. Take, for example, wheat produced in the United States and cork produced in Spain. Both countries can produce each product, but because of climate and old native stands of cork oak in Spain, the cork would cost considerably more to produce in the United States than in Spain. Conversely, wheat costs considerably more to produce in Spain than in the United States. Therefore, assuming that the difference

---

BOX 3–1: Two points of view

Seen from the United States, Japan has a record—and mounting—surplus in her balance of payments and in her international trade. Seen from Japan, this "surplus" looks more like a record write-off of massive inventory losses.

Seen from the United States, the Japanese economic policy looks only too successful—a commercial juggernaut that knows no bounds. Seen from Tokyo, Japan is now beginning to face up to the consequences of monumental economic and business blunders that threaten to sink, or at least slow, the juggernaut.

Source: Peter F. Drucker, "A Troubled Japanese Juggernaut," Reprinted with permission of *The Wall Street Journal*, © Dow Jones & Company, Inc. (1977). All Rights Reserved.

---

[4] For those interested in more extensive coverage of the topic, see Friedrich Klaus, *International Economics* (New York: McGraw-Hill, 1977), 322 pp.

in efficiency (and cost) is greater than the cost of transportation, it would be advantageous for the two countries to exchange products.

It is interesting to note, incidentally, the transitory nature of a nation's advantage. Despite the fact that cork oaks do not reach maximum productivity until they are 50 years old, California cork is now being commercially grown and harvested and has underpriced and supplanted Spanish cork in many applications.

Comparative cost advantage

The principle of comparative advantage applies when one country can produce both goods or all goods more cheaply than another country.[5] International trade can take place beneficially even though one country produces both products more cheaply; in fact, much world trading is done in products in which there is a comparative rather than an absolute advantage. Each country produces and trades the goods in which it has the advantage. The gains come from concentrating productive effort in each country on the products that it can produce best. As the following examples show, the total output will be greater with specialization than without, so there will be more goods to share if there is specialization and trade. The same principle applies to regions and to nations.

In its simplest form comparative advantage may be related to division of skills and labor. Consider the case of a well-known brain surgeon whose fees exceed $100 per hour. The same dexterity and manual skills which make his time so valuable have given him a reputation as an outstanding cabinetmaker; he is probably a better cabinetmaker than the great majority of professional cabinetmakers. Still, although he makes fine cabinets as a hobby, it would be foolish of him to sell any of his time at the cabinetmaker rate of $15 per hour. One exception: he may profitably engage in both activities if he is unable to sell all of his medical time. The factor of surplus labor is often overlooked in the application of comparative advantage.

Perhaps the concept of comparative advantage will be most easily understood through a series of examples. For the following situations, imagine two primitive island societies in which the only goods of value traded are clay pots and woven sifters. Assume that maximum productivity is desired because the pots and sifters wear out rapidly or are hoarded as signs of wealth. Assume further that island Abu can produce both products more efficiently than neighboring island Bua. More specifically, the inhabitants of Abu (Abus) have natural advantages which make it possible for one worker to produce either *three pots or three sifters per day*. The Buans

---

[5] For an interesting application see Harold J. Hoy and John J. Shaw, "The United States Comparative Advantage and Its Relationship to the Product Life Cycle Theory and the World Gross National Product Market Share," *Columbia Journal of World Business*, Spring 1981, pp. 40–50.

(inhabitants of Bua) have a productivity rate of *two pots or one sifter per day*. Each country happens to have 10 persons of working age.

Illustration 1 assumes no world trade or specialization and further assumes that productive labor is allocated equally to pots and sifters. Total production is twice as high in Abu as in Bua. Total production for the two-island economy is 45 pots and sifters per day. The real income of the Abus is twice that of the Buans. Illustration 2 assumes that Buans attempt to specialize in their least-advantageous product—sifters.

ILLUSTRATION 1: Production per working day

	Pots	Sifters	Total
Abu	15	15	30
Bua	10	5	15
Total	25	20	45

ILLUSTRATION 2: Production per working day

	Pots	Sifters	Total
Abu	15	15	30
Bua	0	10	10
Total	15	25	40

Because of this ill-chosen specialization, the total production of the two economies declines. The Buans are even poorer relative to the Abus than in the first illustration and the Abu:Bua standard of living ratio becomes 3:1. Trade can take place as long as Buans want pots, but the real income of the Buans will still be lower than if they produced both products themselves.

Illustration 3 assumes that Bua specializes in its most advantageous product (pots) and trades with Abu for its sifters. Assume that Abu still divides its production equally between pots and sifters. If there is no positive preference for one product over another, world trade need not result, but trade will be advantageous if inhabitants of Bua desire both products. It does not matter to Abus whether they make pots or sifters since they make both equally well, so prices (barter ratios, that is) will depend on the relative trading abilities of inhabitants of the two countries. If the Abus will trade

ILLUSTRATION 3: Production per working day

	Pots	Sifters	Total
Abu	15	15	30
Bua	20	0	20
Total	35	15	50

on a one-for-one basis, the relative standards of living will be 3:2. Note that production at a level of 50 units per day is available for sharing, whereas it was only 45 per day without trade.

Illustration 4 shows the optimum production mix for both countries if the market *desires equal numbers* of pots and sifters. Obviously, Bua should specialize and produce only pots. The Buans still cannot supply half of the two societies' pots; Abu will divide its production between the two products. It has the greatest relative advantage (3:1) in sifters so will emphasize sifter production; in fact, five sixths of its effort will be devoted to sifters and one sixth to pots.

ILLUSTRATION 4: Production per working day

	Pots	Sifters	Total
Abu	5	25	30
Bua	20	0	20
Total	25	25	50

As in Illustration 3, one cannot determine exactly the final allocation of the pots and sifters. Even in such a primitive society the division of products between the two countries will depend on "marketing" skills. Abu will never have to trade on less than a one-for-one basis, because it can produce at this level itself. At the extremes it may be possible for either country to derive the full benefits from trading: Abu could end up with 35 units of production and Bua with 15. Alternatively, Buans could gain up to 20 units. Probably the two countries would share the gains.

In addition to the existence of demand, a few other conditions may be necessary before actual trading would take place.

1. Production gains must be greater than the costs of trading and shipping.
2. Products must be identical or equally acceptable in the minds of middlemen and consumers, regardless of national origin.
3. There must be a sufficiently effective market information network so that traders in both countries are aware of cost differentials.
4. The differential must be sufficient to interest an entrepreneur in trading, that is, provide a profit.
5. Tariffs must not exist or must not exceed the difference in costs after transportation and profit are considered.
6. No other governmental or financial restrictions inhibit the products and trading of those products.

In summary, remember that the economic basis of international trade is no different than that of interregional trade. Goods may be shipped beneficially from one region or one country to another whenever there is a situation of comparative advantage. Commodities or goods will be imported from one place to another if the imported price plus the cost of transportation and any other costs (such as tariffs) are less than the domestic price. However, trading will occur only if the costs differ by an amount which is great enough to make trading worthwhile. The last idea, essentially the element of profit, has often been neglected in the theoretical analyses of economists; but, profit must be present and adequate to justify shipment of goods from one geographic location to another.

Businesses of one country trade with businesses of another. It is the business firm which is the decision-making force behind most international trade. Naturally, businesses engage in international trade to make a profit but the task is not always an easy one since a country's economic goals do not always include a foreign firm's need for profits. Governments frequently protect their markets from intrusion by foreign companies.

MARKET PROTECTION

The theoretical and logical arguments for free trade have equal validity in all countries, yet international businesses must face the reality that they live in a world of tariffs, quotas, and nontariff barriers. All governmentally imposed barriers are imposed through the political pressures of business for protection of their markets.

Despite, or perhaps because of, the fact that the free marketplace is such an effective regulator of competition and prices, there is a tendency for individual executives, and nations as well, to attempt to escape the dominance of the marketplace in international trade. Nations utilize legal barriers, exchange barriers, and psychological barriers to restrain entry of unwanted goods. Businesses work together to establish private market barriers, and the market itself may provide formidable barriers to imported goods.

Protection logic and illogic

There are countless reasons for maintenance of governmental restrictions on trade espoused by protectionists, but essentially all arguments can be classified under the following headings: (1) protection of an infant industry, (2) protection of the home market, (3) need to keep money at home, (4) encouragement of capital accumulation, (5) maintenance of the standard of living and real wages, (6) conservation of natural resources, (7) industrialization of a low-wage nation, (8) maintenance of employment and reduction of unemployment, (9) national defense, (10) increase of business size, and (11) retaliation and bargaining. Economists in general have recognized as valid only the arguments for infant industry, national defense, and industrialization of underdeveloped countries. The resource conservation argument becomes increasingly valid in an era of environmental consciousness and worldwide shortages of raw materials and agricultural commodities.

There might be a case for *temporary* protection of markets with excess productive capacity or excess labor when such protection could facilitate an orderly transition. Unfortunately, however, such protection becomes long term and contributes to industrial inefficiency while detracting from a nation's realistic adjustment to its world situation. Even the admission of these protectionist arguments is severely restricted and applies only in limited circumstances.

Because of their acceptability, most protectionists will argue the need for tariffs on one of these three premises whether or not they are relevant to their products. When arguing a case for protection of a particular industry, proponents are also likely to call on the maintenance-of-employment argument because it has substantial political appeal. The ludicrous aspect of the situation is that these arguments are used even though they are completely irrelevant to the product in question. Sugar and textiles are good examples of protected industries in the United States which cannot be justified by any of the three arguments. When arguing for protection, the basic economic advantages of international trade are ignored. The fact that the consumer ultimately bears the cost of tariffs and other protective measures is conveniently overlooked. Sugar is a good example of the illogic of protection. U.S. sugar prices are artificially held higher than world prices for no sound economic reason. Regardless of the logical or illogical nature of protectionism, trade barriers do exist.[6]

Trade barriers

To encourage development of domestic industry and protect existing industry, governments may establish a whole host of barriers to trade including tariffs, quotas, boycotts, monetary barriers, nontariff barriers, and market barriers. Barriers are imposed not only against imports, but against foreign businesses as well. The inspiration for such barriers may be economic or political, but they are typically encouraged by local industry. Whether or not the barriers are economically logical, the fact remains that they do exist.

Tariffs. The tariff, simply defined, is a tax imposed by a government on goods entering at its borders. Tariffs are used as a revenue-generating tax or to discourage the importation of goods. In Mexico, for example, the tariff on foreign fabricated auto parts ranges from 60–80 percent of the item's value; obviously, this tariff is designed to protect local industry. In general, tariffs:

Increase Inflationary pressures.
Special interests' privileges.
Government control and political considerations in economic matters.
The number of tariffs (they beget other tariffs).

---

[6] For a discussion of this issue see John Hein, "Paging Adam Smith—," *Across The Board,* January 1981, pp. 44–48.

Weaken   Balance-of-payments positions.
           Supply-and-demand patterns.
           International understanding (they can start trade wars).
Restrict Manufacturers' supply sources.
           Choices available to consumers.
           Competition.

In addition, tariffs are arbitrary, discriminatory, and require constant administration and supervision.

In addition to tariffs, governments restrict imports in a variety of other ways. All countries impose some nontariff barriers. Among them are restrictions on the quality of goods that may enter a country, sanitary and health requirements, methods of classifying and placing value on imports, and antidumping regulations, border taxes, and domestic subsidies. Nontariff barriers tend to gain importance as import duties are lowered. Some of the more frequently used barriers are quotas, embargoes or boycotts, and standards requirements. Exhibit 3–2 gives a complete list of nontariff barriers.

Quotas. A quota is a specific numerical or dollar limit applied to a particular type of good. For example, there is a limit on imported television sets in Great Britain, German quotas on Japanese ball-bearings, Italian restrictions on Japanese motorcycles, and Japanese quotas on citrus fruits and other agricultural items. Quotas are designed to put an absolute restriction on a variety of items being imported into a country. In addition, items limited by quota may have tariffs imposed as well. Like tariffs, quotas tend to increase prices. For example, a U.S. honeydew mellon which is under a strict quota retails for $35 in Tokyo.[7]

Boycott. A government boycott is an absolute restriction against the purchase and importation of certain goods from other countries. A public boycott can be either formal or informal and may be government sponsored or sponsored by an industry. It is not unusual for the citizens of a country to boycott goods of other countries at the urging of their government or civic groups. Sometimes executives in a particular industry will attempt to rouse public sympathy for that industry and induce a voluntary boycott against imported competitive goods. During the past decade, for example, the U.S. steel industry has been engaged in a campaign to urge steel users to purchase domestic steel products—solely because they are domestic.

An informal limitation, the Buy-American Act of 1933, was legislated as an antidepression measure. It is still on the books today. Interestingly, it is now under attack while other countries are initiating similar legislation and emphasizing their administration of nonlegislated buy-national policies. In the United Kingdom, for example, there is pressure not to buy imported capital goods; there is even pressure against buying goods made in the

---

[7] Louis Kraar, "Inside Japan's 'Open' Market," *Fortune,* October 5, 1981, p. 119.

EXHIBIT 3–2: Types of nontariff barriers

Specific limitations on trade:
  Quotas
  Import licensing requirements
  Proportion restrictions of foreign to domestic goods
  Minimum imports price limits
  Embargoes
Customs and administrative entry procedures:
  Valuation systems
  Antidumping practices
  Tariff classifications
  Documentation requirements
  Fees
Standards:
  Standard disparities
  Intergovernmental acceptances of testing methods and standards
  Packaging, labeling, marking standards
Government participation in trade:
  Government procurement policies
  Export subsidies
  Countervailing duties
  Domestic assistance programs
Charges on imports:
  Prior import deposit requirements
  Administrative fees
  Special supplementary duties
  Import credit discriminations
  Variable levies
  Border taxes
Others:
  Voluntary export restraints
  Orderly marketing agreements

Source: A. D. Cao, "Non-Tariff Barriers to U.S. Manufactured Exports," *The Columbia Journal of World Business*, Summer 1980, p. 94.

United Kingdom by foreign-owned corporations when similar goods are available from locally owned companies.

A particularly insidious type of boycott has developed in the last decade; the economic boycott used to achieve political ends. In 1978, some products were boycotted by a large number of countries over the issue of black rights. Arab countries boycott Israel and Israel, in return, boycotts them over the Palestine question. Cuba is boycotted by Brazil and South Korea because it supports revolutionary activities in both countries. Portugal is boycotted by a dozen African countries; all communist countries are boycotted by Taiwan; Taiwan is boycotted by China (PRC) and Pakistan; the list goes on and on.[8] Whatever the cause, such trade dislocations are a great

---

[8] For an update on the current status of boycotts see "Boycotts Revisited: Fewer Countries on Lists, But Growing Intensity," *Business International*, April 10, 1981, pp. 113–14.

BOX 3–2: A word for open markets

    Bastiat's century-old farcical letter to the French Chamber of Deputies points up the ultimate folly of tariffs and the advantages of utilizing the superior production advantage of others.

To the Chamber of Deputies:

    We are subjected to the intolerable competition of a foreign rival, who enjoys such superior facilities for the production of light that he can *innundate* our *national market* at reduced price. This rival is no other than the sun. Our petition is to pass a law shutting up all windows, openings, and fissures through which the light of the sun is used to penetrate our dwellings, to the prejudice of the profitable manufacture we have been enabled to bestow on the country.

Signed: Candlestick Makers,
F. Bastiat

---

disservice to the world economy. However, they also point up the vitality of economic forces because they are widely ignored when it is more convenient to do so. South Africa trades openly with many of the countries boycotting it and covertly with others. One diplomat says, "Hypocrisy is the main ingredient on this continent . . . it's the market forces at play. Most African countries are so poor they can't afford to be moral in their transactions." As of 1978, a new U.S. export administration act prohibits U.S. "persons" from supporting, furthering, or complying with boycotts not approved by the United States government. For many companies this poses further problems in their attempts to deal effectively with Arab countries whose boycott of Israel is not sanctioned.

Monetary barriers. A government can effectively regulate its international trade position by various forms of exchange-control restrictions. A government may enact such restrictions to preserve its balance-of-payment position or specifically for the advantage or encouragement of particular industries. Three types of barriers should be considered: blocked currency, differential exchange rates, and governmental approval requirements (for securing foreign exchange). *Blocked currency* is used as a political weapon or as a response to difficult balance-of-payment situations. In effect, blockage cuts off all importing or all importing above a certain level. Blockage is accomplished by refusing to redeem national currencies in the world financial marketplace.

The *differential exchange rate* is a particularly ingenious method of controlling imports. It encourages the importation of goods the government deems desirable and discourages importation of goods the government does not want. The essential mechanism requires the importer to pay varying amounts of domestic currency for foreign exchange with which to purchase products in different categories. For example, the exchange rate for a desirable category of goods might be one unit of domestic money for one unit of a specific foreign currency. For a less-desirable product, the exchange rate might be two domestic currency units for one foreign unit. For an undesirable product, the exchange rate might be three domestic units for one foreign unit. An importer of an undesired product has to pay three times as much for the foreign exchange as the importer of a desired product. This device has been used by several South American countries.

Governmental approval to secure foreign exchange is growing in importance. Most Latin American and East European countries require all foreign exchange transactions to be approved by a central minister. Thus, importers who want to buy a foreign good must apply for an exchange permit, that is, permission to exchange an amount of local currency for foreign currency. The exchange permit may also stipulate the rate of exchange which can be an unfavorable rate depending on what the government desires. In addition, the exchange permit may stipulate that the amount to be exchanged must be deposited in a local bank for a set period prior to the transfer of goods. For example, Brazil has a program that requires funds to be deposited 360 days prior to the import date. This is extremely restrictive since funds are out of circulation and subject to the ravages of 36–50 percent inflation. Such policies cause major cash flow problems for the importer and greatly increase the price of imports. Needless to say, these currency-exchange barriers constitute a major deterrent to trade.

Standards. Nontariff barriers of this category include standards to protect health, safety, and product quality. The standards are sometimes used in an unduly stringent or discriminating way in order to restrict trade, but the sheer volume of regulations in this category is a problem in itself. Fruit content regulations for jam vary so much from country to country that one agricultural specialist says, "A jam exporter needs a computer to avoid one or another country's regulations." Plant and animal quarantine regulations serve an important function, but often are used solely to keep out foreign products. Although all countries use standards to some extent, Japan has raised the process to the level of art. Differing standards is one major disagreement between the United States and Japan.[9] American companies are often confronted by government standards that make it almost impossible to import any goods not tested in Japan. This is dramatically evident with autos. Before an American car can be sold in Japan, its government requires six volumes of documents on standards for each auto plus local testing of nearly every vehicle. This adds as much as $500 to the retail price of a U.S. car in Japan. In contrast, Japanese exports into the United States require only the manufacturer's label certifying the cars meet American safety standards. While many standards may not be maliciously intended to keep

---

[9] In response to criticism leveled against Japanese import procedures, the Ministerial Conference for Economic Measures is simplifying or examining 99 Japanese standards and procedures. For a summary of the decisions see JETRO Special Report, "Japan Improves Import Procedures," January 30, 1982.

out imports, they do so by being so arbitrary or obtuse that importers become discouraged. Sweden, for example, insists on testing all foreign electrical appliances in its own labs, a costly and time-consuming bottleneck.[10]

Not to be overlooked in this category are the FDA (Federal Drug Administration) requirements for the sale of pharmaceutical drugs in the United States. On the average, it takes 12 years of testing before a new drug product will be licensed for sale in the United States. Although this precaution may not have been designed to limit the importation of pharmaceutical drugs, it does, in fact, result in such.

BOX 3–3: Not quite blocked

. . . the mysterious market in which blocked accounts—funds trapped by government fiat within a given country—changed hands. There are billions of dollars worth of blocked accounts around the world, much of it owned by U.S. corporations. A buying-and-selling market exists to make use of these funds, sometimes in deals arranged directly between companies, sometimes through a bank as an intermediary. But often, buyer and seller are brought together by foreign-money brokers in a murky gray area. . . . Brokers tell of markdowns ranging from 2 percent to 50 percent, depending mostly on the eagerness of the seller.

The countries in which blocked funds are held range from underdeveloped nations like Ghana and Zaire to fully industrialized ones like Italy and France. There are many degrees of blockage, from the mildest regulation of the outflow of money to ironclad embargoes. Some blockages last for a relatively short time. Others go on for years; U.S.-based multinational corporations have had accounts in Greece blocked since World War II. Many blockages, of course, stem from political upheavals or from a new regime coming into power. On the other hand, funds may be blocked because of a dispute between a company and the government over an issue far removed from currency regulations. Or the blockage may grow out of a wider problem, such as a nationwide shortage of foreign exchange or chronically weak domestic currencies. That is why blockage is most prevalent in underdeveloped countries, such as India and many younger African nations.

Source: "The Mysterious Market in Blocked Accounts." Reprinted with special permission of *Dun's Review*, October 1976. © 1976 by Dun & Bradstreet Publications Corporation.

Imports are not the only target of discrimination in international business. Many countries make it difficult or impossible to establish foreign production subsidiaries that might compete with local business. For years Japan held foreign investors at bay, and virtually no important industries in that country may be 100-percent foreign owned. Many countries, of course, require substantial local participation. Strict capital and profit repatriation rules can have a nearly identical effect. European countries have bristled at foreign mergers that would mean takeover of local companies; numerous major

---

[10] Peter Nulty, "Why the 'Tokyo Round' Was a U.S. Victory," *Fortune*, May 21, 1979, p. 133.

mergers have been stopped at the last minute by various national governments. Governments can easily exclude foreign goods from the marketplace by refusing to award public contracts to any plants or producers who have purchased foreign goods against the government's wishes.

Foreign restrictions abound and the United States can be counted among those governments using restrictions. For over a decade, U.S. government officials have been arranging "voluntary" agreements with the Japanese steel industry to limit sales to the United States. Similar negotiations with the governments of major textile producers have limited textile imports into the United States.

In the 10 years before 1978, imported shoes captured 46 percent of the U.S. market, closing 300 American shoe factories. U.S. trade negotiators were dispatched to Taiwan, South Korea, Spain, Brazil, and Uruguay to reach informal agreements that would restrain shoe exports to the United States.

Market barriers

The location, size, and structure of a market may deter international goods from entering a given marketplace. Just as large companies in the domestic market tend to ignore villages and hamlets in their marketing plans, so companies engaged in international business are likely to overlook small markets when the vastly broader potential of larger ones remains untapped. A country may be denied possible benefits of international trading because size or remote location make it unprofitable as a market. Distance and aggregate purchasing power or market potential for a given product are key considerations, but they too may be modified by the extent and level of competition within a country. One market may be relatively untapped while another is beyond consideration because competition has preempted it. Very lucrative markets may be closed to international competition because of cartels or other privately imposed market barriers.

Even the habit patterns of consumers in world markets build market barriers. Companies are reluctant to enter markets with unfamiliar local customs and purchasing behavior because of the high possibility of failure. Inadequate channels of distribution can also provide natural market barriers to companies wishing to operate at a mass-distribution level.

In the final analysis, natural market barriers are probably the more formidable deterrents to international trade. If markets appear to offer promise of great profits, most governmental, exchange, and psychological barriers can be surmounted by ingenious businesses. Even though countries tend to instigate barriers to trade, they also appreciate the interdependence of the world's economies and thus strive to lower barriers in a controlled and equitable manner. The General Agreement on Tariffs and Trade (GATT) is one such attempt by countries working together to promote world trade.

**"DO SOMETHING. THAT FOREIGNER IS COMPET-
ING WITH ME."**

Source: *The Colorado Daily*, December 7, 1977, p. 6.

EASING TRADE RESTRICTIONS

Shrinking communication and transportation barriers throughout the world have focused attention in recent years on methods of breaking down artificial barriers, such as tariffs and boycotts, which exist between otherwise natural markets. Contributing to this desire for easier trade has been a high level of productive capacity of various nations, particularly the industrialized nations. If a firm or nation has adequate markets at home, it is not inclined to seek markets elsewhere; but when the productive capacity outruns domestic consumption there is a natural desire to extend the borders of the marketplace. Two major activities to ease trade restrictions have occurred in recent years: (1) development of trade and commercial treaties; and (2) the improvement of international monetary systems.

General Agreement on Tariffs and Trade

Historically, trade treaties were negotiated on a *bilateral* (between two nations) basis, with little attention given to relationships with other countries.

Further, there was a tendency to raise barriers rather than extend markets and restore world trade. The United States and 22 other countries signed the General Agreement on Tariffs and Trade (GATT) shortly after World War II. Although not all countries participated, this agreement paved the way for the first effective worldwide tariff agreement. The original agreement provided a process to reduce tariffs and created an agency to serve as watchdog over world trade. The GATT agency director and staff offer nations a forum for negotiating trade in related issues. Member nations (85 in 1981) seek to resolve their trade disputes bilaterally, but if that fails, special GATT panels are set up to recommend action. The panels are only advisory and have no enforcement powers.

The GATT treaty and subsequent meetings have produced agreements significantly reducing tariffs on a wide range of goods. Periodically member nations meet to reevaluate trade barriers and establish international codes designed to foster trade among members. In general, the agreement covers these basic elements: (1) trade shall be conducted on a nondiscriminatory basis; (2) protection shall be afforded domestic industries through customs tariff, not through such commercial measures as import quotas; and (3) consultation shall be the primary method used to solve global trade problems. Under GATT, there have been 7 "rounds" of intergovernmental tariff negotiations since its inception. The most recent was the "Tokyo Round" which was concluded in 1979.

Earlier GATT agreements focused on tariff reductions while the Tokyo Round addressed tariff restrictions and a strong assault was made on the more insidious protectionist devices, nontariff barriers.[11] During negotiations of the Tokyo Round, the world economies were suffering from severe inflation and recessions because of increased prices for petroleum products. As a result, many countries resorted to various protectionist devices. For example, the United Kingdom imposed quota limits on imports of polyester filaments and cotton yarn from the United States, textile imports into Italy could enter the country only through 10 specified ports, and delays in documentation necessary to export sweaters to France happened to coincide with the buying season. These and other nontariff barriers were a major focus of the Tokyo Round.

While the biggest breakthrough in the Tokyo Round was in agreements to restrict nontariff barriers, there was also an agreement to cut world tariffs by an average of 33 percent on some 5,700 items over an eight-year period. Previous rounds of trade talks (the Tokyo Round was the seventh since GATT was formed in 1947) have lowered tariffs to the point where, for many industries, they represent little or no trade impediment at all. The average level of tariffs is 8.3 percent in the United States, 9.8 percent in

---

[11] "The Growing Perils of Protectionists," *International Management*, May 1980, pp. 16–19.

the European community, 10.9 percent in Japan, and 15.5 percent in Canada. That is considerably lower than the 50 and 60 percent levels which were in force during the height of protectionism in the 1932 depression era. When the Tokyo Round cuts become fully effective by 1988, the average tariff will be 4.3 percent in the United States and only 2.5 percent in Japan.[12]

The adoption of rules or codes to curb the growing use of nontariff barriers was the most significant outcome of the Tokyo Round. This breakthrough has the greatest potential for spurring trade. As tariffs have come down since the beginning of GATT, these nontrade barriers have become the main impediment to international commerce. The areas of agreement are:

1. Control of various subsidies that shield inefficient domestic industries from import competition. The code does not seek to eliminate these subsidies, but only to control the types of subsidies used and their impact on traditional patterns of trade.

2. The "procurement code" designed to make government contracts available to competition. Presently, most countries, including the United States, have "buy-America" policies (i.e., buy home-manufactured goods only) for all government contracts. This procurement code will mean that some government purchases will be open to foreign suppliers.

3. A code to control arbitrary product standards that tend to discourage imports. Perhaps this code is the most significant one in the Tokyo Round. The new code does not dictate the standards a country uses for goods it imports, but it does call for open procedures in adopting standards and sets up a review procedure for settling disputes. One of the more restrictive barriers in trade are standards such as health requirements, performance requirements, and tests required before a product can be imported into a country.

4. A code to standardize the valuation of imported goods to curb counterfitting of merchandise and to simplify import licensing procedures.

5. A code that temporarily will extend "safeguards" (mostly quotas) to any importing country when one of its industries is suffering because of a sudden surge of imports. The safeguards could be invoked even though the imports were priced fairly, that is, imports neither subsidized nor sold at prices below production costs.[13]

On balance, this new round of treaties has been well received by member nations; however, there are those who wonder how effectively they will be enforced if worldwide recession continues and countries can push exports at almost any price.[14] When such conditions occur, protectionism tends to

---

[12] Peter Nulty, "Why the 'Tokyo Round' Was a U.S. Victory," *Fortune,* May 21, 1979, p. 131.

[13] Clyde Hartz, "The New GATT—Successor to the Kennedy Round: Part 1—The Nontariff Agreements," *Business Economics,* May 1979, pp. 5–8.

[14] See, for example, "Tokyo Agreement Revisited: Lack of Wide Application Confuses Rules for MNCs," *Business International,* March 21, 1980, p. 89.

increase and nontariff barriers are the most difficult trade impediments to control.

International Monetary Fund

Inadequate monetary reserves and unstable currencies are particularly vexing problems in world trade. So long as these conditions exist, world markets will not develop and function as effectively as they should. To overcome these particular market barriers, which plagued international trading before World War II, the International Monetary Fund (IMF) was formed. Among its objectives was the stabilization of foreign exchange rates and the establishment of freely convertible currencies. Later, the European Payments Union was formed to facilitate multinational payments. While the International Monetary Fund has some severe critics, most agree that it has performed a valuable service and at least partially achieved many of its objectives.

To cope with universally floating exchange rates, the IMF developed special drawing rights (SDRs), one of the more useful inventions of the IMF. Since both gold and the U.S. dollar have lost their utility as the basic medium of financial exchange, most monetary statistics relate to SDRs rather than dollars. The SDR is, in effect, "paper gold" and represents an average base of value derived from the value of a group of major currencies. Rather than being denominated in the currency of any given country, trade contracts are written more frequently in terms of SDRs because they are much less

GATT—a projected overpass

Philadelphia Evening Bulletin

susceptible to exchange rate fluctuations. Even floating rates do not necessarily accurately reflect exchange relationships. Some countries permit their currencies to float cleanly without manipulation (clean float) while other nations systematically manipulate the value of their currency (dirty float), thus modifying the accuracy of the monetary market place.[15]

Although the motivation for economic and technical assistance in this cold war age is undoubtedly more political than economic, the results have been to upgrade the economies of many nations and to bring many new, small, and underdeveloped nations into the world marketplace. Many of the developing nations represent potential growth markets of the future and should be considered in any evaluation of world markets.

SUMMARY

Regardless of the theoretical approach used in defense of international trade, it is clear that the benefits from absolute or comparative advantage can accrue to any nation. Open markets are needed if world resources are to be developed and utilized in the most beneficial manner. It is true that there are circumstances when market protection may be needed and may be beneficial to national defense or the encouragement of infant industries in developing nations. The temptation, however, is always toward excessive market protection or, more correctly, excessive producer protection, because the consumer seldom benefits from such protection. Because free international markets can help underdeveloped countries become self-sufficient and because open markets provide new customers, most industrialized nations have, since World War II, cooperated in working toward freer trade. Such trade will always be partially threatened by various governmental and market barriers which exist or are created for the protection of local businesses, although the trend in the past few decades has been toward freer trade.

QUESTIONS

1. Define:

Absolute advantage	Exchange rate fluctuation
Relative advantage	Tariff
GATT	IMF
Market mechanism	Psychological market protection

2. Differentiate between:
    Balance of payments and balance of trade.
    Exchange barriers and market barriers.

3. Why is the actual analysis of international economic behavior so complex?

---

[15] See Chapter 21 for a more detailed discussion of international financial management.

4. Differentiate among the three main areas of theoretical analysis of international economics.

5. Explain the role of price as a free market regulator.

6. "Theoretically, the market is an automatic, competitive, self-regulating mechanism which provides for the maximum consumer welfare and which best regulates the use of the factors of production." Explain.

7. Review the economic gains that can be accomplished through world trade. Cite specific examples.

8. Interview several local business people to determine their attitudes toward world trade. Further, learn if they buy or sell goods produced in foreign countries. Correlate the attitudes and report on your findings.

9. What is the role of profit in international trade? Does profit replace or complement the regulatory function of pricing? Discuss.

10. Explain the economics of the situation when one country can trade with another that can produce all products more cheaply than the first.

11. What special conditions need to be fulfilled before trade will actually take place in the situation of comparative advantage?

12. Why does the balance of payments always balance even though the balance of trade does not?

13. Enumerate the ways in which a nation can overcome an unfavorable balance of trade.

14. Support or refute each of the various arguments commonly used in support of tariffs.

15. Can central planning be appropriately applied to economies of such diverse countries as the United States, the USSR, Ghana, and Brazil?

16. France exports about 18 percent of its GDP, neighboring Belgium exports 46 percent. What areas of economic policy are likely to be affected by such variations in exports?

17. Does widespread unemployment change the economic logic of protectionism?

18. Review the economic effects of major trade imbalances such as those caused by petroleum imports.

19. The Tokyo Round of GATT has emphasized the reduction of nontariff barriers. What does this mean and what is the importance of nontariff barriers in international trade?

20. Why will the 1980s be known as the decade of the "new protectionism"?

CASES—PART ONE

Case I-1

When is a company multinational?*

One definition of a multinational company stresses the *structural* element; the criterion for defining multinationality is the number of countries in which a firm is doing business.

An alternative definition of multinational, still based on structural consider- ations, emphasizes ownership, not the operations of the company. A *multina- tional firm* means a firm owned by persons from many nations; *multi* usually means consisting of many, and multinational therefore is "consisting of many nations."

Another structural definition of multinationality could be based on the national composition of the top decision makers. Thus, it may be argued that a multinational firm is one whose top management is composed of nationals of various countries. Such a firm will presumably be less likely to keep the interest of one country above that of every other and will have a "pure" worldwide outlook.

A final possible definition of multinationality using structural characteristics is to look at the organizational structure of the company. This possibility is somewhat like that of the composition of top management. Surely, it may be argued, a multinational firm will structure its organization in a manner best suited to reflect its worldwide network of activities. There is a distinct trend within companies that are very active in the international investment field to realign the company's organizational responsibilities on the basis of a worldwide concept of operations.

The performance school would define a firm as multinational according to performance characteristics such as earnings, sales, or assets, and the number of employees—sometimes advocated as absolute, sometimes as rela- tive. The absolute measure will classify a corporation as multinational if it has committed a certain *amount of resources* to foreign operations. The relative measure asserts that a firm is multinational if it has committed a

---

* From Yair Aharoni, "On the Definition of a Multinational Corporation," *Quarterly Review of Economics and Business,* October 1971, pp. 28–35.

significant *portion* of its financial, technological, and human resources to overseas operations. In other words, a company is multinational if it does business in several countries in such volume that its well-being and growth rest in more than one country.

Using a behavioral criterion, a multinational firm is one whose top management "thinks internationally." Thus, according to Peter Drucker, a multinational firm is one

> with corporate headquarters in the United States but in their organization, their business, their scope, they are worldwide. . . . Corporate top management is not concerned with any one region or territory . . . an international business demands of its management people that they think and act as international businessmen in a world in which national passions are as strong as ever.

A multinational firm, therefore, is a firm whose top management thinks like international business people. Presumably, an international business person is one who always weighs alternative investment possibilities on a worldwide basis and who does not discard an investment opportunity abroad simply because it is not in the United States. Certain definitions stress structural elements, whereas others emphasize performance, and still other behavioral elements. The three are not correlated and each definition leads to the inclusion of some and the exclusion of other corporations active in the international field. It seems clear that the differences are not merely a question of semantics, but that there are several kinds of so-called multinational companies.

For example, there are distinct differences between a company such as Unilever with manufacturing subsidiaries in dozens of countries; a company such as Trans World Airlines which also operates in dozens of countries but with distinctly different operations; a company such as Bethlehem Steel with mining operations in several countries, all supporting the company's manufacturing activities in the United States; a company such as Gulf Oil which owns and operates oil fields in several countries, transports oil, and markets oil; and a company such as Omega Watches, with manufacturing operations in one country, but an export network and sales and service outlets all over the world.

So when is a company multinational? Listen to four senior executives of the world's largest firms with extensive holdings outside the home country speak[1]

Company A: "We are a multinational firm. We distribute our products in about 100 countries. We manufacture in over 17 countries and do re-

---

[1] Reprinted with permission from Howard V. Perlmutter, "The Tortuous Evolution of the Multinational Corporation," *Columbia Journal of World Business*, January/February 1969, pp. 9–10, and Pergamon Press.

search and development in three countries. We look at all new investment projects—both domestic and overseas—using exactly the same criteria."

The executive from Company A tells us that most of the key posts in Company A's subsidiaries are held by home-country nationals. Whenever replacements for these people are sought, it is the practice, if not the policy, to "look next to you at the head office" and "pick someone (usually a home-country national) you know and trust."

Company B: "We are a multinational firm. Only 1 percent of the personnel in our office companies are non-nationals. Most of these are U.S. executives on temporary assignments. In all major markets, the affiliate's managing director is of the local nationality."

The executive from Company B does not hide the fact that there are very few non-Americans in the key posts at headquarters. The few who are there are "so Americanized" that their foreign nationality literally has no meaning. The explanation for this paucity of non-Americans seems reasonable enough: "You can't find good foreigners who are willing to live in the United States, where our headquarters are located. American executives are more mobile. In addition, Americans have the drive and initiative we like. In fact, the European nationals would prefer to report to an American rather than to some other European."

Company C: "We are a multinational firm. Our product division executives have worldwide product responsibility. As our organizational charts show, the United States is just one region on a par with Europe, Latin America, Africa, etc., in each product division."

The executive from Company C goes on to explain that the worldwide product-division concept is rather difficult to implement. The senior executives in charge of these divisions have little overseas experience. They have been promoted from domestic posts and tend to view foreign consumer needs "as really basically the same as ours." Also, product-division executives tend to focus on the domestic market because the domestic market is larger and generates more revenue than the fragmented European markets. The rewards are for global performance, but the strategy is to focus on domestic. The executive's colleagues say "one pays attention to what one understands—and our senior executives simply do not understand what happens overseas and really do not trust foreign executives in key positions here or overseas."

Company D (*non-American*): "We are a multinational firm. We have at least 18 nationalities represented at our headquarters. Most senior executives speak at least two languages. About 30 percent of our staff at headquarters are foreigners."

The executive from the European Company D begins by explaining that since the voting shareholders must by law come from the home country, the home country's interests must be given careful consideration. In the final analysis the executive insists: "We are proud of our nationality; we shouldn't be ashamed of it," and cites examples of the previous reluctance of headquarters to use home-country ideas overseas, to their detriment—

especially in their U.S. subsidiary. "Our country produces good executives, who tend to stay with us a long time. It is harder to keep executives from the United States."

QUESTIONS

1. Discuss the degree of international involvement of each of the companies.
2. Which is a multinational corporation? Why?

Case I–2

Computers USA, Inc.—trading with the enemy

The French subsidiary of Computers U.S.A., Inc., (a U.S. manufacturer) had signed a $20 million contract to supply computer components to Cuba. The computer components were to be attached to a French-made computer system which the Cubans had ordered.

The parent firm in the United States was shocked to learn that its subsidiary was, as the firm saw it, violating the Trading With The Enemy Act by dealing with the Cubans. Computers U.S.A., Inc., canceled the deal.

The president of the French affiliate, a Frenchman, went to court, got a receiver appointed for the subsidiary, and obtained a court order saying in effect that Americans had no right to interfere with the French affiliate and requiring that the contract be executed. The computer components were delivered; then the receiver turned Computers Europe, Inc., back to Computers U.S.A., Inc.

The repercussions are still being felt by U.S. multinationals. When they try to invest in France, and frequently in other countries, the questions are raised: What about sales to China? to Russia? to Cuba? to Vietnam?

QUESTIONS

1. How would you answer the questions raised above? Defend your replies.
2. When can U.S. law be enforced against a U.S. firm in another country?

3. Why do you suppose Computers U.S.A., Inc., canceled the original contract of its French subsidiary?

4. Suppose Computers U.S.A., Inc., had wanted to sell computer components manufactured and shipped from the United States; under the circumstances what would probably have happened?

Case I-3

Fasteners, Inc.—equal opportunity for women in the International Business Division

Fasteners, Inc., manufactures a complete line of industrial fasteners which are used in the manufacture of almost all products. For example, a typical telephone uses 78 fasteners, a gas range 150, and a refrigerator 211. The appliance industry alone uses some 5 billion fasteners a year. Fasteners, Inc., makes several thousand different types and sizes of spring steel, plastic, and threaded fasteners, snap and steel retaining rings. They also design and produce special-order fasteners to fit the particular needs of a manufacturer. The market for fasteners consists, quite literally, of any manufacturer who produces a product which must be assembled and held together in any way other than welding, soldering, or gluing. Total sales last year were $185 million.

Until a few years ago, Fasteners had been primarily a domestic U.S. company. In 1976, however, they began exporting to several European customers, and their sales abroad have grown to about 11 percent of their total profits. They had not concentrated much time on their export division but a recent forecast and study by a management consulting firm convinced them that their markets abroad would grow substantially within the next 15 years. In order to capitalize on the potential, they would have to make a definite management commitment to their international markets. The board of directors studied the report and agreed that they should reorient their emphasis and begin looking at the world as a market. In Western Europe, where 80 percent of their foreign sales existed, the consulting report indicated continued growth; in the Mideast, the Far East, and Latin America, where they have not marketed, the future demand would be even larger than in Europe. One result of their expansion plans would be the need to increase substantially their international-division personnel. Although they currently have about 100 employees in International, most of whom work in the United States, they rely heavily on foreign distributors in their European market for present sales. Part of the expansion plans would include efforts to establish their own sales and marketing subsidiaries in England, Germany, Italy, and Spain and to continue expansion into new markets with wholly owned divisions wherever feasible. They have estimated an increase of 200 to 300 new employees in the International Division as planned expansion occurs over the next five years. Many of the new employees would be experienced nationals recruited from other international firms within their home countries; others would come from the company's normal recruiting pool, young MBAs, and others.

In discussing long-range development plans for the International Division, the issue of equal opportunity for women was raised at one of the board meetings by Ms. Judy Sellridge. Ms. Sellridge, vice president of personnel, wanted to know what action the company would take to insure women an equal opportunity in the company's expansion plans. Fasteners has been totally committed to affirmative action/equal opportunity goals; in fact, Fasteners has taken pride in having, on the average, more women and minority executives than other equal-sized companies within the industry. The president of Fasteners has insisted on strict adherence to affirmative action/equal opportunity guidelines. Ms. Sellridge's question resulted in a lengthy discussion on the issue of equal opportunity in international business. The vice president of the International Division questioned whether Fasteners should actively recruit women for the International Division when expected career paths would not lead beyond the secretarial level or a position in personnel in the New York corporate offices. He claimed there would be no room in the International Division for women executives or for women to represent the company in foreign countries. He also felt that women would be rejected by their foreign contacts. Cultural differences in most other countries of the world do not allow for the equal treatment of women in business efforts. Ms. Sellridge countered his point by referring to a recent *Business Week* article which emphasized that while the world, "is not yet quite their oyster," substantial numbers of women managers are beginning to pry open the shell. Women head Latin American operations for the Sunoco overseas subsidiary of Sun Co. and for Southeast First Bank of Miami. Women represent GE in Moscow, and Bank of America in both Tokyo and Beijing.[1]

Fasteners' president admitted he had not given much attention to the women's issue in terms of the International Division and that there were no women presently in managerial positions in that division. Because of its relatively small size, no problems had arisen; however, with the expected commitment to growth, the question of equal opportunity in the International Division must be discussed. Top management split on the issue. The vice president in charge of the International Division, who had 25 years of experi-

---

[1] "A Rush of Recruits for Overseas Duty," *Business Week*, April 20, 1981, pp. 120–127.

ence in foreign assignments and had been with Fasteners for about five years, opposed the idea of women in any managerial position that would put them in contact with foreign customers. He said their career paths would be shunted to lower levels within the company. He felt there was no future for them in International and he did not want to mislead anyone in order to appear as if the company were complying with the law. Other top management people in domestic operations did not totally agree with this viewpoint.

The president was firmly committed to the idea of women in International, but he did not want to override the judgment of those in charge of that division. Basically, the president wanted to find some compromise position that would allow them to hire women for meaningful international management positions and at the same time avoid situations that would be dysfunctional for the division.

Arguments against hiring women for managerial positions in International were based on cultural differences that exist throughout most of the world. In many countries women are not permitted in business, especially not in supervisory or sales positions above the lowest levels. In the Mideast and in some Latin American countries, the woman's role is definitely not in business, and women are not accepted in management positions except in rare situations. The vice president of International had no first-hand experience of how a woman would be received since he had never, as he said, "seen a female executive or anyone above the level of executive secretary in any of the companies I know of." He felt strongly, however, that he could not place a woman in a position to represent Fasteners, to be in a supervisory position of salesmen, be in sales, or in any position that required contact with locals in another country. To support his position, he asked his assistant to contact other international companies for their experiences with women executives. No company would give concrete figures on how many women they employed in international managerial and sales positions. Because of this reluctance to report hard information, the vice president was suspicious that women did not have equal opportunity in other international divisions either, but since they were all equal opportunity employers they would be reluctant to discuss the issue. Some information on the role of women in business in various countries was available; a brief summary by country or area follows.

Japan and Hong Kong

In a 1980 survey of Japanese firms, 49.9 percent had no women employees in the lowest management ranks.

A 1979 report on female employment in Japan concluded that Japanese women are more self-effacing in their career ambitions than women in other countries. In a survey of 700 graduate females, 95 percent thought that there was "a clear difference of ability and aptitude between men and women."

Thirty-two percent of all business establishments in Japan deny female workers even the chance to be promoted to a responsible position. Only 4.8 percent of all managerial job holders in Japan are women. In government positions, only 0.6 percent of all Japanese public-service employees holding posts of assistant director or higher are women.

Japanese men responded that the reason women were treated as second-class citizens was because they would not stay in a job any longer than they needed to find a good husband; thus they were not worth having.

One personnel director indicated that while Japanese women were not accepted in Japanese business, the character of the Japanese is such that they would not reject a U.S. woman in a responsible position, at least not obviously.

"In Hong Kong," comments Xerox's China operations director, "Chinese businessmen express amazement, not so much at my job but at the fact that, as a woman, I travel and I'm away from home so much."

Europe

Article 119 of the Treaty of Rome (1957) states, "Each member state shall . . . ensure and . . . maintain the application of the principle of equal remuneration for equal work as between men and women workers."

A 1976 European Court order to member countries to comply with Article 119 was met with resistance. One interesting response in Ireland was an advertisement by the government for an *equal pay enforcement officer,* offering different pay rates for men and women.

In Norway, Statoil, Norway's state-owned oil company has allocated $82,000 for training courses and grants for women who wish to compete for higher managerial positions in its technical and economic areas. Further, the company has a policy to choose a woman over a man when two candidates have the same qualifications.[2]

Male resistance to women executives is far stronger in Europe than in the United States. One British advertising executive says, "Of course, there's a place for women in business. They're good at all things that are too boring for machines."

Just five or six years ago women executives were nonexistent except for female-dominated industries such as cosmetics and fashion.

A chief executive of a food company says, "I simply will not have women executives in our firm, but all the same, there is one woman director

[2] "Women—Enrichers of the Environment," *World Business Weekly,* August 10, 1981, p. 41.

we deal with at a supplier company who is a superb manager, and makes a major contribution to discussions."

European women believe that companies are deliberately barring them from line management positions, such as running a plant or a subsidiary, because women would have problems supervising large numbers of men or women.

In France, the proportion of women in managerial and professional staff positions in the insurance industry rose to 29 percent in 1976 from 13 percent in 1955.

The European Institute of Business Administration (INSEAD) in France has 38 women in its current MBA (1981) program. These women represent 15.5 percent of INSEAD's enrollment, more than double that of a year ago.[3]

A French woman executive who made it to the top as president of the firm she inherited said she gets all the qualified women she needs since "women want to work for me because they get such hard times in other French companies." The financial director of her company remarked that she was pregnant when she applied for the post of director of finance and had she been interviewed by a man she never would have gotten the job.

Germany is perhaps the strongest bastion of male chauvinism; German companies always prefer to hire men. One major consulting firm reports that German clients have refused to accept female consultants.

In Spain, women have a long way to go. They still cannot get divorces, and there is no guarantee of equal pay; they have few rights. The position of women and the position of men is best illustrated by a 1978 movie hit called "La Mujer es Cosa de Hombres" ("Woman Is a Thing of Men").

Most top women executives in Europe are with North American firms— particularly U.S. firms. This is influencing European communities. In Britain, banks are increasingly hiring women for key posts, partly because they have seen women performing well in rival U.S. banks.

One U.S. chemical firm has a European branch with a women's equal job opportunity program aimed at training and promoting women into administrative functions within the company. While there were some male prejudices initially, there has been progress. For example, in four years, the number of women in junior and middle management positions has risen from 3 percent to 9 percent of their total European management staff. They have placed women process development

---

[3] "Is There Enough Room At The Top For Women Managers?" *International Management,* April 1981, pp. 17–22.

engineers in Germany, Sweden, and Holland; a project engineer in Holland; attorneys in Spain; and a product-floor manager in Greece.

Latin America and the Mideast

The sex roles in Latin America are just about the same as in Spain—"machismo" is the law.

In Saudi Arabia women are expected to keep the strict *purdah* (seclusion from all public observation). While Western women are not bound by the strict *purdah,* no woman can drive a car, under penalty of her husband's arrest, and in many places she is cautioned against going about alone in public even in the daytime. Further, Moslem practice in Saudi Arabia forbids men and women to work within sight of each other. Dress is also quite restricted. One businessman called it "Koran chic": high necklines, arms covered to the wrist, and skirts down to the ankles.

Companies simply assumed that foreign businessmen, accustomed to more patriarchal cultures, would shy away from doing business with U.S. women but they discovered they had been wrong. Most foreign businessmen are no more reluctant to do business with an American woman than with an American man, recent experience has shown. Yet in some parts of the world the concern is realistic. In Saudi Arabia, a woman would have difficulty even getting a visa.

All the information was given to the president who remained committed to the principle of equal opportunity. He did not want to jeopardize the effectiveness of the proposed expansion of the International Division, but at the same time, he was concerned with four issues.

1. If the five-year goals of the proposed expansion were achieved, the number of U.S. citizens employed in International would equal or be exceeded by those in the domestic division. If no women were employed in the International Division above the secretarial or clerk position, would Fasteners, Inc., be in an undesirable position if challenged on equal opportunity?
2. The report from personnel directors indicated that the European community was beginning to enforce equal opportunity and he was concerned with the impact on Fasteners.
3. Many of the new positions to be created in the next few years would provide opportunities for domestic employees. In fact, International would look to domestic employees for experienced personnel for foreign assignments. Some of the women presently employed by Fasteners would be qualified. What could the company do if any one of the several qualified women applied for transfers?
4. As International develops and it becomes clear that the career path to the top must include some international experience, what would they

do when an experienced, qualified woman in the domestic division applied for a transfer and/or promotion to an opening in International?

You have been asked by the president to examine the problem and write a confidential position paper on women in international jobs. You are to deal with positions that require the person to travel for extended periods in foreign countries; permanent positions which require extensive contact with nationals; positions that may be in direct sales requiring contact with nationals, including supervisory positions over national salesmen. Also, consider problems which may exist for women in dealing primarily on a staff rather than a line position. Basically, the president must know if there would be any real basis for not accepting women in the International Division. He pointed out that before any new employees would be ready to move into a foreign-country position they would have to have four or five years experience. However, since Fasteners, Inc., has experienced women executives in their domestic divisions, there could be requests in the near future for intracompany transfers to positions in International. If the company were to turn down such a request, there would be likelihood of a challenge of the equal opportunity question. It is at that point that they must be able to defend their situation, either by justifying not having female employees or by proceeding with an action plan to provide equal opportunity to women.

PART TWO

THE WORLD MARKETING ENVIRONMENT

CHAPTERS:

4. Cultural dynamics in assessing world markets
5. Business customs and practices in world marketing
6. Political considerations in assessing world markets
7. The international legal environment
8. Geography

CASES:

II–1. Starnes-Brenner Machine Tool Company—to bribe or not to bribe

II–2. Hot Chips, Inc.—manufacturing joint venture and know-how license

II–3. When international buyers and sellers disagree

II–4. Gasselsmann GmbH Mining and Smelting—paying a ransom

Chapter 4

Cultural dynamics in assessing world markets

Humans are born creatures of need. As they mature, want is added to need. Economic needs are spontaneous and, in their crudest sense, limited. Humans, like all living things, need a minimum of nourishment; like a few other living things, they need a type of shelter; and, unlike any other being, they need essential clothing. Economic wants, however, are for nonessentials and, hence, are limitless. Unlike basic needs, wants are not spontaneous and not characteristic of the lower animals; they arise not from an inner desire for preservation of self or species but from a desire for satisfaction above the level of absolute necessity. To satisfy their material needs and wants, humans consume.

The manner in which people consume, the priority of needs and the wants they attempt to satisfy, and the manner in which they satisfy them are functions of their culture which temper, mold, and dictate their style of living. Culture is the human-made part of human environment—the sum total of mankind's knowledge, beliefs, art, morals, laws, customs, and any other capabilities and habits acquired by humans as members of society. It is the "distinctive way of life of a group of people, their complete design for living"—a mosaic of human life.

Since culture deals with a group's "design for living," it is pertinent to the study of marketing, especially foreign marketing.[1] If you consider for a moment the scope of the marketing concept—"the satisfaction of consumer needs and wants at a profit"—it becomes apparent that the marketer must be a student of culture. What is constantly being dealt with when operating as a marketer but the culture of the people (the market)? When a promotional message is written, symbols recognizable and meaningful to the market (the culture) must be used. When designing a product, the style, uses, and all the other related marketing activities must be made culturally acceptable, that is, acceptable to the present society, if they are to be operative and meaningful. In fact, culture is pervasive in all marketing activities—in pricing, promotion, channels of distribution, product, packaging, and styling—and

---

[1] See Mushtaq Luqmani, Zahir A. Quraeshi, and Linda Delene, "Marketing in Islamic Countries: A Viewpoint," *MSU Business Topics*, Summer 1980, pp. 17–25 for an interesting article which illustrates the impact of culture on marketing.

the marketer's efforts actually become a part of the fabric of culture. The marketer's efforts are judged in a cultural context for acceptance, resistance, or rejection. How such efforts interact with a culture determines the degree of success or failure of the marketing effort.

The individual's frame of reference when studying marketing should be that *markets are not* (static), *they become* (change); they are not static but change, expand, and contract in response to marketing effort, economic

---

BOX 4–1: Two cultures meet—at the fast food restaurant

McDonald's came to Singapore in 1980; one in the tourist section of Singapore and the other in People's Park, a chaotic bazaar in Chinatown where hundreds of hawkers shovel out Singapore's celebrated street food. Under a haze of charcoal smoke, People's Park is steamy and redolent, ringing with the noise of crashing dishes, sputtering fat, and bawling waiters. Its customers have a special appetite for entrails.

In McDonald's, a customer hears not Chinese music but a Ray Charles song. It is air conditioned, decor by "plastic," with everything down to the floor tiles imported from the United States. Through McDonald's plate-glass window, flames are visible leaping under the woks of the Min Ho restaurant 30 feet away. A monkey sits on a table outside the open-ended kitchen eating peanuts. An old man washes dishes in a wooden tub while a youth pulls roasted ducks from a barrel-shaped oven. Baskets of noodles and vegetables are stacked here and there. Eels slither in a tank.

Here, in direct confrontation, are two great philosophies of fast food. One uses the freezer, the computer, and the business school to manufacture a few simple dishes in less than 100 seconds. The other relies on the markets of Chinatown; the abacus; and a covey of cousins, aunts, and grandmothers to create a profusion of complicated dishes in a minute or two. McDonald's is fast for cook and customer, the other is fast for the customer, but not for the cook.

McDonald's has rhythm: at 9 a.m. spatulas are sharpened, tartar sauce cartridges are sanitized at 2 p.m., and reconstituted onion is mixed at 10 p.m. The grill beeps when it's time for the uniformed cook to flip a hamburger; the bun toaster beeps when the buns are done; the "fish-fillet" cooking computer beeps when the fish is finished.

Across the alley, two cooks stand in fiery heat before six woks, furiously working six orders at once—plunging crabs into boiling oil, ladling chicken stock over steaming greens, pausing only to wipe the sweat off their arms. The menu has everything; flying foxes, furry bats, and they boast, "if you want it, we will cook it."

The choice between the two fast food restaurants comes down to a matter of taste. Two Americans from New York sit in the People's Park McDonald's eating Big Macs. Wouldn't they like to try some of this city's famous stall food?

"My wife has a weak stomach," says the husband. The wife responds, "I don't like Chinese food. The smell. I can't stand to see it prepared."

Over at the stall restaurant, two Chinese are having lunch. One has a plate of noodles fried with pig's intestines and the other a bowl of pig's-brain soup.

One comments, "Just a piece of meat between two pieces of bread, that's all a McDonald's is." "Here try some guts." The other savors a spoonful of pig's brains. "I've had a hamburger," he says. "I don't know. If I eat too much Western food, I get sick."

Source: Adapted from Barry Newman, "Singapore Fast Food: Try Pig Intestines—or Maybe a Big Mac," *The Wall Street Journal*, January 20, 1981, p. 1.

conditions, and other cultural influences. Markets and market behavior are part of a country's culture. One cannot truly understand how markets evolve or how they react to a marketer's effort without appreciating that markets are a result of culture. Markets are dynamic not only in response to economic change but also in response to changes in other aspects of the culture as well. Markets are living phenomena, expanding and contracting in response to cultural change. Markets are the result of the triune interaction of a marketer's efforts, economic conditions, and all other elements of the culture. Marketers are constantly in the process of adjusting their efforts to cultural demands of the market, but they are also acting as agents of change whenever the product or idea being marketed is innovative. Whatever the degree of acceptance in whatever level of culture, the use of something new is the beginning of cultural change and the marketer becomes a change agent.

This chapter's purpose is to highten the reader's sensitivity to the dynamics of culture. By no means is it a treatise to which one can refer when in doubt about a particular country; rather, it is designed to emphasize the need for study of each country's culture and to point up some of the more relevant aspects that should be examined. The chapter explores briefly the concept of culture related to foreign marketing, while subsequent chapters will deal with particular features of each of the cultural elements as they affect the marketing process.

CULTURAL KNOWLEDGE

There are two classifications of knowledge regarding cultures a marketer should possess to cope with the problems of a different culture. One is factual knowledge about a culture that is usually obvious and must be learned. Different meanings of color, different tastes, and other traits indigenous to a culture are facts which a marketer can anticipate, study, and learn. The other is interpretive knowledge, an ability to understand and to appreciate fully the nuances of different cultural traits and patterns. The meaning of time, attitudes toward other people and certain objects, the understanding of one's role in society, and meanings of life illustrate aspects of a culture which can differ considerably from one culture to another and which require more than factual knowledge to be fully appreciated.

Frequently, factual knowledge has meaning as a straightforward fact about a culture but assumes additional significance when interpreted within the context of the culture. For example, that Mexico is 98 percent Catholic is an important bit of factual knowledge. But equally important is what it means to be a Catholic within Mexican culture versus being Catholic in Spain or Italy. Each culture practices Catholicism in slightly different ways. For example, All Soul's Day is an important celebration among Catholics. In Mexico, however, the celebration receives great emphasis and is much different than in most other Catholic countries. The Mexican observance is a strange combination of pagan (mostly Indian influence) and Catholic tradition. On "The Day of the Dead," as All Soul's Day is called by many in Mexico, it is believed the dead return to feast. Hence, many Mexicans visit the graves of their departed, taking the dead's favorite foods to place on the graves for the dead to enjoy. Prior to All Soul's Day, bakeries pile their shelves with bread shaped like bones and coffins and candy stores sell sugar skulls and other special treats to commemorate the day. As the souls feast on the food, so do the living celebrants. While the prayers, candles, and the idea of the spirit of the soul are Catholic, the idea of the dead feasting is very pre-Christian Mexican. Thus, a Catholic in Mexico observes All Soul's Day quite differently from a Catholic in Spain. This interpretative, as well as factual, knowledge about religion in Mexico is necessary to fully understand the Mexican culture.[2]

Interpretive knowledge requires a degree of insight which may best be described as a "feeling." You must be able to project yourself into the situation. It is the kind of knowledge most dependent on past experience for interpretation and most frequently prone to misinterpretation if one's home-country frame of reference (SRC) is used. Ideally, the foreign marketer should possess both kinds of knowledge about a market. Generally, most facts about a particular culture can be learned by researching published material dealing with that culture. This effort can also transmit a small degree of empathy, but to appreciate the culture fully it is necessary to live with the people for some time. Since this ideal solution is not practical for a marketer, other solutions are sought. Consultation and cooperation with bilingual nationals with marketing backgrounds would be the most effective answer to the problem. This would have the further advantage of helping the marketer acquire an increasing degree of empathy through association with people who understand the culture best— natives.

The successful foreign marketer must become culturally sensitive—attuned to the nuances of culture so the other culture can be objectively

---

BOX 4–2: The hand sign for "okay" has two meanings

Hand gestures are far from international. Italians wave goodbye with palm up and fingers moving back and forth—a beckoning signal to Americans. But when people wave the fingers with the palm down in China, Japan, and other Oriental areas, it's not goodbye—they mean "come here."

People who speak a romance language use more hand gestures than most Americans, but you can go wrong imitating them. For example, if you form a circle with thumb and forefinger, most Europeans will know you mean "it's the best," or "okay." But in some Latin American countries the same gesture has a vulgar connotation.

Bradley Hitchings, ed., "Personal Business." Reprinted from the December 12, 1977 issue of *Business Week* by special permission. © 1977 by McGraw-Hill, Inc.

---

[2] Lawrence Rout, "To Understand Life in Mexico, Consider the Day of the Dead," *The Wall Street Journal*, November 4, 1981, p. 1.

seen, evaluated, and appreciated. Cultural empathy must be cultivated; perhaps the most important steps toward cultural empathy and objectivity are the recognition of the need for empathy and the acquisition of knowledge of a culture. Further, marketers may find it necessary to reinvestigate the assumptions on which they base their judgments, especially if these frames of reference are strictly from their own culture. One major U.S. firm could have avoided a multimillion dollar mistake in Japan had it not relied on an American frame of reference and assumed that all Japanese homes had ovens in which to bake cakes made from the mixes the company unsuccessfully attempted to market.[3] From the U.S. firm's perspective, who would have even asked if Japanese homes had ovens? As one expert warns, the success or failure of operations abroad depends on an awareness and understanding of the fundamental differences in culture and the willingness of the international executive to discard as excess baggage cultural elements of the American frontier.[4]

CULTURE AND ITS ELEMENTS

A point of departure in the study of cultural dynamics for assessing world markets is a brief discussion of the concept of culture. To many, the term *culture* implies a value judgment of another's way of life, knowledge, or social manners. A person is either "cultured" or "uncultured," the difference being that the cultured person has acquired a certain ability in specialized fields of knowledge—usually in art, music, or literature, plus good manners. Historians often use culture to mean those specific features of a civilization in which one society may have excelled; for example, Greek culture is associated with its art and literature. For the foreign marketer, these meanings of culture are much too narrow. The student of foreign marketing should approach an understanding of culture from the viewpoint of the anthropologist. Every group of people or society has a culture since culture is the entire social heritage of the human race—"the totality of the knowledge and practices, both intellectual and material of society . . . [it] embraces everything from food to dress, from household techniques to industrial techniques, from forms of politeness to mass media, from work rhythms to the learning of familiar rules."[5] Culture exists in New York, London, and Moscow just as it does among the Navahos, the South Sea Islanders, or the aborigines of Australia.

It is imperative for foreign marketers to learn the intricacies of cultures different from their own if they are to be effective in a foreign market. A place to begin is a careful study of the elements of culture.

---

[3] "Expert Terms Japan Deficit 'Whipping Boy'," *United Press International* news release, December 1, 1980.

[4] For a fascinating discussion of cultural implications, see Edward T. Hall, *Beyond Culture* (New York: Anchor Press-Doubleday, 1976).

[5] Colette Guillaumin, "Culture and Cultures," *Cultures,* vol. 6, no. 1, 1979, p. 1.

Elements of culture

The anthropologist studying culture as a science must investigate every aspect of a culture if an accurate, total picture is to be obtained. To meet this purpose there has evolved a "cultural scheme" which embodies all the various parts of culture. That same thoroughness is necessary if the marketing consequences of the cultural differences that can exist within a foreign market are to be accurately assessed.

Culture includes all parts of life. The scope of the term *culture* to the anthropologist is illustrated by the elements included within the meaning of the term. They are:

1. Material culture
   Technology
   Economics
2. Social institutions
   Social organization
   Education
   Political structures
3. Man and the universe
   Belief systems
4. Aesthetics
   Graphic and plastic arts
   Folklore
   Music, drama, and dance
5. Language[6]

In the study of humanity's way of life, the anthropologist finds these five dimensions of culture useful because they encompass all the activities of social heritage which constitute culture. They serve as a framework or pattern for the study and analysis of different cultures. Similarly, foreign marketers may find such a cultural scheme a useful framework in evaluating a marketing plan or in studying the potential of foreign markets; all elements are instrumental to some extent in the success or failure of a marketing effort since they constitute the environment within which the marketer operates. Furthermore, we automatically reacted to many of these factors in our native culture so they must purposely be learned in another. Finally, these are the factors with which marketing efforts interact and which are basic in the understanding of the character of the marketing system of any society. Since each of these dimensions of culture has some influence on the marketing process, it is necessary to study the implications of all the differences of these dimensions in analysis of a specific foreign market. A brief examination of each of these elements will illustrate the variety of ways that marketing and culture are interwoven.

---

[6] Herskovits, *Man and His Works* (New York: Alfred A. Knopf, Inc., 1952), p. 634.

Material culture. This is divided into two parts, technology and economics. Technology includes the techniques used in the creation of material goods; it is the technical know-how possessed by the people of a society. Economics is the manner in which people employ their capabilities and the resulting benefits. Included in the subject of economics are the production of goods and services, their distribution, consumption, means of exchange, and the income derived from the creation of utilities. Material culture affects the level of demand, the quality and types of products demanded, and their functional features, as well as the means of production of these goods and their distribution. The marketing implications of the material culture of a country are obviously many. Electrical appliances will sell in England or France but have few buyers in countries where less than 1 percent of the homes have electricity. Even where electricity is available, economic characteristics, such as the level and distribution of income, may limit the desirability of products. Electric toothbrushes and electric carving knives are totally acceptable in the United States, but, in less-affluent countries, not only are they unattainable and probably unwanted, they are probably considered a spectacular waste since disposable income could be spent more meaningfully on better houses, clothing, or food.

Social institutions. Social organization, education, and political structures are concerned with the ways in which people relate to one another, organize their activities in order to live in harmony with one another, teach acceptable behavior to succeeding generations, and govern themselves. The positions of men and women in society, the family, social classes, group behavior, and age groups are interpreted differently within every culture. Each institution has an effect on marketing because each influences behavior, values, and the overall patterns of life. In cultures where the social organizations result in close-knit family units, for example, it is more effective to aim a promotional campaign at the family unit than at an individual family member.[7] Travel advertising in culturally divided Canada pictures a wife alone for the English audience but a man and wife together for the French segments of the population, since the French are traditionally more closely bound by family ties.

The roles and status positions found in a society are influenced by the dictates of social organizations. A woman typically has overlapping family roles in most societies; she is a wife, mother, grandparent, or child. Rules for each of these roles vary from culture to culture. Compare, for example, the U.S. housewife with the Swiss housewife; the Swiss considers washing dishes or cleaning floors as central to her role and rejects commercial appeals emphasizing time and effort saved in performing these household tasks.[8]

---

[7] Roderick J. Lawrence, "Houses and People: A Cross-Cultural Perspective," *Cultures* 7, no. 2 (1980), pp. 150–63.

[8] Susan Douglas and Bernard Dubois, "Looking At the Cultural Environment for International Marketing Opportunities," *Columbia Journal of World Business*, Winter 1977, p. 103.

The social institution of education affects literacy which affects marketing promotion. In countries with low literacy rates, conventional forms of printed promotion cannot be used successfully, therefore, more radio and movie advertising is employed in promotional strategy. Certain types of political institutions hinder development of marketing organizations as well as the marketing of politically vulnerable products. Legal structures differ too; certain business activities permitted in some European countries are forbidden in others.

Mankind and the universe. Under this area come religion, belief systems, superstitions, and their related power structures. The impact of religion on the value systems of a society and the effect of value systems on marketing must not be underestimated.[9] Religion has considerable influence on people's habits, their outlook on life, the products they buy, the way they buy them, even the newspapers they read. In Belgium and the Netherlands, the population is divided between Roman Catholics and Protestants and each group has its own newspapers. Logically enough, media selection can be based on the politics and/or religion of certain target-market groups. Religion extends well beyond the individual or even the family in many countries such as Latin America where the family, the individual, and the community are deeply involved with the church. Acceptance of certain types of food, clothing, and behavior are frequently affected by religion, and such influence can extend to the acceptance or rejection of promotional messages as well. For example, in some countries, if too much attention to bodily functions is featured in advertisements, the behavior would be judged immoral or improper and the products would be rejected.

Superstition plays a much larger role in a society's belief system in other parts of the world than it does in the United States. What might be considered by an American as superstition can be a critical aspect of a belief system in another culture. For example, in parts of Asia, ghosts, fortune-telling, palmistry, head-bumps reading, phases of the moon, demons, and soothsayers are all integral parts of understanding some cultures.[10] Astrologers are routinely called on in Thailand to determine the best location for a structure. The Thais insist that all wood in a new building must come from the same forest, otherwise the boards will quarrel with each other. Houses should have an odd number of rooms for luck, and they should be one story because it is unlucky to have another's foot over your head.

One incident reported in Malaysia involved mass hysteria from a fear of "evil spirits." Most of the factory laborers were involved, and production ground to a halt until a "bomoh" was called, a goat sacrificed, its blood

---

[9] For a complete treatment of the impact of Islamic religion on marketing, see Mushtaq Luqmani, Zahir A. Quraeshi, and Linda Delene, "Marketing in Islamic Countries: A Viewpoint."

[10] Richard Critchfield, "Encountering Asia's Ghosts and Goblins," *The Asian Wall Street Journal Weekly*, February 23, 1981, p. 10.

sprinkled on the factory floor, then roasted and eaten. The next day the hysteria was over, and everyone was back at work.[11]

It is easy to make light of superstitions in other cultures, but when doing business in these cultures it can be an expensive mistake. To make a fuss about being born in the right year under the right phase of the moon and to rely heavily on handwriting and palm-reading experts as in Japan can be worrisome to a Westerner who seldom sees a 13th floor in a brand new building, refuses to walk under a ladder, or worries about the next seven years after breaking a mirror.

Aesthetics. Closely interwoven with the effect of people and the universe are a culture's aesthetics, that is, the arts, folklore, music, drama, and dance. Aesthetics are of particular interest to the marketer because of their role in interpreting the symbolic meanings of various methods of artistic expression, color, and standards of beauty in a particular culture. Without the culturally correct interpretation of a society's aesthetic values, product styling is seldom successful. Insensitivity to aesthetic values not only leads to ineffective advertising and package design, but it can also lead to offending the proposed customer or creating a negative impression. Closely interrelated to folklore and religion, symbolism is paramount in nonverbal communication. The uniqueness of a culture can be quickly spotted in its symbols with their distinct meanings. The Japanese, for example, revere the crane as being very lucky for it is said to "live a thousand years"; however, the use of the number four should be completely avoided since the word for four, "shi," is also the Japanese word for death. In the United States, the deer has a positive connotation, even overtones of masculinity when associated with hunting and the outdoors. In Brazil, the animal's name is the slang word for homosexual.

Language. The importance of understanding the language of a country cannot be underestimated. The successful marketer must achieve expert communication which requires a thorough understanding of the language as well as the ability to speak it. Advertising copywriters should be concerned less with obvious differences between languages and more with the idiomatic meanings expressed.

A dictionary translation is not the same as an idiomatic interpretation, and seldom will the dictionary translation suffice. "A national producer of soft drinks had the company's brand name impressed in Chinese characters which were phonetically accurate. It was discovered later, however, that the translation's literal meaning was 'female horse fattened with wax,' hardly the image the company sought to portray."[12] Pepsi's familiar "come alive

---

[11] Barry Newman, "Malaysian Malady: When the Spirit Hits, a Scapegoat Suffers," *The Wall Street Journal,* March 7, 1980, p. 1.

[12] Jose de la Torre, "Product Life Cycle Is a Determinant of Global Marketing Strategy," *Atlanta Economic Review,* September–October 1975, p. 13.

with Pepsi" translated into German conveyed the idea of coming alive from the grave, again not the intent of the original statement. Schwepps was not pleased with their tonic water translation into Italian: "Il Water," idiomatically means the bathroom.[13] Carelessly translated advertising statements not only lose their intended meaning but can suggest something very different including something obscene, offensive, or just plain ridiculous. For example, in French-speaking countries the trademark toothpaste brand name, "Cue," was a crude slang expression for derriere; not an image the company had in mind for their toothpaste. The intent of a major fountain pen company advertising in Latin America suffered in translation when their new ink was promoted to "help prevent unwanted pregnancies."[14] The poster of an engineering company at a Russian trade show did not mean to promise that its oil well completion equipment was dandy for "improving a person's sex life."[15]

BOX 4–3:   You want a telephone?—Wait!

Telephone service in the United States may be annoying at times, but it's the best in the world.

Currently there are 657 telephones per 1,000 inhabitants in the United States, compared with 594 in Sweden, 350 in Great Britain, 217 in France, and 200 in Greece.

The average installation time after a customer's request is less than a week in the United States. It takes two years in Norway, 18 months to five years in France, and a month in Greece.

The average telephone rate is $10 a month in the United States. In Greece and Italy, it costs $140 to have a phone installed. In Japan, a $500 bond must be purchased in addition to a $167 installment fee. In France, it costs $182 for installation, $8.50 a month, and 9 cents a call. In Guatemala, a new phone line costs $1,000.

Of all the cultural elements a marketer should study to gain some degree of empathy, language may be one of the most difficult to master. Many believe that to fully appreciate the true meaning of a language it is necessary to live with the language for years. Whether or not this is the case, foreign marketers should never take it for granted that they are effectively communicating in another language. Until a marketer can master the vernacular, the aid of a national within the foreign country should be enlisted; even then the problem of effective communications may still exist. One authority suggests a cultural translator, a person who translates not only among languages but also among different ways of thinking, among different cultures, as a means of overcoming the problem.[16]

---

[13] David A. Ricks et al., "Pitfalls in Advertising Overseas," *Journal of Advertising Research,* December 1974, p. 48.

[14] Oscar S. Cornejo, "Avoid Embarrassments in Latin America," *International Advertiser,* May/June, 1981, p. 12.

[15] "More Firms Turn to Translation Experts to Avoid Costly, Embarrassing Mistakes," *The Wall Street Journal,* January 13, 1977, p. 32.

[16] Sir Horace Phillips, "Language, the Passport to Global Business," *The Asian Wall Street Journal Weekly,* March 23, 1981, p. 11.

BOX 4–4: Others make translation errors, too!

Faulty translations are not exclusively an American problem. Translating any language to any other language has its pitfalls. Here are a few translations collected by a travel correspondent. In Thailand, a sign advertising donkey rides for tourists said, "Would you like to ride on your ass?" In a Kowloon hotel, one sign announced to American tourists, "It is forbidden to steal hotel towels, please if you are not person to do such is please not to read notice." On a Japanese monorail ticket-dispensing machine a plaque read, "When ticket do not come out, push the button to back your money." Also in Japan were warnings such as, "Prohibit with shoes on," "No passage this way for the walker," and among the best was a poster in a Japanese garden which informed visitors that, "Japanese garden is the mental home of the Japanese." Another winner in a Tokyo hotel informed guests that "The flattening of underwear with pressure is the job of the chamber maid. To get it done, turn her on." But the place we all want to go is a Thailand bar which advertised itself as, "The shadiest cocktail bar in Bangkok." It was next door to the department store which advised you to "Visit our bargain basement, one flight up."

Source: Adapted from Nino Lo Bello, "Something Funk Would Never Tell Wagnalls," *The Denver Post*, May 1, 1977, p. 45.

Analysis of elements

In an analysis of a potential market, it is advisable to consider the elements of the culture and evaluate each in light of how it could affect a proposed marketing program. Although some may not have a direct impact, others may be totally involved. As a broad generalization, it could be said that the more complete the marketing involvement or the more unique the product, the more need there is for thorough study of each cultural element. If a company is simply marketing an existing product in an already developed market, the need for studying the total culture is certainly less than for the marketer involved in total marketing—from product development, through promotion, to the final selling.

While the analysis of each cultural element vis-à-vis a marketing program is a practical approach to ensure that each facet of a culture is included, it should not be forgotten that culture is a total picture, not a group of unrelated elements. Culture cannot be divided into separate parts and be fully understood. The facets of culture are intricately intertwined and cannot be viewed singly; they must be considered for their synergistic effects. The ultimate personal motives and interests of people are determined by all the interwoven facets of the culture rather than by the individual parts. While some specific cultural elements have a direct influence on individual marketing efforts and must be viewed individually in terms of their potential or real effect on marketing strategy, the whole of cultural elements is manifested in a broader sense on the basic cultural patterns. For example, in marketing, the basic behavior patterns for consumption, that is, who buys, what they buy, frequency of purchases, size purchased, and so on, are established by cultural values of right and wrong, acceptable and unacceptable. The basic motives for consumption which help define fundamental needs and the different forms of decision making have strong cultural underpinnings that are critical knowledge for the marketer. Exhibit 4–1 illustrates one approach to cross-cultural analysis of consumer behavior which should identify aspects of a culture critical in developing an effective marketing strategy.

The different elements of culture have been emphasized but not its dynamic nature; cultures are not static but are living processes. That change is constant seems paradoxical in that another important attribute of culture is that it is conservative and resists change. The dynamic character of culture is significant in assessing new markets even though changes occur in the

---

EXHIBIT 4–1: Outline of cross-cultural analysis of consumer behavior

1. *Determine relevant motivations in the culture:*

     What needs are fulfilled with this product in the minds of members of the culture? How are these needs presently fulfilled? Do members of this culture readily recognize these needs?

2. *Determine characteristic behavior patterns:*

     What patterns are characteristic of purchasing behavior? What forms of division of labor exist within the family structure? How frequently are products of this type purchased? What size packages are normally purchased? Do any of these characteristic behaviors conflict with behavior expected for this product? How strongly ingrained are the behavior patterns that conflict with those needed for distribution of this product?

3. *Determine what broad cultural values are relevant to this product:*

     Are there strong values about work, morality, religion, family relations, and so on, that relate to this product? Does this product connote attributes that are in conflict with these cultural values? Can conflicts with values be avoided by changing the product? Are there positive values in this culture with which the product might be identified?

4. *Determine characteristic forms of decision making:*

     Do members of the culture display a studied approach to decisions concerning innovations or an impulsive approach? What is the form of the decision process? Upon what information sources do members of the culture rely? Do members of the culture tend to be rigid or flexible in the acceptance of new ideas? What criteria do they use in evaluating alternatives?

5. *Evaluate promotion methods appropriate to the culture:*

     What role does advertising occupy in the culture? What themes, words, or illustrations are taboo? What language problems exist in present markets that cannot be translated into this culture? What types of salesmen are accepted by members of the culture? Are such salesmen available?

6. *Determine appropriate institutions for this product in the minds of consumers:*

     What types of retailers and intermediary institutions are available? What services do these institutions offer that are expected by the consumer? What alternatives are available for obtaining services needed for the product but not offered by existing institutions? How are various types of retailers regarded by consumers? Will changes in the distribution structure be readily accepted?

Source: James F. Engel et al., *Consumer Behavior,* 4th ed. (Hinsdale, Ill.: Dryden Press, 1982), p. 97.

face of resistance. In fact, any change in the currently accepted way of life meets with more initial resistance than acceptance. Since the marketer is usually trying to introduce something completely new or to improve what is already in use, how cultures change and the manner in which resistance to change occurs should be thoroughly understood.

BOX 4–5: And so, what does Thanksgiving mean to you?

If this is what foreigners know about Thanksgiving Day, how wrong are we about their holidays? A variety of people in other countries were asked what Thanksgiving holiday meant in America. Here are some responses:

1. Americans arranged Thanksgiving Day to hail the election of Ronald Reagan, and they celebrate it by riding around in cars, putting pumpkins on their heads, and feasting on bread and wine.
2. "Indians?" asked a puzzled Hong Kong school teacher. "What do Indians have to do with Thanksgiving? Indians eat curry. Whoever heard of curried turkey?"
3. An eight-year-old Indian girl replied, "It is when Americans pray to their gods because they got so rich."
4. A cafe owner near the Trevi fountain in Rome said, "They are giving thanks for winning the Civil War."
5. A radio producer in Paris said, "Thanksgiving is the anniversary of the foundation of the federation of the United States."

Source: "Yes, Thanksgiving Day Is For Americans Only," United Press International, November 28, 1980.

CULTURAL CHANGE

One view of culture sees it as the accumulation of a series of the best solutions to problems faced in common by members of a given society. In other words, culture is the means used in adjusting to the biological, environmental, psychological, and historical components of human existence. There are a variety of ways a society solves the problems created by its existence.[17] Accident has provided solutions to some problems; invention has solved many other problems; and, more commonly, societies have found answers by looking to other cultures from which they can borrow ideas. Cultural borrowing is common to all cultures. Take for example, the ubiquitous blue jean. This garment has made its way into almost all cultures. In fact, demand is so great in Eastern European countries that Levi Strauss & Co. was invited by the East Germans to ship emergency supplies of its blue denim to satisfy the country's Christmas holiday demand.[18] Although each society has a few truly unique situations facing it, most problems confronting all societies are similar in nature with circumstances altered for each particular environment and culture.

---

[17] One account of an attempt by industry to forecast social change is reported in "Forecasters Focus on the People Factor," *International Management,* April 1981, pp. 10–14.

[18] "Western Companies Vie to Dress East Europeans in Blue Jeans," *World Business Weekly,* February 23, 1981, p. 10.

Cultural borrowing

Cultural borrowing is a responsible effort to borrow those cultural ways seen as helpful in the quest for better solutions to a society's particular problems. If what it does adopt is adapted to local needs, and once the adaptation becomes commonplace, it is passed on as cultural heritage. Thus, cultures unique in their own right are the result, in part, of borrowing from others. Consider, for example, American culture (United States) and the typical United States citizen who

> begins breakfast with an orange from the eastern Mediterranean, a cantaloupe from Persia, or perhaps a piece of African watermelon. . . . After his fruit and first coffee he goes on to waffles, cakes made by a Scandinavian technique from wheat domesticated in Asia Minor. Over these he pours maple syrup, invented by the Indians of the Eastern woodlands. As a side dish he may have the eggs of a species of bird domesticated in Indo-China, or thin strips of the flesh of an animal domesticated in Eastern Asia which have been salted and smoked by a process developed in northern Europe. . . . While smoking, he reads the news of the day, imprinted in characters invented by the ancient Semites upon a material invented in China by a process invented in Germany. As he absorbs the accounts of foreign troubles he will, if he is a good conservative citizen, thank a Hebrew deity in an Indo-European language that he is 100 percent American.[19]

Actually, the American just discussed was correct to assume he was 100 percent American because each of the borrowed cultural facets has been adapted to fit his needs, molding them into uniquely American habits, foods, and customs. Americans behave as they do because of the dictates of "their culture." Regardless of how or where solutions are found, once a particular pattern of action is judged acceptable by society, it becomes the "approved way" and is passed on and taught as part of the group's cultural heritage. Cultural heritage is one of the fundamental differences between humans and other animals. Culture is learned; societies pass on to succeeding generations solutions to problems, constantly building on and expanding the culture so that a wide range of behavior is possible. The point is, of course, that although much behavior is borrowed from other cultures, it is combined in a unique manner which becomes typical for a particular society. To the foreign marketer, this "similar but different" feature of cultures has important meaning in gaining cultural empathy.

Similarities: An illusion

For the inexperienced marketer the similar-but-different feature of culture creates an illusion of similarity which usually does not exist. Several nationalities can speak the same language or have similar race and heritage, but

---

[19] R. Linton, *The Study of Man* (New York: Appleton-Century-Crofts, 1936), p. 327.

BOX 4–6: Cultural shock—American style

A Chinese accountant newly arrived in the United States to study accounting systems suffered from cultural shock: cold oil-and-vinegar soup, a supermarket selling dog food, and the mysteries of tipping.

His first meal aboard the flight to the United States was foreign to him. Most puzzling, however, were the glass of cold water and the small cup of salad dressing that came with the meal tray.

Having no familiarity with American salads, he thought the oil and vinegar was a soup mix which he poured into the water and drank. "It wasn't very delicious," he recounted on his arrival.

He spoke English, but his fluency was limited. At the hotel he ordered grapefruit for breakfast and was unhappy to be served what he called a "sour orange" instead of the grapes he thought he had ordered.

Asking to visit a supermarket, he said, "I read a rumor in a Chinese newspaper that they sell dog food in American supermarkets," not that he really believed such malicious gossip. When told that supermarkets did indeed sell dog food, he couldn't suppress his astonishment. "It's unbelievable! The dogs and cats in America eat better than people in Asian countries." In China, he confided, dogs weren't ordinarily kept as pets; they must fend for themselves and are more likely to be eaten than to enjoy a good meal.

Many of the questions raised by the Chinese accountant proved difficult for the host to answer. After listening to advice about tipping, the Chinese accountant wanted to know why, if Americans want better service, they don't tip barbers or waiters before they perform their services rather than after. The host acknowledged that that made sense but admitted "we don't do it that way."

Source: Adapted from Dean Rotbart, "Chinese Accountants Find that America is Hard to Figure," *The Wall Street Journal*, June 5, 1981, p. 1.

---

it does not follow that similarities exist in other respects, that a product acceptable to one would be readily acceptable to another, nor that a promotional message that succeeds in one country would succeed in another. Even though they started with a common idea or approach, the cultural assimilation of the borrowed process developed it to meet individual needs and translated it into something quite different. A common language does not guarantee a similar interpretation of even a word or phrase. Both the Englishman and the American speak English, but their culture is sufficiently different so that a single phrase will have different meanings to the two and can even be completely misunderstood. In England, one asks for a "lift" instead of an elevator and an American, when speaking of a garden, generally refers to a vegetable garden while in England a garden is a flower garden. Also, the English woman "hoovers" a carpet whereas the American vaccuums. Among the Spanish-speaking Latin American countries, the problem becomes even more difficult because the idiom is unique in each country, and national pride tends to cause a mute rejection of any "foreign-Spanish" language. In some cases, an acceptable phrase or word in one country is not only unacceptable in another, it can very well be indecent or vulgar. In Spanish, *coger* is the verb "to catch," but in some countries it also has another more basic and crude meaning.

Furthermore, it should not be assumed that differences exist only among national cultures. A single geopolitical boundary does not necessarily mean a single culture; Canada is divided culturally between its French and English heritages although it is politically one country. Within each culture there are many subcultures that can have marketing significance. A successful marketing strategy among the French Canadians may be certain failure among the remaining Canadians. Even the United States has many subcultures that today, with mass communications and rapid travel, defy complete homogenization. It would be folly to suggest that the South is in all respects culturally the same as the northeastern or midwestern parts of the United States. The possible existence of more than one culture in a country, as well as subcultures, should be explored before a marketing plan is decided on.

Marketers must examine each country thoroughly in terms of the proposed products or services and never rely on an often-used axiom that if it sells in one country, it will surely sell in another. The scope of culture is very broad and covers every aspect of behavior within a country or culture. The task of foreign marketers is to adjust marketing strategies and plans to the needs of the culture in which they plan to operate. Whether innovations are developed internally through invention, experimentation, or by accident, or introduced from outside through a process of borrowing, cultural dynamics always seem to take on a positive and, at the same time, negative aspect.

Resistance to change

A characteristic of human culture is that change occurs. That people's habits, tastes, styles, behavior, and values are not constant but are continually changing can be verified by reading ten-year-old magazines. This gradual cultural growth does not occur without some resistance. New methods, ideas, and products are held to be suspect before they are accepted, if ever, as the "right way or thing."

The degree of resistance to a new pattern varies; in some situations new elements are accepted completely and rapidly, and in others, resistance is so strong that acceptance is never forthcoming. Studies show the most important factor in determining what kind and how much of an innovation will be accepted is the degree of interest in the particular subject, as well as how drastically the new will change the old, that is, how disruptive the innovation will be to presently acceptable values and patterns of behavior, and so forth. Observations indicate that those innovations most readily accepted are those that hold the greatest interest within the society and are the least disruptive. For example, rapid industrialization in parts of Europe has changed many long-honored attitudes involving time and working women. Today, there is an interest in ways to save time and to make life more productive; the leisurely continental life is rapidly disappearing. With this time consciousness has come the very rapid acceptance of many innovations which might have been resisted by most just a few years ago. Instant foods, labor-saving devices, McDonald's in France, and all sorts of products supportive of a changing attitude toward work and time are rapidly gaining acceptance.

Although a variety of innovations are completely and quickly accepted, others meet with firm resistance. For over 20 years, India has been engaged in intensive population control programs to reduce the birth rate. But the process has not worked and India's population remains among the highest in the world; it is now at 600 million and could exceed 1.1 billion by the year 2000. Why has birth control not been accepted? Most attribute the failure to the nature of Indian culture. Among the influences which help to sustain the high birth rate are early marriage, the Hindu religion's emphasis on bearing sons, dependence on children for security in old age, and a low level of education among the rural masses. All are important cultural patterns at variance with the concept of birth control. Acceptance of birth control would mean rejection of too many fundamental cultural concepts. For the Indian people it is easier and more familiar to reject the new idea.

Japan is experiencing a revolution in the acceptance of Western ways, such as the world's most advanced electronically controlled commuter trains, television receivers, eating habits,[20] and Western dress, but resistance is still strong to the reform of their archaic script. Japan's "simplified" alphabet has 2,304 symbols, making the typewriter so complex that few Japanese have ever mastered it, yet suggestions for reform meet resistance. In fact, an influential Japanese magazine once published two articles denouncing any proposed change and further demanded that the characters which children must memorize as part of their education be increased from 1,850 to 3,000. In another instance, it appeared that modern Japanese were spurning the traditional arranged marriage but evidence suggests that even though dating habits have changed and young people date freely, when it comes to marriage, they rely on parents to select their spouses.[21] Vigorous reaction to changes that affect our cultural character is found in every society; changes that might alter that character most radically usually meet the strongest resistance.

This process of change and the reactions to it are relevant to the marketer, whether operating at home or in a foreign culture, for marketing efforts are more often than not cultural innovations. As one anthropologist points out, "the market survey is but one attempt to study this problem of acceptance or rejection of an internal change . . . [and] in every attempt to introduce,

---

[20] Nobuko Hashimoto, "Sushi Chains Satisfy Japan's Appetite for Traditional Fare, Fast-Food Flair, *Asian Wall Street Journal Weekly*, May 18, 1981, p. 3.

[21] For an interesting discussion of courting and marriage in Japan see: "Marriage-Minded Japanese Turn to Mama," *The Asian Wall Street Journal Weekly*, August 24, 1981, p. 13.

in a foreign society, a new idea, a new technique, a new kind of goods, the question [of acceptance or rejection] must be faced."

Most cultures tend to be ethnocentric; that is, they have intense identification with the known and the familiar of their culture and tend to devalue the foreign and unknown of other cultures. Ethnocentrism produces a feeling of superiority about one's own culture and, in varying degrees, generates inferior, barbaric, or at least peculiar feelings about other cultures which complicate the process of cultural assimilation. Ethnocentric feelings generally give way if a new idea is considered necessary or particularly appealing.

There are many reasons cultures resist new ideas, techniques, or products. Even when an innovation is needed from the viewpoint of an objective observer, a culture may resist that innovation if the people lack an awareness of the need for it. If there is no perceived need within the culture then there is no demand. Ideas may be rejected because local environmental conditions preclude functional use and thus useful acceptance, or they may be of such complex nature that they exceed the ability of the culture either to effectively use them or to understand them. Other innovations may be resisted because acceptance would require important values, customs, or beliefs to be modified.

Imagine the problems facing the French government in mounting a campaign to persuade the French to drink apple or grape juice, or even water in place of wine and other alcoholic beverages. Their concern is the high incidence of alcoholism in France where the per capita consumption of alcohol is the highest in the world. The French citizen—man, woman, and child drinks 16 liters per year, twice that of U.S. consumption. Success is possible only if values and customs can be changed. Such changes will be especially difficult to accomplish in a country where many pour brandy into morning coffee, drink wine with a mid-morning snack, and wash down lunch and dinner with two liters of wine. Add aperitifs before meals and brandy afterward, rare public water fountains, and bottled water that costs more in a restaurant than beer or wine and the scope of the problem begins to emerge. As one Frenchman commented, "We French think tap water is something to wash your hands in." This is not the first time the government has attempted to change French drinking customs; in 1955, a campaign to get the French to drink milk failed. Perhaps grape juice will succeed although the farmers and vintners who produce the vins ordinaires will also resist the change, making the task all the more difficult.[22]

All facets of a culture are interrelated, and when the acceptance of a new idea necessitates the displacement of some other custom, threatens its sanctity, or conflicts with tradition, the probability of rejection is greater. Although cultures meet most newness with some resistance or rejection, that resistance can be overcome. Cultures are dynamic and change occurs

---

[22] "A War Against the Genie in the Bottle," *World Business Weekly,* January 17, 1981, p. 38.

BOX 4–7: Why wouldn't you buy Fang Fang lipstick?

With more and more trade between China and the United States, one of the problems facing the Chinese is the translation into English of Chinese brand names. When translated, perfectly acceptable brand names to the Chinese take on a somewhat different connotation. For example, they introduced a new sewing machine for the export market with the brand name "Typical." When told that it was a bad name because it meant undistinguished, they replied that the United States had companies with similar names, like "Standard Oil." Other brands that didn't translate well were: "White Elephant Auto Parts," "Pansy Men's Clothing," "Junk Chemicals," and "Fang Fang Lipstick."

---

when resistance slowly yields to acceptance so the basis for resistance becomes unimportant or forgotten. Gradually there comes an awareness of the need for change, ideas once too complex become less so because of cultural gains in understanding, or an idea is restructured in a less complex way, and so on.

Once a need is recognized, even the establishment may be unable to prevent the acceptance of a new idea. It is doubtful that Pope Paul V's Sixth Proclamation which cautioned women to be on their guard against movements of equality that run the risk of "virilizing and depersonalizing" them will have much affect on the Women's Liberation Movement among Catholic women in the United States, although among Italian women it may have a significant effect. According to the pontiff, the movement would equalize men and women and deprive woman of her essential role of motherhood.[23] For some ideas, solutions to problems, or new products, resistance can be overcome in months; for others, approval may come only after decades or centuries.

An understanding of the process of acceptance of innovations is of crucial importance to the marketer since many of the products or marketing programs introduced into another culture will face resistance. The marketer cannot wait centuries or even decades for acceptance but must gain acceptance within the limits of financial resources and projected profitability periods. Possible methods and insights are offered by social scientists who are concerned with the concepts of planned social change. Historically, most cultural borrowing and the resulting change has occurred without a deliberate plan but, increasingly, changes are occurring in societies as a result of purposeful attempts by some acceptable institution to bring about change, i.e., planned change.

PLANNED CULTURAL CHANGE

The first step in bringing about planned change in a society is to determine which cultural factors conflict with an innovation and create resistance to

---

[23] "Pope Cautions against Women's Lib," *Associated Press*, February 1, 1976.

its acceptance. The next step is an effort to change those factors from obstacles to acceptance into stimulants for change. The same deliberate approaches used by the social planner to gain acceptance for hybrid grains, better sanitation methods, improved farming techniques, or protein-rich diets among the peoples of underdeveloped societies can be adopted by marketers to achieve marketing goals.[24]

Marketers have two options when introducing an innovation to a culture. They can wait, or they can cause change. The former requires hopeful waiting for eventual cultural changes that will prove their innovations of value to the culture; the latter involves introducing an idea or product and deliberately setting about to overcome resistance and to cause change that will accelerate the rate of acceptance.

Obviously not all marketing efforts require change in order to be accepted. In fact, much successful and highly competitive marketing is accomplished by a *culturally congruent strategy.* Essentially this involves marketing products similar to ones already on the market in a manner as congruent as possible with existing cultural norms, thereby minimizing resistance. However, when marketing programs require cultural change to be successful, a company may decide to leave acceptance to a *strategy of unplanned change,* or to employ a *strategy of planned change,* that is, deliberately setting out to change aspects of the culture which are offering resistance to predetermined marketing goals. With the use of these last strategies the marketer becomes a change agent. While culturally congruent strategy, strategy of unplanned change, and strategy of planned change are not clearly articulated in international business literature, the three situations occur. The marketer's efforts become part of the fabric of culture, planned or unplanned.

Take, for example, the change in diet that has occurred in Japan since the introduction of milk and bread soon after World War II. The average Japanese, who are predominately fish eaters, have increased their intake of animal fat and protein to the point that fat and protein exceeded vegetable intake for the first time in 1981. As many MacDonald's hamburgers are apt to be eaten in Japan as the traditional rice ball wrapped in edible seaweed. Along with the westernized diet many Japanese have accepted comes overweight. To counter this, the Japanese are buying low-calorie, low-fat foods to help shed excess weight and are flocking to health studios. This all began when the occupation forces introduced bread, milk, and steak to Japanese culture.[25]

Marketing strategy is judged culturally in terms of acceptance, resistance, or rejection. How marketing efforts interact with the culture will determine

---

[24] For an interesting text on change agents see Gerald Zaltman and Robert Duncan, *Strategies for Planned Change* (New York: John Wiley & Sons, 1979), 404 pp.

[25] Geoffrey Murray, "While Rice Rots, Japanese Eat Western Food," *Christian Science Monitor* News Service, January 5, 1981.

the degree of success or failure, but even failures leave their imprint on a culture. All too frequently marketers are not aware of the scope of their impact on a host culture. Further illustration of the use of these ideas will be included in the chapter on product development.[26]

BOX 4–8: Cultural differences

There is nothing common about the Common Market. The European community is not a cultural entity which has identical patterns of thought, attitudes, and behaviour throughout. Mark Abrams has described three Europes: the "new Europe" of big cities like Paris, London, Hamburg, Stockholm, and their conurbations, together with areas of high-density population such as Switzerland and northwest Italy. The "emerging Europe" of his second classification is composed of areas such as the semiurbanised hinterlands of southern France, northern Italy, and southwest Germany. His third grouping, termed "old Europe," refers to the "marginal" farming lands to be found in parts of Spain, Portugal, and NW Scotland. Purchase decisions are influenced by cultural patterns of behaviour. The status of women in society will be of significant interest, for instance, to manufacturers of domestic labour-saving equipment. A few years ago, Singer found that in selling sewing machines in Middle Eastern countries, the husband rather than the wife had to be approached with the argument that the ownership of a sewing machine would make his wife more efficient and useful, not merely save *her* personal trouble and time. In his 1972 report to shareholders, the Unilever Chairman commented that the price of success in multinational trading is "endless readiness to adapt. We must recognize that the Irish like a different flavour in margarine from the English; that in the UK we can build up our own distribution of frozen food direct to the shop but, in Germany, we also use the existing wholesaler distribution; that, in Switzerland, fabrics may be washed in an automatic washing machine at 85°C which in Portugal will be washed by hand at 40°C."

Source: P. M. Chisnall, Manchester Business School, UK, "International Marketing: A Strategic and Tactical Analysis," *Quarterly Review of Marketing*, Winter 1975, p. 8.

SUMMARY

A complete and thorough appreciation of the dimensions of culture may well be the single most important gain to a foreign marketer in the preparation of marketing plans and strategies. Marketers can control the product offered to a market—its promotion, price, and eventual distribution methods, but they have only limited control over the cultural environment within which these plans must be implemented. Since they cannot control all the influences on their marketing plans, they must attempt to anticipate the eventual effect of the uncontrollable elements and plan in such a way that these elements do not preclude the achievement of marketing objectives. They can also set about to effect changes that will lead to quicker acceptance of their products or marketing programs. Planning marketing strategy in terms of

---

[26] For a very comprehensive and meaningful article on the effects of MNCs in LDCs, see John S. Hill and Richard R. Still, "Cultural Effects of Technology Transfer by Multinational Corporations in Lesser Developed Countries," *Columbia Journal of World Business*, Summer 1980, pp. 40–51.

the uncontrollable elements of a market is necessary in a domestic market as well, but when a company is operating internationally, the task is complicated by a new environment influenced by elements unfamiliar and sometimes unrecognizable to the marketer. For these reasons, special effort and study are needed to absorb enough understanding of the foreign culture to cope with the uncontrollable features. Perhaps it is safe to generalize that of all the tools the foreign marketer must have, those that help generate empathy for another culture are the most valuable. Each of the cultural elements will be explored in depth in subsequent chapters.

QUESTIONS

1. Define:

   Cultural empathy   Strategy of planned change
   Culture   "Cultured"
   Culture scheme   "Similar but different"
   Ethnocentrism   Material
   Design for Living   Aesthetics
   Culturally congruent strategy   Frame of reference
   Strategy of unplanned change   Cultural translator

2. What role does the marketer play as a change agent?

3. Discuss the three cultural change strategies a foreign marketer can pursue.

4. "Culture is pervasive in all marketing activities." Discuss.

5. What is the importance of cultural empathy to foreign marketers? How do they acquire cultural empathy?

6. Why should a foreign marketer be concerned with the study of culture?

7. What is the popular definition of culture? What is the viewpoint of cultural anthropologists? What is the importance of the difference?

8. It is stated that members of a society borrow from other cultures to solve problems which they face in common. What does this mean? What is the significance to marketing?

9. "For the inexperienced marketer the 'similar but different' feature of culture creates an illusion of similarity which usually does not exist." Discuss and give examples.

10. Outline the elements of culture as seen by an anthropologist. How can a marketer use this "cultural scheme"?

11. What is material culture? What are its implications for marketing? Give examples.

12. Social institutions affect marketing in a variety of ways. Discuss, give examples.

13. Discuss the implications and meaning of the statement, "Markets are not, they become."

14. "Markets are the result of the triune interaction of a marketer's efforts, economic conditions, and all other elements of the culture." Comment.

15. What are some particularly troublesome problems caused by language in foreign marketing? Discuss.

16. Suppose you were requested to prepare a cultural analysis for a potential market, what would you do? Outline the steps and comment briefly on each.

17. Cultures are dynamic. How do they change? Are there cases where changes are not resisted but actually preferred? Explain. What is the relevance to marketing?

18. How can resistance to cultural change influence product introduction? Are there any similarities in domestic marketing? Explain, giving examples.

19. Prepare a cultural analysis for a specific country and product.

Chapter 5

Business customs and practices in world marketing

An integral component of cultural environment is the manner in which people transact business. Business customs are as much a cultural element of a society as is the language. In fact, most of the cultural elements discussed in the preceding chapters are manifest in business customs. A lack of empathy for and knowledge of foreign business practices are serious deterrents to world trade. An even more serious threat to successful international marketing occurs when business people stumble ahead assuming that other business cultures are similar to their own without realizing their lack of knowledge or comprehension. Even a company successfully doing business overseas may find it is paying a stiff penalty for its lack of cultural adaptation. Only the most naive and unsophisticated would attempt to sell a consumer product abroad without trying to understand the ways of the foreign customer, yet a frequently held misconception is that business counterparts in other countries are moved by similar interests and motivations. Nothing can be further from the truth.

The tragedy of this misconception is that the marketer's channel to the final consumer is through foreign executives and managers whose unresponsiveness may prevent an otherwise acceptable product from ever reaching the market. Because an international marketer must deal first with a variety of foreign intermediaries, a lack of understanding of business customs can create insurmountable barriers.

Even though many obstacles lie in the way of the international marketer, a knowledge of business culture, management attitudes, and business methods can remove many of the obstacles. One authority comments that "without flexibility in one's own attitudes in accepting or at least tolerating differences in such matters as bathing, flavors of food, modes of dress, and basic patterns of thinking, the visiting business person will seldom be able to negotiate a satisfactory conclusion." Obstacles take many forms, but it is not unusual to have a situation in which one negotiator's business proposition is accepted over another's because "that one understands us."

The dominant role of the general culture in developing the business culture should be recognized; this chapter will focus on matters more specifically related to the business environment. Besides an analysis of the need for adaptation, the present chapter explores the complex problems of marketing in various business cultures and reviews the structure of international business processes. Structual elements, attitudes, and behavior are examined, along with patterns of competition and the modes of doing business.

REQUIRED ADAPTATION

Adaptation is a concept in international marketing, and willingness to adapt is a crucial attitude. Adaptation, or at least adaptability, is required on small matters as well as large ones. In fact, the small, seemingly insignificant situations are the most crucial. One writer comments that more than tolerance of an alien culture is required, there is a need for affirmative acceptance of "different but equal." Through such affirmative acceptance, adaptation becomes easier because empathy for another's point of view naturally leads to ideas for meeting cultural differences.

Every trading country throughout history has learned that it must adapt. In ancient Greece, Solon, the lawgiver (c. 639–559 B.C.), persuaded fellow Athenians to adopt the Euboic system of weights and measures to facilitate commerce with Asia Minor. It has taken American business a long time to learn it must adapt not only personal relationships but products and promotional materials to the needs of the customer country. One frequently encounters instances where Latin American countries have purchased goods from Italy or Germany rather than from the United States because U.S. business insisted on providing English instructions and using nonmetric weights and measures. Fortunately for the U.S. balance of payments, American business is learning to adapt.

As a guide to adaptation, one article lists "10 basic criteria that all those who wish to deal with individuals, firms, or authorities in foreign countries should be able to meet." The 10 are (1) tolerance, (2) flexibility, (3) humility, (4) justice and fairness, (5) adjustability to varying tempos, (6) curiosity and interest, (7) knowledge of the country, (8) liking for others, (9) ability to command respect, and (10) ability to integrate oneself into the environment. In short, add the quality of adaptability to the qualities of a good executive for a composite of the perfect international marketer.

Degree of adaptation

Adaptability and adaptation do not require the business executive or representative to give up native ways or change to conform with local customers. It is impossible as well as undesirable for an expatriate, particularly one in the country for a short time, to conform too completely. An English manager does not expect a German to act, speak, and live as though he or she were English. On the other hand, an expatriate manager must not expect local workers to adapt to foreign ways either. When Japanese managers of a Honda manufacturing plant in the United States expected American workers to accept company uniforms and be willing to sing the company

song, they encountered resistance. They quickly realized that although it
worked in Japan, it was counter to U.S. workers' customs. Cultural adaptation
is a requirement of *any* foreign marketer working in *any* foreign environment. American business people do not hold an exclusive right on misunderstanding the ways of strangers.[1]

BOX 5–1:   Doing it my way

   I never cease to admire the calm with which Japanese businessmen deal with
the unpredictable. You might even say they expect the unexpected. They're neither
shocked nor surprised that things are different in the Middle East. Their flexible attitude
of adapting policy to meet local requirements is forcing other countries to be more
sensitive also. If American companies refuse to show the same flexibility, they're
likely to lose out in the long run.
   The Western attitude that gets you strictly no place in the Middle East can be
summed up in the phrase "It's our policy." Translated it means "Sorry, we can't
do this. If you want to do business with us, you'll have to do it our way."

   Source: Katayba Alghanim, "How to Do Business in the Middle East," *Management Review*,
August 1976, p. 20.

Imperatives, adiaphora, and exclusives

   When one becomes aware of the possibility of cultural differences and
the probable consequences of failure to adapt, the seemingly endless variety
of customs can be overwhelming. Where does one begin, what customs
should absolutely be adhered to, what others can be ignored? Answers
to these questions are important. The international marketer must give up
ways that are offensive to customers and business associates. An international
marketer must appreciate the nuances of cultural imperative, cultural adiaphora, and cultural exclusives.
   Cultural imperative refers to the business customs and expectations that
must be met and conformed to. For example, when doing business with a
Mid-Eastern businessman, time spent in small talk and visiting before getting
"down to business" is an absolute necessity. It may seem like a waste of
time to a Westerner but it is a Mid-Eastern custom absolutely necessary to
observe or risk never earning trust and acceptance in that culture. The
Mid-Eastern manager puts much stronger emphasis on personal contact
than does the U.S. manager, and earning the Mid-Easterners trust and acceptance are basic cultural prerequisites for developing and retaining effective
business relationships.[2]
   Cultural adiaphora relates to areas of behavior or to customs which cultural aliens may wish to conform to or participate in but that are not required.

---

[1] "Kearney's Marvin Schiller: The Lessons of Going Global," *World Business Weekly*, August 10, 1981, p. 21.

[2] M. K. Badawy, "Styles of Mid-Eastern Managers," *California Management Review*, Spring
1980, p. 57.

It is not particularly important, but it is permissible to follow the custom in question; the majority of customs fit into this category. One need not adhere to local dress, greet another man with a kiss (a custom in some countries), or eat foods which disagree with the digestive system so long as the refusal is gracious.

BOX 5–2: How to play your cards right in Japan
or
Would you imagine that presenting a business card was so involved?

In Japan, the business card is the executive's trademark. It is both a mini-resume and a friendly deity which draws people together. As a consequence, there is a certain gamesmanship or etiquette which has evolved.

Take, as an example, the following instructions given to Japanese businessmen. First of all, have plenty of cards on hand when attending a large meeting of Japanese businessmen. A participant must have at least 40 cards for each meeting. Participants often exchange cards more than once since the single exchange may not make a lasting impression. For a businessman to make a call or receive a visitor without a card is like a Samurai going off to battle without his sword. It is bad form to greet someone and then, flipping through a card holder, apologize for being out of cards.

The card holder is also a mark of distinction. It should be of good quality and appropriate. A secretary may keep her cards in a handbag, but it makes a bad impression when a young executive pulls a card out of a cheap plastic case used for commuting tickets.

Always stand up when giving or receiving a business card. This iron rule applies regardless of age or status. There are a variety of ways to present a card, depending on the giver's personality and style:

Crab style—held out between the index and middle fingers.

Pincer—clamped between the thumb and index finger.

Pointer—offered with the index finger pressed along the edge.

Upside down—the name is facing away from the recipient.

Platter fashion—served in the palm of the hand.

Not only is there a way to present a card, there is also a way of receiving a card. It makes a good impression to receive a card in both hands, especially when the other party is senior in age or status.

You may put a business card away immediately upon receiving it; however, it is an inexcusable fax pas to put a card away with a brief glance and then, while offering a chair, peek into your pockets to recall his business name.

Source: Adapted from Sakio Sakagawa, "How to Play Your Cards Right in Japan," *The Asian Wall Street Journal Weekly*, June 15, 1981, p. 11.

Executives should also recognize certain *cultural exclusives;* that is, customs or behavior from which the foreigner is excluded. It is not appropriate, for example, for a Christian to attempt to act like a Muslim. Such an attempt would be repugnant to a follower of Muhammad.

Frequently, cultural adiaphora are the most visibly different customs and thus more tempting for the foreigner to try to adapt to when, in fact, adaptation is unnecessary and frequently unwelcome. By concentrating on the wrong customs, they may ignore the more important cultural imperatives which they must abide by and the cultural exclusives they must avoid. A foreign manager must have the perception to know when he is dealing with an imperative, an adiaphora, and with exclusives and the adaptability to deal with each. There are not many imperatives or exclusives, but most offensive behavior results from not recognizing them. When in doubt, rely on good manners and respect for those with whom you are associating.

THE COMPLEXITY OF THE PROBLEM

In this age of shrinking distances between world markets and of rapid change, confusion seems to be the predominant state of mind for a business person contemplating overseas business relationships. It is difficult to cope with so many problems and such a rapidly changing environment. Even the international marketing expert specializing in a single foreign country finds it necessary to be especially alert and perceptive to be attuned to the spirit of the time. The complexity of the situation rests on three points. First, business customs are derived from the basic culture in which the business person operates. Such cultures may be, and usually are, complex themselves. Second, there is great behavioral diversity not only among nations but also within national subcultures. Third, all cultures, particularly the business segments, are constantly changing.

Relationship between culture and business customs

The behavior of business and the culture of a nation are inextricably intertwined.[3] Although culture is modified by the presence of foreign business, we generally think of this interrelationship in terms of business customs and practices being influenced by the culture of the nation or region in which the foreign business operates. Certainly this is the appropriate place for emphasis, but also bear in mind that in today's business-oriented world economy, the cultures themselves are being significantly influenced by business activities and business practices. Cultural anthropologists know that the intermarriage of foreign traders has significantly affected the private as well as the business customs of the adopted country. Indeed, nations such as Germany have been formed to facilitate interregional and intergroup trading relationships.

Most languages, both historical and modern, contain examples of intercultural effects of international marketing relationships; the words Caterpillar, Coca-Cola, and Ford are accepted parts of the local idiom in large parts of the world. And although the effect of business intercourse on the basic

---

[3] For an excellent study of cultural affects on management, see Lane, Kelley and Reginald Worthley, "The Role of Culture in Comparative Management: A Cross Cultural Perspective," *Academy of Management Journal*, no. 1 (1981), pp. 164–73.

culture is acknowledged, it in no way detracts from the fact that the more common cultural relationship is that of business accommodating itself to the native culture. Because individual orientation and cultural patterns change slowly, the domination of a culture in a business situation is inescapable.[4]

Culture not only establishes the criteria for day-to-day behavior but also forms general patterns of attitude and motivation. In the United States, for example, the historical perspective of individualism and "winning the West" today seem to manifest themselves as individual wealth or corporate profit being dominant measures of success. Japan's lack of frontiers and natural resources and its dependence on trade have focused individual and corporate success criteria in terms of uniformity, subordination to the group, and society's ability to maintain high levels of employment. The recent feudal background of southern Europe tends to emphasize maintenance of both individual and corporate power and authority, but blends those feudal concerns with paternalistic concern for minimal welfare for workers and other members of society. Various studies have identified North Americans as individualists; Japanese as consensus oriented and committed to their group; central and southern Europeans as elitists and rank conscious (these descriptions, of course, represent stereotyping and illustrate both the best and worst of that process). Spanish sociologist, Travessi Anderes, contrasts the hierarchical theological influence of the Roman Catholic way of thinking where profits are considered almost sinful and individualism suspicious with the Anglo-Saxon Protestant view that profit is the evidence of rational action by the all-important individual.

Executives, at least partially, are captives of their cultural heritages and cannot escape religious backgrounds, language heritage, or political and family ties. Business customs and daily habits are more likely to be those of one's own people.[5] Such ethnocentrism causes problems when: (1) communicating with company headquarters, (2) adapting to local cultures, or (3) keeping up with political and economic change.

The business person must be aware that foreign counterparts measure standard of living by peer comparison; these peers also provide a motivational frame of reference. Although internationally minded executives might take on the trappings and appearances of business behavior from other countries, their basic frames of reference will still be their own cultures. In fact, culture tends to dominate the domestic business person as well as the foreign visitor.

Prolonged military occupations historically have been characterized by the invading troops being partially assimilated into local cultures as they

---

[4] George W. England, "Managers and Their Value Systems: A Five Country Comparative Study," *Columbia Journal of World Business,* Summer 1978, pp. 35–44.

[5] "Once a Frenchman Always a Frenchman," *International Management,* June 1980, pp. 45–46.

adopt the foreign ways that add convenience or pleasure to their lives. Perhaps such an assimilation of visiting business executives is inevitable as well as desirable.

Stereotyping

One of the most dangerous but beneficial devices in dealing with an alien country is stereotyping: making broad generalizations about a group that includes many diverse elements. (*Stereotype* literally means "to repeat without variation.") Without generalizing or stereotyping it is difficult to cope with the diversity of cultural elements which bombard the business person in international situations. The stereotype can provide an overall understanding—some handholds with which to grasp the broad cultural scheme. Once a basis has been established, the individual must be dealt with as such and stereotypes must be abandoned. Even in the most homogeneous culture the individual prevails and must be analyzed and dealt with separately.

Predominance of local cultures in international business customs implies as great a diversity in business as in personal customs. Such diversity exists not only among countries but *within* countries. There is a tendency to want to regard countries as simple units of similar components, but this is seldom the case. The same individual who would avoid generalizations about national peers is often tempted to generalize concerning countries about which far less is known. It is always appropriate to look for areas of homogeneity to aid understanding but within that context one must always look for the heterogeneity of the individual.

We find diversity not only among countries but among businesses and persons of different ages, rank, and sex. Variations deal with personal charac-

---

BOX 5–3:   Shaking hands, tak, skål, and hygge

In Denmark, spades are spades; verbal camouflage has never been popular. Statements are often very direct—but that does not mean they are intended to insult.

Danes may not have invented the custom of shaking hands, but they certainly have adopted it with rare enthusiasm. At most social gatherings there is a gauntlet to be run, handshakes for all present. And the process is repeated when one leaves, normally at 11 p.m. or later, and not immediately after a dinner is over.

Three essential Danish words are *tak, hygge,* and *skål.* Tak means thank you, and is used frequently—by this writer's count up to 11 times in merely buying a loaf of bread and getting the change.

Skål, the Scandinavian toast, involves lifting the glass and exchanging glances before drinking, and again afterwards. Every time!

Hygge is, as any Dane knows, the untranslatable Danish concept for which "cozy" and "snug" are but pale shadows. It can be and often is used to describe virtually anything in this world. Books could be written about this custom.

Source: "Getting Along with the Danes," *Denmark Review,* The Royal Danish Ministry of Foreign Affairs, Copenhagen, 1980, pp. 20–21.

teristics and include motivation, attitude, and behavior; three classifications which cover just about every aspect of the individual. Along with diverse management outlooks at different levels of business, every personal outlook and management practice is likely to be found.[6] All aspects of business activity must constantly be analyzed, classified, and generalized if foreign business and its environment are to be understood. For example:

In: The Orient	*One:* Makes points without winning arguments; thus the adversary need not "lose face."
Italy	Argues to win; thus is taken seriously.
Switzerland	Speaks precisely and will be taken quite literally.
Great Britain	Uses the "soft sell" approach.
Germany	Uses the "hard sell" approach.
Mexico	Emphasizes the price of the goods.
Venezuela	Emphasizes quality of goods.

Cultural awareness follows commerce; for North Americans one could characterize the time following World War II as the European period and the 1970s as Japanese. The 1980s will certainly be known for the growth of awareness of the Arabian, and consequently Muslim cultures. Seemingly, in U.S. minds, Latin America is incidental and Africa has not yet been discovered.

Already outdated!

Problems of change

The commercial frontier today is a montage of old and new. A study by the Foessa Foundation in Madrid highlights conflict in the managerial elite between "traditional" and "modern" values, the former emphasizing personal feelings and values and the latter, rationality and data. The traditionalist is more likely to be concerned with human values, the modernist with technology. Young persons tend to do business one way, the older persons another way. Within a country even local personnel are in a quandary over which culture they should follow.

The broadening and democratizing of European management functions represents the real Americanization of Europe. Business managers of the world collect good ideas regardless of their source; such idea collecting often results in business customs that blend Oriental, European, and American business behavior. This type of eclectic borrowing has resulted in a certain amount of confusion and chaos.

If possible, the problem of dealing with changing conditions is even

---

[6] See Dennis Anastos, Alexis Bédos and Bryant Seaman, "The Development of Modern Management Practices in Saudi Arabia," *Columbia Journal of World Business,* Summer 1980, pp. 81–92.

more complex and difficult than that of dealing with the cultural diversity of business. The tempo and scope of change in the international business scene can be observed best at a distance. Significant changes take place within even a single decade which completely differentiate the managers of each period. Reliance on earlier information is in many cases irrelevant and, in some cases, downright misleading. In recent years in England, for example, business leadership has shifted gradually from family to professional management. Marketers can be led astray if they rely on old information and fail to allow for changes. It must be kept in mind that changes are gradual and seldom even throughout a culture. There is no doubt that the Japanese are becoming more westernized in many of their business ways, but as some contend, they are Western from "9 to 5" only.[7]

BUSINESS STRUCTURE

The same patterns of diversity and change that characterize business customs and habits are apparent in the structure of business firms. It is difficult, if not impossible, to evaluate and describe fully the structural patterns in different countries. The chief significance of structural forms is how they will affect decision making and authority patterns among customers. Elements which should be evaluated are size, ownership, relationship of the business to its various publics, and the authority patterns.

Size

Size is significant in business structure analysis for purposes of comparison. One method of analyzing business behavior patterns compares businesses of similar size in different countries. Briefly, we can simply classify businesses into large-, medium-, and small-scale firms, neglecting the more esoteric and academic discussions of what constitutes a large, medium, or small business. At a given size level, the managerial outlook from country to country might be fairly similar. Large organizations are probably most homogeneous from country to country because of professional management and the adaptation of American business methods. Business managers in medium-sized and small firms are less likely to have felt the impact of management practices from other countries. Management in smaller firms is likely to be more closely tied to the customs and attitudes of the country than to the attitudes of counterpart managers in other countries.

The composition of business firms classified by size varies greatly from country to country. Nearly every industrial country has some extremely large business firms, and every nation has large numbers of small and very small businesses. It should be noted that actual size is hard to measure in situations

---

[7] Peter F. Drucker, "How Westernized are the Japanese?" *The Wall Street Journal*, August 21, 1980, p. 25.

of interlocking directorates, financial leverage, or other tying arrangements that combine nominally separate firms into de facto unity. Consider some of the industrial-financial-commercial combines of Japan, for example. Mitsui & Company is a trading company with sales of some $20 billion. It is affiliated with industrial and financial firms and has direct (and mostly exclusive) trading rights for over 1,000 other Japanese companies.

BOX 5–4: Old customs never die they just fade away

"Young Ohira will be the chief executive of this company in 10 to 15 years," I had been told repeatedly by the chairman of one of the leading high-technology firms. But when I inquire about Ohira on my latest Japanese trip, there is embarrassed silence. "We had to let him go," the chairman says. "He is an oldest son and his father, who owns a small wholesale business in Kobe, demanded that he take over the family company. We tried to talk the old man out of it, but he is stubborn and so we had to let Ohira go."

"Did he want to leave?" I ask. "Of course not, but he had no choice. He could never have been promoted if he had stayed. Executives, after all, have to set an example—and in Japan an oldest son is still expected to follow his father in his business."

Peter F. Drucker, "How Westernized are the Japanese?" *The Wall Street Journal,* August 21, 1980, p. 12. From *The Changing World of the Executive,* Peter F. Drucker (Times Books, New York, 1982).

The significant question is not that of the range between the large and small but the composition of the business community. *Fortune* magazine regularly compiles a list of America's 1,000 and the world's 500 largest industrial firms. The United States has about the same number of firms as the rest of the free world in the over-$500-million sales bracket (372 U.S. versus 416) and about the same ratio in the over-$250-million sales bracket. Similar data are not readily available or comparable for other sectors of the economy, but business firms in the United States generally are larger in size than they are in other parts of the world.

Management behavior and customs—or more specifically, management skills, orientation, and operational patterns—will vary greatly in organizations of different size. Awareness of the industry structure for a given country can provide significant clues to management behavior.

Business size will affect the volume of sales to an individual firm, the type of representation required, the number of outlets for market coverage, and the number of sales representatives to cover a given industry segment, and will have numerous other marketing implications.

Ownership

Foreign business ownership patterns vary significantly from the ownership patterns of American business. In the United States, businesses tend to be privately owned by first- or second-generation business people or by private investors who have purchased stock and vested management in professional managers. Public ownership of major companies throughout the world is becoming more common. Capital demands of rapid growth, increased availability of investor funds, and merger activities all emphasize the shift from family to public ownership.

Ownership varies from country to country but three patterns of some importance in the United States may be identified. They are: government ownership, family (clan) ownership, and cooperative ownership. Government plays a large (perhaps a dominant) role in business ownership in many free countries. There are few, if any, countries which have so little government investment in business as the United States. For example, some 40 percent of Brazilian business capital is government owned; in Norway, the government's investment approaches some 70 percent of productive enterprise.

In some nations, complete industries have been nationalized and are owned directly by the government. Italy's ENI (Enté Nazionale Idrocarburi) petroleum monopoly is an example of this type of operation. Even before the Socialist Party came to power in France, one third of the 21 largest multinational companies were owned wholly or in part by the government. Since Mitterrand became president of France, the government has moved to nationalize several major sectors of the economy. Government-controlled enterprise is a major form of ownership in most European countries.[8]

The family business dynasty is a second ownership pattern in many countries. A combination family-government pattern is emerging in many of the Middle Eastern countries where there is a strange amalgam of shah, king, prince, brother relationship between business and government.

In some countries, three or four families dominate the entire business and financial scene, and a favorable position with these families is essential to succeed in business. Such family holdings are in some cases the residuals of a feudal age when land wealth was concentrated in the hands of a very few. In other cases, family fortunes are based on generations of expansion from humble industrial or financial enterprises. In many instances, an entire industry will be controlled by a single family group. In Germany, for example, the name Krupp is synonymous with steel; the Indian family Ghanshyamdas Birla controls some 350 Indian business concerns. One of the world's great family-owned concerns is the European empire of the Rothschilds; in Japan, Mitsubishi Iwasaki, Mitsui, Sumitomo, and other families dominate the industrial scene. The trend to concentrate power exists even in rapidly developing economies. An informed executive in the Arab countries can usually tell you which families dominate various industries; such matters are essentially common knowledge.

Except for the agricultural co-op, cooperative enterprises have made little

[8] Renato, Mazzolini, "European Government-Controlled Enterprises: An Organizational Politics View," *Journal of International Business Studies*, Spring/Summer 1980, pp. 48–58.

headway on the American business scene. Quite the reverse is true in Europe where many of the larger businesses are cooperatives. Such general ownership is likely to further contribute to the utilization of professional managers. An outstanding example of this third form of enterprise is the Migros cooperative in Switzerland. Migros accounts for a majority of all retail food sales in Switzerland and has significant market shares in other countries and other product areas.

Various business publics

The policies and behavior of business are affected by the degree to which they are held accountable by the various business publics—government, consumers, labor, and stockholders. Assessments and generalizations about business responsibility are subject to the same hazards of diversity and change that plague any cultural evaluation. The social relationships of business are in a particularly active period of ferment and change in today's age of industrial awakening, growth, and world consciousness. The predominant direction of change has been from narrow self-seeking or owner-serving to greater responsibility to the public at large. American business seems generally to be characterized by a basic loyalty to stockholders with considerable emphasis on the consumer; the marketplace is a key regulator of action.

In some countries, all business bows to the government; in others, the financial community dominates all other business. Labor, in many nations, occupies a particularly warm place in the hearts of business managers and owners. Militant labor groups in many Latin American countries are able to *demand* worker rights. As with diversity found in every phase of business, European employers may be indifferent to worker rights or extremely paternalistic. A recent development, characterized as *codetermination,* is to have workers or representatives of unions or labor councils sit on company boards of directors or, at least, on advisory boards. Increasingly, even in Germany where it is called *Mitbestimmung,* worker participation in management decisions has become a major factor in labor negotiations and an item of special interest to government agencies and to the European community. It is interesting that the varying national attitudes toward responsibility to labor were stumbling blocks in the early formation of the European Common Market. France, Italy, and Belgium were traditionally more welfare oriented than Germany and the Netherlands. Guaranteed lifetime employment is common in many welfare-oriented economies where governments avidly protect workers' rights.

In most countries, it appears that the consumer is the only business public without a preferential position in the eyes of business. Only by exerting force through the marketplace does the consumer receive full consideration. The lack of consumer representation is beginning to change with the growing worldwide interest in consumerism. Product warranties, product liability, and truthfulness in advertising—all issues important in U.S. consumerism movements—are also issues in other countries around the world.[9]

The relationship of business to its various publics significantly affects the attitudes and behavior of foreign business people and should be understood by the marketer.

Sources and level of authority

Business size, ownership, and public accountability combine to influence the authority structure of business. The diversity characterizing each element naturally creates a diversity in authority structure. Knowledge of authority patterns is crucial to an international marketer who must be perceptive and discerning to successfully consummate negotiations in international trade. Each company, indeed each decision, relates to a somewhat different authority structure, but it is useful to examine three typical authority patterns: top-level management decisions, decentralized decisions, and committee decisions.

Top-management decision making. The prerogative of decision making is usually reserved by top management in situations where family or close ownership gives absolute control to the managers and where business size is small enough to make such decision centralization possible. Management in most industrially developing countries prefers to make its own decisions wherever possible. Historically, this also appears to have been the dominant pattern in American business until World War I. Writers commenting on European business agree that European management has limited decision-making authority and that such authority is guarded jealously by top managers. Typically, the number of persons in management is relatively small and decision making is highly centralized. One authority suggests that personalities rather than objectives seem to be the primary organizational foci. Another commentator suggests that European companies "tend to put up restrictive barriers between departments" to force decisions up to the top level.

A recent study by a group of organizational theorists indicates that managers in most countries have a basic conviction that subordinates are generally inadequate people. Such a conviction naturally tends to decrease the amount of authority that will be delegated. The researchers further stated that "in all countries there universally is far more belief in shared objectives participation and in individual control than there is in the capacity of others for initiative, individual action, and leadership." They found that managers in European countries have particular scorn for the abilities of subordinates and, therefore, favor centralized decision making.

Brazil and other countries with a semi-feudal land-equals-power heritage

---

[9] For a comprehensive report on consumer protection, see E. Patrick McGuire, *Consumer Protection Implications for International Trade* (New York: The Conference Board, Inc., 1980), 63 pp.

tend to exclude decision-making participation by middle management and deemphasize upward mobility. Management decisions are made by family members who dominate the various businesses.

In Middle Eastern countries, there is no question that the top man makes all decisions and prefers to deal only with executives with decision-making powers. (See Exhibit 5–1.) A foreign company would be well advised to send top executives to conduct business negotiations in the Middle East.[10]

EXHIBIT 5–1: Differences in Mideastern and Western management

Managerial function	Mideastern stereotype	Western stereotype
Organizational design	Highly bureaucratic, over-centralized with power and authority at the top. Vague relationships. Ambiguous and unpredictable organization environments.	Less bureaucratic, more delegation of authority. Relatively decentralized structure.
Patterns of decision making	Ad hoc planning, decisions made at the highest level of management. Unwillingness to take high risk inherent in decision making.	Sophisticated planning techniques, modern tools of decision making, elaborate management information systems.
Performance evaluation and control	Informal control mechanisms, routine checks on performance. Lack of vigorous performance evaluation systems.	Fairly advanced control systems focusing on cost reduction and organizational effectiveness.
Manpower policies	Heavy reliance on personal contacts and getting individuals from the "right social origin" to fill major positions.	Sound personnel management policies. Candidate qualifications are usually the basis for selection decisions.
Leadership	Highly authoritarian tone, rigid instructions. Too many management directives.	Less emphasis on leader's personality, considerable weight on leader's style and performance.
Communication	The tone depends on the communicants. Social position, power, and family influence are ever-present factors. Chain of command must be followed rigidly. People relate to each other tightly and specifically. Friendships are intense and binding.	Stress usually on equality and a minimization of differences. People relate to each other loosely and generally. Friendships not intense and binding.
Management methods	Generally old and outdated.	Generally modern and more scientific.

M. K. Badawy, "Styles of Mideastern Managers," *California Management Review*, Spring 1980, p. 57. © 1980 by permission of the Regents.

---

[10] M. K. Badawy, "Styles of Mideastern Managers," *California Management Review*, Spring 1980, p. 58.

Decentralized decision making.   When executives at various levels of management are given decision-making authority over their own function, the decision pattern is characterized as decentralized. England's colonial and civil service heritage seems to have placed considerable emphasis on decentralized decision making. The large scale of businesses and the highly developed management systems of American business also are conducive to decentralized decision making. Pragmatism and philosophy clash in Greece, where it is reported that managers favor democratic and decentralized management but lack faith in subsidiaries' decision-making abilities. Attitudes favoring decentralized management decisions are bound to permeate other cultures as businesses grow and professional management ranks develop.

Committee decision making.   Management by group decision or by consensus may be called *committee decision making.* Committees may operate on a centralized or decentralized basis, but the concept of committee management implies something quite different from the individualized functioning of top management and decentralized decision-making arrangements just discussed. Because Far Eastern cultures and religions tend to emphasize harmony and the perfectability of humans, it is not surprising that group decision making predominates there. Despite the emphasis on rank and hierarchy in Japanese social structure, business emphasizes group participation, group harmony, and group decision making—but at top management level.

When Oriental ways were introduced in the United States through Japanese manufacturing plants, many U.S. executives were upset over the committee approach which they considered bothersome because of the time required to reach a decision. One individual with a similar complaint later indicated he appreciated the approach because it resulted in solutions that worked from the outset. The production manager of another Japanese-owned U.S. plant said "it makes you think about everything you do."[11]

The demands of these three types of authority systems on a marketer's ingenuity and adaptability are quite evident. In the case of the authoritative and delegated societies, the chief problem would be to identify the individual with authority. In the committee decision setup, it is necessary that every committee member be convinced of the merits of the proposition or product in question. The marketing approaches to each of these situations will be varied.

MANAGEMENT ATTITUDES AND BEHAVIOR

The training and background, that is, cultural environment, of managers significantly affect their personal and business outlook. Society as a whole establishes the social rank or status of management, and cultural background

---

[11] "Japan's Risk-Taking Middle Managers," *World Business Weekly,* July 13, 1981, p. 52.

dictates patterns of aspiration and objectives among business people. All these influences relate to the attitude of managers toward innovation, new products, and conducting business with foreigners. The results of such management attitudes and objectives are directly reflected in the development of the individual, business, and nation.

There is, indeed, validity to the concept of national character. Descriptions of such character may be overgeneralized, partially inaccurate, and misapplied to individuals; nevertheless, descriptions of national character can provide an introductory level of understanding of some generalized cultural traits with the caveat that all must be subjected to field observation and real-life verification.[12]

Personal background

Successful foreign marketers are always aware that business executives are subject to their own cultures and religions. They also know that foreign customer objectives and aspirations are further tempered by their training and broadening cultural horizons. Some managers learn their skills on the job and limit themselves to the industry where those skills best apply; others are trained in management and are less restricted in the application of their skills.

Sources of managers vary widely from country to country. One study revealed that only 6 percent of Italian personnel managers are sons of blue collar workers; whereas, in the United States, 38 percent of personnel

---

BOX 5–5: Then (1934) and now (1983)—better than the best

In the feudal days of Japan, it was the ambition of every samurai or warrior to serve his lord better than did any of his fellow samurai, and every local lord made efforts to stand higher in the favour of the Shogun and the Emperor than did any other lords in the country. Now that she has entered the world arena, it is her greatest ambition to be better than the best in the world in any line of culture. In the pre-war days the world charged Japan with exporting commodities cheaper than their manufactures would cost in other countries. She was not dumping them at all, but, on the contrary, she endeavoured to supply the world with cheaper articles than were supplied by any other countries in the world. In art, science, literature, trade, industry and what-not does every single Japanese aspire to stand higher in his own profession and occupation than anybody else, and in her effort to be better than the best lies indeed the secret of the great progress that Japan has made and will make to rise up from her defeated ruins. (Hakone, Japan, 1934.)

Source: "Secret of Japan's Progress" in *We Japanese, Being Descriptions of Many of the Customs, Manners, Ceremonies, Festivals, Arts and Crafts of the Japanese* (Miyanoshita, Hakone, Japan: Fujiya Hotel, Ltd., 1934). Reprinted in *Harvard Business Review*, January/February 1981, p. 90.

---

[12] For an interesting study of national character and management, see Jack L. Simonetti and Frank L. Simonetti, "When in Rome, do as the Romans Do," *Management International Review*, no. 3 (1978), pp. 69–74.

officers studied came from labor origins. In Thailand, where men prefer to enter the civil service and the legal profession, businesswomen play a major role in all segments of business. British managers are drawn from a broad population base, but the French are selected from top graduates of the elite educational institutions. One scholar suggests that the latter function more effectively as middle managers.

In most parts of the world, an official goes to work for a company expecting to spend an entire life there working up through the business hierarchy. How different will be the outlook of such a company-oriented person from that of the professional managers being developed in business schools throughout the world and who appear to be forming the nucleus of the world's new business elite.

Business status

The role of business people has been questioned in nearly every society, and social status has often been denied this group. In recent years, executives throughout the world have been expressing concern about their status. Because managers from different countries and cultures have different outlooks on status, experienced international marketers remain alert to differing viewpoints. In Japan, status seeking is learning the status of others in order to pay them suitable respect. In some countries, individuals actually prefer a lower status. It is not unusual to find individuals who would rather work at lower wages and under more difficult conditions than be managers. As supervisors they would be out of the class of their friends and be required to give up a secure (if low) status position. In most countries, executives are actively striving to overcome these barriers.

European marketers have traditionally been suspect in the eyes of their customers and fellow managers, but this is changing. The current European economic boom, which owes so much to efficient international marketing, has been so successful that society's image of European business is changing. The image of business in America has also moved upward in the past few decades. In India, with its highly structured caste system, executives and young people are aspiring to higher classes. One source comments about members of the Marwari caste (in India), indicating that "many Marwaris respected only for their business shrewdness now long for the social standing that Burla (a business leader from that caste) has earned for himself."

Objectives and aspirations

The objectives and aspirations of individual managers are usually reflected in the goals of the business organization and in the practices that prevail within the company. In dealing with foreign business, a marketer must be particularly aware of the varying objectives and aspirations of management. In the United States, we emphasize profit or high wages while in other countries, managers are more likely to emphasize security, good personal life, acceptance, status, advancement, or power. Individual goals are highly personal in any country, so one cannot generalize to the extent of saying that managers in any one country will hold a specific orientation. Managers are not homogeneous; neither is an individual manager necessarily consistent over time. Aspirational patterns may change at different stages of a career or life cycle. Nevertheless, it is still useful to identify patterns which may prevail within a given country.

As with individuals, national patterns may change. A professor in Tokyo tells how the old story of the tortoise and hare was rewritten after World War II to stress cooperation. At that time, the version had the tortoise awaken the hare and cross the finish line hand in hand with him. Years later, with an enhanced sense of competition, the story was changed back to the original Western version to show how consistent performance would overcome.[13]

Besides the differences based on national heritage, an individual's goals also depend partly on possessions (what one already has), age, position in management, and the structure of the business where employed. In general, middle-management personnel are not highly concerned about the profit position of the company because they have no direct responsibility or control over it.

Security and mobility. Personal security and job mobility relate directly to basic human motivation and therefore have widespread economic and social implications. The word *security* is somewhat ambiguous and this very ambiguity provides some clues to managerial variation. To some, security means good wages and the training and ability required for moving from company to company within the business hierarchy; for others, it means the security of a lifetime position with their company; to still others, it means an adequate retirement plan and other welfare benefits. In European companies, particularly in the countries which were late in industrializing, such as France and Italy, there is a strong paternalistic orientation, and it is assumed that individuals will work for one company for the majority of their lives.

The cultures of Japan and other Eastern countries also incorporate such paternalistic notions, and the employer feels full responsibility for guaranteeing employment security to personnel. In fact, the security offered by a Japanese company promotes the kind of loyalty found among their employees. Japan has no social security or welfare system similar to that of the United States, hence, the Japanese employee must rely on his or her company for protection. There are some who attribute much of Japan's economic success to the loyalty and reduced mobility that results. However, even in

---

[13] Analysis of children's stories has been used as a major device to evaluate achievement orientation. For some interesting generalizations relative to comparative achievement patterns in different nations, see David McClelland, *The Achieving Society* (Princeton, N.J.: Van Nostrand Reinhold, 1961) and also his *Motivating Economic Achievement* (Riverside N.J.: Free Press, 1969).

BOX 5–6:   Doing business in Africa

There is only one rule about doing business in Africa—that is, there are no rules. The businessman who wants to succeed must be flexible, patient, and ready to adapt to local whims, changing circumstances, and what must often seem to be the capricious will of Allah.

If you wait long at an African airport (as you undoubtedly will) you can easily spot the people who are going to fail. They disembark briskly, wearing immaculate suits, striped ties, and brittle smiles; they normally carry lockable briefcases along with some other gadget like a portable dictaphone. Their smiles freeze a bit when they realize they have not been met, become even more fixed after they have lost three coins in the telephone box, and disappear when they look impatiently at their watches. This last gesture reveals their fatal flaw: they are still running on "European time."

For a Westener, to be "on time" is a virtue and usually a necessity. That is because it is normally possible for Westeners to predict when a train will arrive, how long it will take a taxi to go from A to B, and things like that. These assumptions are more difficult to make in Africa. Lagos' famous "go slows" (traffic jams) confound the best-laid plans; flash floods can wash away roads in seconds; airplanes are frequently grounded for climatic reasons; and heads of families are often called away to attend to family matters.

When Europeans arrange a meeting for 12 o'clock they probably imagine extreme perimeters of 11:50 and 12:10. For an African the meeting is roughly in the middle of the day. One of the first lessons, then, is to adjust to "African time." The system does, after all, work to your advantage as well, for if you are late no one is surprised or thinks you rude.

Source: By Alan Hutchinson, reprinted from "African Guide," London, in *Atlas World Press Review*, December 1977, p. 46.

---

the Japanese system about a third of the employees are maintained on "temporary status" that is, they have no real job security and are paid significantly less than their fully employed counterparts. When a company assumes the responsibility of lifetime security for its employees, it is not unusual for it to rely on temporary help for peak periods of employment.

Much has been made of the weakening of the lifetime employment system in Japan. A continuing analysis indicates that a very small percentage of Japanese executives seek job mobility. While it is true that there is more mobility among Japanese managers today than existed just 10 years ago, the Japanese system still is a traditional one.[14]

Company and individual attitudes regarding employment security are changing rapidly, particularly in Western European countries where peace and prosperity have dimmed the memories of the insecurities of the world wars. Labor shortages have encouraged middle management shifts from company to company, thus partially relieving the parent company of its paternalistic role. It is safe to say that in most countries businesses are more involved with the everyday lives of their employees than is the case in

---

[14] Peter F. Drucker, "How Westernized are the Japanese?" *The Wall Street Journal*, August 21, 1980, p. 22.

the United States. This is either because of tradition, as in Japan, or by law, as in many South American countries.

Personal life.   For many individuals, a good personal life takes priority over profit, security, or any other goal. In his worldwide study of individual aspirations, David McClelland discovered that the culture of some countries stressed the virtue of a good personal life as being far more important than profit or achievement. The hedonistic outlook of ancient Greece explicitly included work as an undesirable thing that got in the way of the search for pleasure or a good personal life. Perhaps at least part of the standard of living which we enjoy in the United States today can be attributed to the hard-working Protestant ethic from which we derive much of our business heritage.

To the Japanese, their personal life is their company life. Many Japanese workers regard their work as the most important part of their overall lives. Metaphorically speaking, such workers may even find themselves "working in a dream." The Japanese work ethic—maintenance of a sense of purpose—derives from company loyalty and frequently results in the Japanese employee maintaining identity with the corporation.[15]

Jews have been persistently persecuted and suppressed but have persistently succeeded in the commercial world. The Roman Catholic perspective emphasizes the law but relates it to the outcome of eternal life rather than to material goods; in general, Roman Catholic nations have tended to falter commercially. Moslem and Hindu religions stress both the irrelevance of temporal life and the importance of future life; these religions have often been blamed for the lack of economic progress of many countries where they prevail.

Family ownership patterns prevalent in most countries of the world would imply that objectives of the firm are likely to be the objectives of the owners.[16] As one author comments, the business "exists by and for the family, and the honor, the reputation, and wealth of one (the business) are the honor, wealth, and reputation of the other." The unimportance of wealth as compared to a good personal life in some of the developing countries is provided in a commentary by a student from Kenya. He says, "Among Africans, there is not such a thing as keeping up with the people next door. Each individual is satisfied with what he has, and if he can get more, well and good; if not, he keeps up with what he has. We do not see things in terms of wealth as being that important."

Social acceptance.   In some countries, acceptance by neighbors and fellow workers appears to be a predominant goal within business. The Oriental outlook is reflected in the group decision making that is so important

---

[15] Yoshimatsu, Anonuma, "A Japanese Explains Japan's Business Style," *Across the Board*, February 1981, p. 44.

[16] C. N. S. Nambudiri and Mirza S. Saiyadain, "Management Problems and Practices— India and Nigeria," *Columbia Journal of World Business*, Summer 1978, p. 63.

in Japan, and the Japanese place high importance on fitting in with their group. Group identification is so strong in Japan that when a worker is asked what he does for a living, he generally answers by telling you he works for Sumitomo or Mitsubishi or Matsushita rather than that he is a chauffeur, an engineer, or a chemist.[17]

In Java the emphasis is on group harmony. As mentioned earlier, native supervisors there do not want authority over others lest it reduce their acceptance by colleagues. In more situations than U.S. executives would like to admit to, they are finding similar preferences in the U.S. work force.

Advancement.   In younger businesses in many nations, executives are changing old business standards by seeking more rapid advancement than has been traditionally acceptable. Such audacity derives, in part, from expanded promotional opportunities which are developing throughout the world. As in the United States, an increasing amount of attention seems to be given to aggressive young managers who feel they should be compensated or promoted on the basis of merit rather than by the paternalistic, family hierarchy of the past. Still, in most countries, advancement is limited to the elite, the highly educated, especially gifted, or more commonly, the scion of permanent business or political families. A recent study in Spain indicated that a great majority of firms are family owned and, of those studied, only 10 percent of the general managers did not belong to the owner's family.

Power.   Although there is some power seeking by many business managers throughout the world, power seems to be an important motivating force in South American countries. In these countries, many business leaders are not only profit oriented but use their business positions to become social and political leaders.

Patterns of competition

Competitive patterns are a function of level and intensity of competition, government regulation, public opinion, and cultural background.

Avoidance.   Except in the United States, 20th-century orientation toward competition has been to avoid it whenever possible. The prevailing pattern has been to share markets instead of expanding, but as legislation and intensified competition make the world a single marketplace, this pattern is gradually giving way to more aggressive international and national competition. Nonetheless, cartels and other restrictive practices still abound. Cartels are private business agreements—usually among firms in different countries—to share markets, control production, and set prices. Cartels were a highly developed part of European business before World War I. Between the two world wars, the cartelization of European industry was intensified and is now flourishing.

---

[17] Kyonosuke, Ibe, "It Took the Japanese to Build Japan," *Business Week*, October 6, 1980, p. 17.

Participation in worldwide markets, and particularly development of the European community, have been major influences in development of free-trade orientation in Europe. Japanese business has a tendency to prefer to share markets and control prices rather than indulge in what the Japanese call "wasteful competition." In the past the government has protected domestic manufacturers but is now opening up to freer competition. The Japanese are aggressive competitors in the world marketplace but, like most business people, compete only if they have no other alternative.

Government action.   Government action is significant in shaping the patterns of competition within a country. Common Market countries have a clause in their charter prohibiting agreements, mergers, and other concerted practices that tend to restrict free trade. The United States has antitrust legislation, and other countries have similar laws supporting competition, but many foreign governments act as a deterrent to competition.

Friendships.   Personal friendships and national sympathies can significantly affect competitive relationships in the international marketplace. Interestingly, Europeans tend to be more suspicious of each other than of outsiders. It is said that when a French company looks for a partner, it prefers an American to a European or another French company.

Friendships, of course, always play a part in business relationships; but in many foreign countries, personal friendship for a vendor or a feeling of allegiance to a vendor's country may be of major importance in a business situation—even when other things are not equal. Such relationships and trusts often take precedence over price and quality. Highly developed reciprocal relationships are a fairly logical extension of the friendship concept, and eventually even commercial bribery may enter the picture. In many foreign countries, bribery is considered a routine business function and, if not generally condoned, at least generally overlooked.

Intensification.   Worldwide overproduction, underemployment, and quest for profits have caused an intensification of competitive levels. A business which formerly had to deal with only a few competitors from its own country now may be faced with several competitors from each of a half dozen countries. Differential wage rates have been combined with convenient worldwide transportation to transform theoretical concepts of comparative advantage into realities. Business migrates toward maximizing profit opportunities through economies of production in low-wage countries and via entry into more lucrative markets.

Into the arena of worldwide competition, once dominated by U.S. multinationals and a few others, have come an array of new competitors ranging from non-U.S. multinationals (from Japan, France, and Canada) to government-owned enterprises that do business beyond their national borders.[18] Among the more powerful competitors are state-owned enterprises (SOEs)

---

[18] David A. Heenon, "Moscow Goes Multinational," *Harvard Business Review*, May/June 1981, pp. 48, 52.

which traditionally limited their efforts within their national boundaries but have gone international in recent years. These SOEs account for more than 15 percent of world trade and a significant number are listed among *Fortune's* list of 500 largest non-U.S. industries. Their critics see them as awesome competitors since state ownership means less emphasis on costs, profits, access to cheaper capital, and a tendency toward price cutting. Employment may be a state welfare issue and price cutting to insure volume and production is an avenue to full employment.[19]

In addition to the SOEs, some developing countries have spawned MNCs from joint ventures between host governments and third-nation multinationals. In 1981, the Brazilian government, in partnership with a Japanese MNC, built more ships than any other country in the world except Japan. In addition, they have become major exporters of automobiles to other Latin American countries. Korea, Taiwan, and Singapore have spawned Third-World MNCs whose production of electronics and textiles have made them major competitors for worldwide markets.

No discussion of world competition can exclude the Japanese trading companies which have long been major competitors. A new dimension has been added by the trading firms who not only provide for world consumption, but are now evolving as important middlemen for foreign buyers and sellers. For example, Sumitomo Corporation arranged the export of a Du Pont factory from the United States to the Soviet Union in 1975. Today such "third-nation" or "offshore" deals comprise a growing part of these companies' business. Mitsui and Company helped export American grain to Europe; Nisshoiwa arranges for athletic shoes to be manufactured in South Korea and Taiwan for Nike, Inc. of Beaverton, Oregon.[20] With the Japanese trading company serving as middleman for non-Japanese producers, companies not otherwise large enough to be serious worldwide competitors now have a competitive impact.

Although the Japanese trading company is branching out, it continues to be involved in growth markets. They have made their mark in automobiles and electronics, and now have expanded their influence to home computers and pharmaceuticals.[21] As one observer noted, "The Japanese view competition as a world game and are quite aggressive in global/economic competition."[22]

Intensive competition has many advantages, but, unfortunately, it also spawns unsavory practices: bribery, to influence purchases against competi-

---

[19] Yair Aharoni, "The State Owned Enterprise as a Competitor in International Markets," *Columbia Journal of World Business*, p. 16.

[20] "Japan's Big and Evolving Trading Firms: Can the U.S. Use Something Like Them?" *The Wall Street Journal*, December 17, 1980, p. 48.

[21] "Japan's Drug Makers Try World Market, Challenging U.S. and Europe Producers," *Asian Wall Street Journal*, August 1981, p. 4.

[22] William Miller, "Internationalizing the Challenge of Global Competition," *Stanford Graduate School of Business*, Fall 1980–1981, p. 17.

tors; industrial espionage, to gain a little competitive edge; dumping, to gain marginal revenue; and wasteful competition in some markets. Generally, intensive competition leads to market preservation activities.

The 1980s will probably be characterized as the era of new protectionism. Reports of a revival of protectionism come from industrialized and developing countries alike. The European community is opening in favor of what it calls *systematic protectionism,* that is, protection of key industries.[23] While the United States openly advocates free trade, it isn't above "twisting arms" to encourage "voluntary" export quotas from Japan for automobiles and other products. To counter this rise in protectionism, many multinationals are making significant production investment in some of their major foreign markets to protect their market positions from increased import taxes, quotas, and other protectionism devices.[24]

MODE OF DOING BUSINESS

Because of the diverse structures, management attitudes, and behavior encountered in international business, there is considerable variation in methods of doing business. No matter how thoroughly prepared when approaching foreign markets, there is a certain amount of cultural shock when the uninitiated trader encounters actual business situations. In conducting business negotiations, the international marketer becomes aware of the differences in contact level, communications emphasis, and tempo and formality of foreign businesses. Ethical standards are likely to differ, as will the negotiation emphasis. In most countries, the foreign trader is likely to encounter a fairly high degree of government involvement.

Level of contact

Business customs in a given country seem to emphasize one of three kinds of contact: top-level, middle-management, or group contact. In most countries, including Arab and European, executives are reluctant to relinquish their authority so business contacts are made at a relatively high level of management. The situation is modified in the United States where there is considerable delegation of authority. A trader in the United States is likely to be dealing with middle management. In Central and South America, middle or lower management or government employees tend to aggrandize their positions by attempting to participate, or appear to participate, in decisions over which they have no jurisdiction.

A trader from the Far Eastern cultures that stress cooperation and group decision making prefers to deal with a group rather than an individual.

---

[23] "In Favor of Protectionism," *World Business Weekly,* July 27, 1981, p. 42.

[24] "The Japanese Are Coming, and the British Are Pleased," *World Business Weekly,* February 16, 1981, pp. 10–13.

Title or position takes precedence over the individual holding the job, and many firms allow no correspondence with a person's name that is legible. Business replies are made to a file number or a specific title because communications are between companies, not individuals working for companies. In some companies, a functionary called a *disponent* oversees the handling of all correspondence. Direct mail will not get through unless sent to the correct title or is carrying a proper code number. In the Middle East, the situation is likely to be the opposite. In the Levantine situation, one always does business with an individual per se rather than an office or title.

BOX 5–7: The owner is busy

Except in special circumstances, even when local regulations permit, it is unwise to do business in the Arab market without a local partner or sponsor. He is the key figure to business success in the area and must accordingly be selected with great care. As a general rule, greater success is achieved with members of the established business families who although they may demand a greater share of profit, have the contacts and experience required.

As I mentioned, special care must be taken to build a personal relationship with a partner or sponsor and he must be approached with the respect due to a person who is probably personally operating a multimillion dollar business enterprise. This often explains the large delays reported by businessmen in seeking interviews; one would not expect an immediate interview with, for example, the chief executive of General Motors: and he is probably poorly paid compared to the profits earned by the successful Arab. Time is at a premium for him and he will appreciate a comprehensive presentation of the proposed project. He will often make a decision quicker than thought possible in the West where board meetings and committees are involved.

Source: Ian K. Huntington, "Doing Business in the Arab Middle East." © *World*, Peat, Marwick, Mitchell & Co.

Finding the right person, the decision maker, is difficult in almost all societies, but especially so when business customs are unfamiliar or the structure of the business is unfamiliar. One American marketer dealing in Eastern Europe spent six months trying to determine to whom he should be talking.

Companies attempting to do business in the oil-rich markets of the Middle East are admonished to do business through an intermediary who knows the right people. One such intermediary, a Saudi Arabian named Adnan Khashoggi, calls himself a "connector." His connecting seems to have paid off handsomely; he claims to have expedited sales totaling $11.5 billion with commissions to him of $575 million in six years. Although his earnings are unusual, Khashoggi's role is not. There are hundreds or perhaps thousands of contact makers flourishing in the Middle East and throughout the world.[25]

---

[25] Lewis Krarr, "The Super Connector from Saudi Arabia," *Fortune*, June 1977, p. 109, is a fascinating account about a Stanford dropout supersalesman.

Communications emphasis

Language is the basic communication tool of marketers trading in foreign lands; yet managers, particularly from the United States, often fail to develop even a basic understanding of a language, much less master the linguistic nuances that reveal unspoken attitudes and information. One writer comments that "even a good interpreter doesn't solve the language problem." Besides conceptual differences between them, English and Japanese inter-translate badly by nature and structure. Seemingly similar business terms in English and Japanese often have different meanings. Lesser-known languages pose particular problems because it is difficult to find business representatives who can handle more than three or four major languages. Educated Britons tend to be at least bilingual; yet one Italian buyer, an anglophile of long standing, summed up the attitude of many British firms by attributing to them the saying: "Speak English or be damned!"

Probably no language readily translates into another as the meanings of words differ widely among different languages. Japanese do not like their contracts written in the Japanese language because, among other things, it has a tendency to be too vague and nonspecific. The Japanese prefer English-language contracts where words have specific meaning.

Linguistic communication, no matter how imprecise, is explicit but much business communication depends on implicit messages which are not verbalized. Call it a silent language, body language, or nonverbal communication; it does exist. E. T. Hall, Professor of Anthropology and, for decades, consultant to business and government on intercultural relations says, "In some cultures, messages are explicit; the words carry most of the information. In other cultures . . . less information is contained in the verbal part of the message since more is in the context."[26] Hall divides cultures into high-context and low-context cultures. Communication in a high-context culture depends heavily on the context or nonverbal aspects of communication, whereas the low-context culture depends more on explicit, verbally expressed communications. Managers in general probably function best at a low-context level because they are accustomed to reports, contracts, and other written communications.

In a low-context culture, you get down to business very quickly. The high-context culture takes considerably longer to conduct business because the people have developed a need to know more about you before a relationship can develop. You might say they simply do not know how to handle a low-context relationship with other people. Hall suggests that, "in the Middle East, if you aren't willing to take the time to sit down and have coffee

---

[26] "Learning the Arab's Silent Language," *Psychology Today*, August 1979, pp. 45–53. Hall has three remarkable books which should be read by everyone involved in international business: *Beyond Culture* (New York: Anchor Press-Doubleday, 1976); *The Hidden Dimension* (New York: Doubleday & Co., 1966); and *The Silent Language* (New York: Doubleday & Co., 1959).

BOX 5–8: You say you speak English?

The English speak English, North Americans speak English, but can we communicate? It is difficult unless you understand that in England:

Newspapers are sold at *book stalls*.

The *ground floor* is the main floor, while the first floor is what we call the second, and so on up the building.

An apartment house is a *block of flats*.

You will be putting your clothes not in a closet, but in a *cupboard*.

A closet usually refers to the W.C. or water closet which is the toilet.

When one of your British friends says she is going to "spend a penny," she is going to the ladies' room.

A *bathing dress* or *bathing costume* is what the British call a bathing suit, and for those who want to go shopping, it is essential to know that a *tunic* is a blouse; a *stud* is a collar button, nothing more; and garters are *suspenders*.

Suspenders are *braces*.

If you want to buy a sweater, you should ask for a *jumper* or a *jersey* as the recognizable item will be marked in British clothing stores.

A *ladder* is not used for climbing but refers to a run in a stocking.

If you *called up* someone, it means to your British friend that you have drafted the person—probably for military service. To *ring someone up* is to telephone them.

Queer when used by a British person means only feeling funny.

Any reference by you to an *M.D.* will probably not bring a doctor. The term means *mental deficient* in Britain.

When the desk clerk asks what time you want to be *knocked up* in the morning, he is only referring to your wake up call.

Source: Adapted from Margaret Zellers, "How to Speak *English*," *Denver Magazine*, date unknown, pp. 44–100.

---

with people, you have a problem. You must learn to wait and not be too eager to talk business. You can ask about the family or ask 'how are you feeling?' but avoid too many personal questions about wives because people are apt to get suspicious. Learn to make what we call chit-chat. If you don't, you can't go to the next step. It's a little bit like a courtship, and without all the preliminaries, sex becomes just like rape."[27]

Even in low-context cultures our communication is heavily dependent on our cultural context. Most of us are not even aware how dependent we are on the context, and, as Hall suggests, "since much of our culture operates outside our awareness, *frequently we don't even know what we know.*" Exhibit 5–2 shows a rough interpretation of the contextual relationship of different countries.

Ashok Kapoor, an international business professor, relates how "American executives negotiating a contract in the Middle East found there wasn't

---

[27] "Learning the Arabs' Silent Language," *Psychology Today*, August 1979, p. 54.

EXHIBIT 5–2: Contextual background of various countries

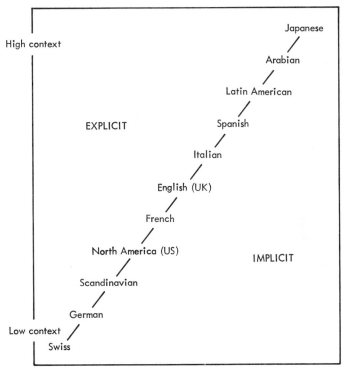

High context

EXPLICIT

Japanese

Arabian

Latin American

Spanish

Italian

English (UK)

French

North America (US)

IMPLICIT

Scandinavian

German

Low context

Swiss

Note: Patterned after E. T. Hall.

time to have their revised negotiating proposal typed, submitted a handwritten version, and thought nothing of it. But the Arabs across the bargaining table considered the gesture so bizarre that they began to analyze it intensely, seeking significant messages. Some concluded the Americans were trying to imply that they considered the whole contract unimportant."[28]

Probably every business person from America or other relatively low context countries who has had dealing with counterparts in high-context countries can tell stories about the confusion on both sides because of the different perceptual frameworks of the communication process. It is not enough to master the basic language of a country; the astute marketer must also gain a complete mastery over the language of business as well as the silent languages of nuance and implication. Communication mastery, then, is not only the mastery of a language but a mastery of customs as well. Such mastery can be developed only through long association.

---

[28] C. Roger Ricklets, "For a Businessman Headed Abroad, Some Basic Lessons," *The Wall Street Journal*, January 16, 1978.

BOX 5–9: You don't have to be a Hollywood star to wear dark glasses

Arabs may even watch the pupils of your eyes to judge your responses to different topics.

A psychologist at the University of Chicago discovered that the pupil is a very sensitive indicator of how people respond to a situation. When you are interested in something, your pupils dilate; if I say something you don't like, they tend to contract. But the Arabs have known about the pupil response for hundreds if not thousands of years. Since people can't control the response of their eyes, which is a dead giveaway, many Arabs wear dark glasses, even indoors.

These are people reading the personal interaction on a second-to-second basis. By watching the pupils, they can respond rapidly to mood changes. That's one of the reasons why they use a closer conversational distance than Americans do. At about five feet, the normal distance between two Americans who are talking, we have a hard time following eye movement. But if you use an Arab distance, about two feet, you can watch the pupil of the eye.

Direct eye contact for an American is difficult to achieve since we are taught in the United States not to stare, not to look at the eyes that carefully. If you stare at someone, it is too intense, too sexy, or too hostile. It also may mean that we are not totally tuned in to the situation. Maybe we should all wear dark glasses.

Source: Adapted from "Learning the Arabs' Silent Language," *Psychology Today*, August 1979, pp. 46–48.

Formality and tempo

Breezy informality and haste seem to characterize the American business relationship, but these behavior patterns seem to be an American exclusive which business people from other countries not only fail to share but fail to appreciate. The apparent informality does not indicate a lack of commitment to the job. Comparing British and American business managers, an English executive commented about the American manager's compelling involvement in business: "At a cocktail party or a dinner the American is still 'on duty.' If a young guest's command of the subject or facility in selling an idea is impressive, the American is quite likely to mark the young person down as a potential recruit, and act on that assumption."

While Northern Europeans seem to have picked up some American attitudes in recent years, don't count on it. As one writer says, "while using first names in business encounters is regarded as an American vice in many countries, no where is it found more offensive than in France." Formalities still reign in that country. It is said that those who work side by side for years still address one another with formal pronouns.

Marketers who expect maximum success must be prepared to deal with foreign executives in a way that is acceptable to them. The Latin American depends greatly on friendships in business relationships but establishes these friendships only in the South American way: slowly, over a considerable period of time. A typical Latin American is highly formal until a genuine relationship of respect and friendship is established. Even after such a relationship has been established, the Latin American is slow to get down to business and will not be pushed. In keeping with the culture, mañana is good enough. One side of Latin American formality is that there is no involving business in personal life.

The Japanese are more likely to intermix business and personal life but are also unharried in business relationships—so unharried, in fact, that Americans or Europeans are likely to lose patience and composure in dealing with the Japanese. Japanese executives are exceedingly courteous but may, in fact, use courtesy and lavish treatment on guests as a future competitive weapon. The patient attitude is derived from indifference to the future. As explained in a classic statement.

> The Japanese do not have any notion of time because they do not have any notion of self. Indeed, time exists only by reference to a term, or definite extent. But, according to the Japanese conception, there is no term, there is only continuous flow. There is no past, no future: time is what measures an action, or rather time is marked by the change of action. It seems that time is an immense reservoir from which you can help yourself. Time belongs to nobody, it is at the disposal of everybody. Everybody can dip and the supply is inexhaustible. Time is what marks life, chiefly the psychological life, which is run, as it has been surmised, by all the others. To appropriate time would be to make it "mine." To direct time supposes a self. Time is simply the dimension in which the Japanese live; they do not own it. This is one explanation for not keeping appointments, set with so much eagerness and seriousness. Time possesses them, not the contrary![29]

BOX 5–10: The Marco Polo Complex

Most foreign businessmen suffer from the "Marco Polo Complex"—a fascination with China and an eagerness to do business there. The Chinese, keenly aware of this, are not above taking advantage of it with games-manship tactics.

For the Chinese, bargaining is an art that requires great skill and patience. Westerners, particularly Americans, tend to view it as a somewhat distasteful task that should be completed as quickly as possible.

"What is extremely frustrating to an American is to go halfway around the world and sit down and the Chinese won't talk business. I've gone in there and by the third meeting I still haven't talked business. I wanted to take my fist and punch these guys out."

In some cases, the Chinese appear to drag out negotiations because they recognize that time is on their side: the foreign businessman is staying in a strange hotel, eating strange food, seeing strange things. He misses his wife. He wants to conclude his business and go home.

Realizing this, the Chinese may act pessimistic about purchasing a salesman's goods and draw out the talks by asking about his house, his children, and the like.

Several frustrated Americans have checked out of their hotels in despair and gone to the airport to leave China—only to get a phone call at the last minute saying, "Come back. We want to talk."

Source: "China Frustrating to Businessmen," *United Press International* news release, March 3, 1981.

---

[29] Maurice Bairy, "Japanese Ways," in *Doing Business in Japan*, ed. R. J. Ballon (Tokyo: Sophia University, 1967), p. 15. Reproduced by permission.

Haste and impatience are probably the most common mistakes of North Americans attempting to trade in the Middle East. Most Arabs do not like to embark on serious business discussions until they have had two or three opportunities to meet the individual they are dealing with; negotiations are likely to be prolonged. Even though Arabs may make rapid decisions once they prepare to do so, they do not like to be rushed and they do not like deadlines.[30] The managing partner of the Kuwait office of Peat, Marwick, Mitchell & Co. says of the "flying-visit" approach of many American business-men, "what in the West might be regarded as dynamic activity—the 'I've only got a day here' approach—may well be regarded here as merely rude."[31]

Business ethics

The moral question of what is right and appropriate poses many dilemmas for domestic marketers. Even within a country, ethical standards are not defined, and there is no common frame of reference. The problem of business ethics is infinitely more complex in the international marketplace because opinions of what is right are spread more widely because of basic cultural diversity. What is commonly accepted as right in one country may be completely unacceptable in another. Giving business gifts of high value, for example, is generally condemned in the United States, but in most countries of the world, gifts are not only accepted but expected.

When a gift becomes a bribe it raises another issue. The statement, "Bribery is not condoned anywhere in the world, even in countries where it is a general practice," seems to reflect the consensus of those most familiar with international business. There is a world of difference between a tip and a million-dollar bribe. That range still leaves plenty of room for argument. What about the ethics of the perfectly legal stipulation tying a $125,000 contribution to a children's hospital to a contract for construction of a meat processing plant?

The question of international business standards of morality is one that will not be dealt with adequately until greater cultural homogenization has occurred through business, political, and social intercourse.

The ethical customs of competitors must be taken into account if a company is to stay in the running. The French aircraft industry reportedly was delighted when the Lockheed scandal erupted in the United States. One magazine commented, "American bad luck may turn out to be good luck for France. It's not likely that we'll see any Parliamentary inquiries probing the details of how France sells its arms." The Italian government considers

---

[30] William H. Miller, "Mideast Is No Easy Mark," *Industrial Week,* October 24, 1977.

[31] Ian K. Huntington, "Doing Business in the Arab Middle East," *World,* Spring 1977, p. 14.

the use of bribes to secure foreign contracts a legitimate business practice so long as the funds are not directed to Italian residents.[32]

It is easy to generalize and moralize about business ethics, but it is much harder to face the decision of whether to withhold or "invest" a million dollars in some dictator's pet project in order to preserve assets or the ability to do business in a country. As one Italian official was quoted, "it may not be ethics, but it is business." Such attitudes make it difficult for U.S. companies who must operate abroad under restraints imposed by the Foreign Corrupt Practices Act. Ultimately, as with all ethical questions, the decision rests on an individual's or board of directors' perception of the difference between pragmatism and absolute morality.[33]

Negotiation emphasis

Basic elements of negotiation are the same in any country: they relate to the product, its price and terms, services related to the product, and, finally, friendship between the vendor and the customers. The differences between traders from various nations relate not to different negotiation elements but rather to a hierarchy of values and to varying emphasis among the elements.

Government is virtually a third party to all international business agreements because it is a measurable force in negotiations in foreign countries. The government may be directly represented or it may be indirectly represented through the marketer's awareness of governmental policy, position, or attitude. Currency availability, admission of goods, physical properties and packaging, advertising, employment conditions, reparation of profits, and other factors are likely to be closely regulated by the government in dealings with foreign countries. (See the chapter on pricing [17] for additional insights on negotiation processes.)

SUMMARY

Business customs and practices in different world markets vary so much that it is difficult to make valid generalizations about them; it is even difficult to classify the different kinds of business behavior that are encountered from nation to nation. The only safe generalizations are that the business person working in another country must be sensitive to the business environment and must be willing to adapt when necessary. Unfortunately, it is seldom easy to know when such adaptation is necessary because in certain instances adaptation is optional and, in others, it is actually undesirable.

---

[32] "Italy Takes Steps to Legalize Bribes to Secure Overseas Bids," *Business International,* May 30, 1980, pp. 171–72.

[33] "Ethics in the 1980s: Corporations will feel Pressures from Within," *Business International,* March 20, 1981, pp. 89–90.

Business behavior is derived in large part from the basic cultural environment in which the business operates; and as such, is subject to the extreme diversity encountered among various cultures and subcultures. Environmental considerations significantly affect the attitudes, behavior, and outlook of foreign business people. Motivational patterns of such business people depend in part on their personal backgrounds, their business positions, sources of authority, and their own personalities.

Varying motivational patterns inevitably affect methods of doing business in different countries. Marketers in some countries thrive on competition, while in others they do all possible to eliminate it. The authoritarian, centralized decision-making orientation in some nations contrasts sharply with democratic decentralization in others. International variation characterizes contact level, ethical orientation, negotiation outlook, and nearly every part of doing business. The foreign marketer can take no phase of business behavior for granted.

The new breed of international business person that has emerged in recent years appears to have a heightened sensitivity to cultural variations. Sensitivity, however, is not enough; the international trader must be constantly alert and prepared to adapt when necessary. One must always realize that, no matter how long in a country, the outsider is not a native; and, in many countries, may always be treated as an outsider. Finally, one must avoid the critical mistake of assuming that a knowledge of one culture will provide acceptability in another.

QUESTIONS

1. Define:

Cultural imperative	Eclectic borrowing
Cultural adiaphora	Cartel
Cultural exclusive	Silent language
Stereotyping	National character

2. "More than a toleration of an alien culture is required, . . . there is a need for 'affirmative acceptance as different but equal.' " Elaborate.

3. "We should also bear in mind that in today's business-oriented world economy, the cultures themselves are being significantly affected by business activities and business practices." Comment.

4. "In dealing with foreign businesses, the marketer must be particularly aware of the varying objectives and aspirations of management." Explain.

5. Suggest ways in which persons might prepare themselves to handle unique business customs that may be encountered in a trip abroad.

6. Business customs and national customs are closely interrelated. In what ways would one expect the two areas to coincide and in what ways would they show differences? How could such areas of similarity and difference be identified?

7. Identify both local and foreign examples of cultural imperatives, adiaphora, and exclusives. Be prepared to explain why each example fits into the category you have selected.

8. Contrast the authority roles of top management in different societies. How will the differing views of authority affect marketing activities?

9. Do the same for aspirational patterns.

10. What effects on business customs might be anticipated from the recent rapid increases in the level of international business activity?

11. Interview some foreign students to determine the types of cultural shock they encountered when they first came to your country.

12. Differentiate between:

> Private ownership and family ownership
> Decentralized and committee decision making

13. In what ways will the size of a customer's business affect business behavior?

14. Identify and explain five main patterns of business ownership.

15. Compare three kinds of decision-making authority patterns in international business.

16. Explore the various ways in which business customs can affect the structure of competition.

17. Why is it important that the business executive be alert to the significance of business customs?

18. Suggest some cautions that an individual from a high-context culture should take when dealing with someone from a low-context culture. Do the same from low- to high-context situations.

READING

The following article is a classic. It was first published some 20 years ago, but these truths, like most cultural concepts, change slowly. Although some specifics may vary, the underlying message of sensitivity to nonverbal communication is timeless. Equally timeless seems to be the individual's capacity for blundering and insensitivity when dealing with foreign cultures.

The silent language in overseas business*
Edward T. Hall

With few exceptions, Americans are relative newcomers on the international business scene. Today, as in Mark Twain's time, we are all too often "innocents abroad,"

* Reprinted with special permission from *Harvard Business Review*, May/June 1960, pp. 87–96. © 1960 by the President and Fellows of Harvard College; all rights reserved.

in an era when naiveté and blundering in foreign business dealings may have serious political repercussions.

When the American executive travels abroad to do business, he is frequently shocked to discover to what extent the many variables of foreign behavior and custom complicate his efforts. Although the American has recognized, certainly, that even the man next door has many minor traits which make him somewhat peculiar, for some reason he has failed to appreciate how different foreign businessmen and their practices will seem to him.

He should understand that the various peoples around the world have worked out and integrated into their subconscious literally thousands of behavior patterns that they take for granted in each other.[1] Then, when the stranger enters, and behaves differently from the local norm, he often quite unintentionally insults, annoys, or amuses the native with whom he is attempting to do business. For example:

In the United States, a corporation executive knows what is meant when a client lets a month go by before replying to a business proposal. On the other hand, he senses an eagerness to do business if he is immediately ushered into the client's office. In both instances, he is reacting to subtle cues in the timing of interaction, cues which he depends on to chart his course of action.

Abroad, however, all this changes. The American executive learns that the Latin Americans are casual about time and that if he waits an hour in the outer office before seeing the Deputy Minister of Finance, it does not necessarily mean he is not getting anywhere. There people are so important that nobody can bear to tear himself away; because of the resultant interruptions and conversational detours, everybody is constantly getting behind. What the American does not know is the point at which the waiting becomes significant.

In another instance, after traveling 7,000 miles an American walks into the office of a highly recommended Arab businessman on whom he will have to depend completely. What he sees does not breed confidence. The office is reached by walking through a suspicious-looking coffeehouse in an old, dilapidated building situated in a crowded non-European section of town. The elevator, rising from dark, smelly corridors, is rickety and equally foul. When he gets to the office itself, he is shocked to find it small, crowded, and confused. Papers are stacked all over the desk and table tops—even scattered on the floor in irregular piles.

The Arab merchant he has come to see had met him at the airport the night before and sent his driver to the hotel this morning to pick him up. But now, after the American's rush, the Arab is tied up with something else. Even when they finally start talking business, there are constant interruptions. If the American is at all sensitive to his environment, everything around him signals, "What am I getting into?"

Before leaving home he was told that things would be different, but how different? The hotel is modern enough. The shops in the new part of town have many more American and European trade goods than he had anticipated. His first impression was that doing business in the Middle East would not present any new problems. Now he is beginning to have doubts. One minute everything looks familiar and he is on firm ground; the next, familiar landmarks are gone. His greatest problem is that so much assails his senses all at once that he does not know where to start looking for something that will tell him where he stands. He needs a frame of reference—a way of sorting out what is significant and relevant.

---

[1] For details see my book, *The Silent Language* (New York: Doubleday & Co., 1959).

That is why it is so important for American businessmen to have a real understanding of the various social, cultural, and economic differences they will face when they attempt to do business in foreign countries. To help give some frame of reference, this article will map out a few areas of human activity that have largely been unstudied.

The topics I will discuss are certainly not presented as the last word on the subject, but they have proved to be highly reliable points at which to begin to gain an understanding of foreign cultures. While additional research will undoubtedly turn up other items just as relevant, at present I think the businessman can do well to begin by appreciating cultural differences in matters concerning the language of time, of space, of material possessions, of friendship patterns, and of agreements.

Language of time

Everywhere in the world people use time to communicate with each other. There are different languages of time just as there are different spoken languages. The unspoken languages are informal; yet the rules governing their interpretation are surprisingly *ironbound*. In the United States, a delay in answering a communication can result from a large volume of business causing the request to be postponed until the backlog is cleared away, from poor organization, or possibly from technical complexity requiring deep analysis. But if the person awaiting the answer or decision rules out these reasons, then the delay means to him that the matter has low priority on the part of the other person—lack of interest. On the other hand, a similar delay in a foreign country may mean something altogether different. Thus:

In Ethiopia, the time required for a decision is directly proportional to its importance. This is so much the case that low-level bureaucrats there have a way of trying to elevate the prestige of their work by taking a long time to make up their minds. (Americans in that part of the world are innocently prone to downgrade their work in the local people's eyes by trying to speed things up).

In the Arab East, time does not generally include schedules as Americans know and use them. The time required to get something accomplished depends on the relationship. More important people get fast service from less important people, and conversely. Close relatives take absolute priority; nonrelatives are kept waiting.

In the United States, giving a person a deadline is a way of indicating the degree of urgency or relative importance of the work. But in the Middle East, the American runs into a cultural trap the minute he opens his mouth. "Mr. Aziz will have to make up his mind in a hurry because my board meets next week and I have to have an answer by then," is taken as indicating the American is overly demanding and is exerting undue pressure. "I am going to Damascus tomorrow morning and will have to have my car tonight," is a sure way to get the mechanic to stop work, because to give another person a deadline in this part of the world is to be rude, pushy, and demanding.

An Arab's evasiveness as to when something is going to happen does not mean he does not want to do business; it only means he is avoiding unpleasantness and is side-stepping possible commitments which he takes more seriously than we do. For example:

The Arabs themselves at times find it impossible to communicate even to each other that some processes cannot be hurried, and are controlled by built-in schedules. This is obvious enough to the Westerner but not to the Arab. A highly placed official in Baghdad precipitated a bitter family dispute because his nephew, a biochemist, could not speed up the complete analysis of the uncle's blood. He accused the nephew of putting other less important people before him and of not caring. Nothing could sway the uncle, who could not grasp the fact that there is such a thing as an *inherent* schedule.

With us, the more important an event is, the further ahead we schedule it, which is why we find it insulting to be asked to a party at the last minute. In planning future events with Arabs, it pays to hold the lead time to a week or less because other factors may intervene or take precedence.

Again, time spent waiting in an American's outer office is a sure indicator of what one person thinks of another or how important he feels the other's business to be. This is so much the case that most Americans cannot help getting angry after waiting 30 minutes; one may even feel such a delay is an insult, and will walk out. In Latin America, on the other hand, one learns that it does not mean anything to wait in an outer office. An American businessman with years of experience in Mexico once told me, "You know, I have spent two hours cooling my heels in an executive's outer office. It took me a long time to learn to keep my blood pressure down. Even now, I find it hard to convince myself they are still interested when they keep me waiting."

The Japanese handle time in ways which are almost inexplicable to the Western European and particularly the American. A delay of years with them does not mean that they have lost interest. It only means that they are building up to something. They have learned that Americans are vulnerable to long waits. One of them expressed it, "You Americans have one terrible weakness. If we make you wait long enough, you will agree to anything."

Indians of South Asia have an elastic view of time as compared to our own. Delays do not, therefore, have the same meaning to them. Nor does indefiniteness in pinpointing appointments mean that they are evasive. Two Americans meeting will say, "We should get together sometime," thereby setting a low priority on the meeting. The Indian who says, "Come over and see me, see me anytime," means just that.

Americans make a place at the table which may or may not mean a place made in the heart. But when the Indian makes a place in his time, it is yours to fill in every sense of the word if you realize that by so doing you have crossed a boundary and are now friends with him. The point of all this is that time communicates just as surely as do words and that the vocabulary of time is different around the world. The principle to be remembered is that time has different meanings in each country.

Language of space

Like time, the language of space is different wherever one goes. The American businessman, familiar with the pattern of American corporate life, has no difficulty in appraising the relative importance of someone else, simply by noting the size of his office in relation to other offices around him:

Our pattern calls for the president or the chairman of the board to have the biggest office. The executive vice president will have the next largest, and so on down the line until you end up in the "bull pen." More important offices are usually located at the corners of buildings and on the upper floors. Executive suites will be on the top floor. The relative rank of vice presidents will be reflected in where they are placed along "executive row."

The French, on the other hand, are much more likely to lay out space as a network of connecting points of influence, activity, or interest. The French supervisor will ordinarily be found in the middle of his subordinates where he can control them.

Americans who are crowded will often feel that their status in the organization is suffering. As one would expect in the Arab world, the location of an office and its size constitute a poor index of the importance of the man who occupies it. What we experience as crowded, the Arab will often regard as spacious. The same is true in Spanish cultures. A Latin American official illustrated the Spanish view of this point while showing me around a plant. Opening the door to an 18-by-20-foot office in which seventeen clerks and their desks were placed, he said, "See, we have nice spacious offices. Lots of space for everyone."

The American will look at a Japanese room and remark how bare it is. Similarly, the Japanese look at our rooms and comment, "How bare!" Furniture in the American home tends to be placed along the walls (around the edge). Japanese have their charcoal pit where the family gathers in the *middle* of the room. The top floor of Japanese department stores is not reserved for the chief executive—it is the bargain roof!

In the Middle East and Latin America, the businessman is likely to feel left out in time and overcrowded in space. People get too close to him, lay their hands on him, and generally crowd his physical being. In Scandinavia and Germany, he feels more at home, but at the same time the people are a little cold and distant. It is space itself that conveys this feeling.

In the United States, because of our tendency to zone activities, nearness carries rights of familiarity so that the neighbor can borrow material possessions and invade time. This is not true in England. Propinquity entitles you to nothing. American Air Force personnel stationed there complain because they have to make an appointment for their children to play with the neighbor's child next door.

Conversation distance between two people is learned early in life by copying elders. Its controlling patterns operate almost totally unconsciously. In the United States, in contrast to many foreign countries, men avoid excessive touching. Regular business is conducted at distances such as 5 feet to 8 feet; highly personal business, 18 inches to 3 feet—not 2 or 3 inches.

In the United States, it is perfectly possible for an experienced executive to schedule the steps of negotiation in time and space so that most people feel comfortable about what is happening. Business transactions progress in stages from across the desk to beside the desk, to the coffee table, then on to the conference table, the luncheon table, or the golf course, or even into the home—all according to a complex set of hidden rules which we obey instinctively.

Even in the United States, however, an executive may slip when he moves into new and unfamiliar realms, when dealing with a new group, doing business with a new company, or moving to a new place in the industrial hierarchy. In a new country the danger is magnified. For example, in India it is considered improper to discuss business in the home on social occasions. One never invites a business acquaintance to the home for the purpose of furthering business aims. That would be a violation of sacred hospitality rules.

Language of things

Americans are often contrasted with the rest of the world in terms of material possessions. We are accused of being materialistic, gadget crazy. And, as a matter of fact, we have developed material things for some very interesting reasons. Lacking a fixed class system and having an extremely mobile population, Americans have become highly sensitive to how others make use of material possessions. We use everything from clothes to houses as a highly evolved and complex means of ascertaining each other's status. Ours is a rapidly shifting system in which both styles and people move up or down. For example:

The Cadillac ad men feel that not only is it natural but quite insightful of them to show a picture of a Cadillac and a well-turned out gentleman in his early fifties opening the door. The caption underneath reads, "You already know a great deal about this man."

Following this same pattern, the head of a big union spends in excess of $100,000 furnishing his office so that the president of United States Steel cannot look down on him. Good materials, large space, and the proper surroundings signify that the people who occupy the premises are solid citizens, that they are dependable and successful.

The French, English, and the Germans have entirely different ways of using their material possessions. What stands for the height of dependability and respectability with the English would be old-fashioned and backward to us. The Japanese take pride in often inexpensive but tasteful arrangements that are used to produce the proper emotional setting.

Middle East businessmen look for something else—family, connections, friendship. They do not use the furnishings of their office as part of their status system; nor do they expect to impress a client by these means or to fool a banker into lending more money than he should. They like good things, too, but feel that they, as persons, should be known and not judged solely by what the public sees.

One of the most common criticisms of American relations abroad, both commercial and governmental, is that we usually think in terms of material things. "Money talks," says the American, who goes on talking the language of money abroad, in the belief that money talks the *same* language all over the world. A common practice in the United States is to try to buy loyalty with high salaries. In foreign countries, this maneuver almost never works, for money and material possessions stand for something different there than they do in America.

Language of friendship

The American finds his friends next door and among those with whom he works. It has been noted that we take people up quickly and drop them just as quickly. Occasionally a friendship formed during schooldays will persist, but this is rare. For us there are few well-defined rules governing the obligations of friendship. It is difficult to say at which point our friendship gives way to business opportunism or pressure from above. In this we differ from many other people in the world. As a general rule, in foreign countries friendships are not formed as quickly as in the United States but go much deeper, last longer, and involve real obligations. For example:

It is important to stress that in the Middle East and Latin America your "friends" will not let you down. The fact that they personally are feeling the pinch is never an excuse for failing their friends. They are supposed to look out for your interests.

Friends and family around the world represent a sort of social insurance that would be difficult to find in the United States. We do not use our friends to help us out in disaster as much as we do as a means of getting ahead—or, at least, of getting the job done. The United States systems work by means of a series of closely tabulated favors and obligations carefully doled out where they will do the most good. And the least that we expect in exchange for a favor is gratitude.

The opposite is the case in India, where the friend's role is to "sense" a person's need and do something about it. The idea of reciprocity as we know it is unheard of. An American in India will have difficulty if he attempts to follow American friendship patterns. He gains nothing by extending himself in behalf of others, least of all gratitude, because the Indian assumes that what he does for others he does for the good of his own psyche. He will find it impossible to make friends quickly and is unlikely to allow sufficient time for friendships to ripen. He will also note that as he gets to know people better, they may become more critical of him, a fact that he finds hard to take. What he does not know is that one sign of friendship in India is speaking one's mind.

Language of agreements

While it is important for American businessmen abroad to understand the symbolic meanings of friendship rules, time, space, and material possessions, it is just as important for executives to know the rules for negotiating agreements in various countries. Even if they cannot be expected to know the details of each nation's commercial legal practices, just the awareness of and the expectation of the existence of differences will eliminate much complication.

Actually, no society can exist on a high commercial level without a highly developed working base on which agreements can rest. This base may be one or a combination of three types:

1. Rules that are spelled out technically as law or regulation.
2. Moral practices mutually agreed on and taught to the young as a set of principles.
3. Informal customs to which everyone conforms without being able to state the exact rules.

Some societies favor one, some another. Ours, particularly in the business world, lays heavy emphasis on the first variety. Few Americans will conduct any business nowadays without some written agreement or contract.

Varying from culture to culture will be the circumstances under which such rules apply. Americans consider that negotiations have more or less ceased when the contract is signed. With the Greeks, on the other hand, the contract is seen as a sort of way station on the route to negotiation that will cease only when the work is completed. The contract is nothing more than a charter for serious negotiations. In the Arab world, once a man's word is given in a particular kind of way, it is just as binding, if not more so, than most of our written contracts. The written contract, therefore, violates the Moslem's sensitivities and reflects on his honor. Unfortunately, the situation is now so hopelessly confused that neither system can be counted on to prevail consistently.

Informal patterns and unstated agreements often lead to untold difficulty in the cross-cultural situation. Take the case of the before-and-after patterns where there is a wide discrepancy between the American's expectations and those of the Arab:

In the United States, when you engage a specialist such as a lawyer or a doctor, require any standard service, or even take a taxi, you make several assumptions: (*a*) the charge will be fair; (*b*) it will be in proportion to the services rendered; and (*c*) it will bear a close relationship to the "going rate."

You wait until after the services are performed before asking what the tab will be. If the charge is too high in light of the above assumptions, you feel you have been cheated. You can complain, or can say nothing, pay up, and take your business elsewhere the next time.

As one would expect in the Middle East, basic differences emerge which lead to difficulty if not understood. For instance, when taking a cab in Beirut it is well to know the going rate as a point around which to bargain and for settling the charge, which must be fixed before engaging the cab.

If you have not fixed the rate *in advance,* there is a complete change and an entirely different set of rules will apply. According to these rules, the going rate plays no part whatsoever. The whole relationship is altered. The sky is the limit, and the customer has no kick coming. I have seen taxi drivers shouting at the top of their lungs, waving their arms, following a red-faced American with his head pulled down between his shoulders, demanding for a two-pound ride 10 Lebanese pounds which the American eventually had to pay.

It is difficult for the American to accommodate his frame of reference to the fact that what constitutes one thing to him, namely, a taxi ride, is to the Arab two very different operations involving two different sets of relationships and two sets of rules. The crucial factor is whether the bargaining is done at the beginning or end of the ride! As a matter of fact, you cannot bargain at the end. What the driver asks for he is entitled to!

One of the greatest difficulties Americans have abroad stems from the fact that we often think we have a commitment when we do not. The second complication on this same topic is the other side of the coin, that is when others think we have agreed to things that we have not. Our own failure to recognize binding obligations, plus our custom of setting organizational goals ahead of everything else, has put us in hot water far too often.

People sometimes do not keep agreements with us because we do not keep agreements with them. As a general rule, the American treats the agreement as something he may eventually have to break. Here are two examples:

Once while I was visiting an American post in Latin America, the Ambassador sent the Spanish version of a trade treaty down to his language officer with instructions to write in some "weasel words." To his dismay, he was told, "There are no weasel words in Spanish."

A personnel officer of a large corporation in Iran made an agreement with local employees that American employees would not receive preferential treatment. When the first American employee arrived, it was learned quickly that in the United States he had been covered by a variety of health plans that were not available to Iranians. And this led to immediate protests from the Iranians which were never satisfied. The personnel officer never really grasped the fact that he had violated an ironbound contract.

Certainly, this is the most important generalization to be drawn by American businessmen from this discussion of agreements: there are many times when we are vulnerable *even when judged by our own standards.* Many instances of actual sharp practices by American companies are well known abroad and are giving American business a bad name. The cure for such questionable behavior is simple. The companies concerned usually have it within their power to discharge offenders and to foster within their organization an atmosphere in which only honesty and fairness can thrive.

But the cure for ignorance of the social and legal rules which underlie business agreements is not so easy. This is because:

The subject is complex.

Little research has been conducted to determine the culturally different concepts of what is an agreement.

The people of each country think that their own code is the only one, and that everything else is dishonest.

Each code is different from our own; and the farther away one is traveling from Western Europe, the greater the difference is.

But the little that has already been learned about this subject indicates that as a problem it is not insoluble and will yield to research. Since it is probably one of the more relevant and immediately applicable areas of interest to modern business, it would certainly be advisable for companies with large foreign operations to sponsor some serious research in this vital field.

Chapter 6

Political considerations in assessing world markets

"The People's Republic of China Now Permits Full Foreign Ownership," "Coca-Cola Ordered by India to Disclose Formula For Drink," "British Petroleum Company Nationalized by Nigeria," "Mitterrand Announces Plan to Nationalize French Banks," "Quebec Moves to Expropriate General Dynamic's Asbestos Corporation Unit," "Cerro Takes Loss of $45.6 Million in Peru Seizure." These are all recent headlines indicative of the complex and dynamic political environment facing the international marketer.

An undeniable and crucial fact of doing business in a foreign country is that permission to conduct business is controlled by the government of the host country. A fundamental point in assessing the political climate toward business in another country is that each independent state has the recognized right to either grant or withhold permission to do business within its political boundaries.[1] The host government can and does control and restrict a foreign company's activities by encouraging and offering support or by discouraging and banning its activities—depending on the pleasure of the host. A foreign business operates only as a guest and at the convenience of its host. In recent years, there has been a strongly expressed desire for cooperation among LDCs to control programs which will lead to the redistribution of income and wealth from developed countries.[2]

The New International Economic Order (NIEO), a resolution of the United Nation's Charter of Economic Rights and Duties of the States, is an attempt to establish a consensus on how the "new world economy" will function. The proposed NIEO includes "reform of compensatory financing, the international monetary system, new trade preferences, commodity programs (already agreed on), additional aid (especially in stretching out existing debt repayments), global resource management, preferential access to technol-

---

[1] An exception to this, of course, may be the Communist-bloc countries, where a government other than the host country may be involved. A somewhat similar situation also exists in "free world" nations, as under the Battle Act of the United States, so far as trade with Communist nations is concerned.

The recent requirement by Mexico that computers be manufactured in Mexico is a good example. See Lawrence Rout, "Mexico Limits U.S. Makers of Computers," *The Wall Street Journal*, January 29, 1981, p. 1.

[2] Jack N. Behrman, "Transnational Corporations in the New International Economic Order," *Journal of International Business Studies*, Spring/Summer 1981, pp. 29–41.

ogy, assistance in creating indigenous capabilities in science and technology, industrial self-reliance, and strengthening trade and economic cooperation among LDCs themselves."[3]

In short, the intention of the NIEO is to establish a unified front to MNCs and advanced nations to effect vast economic changes that will improve the LDCs' lot. Whether or not cooperation among LDCs will produce a unified front is debatable; but certainly the expectations of a new international economic order will influence the attitude of most LDCs towards MNCs and result in greater control over their activities.[4]

National environments differ widely: some countries are economically developed, some underdeveloped; some countries have an abundance of resources, others few or none; some countries are content with the status quo, others seek drastic changes to improve their relative positions in the world community. Of primary importance is that a government reacts to its environment by initiating and pursuing policies deemed necessary to solve the problems created by its particular environment. Reflected in its policies and attitudes toward foreign business are a government's ideas of how best to promote the national interest considering its own resources and political philosophy. The government is an integral part of every foreign business activity—a silent partner who has nearly total control. Therefore, the host country will judge every foreign business venture by standards as variable as there are nations, political philosophies, degrees of economic development, and environmental factors affecting human needs and wants.

Before a company commits itself to operating within a country, it should exert considerable effort in assessing the dominant political climate. Such an assessment should cover at least the following: (1) the current form of government, (2) current political party system, (3) stability and permanency of government policy, and (4) the risks or encouragements to foreign business from political activity. The fundamental policies and attitudes toward foreign business will differ drastically as a result of the different directions taken to achieve national goals. Errors are made by foreign marketers in not appraising correctly, if at all, the significance of the role of government in the success of their business ventures. The purpose of this chapter is to explore some of the more salient political considerations in assessing world markets.[5]

GOVERNMENTS AND POLITICAL PARTY SYSTEMS

A realistic appraisal of the political climate begins with a thorough study of the basic factors of the structures of government. What type of government

[3] Behrman, "Transnational Corporations in the New International Economic Order," p. 29.

[4] Joel Davidow, "Multinationals, Host Governments and Regulation of Restrictive Business Practices," *Columbia Journal of World Business,* Summer 1980, pp. 14–19.

[5] For a provocative article on the intertwining of business and politics see Richard Whalen, "No American Business is an Island," *Across the Board,* July 1980, pp. 40–51.

does the country have? Is it primarily a democracy, dictatorship, monarchy, socialistic or communistic state, or does it have tendencies in the direction of any one of these forms of government? With knowledge of the form of government, the observer will gain some insight into the impending business-political environment.[6]

Types of governments

The type of government is determined by the procedure through which the citizens form and express their will and the extent to which their will controls the composition and policy of government.

Most states can be classified as having either parliamentary or absolutist governments. Parliamentary governments can be further subdivided into either republics or constitutional monarchies, and absolutist governments include absolute monarchies and dictatorships.

Under parliamentary government the people are consulted from time to time to ascertain the majority will, and, therefore, policies of the government theoretically reflect the majority opinion of the population. Under absolutist government, the ruling regime dictates government policy without specifically consulting the needs and wants of the people.

Vital to foreign business is the makeup of the current government and the predominant philosophy toward business in general and foreign business in particular. Is the government conservative, middle of the road, or leftist? Does the existing business climate include support of the free enterprise system or does state ownership of industry prevail? Answers to these questions can be determined by examining the philosophy of the political party in power.

Political parties

Under parliamentary government, where public opinion is influential in forming policy, political parties must crystallize public opinion around definite legislative and administrative measures. The marketer should be concerned with political parties because of their influence on the prevailing attitudes of the government toward business; and, more specifically, because they are instrumental in determining the role foreign business will play within the economy.

Political party systems within a government can be divided into four types: two-party system, multiparty system, single-party system, and dominated one-party system. The two-party system consists of two strong parties that typically succeed each other in control of the government. The two

---

[6] An interesting article on the relationship between companies and host countries is "Are Multinationals Aliens to the Third World," *International Management,* January 1981, pp. 12–16.

parties have different philosophies, and when they succeed one another, the impact on business and government relations can be more drastic on foreign firms than on domestic firms.

The government of Great Britain is a good example. In an interview with a spokesman for the British Labor Party, some fundamental differences in attitude toward foreign business between the Labor and Conservative parties were shown. The discussion involved how the Labor Party proposed to handle problems with the balance-of-payments when that party was in power and the spokesperson was the prime minister. It was made known there would be no hesitation about placing temporary limitations on imports of manufactured goods plus extending exchange controls if necessary. This approach was in direct contrast to the philosophy of the then ruling Conservative Party which had been gradually liberalizing the controls on foreign businesses for several years. Later, when the Labor Party came to power, there were indeed some significant changes made; among other controls, a 15 percent surcharge on imports was instituted. When the Labor Party was later replaced by the Conservative Party, a liberalization of controls was instituted and the Conservative Party's policies were again put into place. A foreign firm doing business in Great Britain during this period was see-sawed between the liberal trade policies of the Conservatives and the restrictive ones of the Liberals.

In the multiparty system, no single party is strong enough to gain control of the government, and the government is formed through coalitions of various parties. In contrast to the two-party system, the multiparty system has frequent and continuous changes of coalition parties, since the longevity of each coalition is dependent on the cooperation of each one of its partners—all of whom are typically at philosophical odds. The multiparty system with all its problems is best typified by Italy. Other modern governments with multiparty systems are Germany, France, Belgium, the Netherlands, and Israel.

At the other extreme from the multiparty system is the single-party system with one political party dominating to such an extent that no other party has any chance of gaining control in an election. Such situations generally exist in young countries early in the development of a parliamentary system. As they advance, significant changes occur and a multiparty system generally develops. Mexico is a good example of a single-party system: the PRI Party (revolutionary party) is virtually guaranteed election in every national vote. Open elections are held, but the opposing party's slate of candidates (PAN Party) seldom pull more than a nominal vote since the PRI has the support of the vast majority of the electorate. For a young country in the throes of economic development, a sound one-party system may provide a degree of stability and continuity of development that is necessary, or at least helpful, for rapid growth.

The fourth political party system is a very different version of the one-party political system. In this type, the dominant party actively quells any true opposition and inhibits the growth and normal operations of other parties. Instead of the dominant party having the support of the majority in open and free competition, all competition is severely restricted, and the controlling party gets support because no effective opposition is permitted. Instead of the dominated one-party system developing into a two-party or multiparty system, it may gradually be transformed into a dictatorship.

Knowledge of party philosophy

Particularly important to the marketer is the prevailing attitude of government toward foreign business. Equally important are all the basic philosophies of parties represented within the country since any one of them might come into power, thereby altering prevailing attitudes. In addition, it is important to study the overall political system of a country because each party's philosophy can have significant effect on the general direction of the political policies of the government. It is not unusual for a winning party in an election to consider the policies advocated by the other party or parties.[7] In a multiparty system this is usually more the case than the exception since a coalition is required in order to form a government.

Even in a single-party system, as in Mexico where the PRI Party is always in power, attitudes and philosophies of the other parties remain important. This is especially true since the electoral reform law of 1963 provides that any party receiving at least 2.5 percent of the total Mexican national vote will receive no less than five seats in the Chamber of Deputies and can receive up to 20 seats.

In summary, a firm assessing the political climate of a foreign government should consider existing governmental philosophy as well as the long-range direction of its political development whenever possible. The latter requires a knowledge of the various political parties and their attitudes toward business and government, and, more important, their attitudes toward foreign business and government.

THE PERMANENCY OF GOVERNMENT POLICY

Foreign business finds the stability or instability of a government's policies in the country within which it operates to be of prime importance since stability directly affects the permanency of the policies applicable to operations. While government policy is always in a state of gradual change, business is primarily concerned with radical changes in policy which create a climate of uncertainty. Such radical changes may be defined as *instability*.

---

[7] See, "Australia, a New Political Turn Worries Multinationals," *Business Week*, November 3, 1980, p. 51 for a report of this occurring in Australia.

Instability usually results from a change in form of government and/or a shift in political parties at the head of the government. Inherent in these shifts are changes in philosophy that result in drastic readjustments of policy toward foreign business.

The most drastic changes in government-business relations occur when one type of government is replaced by another. In many instances retaliation against "exploiting foreign businesses" becomes the political battle cry of the reform government. Thus, foreign business becomes the scapegoat against which both social discontent and national frustrations can be aimed. Once in power, the reform government can create a public image of success and spectacular accomplishment by instituting reprisals against foreign "exploiters."

Although government policy may alter the potential of some markets, foreign investments can be profitable under any type of government as long as there is some long-run predictability and stability. For example, PepsiCo operates profitably in Russia under one of the more extreme political systems. It is the unpredictable and drastic shifts in government tactics that deter investments. The rise to power of an unpredictable, radical reform government seems to worsen the investment climate and to deter new investment more than government corruption or hostility toward specific foreign businesses. It was reported that billions of dollars worth of business decisions were halted as multinational executives in France and around the world tried to determine what the stunning presidential victory of Socialist Mitterrand meant for foreign business.[8] Although the government under Giscard d' Estaing had Europe's most formidable array of government controls on business, that situation was predictable, whereas Mitterrand's policies were unknown. This kind of uncertainty is difficult for businesses to deal with.[9]

Changes in political parties that head a government also can result in unstable conditions, although not so severe as an overthrow of the government. Generally, changes in policy are made so that the operation of foreign businesses is more in line with the philosophy of the new party. In some instances, a new political party at the helm can result in action as severe as nationalization or expropriation of an industry; however, the usual results are tightening or lessening of various government controls.

Not all government change necessarily means more controls and harrassment for the MNC—quite the opposite can occur. For example, the change in the Chinese government that occurred at the death of Chairman Mao has resulted in easing of restrictions on foreign businesses to the extent of allowing wholly-owned branches and subsidiaries within the country.[10]

---

[8] "France Businesses Feeling a Mitterrand Shock," *Business Week*, May 25, 1981, p. 66.

[9] "France Under Mitterrand: Business Hopes and Fears," *World Business Weekly*, May 25, 1981, pp. 6–7.

[10] "China Now Permits Full Foreign Ownership," *The Asian Wall Street Journal Weekly*, June 15, 1981, p. 3.

NATIONALISM

While shifts in political parties and types of government philosophies may cause instability and changes in government-business relations, the wave of intensive economic nationalism that is spreading throughout the world may prove to be the most critical political factor affecting international business for the remainder of this century. If not properly coped with, this militant nationalism, which "has as one of its central aims, the preservation of national economic autonomy," may make the early history of nationalism and foreign investment pall by comparison.

For a state to survive more than a fleeting historical moment it must enjoy the loyalty of most of its residents. In other words, most residents must identify their interest more with the preservation of the sovereignty of the state in which they reside than with any other. Some would call this *personal identification* or *loyalty nationalism*, others, *patriotism*.

BOX 6–1: Economic revolution—Marxist or nationalist?

The Chief of the Joint Staffs of the Peruvian military says:

"We are fighting for the dignity and sovereignty of Peru. How can we, in this country, accept that the rich should grow richer and the poor grow poorer? Shouldn't the foreign companies be ashamed to reap high profits when a great part of the population lacks the necessities of life? We want to fight against unpardonable privileges of the oligarchy and we are determined to use all our energies to crush those who oppose the indispensable change in Peru's social structure. . . . Our revolution is not Marixist. It is nationalist."

Source: Peter Nehemkis, "Latin America: Testing Ground for International Business," © by The Regents of the University of California. Reprinted from *California Management Review* 13, no. 4, p. 90, by permission of The Regents.

In order to understand the conflicts and pressures inherent in the international movement of capital, skills, technology, and goals, an appreciation for the essential nature of nationalism and the cluster of interests represented in that notion is needed. Regardless of the objectivity of one's view, it is necessary to appreciate that no nation-state, however secure, will tolerate unlimited penetration by a foreign company into its market and economy if control of management is in another country. This is especially true if the decisions made are perceived as insensitive to the social/economic priorities of the host country.

This attitude is probably best illustrated by the sharp public criticism of foreign MNCs in Brazil. A "manifesto" recently published states that even though MNC investment had substantial impact on Brazil's rise to the world's eighth largest economy, continued investment would lead to "serious political and social distortion." Some of the unfavorable results listed were the "division of the country's industrial establishment among the leading multinational companies;" deterioration of the educational system; increasing foreign indebtedness; and the "progressive occupation by foreign companies of considerable portions of national territory."[11] The manifesto argues that the country must "recover the command of its own destiny" and national identity.

The confrontation is inevitable since the policy functions of government— allocation of resources, stabilization, and distribution—and the interests of the multinational corporation will be in conflict at some point. Because the corporation operates outside the political boundaries of the host country, it can frequently avoid national redistribution policies; further, it participates in an international distribution of income and wealth that can be controlled only imperfectly, if at all, by national governments.

This concern over the position of foreign investment in a country may be easier to understand if the perspective of the host country is appreciated. Consider, for example, the situation in Canada where a strong feeling among Canadians is that too much of their economy is dominated by U.S. investors. In 1981, the majority of the ownership of Canada's oil industry was held by U.S. companies. U.S. companies also own 32 percent of the pulp and paper industry, 36 percent of the mining and smelting industry, and 39 percent of manufacturing as a whole. Of the 100 largest companies in Canada, 37 are U.S. owned or controlled. It is understandable for many Canadian citizens to consider these figures intolerable and to show considerable concern about the involvement of foreign business in the economy of their country.[12]

Even in the United States, where foreign ownership of U.S. business is relatively small compared to Canada and most other countries of the world, concern is still voiced by Congress. A House government-operations committee has recently called for "a screening agency, similar to agencies in other countries, which would be empowered not only to bar harmful investments but to extract substantial benefit to the U.S. economy from all others."[13]

As nation-states are challenged by the multinational corporation, it gives rise to a xenophobic economic nationalism in developing nations as well as in developed ones. One reason given for this attitude by both developed and underdeveloped countries is the control and protection of the nation's sovereignty.

We are accustomed to the idea of rigid regulation of investments and even expropriation in underdeveloped countries, but the idea of economic nationalism among developed Western nations seems unusual. However, even the United States, which customarily has had an open-door policy toward investments (in fact, until recently holding seminars to encourage

---

[11] "Brazilian Critics Censure the Role Of MNCs in Economy," *Business Latin America,* January 14, 1981, pp. 13–14.

[12] Herbert Meyer, "Trudeau's War on U.S. Business," *Fortune,* April 6, 1981, pp. 74–78; and Barry Newman, "Australia Fears Effect of Foreign Investment as its Economy Booms," *Wall Street Journal,* October 2, 1980, p. 1.

[13] Dave Bartel, "Foreign Investments Pose U.S. Threat," *Knight-Ridder News Service,* August 8, 1980.

foreign investment) has been offering resistance and raising questions about skyrocketing foreign investment. As foreign banks have increased their holdings in U.S. banks, opposition is being voiced by banking groups as well as by Congress. At least three congressional committees have been set up to study the problem of foreign investment and to determine if new legislation is necessary for the regulation of foreign control of critical industries. Canada, Great Britain, Germany, and many other countries are raising similar questions and contemplating either laws to control foreign investment or stricter enforcement of existing controls.[14]

BOX 6–2:   Nationalism in U.S.?

Nearly half the states in the United States restrict the purchase of foreign-made goods.

That's the finding of a survey undertaken by the United States—Japan Trade Council Inc. The report is contained in a 12-page booklet titled "State Barriers to World Trade." It notes that "at least 23 states currently impose substantial restrictions on the purchase of foreign-made goods for public projects." It goes on: "Businessmen seeking to supply foreign materials to a state project are confronted by an array of bureaucratic practices that lack uniformity and are often arbitrarily administered."

Alabama, Massachusetts, and Illinois, the report complains, "virtually ban the purchase of certain foreign-made materials, particularly fabricated steel products." Alaska, Arkansas, and New Mexico, it adds, give "preferential treatment to in-state materials and suppliers." Among major states with "intentional buy-American policies," according to the survey, are New York, New Jersey, and Pennsylvania.

Source: "Global Report," *The Wall Street Journal.*

The effects of nationalism on the multinational company are the same whether the country is industrialized or among the lesser developed nations. Most variation would be in degree of intensity, but all countries will demand control of profits and borrowing within the host country, control of the impact on the local company (i.e. curtailment of imports in favor of locally made products, and pushing of exports of locally made products), control over foreign investment in established and locally owned business, local ownership of equity, in part at least, by nationals, and the replacement of expatriate management by local citizens.

Strong feelings of nationalism, changes in governments, and shifts in political parties all lead to conditions which create unstable relations between governments and foreign businesses. The following discussion deals with how political climate affects a product's vulnerability.

---

[14] Leonard Urry and James Hildreth, "A Flood of Japanese Products Challenges U.S. Industry," *Denver Post—Newhouse Service,* October 5, 1980; and "U.S., Japanese Export Assault on Europe Stirs Protectionist Cries in Common Market," *The Wall Street Journal,* December 24, 1980, p. 10.

ASSESSING POLITICAL VULNERABILITY

Some products appear to be more politically vulnerable than others, that is, because of particular circumstances they receive special governmental attention, either favorable or unfavorable depending on the product. Favorable political attention can mean protection, reduced tax rates, exemption from quotas, control of competition, and other concessions.

This is illustrated by the Sudan's attempts to encourage investments in high-priority industry by exempting investors from corporate taxes for five years, from customs duties and surcharges on machinery and equipment, giving priorities in financing from local banking institutions, and protecting them from foreign competition through quotas or increased duties on imported goods.

Political vulnerability, however, also can lead to labor agitation, public regulations, price fixing, allocation quotas, expropriation, regulation and control, or other forms of government harassment if the product is considered to be nonessential or undesirable. For example, a group of competitors of Dow Chemical Company successfully blocked that company's plans to build a giant new petrochemical facility in Brazil without local partners. Protests from Brazilian competitors charged that Dow would dump a large portion of the increased output in their home market. They joined with politicians who used the government's proposed action on the Dow project as a way of attacking the government itself.[15] In Colombia, a tobacco monopoly with government sanction managed to keep machinery for a new British-American tobacco company plant on the dock for nearly two years, effectively killing the project.

Attitudes toward politically vulnerable products can change from unfavorable to favorable overnight with a change in attitude of the government. Indian bureaucrats blocked three American firms from building a $40 million fertilizer plant. Yet, a year later, the change in political climate was such that another firm was able to come to terms with the government and secure the necessary permits in a day and a half. The Indian government came to the realization that foreign investment was necessary to the industry for the sake of agriculture. In another instance, some four years after the passage of an investment law which encouraged IBM to invest in computer manufacturing, Indian bureaucrats must have felt the computer industry was not a necessary contribution to the economy; through insistence on new ownership requirements, the bureaucrats caused IBM to curtail production in India.

There are at least as many reasons for a product's political vulnerability as there are political philosophies, economic variations, and cultural differences. Unfortunately, there are no set rules a marketer can follow to deter-

---

[15] "Brazil: Local Industry Stops a big Dow Expansion," *Business Week*, August 25, 1980, p. 46.

BOX 6–3: Coke's got a secret—and they aren't going to tell

For 91 years, the formula for making Coca-Cola has been a closely guarded secret. Now the government of India has ordered Coca-Cola to disclose it or cease operations in that country. This secret ingredient called 7-X supposedly gives Coke its distinctive flavor. The government's Minister for Industry told the Indian parliament that Coca-Cola's Indian branch would have to transfer 60 percent of its equity shares to Indians and hand over its know-how by April 1978, or shut down. Indian sales account for less than 1 percent of Coca-Cola's worldwide sales. The potential market, however, in India, a country of over 586 million, is tremendous.

The government has refused to let the branch import the necessary ingredients since March (1977), and Coke—once as abundant as bottled drinking water sold in almost every Indian town of more than 50,000—is nearly gone throughout India. The Minister for Industry said Indian scientists had developed a concentrate for a substitute soft drink, and he expected Indian bottlers to take advantage of this new development. "The Minister feels the activities of Coca-Cola in India 'furnish a classic example of how multinational corporations operating in a low-priority, high-profit area in a developing country attain run-away growth and, in the absence of alertness on the part of the government concerned, can trifle with the weaker indigenous industry in the process.' " Coke said they wouldn't give up the formula and India said they had to leave. You can't buy Coca-Cola in India today, Coke packed up their bags and left the country.

Source: Adapted from "Coca-Cola Ordered by India to Disclose Formula for Drink," *The Wall Street Journal*, August 13, 1977, p. 11; "Indians Want Coke Know-How," *New York Times*, August 10, 1977; and Ranjan Das, "Impact of Host Government Regulations on MNC Operation: Learning From Third World Countries," *Columbia Journal of World Business*, Spring 1981, p. 89.

---

mine definitely whether or not a product will be subject to political attention. By answering the following questions, however, a marketer may detect clues to a product's vulnerability.

1. Is the availability of supply of the product ever subject to important political debates? (sugar, salt, gasoline, public utilities, medicines, foodstuffs)

2. Do other industries depend on the production of the product? (cement, power machine tools, construction machinery, steel)

3. Is the product considered socially or economically essential? (key drugs, laboratory equipment, medicines)

4. Is the product essential to agricultural industries? (farm tools and machinery, crops, fertilizers, seed)

5. Does the product affect national defense capabilities? (transportation industry, communications)

6. Does the product include important components that would be available from local sources and that otherwise would not be used as effectively? (labor, skills, materials)

7. Is there local competition or potential local competition from manufacturers in the near future? (small, low-investment manufacturing)

8. Does the product relate to channels of mass communication media? (newsprint, radio equipment)
9. Is the product primarily a service?
10. Does the use of the product, or its design, rest on some legal requirements?
11. Is the product potentially dangerous to the user? (explosives, drugs)
12. Does the product induce a net drain on scarce foreign exchange?[16]

Depending on how these questions were answered and the particular philosophy of those in power at the time, a company might expect to receive favorable political attention if they contributed to the achievement of national goals; or conversely, unfavorable attention if they were nonessential in view of current national needs. For products judged nonessential, the risk would be great, but for those thought to be making an important contribution, encouragement and special considerations generally would be available.

In addition to these qualitative measures of political vulnerability, a growing number of firms are employing more systematic methods of measuring political risk. *Political risk assessment* is an attempt to forecast political instability and thus alter the "rules of the game" under which a firm makes its decision to enter a market. There are three uses for political risk assessment: (1) to provide a framework for evaluating the political risk associated with countries, (2) to identify those elements of political risk associated with foreign businesses and to provide sufficient warning of mounting political risk to allow a firm to protect or at least minimize its exposure, and (3) to allow a company to identify and examine countries where risks were once high but where risk has decreased so that they now present good investment opportunities.

There are a variety of methods used to measure political risk. They range from having in-house political analysts[17] to using external sources that specialize in analyzing political risk.[18] Presently, all methods are far from being perfected; however, the very fact a company attempts to systematically examine the problem is significant.[19]

For a marketer doing business in a foreign country, a necessary part of any market analysis is an assessment of the probable political consequences

---

[16] Richard D. Robinson, "The Challenge of the Underdeveloped National Market, *The Journal of Marketing,* October 1961, pp. 24–25. Reprinted from *The Journal of Marketing,* published by the American Marketing Association.

[17] Ronald Alsop, "More Firms are Hiring own Political Analysts to Limit Risks Abroad," *Wall Street Journal,* March 30, 1981, p. 1.

[18] "Risk/Opportunity Index Projects Better Times for World Economy," *Business International,* June 5, 1981, pp. 179–80.

[19] For a comprehensive review of risk assessment, see Stephen J. Kobrin, "Assessing Political Risk Overseas," *The Warton Magazine,* Winter 1981–1982, pp. 25–31; Edwardo Lachica, "Firms That Assess Overseas Business Climate Find Political Predictions a Risky Business," *The Asian Wall Street Journal Weekly,* May 25, 1981, p. 18; and Thomas L. Brewer, "Political Risk Assessment for Foreign Direct Investment Decisions: Better Methods for Better Results," *Columbia Journal of World Business,* Spring 1981, pp. 5–12.

of a marketing plan—some marketing activities are more susceptible to political considerations than others. Basically, it boils down to evaluating the essential nature of the immediate activity. The following section explores some risks that face a business whose products and activities are politically vulnerable.

CONFISCATION, EXPROPRIATION, DOMESTICATION, AND OTHER RISKS

Risks resulting from the political implications of a company's activities can range from confiscation, the most severe, through many lesser but still significant government activities such as exchange controls, important restrictions, price controls, and labor policy. *Confiscation, expropriation, domestication,* and *nationalization* of foreign investments are terms frequently used and incorrectly defined in the literature on political vulnerability. *Confiscation* occurs when a foreign investment is taken over by a government without any reimbursement. *Expropriation* occurs when a foreign investment is taken over by government but some form of reimbursement is made. The reimbursement may not be the full value of the investment from the viewpoint of the company being expropriated, but, nonetheless, some attempt to reimburse foreign investment is made. Expropriation also implies that though reimbursement was made, the original owners of the company did not willingly sell.[20]

While confiscation and expropriation deal with the taking of property, *nationalization* technically refers to ownership by the government. For example, a firm's property may be expropriated and subsequently turned over to the private sector within the country, or it may be confiscated or expropriated and operated by the government. In the latter situation, it is correct to say that the business was nationalized. Generally, nationalization affects an entire industry rather than a single company. For example, the British nationalized the railways, that is, railroads in Britain are owned and operated by the British government; the French government nationalized all banks in 1981.

Domestication is defined as that process whereby a government, by various means, forces a foreign-held corporation to relinquish control, including actual ownership, on several fronts to nationals. This process will be discussed in more detail later in the chapter. Each of the politically and/or economically inspired sanctions against foreign business is sufficiently important and occurs with enough frequency to require the special consideration of foreign marketers; in most foreign business ventures, one or all of these risks are incurred to some degree and must be accepted as political realities of the environment when marketers are doing business overseas.

---

[20] For an interesting discussion of the problems of multinational firms and national goals see, Thomas N. Gladwin and Ingo Walter, *Multinationals Under Fire: Lessons in the Management of Conflict* (New York: John Wiley & Sons, 1980), 688 pp.

Confiscation and expropriation

Confiscation or expropriation of foreign business are probably the most frequently used and most critical politically induced risks of foreign business. Modern economic history is replete with cases of confiscation and expropriation. Some better known examples are Mexico's takeover of the foreign-owned railway system in 1937 and the oil industry in 1938; Guatemala's takeover of foreign-owned banana plantations in 1953; the Cuban confiscation and nationalization of all industry in 1960; Brazil's takeover of U.S.-owned electrical power plants; the 1969 expropriation of Standard Oil's holdings and the 1973 expropriation and nationalization of the Cerro holdings by the government of Peru. The World Bank reported that since 1960 a total of 1,535 firms from 22 different capital exporting countries have been expropriated in 511 separate actions by 76 nations. According to this source, approximately 12 percent of all foreign investment in 1967 was nationalized by 1976.[21]

The motivation of a country that expropriates investment is frequently couched in deep sentiments of nationalism. Why does a nation feel that it must seize foreign investment? Many reasons are given, but basically such actions stem from the belief (whether valid or not is immaterial) that the country's national goals and self-interest can best be served by government or national ownership rather than by foreign control of a particular industry.

Confiscation is especially alluring to many underdeveloped countries; as one observer noted, "Since all confiscation requires is a decree by the government, it is relatively easy—dirt cheap—in fact, it costs nothing at all. Further, confiscation seems to transfer national wealth and property from foreign hands to local hands rapidly and with minimum continuing problems. This observation is not completely accurate since history shows foreign business investments to be reluctant to return to a country after assets have been confiscated even though there is also evidence that another person's problems are not necessarily seen as one's own. By 1981, just two years after the revolutionary government of Iran confiscated a substantial portion of foreign investment, European and Japanese auto manufacturers were negotiating with the Iranian government for the right to assemble cars and trucks there.[22]

Expropriation is typically justified on grounds that the industry is critical to national defense, national sovereignty, national wealth and/or national economic growth, and thus the nation's interests require that the industry not be controlled by a foreigner. Certain industries are more susceptible to expropriation than others; public utilities are a frequent target, since it is universally believed they are critical to economic growth as well as being

---

[21] Joseph V. Miscallef, "Political Risk Assessment," *Columbia Journal of World Business,* January 1981, p. 47.

[22] "Car Makers Vie for the Iranian Markets," *World Business Weekly,* July 13, 1981, p. 19.

instrumental in defense capabilities. Mining, oil, and other natural resources are also particularly vulnerable since the nation's wealth is at stake. Other industries that are basic to the country's economy can be just as vulnerable. Another justification used for expropriation is the strong feeling that foreign businesses typically exploit the national wealth of the host country, taking everything from the country and giving nothing in return. There may have been some truth in this observation during the past decade. According to a Peruvian estimate, between 1950 and 1965, $3.90 was taken out of the country as profit, dividends, interest, credit, or as payment for the use of technology, for every $1.00 invested.[23]

Government takeover does not always mean total loss for the foreign investor; in some cases, the government reimburses the investor for the value of losses. The reimbursement is seldom felt to be equitable by the foreign owner, but there is less stigma attached to such government action if some payment is made.

Some authorities believe that the risks of confiscation and expropriation will lessen in the future for three reasons. One, governments are coming to realize investment is necessary for achievement of desired growth potential. Furthermore, past experience has shown that government or local ownership does not always yield the desired results; in some cases, experience has shown an industry has faltered and its contribution to the national economy has decreased after expropriation. A second fact which may alter future attempts at confiscation and expropriation is the more stringent economic pressure being levied against offending nations by the country of the affected firm when equitable reimbursement is not made. Although in the opinion of one international legal authority, "the traditional international rules on property protection are outdated . . . international law is indifferent to expropriation of aliens."[24] The third reason is that investing firms are trying to make themselves indispensable and less vulnerable in a host country. Such activities include encouraging nationals to invest in the business venture, training nationals for important management positions, borrowing capital from local or third country banks to which the host government is indebted, and generally attempting to erase the constant[25] suspicion that the foreign firm is somehow exploiting the host country.

Although the threat of confiscation or expropriation may be abating, it still persists and is of prime significance as a political risk in doing business abroad. Another, and perhaps more insidious, way for a government to take over a company is a process of systematically restricting a company and forcing step-by-step liquidation, resulting in the investment being con-

---

[23] "Are Multinationals Aliens in the Third World?" *International Management,* January 1981, p. 14.

[24] Rudolf Dolzer, "Expropriation and Aliens: Customary International Law and Transition," *CTC Reporter,* 1, no. 9 (Winter 1980), pp. 38–39.

[25] "Insuring Against Risk Abroad," *Business Week,* September 14, 1981, p. 63.

BOX 6–4: Expropriation means loss?—Depends on the view

The meaning of "failure" is confused by a basic difference in investment philosophy. One writer explains:

"The United States investors view their foreign investment perspectively—they look at the investment today and project various inputs in the future that can contribute to the value of the total investment. On the other hand, many Latin American hosts view an investment 'historically'—they look back at what the investor has already exacted from his investment and therefore value his present-day investment at a much lower figure. These diverse views of valuation result in the initial positions (investor's and host's) being far apart."

Even the Anaconda and Kennecott expropriations in Chile cannot really be described as failures if one considers the profits gained since the early 1900s, before the companies were finally expropriated. A true failure is a company which shows a net loss from its Latin American ventures—and these are very few.

Source: Jon B. Utley, "Doing Business With Latin Nationalists," *Harvard Business Review* 51, no.1, p. 80.

---

trolled by nationals. This process of "domestication" can be as lethal as confiscation.[26]

Domestication

Increasingly, more host countries are attempting to transfer control of foreign investment to national ownership and bring the firm's activities in line with national interests through *domestication*.[27]

Rather than outright confiscation or expropriation, concern over foreign investment is manifested more subtly in the gradual encroachment on the freedom to operate within the country. In essence, governments seek to *domesticate* the foreign investor rather than confiscate or expropriate.

Domestication entails:

A transfer of ownership in part or totally to nationals.

The promotion of a large number of nationals to higher levels of management.

Greater decision-making powers resting with nationals.

A greater number of products locally produced rather than imported for assembly.

Specific export regulations designed to dictate participation in world markets.

---

[26] For a comprehensive study of expropriation see, Adeoye A. Akinsany, *The Expropriation of Multinational Property in The Third World*, (New York: Praeger Publishers, 1980) 386 pp.

[27] Parts of this section are from Philip R. Cateora, "The Multinational Enterprise and Nationalism," *MSU Business Topics* 19, no. 2.

Domestication is the process whereby a government forces foreign-held enterprise to relinquish control on several fronts to nationals. For example, the Malaysian government, through a series of legislative moves, required the following to be carried out by foreign investors in Malaysia:

1. Malaysians' shares of industrial assets increased from the then current 3 percent to 30 percent by 1980.
2. Foreign control of industry and commerce reduced from 60 percent to 30 percent by 1980.
3. Preferential hiring and promotion consideration given Malays.
4. State-owned companies to have equity in the form of special management shares each to carry 300 votes and be significant in the management operation of the foreign subsidiary.[28]

BOX 6–5: Two sides to the story?

The news from Peru was typically something like this: "Peru has seized its largest oil company, telephone utilities, banks, and sugar plantations and has ordered eight auto assembly plants to close."

In fact, these actions were not as prejudicial to business as the reporting made them appear:

The oil company, belonging to Standard Oil Company (New Jersey), was indeed expropriated. On the other hand, international Telephone & Telegraph, which had owned the telephone company, traded it for a luxury Sheraton hotel and a joint venture with the government to manufacture communications equipment.

As for the banks, one, the Banco Popular, was on the verge of failure; while the other, belonging to Chase Manhattan, was paid for in hard cash.

The sugar plantations were turned over to worker cooperatives under the agrarian reform, and the former owners received bonds which offered them special concessions if they would use the bonds to establish industries.

In the case of the assembly plants, a thoughtful reader might have wondered what kind of distorted "capitalism" must have existed in a small country like Peru to permit so many auto factories in the first place.

Source: Utley, "Business with Nationalists," *Harvard Business Review*, 51, no. 1, p. 78.

Effects of government-initiated domestication

The effects of government-initiated domestication of a foreign firm can be disastrous; in fact, the effect can be the same as confiscation. Consider an established foreign investor with 100 percent ownership of a firm facing an ultimatum to sell 51 percent or more of that ownership to local nationals by a specific date. Even if the local capital were available, it would be almost impossible to sell the stock at a fair, equitable price since perspective purchasers know a forced sale means they can negotiate the price to an expropriative level and the foreign investor has no recourse.[29] Even when

---

[28] "Malaysia, a Get Tough Policy on Foreign Control," *Business Week*, July 7, 1975, p. 32.

[29] "Insuring Against Risk Abroad," *Business Week*, September 14, 1981, p. 62.

equity is sold at reasonable prices, a basic conflict of interest between the foreign investor and the national stockholder frequently arises. A forced sale is generally made to a small group interested in an immediate return on investment rather than the reinvestment of profits necessary for continued market development and capital growth.

Equally calamitous can be government directives requiring a certain percentage of top level management to be nationals. Unless adequately trained nationals who are willing to follow corporate guidelines can be appointed to fill these positions, companies find they are unable to maintain control over their investments. In many instances, companies have no adequately trained nationals within the company to transfer to higher level positions so they must seek others outside the business. They then find there are few available who have the depth of experience necessary, and the competition for those few is fierce. Equally troublesome is the fact that new owners may force the hiring of "loyal" nationals with little capability for the position and more interest in protecting the personal interests of the national stockholder than in implementing long-term corporate plans. In either case, personnel in executive positions are unable or unwilling to make decisions commensurate with positions they hold.[30]

Further complications and costly problems for the foreign investor come with requirements that supplies, raw materials, and perhaps component parts be purchased locally. In most cases, when a government requires raw materials and supplies be of local origin, they are not readily or economically available. If fact, the intent of the government is to force the foreign owner to create local demand, thus stimulating local production. The company then finds that not only are supplies unavailable, but, in order to create local supplies, they must provide the primary investment capital for local industries as well as train and provide necessary expertise. With established supply sources, experience, and/or local financing completely lacking, the foreign investor must find ways (frequently at enormous expense and time lapse) of producing locally.

Foreign investors of the future face changing conditions directly affecting their interest in foreign countries. Unless the multinational investor of the 1980s exhibits concern with the host country's total economy, the growing animosity to U.S. dollars throughout the world will continue to show itself in government-initiated domestication, confiscation, or expropriation of U.S. investments. In order to avoid the economic pitfalls of these policies, global investment strategies will have to include a social awareness of local needs and wants. The investment must be designed to become a fully-integrated part of the domestic economy.

Although confiscation, expropriation, and government-initiated domestication frequently cause substantial loss of investment, a more common risk

---

is the multitude of minor but costly harassments encountered when a marketer does business in another country.

Other risks

Confiscation, expropriation, or domestication of a foreign business are extreme actions for any government. Most businesses abroad are faced with less drastic risks of politically condoned or inspired controls and pressures exerted against foreign operators. Political objectives under the banner of national security and/or the protection of infant industry are demanded despite the cold economic facts involved.

Exchange controls.   Exchange controls stem from shortages of foreign exchange held by a country. When a nation faces shortages of foreign exchange, controls may be leveled over all movements of capital or, selectively, against the most politically vulnerable companies in order to conserve the supply of foreign exchange for the most essential uses. A recurrent problem for the foreign investor is getting profits and investments into the currency of the home country.

Exchange controls are also extended to products by applying a system of multiple exchange rates to regulate trade in specific commodities classified as necessities or luxuries. Necessary products are placed in the most favorable (low) exchange categories, while luxuries are heavily penalized with high foreign exchange rates.

In countries with an especially difficult balance-of-payments problem, earnings as well as principal have been frozen for considerable periods of time. Such extreme measures are infrequent, as are cases of countries limiting profit remittance to a small, fixed percentage of net assets.

Currency convertibility is a continuing problem since most countries maintain regulations for control of currency and, in the event that an economy should suffer an economic setback or foreign exchange reserves suffer severely, the controls on convertibility are imposed rapidly.

Import restrictions.   Selective restrictions on the import of raw materials, machines, and spare parts are a fairly common strategy to force foreign industry to purchase more supplies within the host country and thereby create markets for local industry.[31] One such move by the Brazilian government required that before issuing an import permit for parts not made in Brazil, a 360-day import deposit was required prior to importation of the goods. The net result was at least a 50 percent increase in import costs to that particular firm. Although this is done in an attempt to support the development of domestic industry, the result is often to hamstring and sometimes interrupt the operations of established industries. The problem becomes critical when there are no adequately developed sources of supply within the country.

---

[31] "Mexican Government will Require Permits for 90% of Imports," *The Wall Street Journal,* July 2, 1982, p. 27.

BOX 6–6: Drink wine, not coke

Italy: A simple case in protectionism, observers say, is behind last week's Tempest in a Coke bottle. Genoa's public prosecutor ordered 100 million bottles of Coca-Cola withdrawn from sales outlets because ingredients were illegally listed on the bottle cap. The next day, however, the prosecutor relented, allowing bottled Coke to be sold as long as retailers display ingredients on a window poster. But growing evidence that Italian youth is forsaking the traditional meal-time glass of vino for Coke, say observers, is the real reason the soft drink is under pressure.

"World Round-Up." Reprinted from the December 5, 1975 issue of *Business Week* by special permission. © 1975 by McGraw-Hill, Inc.

Tax controls. Taxes must be classified as a political risk when used as a means of controlling foreign investments. In such cases, they are raised without warning and in violation of formal agreements. A squeeze on profits results from raising taxes significantly as a business becomes established. In those underdeveloped countries where the economy is constantly threatened with a shortage of funds, unreasonable taxation of successful foreign investments appears to be the handiest and quickest means of finding operating funds.

Price controls. Essential products that command considerable public interest, such as drugs, medicines, food, gasoline, and cars, are often subjected to price controls. Such controls may be applied during inflationary periods to control the cost of living and frequently are used by a government to force foreign companies to sell equity to local interests. In Venezuela, for example, Heinz de Venezuela and William Underwood Company have been under restrictive price controls for a number of years. The Underwood Company has not been able to increase the price of its popular deviled ham for over 10 years. Considering the inflation rate in Venezuela for the last 10 years, these price controls are very costly.[32]

Labor problems. In many countries, labor unions have strong government support which they use effectively in obtaining special concessions from business. Layoffs may be forbidden; profits may have to be shared; and an extraordinary number of services may have to be provided. In fact, in many countries, foreign firms are considered fair game for the demands of the domestic labor supply.

In France, the belief in full employment is almost religious in fervor; layoffs of any size, especially by foreign-owned companies, are regarded as national crises. When, as a result of cutbacks in demand, both General Motors and Remington Rand attempted to lay off workers in their French plants, the French Minister of Industry reprimanded them and stated he would not allow "certain isolated enterprises to practice an irresponsible policy that does not respect the social contract linking a financially powerful enterprise

---

[32] "Venezuela Beckons Foreign Investors, but Credibility Gap Obstructs Reentry," *The Wall Street Journal,* December 31, 1980, p. 10.

to the labor it employs." Although both General Motors and Remington Rand were privately assured that the minister's remarks were for public consumption, the reaction is indicative of the relationship between government and labor in many countries. The same conditions that forced General Motors and Remington Rand to lay off workers were causing domestic French industry to lay off personnel also, but apparently that situation went unnoticed by the government.

Throughout Europe, the strength of labor and its desire to influence business decisions which may have an effect on labor is causing concern among the MNCs. The European Parliament, for example, is considering a proposal to force multinational companies with European-based subsidiaries to make disclosures of global operations to local labor unions twice a year. The basic thrust of the proposal would be that decisions made by any multinational which might affect European labor must be disclosed prior to the actions being taken. Thus, multinationals would be restricted worldwide if, in the opinion of European labor, the proposed actions would cause any economic loss to labor.[33]

In Mexico, not only is the freedom to fire restricted, but recent constitutional amendments legally obligate companies to share profits with their employees. A "national committee" has been set up to determine the amount of a firm's profits and the extent to which they must be shared with labor. The committee is composed of representatives of government, management, and labor, each with equal representation. It is felt the representation is not fairly balanced since labor unions are regarded as arms of the Mexican government, outnumbering management two to one.

Another labor problem is the restrictions on entry into a country of key technicians. To force the hiring of nationals some countries will not provide work permits for technically trained personnel regardless of whether or not similar talents are available within the country.

Violence.   Although not government initiated, violence is another related risk that multinational companies must consider in assessing the political vulnerability of their activities.[34] Violence against governments, as well as against multinational firms, has increased during the 1970s. In fact, between 1970 and 1978, violence was directed against business targets in 2,427 cases out of a total of 5,529 terrorist incidents. The losses reached over $500 million in material damage, ransom paid in abductions, and funds taken in robberies. Moreover, thousands of business executives and personnel were held hostage, wounded, or killed.[35]

---

[33] "Common Market: A Call for Multinationals to Tell Labor Their Plans," *Business Week*, January 12, 1981, p. 40; and Richard I. Kirkland, Jr., "Bad News Brewing—the European Community may Soon Expose Management's Plans to the Slings and Arrows of Outraged Workers," *Fortune*, December 14, 1981, pp. 142–46.

[34] For a comprehensive discussion of violence and business, see Yonah Alexander and Robert A. Kilmarx, *Political Terrorism and Business* (New York: Praeger Publishers, 1979), 345 pp.

[35] "The Fear That Haunts Corporate America," *Across the Board,* May 1981, pp. 47–50.

Further, terrorist activities have increased steadily over the past eight years. In fact, 58.2 percent of all terrorist activities recorded since January, 1970 have taken place in a three-year period from 1976 to 1979. Out of an eight-year total of 4,899 acts of violence, 2,851 of them occurred in that three-year period.[36] Frequently, violence is directed to embarrass a government and its relationship with multinational firms; it forces the government to take action against the multinational to placate leftist groups who instigate the violence.[37]

ENCOURAGING FOREIGN INVESTMENT

Many governments encourage foreign investment. In fact, within the same country, some foreign businesses fall prey to politically induced harassments while others may be placed under a government umbrella of protection and preferential treatment. The difference lies in the evaluation of a company's contribution to the nation's self-interest.[38]

Foreign governments

The most important reason to encourage foreign investment is that it affords the most rapid means of providing necessary goods and services. Actually, foreign investment can be instrumental in accelerating the development of an economy. Many countries are coming to realize that foreign investment, properly controlled, need never be discouraged because the benefits outweigh most of the disadvantages involved.

One underdeveloped country has openly invited investors to literally take over the industrialization of that country. The many inducements include tax exemptions, protection against competing imports, unimpeded movement of capital and profits, and a multitude of other concessions. Naturally, direct contribution to the economy is a necessary prerequisite for the special treatment. Colombia's most recent 10-year-development plan allows for special considerations to foreign investors, including income tax exemptions up to 100 percent, providing the company's "sole business is the development of a basic industry necessary for Colombia's development."[39]

Along with direct encouragement from the host country an American company can receive assistance from the U.S. government. The intent is to encourage investment by helping to minimize and shift some of the risks from foreign political considerations.

---

[36] Alexander and Kilmarx, *Political Terrorism and Business* p. 281.

[37] For a discussion of how companies are relating to violence, see John K. Ryans, Jr. and William L. Shanklin, "Terrorism and the MNC," *Business*, March/April, 1980, pp. 2–7.

[38] "Concessions and Restrictions: Some Unusual Results of Major Data Study," *Business International*, August 14, 1981, pp. 257–59.

[39] "Foreign Countries Offer Wide Range of Incentives to Invest," *Asian Wall Street Journal Weekly*, August 24, 1981, pp. 12–14.

United States government

The U.S. government is motivated for economic as well as political reasons to encourage American firms to seek business opportunities in other countries. This has resulted in a variety of services and inducements intended to prompt American firms to go overseas. The kinds of assistance can be divided into two areas: activities designed to create favorable climates for foreign investment, and activities designed to assist day-to-day operations.

Part of the government's efforts to create favorable climates for overseas investment are the various activities designed to minimize some of the more troublesome politically motivated risks of doing business abroad. The government provides assistance against risks from deliberate activities of foreign governments such as losses arising from confiscation, expropriation, revolutions, war, and the inability to transfer profits and capital because of exchange restrictions.

Government support in minimizing political risks comes in at least two ways. One is through various agencies which offer guarantees against specific types of risks. In essence, the government provides the means for a foreign investor to purchase insurance against a particular risk. Another means of help covers the most severe political risk, confiscation; limitations have been placed on the granting of U.S. aid to those countries which have seized American-controlled property without equitable restitution.

The Export-Import Bank (Eximbank) is a U.S. government agency whose purpose is to underwrite, financially, international trade and investment activities of American firms. It also provides for guarantees against certain kinds of political risks. For a cost of one half of 1 percent per year of the guarantee coverage, a foreign investor can get coverage of up to 95 percent of loss because of political risks. Those insurable risks include inconvertibility, war, confiscation, civil disturbances, and the cancellation or restriction of export or import licenses.[40]

The Agency for International Development (AID), in conjunction with its aid to underdeveloped countries, has provisions for limited protection in support of "essential" projects in approved countries and for approved products. The costs of coverage are similar to those of the Eximbank and coverage extends to the basic political risks of convertibility, confiscation or expropriation, and war.

A broader-risk insurance coverage was provided in 1969 when the Foreign Assistance Act authorized creation of the Overseas Private Investment Corporation (OPIC) to provide "political-risk insurance for companies investing in less developed countries."

Besides the guarantees offered by the various insurance programs, the Hickenlooper Amendment to the Foreign Assistance Act of 1961 also provides assistance in case of confiscation or inadequately reimbursed expropri-

---

[40] Clarence I. Blau, "U.S. Government Resources in the Management of Foreign Operations," International Management Series, no. 1, p. 59.

BOX 6–7: Praise of the MNC from an LDC

While many countries, particularly less developed ones, perceive international companies as a threat, Singapore feels they have helped preserve the island's national identity and build its future. This is the theme of a brief study of the impact of MNCs on his country written by Dr. Lee Soo Ann, professor of economics at Singapore University.* With virtually no resources but its people, Singapore today has a living standard that is high by world, as well as Asian, standards. Its fastest era of growth came after 1966, when it consciously adopted the policy of becoming "a global city," and redoubled its efforts to attract investment from major MNCs and financial institutions to strengthen its links with the world economy.

* *Singapore Goes Transnational: A Study of the Economic Impact of Investment by Multinational Corporations in Singapore* (Singapore: Eastern Universities Press.)

Source: Reprinted from the May 27, 1977 issue of *Business International* with permission of the publisher, Business International Corp. (New York).

---

ation through direct economic action against an offending country. The Hickenlooper Amendment to the Foreign Assistance Act was designed to retaliate against confiscation or expropriation. In addition to government-sponsored insurance against political risk, there are private sources from which political risk insurance can be purchased. Lloyds of London, for example, provided NBC-TV with insurance for the 1980 Olympic Games. The contract provided for losses due to contract frustration, or outright repudiation by the Russians; in addition, it provided coverage of any political act that might be carried out by the United States for whatever reason including a human rights issue. This is the coverage that gave NBC a claim for $66 million resulting from the Russian invasion of Afghanistan and the subsequent U.S. decision not to enter the 1980 Olympic Games.[41]

BOX 6–8: Whatever you call it—Its still a bribe

U.S. expressions, such as *bribe, payoff,* all sound a little stiff and cold. In some countries the terms for the same activities have a little more character.* For example,

Country	Term	Translation
Japan	Kuroi kiri	Black mist
Germany	Schmiergeld	Grease money
	Nutzliche abgabe	Useful contribution
Latin America	El soborno	Payoff
Mexico	La mordida	The bite
Middle East	Baksheesh	Tip, gratuity
France	Pot-de-vin	Jug of wine
East Africa	Chai	Tea
Italy	Bustarella	Little envelope

* Other terms are *wairo* (Japan), *dash* (Nigeria), and *backhander* (India).

---

[41] See Richard Peterson, "Can Multinationals Survive in Today's World?" *Risk Management,* February 1981, p. 35.

SUGGESTIONS TO REDUCE POLITICAL VULNERABILITY

Even though a company cannot directly control or alter the political environment of the country within which it operates, there are measures that can lessen the degree of susceptibility of a specific business venture to politically induced risks.

Foreign investors frequently are accused of exploiting a country's wealth at the expense of the national population and for the sole benefit of the foreign investor. This attitude is best summed up in this statement made by a recent president of Peru: "We have had massive foreign investment for decades but Peru has not achieved development. Foreign capital will now have to meet government social goals."

These charges are not wholly unsupported by past experiences, but today's enlightened investor is seeking a return on investments commensurate with the risk involved. To achieve such returns, hostile and generally unfounded fears must be overcome; countries, especially the less developed, fear foreign investment for many reasons. They fear the multinationals' interest is only to exploit their labor, markets, or their raw materials and leave nothing behind except the wealthy who become wealthier.[42]

As long as fears of this sort persist, the political climate for a foreign investor will continue to be hostile. Are there ways of allaying the fears expressed above? A list of suggestions made some 20 years ago is still appropriate for a company which intends to be a good corporate citizen and thereby minimize its political vulnerability. A company is advised to remember:

1. It is a guest in the country and should act accordingly.
2. The profits of an enterprise are not solely any company's; the local "national" employees and the economy of the country should also benefit.
3. It is not wise to try to win over new customers by completely "Americanizing" them.
4. Although English is an accepted language overseas, a fluency in the language of the international customer goes far in making sales and cementing good public relations.
5. It should try to contribute to the country's economy and culture with worthwhile public projects.
6. It should train its executives and their families to act appropriately in the "foreign" environment.
7. It is best not to conduct business from the United States but to staff foreign offices with competent nationals and supervise the operation from home.

---

[42] An interesting history of a U.S. multinational in Latin America which may shed some light on the general feeling of many LDCs toward foreign investment is Thomas McCann, *An American Company: The Tragedy of United Fruit* (New York: Crown Publishers, 1976), 244 pps.

Manifestations of the suggestions listed include such examples as Pepsi-Cola sponsoring opera and ballet in Argentina; Proctor & Gamble, IBM, and others supporting educational programs in Asia; Gulf Oil fighting small-pox in Nigeria; General Electric providing music in hospitals and jails; Xerox Corporation sponsoring Sesame Street in Latin America and Cargill funding agricultural research in Brazil.[43]

There are many companies which survive even the most hostile environments; through their operating methods they have been able to minimize their political vulnerability. Sears Roebuck & Co., for example, has a favorable image throughout Latin America, and thus is able to survive wave after wave of nationalistic attack. Sears developed its favorable image in a variety of ways, including a successful profit-sharing program. They voluntarily offer profit participation to all employees, and today their employees have a substantial vested interest in the company. Thus, employees and their families are among Sears' most ardent defenders.

In addition, Sears has pioneered programs to develop local industry. They have, as corporate policy, a program to buy at least 20 percent of all merchandise sold in their stores from local manufacturers; today, they are operating closer to 90 percent. The results of such policy are that Sears buys from over a thousand local sources throughout Latin America, suppliers who owe their very existence to Sears' activities. It is estimated that some 400 companies have been founded directly on the basis of Sears' guarantees of markets.

Although many of those interested in doing business overseas may not feel they can go as far as Sears, there is certainly much to be said for attempting to become more closely identified with the ideals and desires of the host country. To do so might render a marketer's activities and products less politically vulnerable; and although it would not eliminate all the risks of the political environment, it might reduce the likelihood and frequency of some politically motivated risks.

In an attempt to persuade host governments that a company's investments make a positive contribution to the country's economy, one suggestion is to prepare a "balance sheet" to illustrate the net contribution a subsidiary makes. Exhibit 6-1 is an example of one developed by Clark Equipment Company to portray the contributions of their Argentine and Brazilian subsidiaries (EXIMIA and ECSA). They report that the information summarized in the balance sheet has been helpful in obtaining government approval for activities, including import licenses and expansion permits. A further benefit of such a balance sheet is to make those concerned with operations within the company more aware of local aspirations and thus, more responsive.

In spite of efforts at being a "good citizen" new modes of investment

---

[43] "Cargill in Brazil Shows How MNCs Can Aid Development," *Business Latin America*, October 14, 1981, pp. 321–28.

which render the venture less risky initially may be the only long-range solution to hostile political environments as nationalism continues to increase.[44]

In addition to corporate activities focused on the social and economic
goals of the host country and good corporate citizenship as discussed, there
are other strategies that MNCs can use to minimize political vulnerability
and risk.

Joint ventures typically have been less susceptible to political harassment.
Joint ventures can be with either locals or other third country multinational
companies; in both cases, a company's financial exposure is limited. A joint
venture with locals helps minimize anti-MNC feelings, and a joint venture
with another MNC adds the additional bargaining power of a third country.

Expanding the investment base to include several investors and banks
in financing any investment in the host country is another strategy. This
has the advantage of engaging the power of the banks whenever any kind
of government takeover or harassment is threatened. This strategy becomes
especially powerful if the banks have made loans to the host country; if
the government threatens expropriation or other type of takeover, the financing bank has substantial power with the government.

Marketing and distribution control located outside the country can be
used effectively if an investment should be expropriated; the host country
would then lose access to world markets. This has proved especially useful
for MNCs in the extractive industries where world markets for iron ore,
copper, and so forth are crucial to the success of the investment. Peru found
that when Marcona Mining Company was expropriated the country lost
access to iron ore markets around the world and ultimately had to deal
with Marcona on a much more favorable basis than first thought possible.

Licensing technology is a strategy some firms find eliminates almost all
risks. It can be especially effective in situations where the technology is
unique and the risk is high.

The strategies just discussed can be effective in forestalling or minimizing
the effect of a total takeover. However, in those cases where an investment
is being domesticated by the host country, the most likely long-range solution
is a planned phasing out, that is, a predetermined domestication. While
this idea is not a favorite business practice, the alternative of government-
initiated domestication can be as disastrous as confiscation. As a feasible
response to rising nationalism, predetermined domestication is a system
which can be profitable and politically acceptable to the host country as
well as profitable and operationally expedient for the foreign investor.[45]

---

[44] Yzes Ldoz and C. K. Prahalad, "How MNCs Cope With Host Governments Interventions,"
Harvard Business Review, March/April 1980, pp. 149–57.

[45] Randall J. Jones, Jr., "A Model for Predicting Expropriation in Latin America Applied
to Jamaica," *Columbia Journal of World Business,* Spring 1980, pp. 74–80.

EXHIBIT 6–1: Clark Equipment Company foreign investment balance sheet (financial figures in U.S. $ millions)

	1972 EXIMIA*	1972 ECSA†	1973 EXIMIA	1973 ECSA	1974 EXIMIA	1974 ECSA
A. Employment benefits:						
Total employees	332	3,310	331	4,934	381	4,890
Salaried						
Transferred from foreign operation	—	6	—	6	—	4
Local residents	151	1,081	180	1,516	213	1,647
Hourly						
Transferred from foreign operation	—	—	—	—	—	—
Local residents	181	2,223	151	3,412	168	3,239
Expenditure for training personnel	$ —	$ 97	$ —	$ 147	$ —	$ 203
Number of personnel trained	—	188	—	264	—	318
B. Contribution to local economy:						
Total salaries and wages (including fringes)	$ 932	$ 9,830	$1,350	$16,062	$ 2,187	$23,020
Total taxes	$ 519	$ 9,514	$ 854	$13,251	$ 1,391	$16,141
Total import duties	$ 589	$ 1,298	$ 579	$ 2,364	$ 846	$ 3,301
Total value of local purchases (including fixed assets)	$2,457	$21,355	$3,418	$39,029	$5,678	$48,569
Number of local suppliers	1,206	974	1,441	1,143	1,656	1,125
Credit granted to local customers	$3,265	$28,387	$3,722	$45,173	$ 6,536	$68,340
C. Balance-of-payments contribution:						
Exports (f.o.b.)	$ 107	$ 598	$1,262	$ 1,328	$ 3,970	$ 4,953
Imports (f.o.b.—including fixed assets)	$1,887	$ 8,750	$1,662	$11,546	$ 1,535	$19,390
Dividends, interest and fees remitted to foreign entities	$ 660	$ 273	$ 209	$ 546	$ 261	$ 5,647§
Import substitution value of local production‡	$4,214	$24,147	$6,169	$37,113	$10,811	$49,328
Capital increase from foreign sources	$ —	$ —	$ (139)	$ —	$ 647	$ —
Loans from foreign sources	$1,650	$ 6,055	$1,650	$ 3,000	$ 950	$23,115
Total BOP contribution	**$3,424**	**$21,777**	**$7,071**	**$29,349**	**$14,582**	**$52,359**

* EXIMA—Eximia Industrias Clark Argentina SA.
† ECSA—Equipamentos Clark SA (Brazil).
‡ Estimated at 66 percent of sales.
§ Includes payment of loans.
Source: Reproduced from the June 20, 1975 issue of *Business International* with permission of the publisher, Business International Corp. (New York).

Predetermined domestication: An alternative

Predetermined domestication is, in essence, a gradual, planned process of participating with nationals in all phases of company operations. Initial investment planning would include steps to:

1.   Sell equity to nationals at fair prices over a number of years.
2.   Prepare nationals for top decision-making positions.
3.   Integrate local companies (where feasible) into worldwide marketing programs.
4.   Develop local companies as sources of supply.
5.   Put on a sound economic base or make unnecessary any government concessions initially needed for successful investment.

Initial investment planning should provide for eventual sale of a significant interest (perhaps even controlling interest) to nationals and incorporation of national economic needs and national managerial talent into the business as quickly as possible. Such a policy is more likely to result in reasonable control remaining with the parent company even though nationals would hold important positions in management and ownership. If company plans include training and developing nationals to hold major positions, it would ensure that those reaching top positions would be qualified and in harmony with corporate objectives. Such company-trained nationals would be more likely to have a strong corporate point of view rather than just a country (national) point of view.

BOX 6–9:   Predetermined domestication

The Dominican Republic subsidiary of Gulf & Western Industries has begun to transfer land to its workers in a move toward an employee-owned company. Gulf & Western holds 267,000 acres in the Caribbean nation, about 120,000 acres of which are in sugar cane production. The company also is involved in cattle ranching, citrus farming, and hotel keeping. According to a company spokesman, workers will be eligible to buy shares in the new worker-owned corporation "based on the seniority system." They also will offer training and technical assistance to the new owners. Crops grown by the new company will be for the Dominican Gulf market and for export. Gulf & Western said more than 200 Dominican employees had received shares in the new corporation which is called Agricultural Company of Central Romana Employees and Workers. The plan calls for the company to eventually transfer more than 30,000 acres of arable land to the worker-owned unit.

The company feels its unique program of worker ownership will be a positive economic force in the Dominican Republic. However, some Dominicans claim Gulf & Western is trying to buy time in an increasingly nationalistic nation. The transfer, according to Gulf & Western, will take between 5 and 10 years and benefit about 4,000 employees. The company which employs close to 19,000 at the peak of the sugar cane cutting season, acknowledged that 15,000 seasonal sugar cane cutters will not be eligible to become shareholders.

Adapted from "Gulf & Western Dominican Unit Begins Program to Become Worker-Owned Firm," *The Wall Street Journal*, February 8, 1977, p. 12.

If initial development specified the use of local supplies, it would eliminate sudden short-term crash programs to provide supplies. Local suppliers developed over a period of time could ultimately handle a significant portion of total needs, thus meeting government demands for encouraging local business and industry. Further, a sound, sensible plan to sell ownership over a number of years would insure a fair and equitable return on investment, in addition to encouraging ownership throughout the populace and discouraging attempts by a few to exert undue corporate control. Finally, if government concessions and incentives essential in early stages of investment were rendered economically feasible or unnecessary, the company's political vulnerability would be lessened considerably.

While predetermined domestication may not be the ideal investment plan, it is a practical, workable alternative to government-initiated domestication or expropriation. There is no doubt that more and more governments will establish policies for domesticating foreign investments since it enables the host country "to have its cake and eat it too." Government-initiated domestication becomes one more condition which must be considered in developing an overall strategy for foreign investment.[46]

Political payoffs

One approach to dealing with political vulnerability is the political payoff—attempting to lessen political risks by paying those in power to intervene on behalf of the multinational company. Political payoffs or bribery have been used to lessen the negative effects of a variety of problems. Paying heads of state to avoid confiscatory taxes or expulsion, paying fees to agents to insure the acceptance of sales contracts, and providing monetary encouragement to an assortment of people whose actions can affect the effectiveness of a company's programs are decisions which frequently confront multinational managers and raise ethical questions.

The decision to pay a bribe creates a major conflict between what is ethical and proper and what is profitable and sometimes necessary for business. International payoffs are perceived by those involved as a means of accomplishing business goals.

For U.S. businesses bribery became a national issue during the mid-70s with public disclosure of political payoffs to foreign recipients by U.S. firms. Amounts paid were as high as $70 million and included such companies as Lockheed Aircraft, United Brands, Gulf Oil, and other major multinational firms. An SEC-sponsored study released in 1977 estimated that between 1970 and 1976 almost $412 million in questionable payments were made by U.S. corporations. At the time, there were no U.S. laws against paying

---

[46] For a complete discussion of how MNCs deal with political uncertainty, including case studies, see Stephen Blank et al., "Assessing the Political Environment: "An Emerging Function of International Companies" (New York: The Conference Board Inc., report no 794, 1980), 72 pp.

bribes in foreign countries, but for publicly held corporations, the Securities and Exchange Commission rules required accurate public reporting of all expenditures. Since the payoffs were not properly disclosed, many executives were faced with charges of violating SEC regulations.

The issue took on proportions greater than one of nondisclosure, however, to spotlight the basic question of ethics. Business's defense was primarily that payoffs were a "way of life" throughout the world; if you didn't do it, you lost out. They illustrated their dilemma with the case of an aircraft company: What would you do when a $10 million payoff would assure a $200 million sale? In answering that question, it must be kept in mind that your foreign competition would be willing and able to pay and you would lose the sale and a $20 million profit. The difficulty with such a defense is that even in those countries where it is general practice, it really is not sanctioned. The result of the public disclosures resulted in several U.S. executives being dismissed from their positions, and at least one country's prime minister and many other lesser ministers and officials being removed from office. By 1981, the Japanese courts had sentenced two of the officials to prison terms and the prime minister is still being tried.[47]

The issue of payoffs is hotly debated by U.S. business people. The major complaint is that other countries do not have legislation as restrictive as the United States.[48] Indeed, in some countries, not only is bribery legal, in some cases (e.g., West Germany), payments can be deducted as business expenses for tax purposes. Although payoffs are not illegal in West Germany, the governments where payments are received do not always ignore such activities, especially when payments go to top level government officials. Siemens, a West German electrical manufacturer, allegedly paid bribes to government officials in Austria and Indonesia. The Austrian government has charged Siemens and others with paying bribes, as has the government of Indonesia.[49]

In each case, top government officials responsible for awarding major contracts were involved. One point seems clear; even in countries where bribery is tolerated, those exposed usually are prosecuted. It is especially interesting that in Italy and West Germany where it is not illegal to pay bribes, the laws clearly state that they only apply to transactions outside the country.[50]

The definition of bribery can range from the relatively innocuous payment of a few cents to a minor official or business manager to expedite the process-

---

[47] "Japanese Court Finds Two Guilty in Lockheed Case," *The Wall Street Journal,* November 6, 1981, p. 31.

[48] "U.S. Firms Say '77 Ban on Foreign Payoffs Hurts Overseas Sales," *The Wall Street Journal,* August 2, 1979, p. 1.

[49] "West German Concern Faces Bribery Charges in Contracting Abroad," *The Wall Street Journal,* February 17, 1981, p. 1.

[50] "Italy Takes Steps to Legalize Bribes to Secure Overseas Bids," *Business International,* May 30, 1980, pp. 171–72.

ing of papers or the loading of a truck, to the extreme of paying millions of dollars to a head of state to ensure your company preferential treatment. The law concerning bribery in the United States deals exclusively with the issue of bribery of high political officials, but the issue is confused and compounded by other types of payments.

In dealing with bribery it must be defined as there appear to be limitless variations. First, the difference between bribery and extortion must be established. Voluntarily offered payments by someone seeking unlawful advantage is bribery; payments extracted under duress by someone in authority from a person seeking only what they are lawfully entitled to is extortion.[51] An example of extortion would be a finance minister of a country demanding heavy payments under the threat that millions of dollars of investment would be confiscated.

BOX 6–10: How the Russians deal with bribery

The Soviet government has just served notice that bribery in connection with Russia's growing trade with the Western countries is risky business.

The death sentence has been meted out to a Soviet official who was found guilty of soliciting and receiving bribes in return for placing contracts with a foreign supplier. And the Swiss businessman who was convicted of making the payments has been sentenced to 10 years in prison.

News of the bribery case—said to be the first of its kind involving foreign trade—appeared in a government weekly magazine, *Nedelya,* which gave these details:

Yuri S. Sosnovsky, director of a Russian government furniture-manufacturing organization, approached the businessman, Walter Haefelin, at a trade exhibition in the Soviet Union in 1973. They agreed that the Russian agency would purchase machinery through Haefelin and that Sosnovsky would receive payments concealed in the price of the equipment.

On the first contract, Sosnovsky received about $140,000 in rubles plus about $7,000 worth of goods.

In July, 1974, Haefelin was arrested at the Moscow airport on a flight from Prague, Czechoslovakia. He was carrying about $65,000 in rubles as a first payment to Sosnovsky on another contract.

Source: "How the Russians Deal with Bribery," Reprinted from *U.S. News & World Report,* June 2, 1975, p. 58. Copyright 1975 U.S. News & World Report, Inc.

A variation of bribery that should be defined is the difference between "lubrication" and "subornation."[52] Lubrication involves a relatively small sum of cash, gift, or service made to a low-ranking official in a country where such offerings are not prohibited by law; the purpose of such a gift being to facilitate or expedite the normal, lawful performance of a duty by that official (a practice common in many countries of the world). "Suborna-

---

[51] Jack G. Kaikati, "The Phenomenon of International Bribery," *Business Horizons,* February 1977, pp. 25–37.

[52] Hans Schollhammer, "Ethics in an International Business Context," *MSU Business Topics,* Spring 1977, pp. 53–63.

tion," on the other hand, generally involves large sums of money, frequently not properly accounted for, designed to entice an official to commit an illegal act on behalf of the one paying the bribe. Lubrication payments accompany requests for a person to do a job more rapidly or more efficiently, whereas subornation is a request for officials to turn their heads, not do their job, or to break the law.

A third type of payment which can appear to be a bribe but may not be, is an agent's fee. When a business person is uncertain of a country's rules and regulations, an agent may be hired to represent the company in that country. This would be similar to hiring an agent in the United States, for example, an attorney, to file an appeal for a variance in a building code on the basis that the attorney will do a more efficient and thorough job than someone unfamiliar with such procedures. Similar services may be requested of an agent in a foreign country when problems occur. However, a part of that agent's fees may be used to pay bribes; it is usually impossible to determine whether the intermediary's fees are being used unlawfully. There are many "middlemen" (attorneys, agents, distributors, etc.), who function simply as conduits for illegal payments. The process is further complicated by legal codes which vary from country to country; what is illegal in one country is "winked at" in another and is legal in a third. In the United States it is illegal to pay bribes. In 1977, the Foreign Corrupt Practices Act (FCPA) was passed. This law makes it illegal for companies to bribe foreign officials, candidates, or political parties. Stiff penalties also can be assessed against executives found guilty of having "a reason to know" that a company's independent agents are paying bribes.[53]

The law also requires publicly held U.S. companies to adopt accounting procedures designed to help top company officers spot illegal payments; companies violating the new law can be fined up to $1 million. Company officials, directors, employees, or agents breaking this law are subject to a five-year sentence and a fine of up to $10,000. The immediate reaction to this law from those knowledgeable about international business indicated that U.S. businesses would be at a definite disadvantage in international business dealings. Further, the law deals only with political payoffs and does not address itself to other kinds of payoffs which exist in other countries. Such activities are euphemistically referred to as *baksheesh, squeeze,* or *mordida;* it seems every country has its own name to cover "the grease" necessary to expedite business activity. One difficulty in dealing rationally with the ethical question of bribery is the range of activities generally classified under the broad term *bribery.* Because the FCPA law lacks clarity, some early interpretations by business were so extremely narrow that simple payments to expedite activities were not made. A good deal of confusion

---

[53] A complete discussion of the FCPA and international marketing can be found in Jack G. Kati and Wayne L. Label, "American Bribery Legislation: Obstacle to International Marketing," *Journal of Marketing,* Fall 1980, pp. 38–43.

arose and several interpretations of the law were extant, primarily dealing with the kinds of payments not considered under the law.[54]

BOX 6–11: Is it still a bribe when it's entertainment?

With international attention focused on bribery, here is a short list of the ways bribes are handled.

In Africa, one reserves a hotel room in Paris for two weeks or loans a large car which is never returned. The director of an international firm noted that, "a Nigerian official cost us $30,000 for a twelve-day stay in Paris."

Bribing in Mexico is done with the stylized flair of a Latin seduction, beginning with dinner at an expensive restaurant and climaxing with a weekend jet jaunt to Cancun or Acapulco.

For really big South American deals, one Italian company is building an entire luxury real estate development in Uruguay; no units are for sale to the public, but plots are doled out to favored Latin American officials.

For big bucks, it was alleged that European managers had unlimited authority to pay cash to half a dozen Swiss bank accounts on behalf of Latin American officials responsible for the $10 billion dam being built on the Brazilian and Paraguayan border. A reported $140 million was paid.

In Malaysia, businessmen trade on the Malaysian's mania for gambling. Common approaches are to invite a minister to an afternoon of golf, bet heavily, and then spend the next three hours swatting the ball into sand traps, or get into an after-dinner poker game with a key civil servant and lose heavily.

Source: Adapted from Pierre Beaudeux, "The Bribery Business," *World Press Review*, February 1981, p. 54; "A Taste for the Take," *Time*, June 15, 1980, p. 46; and "Big Profits in Big Bribery," *Time*, March 16, 1981, pp. 58–67.

The other major cause for concern among U.S. executives about the FCPA is the provision that they are liable whether or not they have any reason to know that an agent in their employ indeed paid a bribe. The restrictiveness of the law, as interpreted by many, is such that there is a general feeling that U.S. firms are not able to effectively compete in markets where such payments are routine. Many U.S. firms are restricting their agents from "business as usual" for fear that they are paying bribes. Because of the restrictiveness and uncertainty of the original bill, there is a new bill which has passed the Senate and is now before the House to clarify the provisions in question. The version which has passed the Senate specifies that illegal foreign bribery means only willful bribery. This will end prosecution of U.S. businessmen for having "reason to know" their companies pay bribes abroad. Now they must knowingly authorize bribes to be subject to the conditions of the FCPA. In addition, the bill also states that payments made to facilitate a sale, if lawful in the country involved, do not constitute a bribe. One final provision of the Senate bill softens the name of the act

---

[54] "Misinterpreting the Anti-Bribery Law," *Business Week*, September 3, 1979, pp. 150–51.

from the Foreign Corrupt Practices Act to the Business Practices and Records Act.[55]

It is obvious from this discussion that the answer to the question of bribery is not an unqualified one. It is easy to generalize about the ethics of political payoffs and other types of payments; it is much more difficult to make the decision to withhold payment of money when the consequences of not making the payment may affect the company's ability to do business profitably or at all. With the variety of ethical standards and levels of morality which exist in different cultures, the dilemma of ethics and pragmatism which faces international business cannot be resolved until more countries decide to effectively deal with the issue. Perhaps the United States' stand on making bribery illegal is a step in that direction.[56]

MANAGING EXTERNAL AFFAIRS

Regardless of how well multinational companies lessen political vulnerability through investment and business decisions, a problem which all face is one of public image. Reading the popular press in the United States, or anywhere in the world, could lead one to believe that almost everything evil is caused by multinational companies (MNCs) and that the little good done are self-serving acts. In other words, on top of everything else, MNCs have a bad press—a poor image—and based on a recent study of United States-owned MNCs, most do not have a specific worldwide external affairs program to deal with the problem. There is growing concern over this issue and many companies have begun specific actions to improve their public images.[57]

There are several issues involved which shape the external affairs programs, or absence thereof, of multinational companies. One important consideration is whether to maintain a low profile and react to criticisms as they develop or to actively meet and perhaps forestall challenges before they develop. Advocates of a low profile support their position on the basis that it is better to attract minimum attention and avoid criticism. Further, they feel that a company that attracts attention might also attract political harassment and the potential for violence against the company and employees. Those who support a more active external affairs program suggest that ignoring the public image of MNCs will allow it to get worse instead of better; that by not being active in their public pronouncements and actions, the MNC always will be on the defensive, never having the opportunity

---

[55] "Senate Amends Bribery Act," *Associated Press,* November 24, 1981.

[56] For a discussion of how corporate audit committees deal with the problem of illegal payments see Frederick L. Neumann, "Corporate Audit Committees and the Foreign Corrupt Practices Act." *Business Horizons,* June 1980, pp. 62–71.

[57] For case studies of how MNCs manage public affairs, see S. Watson Dunn, Martin F. Cahill, and J. J. Boddewyn, *How Fifteen Transnational Corporations Manage Public Affairs* (Chicago: Crain Books, 1979), 115 pp.

to present positive achievements of the company.[58] Further, there is little evidence of the effectiveness of being passive and maintaining a low profile.

Another issue which affects a MNC's public relations program is centralized versus decentralized management. Many feel that external affairs issues are local, that is, country oriented, and the subsidiary should be responsible for dealing with local issues. Indeed, who could better deal with PR problems than those on the spot? This study revealed that few of the headquarters divisions provided any *guidelines* to help subisidiaries deal with regional or global public affairs problems. The implication was that a company is represented haphazardly and, perhaps, infrequently. The most critical reason for centralized management of worldwide public relations activities is that much of the corporate image is not just country oriented. In fact, today threatening pronouncements come from international and regional groups as well as individual countries.

The United Nations, Andean Common Market, and EC have strong public opinions about multinational companies which affect the present as well as the future potential environment for the MNC. In addition, there are private organizations such as international trade unions and the very active international trade secretariats which have specific opinions about the MNCs and their roles relative to their specific interest groups.[59] Some of the private groups can cause major problems. An example is the Third World Working Group which published a report alleging that an international milk company and others were mass murderers of babies in less developed countries as a result of their advertising and marketing. The company sued the Third World Working Group and ultimately won; but the PR cost was high.

While there may be some support and rationale for maintaining a low profile,[60] the evidence suggests that MNCs should have a worldwide headquarters-managed external affairs program that is regionally and internationally oriented.

Organization for such a program will necessarily vary from company to company but the principal elements are delineated in Exhibit 6–2. The major inputs for a practical program, how and by whom the inputs are developed into programs, and how they can be transformed into actions are shown. The most effective programs come from the top and involve both corporate policy and image.[61] To develop and maintain a global image, an effective communication strategy is also necessary. One recommendation

---

[58] "Multinationals Seeking Ways to Answer Their Critics," *World Business Weekly*, December 22, 1980, p. 8.

[59] "Corporate Critics Build Steam for Anti-MNC Campaigns Throughout Third World," *Business International*, October 17, 1980, pp. 329–31.

[60] "MNCs Seek Low Profile in Face of Challenges from Political, Social, Governmental Sectors," *International Marketing Report* 1, no. 9 (March 1977), p. 1.

[61] David H. Blake, "How to Get Operating Managers to Manage Public Affairs in Foreign Subsidiaries," *Columbia Journal of World Business*, Spring 1981, pp. 61–67.

EXHIBIT 6–2:   Organizing for worldwide external affairs

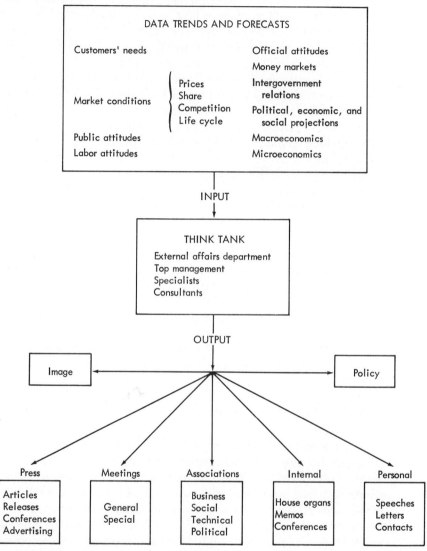

Source: Reproduced from the December 12, 1975 issue of *Business International*, with permission of the publisher, Business International Corp. (New York).

suggests five fundamental tasks to develop an effective communication strategy that will deal with the company's global image.

Fundamental Task 1: The clear articulation and acceptance of a managerially relevant social concept of the MNC.

Fundamental Task 2: The measurement and evaluation of how the MNC affects the host state:

1. Development of a *social and economic impact statement.*
2. Inventory of social programs and analysis of their management.
3. *World profile*—host state perceptions of MNC impact.
4. Analysis of management of corporate social policy.

Fundamental Task 3: The determination of the content and targets of a communications strategy:

1. Identify the major problem areas regarding MNC impact.
2. Forecast what the future major problems are likely to be.
3. Determine those MNC activities and effects which contribute to the host state.
4. Select various groups or publics as targets for communications efforts on the basis of:
    a. Nature of probable issues.
    b. Positive and negative impacts of MNC on issues and on groups.
    c. Importance of these groups to MNC success or failure.

Fundamental Task 4: (from the headquarters point of view). Development and implementation of the communications effort:

1. Require the setting of objectives.
2. Help design and give counsel on specific communications strategies.
3. Aid subsidiaries in determining costs of efforts.
4. Recommend ways to measure the impact of such efforts.
5. Insist that subsidiaries keep headquarters informed of activities and reactions of host country groups.
6. Develop subsidiary management skills in this area.

Fundamental Task 5: Direct headquarters management of communications strategies at the regional and international levels.[62]

Implicit in the fundamental tasks outlined is that the firm knows its publics. Column 1 of Exhibit 6–3 are the publics from which criticism may come and to whom the company must communicate if criticisms are to be overcome or forestalled. Column 2 are issues frequently raised. By nature of the problem there may be many more publics and issues than those included. Indeed, any one or a group of publics may raise one or a combination of the topics listed.

An external affairs program, however well designed and executed, is never better than the behavior of the company. Most companies today strive to become good corporate citizens in their host countries; but because of overheated feelings of nationalism or political parties seeking publicity or scapegoats for their own failures, the negative aspects of MNCs, whether true or false, are the ones which frequently reach the public. The only effective defense for the multinational company is to actively tell its own story. As one authority states, "Passivity is passé. It is high time for a high profile."

---

[62] Source: "The Global Image Makers." Reprinted with permission from the June 1976 issue of *Public Relations Journal,* Copyright 1976.

EXHIBIT 6–3: The MNC's publics and issues

Publics	*Issues**
Church	Nationalism
Labor	Industrial democracy
Suppliers	Environment protection
Customers	Energy and raw materials
Competitors	Taxes
Pressure groups	Incentives and restrictions
Stockholders	Investemtn approvals and permits
Academia	Personnel relations
General public	Attracting personnel
Minority groups	Mergers and acquisitions
Public media	Money and credit
Governments and agencies	Legitimacy
Conservationists	Prices and profits
Financial community	Image (company and product)
	Consumerism
	Women's liberation
	Union relations
	Equal opportunities

* The issues do not correspond with the publics listed.

Source: Adapted from "How Embattled MNCs Can Devise Strategies for External Affairs," *Business International*, December 12, 1975, p. 394.

SUMMARY

Vital to every marketer's assessment of a foreign market is an appreciation for the political environment of the country within which he or she plans to operate. Government involvement in business activities, especially foreign-controlled business, is generally much greater than business is accustomed to in the United States. The foreign firm must strive to make its activities politically acceptable, or it may find it is subjected to a variety of politically condoned harassments. In addition to the harassments which can be imposed by a government, the foreign marketer frequently faces the problem of uncertainty of continuity in government policy. As governments change political philosophies, a marketing firm accepted under one administration may find that its activities are completely undesirable under another. The U.S. government may aid American business in its foreign operations, and for those companies which a country considers vital to achieving national economic goals, the host country often provides an umbrella of protection not extended to others. An unfamiliar or hostile political environment does not necessarily preclude success for a foreign marketer if the marketer's plans are such that the company becomes a local economic asset.

QUESTIONS

1. Define:

   Parliamentary government   Confiscation
   "Peoples" republics   Currency convertibility
   Absolutist government   Hickenlooper Amendment
   FCPA   Political vulnerability
   Expropriation   Domestication
   External affairs   Predetermined domestication
   Political risk assessment   NIEO

2. Why would a country rather domesticate than expropriate?

3. How can government-initiated domestication be tantamount to confiscation?

4. Discuss predetermined domestication as an alternative investment plan.

5. "An undeniable and critical fact when doing business in a foreign country is that permission to conduct business is controlled by the government of the host country." Comment.

6. What are the main factors to consider in assessing the dominant political climate within a country?

7. Why is a working knowledge of party philosophy so important in a political assessment of a market? Discuss.

8. What are the most common causes of instability in governments? Discuss.

9. Discuss how governmental instability can affect marketing.

10. What are the most frequently encountered political risks in foreign business? Discuss.

11. Expropriation is considered a major risk of foreign business. Discuss ways in which this particular type of risk has been minimized somewhat as a result of company activities. Explain how these risks have been minimized by the activities of the U.S. government.

12. How do exchange controls impede foreign business? Discuss.

13. How do foreign governments encourage foreign investment? Discuss.

14. How does the U.S. government encourage foreign investment? Spell out the implications in foreign marketing.

15. What is the Hickenlooper Amendment? What role does it play in foreign marketing?

16. Discuss some measures a company might take to lessen its political vulnerability.

17. Why do lesser developed countries fear foreign investment? Is there any evidence that these attitudes are changing? Are there steps a company can take to lessen these fears? Discuss.

18. Select a country and analyze it politically from a marketing viewpoint.

19. The text suggests that violence is a politically motivated risk of international business. Comment.

20. If all the ways suggested to reduce political vulnerability don't work, as was the case with Marcona, then why bother? Discuss.

21. What are the advantages of a Foreign Investment Balance Sheet? Can you add some other items to those in Exhibit 6–1?

22. Political payoffs are a problem; how would you react if you faced the prospect of paying a bribe? If you knew that by not paying you would not be able to complete a $10 million contract?

23. Differentiate among the following:
     subornation
     lubrication
     extortion
     bribery

24. Exhibit 6–3 lists the various publics and issues frequently confronting a multinational; see how many more you can add to the lists.

Chapter 7

The international legal environment

Among the many components of a marketer's operating environment and an integral part of a country's culture are the laws which govern business activities. The legal environment for foreign marketers takes on added importance since no single, uniform international commercial law governing foreign business transactions exists. Laws vary from country to country; the marketer is confronted with as many different legal environments as there are countries. Furthermore, in commercial transactions between countries, the marketer is faced with the problem of determining which country's legal system has jurisdiction.

The legal systems of the world are so disparate and complex it is beyond the scope of this text to explore the laws of each country individually. There are, however, legal problems common to most international marketing transactions which must be given special attention when operating abroad.

A summary of these potential problems is found in a checklist by *Business International;* it was compiled as an aid in developing awareness of the legal problems of foreign marketing. The list includes elements related to marketing that are most prone to legal difficulty:

1. Rules of competition on (*a*) collusion, (*b*) discrimination against certain buyers, (*c*) promotional methods, (*d*) variable pricing, (*e*) exclusive territory agreement.
2. Retail price maintenance laws.
3. Cancellation of distributor or wholesaler agreements.
4. Product quality laws and controls.
5. Packaging laws.
6. Warranty and after-sales exposure.
7. Price controls, limitations on markups, or markdowns.
8. Patents, trademarks, and copyright laws and practices.[1]

This list is not a complete compilation of all possible legal problems; it deals only with those problems peculiar to marketing. Marketers must also be concerned with laws that apply to business in general. The purpose of this chapter is to provide the reader with a broad view of the international legal environment with the hope that the reader will appreciate the need

---

[1] "201 Checklists—Decision Making in International Operations," *Business International,* 1980, pp. 103–04.

for knowledge of legal systems and the necessity of securing expert legal advice when doing business in a foreign country.

BASES FOR LEGAL SYSTEMS

The legal systems of the countries of the world stem from one of two common heritages—the *common law,* derived from English law and found in England, the United States, Canada, and other countries which have at one time been under English influence; and *civil* or *code* law, which is derived from Roman law and found in the majority of the countries of the world. To the marketer conducting business abroad, the difference between these two systems can be of more than theoretical importance since due process of law varies considerably between code-law and common-law countries.

The basis for common law is tradition, past practices, and legal precedent set by the courts through interpretations of statutes, legal legislation, and past rulings. Common law seeks "interpretation through the past decisions of higher courts which interpret the same statutes or apply established and customary principles of law to a similar set of facts."[2]

Code law is based on an all-inclusive system of written rules (codes) of law. Under code law, the legal system is generally divided into three separate codes: commercial, civil, and criminal. While common law is recognized as not being all inclusive, code law is considered complete as a result of "catchall" provisions found in most code-law systems. For example, under the commercial code in a code-law country, the law governing contracts is made inclusive with the statement that "a person performing a contract shall do so in conformity with good faith as determined by custom and good morals."[3] Although code law is considered inclusive, it is apparent from the foregoing statement that some broad interpretations are necessary in order to include everything under the existing code.[4]

Commercial law can vary in meaning between common-law and code-law countries; under common law, commercial disputes are subject to laws which may be applied to either civil or commercial disputes since there is no specific recognition of commercial problems as such. Code law differs in that there is a separate code specifically designed for business. The commercial code has precedent over other codes when matters of business are before the court. The provision results from historical recognition that the legal problems of merchants are often unique and thus should have special status under the law.

[2] Leslie Llewellyn Lewis, ed., *The Dartnell International Trade Handbook,* 1st ed. (Chicago: The Dartnell Corporation, 1963), p. 513.

[3] *Ibid.,* p. 513.

[4] John Bridge, "National Legal Tradition and Community Law: Legislative Drafting and Judicial Interpretation in England and the European Community," *Journal of Common Market Studies,* June 1981, pp. 351–76.

Steps are being taken in common-law countries to codify commerical law even though the primary basis of commercial law is common law, that is, precedents set by court decisions. An example of the new uniformity and a measure of codification is the acceptance of the Uniform Commercial Code by most states in the United States. Even though U.S. commercial law has been codified to some extent under the Uniform Commercial Code, the philosophy of interpretation is anchored in common law. Similar strides toward a unified commerical code have been made in England.

As shall be discussed later (in the section Protection of Industrial Property Rights), laws governing industrial property rights offer the most striking differences between common- and code-law systems. Under common law, ownership is established by use; whereas under code law, ownership is determined by registration.

In some code-law countries, certain agreements may not be enforceable unless properly notarized or registered; whereas in a common-law country, the same agreement may be binding so long as proof of the agreement can be established.

Although every country has elements of both common and code law, there are sufficient differences between common- and code-law systems regarding contracts, sales agreements, and other legal problems that an international marketer familiar with only one system must enlist the aid of legal counsel even with the most basic legal questions.

An illustration of where fundamental differences in the two systems can cause significant difficulty is in the performance of a contract. Under common law in the United States, it is fairly clear that impossibility of performance does not necessarily excuse compliance with the provisions of a contract unless it is impossible to comply for reasons of an "act of God," such as some extraordinary happening of nature not reasonably anticipated by either party of a contract. Hence, floods, lightning, earthquakes, and similar occurrences are generally considered acts of God. Under code law, acts of God are not limited solely to acts of nature but are extended to include "unavoidable interferences with performance, whether resulting from the elements, forces of nature, or unforeseeable human acts,"[5] including such things as labor strikes and riots.

For example, consider the following two situations. A contract was entered into to deliver a specific quantity of cloth. In one case, before delivery could be made by the seller, an earthquake caused the destruction of the cloth, and compliance was then impossible. In a second case, pipes in the sprinkler system of a warehouse where the material was stored froze and broke, spilling water on the cloth and destroying it. In both cases, loss of the merchandise was sustained and delivery could not be made. The question is whether the parties in these cases were absolved of their

---

[5] Lewis, *The Dartnell International Trade Handbook,* p. 533.

obligations under the contract because of the impossibility of delivery. The answer depends on the system of law invoked.

In the first situation and under both common and code law, the earthquake would be considered an act of God and impossibility of performance would excuse compliance under the contract. In the second situation, the courts in common-law countries would probably rule that the bursting of the water pipes did not constitute an act of God if it happened in a climate where freezing was expected. Therefore, impossibility of delivery would not necessarily excuse compliance with the provisions of the contract. In code-law countries where the scope of impossibility of performance is extended considerably, the destruction might very well be ruled an act of God, and thus release from compliance with the contract could be obtained. When entering a contract with Eastern European countries there are two sensitive areas to consider when wording a detailed act of God statement.[6] One involves the phrase "act of God." Eastern European negotiators prefer "act of nature," and for all practical purposes, the meaning is the same. The other area of sensitivity concerns strikes. East European negotiators tend to look on labor disruptions as an issue readily resolved by their Western partners by meeting workers' demands.

The foreign marketer must be especially concerned with the differences between common- and code-law systems when operating between countries using the two systems; the rights of the principals of a contract or some other legal document under one law may be significantly different from their rights under the other. It should be kept in mind that there are also differences between the laws of two countries using common law as well

---

BOX 7–1: The long reach of U.S. law

If you are a United States firm, you cannot do business with foreigners without the permission of the U.S. government. Permission can be denied at any time. Here are two recent examples of the long reach of U.S. law:

General Electric Co. reported that it will forfeit a $175 million contract to deliver parts for the proposed Soviet natural gas pipeline. Its contract was to supply rotor blades and nozzles for compressor turbines to a West German firm who in turn would sell the turbines to the Soviets. The U.S. government imposed sanctions against Russia in response to the imposition of martial law in Poland.

Fiat Allis, a Fiat (Italy) and Allis-Chalmers (U.S.) joint venture doing business in the United States, announced that it might close if the U.S. government doesn't approve a contract to sell bulldozers to the Soviet Union. All licenses to export high-technology and oil and natural gas equipment to the Soviets had been suspended.

Sources: "GE Says Sanctions Cost It $175 Million Soviet Pipeline Job," *The Wall Street Journal*, January 11, 1982, p. 25; and "Fiat Allis Warns It Might Close if Reagan Refuses to Allow a Contract with Soviets," *The Wall Street Journal*, February 23, 1982, p. 21.

---

[6] "Defining Force Majeure Essential in EE Contracts," *Business Eastern Europe*, July 3, 1981, p. 212.

as differences between two countries using code law. Thus, the problem of the marketer is not only one of appreciating the significance of the basis for the law in a particular country—whether or not it is a common- or code-law country—but also one of anticipating the different laws which regulate business regardless of the legal system of the country.

JURISDICTION IN INTERNATIONAL LEGAL DISPUTES

One of the problems of international marketing is determining which legal system will have jurisdiction when commercial disputes arise. A frequent error is to assume that disputes between citizens of different nations are adjudicated under some supranational system of laws. Unfortunately, there is no judicial body to deal with legal commercial problems arising between citizens of different countries.

In the everyday discussions of foreign business, it is often implied there exists a body of international law to which all foreign trade activities are subject. No such body of international law exists. The confusion probably stems from the existence of international courts, such as the World Court at The Hague and the International Court of Justice, the principal judicial organ of the United Nations. These courts are operative in international disputes between sovereign nations of the world but not between private citizens.

Legal disputes can arise between parties in three different situations: (1) between governments, (2) between a company and a government; and, (3) between two companies. Disputes between governments can be adjudicated by the World Court whereas the other two situations must be handled either in the courts of the country of one of the parties involved or through arbitration. Unless a commerical dispute involves a national issue between states, it will not be handled by the International Court of Justice or any similar world court.

Since there is no body of rules concerned solely with international commercial transactions, thereby constituting an "international commercial law," the foreign marketer must look to the legal system of all the countries involved—the laws of the home country, and/or the laws of the countries within which business is conducted. This, then, is the added dimension of the legal environment which becomes significant in foreign marketing. Every country has its own legal system to which the foreign marketer's operations must be tailored.

Since there is no international commercial law, when international commercial disputes arise the problems must be settled under the laws of one of the countries concerned. The paramount question in a dispute is which law governs. Although this may appear to be an easy question to answer, it is not. Jurisdiction over private, international legal disputes is generally determined in one of three ways: (1) on the basis of jurisdictional clauses included in contracts, (2) on the basis of where a contract was entered into, or (3) on the basis of where the provisions of the contract were per-formed.

The most clear-cut decision can be made when the contracts or legal documents supporting a business transaction state very clearly whose law is to predominate. In fact, it is advisable to include a jurisdictional clause in all contracts to avoid the problem of determining jurisdiction after a dispute arises. A clause similar to the following will, in most cases, establish jurisdiction in the event of future disagreements:

> That the parties hereby agree that the agreement is made in Colorado, USA, and that any question regarding this agreement shall be governed by the law of the state of Colorado, USA.

In the illustration above, it is agreed that should a dispute arise the laws of the state of Colorado would be invoked. If the complaint were brought in the court of another country, it is probable that the same Colorado law would govern the decision. Cooperation and a definite desire to be judicious in foreign legal problems has led to the practice of foreign courts judging disputes on the basis of the law of another country or state whenever applicable. Thus, if an injured party from Colorado brings suit in the courts of Mexico against a Mexican over a contract which included the clause above, it would not be unusual for the Mexican courts to decide on the basis of Colorado law. This is assuming, of course, it was recognized that Colorado law prevailed in this dispute either as a result of a prior agreement by the parties or on some other basis.

A jurisdictional clause does not always solve the legal problem of which laws should be invoked. Even with a specific clause establishing jurisdiction, if the contractual events are not, in effect, entered into or executed within the state indicated, courts have been known to disregard the jurisidictional clause and apply different rules in determining which law governs. In cases where there is no jurisdictional clause, or where such a clause is not effective, decisions are sometimes arrived at on the basis of where the contract was entered into. In such disputes, the laws of the country or state where the contract was created predominate. Other legal disagreements are sometimes settled on the basis of where the provisions of the contract were performed. The laws of the country where the business transaction was actually carried out are invoked in judging a dispute. In all cases where there is no jurisdictional clause, the governing legal system is determined by one of the two methods above. Since there is no clear-cut procedure concerning who has jurisdiction, and since the laws of one country may typically be more favorable than another, it is probably wise to include in all agreements a clause stipulating whose laws are to govern. In most cases, courts will uphold these clauses, provided substantial acceptance or performance of the agreement has actually occurred within the designated state.

LEGAL RECOURSE IN RESOLVING
INTERNATIONAL DISPUTES

When it becomes apparent that the settlement of a dispute cannot be resolved on a private basis, the foreign marketer must resort to more resolute action. Many international business people prefer a settlement through arbitration rather than to sue a foreign industry.

Problems with litigation

Lawsuits in public courts are avoided for a number of reasons. Most observers of litigation between citizens of different countries feel that almost all victories are spurious because the cost, frustrating delays, and extended aggravation which these cases produce are more oppressive by far than any matter of comparable size. The best advice is to seek a settlement, if possible, rather than sue. Other reasons frequently considered as deterrents to litigation are:

1. Fear of creating a poor image and damaging public relations.
2. Fear of unfair treatment in a foreign court. (Although not intentional, there is justifiable fear that a lawsuit can result in unfair treatment since the decision could be made by either a jury or judge not well versed in trade problems and the intricacies of international business transactions.)
3. Difficulty in collecting a judgment which may otherwise have been collected in a mutually agreed settlement through arbitration.
4. The relatively high cost and time required when bringing legal action.
5. Loss of confidentiality.

One authority suggests that the settlement of every dispute should follow three steps: first, try to "placate" the injured party; if this does not work, "arbitrate"; and finally, "litigate." The final step is typically taken only when all other methods fail. Actually, this advice is probably wise whether one is involved in an international dispute or in a domestic one.

Arbitration

Because of the pitfalls of litigation, the majority of international commercial disputes are resolved by arbitration. The usual arbitration procedure is for the parties involved to select a disinterested and informed party or parties as referee to determine the merits of the case and make a judgment that both parties agree to honor. In actual practice, however, formal rules and procedures are established for entering into an arbitration agreement.

Tribunals for arbitration. Although an informal method of arbitration as outlined above is workable, most arbitration is conducted under the auspices of one of the more formal domestic and international arbitration groups organized specifically to facilitate the mediation of commercial disputes. These groups have experienced arbitrators available and formal rules for the process of arbitration and, in most countries, the decisions reached in formal mediation are enforceable under the law.

Among the formal arbitration organizations are:

1. The Inter-American Commercial Arbitration Commission, which conducts arbitration in disputes between the businesses of 21 American republics, including the United States.
2. The Canadian-American Commercial Arbitration Commission, which functions in disputes between Canadian and U.S. businesses.
3. The London Court of Arbitration, which is restricted to those cases that can be legally arbitrated in England. Decisions by the London Court of Arbitration are enforceable under English law and English courts.
4. The American Arbitration Association, which was one of the early arbitration tribunals organized in the United States and was originally concerned only with disputes within the United States. Later, however, its activities were expanded to worldwide scope.
5. The International Chamber of Commerce, which is an affiliation of Chambers of Commerce of many of the world's nations. With its worldwide scope, it has established a Court of Arbitration whose rules are used in conducting arbitration.

International Chamber of Commerce.   The procedures used by formal arbitration organizations are similar. Arbitration under the rules of the International Chamber of Commerce affords an excellent example of how most organizations operate. When an initial request for arbitration is received, the Chamber first attempts a conciliation between the disputants. If this fails, the process of arbitration is started. The plaintiff and the defendant select one person each from among acceptable arbitrators to defend their case, and the ICC Court of Arbitration appoints a third member, generally chosen from a list of distinguished lawyers, jurists, and/or professors.

The arbitrators arrange for a meeting with both parties and after hearing each side present its case, the ICC members make a decision and a award. The history of ICC effectiveness in arbitration has been spectacular; of the more than 200 decisions recorded, only about 20 have been rejected by the litigants. Of the decisions rejected, all but one have had the arbitration decision upheld in the courts when further litigation was pursued.

An example of a case which involved arbitration by the ICC concerned a contract between an English business and a Japanese manufacturer; the English business agreed to buy 100,000 plastic dolls for 80 cents each. On the strength of the contract, the English business sold the entire lot at $1.40 per doll. Before the dolls were delivered, the Japanese manufacturer had a strike; the settlement of the strike increased costs and the English business was informed that the delivery price of the dolls had increased from 80 cents to $1.50 each. The English business maintained that the Japanese firm had committed to make delivery at 80 cents and should deliver at that price. Each side was convinced they were right. The Japanese, accustomed to code law, felt that the strike was beyond control, was "an act of God," and thus compliance with the original provisions of the contract were excused. The English, accustomed to common law, did not accept the Japanese reasons for not complying since a strike can be considered the normal course of doing business and not an act of God. The dispute could not be settled except through litigation or arbitration. They chose arbitration; the ICC appointed a Scandinavian Supreme Court justice who heard both sides and ruled that the two parties would share proportionately in the loss. The case was settled to the satisfaction of both parties, and costly litigation was avoided. Most arbitration is successful, but it must be emphasized that the success of arbitration depends on the willingness of both parties to accept the arbitrator's rulings.

Arbitration clauses. Most authorities recommend that contracts and other legal documents include clauses specifying the use of arbitration in case of dispute. Unless a provision for arbitration of any dispute is incorporated as part of a contract, the likelihood of securing agreement for arbitration after a dispute arises is somewhat reduced. In fact, attempts to refer a dispute to arbitration after disagreement arises frequently fail since one party or the other is unwilling to agree on the form or place of arbitration.

The following is an example of an arbitration clause suggested by the International Chamber of Commerce for inclusion in all legal documents where arbitration may be necessary.

> "All disputes arising in connection with the present contract shall be finally settled under the rules of conciliation and arbitration of the International Chamber of Commerce by one or more arbitrators appointed in accordance with the said rules."

Even though it is suggested that arbitration clauses be included in a contract to avert later problems, there is some question of the legality of enforcing arbitration agreements made prior to a dispute.

Enforcement of arbitration clauses

Arbitration clauses generally require agreement on two counts: (1) the parties agree to arbitrate in case of a dispute according to the rules and procedures of some arbitration tribunal; (2) they agree to abide by the awards resulting from the arbitration. Difficulty arises when the parties to a contract fail to honor the agreements. Companies may refuse to name arbitrators, refuse to arbitrate, or after arbitration awards are made, they may refuse to honor the award. In most countries, arbitration clauses are recognized by the courts and are enforceable by law within those countries.

There is a U.S. federal arbitration law which recognizes the legality of arbitration clauses and establishes the necessary legal procedures to enforce such clauses. Over 56 countries have signed a U.N. Convention on the Recognition and Enforcement of Foreign Arbitral Awards[7] which binds them to uphold foreign arbitrational awards. Previously, a winning party had to sue to enforce a foreign award; under the U.N. Convention, the courts of the signatory countries automatically uphold foreign arbitral awards issued in member countries.

A number of important countries are not signers of the U.N. Convention nor do they have the necessary statutes to enforce arbitration clauses. Included are such countries as the People's Republic of China, Brazil, Canada, Portugal, and Argentina.

Because it establishes the original intent of the parties, an arbitration clause should be included in all international contracts. This alone may be sufficient to convince the parties to arbitrate whether or not the clause is legally enforceable. In some Mid-Eastern countries, if the arbitration clause does not stipulate that arbitration is to be carried out in a Mid-Eastern country, no settlement is enforceable.[8] Experience suggests, however, that arbitration awards or judgments confirming arbitration clauses in contracts are generally enforceable in most foreign courts. This is true even in countries where binding national laws are not in existence. Since laws and procedures vary from country to country, arbitration can be used as a sort of "legal esperanto" to bridge the gap between differing legal systems.[9]

COMMERCIAL LAW WITHIN COUNTRIES

The marketer should always be aware of the different legal systems to be abided by when doing business in more than one country. This problem is especially troublesome for the marketer who formulates a common marketing plan to be implemented in several countries. Although differences in languages and customs may be negated, legal differences between countries may still prevent a standardized marketing program.

Each country has laws regulating activities in promotion, product development and labeling, pricing, and channels of distribution.[10] These laws are very complicated; even the widely accepted practice of using premiums

---

[7] "States That Are Parties as of February, 1980!" *The Arbitration Journal,* September 1980, vol. 35, no. 3, pp. 39–40.

[8] "Settling International Contract Disputes Through Arbitration," *International Management,* May 1981, pp. 45–46.

[9] For the student who wants to read further on the problems and advantages of arbitration, see: Francis J. Higgins et al., "Pitfalls in International Commercial Arbitration," *The Business Lawyer* 35 (April 1980), pp. 1035–51; and "When Contracts Cause Legal Disputes," *World Business Weekly,* June 8, 1981, p. 19.

[10] "Label Language Law Boosts Packaging Costs for Firms in Malaysia," *Business Asia,* July 24, 1981, p. 238.

in a promotional effort can cause problems. In discussing this problem, one marketer commented that "there's no one way to promote a product with premiums throughout Europe." Reference was being made to the diverse and often difficult restrictions found in European countries regarding the use of premiums. A sampling of the different restrictions reveals the following.

In Austria, premium offers to consumers come under the discount law which prohibits any cash reductions that give preferential treatment to different groups of customers. Since it is considered that most premium offers would result in discriminatory treatment of buyers, they normally are not allowed. Premium offers in Finland are allowed with considerable scope as long as the word *free* is not used and consumers are not coerced into buying products. France also regulates premium offers which are, for all practical purposes, illegal since it is illegal to sell for less than cost price or to offer a customer a gift or premium conditional on the purchase of another product. Furthermore, a manufacturer or retailer cannot offer products different from the kind regularly offered (for example, a detergent manufacturer cannot offer clothing or kitchen utensils; the typical cereal premiums would be completely illegal under this law). West German law covering promotion in general is about as stringent as can be found. In fact, the laws are so voluminous and complicated that any advertiser contemplating a promotional campaign should consult a lawyer. Most kinds of promotion are allowed but with severe restrictions.

Another major stumbling block confronting those attempting to advertise across national boundaries are the various laws concerning product *comparison,* a natural and effective means of expression. In Germany, comparisons in advertisements are always subject to the competitor's ability to go to the courts and ask for proof of any implied or stated superiority. In Canada, the rulings are even more stringent; all claims and statements must be examined to insure that any representation to the public is not false or misleading. Such representation can be made verbally in selling or contained in or on anything that comes to the attention of the public (such as product labels, inserts in products, or any other form of advertising including what may be expressed in a sales letter). Courts have been directed by the law to take into account in determining whether a representation is false or misleading the "general impression" conveyed by the representation as well as its literal meaning. In essence, the courts are expected to apply the *credulous man standard* which means that if any reasonable person could possibly misunderstand the representation, the representation is misleading. In essence, "puffery," an acceptable practice in the United States, could be interpreted in Canada as false and misleading advertising. Thus, a statement such as "The strongest drive shaft in Canada" would be judged misleading in Canada, unless there was absolute evidence that the drive shaft was stronger than any other drive shaft for sale in Canada.

The examples illustrate the diversity of laws found among countries. These differences are apparent not only in advertising but in pricing, sales agreements, and other commercial activities. A frequent marketing approach to Europe is to consider the continent as a unified market. Earlier chapters have illustrated the inherent fallacy of this approach. The problems created by differences in laws among countries are no less pronounced than the difficulties arising from the differences found in social custom, taste, and economies existing among foreign nations.

There is some hope, especially among the European Community countries, of having a common commercial code. This has not yet been achieved and those U.S. companies that have operated under the erroneous belief that the Common Market is truly common in all respects have had spectacular failures. Although the EC is a beautiful picture of economic cooperation, for the marketer it is still a matter of dealing with nine different countries, cultures, and languages, as well as nine different legal systems.[11] In fact, there is some indication that a rising nationalistic feeling among members of the European Community is amplifying some differences among countries. For example, the French have become especially concerned with their identity and have passed some rather specific regulations on the mandatory use of the French language on all product labels, in all advertising leaflets, instructional manuals, warranties, and other product information items. While original material in another language is not forbidden, it must be accompanied by a complete French translation.

However, some progress toward unification of a commercial code is being made in Europe as evidenced by the steps taken toward a unified patent law. The European Patent Convention (EPC) discussed in the next section is a good example of attempts toward unification of commercial law among European countries. The EPC would permit companies in any one of the signatory countries to file a patent with a single patent office and have the patent binding in all countries involved instead of the current method of filing patents in each of the countries. This cooperative effort could lead to a unified commercial legal system for all EC countries and eventually for a majority of the trading nations of the world.

In the meantime, however, businesses that decide to invest in a foreign country will have to deal with multiple legal systems as well as purely business considerations. For example, a decision to construct a manufacturing plant in a European country should include an analysis of the legal systems in each country being considered. Corporate laws of countries, the effective tax burden in each country, tax and financial incentives, as well as a broad range of other legal questions must be included in any evaluation of potential building sites since these legal points vary drastically among countries. The same careful investigation of the legal environment is important in planning marketing activities.

---

[11] See, for example, Rudi Portaria, "Product Liability Laws Overseas Are Idling at the Crossroads," *Risk Management,* March 1981, p. 16.

PROTECTION OF INDUSTRIAL PROPERTY RIGHTS—A SPECIAL PROBLEM

Companies spend thousands of dollars establishing brand names or trademarks for their products to symbolize quality and a host of other product features designed to entice customers to buy their brands at the exclusion of all others. Millions of dollars are spent on research to develop industrial properties such as products, processes, designs, and formulas, in order to provide a company with an advantage over competitors. Such industrial properties are among the more valuable assets a company may possess. Names like "Kodak," "Coca-Cola," "Gucci" or rights to processes like xerography, the production of nylon and cellophane, are invaluable. Normally these properties can be legally protected to prevent other companies from pirating or infringing on such assets. Companies must, however, keep a constant vigil for piracy of their products.

BOX 7-2:   When the counterfeit is better than the original, which one is genuine?

When the West German maker of Comtesse-brand high-fashion leather goods decided to do some manufacturing in Hong Kong, it was in for a surprise. In its leased factory space were 10 large boxes left behind by the previous tenant. Inside the boxes were thousands and thousands of Comtesse labels, all fake. The previous tenant had been a Comtesse counterfeiter.

Hong Kong may not be the counterfeit-merchandise center of Asia—many give that dubious honor to Taiwan—but counterfeiting is big business there. Hong Kong copiers prefer luxury goods—Seiko and Rolex watches, Lacoste shirts, Celine bags, and Hermes scarves while their Taiwan counterparts favor automotive spare parts, padlocks, and batteries.

It is estimated that 1 percent of the watch exports from Hong Kong are fakes representing more than $13 million annually. Gucci says counterfeiters are eating up as much as $1 million of its yearly sales in Hong Kong. Fake Gucci bags sometimes can be purchased in Hong Kong's street stalls for less than the cost of a chicken. Another problem involves quality. One luxury-bag manufacturer is concerned about the quality of his brand's counterfeits; the fake bags are better than the European-made ones.

Some shoppers, impressed with a status product's name but depressed by its price, welcome the fakes. One recent tourist, for instance, was delighted to find cut-rate Guccis in a street stall. He knew they were fakes but that didn't bother him. "Why should it?" he asked. "I'll give them to my relatives. They'll never know."

Counterfeiters have become extremely adept at faking labels. Rolls of trademarked labels are so perfectly copied and so commonly available in Hong Kong that some manufacturers buy their own faked labels in street stalls when they run low.

Source: Adapted from Anthony Spaeth, "Hong Kong Counterfeit Trade Thrives but Faked Brands Arouse Genuine Ire." *The Wall Street Journal*, October 29, 1980, p. 35.

It has been estimated that more than 10 million fake Swiss timepieces carrying such famous brand names as Cartier and Rolex are sold every year, netting illegal profits of at least $500 million.[12] Counterfeit trade has

---

[12] "The Push to Out Stamp Fakes," *World Business Weekly*, December 29, 1980, p. 8.

risen to the point that several countries, including the United States, the European Community, and Canada, are seeking a change in GATT rules that would impose severe penalties against countries which permit the manufacture and sale of pirated goods.[13]

Inadequate protection

The failure to adequately protect industrial property rights abroad can lead to the loss of these rights in potentially profitable markets. Because patents, processes, trademarks, and copyrights are valuable in all countries, some companies have found that their assets have been appropriated and profitably exploited in foreign countries without license or reimbursement. Furthermore, they often learn not only that another firm is producing and selling their product or using their trademark, but that the pirating company is the rightful owner in the country where they are operating.

There have been many cases where companies have lost the rights to trademarks and have had to buy back these rights or pay royalties for their use. One of the most unusual cases involved a U.S. citizen residing in Mexico who registered in Mexico, a code-law country, the brand names and trademarks of some 40 companies. Included were such well-known names as "Carter's Little Liver Pills" and "Bromo Seltzer." Although most of the companies were able to regain control of their brand names, the procedure required lengthy litigation and considerable help from the U.S. government. If the culprit had not been so blatant in pirating 40 such well-known brands, he probably would have been successful. Others have had singular success in pirating processes and demanding significant payment from their original owners. Also, it is not uncommon to find situations where manufacturers have licensed local companies to produce products in return for a royalty. This is paid for a few months or a year, then terminated by the licensee. When inquiries about the stopped royalty payments are made, the licensor is told that the particular process is no longer being used. Further inquiry finds the process has been changed minimally and the licensee continues to produce the product without paying the royalty. In most instances, the pirating of processes can be avoided by carefully drawn agreements between the licensee and the licensor.

The problems of inadequate protective measures taken by the owners of valuable assets stem from many causes. One of the more frequent errors is assuming that since the company has established their rights in the United States they will be protected around the world or at least be able to establish rightful ownership should the need arise. Many businesses fail to understand that most countries do not follow the common-law principle of ownership established by prior use.

---

[13] "How U.K., French Firms Are Fighting Back," *Business Europe*, April 17, 1981, pp. 123–24; "The West Lets the Vendor Beware," *World Business Weekly*, February 23, 1981, p. 13.

BOX 7-3: Dealings with Iraq required to be in Arabic language

Iraq instituted a new law requiring use of the classical Arabic language in all dealings with Iraqi government organizations. Law No. 64 of 1977, "Preserving the Purity of the Arabic Language," requires contracts, records of accounts, and other official correspondence with the government to be in Arabic, although foreign translations can be included. The law requires trademarks, patents, and commercial marks to be in Arabic or, if billingual, that the Arabic version be prominent. It imposed a deadline of February 16, 1978, for reregistration of all foreign trademarks and patents. Trademarks and patents not registered as of that date were subject to loss of proprietary rights.

Source: "Dealings With Iraq Required to Be in Arabic Language," *Commerce America*, February 13, 1978, p. 16.

Prior use versus registration

In the United States, a common-law country, ownership of industrial property rights is established by prior use—whoever can establish first use is typically considered the rightful owner. In fact, before trademarks and brand names can be registered, they must actually be in use. In many code-law countries, however, ownership is established by registration rather than by prior use—the first to register a trademark or other property right is considered the rightful owner. Therefore, a company that believes it can always establish ownership in another country by proving it used the trademark or brand name first is under a false impression which can lead to the loss of these assets. However, prior registration may be subject to challenge under certain laws by a person who claims and can prove to have first presented the product to the market. Upon such proof, prior registration may be canceled. To further complicate the problem, countries frequently change their laws from a typical common-law basis to code law. For example, in 1976, Canada, a common-law country, began legislation to change their patent laws giving priority to registration over prior invention as a means of establishing rights to a patent.

Avoiding the possible loss of industrial property rights which may be profitable either for the company to sell directly or to license others to produce and sell in foreign markets is generally a matter of properly registering them within these countries. This task can be facilitated by several international conventions which provide for simultaneous registration in member countries.

International conventions

Many countries participate in international conventions designed for mutual recognition and protection of industrial property rights. There are three major international conventions and a fourth in the making; the United States is a member of three. The four are:

1. The International Convention for the Protection of Industrial Property, commonly referred to as the *Paris Union,* comprises a group of 80 nations, including the United States, which have agreed to recognize the rights of all members in the protection of trademarks, patents, and other property rights. Registration in one of the member countries insures the same protection afforded by the home country in all the member countries.

2. The Inter-American Convention includes most of the Latin American nations and the United States. It provides protection similar to that afforded by the Paris Union.

3. A third important convention is the Madrid Convention, which established the Bureau for International Registration of Trademarks. There are some 24 member countries in Europe which have agreed to automatic trademark protection for all members. Even though the United States is not a participant of the Madrid Convention, if a subsidiary of a U.S. company is located in one of the member nations, the subsidiary could file through the membership of its host country and thereby provide protection in all 24 countries for the U.S. company.

4. The Trademark Registration Treaty (TRT) is designed to make it simpler and less expensive to obtain trademark protection in foreign markets. The TRT provides that for a single fee a trademark application can be filed with the World Intellectual Property Organization (WIPO). The TRT became effective in 1980. The United States signed the TRT, but will have to amend its trademark laws to provide for registration based on intention to use a mark in order to ratify the treaty.

In addition to the four agreements above, there are two new multicountry patent arrangements which will streamline patent procedures in Europe. The Patent Cooperation Treaty (PCT) facilitates the application of patents among its 28 member countries. It provides comprehensive coverage in that a single application filed in the United States will supply the interested party with an international search report on other patents to help evaluate whether or not to seek protection in each of the countries cooperating under the PCT.

The European Patent Convention (EPC) has 11 European-member countries. The EPC establishes a regional patent system allowing any nationality to file a single international application for a European patent.[14]

Once a trademark, patent, or other industrial property right is registered, most countries require that these rights be worked and properly policed. The United States is one of the few countries where a patent can be held by an individual throughout the duration of the patent period without being manufactured and sold. Other countries feel that in exchange for the monop-

---

[14] Vincent D. Travaglini, "Protection of Industrial Property Rights Abroad," *Business America,* September 7, 1981, pp. 3–9.

oly provided by a patent, the holder must share the product with the citizens of the country. Hence, if patents are not produced within a specified period, usually from one to five years (the average is three years), the patent reverts to public domain. This is also true for trademarks; products bearing the registered mark must be sold within the country, or the company may forfeit its right to a particular trademark.

Companies are also expected to actively police their industrial property in bringing to court any violators. Policing can be a difficult task, with success depending in large measure on the cooperation of the country within which the infringement or piracy takes place.

Jurisdiction of U.S. laws

Leaving the legal boundaries of a home country does not necessarily exempt a business from home-country laws. For example, regardless of the nation within which business is done, a U.S. citizen is still subject to the internal revenue laws of the United States, laws which prohibit participating in unauthorized boycotts of friendly nations such as the Arab boycott of Israel; trading with an enemy of the United States; or participating in any commercial venture which adversely affects the United States economy.[15] Thus, at any given time, a U.S. citizen in a foreign country must look not only to the laws of the host country, but simultaneously to the rules of the home sovereign.

The question of jurisdiction of U.S. laws over acts committed outside the territorial limits of the country has been settled by the courts through application of a long-established principle of international law, the "objective theory of jurisdiction." "This concept holds that 'even if an act is committed abroad, that is, outside the territorial jurisdiction of U.S. courts, those courts can nevertheless have jurisdiction over it, if the act produces consequences or effects within the U.S.' "[16]

Technically, an activity on the part of a U.S. firm which is considered by U.S. courts to have a damaging effect on U.S. foreign or domestic commerce or on our national safety is subject to U.S. law. The only exception is that a U.S. citizen would not be punished for violating a U.S. law if the violation occurred within a foreign country as a result of enforced compliance with local foreign law.

As more U.S. firms become multinational and merge or enter into joint ventures with large non-U.S. multinational firms, they find themselves in situations where the question of violation of U.S. law becomes an important issue. Increasingly, U.S. companies find some host countries involving them

---

[15] "Antiboycott Rules Likely to Plaque U.S. Firms Despite New Administration," *Business International,* December 19, 1980, pp. 401–02.

[16] Andre Simons, "Foreign Trade and Antitrust Laws," *Business Topics,* Summer 1962, p. 27.

in trade with foreign countries that the U.S. government has trade embargos against, thus forcing them to trade with "the enemy." For example, the Freuhauf Corporation was caught in the middle when their French subsidiary signed a $20 million contract with the People's Republic of China. At that time, the United States was not trading with China, and any U.S. firm that did was in violation of the Trading with the Enemy Act. Freufauf (U.S.) canceled the contract, but the French government intervened, legally seized the French subsidiary, and the deal went through without U.S. Freuhauf involvement. Since the Freuhauf case, relations between the United States and China have improved considerably and these two nations are trading extensively. Yet, a U.S. company or any of its joint ventures cannot sell to China or any other country without special permission from the U.S. government for certain products. Special permission had to be obtained before a French licensee of Westinghouse nuclear power-plant technology could sell to China; Caterpillar Tractor waited over a year to get permission to sell pipe-laying equipment to Russia.[17] Similar problems have faced U.S. firms in Argentina, Canada, and elsewhere.

Further, there is growing concern among international marketers about the effects of antitrust enforcement by the U.S. government and foreign governments beyond their respective boundaries. Outright purchases, mergers, licensing, and joint ventures with foreign firms have been on the increase in recent years, sparking considerable interest within the antitrust departments of many governments. As a result, jurisdictional issues have become more and more crucial because they raise the question of how and when a country's laws can be enforced outside its political boundaries. Heads of state do not like the idea of possible interference with their national policies, and frequently the multinational firm is caught in the middle. The issue is especially important to U.S. multinational firms since the "long arm" of U.S. legal jurisdiction is causing anxiety among heads of state in Europe, Canada, and Latin America "over the influence of American government policy acting on their own economies through the multinationals."

U.S. ANTITRUST ENFORCEMENT

The question of jurisdiction and how U.S. antitrust laws apply is frequently asked but only vaguely answered. The basis for determination ultimately rests with the interpretation of Sections I and II of the Sherman Act; Section I states that "every contract, combination . . . or conspiracy in restraint of trade or commerce among the several states or with foreign nations is hereby declared to be illegal"; Section II makes it a violation to "monopolize, or attempt to monopolize, or combine or conspire with any other person or

---

[17] "U.S. to Let French Sell Two Reactors with Westinghouse Technology to China," *The Wall Street Journal,* December 27, 1979, p. 6; "Caterpillar Request to Sell Gear to Soviets Splits Reagan Aides Forming Trade Plan," *The Wall Street Journal,* June 4, 1981, p. 7.

persons, to monopolize any part of the trade or commerce among the several states, or with foreign nations."

Antitrust enforcement has two purposes in international commerce. The first is to protect American consumers by insuring that they benefit from products and ideas produced by foreign competitors as well as by domestic competitors. Competition from foreign producers is important when imports are, or could be, a major source of a product or when a domestic industry is dominated by a single firm. This becomes relevant in many joint ventures, particularly if the joint venture creates a situation when a U.S. firm entering a joint venture with a foreign competitor could restrict competition for the U.S. parent in the U.S. market. The second purpose of antitrust legislation is to protect American export and investment opportunities against any privately imposed restrictions. The concern is that all U.S.-based fims engaged in the export of goods, services, or capital should be allowed to compete on merits and not be shut out by restrictions imposed by bigger or less-principled competitors.[18]

The Justice Department recognizes that application of U.S. antitrust laws to overseas activities raises some difficult questions of jurisdiction. It recognizes that U.S. antitrust-law enforcement should not interfere unnecessarily

---

BOX 7-4: Stopping the reach of U.S. law—conflict brewing?

A source of tension between the United States and West Germany has been the foreign activity of American antitrust investigators who were said to have conducted "fishing expeditions" as if they were employees of the German government. Under a new agreement, West Germany will cooperate with the United States in ferreting out restrictive business practices, joint action will be taken, and data will be shared. The National Association of German Industries (BDI) welcomes this agreement because it will channel snooping by U.S. antitrust agents into the German justice system. It will ensure the involvement of the West German government in all investigations of anticompetitive practices that violate commonly agreed upon principles.

Under the new agreement if an antitrust unit of one country requests information on an individual or company of the other, the equivalent agency can provide this data by indicating it has no objection to its release. However, *it can also recommend that the information not be made available.* *

Attorney General Griffin Bell warned multinational corporations that the Justice Department will not hesitate to pursue antitrust violators beyond U.S. borders. . . . In a speech . . . he also chided some foreign governments for refusing to provide U.S. law-enforcement officials with the same kind of cooperation the United States offers foreign investigators. . . . *British, West Germany, Canada, Australia, and the Netherlands are among those countries that have adopted laws designed to regulate the degree of cooperation with U.S. investigations for persons within their territory.* †

* "Antitrust Truce," *Atlas World Press Review*, November 1976, p. 52.
† "Multinational Antitrust Violators Told by Bell They'll Be Pursued Outside U.S.," *The Wall Street Journal*, August 9, 1977, p. 2.

---

[18] This section relies heavily on "Antitrust Guide in International Operations," United States Department of Justice, Antitrust Division, January 26, 1977, 63 pp.

with the sovereign interest of a foreign nation. At the same time, however, the Antitrust Division is committed to control foreign transactions at home or abroad which have a substantial and foreseeable effect on U.S. commerce. When such business practices occur, there is no question in the Antitrust Division of the Department of Justice that U.S. laws apply.

With all due respect to the Justice Department's commitment to protect commerce within the United States, the extraterritorial application of U.S. antitrust laws creates major problems for international companies in the United States and elsewhere. The problems are twofold: (1) the kinds of activities imposed by foreign countries such as joint ventures, licensing requirements, and joint research may be subject to antitrust review. Frequently in these situations, companies are caught between the host government requiring joint ventures to do business within the country and the U.S. Justice Department restricting or forbidding such ventures because of their U.S. anticompetitive effects; (2) the extraterritorial application of antitrust laws can and does cause problems with host countries who are incensed at the influence of U.S. law within their boundaries. Host countries see this influence as further evidence of U.S. interference. This was the situation in France when the United States intervened in the Freuhauf case mentioned earlier. It was also the situation in Germany when the U.S. Department of Justice intervened in the Gillette case.

When the intent of any kind of overseas activity is, indeed, to restrain trade there is no question about the appropriateness of applying U.S. laws. The question arises in situations where the intent is not to restrain trade but simply to conclude a reasonable business transaction. A good example of such a situation is the Gillette Company case which began in 1967 and was finally settled by a consent decree in 1977. In 1967, Gillette Company, a U.S. razor manufacturer, bought controlling interest of Braun A.G., a German manufacturer of appliances whose most successful product is an electric shaver. From a business point of view this acquisition made business sense for Gillette. It gave Gillette an entry into the European electric-shaver market as well as other parts of the world where Braun shavers are sold. It also was important to Braun, who received a fair market price for their company, since it provided them with the financial strength their company needed for continued worldwide expansion. Once the transaction was consummated, the Justice Department entered the picture on the basis that the acquisition would be in violation of the Sherman Antitrust Act.

The Justice Department case was explained as follows: since Braun had an electric shaver and Gillette did not, the acquisition gave Gillette a shaving instrument (that is, an electric shaver) which might tend to lessen competition within the United States. The Justice Department alleged Braun would be eliminated as a potential independent competitor in the U.S. shaving market and Gillette's dominant position in the industry would be enhanced, thereby substantially lessening competition in the United States. Gillette replied that this was, at least in the immediate future, impossible since Braun held cross-patent and license arrangements with Ronson Corporation, precluding Braun from selling their razors in the United States. Rather than accept this as a point in favor of the Gillette-Braun merger, the Justice Department countered that with the merger Gillette would take over Braun's rights to certain Ronson patents and processes which could further lessen the competition between Gillette and Ronson. The Justice Department sued Gillette to compel them to divest their interest abroad. Gillette countered with a suit, and in 1977, the case was finally settled with a consent decree.

Under the terms of the consent decree, Gillette agreed to form a U.S. corporation to produce and market electrical shavers in the United States; further, Gillette and Braun agreed to give the new company all their shaving-instrument technology and know-how as well as the U.S. patent rights; also, Gillette and Braun agreed to provide capital, manpower, and business services needed to make the new company fully operative within two years of the final decree; that within four years after the date of the final judgment, Gillette would divest itself of all its interest in the new company; and finally, Gillette would be forbidden for a 10-year period, beginning with the decree date, from acquiring any interest in any U.S. manufacturing and distribution of electric razors, as well as safety razors and blades without the specific approval of the Justice Department and the court. Thus, the issue was *settled,* competition in the United States was *protected,* and the confusion level of just how antitrust laws apply to U.S. firms was raised another notch.

Similar moves in the antitrust area are causing major problems for the United States and its multinational firms. A reasonable question is, if the government encourages U.S. firms to become multinational in operation, then shouldn't the government take a closer look at antitrust legislation designed to control the actions of *domestic* companies which may not be appropriate in terms of worldwide business practices?

Adding to the confusion are the many foreign countries which are adopting laws similar to the U.S. antitrust laws designed to regulate antitrust activities within the country and, in some instances, to reduce the effect of U.S. competition.

Foreign-country antitrust enforcement

With the exception of the United States, antitrust laws have been either nonexistent or unenforced in most of the world's countries for the better part of the 20th century. However, by the 1970s, the European Community began to actively enforce the Community's antitrust laws patterned after those in the United States.[19] Price discrimination, supply restrictions, and full line forcing are areas where the European Court of Justice of the EC has dealt severe penalties. For example, Michelin was fined $700,000 for

---

[19] Debbie C. Tennison, "IBM Antitrust Suit in Common Market Could Have Widespread Ramifications," *The Wall Street Journal,* March 1, 1982, p. 5.

operating a system of discriminatory rebates to Dutch tire dealers and similar penalties have been assessed against such major companies as United Brands Co. for price discrimination and F. Hoffmann-LaRoche and Company for noncost-justified fidelity discounts to its dealers.[20]

Individual countries are also stengthening their antitrust laws. For example, West Germany is considered to have the toughest and most comprehensive antitrust laws outside the United States. Great Britain recently passed a stiff Competition Bill which details seven areas of competition to be investigated, ranging from supply restrictions of retailers to discriminatory pricing.[21]

Japan is revising and intensifying its antimonopoly laws and while enforcement of these seems to be directed primarily toward the actions of Japanese companies, foreign-company members of joint ventures are affected, also. Even developing countries are becoming more concerned with antitrust problems. While antitrust is commonly considered a preoccupation of developed nations, there has been a substantial increase in concern over restraint of trade among developing countries. In the industrialized world, restraint of trade has typically meant restraint of competition, and, in most instances, refers to restrictions imposed on competition between independent companies. Developing nations see intracorporate limitations imposed by a parent company on its subsidiary within their country as the major violation of free trade. Thus, restraint of trade is more an interpretation of their concern with a parent (multinational) firm restraining the competitive activities of its subsidiary within the country. In all these situations, the multinational firm is confronted with various interpretations of antitrust, and further, its activities in one country may inadvertently lead to antitrust violations in another.

Thus, the foreign marketer is faced with the unique problem of having to consider not only different legal systems but the foreign policy of the United States and the host country, which are frequently in conflict. If the

---

BOX 7-5: Treat all customers alike

Johnson & Johnson has been fined about $282,000 by the European Commission for restricting exports of its Gravindex pregnancy-test kits to West Germany. The Commission found that the firm's British subsidiary, Ortho Pharmaceuticals, stopped shipments of the kits to Germany by request of the firm's German and Swiss subsidiaries, both named Cilag Chemie. At the time, the price of the kits in West Germany was two-and-a-half times more than in Britain. "The export restrictions were undoubtedly intended to protect the high price levels in other EC member states, particularly in Germany, from competition from UK dealers," the Commission commented.

Source: *World Business Weekly*, December 15, 1980, p. 19. By permission of the Financial Times, London.

---

[20] "European Community: The Clamor to Reform Antitrust Enforcement," *Business Week*, June 8, 1981, p. 72 and "The EC Cracks Down on Price Discrimination," *Business Week*, December 7, 1981, p. 45.

[21] "Companies in Britain Are Told: Fight Fair for Your Market Share," *World Business Weekly*, April 28, 1980, pp. 22–23.

scope of operations includes more than one foreign country, the number of legal systems and foreign policies to be considered increases.

SUMMARY

Foreign business faces a multitude of problems in its efforts to develop a successful marketing program. Not the least of these problems are the varying legal systems of the world and their effect on business transactions. Just as political climate, cultural differences, local geography, different business customs, and the stage of economic development must be taken into account, so must such legal questions as jurisdictional and legal recourse in disputes, protection of industrial property rights, extended U.S. law enforcement, and enforcement of antitrust legislation by U.S. and foreign government. A primary marketing task is to develop a plan that will be enhanced or at least not adversely affected by these and other environmental elements.

The myriad questions created by different laws and different legal systems indicate that the most prudent path to follow at all stages of foreign marketing operations is one which leads to competent counsel well versed in the intricacies of the international legal environment.

QUESTIONS

1. Differentiate between common law and code law. Show how the differences may affect marketing activities.
2. How does the international marketer determine what legal system will have jurisdiction when legal disputes arise?
3. Discuss the state of international commercial law.
4. Discuss the limitations of jurisdictional clauses in contracts.
5. What is the "objective theory of jurisdiction"? How does it apply to a firm doing business within a foreign country?
6. Discuss some of the reasons why it is probably best to seek an out-of-court settlement in international commercial legal disputes rather than to sue.
7. Illustrate the procedure generally followed in international commercial disputes when settled under the auspices of a formal arbitration tribunal.
8. What are industrial property rights? Why should a company in international marketing take special steps to protect them?
9. In many code-law countries ownership of industrial property rights is established by registration rather than prior use. Comment.
10. Discuss the advantages to the international marketer arising from the existence of the various international conventions on trademarks, patents, and copyrights.

11. "The legal environment of the foreign marketer takes on an added dimension of importance since there is no single uniform international commerical law which governs foreign business transactions." Comment.

12. What is the "credulous man standard" in advertising and what is its importance in international marketing?

13. Differentiate between the European Patent Convention (EPC) and the Patent Cooperation Treaty (PCT) in their effectiveness in protecting industrial property rights.

14. "In the industrialized world, restraint of trade has typically meant restraint of competition, and, in most instances, refers to restrictions imposed on competition between independent companies." Developing countries view restraint of trade differently. Comment.

15. Discuss why the U.S. Justice Department has become more active in enforcing the Sherman-Antitrust law against U.S. multinationals. What kinds of problems does this create in foreign countries?

Chapter 8

Geography

Geography, the study of the earth's surface, climate, continents, countries, peoples, industries, and products is an element of the uncontrollable environment which confronts the marketer but which generally receives little attention. There is a tendency to study the manifestations of the effect of climate, topography, and available resources rather than to study these geographical factors as important causal agents in the marketing environment. The physical character of a nation is perhaps the principal and broadest determinant of both the characteristics of a society and the means by which that society undertakes to supply its needs. Thus, the study of geography is important for the student of marketing when evaluating marketing and its environment.

The world as a whole will be examined to acquaint readers with the broad scope of world markets and the effect of the diversity of geography on the economic profiles of various nations. The orientation of the chapter is to consider some important geographic characteristics of the world which may affect markets and which should be taken into account when examining the environmental aspects of marketing.

This chapter will discuss some of the characteristics of world markets that must be weighed to effectively establish marketing plans. A secondary purpose is to provide the student of international marketing with a greater awareness of the world, its complexities, and its diversities; an awareness which can mean the difference between success and failure in marketing ventures.

Climate and topography will be examined as some of the broader and more important elements of geography. A brief look at the earth's resources and population—the building blocks of world markets—and a short overview of world trade and world trade routes will complete the presentation of geography and world markets.

CLIMATE AND TOPOGRAPHY

As elements of geography, the physical terrain and climate of a country are important environmental considerations when appraising a market. The effect of these geographical features on marketing can range from the obvious influences on product adaptation to more profound influences on the development of the marketing systems within a country.

Altitude, humidity, and temperature extremes are all climatic features

215

which may affect the use and functionality of products and equipment. Products that perform well in temperate zones may deteriorate rapidly or require special cooling or lubrication to function adequately in tropical zones. Manufacturers found that construction equipment used in the United States required extensive modifications to cope with the intense heat and dust of the Sahara Desert. Within even a single national market, climate can be sufficiently diverse to require major adjustments. In Ghana, a product adaptable to the entire market must be able to operate effectively in extreme desert heat and dehydration as well as in tropical rain forests and consistently high humidity.

By affecting the character of a nation's economy and its economic and social development, geography has an even more direct influence on marketing. South America represents an extreme but well-defined example of the importance of geography in marketing considerations. The economic and social systems that exist there today can be explained partly in terms of the geographical characteristics of the area.

South America is a continent 4,500 miles long and 3,000 miles wide at its broadest point, two thirds of it comparable to Africa in its climate, with 48 percent of its total area made up of forest and jungle and only 5 percent arable.

Mountain ranges cover the west coast for 4,500 miles with an average height of 13,000 feet and a width of 300 to 400 miles. This is a natural, formidable barrier which has precluded the establishment of commercial routes between the Pacific and the Atlantic coasts. Building railroads and highways across the United States was a monumental task, but nothing compared to the requirements of building a railroad from northeast Brazil to the Peruvean West through jungles and mountains.

Once the Andes are surmounted, the Amazon basin of 2 million square miles lies ahead. It is the world's greatest rain forest, almost uninhabitable and impenetrable. Through it runs the Amazon, the world's second largest river which, with its tributaries, has almost 40,000 miles of navigable water. On the east coast is another mountain range covering almost the entire coast of Brazil, with an average height of 4,000 feet.

South America presents a geographic picture of natural barriers that inhibit national growth, trade, and communication. It is a vast land area with a population concentration on the outer periphery and an isolated and almost uninhabited interior. The major cities of South American countries are within 200 miles of the coast, but even the cities are often separated from each other by inadequate roads and poor communication. Thus, national unity and an equal degree of economic development are nearly impossible. Many citizens of South American countries are so isolated they do not recognize themselves as part of the nation that claims their citizenship. Geography has divided South America into secluded communities.

Another characteristic of Latin American countries is the population concentration in major cities. In almost every case, a high percentage of the total population of each country lives in a few isolated metropolitan centers

---

BOX 8–1: Climate and success

A major food processing company had production problems after it built a pineapple cannery at the delta of a river in Mexico. The pineapple plantation was located upstream, and the plan was to barge the ripe fruit downstream for canning, load them directly on ocean liners, and ship them to the company's various markets. When the pineapples were ripe, however, the company found itself in trouble: the time of crop maturity coincided with the flood stage of the river. The current in the river during this period was far too strong to permit the backhauling of barges upstream and thus the plan for transporting the fruit with barges could not be implemented. With no alternative feasible means of transport, the company was forced to close the operation. Their new equipment was sold for 5 percent of original cost to a Mexican group who immediately relocated the cannery. A seemingly simple, harmless oversight of weather and navigation conditions became not only of costly significance, but in fact, the primary cause for major losses to the company.

Source: David Ricks, *Big Business Blunders: Mistakes in Multinational Marketing* (Homewood, Ill.: Richard D. Irwin, 1983), p. 4.

---

with most of the wealth, education, and power. The surrounding rural areas remain almost unchanged from one generation to the next, usually at subsistence levels. In many areas, even the language of the rural people is not the same as that of metropolitan residents.[1]

With the circumstances illustrated in this South American example, a market is rarely homogeneous. In Colombia there are four major population centers separated from one another by high mountains. Even today, these mountain ranges are a major barrier to travel in Colombia. For example, the air time from Bogota' to Medellín, the third largest city in Colombia, is 30 minutes. By highway, that same trip takes 10 to 12 hours. However in 1980, the new president declared that before he leaves office an improved highway will be built and "plans to drive the distance in six or seven hours." Because of the physical isolation, each center has a different dialect, style of living, and population characteristics; even the climates are different. Thus, from a marketing view, the four centers constitute four distinctly different markets.

Although the geography of Latin America may appear extreme, a further study of geography reveals that many areas in the world have extreme topographic and climatic variations. Consider, for example, the physical and/or climatic variations that exist within such countries as China, the Soviet Union, and India.

In Canada, one observer notes that vast distances and extreme winter weather have a major influence on distribution. Reorder points and safety stock levels must be higher than normally expected for given inventories since large cities such as Montreal can be isolated suddenly and completely because of heavy snowfalls. At such times, delivery delays of three to four

---

[1] This discussion is based in part on a monograph of Herbert V. Prochnow, "Economic, Political, and Social Trends in Latin America" (Chicago: The First National Bank of Chicago, n.d.).

days are common. Additionally, shipment delays can result from a shortage
of insulated rail cars and trucks, and the high cost of heating rail cars on
long hauls in such extreme weather can add 10 percent or more to a company's freight bill.

Imagine the formidable problems of appraising market potential or devising a marketing mix that would successfully reconcile the diversities in such
situations. Rolls-Royce found that a fully armor-plated car provided by the
British government for its envoy to Canada required extensive body work
and renovations after just a short time in Canada. It was not the cold that
demolished the cars, but the salted sand spread liberally by municipal authorities to keep the streets passable throughout the four or five months of
virtually continuous snow. The fenders were corroded and rusted, the door-
side panels likewise, the oil system leaked, and the air conditioning and
automatic windows were knocked out by an electrical fault. While this may
be an extreme and isolated case, it illustrates the harshness of a climate
and the need to consider such elements in product development.[2]

The hurdles are not insurmountable but geography cannot be ignored
because of its direct effect on marketing and such activities as communica-

---

**BOX 8–2: Geography, infrastructure, and level of technology—Why won't
the cars and buses run?**

Geography, infrastructure, and level of technology of a market are important uncontrollable elements to which products must be adapted. Here are two incidents where
they were not properly accounted for:

General Motors of Canada sold 25,000 Chevrolet Malibus to Iraq. However, they
were mechanically unfit for Iraq's hot, dusty climate. When the Malibus hit Baghdad's
roads and streets their air filters choked on the dust and their transmissions labored
in the heat and traffic. GM tripled to 36 its fulltime engineers and mechanics in Baghdad
where they are installing supplementary air filters and changing clutches. Iraq refuses
to take any more cars until the 13,500 already delivered are repaired properly.

In Egypt, the problem was with buses whose diesel engines were so loud and
noisy that they were nicknamed the "Voice of America." All 600 buses had to have
replacement mufflers for urban use. But that wasn't all. In less than a year, performance
was so bad that their failure became a source of embarrassment and irritation to
Egyptian and U.S. officials. According to a transportation engineering firm, the trouble
stemmed from a failure to anticipate how roughly they would be used. "With a few
changes to meet American air pollution control standards, they would probably last
for years on American roads with American drivers and American maintenance,"
said one engineer. "But, in Egypt, the driving conditions are appalling, the drivers
are untrained and reckless, and the concept of maintenance is to ignore it until the
bus breaks down. Buses routinely must carry double the load they were meant for.
Whoever approved the original specifications should have known that."

Sources: "GM Runs Into a Middle-East Crisis: It's too Hot and Dusty in Baghdad," *The Wall
Street Journal*, February 23, 1982, p. 29 and "Egypt Angered, not Aided, by Gift of U.S. Buses,"
Los Angeles Times, January 12, 1982.

---

[2] "Rolls-Royce Beaten by Canada's Winters," *World Business Weekly*, April 6, 1981, p.
41.

tions and distribution. Furthermore, there may be indirect effects through the geographical ramifications on the society and culture of the country, all of which ultimately must be reflected in marketing activity. Many of the peculiarities of a country (i.e., peculiar to the foreigner) would be better understood and anticipated if its geography were studied more closely.

The effect of natural barriers on market development also must be considered. Because of the ease of distribution, coastal cities or cities situated on navigable waterways are more likely to be trading centers than are landlocked cities. Cities not near natural physical transportation routes generally are isolated from one another even within the same country. Consequently, when planning distribution systems, it would be unwise to assume that one distribution point might serve a wide territory.

In discussing distribution in Africa, one marketer pointed out that a shipment from Mombasa on the Kenya east coast to Freetown on the bulge of West Africa could require more time than a shipment from New York or London to Kenya over established freight routes. Even within a country more than one distribution center may be necessary; a Nairobi, Kenya, site could not adequately service the Mwanza region on the Tanganyika side of Lake Victoria only a few hundred miles away. As countries expand their economies, natural barriers are adapted to rather than overcome; the task of surmounting natural barriers is left to more affluent generations. Thus, geography, or at least topography and climate, can be of great importance in underdeveloped countries where people have not had the time or economic capability to overcome such obstacles. In Ecuador the road conditions are such that it is hardly possible to drive a car from the port of Guayaquil to the capital of Quito only 200 miles away. Contrast this to the accomplishments of more economically advanced countries where formidable mountain barriers are frequently overcome. A case in point is the 7.2-mile tunnel which cuts through the base of Mont Blanc in the Alps. This highway tunnel brings Rome and Paris 125 miles closer and provides a year-round route between Geneva and Turin of only 170 miles; it was previously a trip of nearly 500 miles when snow closed the highway over the Alps.

Of the world's 20 poorest countries, climate and geography contribute significantly to their plight. As one report suggested, each of the 20 countries has a slim margin between subsistence and disaster,

> all exist in a fragile tropical environment which had been upset by the growing pressure of people. Without irrigation and water management, they are afflicted by droughts, floods, soil erosion, and creeping deserts, which reduce the long-term fertility of the land. Disasters such as drought intensify the malnutrition and ill health of the people, and endemic diseases undermine their vitality. Their poverty, harsh climate, and isolation all make it harder to exploit their resources, especially minerals. The sun, which might be a valuable source of cheap energy, is presently a curse, sapping their vigor while they are forced to use relatively expensive conventional forms of energy.[3]

---

[3] Desiree, French, "Poorest of the Poor," *Forbes,* July 20, 1981, p. 38.

The poverty of these countries is reflected in their economy which, as measured by their gross domestic product, has grown over a 19-year period at an average annual rate of 0.7 percent compared with the 2.9 percent for developing countries as a group. While climate and geography are not the only causes of their economic weakness, they are certainly a major contributing force.

In summary, the marketer should not only consider the effects of climate, altitude, humidity, temperature, and such on the product, but should also examine the more complex effect of geography on general market characteristics, distribution systems, and the state of the economy.

RESOURCES

The availability of minerals and the ability to generate energy are the foundations of modern technology. The location of the earth's resources as well as available sources of energy are geographical accidents, and the world's nations are not equally endowed; nor does a nation's demand for a particular mineral or energy source necessarily coincide with domestic supply.

Energy is necessary to power the machinery of modern production and to extract and process the resources necessary to produce the goods of economic prosperity. In much of the underdeveloped world, human labor still provides the preponderance of energy. The principal supplements to human energy are animals, wood, fossil fuel, nuclear power, and to a lesser and more experimental extent, the ocean's tides, geothermal power, and the sun. Of all the energy sources, petroleum usage is increasing most rapidly because of its versatility and the ease with which it is stored and transported.

Many countries which were self-sufficient during much of their early economic growth have become net importers of petroleum during the last 20 years and continue to become increasingly dependent on foreign sources. A spectacular example is the United States which was almost completely self-sufficient until 1942, became a major importer by 1950, and by 1980 was importing over 50 percent of annual requirements. If present rates of consumption continue, predictions are that the United States will be importing over 70 percent of its needs by the year 2000.

Only since World War II has concern for the limitless availability of seemingly inexhaustible supplies become a prominent factor. The dramatic increase in economic growth in the industrialized world and the push for industrialization in the remaining world has put such tremendous pressure on the earth's resources that at the beginning of the 1980s predictions of exhausted resources threatened many of the necessary building blocks of economic growth and development.[4] Unfortunately, a mineral deposit once

---

[4] "A Strategy for Coping with Mineral Shortages," *International Management,* April 1981, pp. 53–54.

exhausted is gone forever; petroleum, the premium fossil fuel used in energy creation, is rapidly approaching exhaustion according to all current predictions.

As an environmental consideration in world marketing, the location, quality, and availability of resources will affect the pattern of world economic development and trade for at least the remainder of the century.[5] This factor must be weighed carefully by astute international marketers in making worldwide international investment decisions. In addition to the raw materials of industrialization, there must be an available and economically feasible energy supply to successfully transform resources into usable products.

BOX 8–3:   How many slaves work for you?

A healthy, hard-working person can produce just enough energy to keep a 100-watt light bulb burning. This may seem unimportant, but it is a humbling reminder that muscle power is really very puny. . . .

Supplementary energy now exceeds muscle energy in every part of our lives from food production to recreation. It is like a gang of silent slaves who labor continually and uncomplainingly to feed, clothe, and maintain us. The energy comes, of course, from mineral resources such as coal, oil, and uranium, not from real slaves, but everyone on the earth now has "energy slaves." . . . In India the total supplementary energy produced is equivalent to the work of 15 slaves, each working an eight-hour day, for every man, woman, and child. In South America everyone has approximately 30 "energy slaves"; in Japan, 75; Russia, 120; Europe, 150; and in the United States and Canada, a huge 300. The concept of "energy slaves" demonstrates how utterly dependent the world has become on mineral resources. If the "slaves" were to strike (which means if the supplies ran out), the world's peoples could not keep themselves alive and healthy. Reverting to muscle power alone would bring starvation, famine, and pestilence. Nature would quickly reduce the population.

Source: Brian J. Skinner, *Earth Resources,* 2d ed., © 1976, pp. 3–4. Reprinted by permission of Prentice-Hall, Inc., Englewood Cliffs, N.J.

There is great disparity in the location of the earth's resources which generates world trade between those who do not have all they need and those who have more than they need and are willing to sell. Importers of most of the resources are industrial nations which do not have sufficient supplies domestically to meet demand. Aluminum is a good example; three countries, Australia, Guinea, and Brazil account for over 65 percent of the world's reserves, and one country, the United States, consumes 35 percent of all aluminum produced. Of the 20 items listed in Exhibit 8–1, the United States has major reserves in only five but consumes 20 percent or more of the world's total of 16 of the 20 items.

Besides the geographical unevenness with which most resources occur, the continuing availability of supply is a matter of grave concern. For many

---

[5] Robert B. Stobaugh, "Energy Future in an International Trade," *Journal of International Business Studies,* Spring/Summer 1981, pp. 23–28.

EXHIBIT 8–1: Reserves, projected consumption, and principal producers and consumers of selected nonrenewable resources

Resource	Known global reserves, 1974* (A)	Static index (years)† (B)	Probable annual projected rate of growth (percent)‡ (C)	Amount used (1974–2000)§ (D)	Amount of reserves left in the year 2000‖ (E)
Aluminum	3,840 million s.t.	226	5.2	957 million s.t.	2,883 million s.t.
Chromium	577 million s.t.	206	2.8	111 million s.t.	466 million s.t.
Coal	888 billion s.t.	274	1.8	111 billion s.t.	777 billion s.t.
Cobalt	5,404 million lbs.	78	3.3	2,945 million lbs.	2,459 million lbs.
Copper	450 million s.t.	62	3.9	317 million s.t.	133 million s.t.
Gold	1,320 million T.oz.	51	2.6	1,100 million T.oz.	220 million T.oz.
Iron	100 billion s.t.	177	2.8	22,313 million s.t.	77,687 million s.t.
Lead	165 million s.t.	49	2.6	143 million s.t.	22 million s.t.
Manganese	2,013 million s.t.	197	2.8	404 million s.t.	1,609 million s.t.
Mercury	4,930 thousand fl.	21	0.8	7,044 thousand fl.	–
Molybdenum	13 billion lbs.	65	4.4	9,992 million lbs.	3,008 million lbs.
Natural gas	2,146 trillion cu.ft.	46	4.7	2,599 trillion cu.ft.	–
Nickel	60 million s.t.	77	2.6	33 million s.t.	27 million s.t.
Petroleum	665 billion bbls.	32	2.6	883 billion bbls.	–
Platinum group #	561 million T.oz.	93	3.0	245 million T.oz.	316 million T.oz.
Shale oil	50 billion bbls.	909	11.5	8,560 million bbls.	41,440 million bbls.
Silver	6,000 million T.oz.	16	2.0	13,254 million T.oz.	–
Tin	10,120 thousand l.t.	44	1.5	7,587 thousand l.t.	2,533 thousand l.t.
Tungsten	3,924 million lbs.	46	2.7	3,156 million lbs.	768 million lbs.
Zinc	260 million s.t.	41	2.2	230 million s.t.	30 million s.t.

* Data are from U.S. Bureau of Mines, *Mineral Facts and Problems, 1975* (Washington, D.C.: Government Printing Office, 1976); s.t. = short ton, lbs. = pounds, T.oz. = Troy ounce, fl. = flask, ft. = feet, bbls. = barrels, l.t. = long ton.

† The number of years known global reserves (Col. A) will last at current global consumption. Calculated by dividing known reserves (Col. A) by the current annual consumption (*Mineral Facts and Problems*, 1975).

‡ Source: *Mineral Facts and Problems*, 1975.

§ Author's calculations. Amount of reserves used between 1974–2000 at the annual projected rate of growth.

‖ Amount of reserves remaining in the year 2000 (Col. A–Col. D).

Platinum group includes platinum, palladium, iridium, osmium, rhodium, and ruthenium.

minerals, the rate of consumption is multiplying at an alarmingly rapid rate. As populations grow, more minerals are required, and with improvement in the general welfare and economic level, per capita consumption further accelerates demand. The result is an increasing growth rate which portends near exhaustion of most known reserves within this century. Exhibit 8–1 presents two possible rates of depletion. Column A presents the known reserves and Column B gives the number of years known global reserves will last at current rates of consumption. Assuming increased population growth and an increasing rate of per capita consumption, Column D shows the remaining years of supply when consumption grows at projected rates of growth.

Thus, known reserves of mercury at present rates of consumption (Col. B) would last 21 years. At an annual projected growth rate of 0.8 percent, known reserves will be depleted before the year 2000. Exploration for new reserves continues and frequently new reserves are found, but even if reserves are doubled, the extended availability of mercury is still short. Petroleum and natural gas, two of the major sources of energy needed for production, are also in short supply. Petroleum supplies at present usage rates will be near exhaustion by 2000. Costs will also be affected as reserves diminish.

Some of the most potentially critical shortages exist with strategic materials such as cobalt and tantalum and tungsten, a scarcity further aggravated by political instability. The probability of continued political upheavals within the next two decades is very high. Such political crises can interrupt the supply of strategic materials, a major concern of many multinationals who must resort to stockpiling as protection from sudden stoppage of supplies.[6]

One might quarrel with the mathematics used in this illustration and the accuracy of known reserves, but even if the projections in Exhibit 8–1 were doubled, there is no question that the availability of resources is, and will continue to be, a major environmental consideration in international marketing with political as well as economic ramifications.

POPULATION

Although not the only determinant, sheer numbers of people are significant in appraising potential consumer demand. Factors such as current population figures, rates of growth, age levels, and rural/urban population distribution are all closely related to demand for various categories of goods.

Exhibit 8–2 illustrates the present population by major areas and the number of years it will take to double the population. Recent estimates indicate there are almost 4.5 billion people in the world. At current growth

---

[6] "How Dependent Are You on Strategic Materials? Firms Should Take Stock," *Business International,* April 24, 1981; and "Are There Physical Limits to Growth?" *The OECD Observer,* September 1979, p. 11.

EXHIBIT 8-2: World population by major areas—1950, 1981, 2000 (years to double and life expectancy)

	1950 (millions)	1981* (millions)	Years to double	Life expectancy, 1981 (years)	2000* (millions)
World	2,513.0	4,492.0	42	62	6,199.0
Africa	219.0	486.0	24	49	828.0
Asia	1,380.0	2,609.0	40	60	3,612.0
North America	166.0	254.0	95	74	290.0
Latin America	164.0	366.0	29	64	608.0
Europe (including USSR)	572.0	754.0	178	72	832.0
Oceania	12.6	23.0	54	69	27.0

* Estimate.
Source: Population Reference Bureáu, 1981 and Statistical Yearbook, UNESCO, 1981, p. i-7.

rates there will be between 6 and 7 billion by the year 2000. Exhibit 8–2 shows dramatically that the population in the underdeveloped parts is going to increase most rapidly. And it is these poor nations that are least able to support such population increases.[7]

Not only is the world's population growing rapidly, but the population density is shifting from the industrial nations of the North to the developing nations of the South. By the end of this century, population in the developed region is expected to increase by about 200 million whereas the developing areas of Africa, Asia, and Latin America are expected to increase by 2 billion. By the year 2000, World Bank predicts over four fifths of the world's population will be concentrated in developing countries.[8]

Rural-urban shifts

In addition to the population increase, there has been a significant population shift from rural to urban areas all over the world. Many of the ramifications of this trend are of direct importance to marketing.

Shifts of population from rural to urban areas are of recent significance. In the early 1800s, less than 3.5 percent of the world's people were living in cities of 20,000 or more and less than 2 percent in cities of 100,000 or more. The real beginning of worldwide urbanization, starting in Europe, came with the Industrial Revolution; by the 1950s, over one fifth (20 percent) of the people of the world lived in cities of 20,000 or more.

Current trends in urban, rural, and total population are illustrated for selected regions in Exhibit 8–3. Regardless of the state of their economic

[7] "If you Live in Bangladesh and Want Some 40 More Years," *Forbes,* July 6, 1981, p. 24; and Carl Haub, Population Reference Bureau, *Population Migration,* June 28, 1981.

[8] Herman G. van der Tak, "A New Look at the Population Problem," *The Futurist,* April 1980, p. 43.

EXHIBIT 8–3: Urban and rural population by major areas of world regions 1950–2000

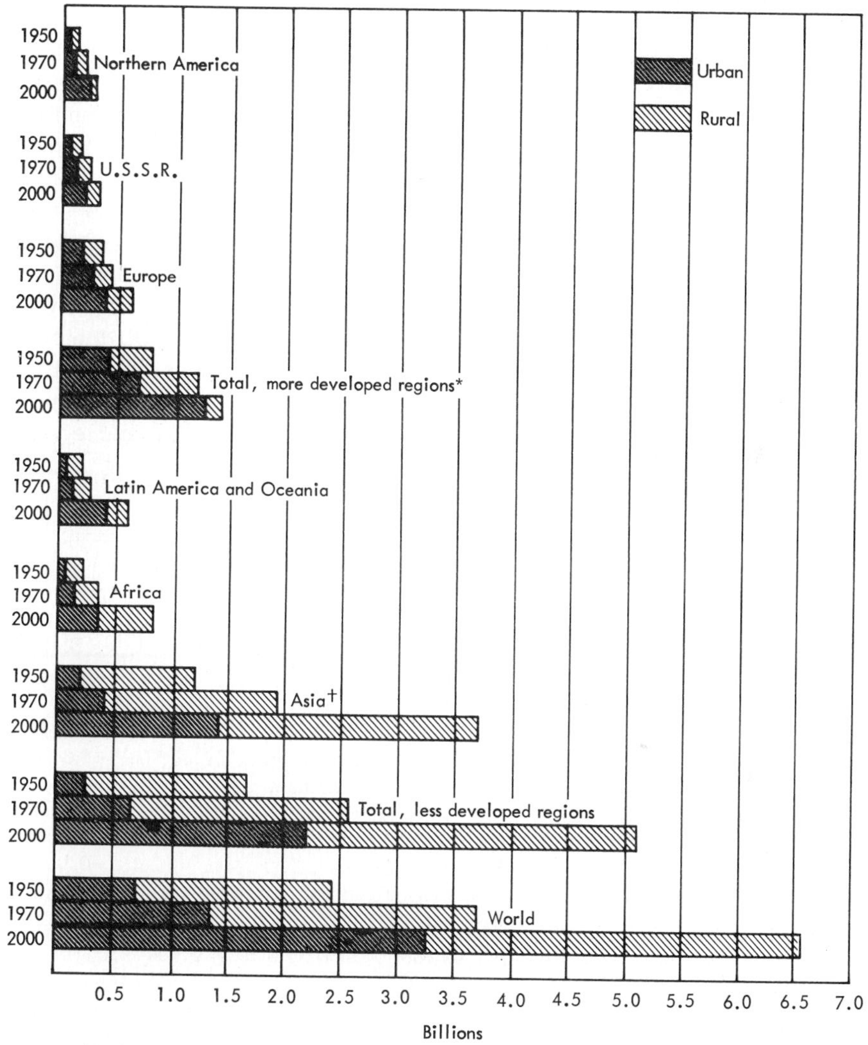

* Includes Japan.
† Excludes Japan.
Source: Adapted from "World Economic and Social Indicators," World Bank Report No. 700/77/04, May/June 1977.

development, the rise in urban population in all regions is extraordinary. Between 1950 and 1975 urban population in the developing countries increased by 311 percent, and it is estimated that between 1975 and 1985 the same countries will have urban population increases of another 155 percent.

By 2000, it is expected that 50 percent of the world's population will live in urban areas compared with the current 36 percent, and that at least 60 cities will have populations of 5 million or more. Present estimates indicate that Mexico City, now the world's third largest city, will be the world's largest with a population of 31 million inhabitants. If current trends continue, within the next 20 years the world will witness a population shift paralleled only once before in history when Europeans left their homes and migrated to North and South America. The growing migration of people from rural to urban areas is largely a result of a desire for greater access to sources of education, health care, and improved job opportunities. However, the reality is that such dreams seldom materialize. The intense migration has led instead to slums populated with unskilled workers living hand to mouth without the most rudimentary elements of water supply, sanitation systems, or adequate food. Many fear that as we approach the year 2000, the bulging cities will become fertile fields for social unrest unless conditions in urban areas are improved. Since most of these increases will be occurring in developing countries, it is anticipated they will face major social and economic problems.

BOX 8–4: The world's 10 fastest-growing areas versus 10 areas with zero population growth

	Annual growth rate (percent)		Annual growth rate (percent)
1. Holy Sea	11.3	1. Faeroe Islands	−0.7
2. Bahrain	10.5	2. Switzerland	−0.4
3. Cocos (Keeling) Islands	10.5	3. Gibraltar	−0.3
4. Western Sahara	8.9	4. West Germany	−0.3
5. United Arab Emirates	8.4	5. East Germany	−0.2
6. Guam	6.2	6. Luxembourg	−0.2
7. Kuwait	6.1	7. Austria	−0.1
8. Quatar	5.7	8. Cyprus	−0.1
9. U.S. Virgin Islands	4.6	9. Turks and Caicos Islands	0.0
10. Ivory Coast	4.3	10. United Kingdom	0.0

Source: *Demographic Yearbook*, 1978 (New York: United Nations, 1979), pp. 98–103.

During this same period it is estimated that the Western industrialized world's population will decline. Birth rates in Western Europe have been decreasing since the early or mid-1960s; women are choosing careers instead of children, and working couples elect to continue a free-spending lifestyle. As a result of these and other contemporary factors, populations in many countries have dropped below the rate necessary to maintain present population levels. For example, West Germany's native population has been falling steadily since 1972 to about 57 million in 1981 and will fall to 52 million by the year 2000. In 1964, the fertility rate was over 2.5, well above the 2.1 replacement rate demographers figure is needed to keep population numbers level over the long run; presently the fertility rate is down to 1.4. The populations of France, Sweden, Switzerland, and Belgium are all expected to begin dropping within a few years. Austria, Norway, Denmark, and several other nations are now at about zero population growth and probably will slip to the minus side in another decade or so.

These trends worry government officials; population decreases do not necessarily produce positive results. The German government has raised family allowances, particularly for second and third children, and substantially liberalized maternity leave pay. Sweden has increased child allowances and lengthened maternity/paternity leaves and the Swedish parliament has ordered a major study of the reasons for recent low fertility rates. Other West European governments have taken similar steps. Many businesses also are beginning to watch demographic developments with concern (see Exhibit 8–4). A spokesman for the Nestlé Company reported they were looking for markets outside Europe because of these trends.

The economic fallout of a declining population has many ramifications. Businesses find their domestic market shrinking for such items as maternity and infant goods, school equipment, and many durables. As a consequence, they must cut production and lay off workers which eventually affects living standards. Europe seems to have a special problem because of the increas-

EXHIBIT 8–4: A comparison of 20 countries

Country	Population	Gross national product per person (U.S. dollars)	Year	Life expectancy (in years) Male	Female
Australia	13,548,472	7,515	1978	67.63	74.15
Belgium	9,650,944	9,025	1978	67.79	74.21
Brazil	92,341,556	1,523	1978	57.61	61.10
Canada	22,992,605	7,572	1978	69.34	76.36
France	52,655,802	7,908	1978	69.73	77.85
Germany FR	60,650,599	9,278	1978	68.99	75.64
India	548,159,652	150	1977	46.40	44.70
Japan	111,939,643	7,153	1978	72.15	77.35
Italy	53,744,736	3,076	1977	68.97	74.88
Netherlands	13,045,785	8,509	1978	72.0	78.40
New Zealand	3,129,383	5,346	1978	68.55	74.60
Norway	3,874,133	7,949	1978	72.31	78.65
Philippines	41,831,045	457	1978	56.90	60.0
South Africa	21,794,328	1,296	1978	56.60	59.40
Sri Lanka	12,689,897	168	1978	64.80	66.90
Sweden	8,208,544	9,274	1978	72.23	78.14
Turkey	40,347,719	873	1975	53.70	53.70
United Arab Emirates	179,126	16,665	1978	51.60	53.80
United Kingdom	55,506,131	4,955	1978	67.81	73.81
United States	203,235,298	8,612	1978	68.77	76.50

Source: *Statistical Yearbook 1979/1980* (New York: United Nations, 1981).

ing percentage of elderly people who must be supported by shrinking numbers of active workers. The elderly require higher government outlays for health care and hospitals, special housing and nursing homes, pension and welfare assistance, but the work force that supports these costs is dwindling. In addition, it is anticipated there will be a shortage of skilled workers in these countries because of decreasing population. In summary, both the trends of increasing population in the developing world with substantial shifts from rural to urban areas, and declining birth rates in the industrialized world will have profound effects on the state of world business and world economic conditions by the year 2000 (see Exhibit 8–5). And although world population may be increasing, multinational firms may see that world markets are decreasing on a relative basis since the monied world is losing numbers and poor nations are gaining numbers. While population numbers are important in marketing, these numbers must have a means to buy to be an effective market.

Opportunities in developing countries

People in former colonial empires, primitive tribes, and more settled communities which have existed in relative isolation and represent more than a billion non-Caucasian peoples are determined to improve their living conditions and share in the opportunities of the world. In a matter of decades, these peoples are seeking and attaining rates of economic growth other

---

EXHIBIT 8–5: The world's largest urban areas (1978) and projections to the year 2000

Rank and urban area (1978‡)		Rank and urban area (2000)	
1. New York–northeastern New Jersey	16,678,818	1. Mexico City (2)*	31,616,000
2. Mexico City	13,993,866	2. Tokyo-Yokohama (3)	26,128,000
3. Tokyo-Yokohama	11,695,150	3. São Paulo (12)	26,045,000
4. Shanghai	10,888,000	4. New York–northeastern New Jersey (1)	22,212,000
5. Los Angeles–Long Beach	10,350,362	5. Calcutta (13)	19,663,000
6. Algiers	9,903,530	6. Rio de Janeiro†	19,383,000
7. Buenos Aires	9,749,000	7. Shanghai (4)	19,155,000
8. Paris	8,547,625	8. Greater Bombay†	19,065,000
9. Moscow	7,909,000	9. Beijing (Peking) (11)	19,064,000
10. Chicago–Gary	7,658,335	10. Seoul (15)	18,711,000
11. Beijing (Peking)	7,570,000	11. Djakarta†	16,933,000
12. São Paulo	7,198,608	12. Cairo-Giza-Imbaba†	16,398,000
13. Calcutta	7,031,382	13. Karachi†	15,862,000
14. London	7,028,200	14. Los Angeles–Long Beach (5)	14,795,000
15. Seoul	6,879,464	15. Buenos Aires (7)	13,978,000

* ( ) = rank in 1978.
† Not in top 15 in 1978.
‡ *Demographic Yearbook*, 1978, 30th Issue (New York: United Nations, Department of Economic and Social Affairs, Statistical Office, 1979), pp. 209–36.

countries have taken centuries to achieve. Population centers that were markets for only the barest necessities of life at the end of World War II are now relatively lucrative markets for industrial goods as well as an increasing variety of consumer goods.

Although absolute numbers of people may not constitute a market, when coupled with rapid economic growth they can produce amazing results. What is occurring in Africa today gives an insight into the future possibilities of such a situation. Nowhere is industry less developed than in Africa; yet a recent United Nations survey estimates that industrial production in Arab, black, and white Africa will double in the next 20 years. Although the industrial base is small and founded primarily on the conversion of agricultural raw materials, the United Nations report noted that Africa was beginning to develop or expand its own metals, machines, chemicals, and textile industries. It is this growth in industrial production that develops the means on which market potential is based.

WORLD TRADE

The basis of world trade can be stated simply as the result of equalizing an imbalance in the needs and wants of a society on one hand and its supply of goods on the other. Countries and societies have demands for many goods which may or may not be available within their own boundaries. Those who have an excess of goods of one kind or another trade for commodities in demand but not economically available or in short supply at home.

Nowhere is this balance of supply and demand more obvious today than with petroleum products. The industrialized world, Europe, Japan, and North America, have inadequate reserves of petroleum (or in the case of the United States, rapidly shrinking reserves), and the highest and most rapidly increasing demand while two thirds of the world's reserves are controlled by a small group of underdeveloped nations. In short, trade is the result of differences among countries. There are at least three reasons countries differ in what they trade for and produce:

1. Differences in culture and skills.
2. Differences in the stage of economic development.
3. Differences in the availability of natural resources.

Differences in people

Different cultural development has provided the people of some countries with skills and talents difficult to duplicate and in demand the world over. The Italians are known for their ability to manufacture stylish shoes, the British for their woolen goods, the Swiss for precision instruments, and the Japanese for well-made automobiles; all products which can be exported and exchanged for products in short supply within their countries. Parisians

EXHIBIT 8–6: Trade of leading 15 world trading countries (in millions of currency)*

Country	Total exports/imports for ranking	Imports			Exports		
		U.S. dollar value of total imports	Dollar value—principal import	Dollar value—sales by leading supplier	U.S. dollar value of total exports	Dollar value—principal export	Dollar value sales to leading customer
United States–Puerto Rico	$396,242	$217,664	Mineral fuels 63,735	Canada 38,458	$178,578	Machines, transport equipment 72,671	Canada 32,176
Federal Republic of Germany	329,287	157,747	Mineral fuels 30,957	Netherlands 19,553	171,540	Machines, transport equipment 77,496	France 21,831
Japan	213,717	110,672	Mineral fuels 45,354	United States–Puerto Rico 20,465	103,045	Machines, transport equipment 58,475	United States–Puerto Rico 26,597
France	205,053	106,994	Machines, transport equipment 23,879	Federal Republic of Germany 19,222	98,059	Machines, transport equipment 35,552	Federal Republic of Germany 16,872
United Kingdom	193,999	102,969	Machines, transport equipment 27,210	Federal Republic of Germany 12,316	91,030	Machines, transport equipment 31,457	Federal Republic of Germany 8,974
Italy	150,212	77,970	Mineral fuels 18,346	Federal Republic of Germany 13,351	72,242	Machines transport equipment 22,089	Federal Republic of Germany 13,662
Netherlands	130,952	67,285	Machines, transport equipment 14,999	Federal Republic of Germany 12,368	63,667	Mineral fuels 11,966	Federal Republic of Germany 19,416
USSR†	122,535	57,773	Machines, nes nonelectric 4,145	German Democratic 54,288	64,762	Crude petro 14,716	German Democratic 5,829

Country	Imports total		Largest import category		Leading supplier	Exports total		Largest export category		Leading customer
Belgium/Luxembourg	116,668	14,715	Machines, transport equipment	13,280	Federal Republic of Germany	56,258	19,169	Basic manufactures	12,637	Federal Republic of Germany
Canada	109,052	25,845	Machines, transport equipment	37,945	United States–Puerto Rico	55,660	16,598	Machines, transport equipment	37,493	United States–Puerto Rico
Switzerland	55,861	7,202	Machines, transport equipment	8,393	Federal Republic of Germany	26,507	8,419	Machines, transport equipment	5,199	Federal Republic of Germany
Sweden	55,728	7,879	Machines, transport equipment	4,948	Federal Republic of Germany	27,240	11,318	Machines, transport equipment	3,178	United Kingdom
Spain	43,335	7,674	Mineral fuels	3,133	Federal Republic of Germany	17,903	5,345	Basic manufactures	2,943	France
Australia	39,037	6,256	Machines, transport equipment	3,779	United States–Puerto Rico	22,605	6,003	Food/live animals	5,207	Japan
Austria	35,737	6,065	Machines, transport equipment	8,570	Federal Republic of Germany	15,483	5,646	Basic manufactures	4,687	Federal Republic of Germany

* Order determined by total $ value of imports and exports.

† 1975 was the last year for which complete data were available. The above information is for 1978 as opposed to 1979 for all other countries. Total imports, exports, and exports/imports are 1979 figures.

Source: *Yearbook of International Trade Statistics* (New York: United Nations Publishing Service, 1980).

have a cultural heritage for producing high-fashion women's clothing which sets style for much of the world. Differences of this nature usually result in world trade.

Differences in economies

The various economies of the world are all at different stages of development with diverse needs and wants. At one end of the scale are many Latin American countries and many African nations all eager for industrialization. They have little or no industry and no means to produce products necessary to meet the industrial needs dictated by their aspirations. The products from highly developed industrial economies are necessary; therefore, they trade with France, the United States, and other industrialized countries for the equipment necessary to create their own industrial base. At the other end of the development scale are nations with mature economies and sizable populations which can afford the luxuries of an affluent society and whose wants have long been satisfied with products from around the world. Many of these products are from lesser developed countries; thus, trade is created.

Economic changes do occur over time and trade patterns shift. For example, 20 years ago Brazil was a net importer of automobiles, today Brazil exports automobiles. In the United States, automobiles were not even included in the top 20 products imported in 1955, by 1980, autos appeared as one of the United States' most important imports. Thus, trade shifts as a result of changes in the economic conditions among trading nations.

Differences in natural resources

Some countries are better endowed than others with natural resources. Most of the tin in the world is found in the tropics, and most of the coffee, which requires a special climate, is grown in just a few countries; yet these products are consumed by most of the world. All countries have wants and needs they cannot gratify domestically; hence, world trade must satisfy these desires. The different bases of world trade are vividly pointed up in Exhibit 8–6.

The United States is the largest world trader. The 1979 figures of dollar value of exports and imports (Exhibit 8–6) show that the value of foreign trade in the United States was $396 billion, up from $203 billion in 1975.

Exhibit 8–7 shows the composition of foreign trade for the United States. Notice that exports are products in which the United States excels either in talent or abundance and that imports are typically raw materials in short supply but vital to the economy or to manufactured goods. Most countries engage in some form of trade, some more than others, as their needs differ.

EXHIBIT 8–7: Composition of U.S. foreign trade (equalizing imbalances)

IMPORTS

Oil, Petroleum Products
Bananas, Spices
Copper, Mercury, Coffee
Mahogany, Chrome, Zinc
Tungsten, Rubber, Hides
and Skins, Tin, Tea
Tungoil, Manganese
Bauxite, Newsprint
Cane Sugar, Pepper
Coconut Oil
Wines and Spirits
Wood Pulp, Diamonds, Nickel, Lead
Manufactured Goods
Semimanufactured Goods
Autos

EXPORTS

APPLES   WHEAT

LUMBER   PAPER AND   BOOKS
              PAPERBOARD
WHEAT   PAINTS
         MEAT   AGRICULTURAL
          SOYBEANS   MACHINERY
CANNED FRUITS   WHEAT
AND VEGETABLES   AUTOMOBILES   STEEL
        MEAT   CORN   AND PARTS
                           COAL
   BEEF   INDUSTRIAL MACHINERY
          PHOTOGRAPHIC
            GOODS   TOBACCO
AIRCRAFT
        PETROLEUM   CIGARETTES
        REFINING
        PRODUCTS   SULFUR   COTTON
                        GOODS
                COTTON
COTTONSEED CAKE   NAVAL STORES
AND MEAL

Original Source: W. S. and E. S. Woytinsky, *World Population and Production* (New York: The Twentieth Century Fund, 1953), p. 183. Revised: *Yearbook of International Trade Statistics* (New York: United Nations Publishing Series, 1980).

WORLD TRADE ROUTES

Major world trade routes have developed between the two most industrialized continents—North America and Europe. It might be said that world trade routes bind the world together, minimizing distance, natural barriers, lack of resources, and the fundamental differences between peoples and economies. Early trade routes were, of course, overland; later came sea routes and, finally, in present times, air routes to connect countries. Regardless of the means of transportation, the main trade routes present a vivid picture of the world's countries attempting to overcome economic and social imbalances created in part by the influence of geography.

The leading sea lanes illustrated in Exhibit 8–8 and world trade figures in Exhibit 8–6 can be compared to show the relationship of the volume of import-export trade and trade route importance. Exhibit 8–8 includes rail

EXHIBIT 8–8:   Surface communications

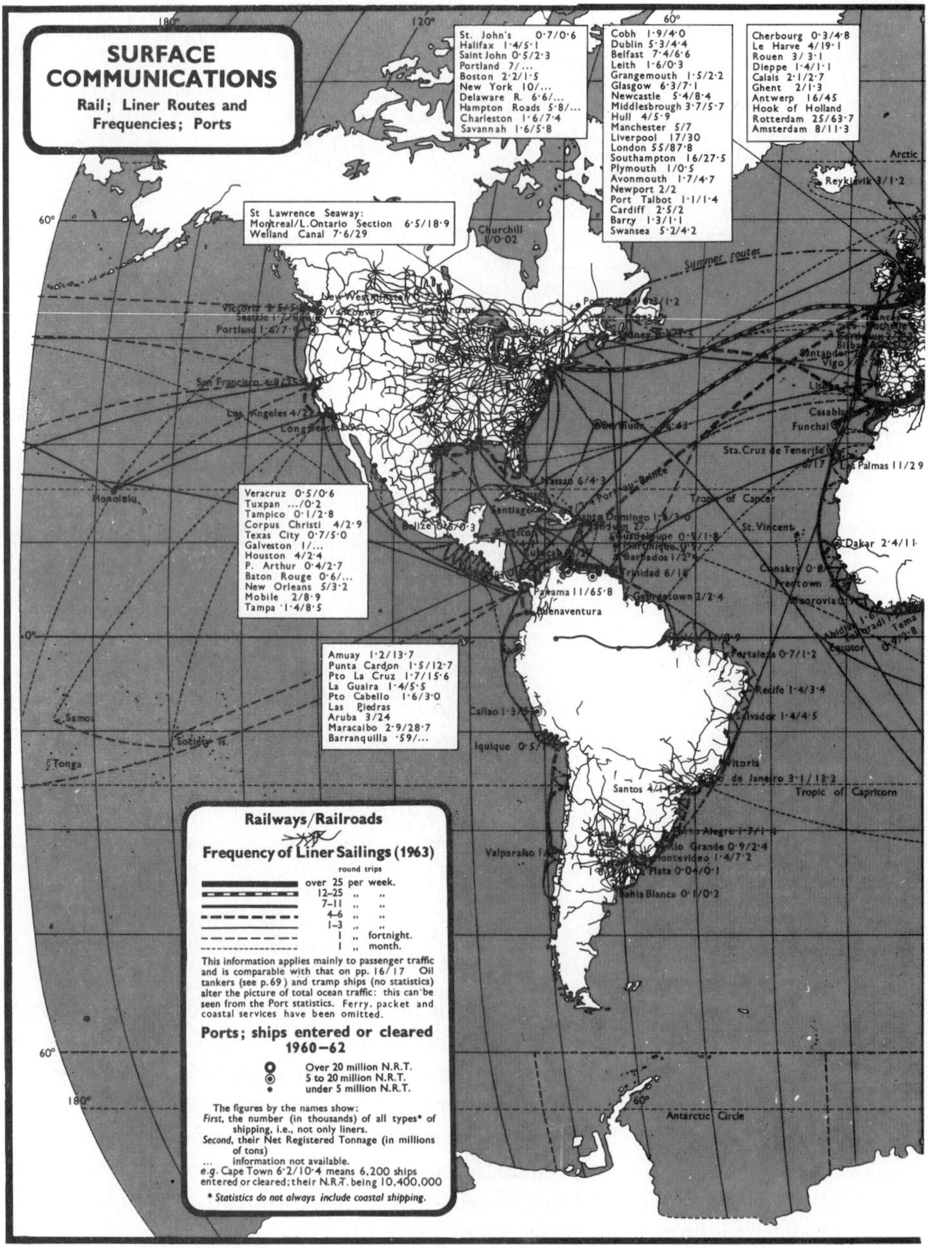

Source: *Oxford Economic Atlas of the World*, 4th ed. Reprinted with permission.

EXHIBIT 8–8 (*concluded*)

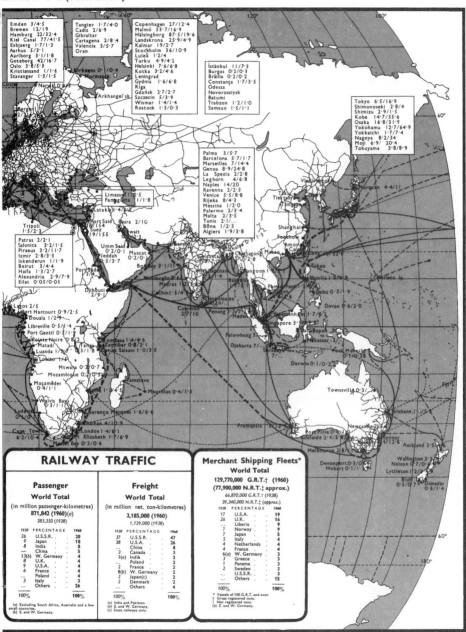

Emden 3/4·5	Tangier 1·7/4·0	Copenhagen 27/12·4
Bremen 12/19	Cadiz 2/6·9	Malmö 33·7/16·9
Hamburg 22/32·4	Gibraltar	Hälsingborg 87·5/19·6
Kiel Canal 77/41·5	Cartagena 2/8·4	Landskrona 25·9/4·9
Esbjaerg 1·7/1·3	Valencia 3/5·7	Kalmar 19/2·7
Aarhus 5/3·1	Oran	Stockholm 36/10·9
Aarlborg 3·1/1·8		Luleå 1·2/4
Goteborg 42/16·7		Turku 4·9/4·2
Oslo 3·8/5·3		Helsinki 7·6/6·8
Kristiansand 1/1·6		Kotka 3·2/4·6
Stavanger 1·3/1·5		Leningrad

İstanbul 11/7·3
Burgas 0·2/0·3
Brăila 0·2/0·2
Constanţa 1·7/3·5
Odessa
Novorossiysk
Batumi
Trabzon 1·2/1·0
Samsun 1·5/1·1

Gydnia 1·6/6·8
Riga
Gdańsk 2·7/2·7
Szczecin 5/3·9
Wismar 1·4/1·4
Rostock 1·3/0·3

Tokyo 6·5/16·9
Shimonoseki 2·8/4
Shimizu 2·9/1·5
Kobe 14·7/55·6
Osaka 16·8/31·9
Yokohama 12·7/64·9
Yokkaichi 1·7/7·4
Nagoya 8·2/34
Moji 6·9/20·4
Tokuyama 3·8/8·9

Palma 3/5·7
Barcelona 5·7/1·7
Marseilles 7/14·4
Genoa 8·9/24·8
La Spezia 2/2·8
Leghorn 4/6·8
Naples 14/20
Ravenna 2/2·3
Venice 5·5/8·8
Rijeka 8/4·3
Messina 1/2·0
Palermo 2/3·4
Malta 2/3·5
Tunis 2/1/...
Bône 1/2·3
Algiers 1·9/3·8

Limassol 1/2·5
Famagusta 1/1·8

Tripoli 1·5/2·3
Port Said 7/... Basra 2/10
Suez 1/54
Kuwait 19/155

Patras 2/2·1
Salonica 3·2/1·5
Piraeus 3·2/1·1·7
Izmir 2·8/3·3
Iskenderun 1/1·9
Beirut 3/4·4
Haifa 1·3/2·7
Alexandria 2·9/7·9
Eilat 0·05/0·05

Umm Said 0·2/0·1
Jeddah 0·2/0·
Muscat 0·2/0·

Djibuti 2/9·1

Lagos 2/5
Port Harcourt 0·9/2·5
Douala 1/2
Libreville 0·5/1·4
Port Gentil 0·7/1·9
Pointe Noire 0·8/2
Matadi 2/...
Luanda 1/7
Lobito 1/7
Mtwana 0·2/0·7
Mozambique 0·2/0·

Moçamēdes 0·4/1·1
Walvis Bay 0·3/1·1

Lüderitz 0·1/0·
Cape Town 6·2/10·4
Port Elizabeth 1·7/6·9
Mossel Bay 0·2/0·6

Mombasa 1·4/4·6
Zanzibar 0·8/2·1
Dar es Salaam 1·0/0·3·5

Mauritius 0·4/1·3

Lourenço Marques 1·6/6·6

Townsville 0·3/...
Darwin 0·1/0·2

Devonport 0·3/0·
Hobart 0·1/1·

Wellington 2/3·3
Nelson 0·7/0·
Lyttleton 1/2·3

Bluff 0·5/0·7
Dunedin 0·5/1·4

Auckland 3·5/1·6

Brisbane 1·7/5·

Newcastle 2/

Sydney

Melbourne 2/8

Adelaide 2·4/5·

Port Pirie 1·4/

Premantle 0·4/...

Singapore 3·4/12·6

Djakarta 7/...

Palembang 3/...

Penang 2·5/10

Colombo 2·5/10

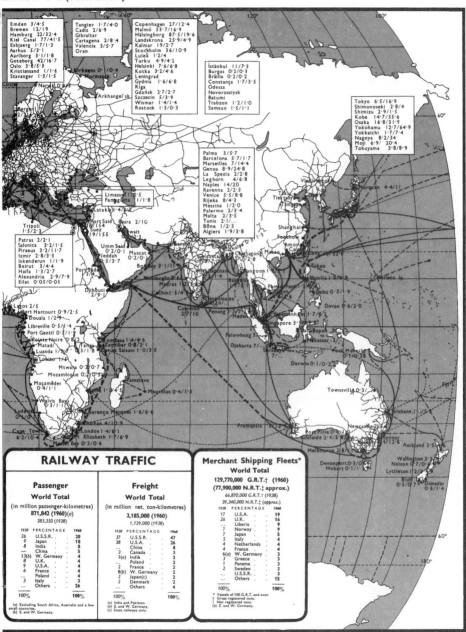

RAILWAY TRAFFIC

Passenger			Freight		
World Total			**World Total**		
(in million passenger-kilometres)			(in million net. ton-kilometres)		
871,842 (1960)(a)			**3,185,000 (1960)**		
383,350 (1938)			1,129,000 (1938)		
1938	PERCENTAGE	1960	1938	PERCENTAGE	1960
26	U.S.S.R.	20	37	U.S.S.R.	47
9	Japan	18	38	U.S.A.	26
8	India	8	...	China	8
—	China	5	3	Canada	3
13(b)	W. Germany	4	3(a)	India	2
8	U.K.	4	...	Poland	2
9	U.S.A.	4	2	France	2
6	France	4	8(b)	W. Germany	2
...	Poland	4	2	Japan(c)	2
3	Italy	3	2	Denmark	2
...	Others	26	...	Others	4
100%		100%	100%		100%

(a) Excluding South Africa, Australia and a few small countries.
(b) E. and W. Germany.

(a) India and Pakistan.
(b) E. and W. Germany.
(c) State railways only.

Merchant Shipping Fleets*
World Total

129,770,000 G.R.T.† (1960)
(77,900,000 N.R.T.‡ approx.)
66,870,000 G.R.T.† (1938)
39,340,000 N.R.T.‡ (approx.)

1938	PERCENTAGE	1960
17	U.S.A.	19
26	U.K.	16
...	Liberia	9
7	Norway	9
7	Japan	5
5	Italy	4
4	Netherlands	4
4	France	4
6(a)	W. Germany	3
3	Greece	3
2	Panama	3
2	Sweden	3
...	U.S.S.R.	3
...	Others	15
100%		100%

* Vessels of 100 G.R.T. and over.
† Gross registered tons.
‡ Net registered tons.
(a) E. and W. Germany.

© Oxford University Press 1972.

as well as sea routes of countries involved in world trade. The most obvious feature is the relationship of industrialization and degree of economic development and the available means of surface communications.

To discuss trade routes and not pay particular attention to air communications would be an oversight. Although airfreight is not extremely important as a percentage of total freight transportation, it is increasing in importance with larger and faster aircraft. For particular commodities (items of high perishability and/or high unit value), it is a major means of transport. A leading airline advertises that it has regularly scheduled cargo flights taking off or landing every 2¼ minutes around the clock and around the globe.

An interesting comparison between surface routes and air routes is air service to the world's less industrialized countries. Although air routes are the heaviest between points in the major industrial centers, they are also heavy to points in less developed countries. The obvious reason is that for areas not located on navigable waters or where the investment in railroads and effective highways is not feasible, air service is often the only answer. Air communications have had the effect of making otherwise isolated parts of the world reasonably accessible.

BOX 8–5: New Zealand, Australia—next door?

Many New Zealand sales are lost because Americans think of Australia and New Zealand as one market and that one Australia-based representative can serve for both, which is about the same air mileage-wise as having one representative for Albuquerque and Pittsburgh. New Zealand is not as close to Australia as many Americans think. Auckland is 1,343 air miles from Sydney (Albuquerque and Pittsburgh are 1,308 air miles apart). Many U.S. firms have granted agency distributor or other representative rights covering New Zealand to companies located in Australia, but the American Consulate in Auckland says many such Australian companies often do not know the New Zealand markets or do not make reasonable efforts to sell the U.S. product there. In addition, shipments incur additional costs by being routed through Australia, and payment complications sometimes ensue because of the different Australian and New Zealand currency values.

Source: "Marketing News," date unknown.

SUMMARY

One British authority admonishes foreign marketers to study the world until "the mere mention of a town, country, or river enables it to be picked out immediately on the map."[9] Although it may not be necessary for the student of foreign marketing to memorize the world map, a prospective

---

[9] Henry Deschampsneufs, *Selling Overseas* (London: Business Publications, Ltd., 1960), p. 46.

international marketer should be reasonably familiar with the world and its climatic and topographic differences. Since geography is an important environmental element, the need for geographical knowledge is greater than being able to discuss the world. For the marketer whose career has been restricted to one country, many of the important marketing characteristics of geography may be completely unknown and thus overlooked when marketing in another country. For someone who has never been in a tropical rain forest with an annual rainfall of at least 60 inches and sometimes more than 200 inches, it is difficult to anticipate the need for protection against high humidity, or to anticipate the difficult problems caused by dehydration in constant 100° plus heat in the Sahara region.

Aside from the simpler and more obvious ramifications of climate and topography there are more complex geographical influences on the development of the general economy and society of a country. In this case, the need for studying geography is to provide the marketer with an understanding of why a country has developed as it has rather than as a guide for adapting marketing plans. In summary, geography is one of the environments of foreign marketing which should be understood and which must be included in foreign marketing plans to a degree commensurate with its influence on marketing effort.

QUESTIONS

1. Study the data in Exhibit 8–1 and briefly discuss the long-term prospects for industrialization of an underdeveloped country with a high population growth and minimum resources.

2. Why study geography in international marketing? Discuss.

3. Pick a country and show how employment and topography affect marketing within the country.

4. Discuss the bases of world trade. Give examples illustrating the different bases.

5. The marketer "should also examine the more complex effect of geography on general market characteristics, distribution systems, and the state of the economy." Comment.

6. The world population pattern trend is shifting from rural to urban areas. Discuss the marketing ramifications.

7. Select a country with a stable population and one with a rapidly growing population. Contrast the marketing implications of these two situations.

8. "The basis of world trade can be simply stated as the result of equalizing an imbalance in the needs and wants of society on one side and the supply and demand of goods on the other." Explain.

9. How do differences in people constitute a basis for trade?

10. ". . . world trade routes bind the world together. . . ." Discuss.

11. Why are air routes so important in less developed countries? Illustrate your answer with examples.

12. What are the marketing ramifications of the population projections for the year 2000 in the developing world?

Case II–1

Starnes-Brenner Machine Tool Company—to bribe or not to bribe

The Starnes-Brenner Machine Tool Company of Iowa City, Iowa, has a small, one-man sales office headed by Frank Rothe in Latino, a major Latin American country. Frank has been in Latino for about 10 years and is retiring this year; his replacement is Bill Hunsaker, one of Starnes-Brenner's top salesmen. Both will be in Latino for about eight months, during which time Frank will show Bill the ropes, introduce him to their principal customers and, in general, prepare him to take over.

Frank has been very successful as a foreign representative in spite of his unique style and, at times, complete refusal to follow company policy when it doesn't suit him. The company hasn't really done much about his method of operation although from time to time he has angered some top company men. As President McCaughey, who retired a couple of years ago, once remarked to a vice president who was complaining about Frank, "If he's making money—and he is (more than any of the other foreign offices), then leave the guy alone." When McCaughey retired, the new chief immediately instituted organizational changes that gave more emphasis to the overseas operations, moving the company toward a truly worldwide operation into which a "loner" like Frank would probably not fit. In fact, one of the key reasons for selecting Bill as Frank's replacement, besides Bill's record as a top salesman, is Bill's capacity as an "organization" man. He understands the need for coordination among operations and will cooperate with the home office so the Latino office can be expanded and brought into the "mainstream."

The company knows there is much to be learned from Frank and Bill's job is to learn everything possible. The company certainly doesn't want to continue some of Frank's practices, but much of his knowledge is vital for continued, smooth operation. Today, Starnes-Brenner's foreign sales account for about 25 percent of the company's total profits, compared with about 5 percent only 10 years ago.

The company is actually changing character from being principally an exporter without any real concern for continuous foreign market representation to worldwide operation where the foreign divisions are part of the total effort rather than "stepchild" operations. In fact, Latino is one of the last operational divisions to be assimilated into the "new" organization. Rather than try to change Frank, the company has been waiting for him to retire before making any significant adjustments in their Latino operations.

Bill Hunsaker is 36 years old with a wife and three children; he is a very good salesman and administrator although he has had no foreign experience. He has the reputation of being fair, honest, and a "straight shooter." Some, back at the home office, see his assignment as part of a grooming job for a top position, perhaps eventually the presidency. The Hunsakers are now settled in their new home after having been in Latino for about two weeks. Today is Bill's first day on the job.

When Bill arrived at the office, Frank was on his way to a local factory to inspect some Starnes-Brenner machines that had to have some adjustments made before being acceptable to the Latino government agency buying them. Bill joined Frank for the plant visit. Later, after the visit, we join the two at lunch.

Bill, tasting some chili, remarks, "Boy! this certainly isn't like the chili we have in America." "No, it isn't, and there's another difference too . . . the Latinos are Americans and nothing angers a Latino more than to have a 'Gringo' refer to the United States as America as if to say that Latino isn't part of America also. The Latinos rightly consider their country as part of America (take a look at a map) and people from the United States are North Americans at best. So, for future reference, refer to home either as the United States, States, or North America, but for gosh sakes not just America. Not to change the subject, Bill, but could you see that any change had been made in those S-27s from the standard model?" "No, they looked like the standard. Was there something out of whack when they arrived?" "No, I couldn't see any problem—I suspect this is the best piece of sophisticated bribe taking I've come across yet. Most of the time the Latinos are more 'honest' about their 'mordidas' than this." "What's a *mordida?*" Bill asks. "You know, *'kumshaw,' 'dash,' 'bustarella,' 'mordida';* they are all the same: a little grease to expedite the action. *'Mordida'* is the local word for a slight offering or, if you prefer, bribe," says Frank.

Bill quizzically responds, "How much bribery does it take to make successful sales anyway?" "Oh, it depends on the situation but it's certainly something you have to be prepared to deal with." Boy, what a greenhorn, Frank thinks to himself, as he continues, "Here's the story. When the S-27s arrived last January, we began uncrating them and right away the 'Jefe' engineer, 'Jefe,' that's the head man in charge, began extra careful examination and declared there was a vital defect in the machines; he claimed the machinery would be dangerous and thus unacceptable if it wasn't corrected. I looked it over but couldn't see anything wrong so I agreed to have our staff engineer check all the machines and correct any flaws that might exist. Well, the 'Jefe' said there wasn't enough time to wait for an engineer to come from the States, that the machines could be adjusted locally, and we could pay him and he would make all the necessary arrangements. So, what do you do? No adjustment his way and there would be an order canceled; and, maybe there was something out of line, those things have been known to happen. But for the life of me I can't see that anything had been done since the machines were supposedly fixed. So, let's face it, we just paid a bribe and a pretty darn big bribe at that—about $200 per machine—what makes it so aggravating is that that's the second one I've had to pay on this shipment."

"The second?" asks Bill. "Yeah, at the border when we were transferring the machines to Latino trucks, it was hot and they were moving slow as blazes. It took them over an hour to transfer one machine to a Latino truck and we had 10 others to go. It seemed that every time I spoke to the dock boss about speeding things up they just got slower. Finally, out of desperation, I slipped him a fistful of pesos and, sure enough, in the next three hours they had the whole thing loaded. Just one of the 'local customs' of doing business. Generally though, it comes at the lower level where wages don't cover living expenses too well."

There is a pause and Bill asks, "What does that do to our profits?" "Runs them down, of course, but I look at it as just one of the many costs of doing business—I do my best not to pay but when I have to, I do." Hesitantly Bill replies, "I don't like it, Frank, we've got good products, they're priced right, we give good service, and keep plenty of spare parts in the country, so why should we have to pay bribes to the buyer? It's just no way to do business. You've already had to pay two bribes on one shipment; if you keep it up, the word's going to get around and you'll be paying at every level. Then all the profit goes out the window—you know, once you start, where do you stop? Besides that, where do we stand legally? Perhaps you've missed all the news back in the States about the United Fruit bribery payment, Japan and Lockheed, the oil companies, laundered money, and so. Congress is mad, countries are mad; in fact, the Foreign Corrupt Practices Act makes paying bribes like you've just paid illegal. I'd say the best policy is to never start; you might lose a few sales but let it be known that there are no bribes; we sell the best, service the best at fair prices, and that's it."

"You mean the Business Practices and Records Act don't you?" Frank asks and continues in a—I'm not really so out of touch—tone of voice, "Didn't Congress soften the old Foreign Corrupt Practices Act?" "Yes, you're right, the law's name and some of the provisions have been changed but what you are doing is still illegal, old law or new," replies Bill.

Oh boy!! Frank thinks to himself as he replies. "First of all, I've heard about all the difficulty with bribing governments, but what I did was just peanuts compared to Japan and Lockheed. The people we 'pay off' are small and, granted, we give good service, but we've only been doing it for the last year or so. Before that I never knew when I was going to have equipment to sell. In fact, we only had products when there were surpluses stateside. I had to pay the 'right' people to get sales and, besides you're not back in the States any longer. Things are just done differently here. You follow that policy and I guarantee that you'll have fewer sales because our competitors from Germany, Italy, and Japan will pay. Look, Bill, everybody does it here; it's a way of life and the costs are generally reflected in the markup and overhead. There is even a code of behavior involved. We're not actually encouraging it to spread, just perpetuating an accepted way of doing business."

Patiently and slightly condescendingly, Bill replies, "I know, Frank, but wrong is wrong and we want to operate differently now. We hope to set up an operation here on a continuous basis; we plan to operate in Latino just like we do in the United States. Really expand our operation and make a long-range marketing commitment, grow with the country!! And, one of the first things we must avoid are unethical. . . ."

Frank interrupts, "But really, is it unethical? Everybody does it, the Latinos even pay mordidas to other Latinos; it's a fact of life—is it really unethical? I think that the circumstances that exist in a country justify and dictate the behavior. Remember man, 'When in Rome, do as the Romans do.' " Almost shouting, Bill blurts out, "I can't buy that. We know that our management practices and techniques are our strongest point. Really all we have to differentiate us from the rest of our competition, Latino and others, is that we are better managed and, as far as I'm concerned, graft and other unethical behavior has got to be cut out to create a healthy industry. In the long run, it should strengthen our position. We can't build our future on illegal and unethical practices."

Frank angrily replies, "Look it's done in the States all the time. What about the big dinners, drinks, and all the other hanky-panky that goes on? Not to mention Gulf Oil, United Fruit, or our own Congress and ABSCAM. How many congressmen went to jail or lost reelection on that one? What is that, if it isn't mordida, the North American way? The only difference is that instead of cash only, in the United States we pay in merchandise and cash." "That's really not the same and you know it. Besides, we certainly get a lot of business transacted during those dinners even if we are paying the bill." "Bull, the only difference is that here bribes go on in the open; they don't hide it or dress it in foolish ritual that fools no one. It goes on in the United States and everyone denies the existence of it. That's all the difference—in the United States we're just more hypocritical about it all.

"Look" Frank continues almost shouting, "we are getting off on the wrong foot and we've got eight months to work together. Just keep your eyes and mind open and let's talk about it again in a couple of months when you've seen how the whole country operates; perhaps then you won't be so quick to judge it absolutely wrong."

Frank, lowering his voice, says thoughtfully, "I know it's hard to take;

probably the most disturbing aspect of dealing with business problems in underdeveloped countries is the matter of graft. And, frankly, we don't do much advance preparation so we can deal firmly with it. It bothered me at first; but, then, I figured it makes its economic contribution, too, since the payoff is as much a part of the economic process as a payroll. What's our real economic role anyway, besides making a profit, of course? Are we developers of wealth, helping to push the country on to greater economic growth, or are we missionaries? Or should we be both? I don't really know, but I don't think we can be both simultaneously, and my feeling is that as the country prospers, as higher salaries are paid, and better standards of living are reached, we'll see better ethics. Until then, we've got to operate or leave and, if you are going to win the opposition over, you'd better join them and change them from within, not fight them."

Before Bill could reply, a Latino friend of Frank's joined them and they changed the topic of conversation.

QUESTIONS

1. Is what Frank did ethical? Who's ethics? Latino's or the United States'?

2. Are Frank's two different payments legal under the Business Practice and Records Act (Foreign Corrupt Practices Act)?

3. Frank seemed to imply that there was a difference between what he was doing and what happened in Japan or with United Fruit. Is there any difference? Explain.

4. Frank's attitude seems to imply that a foreigner must comply with all local customs, but some would say that one of the contributions made by U.S. firms is to change local ways of doing business. Who is right?

5. Should Frank's behavior have been any different had this not been a government contract?

6. If Frank shouldn't have paid the bribe, what should he have done, and what might have been the consequences?

7. What are the company interests in this problem?

8. Explain how this may be a good example of the S.R.C. (self-reference criterion) at work.

9. Do you think Bill will make the grade in Latino? Why? What will it take?

10. How can an overseas manager be prepared to face this problem?

Case II-2

Hot Chip, Inc.—manufacturing joint venture and know-how license

Hot Chip, Inc., is the third largest U.S. manufacturer of certain key transistor parts. It has about 22 percent of the domestic market but has been unsuccessful in its attempts to market its transistor parts in Japan, one of the world's most important markets for the product. In order to surmount this difficulty, it has entered into a joint venture with Japan Manufacturing (JM), one of Japan's largest industrial combines. They have formed a manufacturing joint venture, JZC, using Hot Chip know-how to produce completed transistors. Hot Chip will have 49 percent of the stock and half of the Board of Directors. In return for technology, JM will be responsible for the day-to-day operation of JZC. JM has not been in this particular field, but does manufacture a great deal of electronic equipment. Accordingly, the joint venture company will be operating on know-how licensed by Hot Chip.

Hot Chip is concerned because JZC will have lower manufacturing costs than it has in the United States, and JM and JZC may be sources of disruption to Hot Chip's existing marketing arrangements in Australia, New Zealand, the Philippines, Europe, and the United States. Accordingly, Hot Chip has inserted into the agreement with JM a condition that neither JZC nor JM will export the transistor parts to the United States or other designated markets.

QUESTIONS

1. Discuss the legality of the proposed joint venture under U.S. antitrust law. Be certain to consider all ramifications of the agreement.

2. Review the logic of an alliance with a potential competitor.

Case II–3

When international buyers and sellers disagree*

No matter what line of business you're in, you can't escape sex. That may have been one conclusion drawn by an American exporter of meat products after a dispute with a West German customer over a shipment of pork livers. Here's how the disagreement came about:

The American exporter was contracted to ship "30,000 lbs. of freshly frozen U.S. pork livers, customary merchandisable quality, first rate brands." As the shipment that was prepared met the exacting standards of the American market, the exporter expected the transaction to be completed without any problem.

But when the livers arrived in West Germany, the purchaser raised an objection: "We ordered pork livers of customary merchantable quality— what you sent us consisted of 40 percent sow livers."

"Who cares about the sex of the pig the liver came from?" the exporter asked.

"We do," the German replied. "Here in Germany we don't pass off spongy sow livers as the firmer livers of male pigs. This shipment wasn't merchantable at the price we expected to charge. The only way we were able to dispose of the meat without a total loss was to reduce the price. You owe us a price allowance of $1,000."

The American refused to reduce the price. The determined resistance may have been partly in reaction to the implied insult to the taste of the American consumer. "If pork livers, whatever the sex of the animal, are palatable to Americans, they ought to be good enough for anyone," the American thought.

It looked as if the buyer and seller could never agree on eating habits.

QUESTIONS

1. In this dispute which country's law would apply, that of the United States or of West Germany?

2. If the case were tried in U.S. courts, who do you think would win? In German courts? Why?

---

* Copyright © 1968 by Dun & Bradstreet Publications Corp. Reprinted by special permission from the November 1968 issue of *Business Abroad*.

3. Draw up a brief agreement which would have eliminated the following problems
    before they could occur.

    a. Whose law applies.
    b. Whether the case should be tried in U.S. or German courts.
    c. The difference in opinion as to "customary merchandisable quality."

4. Discuss how S.R.C. may be at work in this case.

Case II–4

Gasselsmann GmbH Mining and Smelting—paying ransom*

Wolf Frankel glanced at the bedside clock as he reached to answer
the telephone. Who could be ringing at 3 a.m.?

"Herr Frankel? It's James Perez. I'm sorry to disturb you but we are supposed to report things like this immediately."

Perez was the second in command in the South American country where
Gasselsmann GmbH, an aluminium smelting and fabricating firm based
in West Germany, mined most of its bauxite. Frankel was the firm's director
of international operations.

Perez explained that Lutz Luneberger, the head of the subsidiary, had
been kidnapped by terrorists.

Frankel was now wide awake. "Go and see what you can do for Frau
Luneberger," he said. "I'll phone our chief of security and get him to fly
out. Have someone meet him at the airport tomorrow. And keep me informed
of developments."

Three days later, Perez phoned Frankel to say that the terrorists had
demanded a ransom. "They want food, medical supplies, and $10 million
in cash or they will kill Luneberger," he said.

The security chief also came on the phone to tell Frankel that the government of the country was proving difficult to deal with and suggesting that
Frankel himself fly out.

As they drove from the airport, Perez told Frankel that a priest had been

* Adapted from "Dilemma and Decision," *International Management,* October 1979, pp.
8–9.

found to act as intermediary with the terrorists. "But first we have a meeting with the minister of state for security," he said.

Frankel knew the minister slightly. He was unprepared, however, for the uncompromising line the man took.

"Although you may talk with these people," the minister said, "there is no question of their demands being met. One cannot compromise with traitors and thugs. You must realize, also, that if your company gives in now, in this part of the world, it will open the flood gates. One cannot afford to be soft with terrorists."

Frankel's meetings with the intermediary were attended by a government representative whose presence inhibited free and frank discussion.

As the weeks passed, Frankel travelled frequently between South America and the corporate headquarters in Dusseldorf. He had as many problems at home as in the field. Some members of the board took a hard line, saying the company should not pay, while others demanded speedier progress. There was also the threat of legal action by the family if the victim was killed.

While attending one of the board meetings, Frankel received a telex from his security man saying that he had arranged direct contact with the terrorists if Frankel wanted to take advantage of it.

Frankel did. He obtained the approval of the board to offer the terrorists a ransom of $1 million if they would drop the request for food and medical supplies, which could not be delivered without the agreement of the government. The money, however, could be transferred through a Swiss bank.

Frankel flew back to South America and after a week of waiting met the terrorist spokesman secretly. At first he did not seem to be making progress, but after hours of talking the terrorists suddenly agreed to the deal.

Frankel was elated. However, when he got back to his hotel he received a phone call from the minister of state, who asked to see him immediately.

The minister said that he knew all about the cash deal. "In this country, nothing is secret for long. I regret that you have gone behind my back in dealing with these people. The government I represent will not allow this deal to go through. Should you attempt to proceed, we will seize your company's assets."

Frankel believed the minister was bluffing. He did not think the government could afford to alienate other international companies with interests in the country. He said as much to the minister.

"That may be," the minister replied. "But remember, we can make life very difficult for you here, from an operating point of view. You will recall, also, that next year your licence to mine and export bauxite comes up for renewal. How would you like to buy your bauxite on the open market?"

That night, Frankel pondered this threat. What should he do? If he paid the money he might save Luneberger's life. But if the company lost its bauxite concession it would cease to be a fully integrated aluminium concern. That could cost a lot more than the $1 million.

If, however, he did not pay, it was practically certain that Luneberger would be killed.

QUESTIONS:

1. How could Frankel save both his colleague and the company?

2. What should the company have done to protect itself against such terrorist acts?

3. What plans could the company make to prepare for any future risks of terrorism?

PART THREE

WORLD MARKET PATTERNS

CHAPTERS:

CASES:

Chapter 9

Researching world markets

The intricacies of international operations and the complexity of the environment within which the international marketer must operate create an extraordinary demand for information. Earlier chapters have illustrated the variety of questions facing the foreign marketing decision maker. Marketing research provides many of the answers that an international marketer must have to develop and successfully execute marketing strategies. Marketing research is the *systematic gathering, recording, and analyzing of data to provide information useful in marketing decision making.* When operating in foreign markets, the need for thorough information as a substitute for uninformed opinion is equally as important as it is in domestic marketing.[1]

International marketing research and *marketing research* are synonymous since research is basically the same whether applied in Hoboken, New Jersey, or Sri Lanka.

Generally, the tools and techniques in foreign and domestic marketing research remain the same, but the environments within which they are applied are divergent, thus creating difficulty. Rather than acquiring new and exotic methods of research, the international marketing researcher must acquire the ability for imaginative and deft application of tried and tested techniques in sometimes totally strange milieus. The mechanical problems of implementing foreign marketing research might vary from country to country, but the overall objectives for foreign and domestic marketing research are basically the same—to answer questions with current, valid information that a marketer can use to design and implement successful marketing programs. Within a foreign environment, the frequently differing emphasis on kinds of information needed, the often limited variety of tools and techniques applicable, and the difficulty in implementing the research process constitute the challenges facing most international marketing researchers.

This chapter deals with the operational problems encountered in gathering information in foreign countries for use by international marketers. Emphasis is on those elements of data generation that usually prove especially

---

[1] For a very complete discussion of marketing research in foreign environments see Susan P. Douglas and C. Samuel Craig, "Marketing Research in the International Environment," in *Handbook of International Business,* ed., Ingo Walter, (New York: John Wiley & Sons, 1982)

troublesome in conducting research in an environment other than the United States. There is also a summary of secondary sources available through public and private agencies, followed by a section on a multinational marketing information system.

BREADTH AND SCOPE OF INTERNATIONAL MARKETING RESEARCH

A basic difference between domestic and foreign market research is the broader scope required for foreign research. Research can be divided into three types based on information needs. These are (1) general information about the country, area, and/or market; (2) specific information used to solve problems arising in advertising, pricing, distribution, and product development; and (3) the forecasting of future marketing requirements by anticipating social, economic, and consumer trends within specific markets or countries. In domestic operations the marketing research department is usually responsible only for the second type, since other departments generally are responsible for such activities as business and economic research.

This difference is reflected in the results of a comparative study of expenditures on research activities between U.S. and Western European firms. Exhibit 9–1 shows that of those topics considered, research to collect general information was ranked first and received 38 percent of the West Europeans' research budget while the U.S. firms spent only 6 percent collecting this type of information. Product research was considered important by both, with U.S. firms ranking it first and West Europeans ranking it second. Another interesting observation is that U.S. firms ranked Syndicated Information (Nielsen studies, etc.) as second in importance, accounting for 23 percent of their research budget, whereas West Europeans spent only 5 percent on this type of information.

In international marketing research, the researcher's activities are frequently much broader than those of a domestic marketer and can involve all types of information essential to conducting business abroad. A foreign market researcher is frequently expected to provide all the information relevant to the question of a firm entering a new market—political stability of the country, cultural attributes, geographical characteristics, market characteristics, and projections of potential economic growth. In addition, a foreign market research department might also be expected to be the source of information necessary to compensate for lack of empathy within a strange environment, probable language deficiencies, and the lack of day-to-day market contact normally maintained in the home market. Sperry Rand Corporation's planning steps call for collecting and assessing data in three major

[2] See Warren J. Keegan, "Multinational Scanning: A Study of the Information Sources Utilized by Headquarters Executives in Multinational Companies," *Administrative Science Quarterly*, September 1974, p. 411.

EXHIBIT 9–1: How U.S. and Western European firms spend research funds*

Types of research project	Western European firms Percent of budget	Rank	United States firms Percent of budget	Rank
General information	38	1	6	5
General market studies				
Trade research studies				
Environmental scanning studies				
Corporate image studies				
Product	36	2	33	1
Product tests				
Package				
Price				
Concepts				
Positioning				
Consumer	12	3	20	3
Advertsing	10	4	18	4
Syndicated information	5	5	23	2
Continuing audits				
(Nielsen, NTMA)				
Warehouse withdrawal data				

* Adapted from Steven E. Permut, "The European View of Marketing Research," *Columbia Journal of World Business,* Fall 1977, exhib. 3, p. 99.

categories: (1) environmental conditions, (2) divisional assessment, and (3) review of strategies. The environmental conditions section includes:

1. Economic. This section includes general data on growth of the economy, inflation, business cycle trends, and the like; profitability analysis for the division's products; specific industry economic studies; analysis of overseas economies; and key economic indicators for the US and major foreign countries.
2. Sociological and political climate. This section is a general noneconomic review of conditions affecting the division's business. In addition to the more obvious subjects, it also covers ecology, safety, leisure time, and their potential impact on the division's business and so on.
3. Overview of market conditions. This section is a detailed analysis of market conditions the division faces by market segment, including international.
4. Summary of the technological environment. This section summarizes the "state of the art" technologically as it relates to the division's business. It too is carefully broken down by product segments.
5. A last section reviews competitors' market shares, methods of market segmentation, products, and apparent strategies on an international scope.[3]

[3] *Corporate External Affairs* (New York: Business International, December 1975), p. 142.

Information of such latitude is necessary for any sound marketing decision. For the domestic marketer, *most* of such information has been acquired after years of experience with a single market, but in a foreign market this basic information must be gathered for every new market.

Once the general information listed is gathered and a position in the market is established, the tasks of a marketing research department in that market become more similar to those of their domestic counterparts. There are many checklists of information or "intelligence" necessary for sound international marketing. While the checklists vary in content, they all agree that an adequate foreign market information system should include "foreign factors" which vary from country to country or from area to area within a country. Some foreign factors to be considered are:

1. Competition (U.S., local, and third country).
2. Transportation.
3. Electrical characteristics.
4. Trade barriers.
5. Economic environment.
6. Business philosophies.
7. Legal systems.
8. Social customs.
9. Languages.
10. Political climate.
11. Consumption patterns.
12. Relevant cultural patterns.
13. Religions and moral backgrounds.
14. Philosophies of major political parties.

In essence, the checklists include the foreign-based uncontrollable factors as discussed in Chapter 1. Naturally, problem-oriented marketing information is also included in any list of international marketing research activities.[4]

There is a basic difference between information ideally needed and that which is collectable and/or used. There are many firms engaged in foreign marketing that do not make decisions with the benefit of the information listed. Cost, time, and the human elements are critical variables. Some firms have neither the appreciation for information nor adequate time or money for implementation of research. As a firm becomes more committed to foreign marketing and the cost of possible failure increases, greater emphasis is placed on research. Consequently, an international firm is or should be engaged in the most sophisticated and exhaustive kinds of research activities, while the infrequent or part-time exporter has less concern even though there is need for market information.

In addition to the degree of need, the cost of research must be considered.

---

[4] See also "201 Checklist: Decision Making in International Operations," Business International Corporation, 1980, p. 114.

When the cost of research, the business risk involved, and the probable profit potential of markets are incompatible, a decision for research may lead to minimal commitment. The cost of original research can outweigh the value of information gathered and must be evaluated accordingly. Less costly secondary information is also available; for example, many export agencies provide information as part of their services to exporters. This type of secondary data is a part of the total research effort. When considering foreign-market information needs, two questions arise: (1) what are the procedures and problems of collecting data? and (2) who should collect the data?[5]

THE RESEARCH PROCESS

The quality of information available to a foreign marketer can vary from uninformed opinion to thoroughly researched fact. The purpose of marketing research is to provide the most accurate and reliable data possible within *limits imposed by time, cost, and the present state of the arts.* The measure of a competent researcher is the ability to utilize the most sophisticated and adequate techniques and methods available within these limits. Research conducted for any problem is always a compromise, but the final results should be the most accurate and reliable within the conditions just described. A systematic and orderly approach to research should follow the same pattern whether applied in Boulder, Colorado, or Bogota, Colombia. A research program should include the following steps:

1. Define the research problem and establish research objectives.
2. Determine the sources of information to fulfill the research objectives.
3. Gather the relevant data from secondary and/or primary sources.
4. Analyze, interpret, and present the results.

The researcher's task is to execute each of these steps with maximum objectivity and accuracy within the limitations of cost, time, and ability.

Although the steps in a research program are similar for all countries, variations and problems in implementation will occur because of differences in cultural and economic development. Subsequent sections will illustrate some frequently encountered problems of the international market researcher. It must be emphasized that these problems vary from country to country. While the problems of research in England or Canada may be similar to those in the United States, research in Germany, South Africa, or Mexico may offer a multitude of very different and difficult distinctions from one another. These distinctions become apparent with the first step in the research process—formulation of the problem.

---

[5] For an interesting report on the state of marketing research in Europe, see Steven E. Permut, "The European View of Marketing Research," *Columbia Journal of World Business,* Fall 1977, p. 94.

DEFINING THE PROBLEM AND ESTABLISHING
RESEARCH OBJECTIVES

The first step in the research process is to define the research problem and establish specific research objectives. The major difficulty here is translating the business problem into a research problem with a set of specific, researchable objectives.[6] This initial stage of research frequently goes amiss because of improper definition. Researchers often embark on the research process with only a vague comprehension of the total problem.

The first step in research is more critical in foreign markets since unfamiliarity with the environment tends to cloud problem definition. Researchers either fail to anticipate the influence of the local culture on the problem or fail to identify the self-reference criterion[7] and treat the problem definition as if it were in the researcher's home environment. Frequently, a student of international marketing will read of a foreign business failure seemingly from a simple error and wonder why the company did not conduct research. In many of those cases, research was conducted, but the questions asked were more appropriate for the U.S. market than for the foreign one. Isolating the self-reference criterion is one of the more crucial steps in the problem formulation stage of international marketing research.

Other difficulties in foreign research stem from failure to establish problem limits broad enough to include all relevant variables. Information on a far greater range of factors is necessary in order to offset the unfamiliar cultural background of the foreign market. Consider proposed research concerning consumption patterns and attitudes about hot milk-based drinks. In the United Kingdom, hot milk-based drinks are considered to have sleep-inducing, restful, and relaxing properties, and are traditionally consumed prior to bedtime. Conversely, people of Thailand drink the same milk-based drinks in the morning on the way to work and see them as being invigorating, energy-giving, and stimulating. If one's only experience is the United States, the picture is further clouded since hot milk-based drinks are frequently associated with cold weather either in the morning or evening and for different reasons at each time of day. Thus the market researcher must be certain that the problem definition is sufficiently broad to cover the whole range of response possibilities.[8]

Once the problem is adequately defined and research objectives established, the researcher must determine the availability of information needed. If the data are available—if they have been collected by some other agency, the researcher should then consult these secondary sources. If no data are available, or the secondary sources appear inadequate, it will be necessary to begin the collection of primary data.

---

[6] For a discussion of problem formulation, see Chapter 7 in Harper W. Boyd et al., *Marketing Research,* (Homewood, Ill.: Richard D. Irwin, 1981), pp. 202–04.

[7] See Chapter 1 for discussion of this concept.

[8] Charles S. Mayer, "The Lessons of Multinational Marketing Research," *Business Horizons,* December 1978, p. 8.

PROBLEMS OF THE AVAILABILITY AND USE OF SECONDARY DATA

The breadth of many foreign marketing research studies and the marketer's unfamiliarity with a country's basic socioeconomic data results in considerable effort being placed on using secondary data. Unfortunately, these data are not as available in foreign markets as in U.S. markets. The U.S. government provides comprehensive statistics for the United States periodic censuses of U.S. population, housing, business, and agriculture have been taken, in some cases, for over 100 years. Current estimates or gross national product and other key U.S. economic indicators, as well as special studies and compendiums of available statistics, are readily available. Commercial sources, trade associations, management groups, and state and local governments also provide the researcher with additional sources of detailed U.S. market information.

Few foreign countries can match data available in the United States. Data collection in many countries only recently has been started. However, data collection is improving substantially through the efforts of organizations

---

BOX 9–1: Ten countries which have gone the longest without a census or population survey

1.	Oman	No census ever.
2.	Qatar	No census ever.
3.	Laos	No census ever; last estimate 1958.
4.	N. Korea	No information available.
5.	San Marino	September 28, 1947; enumerated population 12,100.
6.	Bolivia	September 5, 1950; it is estimated that the population of Bolivia has more than doubled since then.
7.	People's Republic of China	June 30, 1953 (scheduled, 1982); enumerated population 582,603,417. Although censuses have been held since 1953, they are considered inaccurate. In rural areas of China ancestor worship is so strong that it is common practice to retain the names of clan members on official registers after they die.
8.	Andorra	November, 1954; the population of Andorra has quadrupled since, and is now over 26,000.
9.	Guinea	October 1954–April 1955; reported population 2,570,000—considered a gross underestimation.
10.	Zaire	May 1955–February 1958.

Notable also-rans include Nigeria, which has held four censuses since 1952, but none has been considered accurate enough to allow publication of the results; and Saudi Arabia, which held a census in 1962–63, but the results were repudiated by the government. (Another census was held in September 1974, but the official results have not been made public.)

Sources "World Population: Recent Demographic Estimates for the Countries and Regions of the World" (Washington, D.C.: U.S. Bureau of the Census, International Statistical Programs Center, 1975); and Meyer Zitter and Edith McArthur, "Census Bureau International Programs," *American Demographics,* February 1982, p. 31.

such as the United Nations and the Organization for Economic Cooperation and Development (OECD). As a country becomes more involved in international business, a greater interest in basic data and better collection methods develop.

There are generally three critical shortcomings regarding secondary data on foreign markets. First is the paucity of detailed data on many market areas. Until the United Nations began collecting world economic data, little more than rough estimates were available.

Detailed data on the numbers of wholesalers, retailers, manufacturers, and facilitating services are unavailable for many parts of the world as, surprisingly enough, are data on population and income. This appears to be true for even the more developed nations.

A second problem relates to the reliability of some of the available secondary data. Official statistics are sometimes too optimistic, reflecting national pride rather than practical reality. Further, business statistics can be adversely affected by the tax structure and fear of the tax collector. Many Latin American and Far Eastern countries are particularly prone to be both overly optimistic and unreliable in reporting relevant economic data about their countries. As one researcher noted, Saudi Arabian statistics are almost as fluid "as the nation's shifting sands." An American survey team verified that 60 million frozen chickens had been imported into Saudi Arabia in 1975 although official figures reported only 10 million. A Japanese company found that 40,000 air conditioners had actually been imported but official figures were underestimated by 30,000 units.[9] Whether errors of such magnitude are intentional or simply the result of sloppy record-keeping is not always clear.

In the case of the European Community (EC), tax policies can affect the accuracy of reported data. Production statistics are frequently inaccurate because these countries collect taxes on domestic sales. Thus, companies have been known to shave their production statistics a bit to match the sales reported to tax authorities. Conversely, foreign trade statistics may be blown up slightly because each country in the EC grants some form of export subsidy. Obviously, for a marketer who relies on secondary data as a basis for forecasting or estimating market demand, errors of this type are critical.

Researchers should always have a healthy degree of skepticism about secondary data regardless of the source. The economics department of the respectable Organization of Economic Cooperation and Development (OECD) is one of the world's oldest sources of multinational economic data. For the most part, OECD data are among the most accurate to be found; yet it sometimes has been criticized for adjusting forecasts to the official line of its member governments. In fact, several years ago it was charged

---

[9] John F. Maloney, "In Saudi Arabia, Sands, Statistics Can Be Shifty," *Marketing News*, July 2, 1976, p. 6.

that economic reports were so heavily weighed in favor of its wishful thinking government members that an economic upturn was being forecast when in fact world economic conditions were already reflecting a downturn. In this incident, the OECD research staff was able to resist pressures so that accurate data were ultimately reported.

A third problem involves the comparability and currency of available data. In the United States, current sources of reliable and valid estimates of socioeconomic factors and business indicators are readily available. In other countries, especially less developed, data can be many years out of date, as well as having been collected on an infrequent and unpredictable schedule. Naturally, the rapid change in socioeconomic features being experienced in many of these countries makes the problem of currency a vital one. Further, even though many countries are now gathering reliable data,

---

BOX 9–2:   International data: Caveat emptor

The statistics used . . . are subject to more than the usual number of caveats and qualifications concerning comparability than are usually attached to economic data. Statistics on income and consumption were drawn from national-accounts data published regularly by the United Nations and the Organization for Economic Cooperation and Development. These data, designed to provide a "comprehensive statistical statement about the economic activity of a country," are compiled from surveys sent to each of the participating countries (118 nations were surveyed by the UN). However, despite efforts by the UN and the OECD to present the data on a comparable basis, differences among various countries concerning definitions, accounting practices, and recording methods persist. In Germany, for instance, consumer expenditures are estimated largely on the basis of the turnover tax, while in the United Kingdom, tax-receipt data are frequently supplemented by household surveys and production data.

Even if data-gathering techniques in each country were standardized, definitional differences would still remain. These differences are relatively minor except in a few cases; for example, Germany classifies the purchase of a television set as an expenditure for "recreation and entertainment," while the same expenditure falls into the "furniture, furnishings, and household equipment" classification in the United States.

While income and consumption expenditures consist primarily of cash transactions, there are several important exceptions. Both income and expenditures include the monetary value of food, clothing, and shelter received in lieu of wages. Also included are imputed rents on owner-occupied dwellings, in addition to actual rents paid by tenants. Wages and salaries, which make up the largest share of consumer income, include employer contributions to social security systems, private pension plans, life and casualty insurance plans, and family allowance programs. Consumer expenditures include medical services even though the recipient may make only partial payment; if, however, the same services are subsidized wholly by public funds, the transaction is listed as a government rather than a consumer expenditure.

Expenditures, as defined by both the UN and the OECD, include consumption outlays by households (including individuals living alone and private nonprofit organizations. The latter include churches, schools, hospitals, foundations, fraternal organizations, trade unions, and other groups which furnish services to households free of charge or at prices that do not cover costs.

Source: David Bauer, "The Dimensions of Consumer Markets Abroad," *The Conference Board Record,* reprinted with permission.

there are generally no historical series with which to compare the current information.

A related problem is the manner in which data are collected and reported. Too frequently, data are reported in different categories or in categories much too broad to be of specific value. As an example, Germany classifies the purchase of television sets as an expenditure for "recreation and entertainment," while the same item in the United States is classified as "furniture, furnishings, and household equipment." Italians, on the other hand, group all conceivable types of electrical welding equipment including spare parts, welding electrodes, and other welding equipment and accessories under one heading. If a company was interested in establishing a trend or demand for a single product like spot welders, it would be almost impossible to use the Italian statistical grouping as a basis of projection.

A later section in this chapter will deal specifically with sources of secondary data on foreign markets. The possibility of the shortcomings just discussed should be considered when using any source of information even though many countries have the same high standards of collection and preparation of data generally found in the United States. Data from secondary sources from any country (including the United States) must be checked and interpreted carefully. As a practical matter, the following questions should be asked in order to effectively judge the reliability of data sources:

1. Who collected the data? Would there be any reason for purposely misrepresenting the facts?
2. For what purpose were the data collected?
3. How were they collected? (methodology)
4. Are the data internally consistent and logical in light of known data sources or market factors?

In general, the availability and accuracy of recorded secondary data increase as the level of economic development increases. To be sure, there are many exceptions; India is at a lower level of economic development than many Latin American countries, but has more accurate and complete development of government-collected data.

Fortunately, more interest in collecting quality statistical data arises as countries realize the value of extensive and accurate national statistics for orderly economic growth. This interest to improve the quality of national statistics has resulted in remarkable improvement in availability of data over the past 20 years.

SOURCES OF SECONDARY DATA

For almost any marketing research project, an analysis of available secondary information is a useful and inexpensive first step. Although there are information gaps, particularly for detailed market information, the situation on data availability and reliability has rapidly improved through the 1970s.

Data collection and publication programs of public and private sources are being revised with such frequency that a comprehensive list of sources would be impractical for this text. Instead, the principal agencies that collect and publish information useful in international business are presented, with some notations of selected publications.

U.S. government

The U.S. government actively promotes the expansion of U.S. businesses into international trade. In the process of keeping the U.S. business informed of foreign business opportunity, the U.S. government generates a considerable amount of general and specific market data for use by international market analysts. Although information is available from a number of agencies of the U.S. government, the principal source of information is the Department of Commerce which makes its services available to U.S. business in a variety of ways. First, information and assistance are available either through personal consultation in Washington, D.C., or through any of the field offices of the Department of Commerce located in key cities in the United States. Second, the Department of Commerce works closely with trade associations, chambers of commerce, and other interested associations in providing information, consultation, and assistance in developing international commerce. Third, the Department publishes a wide range of information which is available to interested persons at nominal cost.

The principal publications of the Department of Commerce relating to international business are as follows:

1. *Foreign Trade Report,* FT 410; U.S. exports—commodity by country. The FT 410 provides a statistical record of shipment of all merchandise from the United States to foreign countries, including both quantity and dollar value of these exports to each country during the month covered by the report. Additionally, it contains cummulative export statistics from the first of the calendar year. From this report you can learn which of more than 150 countries have bought any of more than 3,000 U.S. products. By checking the FT 410 over a period of 3 or 4 years, it can be determined which countries have the largest and most consistent markets for products.

2. *International economic indicators;* quarterly reports providing basic data on the economy of the United States and seven other principal industrial countries. Statistics included are gross national product, industrial production, trade, prices, finance, and labor. This report measures changes in key competitive indicators and highlights economic prospects and recent trends in the eight countries.

3. *Market share reports;* an annual publication prepared from special computer runs to show U.S. participation in foreign markets for manufactured products during the last 5-year period. The 88 reports in a country's series

represent import values for U.S. and eight other leading suppliers and the U.S. percentage share for about 900 manufactured products.

4.   *International marketing information series;* publications that focus on foreign market opportunities for U.S. suppliers. This series is designed to assemble under a common format a diverse group of publications and reports available to the U.S. business community. The following publications are made available on a continuing basis under this program:

a.   Global market surveys. Extensive foreign market research is conducted on target industries and target business opportunities identified by the Commerce Department. Findings are developed into global market surveys. Each survey condenses foreign market research conducted in 15 or more nations into individual country market summaries.

b.   Country market sectoral surveys. In-depth reports covering the most promising U.S. export opportunities in a single foreign country. About 15 leading industrial sectors usually are included. Surveys currently available deal with Brazil, Nigeria, Venezuela, Indonesia, Iran, and Japan.

c.   Overseas Business Reports (OBR); reports which provide basic background data for business people who are evaluating various export markets or are considering entering new areas. They include both developing and industrialized countries.

d.   Foreign economic trends and their implications in the United States. This series gives in-depth reviews of current business conditions, current and near-term prospects, and the latest available data on the gross national product, foreign trade, wage and price indexes, unemployment rates, and construction starts.

e.   Business America (formerly Commerce America). The Department of Commerce's principal periodical, a weekly news magazine, which provides an up-to-date source of worldwide business activity covering topics of general interest and new developments in world and domestic commerce.

5.   *Trade Opportunities Program (TOP).* Overseas trade opportunities, private and government, are transmitted to the TOP computers through various American embassies and councils. U.S. business firms can indicate the product or products they wish to export, types of opportunities desired (direct sales and representation) in countries of interest. The TOP computer matches the foreign buyer's agent's or distributor's product interest with the U.S. subscriber's interest. When a match occurs, a trade opportunity notice is mailed to the U.S. business subscriber.

In addition to the above publications, the Department of Commerce provides a host of other information services. Exhibit 9–2 will provide the reader with a fairly good indication of the kinds of information available through the Department of Commerce.

Besides the material available through the Department of Commerce, consultation and information are available from a variety of other U.S. agen-

EXHIBIT 9–2:

FAST — MATCH

A quick, easy way to match your
international business requirements
to the appropriate government
programs or services designed to
satisfy those needs

IF YOU ARE SEEKING
INFORMATION REGARDING ➡

USE ⬇

	Potential markets	Market research*	Direct sales leads	Agents/distributors	License	Credit analysis	Financial assistance	Risk insurance	Tax incentives
Foreign Trade Statistics (FT–410)	•								
Global Market Surveys	•	•							
Foreign Market Reports	•	•							
Market Share Reports	•	•							
Foreign Economic Trends	•	•							
Business America	•	•	•	•	•				
Commercial exhibitions	†	†	•	•	•				
Overseas Business Reports (OBR)		•							
Overseas Private Investment Corporation		•					•	•	
Commerce Business Daily			•						
New Product Information Service			•	•	•				
Trade Opportunity Program (TOP)			•	•	•				
Industry trade lists			•	•	•				
Special trade lists			•	•	•				
Export Mailing List Service (EMLS)			•	•	•				
Agent/Distributor Service (ADS)				•					
World Traders Data Reports (WTDR)						•			
Export–Import Bank							•	•	
Foreign Credit Insurance Assoc. (FCIA)								•	
Domestic International Sales Corporation (DISC)							•		•

* Foreign trade outlook market profiles; industry trends; distribution and sales channels;
transportation facilities; local business practices and customs; investment criteria; import
procedures and trade regulations; and industrial property rights.

† Research material developed regarding a planned exhibition and released to support
promotional activities. Cost of services may be obtained from Commerce District Offices.

cies. For example, the Department of State, Bureau of the Census, and
the Department of Agriculture can provide valuable assistance in the form
of services and information for an American business engaged in international operations.[10]

International organizations

A number of international organizations, particularly those formed since
World War II, provide information and statistics on international markets.

[10] For more specific detail, see *Export Marketing for Smaller Firms*, 3d. ed. (Washington,
D.C.: Small Business Administration, August 1981), Appendix 2, pp. 109–23.

The *Statistical Yearbook,* an annual publication of the United Nations, provides comprehensive social and economic data for more than 250 countries around the world. Many regional organizations, such as the Organization for Economic Cooperation and Development (OECD), Pan American Union, and the European Economic Community publish information statistics and market studies relating to their respective regions.

Governments of foreign countries

Most of the industrially developed nations of the world and many of the underdeveloped nations actively promote the collection and dissemination of market information and statistics. Information about such publications is available from each country's consulate-general.

Chambers of commerce

In addition to government and organizational publications, many foreign countries maintain chamber of commerce offices in the United States that function as a type of permanent trade mission. These foreign chambers of commerce generally have research libraries available and are knowledgeable regarding further sources of information on specific products or marketing problems. There are also American chambers in most major trading cities of the world. Often the American Chamber of Commerce in Paris can give more current information and lists of potential business contacts in France than are available from any other source. A listing of chambers of commerce and other government and nongovernment agencies can be found in *A Directory of Foreign Organizations for Trade and Investment Promotion* published by the U.S. Department of Commerce. The United Chamber of Commerce publication *Foreign Commerce Handbook: Basic Information and a Guide to Sources* is an excellent reference source for foreign trade information.

Trade, business, and service organizations

Foreign trade associations are particularly good sources of information on specific products or product lines. For example, *Self-Service 1970* was published by the International Self-Service Organization in three languages. Besides a survey of international self-service operations, it includes a bibliography and membership list. Many associations perform special studies or continuing services in collecting comprehensive statistical data for a specific product group or industry. Although some information is proprietary in nature and available only to members of an association, nonmembers frequently have access to it under certain conditions. Membership lists which provide valuable up-to-date lists of potential customers or competitors are often available to anyone requesting them, and a listing of foreign trade associations is usually annotated at the end of a specific *Trade List*.

Foreign service industries also supply valuable sources of information useful in international business. Service companies—such as commercial and investment banks, international advertising agencies, foreign-based research firms, economic research institutes, foreign carriers, shipping agencies, and freight forwarders—generally regard the furnishing of current, reliable information as part of their service function. The banking industry in foreign countries is particularly useful as a source of information on current local economic situations. The Chase Manhattan Bank in the United States periodically publishes a newsletter on such subjects as the European Common Market. There are several good independently published reports on techniques, trends, forecasts, and other such current data.[11] Many foreign banks publish periodic or special review newsletters relating to the local economy, providing a firsthand analysis of the economic situation of specific foreign countries. For example, the Kretiet Bank in Brussels published *Belgium, Key to the Common Market* and the Banco National Commercio Exterior in Mexico published *Mexico Facts, Figures, Trends*. While these publications are sometimes available without charge they usually must be translated.

A number of research agencies specializing in detailed information on foreign markets have developed in the past few years. Their services are available either on a subscription basis for an entire series or in specific series relating to an individual foreign country. A listing of commercial and investment banks in foreign countries, as well as a fairly detailed list of special-purpose research institutes, can be found in *The Europa Yearbook*.

PROBLEMS OF GATHERING PRIMARY DATA

When there are no adequate sources of secondary data, the market researcher must collect primary data. The problems in foreign primary-data collection are different from those in the United States only in degree. The most significant factor affecting the success of a survey hinges on the willingness of the respondent to provide the desired information, or the ability to articulate what he or she knows, that is, the ability of the researcher to get an unwilling respondent to provide correct and truthful information.

Cultural differences offer the best explanation for the unwillingness or the inability of many to respond to research surveys. For instance, in some countries the husband not only earns the money but dictates exactly how it is to be spent. Since the husband controls the spending, it is he and not the wife who should be questioned to determine preferences and demand for many consumer goods. In such a situation, not only might the

---

[11] An excellent information service is *Business International*, which also publishes *Business Europe, Business Asia, Business Latin America*, and *Business China*.

researcher not properly identify the "correct" source of information but may also find varying degrees of unwillingness to answer personal or gender-related inquiries.

Unwillingness to respond

Citizens of many countries do not feel the same legal and moral obligations to pay their taxes as we do in the United States. Tax evasion is an accepted practice for many and a source of pride for the more adept. Where such an attitude exists, taxes are arbitrarily assessed by the government and anyone asking questions about income, personal possessions, or any topic from which tax assessment could be inferred, is immediately suspected of being a tax agent and provided with incomplete or misleading information. One of the problems reported by the government of India in a recent population census was the underreporting of tenants by landlords trying to hide the true number of people living in houses and flats. The landlords had been subletting accommodations illegally and were concealing their activities from the income tax department.[12]

The European business person has traditionally been much more concerned with competitive secrecy than a U.S. counterpart. In the United States, publicly held corporations are compelled by the SEC to disclose certain operating figures on a periodic basis. In Europe, such information is seldom if ever released and then most reluctantly. Attempts to enlist the cooperation of a number of European merchants in setting up a store sample for shelf inventory and sales information ran into strong resistance because of suspicions and a tradition of competitive secrecy. The resistance was overcome by the researcher's willingness to approach the problem step by step. As the retailer gained confidence in the researcher and realized the value of the data gathered, more and more necessary information was provided. Besides the reluctance of businesses to respond to surveys, local politicians in underdeveloped countries may interfere with studies in the belief they might be subversive and must be stopped or hindered. A few moments with local politicians can prevent days of delay.

In some cultures, women would never consent to an interview by a male or any stranger. A French-Canadian woman does not like to be questioned and is likely to be reticent. She prefers privacy for herself and her family. In some societies, a man would certainly consider it beneath his dignity to discuss shaving habits or brand preference in personal clothing with anyone; and most emphatically not with a female interviewer. There is also growing resistance to surveys everywhere because of the misuse of interviewing by door-to-door salespeople who claim to be doing marketing research when, in fact they are selling household items.

---

[12] Peter Niesewand, "India Overcrowding Worse Than Thought," *The Guardian,* March 13, 1981.

The paucity of available information may also stem from the inability of the respondent to articulate the answer. The ability to express attitudes and opinions about any product depends on the respondent's ability to recognize the usefulness and value of such a product. It is difficult for a respondent to formulate needs, attitudes, and opinions about goods whose use may not be understood, which have never been available, or which are not in common use within the community. In fact, it may be impossible for someone who has known only iceboxes to express accurate feelings or provide any reasonable information about purchase intentions, likes, or dislikes concerning electric refrigerators. Under these circumstances, the creative capabilities of the foreign marketing researcher undergoes thorough testing.

BOX 9–3: Telephone survey in Cairo

Neither Cairo nor Tehran—one with a population of 8 million, the other with nearly 5 million—has a telephone book. In some cities in Saudi Arabia, streets have no names and houses have no numbers—posing interesting questions about how to bill and collect [or conduct a field survey]. In Oman, business people hire small boys to sit at the phone all day, trying to get a line and then dialing, over and over, in mostly futile efforts to complete a few calls. Planes from Cairo to Athens are crowded with business people making the trip in order to place international calls from Athens hotels. . . . With around 250,000 lines for a population of 8 million, the system [in Cairo] is virtually useless during business hours. Anyone lucky enough to get a line then probably wouldn't be in Cairo in the first place.

Source: Walter Guzzardi, "The Great World Telephone War." Reprinted from the August 1977 issue of *Fortune Magazine* by special permission; © 1977 Time, Inc.

Although cultural differences may make survey research more difficult to conduct, it is not impossible. In some communities, it is necessary to enlist the aid of locally prominent people to open otherwise closed doors; in other situations, professional people and local students have been used as interviewers because of their knowledge of the market. As with most of the problems of collecting primary data, the difficulties are not insurmountable to a researcher aware of their existence.

Sampling in field surveys

The greatest problem of sampling stems from the lack of adequate detail of universe characteristics and available lists from which to draw meaningful samples. If current, reliable lists are not available, sampling becomes much more complex and generally less reliable. In many countries, telephone directories, cross-index street directories, census tract and block data, and detailed social and economic characteristics of the universe are not available on a current basis if at all. The researcher has to estimate characteristics and population parameters, sometimes with little basic data on which to build an accurate estimate.

To add to the confusion, in some South American, Mexican, and Asian cities, street maps are unavailable and in some Asian metropolitan areas, streets are not identified nor are houses numbered. In contrast, one of the easier aspects of research in Japan is that names and addresses are normally available from the local *Inhabitants Register,* compiled by the city or town government.[13]

The adequacy of sampling techniques are also affected by a lack of detailed social and economic information. Without an age breakdown, for example, the researcher can never be certain of a representative sample requiring an age criterion, since there is no basis of comparison with the age distribution in the sample. Although a lack of detailed information does not prevent the use of sampling, it does make it more difficult. In place of probability techniques, many researchers in such situations rely on convenient samples taken in market places and other public gathering places. The danger in that solution comes because of differences in the respondents found at public gathering places. Due to the practice of Purdah, shopping mall interviews in Saudi Arabia would produce an all-male sample.[14]

The effectiveness of various methods of commmunications (mail, telephone, and personal interview) in surveys is limited. In many countries, telephone ownership is extremely low, making telephone surveys virtually worthless unless the survey is intended to cover only the wealthy. In Sri Lanka fewer than 3 percent of the residents have telephones and those who do are the wealthy. Even if the respondent has a telephone, the researcher may still not be able to complete a call. It is estimated that in Cairo, 50 percent of the telephone lines can be out of service at the same time, and 75 percent of all dialed calls fail to get through on the first attempt.[15]

Inadequate mailing lists and poor postal service are more problems for the market researcher using the mail to conduct research. In Nicaragua, delays of weeks in delivery are not unusual, and expected returns are lowered considerably because a letter can be mailed only at a post office. In addition to potentially poor service within countries, there is also the extended length of time required for delivery and return when a mail survey is conducted from another country. Surface delivery can require three weeks or longer between some points on the globe, and although airmail reduces this time drastically, it also increases costs considerably.

Adequate lists and population detail may be critically short in some countries, but not everywhere. There are countries where every adult is required by law to register and provide detailed socioeconomic data. In many European countries, as well as in Japan, voter lists, police registration lists, and

---

[13] Andrew Watt, "A Day in the Working Life of a Japanese Interviewer Shows Some Similarities to U.S. and Some Differences," *Marketing News,* May 15, 1981, sect. 2, p. 12.

[14] David C. Pring, "American Firms Rely on Multinational Research Suppliers to Solve Marketing Problems Overseas," *Marketing News,* May 15, 1981, sect. 2, p. 2.

[15] "Cairo's Telephone System Improves," *World Business Weekly,* February 16, 1981, p. 19.

tax records are available for research. In Sweden, the government annually publishes a blue book which lists the incomes of every person in Sweden.

Cross-cultural studies tend to highlight the differences used in marketing research in other countries. To complete a cross-cultural study done on perceived risk in the United States and Mexico, differences in survey methods, respondent selection, and interviewing technique were required.[16] In the U.S. portion of the study, a telephone "criss-cross directory" was used to identify income areas from which streets were randomly selected; then, from the selected streets, one household was randomly picked for a telephone interview. Mexico does not have a comparable source such as a criss-cross directory and it is estimated that 60 percent or more of the upper-middle and upper class families in the city have unlisted telephone numbers. And since Mexican respondents are also reluctant to give information to strangers over the telephone, the research had to be designed differently. First, local, knowledgeable professionals were hired to identify upper-middle and upper class residential sections of the city; from these sections, a sample of blocks was randomly chosen, and interviewers were instructed to begin at a randomly selected corner of each block to contact every third house for an interview.

The adaptations necessary to complete the cross-national study described serve as good examples of the need for resourcefulness in international marketing research. However, growing evidence indicates that insufficient attention has been given to nonsampling errors which leads to the unreliability of data gathered in cross-national research.[17]

Language and comprehension

The most universal survey sampling problem in foreign countries is the language barrier. Differences in idiom and the difficulty of exact translation create problems in eliciting the specific information desired and in interpreting the respondent's answers. The obvious solution of having questionnaires prepared or reviewed by someone fluent in the language is frequently overlooked. In one such case, a German respondent was asked the number of "washers" (washing machines) produced in West Germany for a particular year; the reply reflected the production of the flat metal disc instead of washing machines.

The researcher cannot assume that a translation into one language will suffice in all areas where that language is spoken. Such was the case in a translation done in Mexico for the author. When the author was in Mexico and requested a translation of the word *outlet,* as in "retail outlet," to be

---

[16] Robert J. Hoover, Robert T. Green, and Joe Saeger, "A Cross-National Study of Perceived Risk," *Journal of Marketing,* July 1978, pp. 102–08.

[17] Harry L. Davis, Susan P. Douglas and Alvin J. Silk, "Measure Unreliability: A Hidden Threat to Cross-National Marketing Research?", *Journal of Marketing,* Spring 1981, pp. 98–108.

BOX 9–4: Stumble in Japan or do marketing research first

If you are going to do business in another culture, you must know your market. Marketing research would have helped avoid most of the problems these companies had.

The baby powder company that fretted about the relatively low demand for baby powder until it did some research on how the Japanese live. In their small homes, mothers fear powder will fly around and get into their spotlessly clean kitchens. The company had to settle for selling its product in flat boxes with powder puffs so the mothers could apply it sparingly. Adults won't use it at all. They wash and rinse themselves before soaking in hot baths—after which powder makes them feel dirty again.

The cake mix company that designed a mix to be prepared in electric rice cookers which all the Japanese have rather than ovens which few have. The product flopped. Why? The Japanese take pride in the purity of their rice which they thought would be contaminated by cake flavors. It was like asking an English housewife to make coffee in her teapot.

One company that was ready to launch a new peanut-packed chocolate bar aimed at giving teenagers quick energy during their cramming season for exams found out in time that a Japanese old wives' tale held that eating chocolate with peanuts can give you a nosebleed. The product was never marketed.

Source: From "Learning How to Please the Baffling Japanese," *Fortune*, October 5, 1981, p. 122.

---

used in Venezuela, it was read by Venezuelans to mean an electrical outlet, an outlet of a river into an ocean, and the passageway into a patio. Needless to say, the responses were useless although interesting.

Literacy poses yet another problem; in some less developed countries with low literacy rates, written questionnaires are completely useless. Within countries, too, the problem of dialects and different languages can make a national questionnaire survey impractical. In India there are 14 official languages and considerably more unofficial ones. One report on marketing research in Taiwan points out,

> student interviewers from the universities are often mainland Chinese who have not learned Taiwanese. While they are able to converse effectively in many sections of the larger cities, they are ineffective in most other areas of Taiwan. . . . In addition to the Taiwanese and Mandarin languages, there are small groups speaking Cantonese Chinese, and about 150,000 mountain-dwelling aborigines with their own language. . . . A systematic sampling of the entire population of Taiwan with its diverse languages would require a well-trained, multilingual staff of interviewers. Such a staff is extremely difficult to acquire.[18]

One suggestion designed to deal with semantic problems in question-naires is to use "back translation," that is, have material translated from

---

[18] Roman R. Andurs, "Marketing Research in a Developing Nation, Taiwan: A Case Example," *University of Washington Business Review,* Spring 1969, p. 43. Reprinted with permission.

one language into another language then have a third party translate it back into the original. This pinpoints misinterpretations and misunderstandings before they reach the public. A soft drink company wanted to use a very successful Australian advertising theme, "Baby, it's cold inside," in Hong Kong. They had the theme translated from English into Cantonese by one translator and then retranslated by another from Cantonese into English where the statement came out, "Small Mosquito, on the inside it is very cold." Although "small mosquito" is the colloquial expression for small child in Hong Kong, the intended meaning was lost in the translation.[19]

Because of cultural and national differences, confusion can just as well be the problem of the researcher as the respondent. One classic misunderstanding which occurred in a *Reader's Digest* study of consumer behavior in Western Europe resulted in the report that France and West Germany consumed more spaghetti than did Italy. This rather curious and erroneous finding resulted from a question which asked about purchases of "packaged and branded spaghetti." Italians buy their spaghetti in bulk while the French and West Germans buy branded and packaged spaghetti. Since the Italians buy little branded or packaged spaghetti, the results underreported spaghetti purchases by Italians. However, the real question is what the researcher wanted to find out. Had the goal of the research been to determine how much branded and packaged spaghetti was purchased, the results would have been correct. However, since the goal was to know about total spaghetti consumption, the data were incorrect. Researchers must always verify that they are asking the right question.[20]

BOX 9–5: Hanged or suspended—it's a matter of translation

Be sure that your English original is as clear and unambiguous as possible. An American executive based abroad received a cable about his daughter, a college student in the States: "Daughter hanged for crimes committed in youth." Traced through various translations, the original turned out to be: "Daughter suspended for minor offense." Make the distinction between your hanging and your suspension clear to your translators.

Source: Ms. Donnella Ruiz, *Business America Colorado*, January 1982, p. 7.

One authority warns that even if a phenomenon is similar in different cultures it may manifest itself differently. Consider the concept of affection, an idea frequently expressed in advertising campaigns. While all peoples display some form of affection, the exact form affection takes in different

---

[19] Lee Adler and Charles S. Mayer, "Meeting the Challenge of Multinational Marketing Research," *Multinational Product Management Proceedings* (Cambridge, Mass.: American Marketing Association/Management Science Research Institute Workshop, August 1976, Report No. 76–110), p. xvi–13.

[20] Charles S. Mayer, "The Lessons of Multinational Research," *Business Horizons*, December 1978, p. 11.

cultures will be substantially different.[21] Thus, questions formulated to measure affection can lead to confusion if they are not properly written to reflect the cultural bias.

Modifications in marketing research methods must be made to obtain the desired information for decision making, but the quality of results need not be slighted. Indeed, the reason for modification is to ensure results that will be usable even though methods of application are different. It is the modifications that give the assurance that full communication occurs, which after all is the "cornerstone of a good survey."

PROBLEMS IN ANALYZING AND INTERPRETING
RESEARCH INFORMATION

Once data have been collected, the final step is the analysis and interpretation of findings in light of the stated marketing problem. Both secondary and primary data collected by the market researcher are subject to the many limitations just discussed. In any final analysis, the researcher must take into consideration these factors and, despite their limitations, produce meaningful guides for management.

The meaning of words, the consumer's attitude toward a product, the interviewer's attitude, or the interview situation can each distort research findings. Just as culture and tradition influence the willingness to give information, they also influence the information given. Accepting information at face value in foreign markets is an imprudent practice. Newspaper circulation figures, readership and listenership studies, retail outlet figures, and sales volume can all be distorted through local business practice. To cope with such disparities, the foreign market researcher must possess three talents to generate meaningful marketing information.

First, the researcher must possess a high degree of cultural understanding of the market in which research is being conducted. In order to analyze research findings social customs, viewpoints, semantics, current attitudes,

---

BOX 9–6:   Industry statistics?

Considerable confusion arises, for example, when the prescribed product categories overlap: If the Dutch product classifications for the printing industry specify one group comprising "printed matter for advertising purposes" and another comprising "calendars," where should the million-guilder printing job for the Royal Dutch Shell calendars be reported? One printing company explained. "To balance it off, we reported one way one year and the other way the next."

Source: "European Market Research: Hide and Seek," *Sales Management*, vol. 102, no. 3, p. 46.

---

[21] Robert T. Green and Phillip D. White, "Methodological Considerations in Cross-National Consumer Research," *Journal of International Business Studies*, Fall/Winter 1976, p. 83.

and business customs of a society or a subsegment of a society must be clearly understood.

Second, a creative talent for adapting research findings is necessary. A researcher in foreign markets often flies by the seat of the pants and is called on to produce results under the most difficult circumstances. Ingenuity and resourcefulness; willingness to use "catch as catch can" methods to get facts; patience; a sense of humor; and a willingness to be guided by original research findings even when they conflict with popular opinion or prior assumptions are all considered prime assets in foreign marketing research.

Third, a skeptical attitude in handling both primary and secondary data is helpful. It might be necessary to check a newspaper pressrun over a period of time to get accurate circulation figures, or deflate or inflate reported consumer income in some areas by 25 to 50 percent on the basis of observable socioeconomic characteristics.

These essential capabilities suggest that a foreign marketing researcher should be a foreign national or should be advised by a foreign national who can accurately appraise the data collected in light of the local environment, thus validating secondary as well as primary data.

ESTIMATING MARKET DEMAND

In assessing current product demand and forecasting future demand, reliable historical data are required. As previously noted, the quality and availability of secondary data frequently are inadequate; nevertheless, estimates of market size must be attempted in order to plan effectively. Despite limitations, there are approaches to demand estimation usable with minimum information. The success of these approaches relies on the ability of the researcher to find meaningful substitutes or approximations for the needed economic and demographic relationships. To illustrate, some of the necessary but frequently unavailable statistics for assessing market opportunity and estimating demand for a product are current trends in market demand. When the desired statistics are not available, a close approximation can be made using local production figures plus imports with adjustments for exports and current inventory levels. These data are more readily available because they are commonly reported by international organizations such as the United Nations. One researcher suggests that if exports, imports, and inventory levels are relatively constant over time, production alone will "mirror consumption trends"[22] and thus can be used as a basis for estimating market growth. Once approximations for sales trends are established, the historical series can be used as the basis for projection of growth.

---

[22] For a very complete discussion of estimating demand in East Europe see: A. Coskun Samli, "An Approach for Estimating Market Potential in East Europe," *Journal of International Business,* Fall/Winter, 1978, p. 49.

In any straight extrapolation, however, the estimator assumes that the trends of the immediate past will continue into the future. In a rapidly developing economy, extrapolated figures may not be valid and must be adjusted accordingly.

Another possible technique is to estimate by *analogy*. This assumes that demand for a product develops in much the same way in all countries as comparable economic development occurs in each country. First, a relationship must be established between the item to be estimated and a measurable variable in a country which is to serve as the basis for the analogy. Once a known relationship is established, the estimator then attempts to draw an analogy between the known situation and the country in question. For example, suppose a company wanted to estimate the market growth potential for a beverage in Country X, for which it had inadequate sales figures, but the company had excellent beverage data for neighboring Country Y. In Country Y it is known that per capita consumption increases at a predictable ratio as per capita gross domestic product (GDP) increases. If per capita GDP is known for Country X, per capita consumption for the beverage can be estimated using the relationships established in Country Y. Caution must be used with analogy since the method assumes that factors other than GDP which affect consumption are similar in both countries, such as the same tastes, taxes, prices, selling methods, availability of products, consumption patterns, and so forth. Despite the apparent drawbacks to analogy, it is useful where data are limited.

Income elasticity, which measures the relationship between personal or family income changes and demand for a product, can be used in market-demand forecasting. In income elasticity ratios, the sensitivity of demand for a product to income changes is measured. The elasticity coefficient is determined by dividing the percentage change in the quantity of a product demanded by the percentage change in income. With a result of less than one, it is said that the income-demand relationship is relatively inelastic and, conversely, if the result is greater than one, the relationship is elastic. As income increases, the demand for a product increases at a rate proportionately higher than income increases. For example, if income coefficient elasticity for recreation is 1.20, it implies that for each 1 percent change in income the demand for recreation could be expected to increase by 1.2 percent; or if the coefficient is 0.8, then for each 1 percent change in income, demand for recreation could be expected to increase only 0.8 percent. The relationship also occurs when income decreases, although the rate of decrease might be greater than when income increases. Income elasticity can be very useful, too, in predicting growth in demand for a particular product or product group.

The major problem of this method is that the data necessary to establish elasticities may not be available. However, in many countries income elasticities for products have been determined and it is possible to use the analogy method described above (with all the caveats mentioned) to make estimates for those countries. Income elasticity measurements only give an indication of change in demand as income changes and do not provide the researcher with any estimate of total demand for the product.

As is the case in all the methods described in this section, income elasticity measurements are no substitute for original market research when it is economically feasible and time permits. As more adequate data sources become available, as would be the situation in most of the economically developed countries, more technically advanced techniques like multiple regression analysis or input-output analysis can be used.[23]

RESPONSIBILITY FOR CONDUCTING MARKETING RESEARCH

Depending on size and degree of involvement in foreign marketing, a company in need of foreign market research can rely on an outside foreign-based agency or on a domestic company with a branch within the country in question. It can conduct research using its own facilities or employ a combination of its own research force with the assistance of an outside agency.

Traditionally, the information function has been part of the export manager's job. As both the interest and investment in foreign opportunities increase, the probability of costly errors in foreign business operations increases, and a more organized and systematic method of providing reliable answers to key questions is required.

In many companies, an executive is specifically assigned the research function in foreign operations; they select the research method and work closely with foreign management, staff specialists, and outside research agencies. Other companies maintain separate research departments for foreign operations or assign a full-time research analyst to this activity. For many companies, a separate department is too costly; the diversity of markets would require a large department to provide a skilled analyst for each area or region of international business operations. For these reasons, some companies elect the alternative of parceling out specific marketing research tasks as staff assignments, often employing a marketing technician for support of such staff assignments.

A trend toward decentralization of the research function is apparent. In terms of efficiency, it appears that having "your person in Havana" provides

---

[23] For a more complete description of the techniques discussed here as well as a discussion of a variety of other techniques, see any standard text in sales forecasting and the following. John D. Daniels, Ernest W. Ogram, Jr., and Lee H. Radebaugh, *International Business: Environments and Operations* (Reading, Mass.: Addison-Wesley Publishing, 1979), pp. 330–38; Stefan H. Robock, Kenneth Simmonds, and Jack Zwick, *International Business and Multinational Enterprises* (Homewood, Ill.: Richard D. Irwin, 1977), pp. 377–95; Reed Moyer, "International Market Analysis," *Journal of Marketing Research,* November 1968, pp. 353–60. For an excellent series of articles on international business and forecasting, see *The Columbia Journal of World Business,* Winter 1976. The entire issue is devoted to forecasting.

information more rapidly and accurately than a staff research department. The obvious advantage to decentralization of the research function is that control of the research function rests in hands closer to the market. Field personnel, resident managers, and customers generally have a more intimate knowledge of the subtleties of the market and an appreciation of the diversity which characterizes most foreign markets. The disadvantage of decentralized research management is possible ineffective communications with staff-level executives.

Independent research agencies can be used in conjunction with a firm's own research personnel or as a substitute for a formal research staff. Most major U.S. advertising agencies and many research firms have established multiple branch offices around the world. International business consulting and research firms have shown corresponding increases in activity and a broader range of available services. There also has been a healthy growth in foreign-based research and consulting firms. A significant increase in the activity of international advertising groups, international management associations, newsletters, and association bulletins provide for an interchange of ideas between internationally oriented researchers.

A study of practices among EC companies concluded that the availability of qualified marketing research agencies outside the United States had increased substantially in the last 15 to 20 years and that companies rely more on these agencies to collect data for decision making. The study also indicated there has been a substantial increase in the gathering of research data, especially as a market for particular products shifted from a seller's to a buyer's market. Whether a company utilized an outside agency to conduct research or whether the research was conducted by a domestic research division depend primarily on the kind of product concerned. For consumer nondurables, 58 percent of the companies interviewed indicated they relied on Common Market advertising agencies, and 42 percent relied on research staffs within the local subsidiary for research assistance. For consumer durables, however, 67 percent of the respondents used the marketing research staff located in the United States headquarters for conducting research. Again, in the case of consumer durables, there was heavier reliance on marketing research agencies for conducting research than on advertising agencies. The difference between consumer nondurables and consumer durables in utilization of advertising versus marketing research agencies and utilization of local versus home staff is probably attributable to the cultural implications of nondurable versus durable consumer goods. Nondurables seem to be affected more by the peculiarities of local culture, thereby requiring more local, on-the-spot cultural expertise in the marketing research activity.[24] Involvement with outside agency support can vary from total reli-

---

[24] Dagfinnmoe Hansen and J. J. Boddewyn, *American Marketing in the European Common Market* (Cambridge, Mass.: Marketing Science Institute, Report No. 76–107), August 1976, pp. 92–94.

ance on the agency to selective use for specific problems when competency is needed in unfamiliar countries.

MULTINATIONAL MARKETING INFORMATION SYSTEMS

Increased marketing activity by domestic and multinational firms has generated not only more data but a greater awareness of its need. In addition to the changes in the quantity and type of information needed, there has been an increase in competent agencies (many of them subsidiaries of U.S. marketing research firms) whose primary functions are to gather data. As firms become established, and their information needs shift from those necessary to make initial market investment decisions to those necessary for continuous operation, there is a growing demand for continuous sources of information both at the country operational level and at the worldwide corporate level. However, as the abundance of information increases, it reaches a point of "information overload" and requires some systematic method of interpreting and analyzing data.[25]

A company shift from decisions involving market entry to those involved in managing and controlling a number of different growing foreign markets requires greater emphasis upon *a continuous system designed to generate, store, catalogue, and analyze information from sources within the firm and external to the firm for use as the basis of worldwide and country-oriented decision making.* In short, companies have a need for a *Multinational Marketing Information System* (MMIS).

Conceptually, a MMIS embodies the same principal as any information system, that is, an interacting complex of persons, machines, and procedures designed to generate an orderly flow of relevant information,[26] to bring all the flows of recorded information into a unified whole for decision making.[27] The only differences from a domestic marketing information system are (1) scope—a MMIS covers more than one country—and (2) in levels of information—a MMIS operates at each country level with perhaps substantial differences among country systems and at a worldwide level encompassing an entire international operation. The system (see Exhibit 9–3) includes a subsystem for each country designed for operational decision making— a country-level marketing information system; each country system also provides information to a multinational marketing information system designed to provide for corporate control and strategic long-range planning decisions. In developing a MMIS, it is necessary to design an adequate MIS for each

---

[25] E. D. Jaffe, "Multinational Marketing Intelligence: An Information Requirement Model," *Management International Review* 19, no. 2 (1979), pp. 53–60.

[26] See Philip Kotler, *Principles of Marketing* (Englewood Cliffs, N.J.: Prentice-Hall, 1980), p. 136.

[27] John A. Howard, *Marketing Management*, 3d ed. (Homewood, Ill.: Richard D. Irwin, 1973), p. 145.

EXHIBIT 9–3:

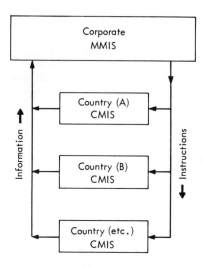

country/market.[28] Because of the vast differences that occur among a company's various markets, each country/market MIS will probably have different data requirements. Once an MIS is set for each country/market, then an overall MMIS for the worldwide operation is designed. Each level of management has substantially different data needs since country/market systems are designed to provide information for day-to-day operations while the MMIS is concerned with broader issues of control and long-range strategic planning. However, the country/market MIS data are used not only for daily operations but are ultimately transmitted to the MMIS to be included in overall planning decisions. Some of the most challenging tasks facing the developer of the MMIS are determining the kinds of data and the depth of detail necessary and analyzing how it should be processed. This implies that models for decision making have been thought through and are sufficiently specific to be functional.

An MMIS can be designed as a basic system which provides only a source of information or as a highly sophisticated system that includes specific decision models. Experience has shown that success is greater when a company begins with a basic system and continues perfecting it to the desired level of sophistication.

In the development of any information system, there are some problems that can be avoided with the proper approach. It is important to appreciate that the same market information system cannot serve all levels of management. As discussed earlier, this is especially true for a MMIS since top management at worldwide corporate levels needs information to make strate-

---

[28] For further discussion of MIS development see Philip Kotler, *Marketing Management: Analysis Planning and Control,* (Englewood Cliffs, N.J.: Prentice-Hall, 1980).

BOX 9–7:   Better check with all competitors

Quite often multinational corporations considering investing in a particular country or region will do some preliminary market research and then dispatch an executive or a team of people on an inspection tour. Local leaders are contacted and conferences held with government officials and businessmen. After surveying the political landscape for several days—even weeks—company representatives return home to apprise senior management of their impressions. This grand tour technique tends to suffer from an overdose of selective information.

A Swiss pharmaceutical company, on the recommendations of its grand tourists, constructed an $8 million manufacturing plant in one Southeast Asian country. Carefully camouflaged from the visiting team and, hence, missing from its market assessment was a powerful but "hidden competitor," the politically sanctioned black market in legitimate drugs, established to supplement the low salaries of government bureaucrats. The Swiss company's failure to take into account this important competitor (with almost a 20 percent market share) resulted in excess capacity and depressed earnings.

Source: R. J. Rummel and David A. Heenan, "How Multinationals Analyse Political Risk," *Harvard Business Review*, January/February 1978, pp. 68–69.

---

gic and control decisions while country-level management needs information for operational decisions. Another problem to avoid is a plethora of detail and *too* broad a range of information: too much information is as bad as too little, and information overload is one of the most frequent reasons given for the nonuse of an information system. The decision maker needs an information system designed to reduce masses of raw data into usable forms. Finally, unless familiar with the scope of the marketing problem, a decision maker may be unable to appreciate the kind of information needed and therefore be unable to use the more sophisticated data a country MIS can provide. Adequate familiarization with the output of a system is mandatory or it may be rejected in its entirety as overwhelming. The masses of raw data generated as a company becomes more involved in a country market, and as a multinational company's breadth of operation expands, require intelligent analysis and interpretation to arrive at more competitive decisions. An MMIS could be the answer.

SUMMARY

The basic objective of the market research function is providing management with information for more accurate decision making. This objective is the same for domestic and international marketing. In foreign marketing research, however, achieving that objective presents some problems not encountered on the domestic front.

Consumer attitudes about providing information to a researcher are culturally conditioned. Foreign market information surveys must be carefully designed to elicit the desired data and at the same time not offend the respondent's sense of privacy. Besides the cultural and managerial constraints involved in gathering information for primary data, many foreign markets have inadequate and/or unreliable bases of secondary information.

Three generalizations can be made about the direction and rate of growth of marketing research in foreign marketing. First, there is an increasing awareness and acceptance on the part of both home-based and foreign management of the importance of marketing research's role in decision making. Second, there is a current trend toward the decentralization of the research function in order to put control closer to the area being studied. Third, the most sophisticated tools and techniques are being adapted to foreign information gathering with increasing success. So successful, in fact, that it has become necessary to develop structured information systems to appreciate and effectively utilize the mass of information available.

QUESTIONS

1. Terms—define and show the significance to international marketing:

    International marketing research   MMIS
    Research process   Back translation
    Comparability and currency of data   Income elasticity
    Overseas business reports   Analogy
    Trade lists

2. Discuss how the shift from making "market entry" decisions to "continuous operations" decisions creates a need for different types of information and data. What assistance does an MMIS provide?

3. Using a hypothetical situation, illustrate how an MMIS might be established and how it would be used at different levels.

4. Discuss the breadth and scope of international marketing research. Why is international marketing research generally broader in scope than domestic marketing research?

5. The measure of a competent researcher is the ability to utilize the most sophisticated and adequate techniques and methods available within these limits" [of time, cost, and the present state of the arts]. Comment.

6. What is the task of the international market researcher? How is it complicated by the foreign environment?

7. Discuss the stages of the research process in relation to the problems encountered. Give examples.

8. Why is the formulation of the research problem difficult in foreign market research?

9. Discuss the problems of gathering secondary data in foreign markets.

10. "In many cultures, personal information is inviolably *private* and absolutely not to be discussed with strangers." Discuss.

11. What are some problems created by language and the ability to comprehend in collecting primary data? How can a foreign market researcher overcome these difficulties?

12. Sampling offers some major problems in market research. Discuss.

13. Select a country. From secondary sources compile the following information for at least a 10-year period prior to the present date:
    Principal imports
    Principal exports
    Gross national product
    Chief of state
    Major cities and population
    Principal agricultural crop

14. "The foreign market researcher must possess three essential capabilities in order to generate meaningful marketing information." Discuss.

15. Discuss the growing need for an MMIS system.

Chapter 10

Multinational markets

Economic cooperation has become an international byword since the conclusion of World War II. Encouraged by the success of the European Economic Community (European Common Market), now officially titled the European Community (EC), many other countries have banded together in various kinds of multinational economic groups in the hope that such organizational forms will help them perform economic miracles.

Essentially, a multinational market is created when a number of individual countries agree to take positive steps to reduce trade and tariff barriers among the participating countries. Organizational form varies widely among market groups, but the universal orientation of such multinational cooperation is economic benefit for the participants. Sometimes political and social benefits accrue, but the dominant motive for affiliation remains economic.

Economic integration through customs unions relates directly to the marketing function of business. Such cooperation facilitates the marketing of one country's goods in another country and facilitates the acquisition of lower-priced goods produced elsewhere. Development of multinational markets and their success is partly a function of the stage of economic development of the participating countries; as nations expand their productive capacities, they also need to expand the boundaries of their markets. Without mass marketing facilities and mass markets, modern mass production capacity (or the surplus productive capacity of relatively inefficient nations) cannot be successfully utilized.

The European Community is the foremost example of economic cooperation. A few others are the Central American Common Market, the British Commonwealth of Nations, the Council for Mutual Economic Assistance, the Afro-Asian Organization for Economic Cooperation, and the newly created Latin American Integration Association.[1]

Multinational market groups form large markets which provide potentially significant opportunities for international business. While it may not be feasible to market into each of a number of separate nations, economic union of those nations may offer a logical market. Be alert to the marketing implica-

---

[1] The Latin American Integration Association replaced the Latin American Free Trade Association in 1980. For a discussion of the causes for the change see "New Latin American Association Carries on Traditions of LAFTA, with Some Important Differences; *Business America*, April 6, 1981, p. 15.

tions of multinational market developments reviewed in this chapter; the impact of such market groupings in world business is greater than ever anticipated in the early days of the markets in question.

STRATEGIC IMPLICATIONS FOR MARKETING

The complexion of the entire world marketplace has been changed significantly by the coalition of nations into multinational market groups. To international business firms, multinational groups spell opportunity in bold letters through access to greatly enlarged markets with reduced or abolished country-by-country tariff barriers and restrictions. Production, financing, manpower, and marketing decisions are affected by the remapping of the world into market groups.

New marketing opportunities are created but so are new problems. World competition has intensified because businesses have grown and become stronger and more experienced in dealing with large markets. The international manager is still confronted by individual national markets with the problems of language, customs, and instability even though packaged under the umbrella of a "common market." Most countries have little in common with their multinational market bedfellows.

Multinational groups have also closed businesses out of many markets. If a company is unwilling to produce within a market area, it may have lost access to the entire market or finds itself restricted in the quantity it can sell. Japan is having problems with exporting its autos and TVs to the European Community. The French have objected to the number of color TVs coming into member countries and eventually being sold to France; as a consequence, they appealed to the EC commission for a ban against Japanese TV sets and the ban was approved.[2]

Regulation of business activities has been intensified throughout multinational market groups; each group now has management and administrative bodies specifically concerned with business. In the process of structuring markets, rules and regulations common to the group are developed which are often more sophisticated than those of the individual countries. They reflect the type of legislation developed to regulate business in the United States and in the European Community. Despite all the problems and complexities of dealing with the new markets, the overriding message to the international marketer continues to be opportunity and profit potential so business continues to aid and encourage multinational market development.

OPPORTUNITIES

Economic integration creates large mass markets for the marketer. Many national markets, too small to bother with individually, take on new dimension

---

[2] "EC Backs French Ban on Japanese TV Sets," *Asian Wall Street Journal* March 9, 1981, p. 2.

and significance when combined with markets from cooperating countries. The European Community exceeds the United States in population and trade volume. The Commonwealth has nearly four times the U.S. population and a similar import volume. The large markets are particularly important to businesses accustomed to mass production and mass distribution. Not only are the markets large in numbers, but they are also rapidly improving in purchasing power. Although not so spectacularly successful, the other multinational markets are improving continually and provide significant marketing opportunities.

Most multinational groups have developed coordinated programs to foster economic growth. Such programs work to the advantage of marketers by increasing purchasing power, improving regional infrastructure, and fostering economic development. Activities of the sort cited, coupled with increased market size have, in fact, opened markets and provided economical market access to countries which were formerly closed because of inefficiency as markets.

Market group countries are improving their marketing institutions; improvement in channels of distribution, advertising, and transportation facilities provide opportunities for aggressive foreign marketers to utilize technical skills and abilities. Today there is reasonable distribution efficiency in countries marketers have overlooked for years because their small size did not warrant the huge efforts and costs associated with entering such markets.

Competition

Multinational market groups have increased world competition. They have accomplished some of this by legislation and regulation, but such activities are trivial compared to the competition created by the lure of large, strong markets. Often individual national markets were ignored by major foreign companies until merged into multinational market groups. Then businesses from every country were attracted by the opportunities for large-scale production and mass distribution. The dominant national producer/marketer which for years had things pretty much its own way is likely to find that counterparts from other countries have suddenly invaded the market. Look at the mathematics. If six countries merge into a market and each has three local producers for a product, there are suddenly 18 competitors. Add to these the marketers from other countries attracted by the size, potential, and economic health of the multinational market. No wonder there is a trend toward market protection when competition has become so intense. The challenge to the international marketer is obvious. With more competition, the manager must become more effective, production must become more economical and all competitors will be brought to a higher level of marketing. Some marketers may be faced with a loss situation because the market cannot support so many competitors, each of whom usually is determined to increase market share. Total consumption is not likely to be larger than the sum of the six, but the total numbers of competitors is likely to be considerably larger.

Market complexity

Common markets are not so common in fact as they are in name. The heterogeneous nature of cooperating countries requires that individual attention be given to the component parts of the multinational groups. Not only is each national market different, but there are regional differences within markets. As one Geneva-based marketing executive said, "Subtleties are so fine and the rate of change so great the headquarters managers have neither the capability nor the budget to keep abreast of the developments by themselves." To date, the common markets have not eliminated language barriers, cultural barriers, advertising media problems, or even completely eliminated tariff and nontariff barriers between countries within a given market group. Life continues to be complicated for the international marketer.

The international manager not only must cope with the economic fluctuations, market variations, and environmental changes in each national market but must deal with the same factors for the multinational market. A new layer of governmental complexity has been added. In one sense it might be said that now each country has two governments: its local national government and the multinational market group which has a sovereignty of its own.

In fact, as the European Common Market has prospered it has moved toward more uniform rules for all its members and a supra-commission speaks for the group. For example, the EC commission is proposing to harmonize trademark law among its members and establish an EC trademark versus trademarks in each member country; further, there is a push to allow lawyers to practice law as EC attorneys, that is, practice in any EC country.[3] Antitrust enforcement is also handled by the European Commission.[4] The only question that remains is when the European Commission will reach the point where it controls more of the economic activity among its members than individual member countries do—the time is probably closer than any realize.

Political power struggles are likely to take place among the various members of the multinational market organizations. Such power struggles can be particularly disruptive to the market, and foreign companies may find themselves in a scapegoat position. The European Community is well established and functioning smoothly; yet one sees and will continue to see headlines such as: "Is EEC Splitting in the Seams?: Franco-German Robbery

---

[3] "European Community File," *World Business Weekly*, January 19, 1981, p. 25.

[4] "Dawn Raids by Anti-trust Probers," *World Business Weekly*, April 20, 1981, p. 27.

Virtually has Killed the Old Concept of 'Community.' " However, as they become more economically interdependent, a split becomes less and less likely.

Market barriers

A major purpose of a multinational market is to protect the businesses which operate within its borders. An expressed goal is to give advantage to the companies in the market in their dealings with various countries of the market group. Analysis of the intraregional and international trade patterns of the market groups indicate that such results have been achieved. Trade does increase among member nations and decrease with nonmember

---

Box 10–1:   Wouldn't it be easier if you spoke only one language?

With the expansion of the European Community to include Greece in 1982 and Spain and Portugal in 1984, language looms as a major problem of economic unity. Common Market regulations require that when any one of the official languages is used at a meeting, interpretation into the others must be available on demand. The official languages include English, Danish, Dutch, French, German, Italian, Greek, and in 1984, Spanish and Portugese. This variety of languages causes major problems with the interpreting services. Interpreters for English, French, and German are relatively easy to find. But Danish, Dutch, and Italian interpreters come at a premium and finding a Greek interpreter is nearly impossible. It is further complicated because the Greek interpreter must be able to translate any of the other nine languages into Greek. Not only is the Greek language difficult, but it is spoken fluently in combination with other languages by very few people, even Greeks. The interpreting service director said "we began recruiting Greek interpreters three years before Greece joined the Economic Community and so far we haven't been very successful." She was able to find nine interpreters to translate into Greek and six others to translate out of Greek. But finding anyone who could turn Greek into Danish seems virtually impossible.

Consider how many interpreters are needed in a typical meeting. Even before the Greek entry into the Common Market, 13 to 16 interpreters were needed to handle a meeting at which all official languages were being used. If Greek, Spanish, and Portugese were also spoken, at least 30 interpreters would be needed for a meeting. In 1979, there were 8,375 meeting where all the official languages needed to be interpreted. Suppose you can't find an interpreter who can translate Danish into Greek. What do you do? One solution is to double-relay your interpretation. For example, one interpreter would translate from Danish into German; this would be picked up by another who could translate German into French; a third would then turn the French into Greek. Most interpreters dislike the relay system; major problems can develop if one interpreter errs. The second interpreter then simply spreads the mistake. With the addition of more languages, double-relays as standard practice would make discussions at certain meetings totally incomprehensible.

Even further in the future lies the possibility that Turkey will join the Common Market. The interpreters simply shake their heads at the thought of having to find Turkish interpreters. "Impossible," one official mutters under his breath.

Adapted from David Brand, "In Brussels Today, a Great Dane is One Who Knows Greek," *Wall Street Journal*, January 12, 1981, p. 1.

nations. U.S. exports to the European Community, for example, were reduced as much as $650 million per year. Such local preferences certainly spell trouble to the exporter located outside the market. Companies willing to invest in production facilities in such markets may be benefitted by such protection as they become a part of the market. Exporters, however, are in a considerably weaker position.

Markets may be closed entirely to foreign-based firms through supranational politics. Some multinational market groups include one country with a producer of a particular good. That producer may have priority access to the entire market closing all countries to foreign competition which previously had access. Economic development programs of some multinational groups designate a specific country or even company as the exclusive producer for a given type of product. So-called sectorial programs may absolutely exclude imports or may reduce their effectiveness through common tariffs.

Such is the case with Japan and the European Community. Japanese steel, T.V.s, and autos have strong export sales in the lucrative common market, but vigorous opposition from EC members with basic industries hurt by Japanese importers has managed to get the European commission to impose quotas, increase import taxes, and raise other barriers to Japanese goods. Despite these restrictions, the EC's trade deficit with Japan was $10 billion in 1980 and growing at a rate of $1 billion per year.[5]

Such deficits increase the cry for greater protection. Fearing continued attacks against Japanese imports, Japan is making investments in Greece to use as a springboard into the EC market.[6] Joint ventures and licensing agreements with Greek partners will enable the Japanese to enter the EC from Greece more easily than as an exporter from Japan or some other non-EC member country.

Regulation

The very process of forming a multinational market group causes new levels of administration and governance to come into being and focuses attention on business practices. The result is often increased regulation of business behavior. Most multinational market groups have established regulations pertaining to mergers, joint ventures, and various relationships between local and foreign business. In many instances, countries which previously had virtually no regulations have become part of a regulatory hierarchy so that businesses are subjected to the new rules. Production activities and labor relations are often included under such strictures. Of special importance to the marketer are regulations concerning pricing, promotion, product

---

[5] "Japan's Rebuff to a Common Market Pact," *Business Week*, December 1, 1980, p. 60.

[6] "Japanese Companies Poised to Use Greece as EEC Springboard," *Business Europe*, January 9, 1981, p. 9.

liability, middleman relationships, and personnel practices. Sometimes the regulations simplify business by setting basic ground rules, but, in other instances, the marketer simply inherits red tape, bureaucracy, and unnecessary problems.

Profit

Because they are dynamic and because they have great growth possibilities, the multinational markets are likely to be especially rough and tumble for the external business. These markets may be more difficult to profit from than some of the apparently less desirable single national markets. The requirements for profitable entry are essentially the requirements of a competitive marketplace anywhere—a high degree of marketing ability, total commitment to the competitive effort, versatility, and fast action. The secretary of a German manufacturers' association said, "We tell our members to get busy now. We tell them, 'Get in there, set up your outlets, hire your agents, prospect for customers—or you will be dead ducks.' " Besides these requirements, the foreign business person must also deal with multinational market problems and complications related to trade restrictions, exchange and financial arrangements, marketing barriers and limitations, as well as the general problems of communications and acculturation in a single but nonhomogeneous market.

Overproduction with resulting price cutting and profit deterioration may become a common phenomenon in some of the multinational market areas. In their eagerness to become established in these areas, some manufacturers will construct production facilities or capacities beyond the short-run market potential. Several such facilities working toward long-term markets can create chaotic market conditions in the short run. In some countries, the cost of entering the market will be too great considering the slow payoff rate. Many manufacturers, therefore, will have to decide between entering an initially unprofitable market or being excluded from it permanently.

HISTORY OF MULTINATIONAL ECONOMIC ORGANIZATIONS

Publicity about the European Community makes many people believe that economic union is a new concept. However, contemporary economic unions have deep roots and are at least partly based on other already existing political and economic unions. Although both political and economic cooperation are required, economic motivations historically have been stronger than political motivations in the formation of many countries. History reveals it was not unusual for a king to arrange the marriage of his daughter or son so that his kingdom and economic power would be extended. The United States of America and, more recently, the Union of Soviet Socialist Republics are both aggregations of individual sovereign states who joined forces not only for political reasons but for economic benefit. Imagine the difficulties if each state in the United States had the power to levy tariffs at its borders; confusion, increased prices, and retarded trade would follow.

The history of all economic unions is marked by toil, turmoil, success and failure, as sovereign nations attempt to homogenize their common interest. A brief review of the history of the European Community, below, offers some insight into the ideas behind some market groups, and characteristics affecting their success or failure.

European Community: A long time coming

In sharp contrast to Britain, which was politically and economically unified as early as 1603, European efforts at meaningful unions defied all serious attempts for many years. There were hopes for a unified or at least partially unified Europe after the War of 1812, but the Peace Congress of Vienna failed at consolidation. Germany, for example, consisted of 39 confederated states with hundreds of customs frontiers retarding economic progress. Prussia finally took the lead toward German unification in the 1830s and formed a Zollverein in which 18 states accepted the Prussian rates of duty and custom procedures. The authority of the Zollverein was not limited to tariffs but included the monetary system, weights and measures, internal taxes, and other economic measures. After three decades of operation, Bismarck's reign replaced the Zollverein, but the economic benefits of the union were highly evident. One writer comments, "the 30 odd years of the Zollverein were a time of quick economic growth for Germany, which was transformed from a technically backward and mainly agricultural society into one of the leading industrial states on the continent." Despite its successes, the Zollverein was a weak instrument, and political unification was necessary for the new Germany to benefit from its partial economic unification.

Germany's subsequent economic and political success caused economic scholars of the time to champion economic union. An influential advocate of the common market concept was Friedrich Naumann who, in his 1919 book *Mitteleuropa,* encouraged immediate economic union between Germany and Austria-Hungary. He saw Mitteleuropa as a nucleus of the European market, including virtually all continental Europe west of Russia. Germany's defeat in World War I did not end thoughts of a unified Europe under German leadership. In 1931, Austria and Germany announced they had formed a new customs union but the international court of justice struck it down as being contrary to the peace treaty.

The idea of union was found all over Europe: Winston Churchill headed a movement for a united Europe, Count Richard Coudenhove-Kalergi convened a meeting of European Union of Federalists constantly sought European federation. A Frenchman, Jean Monnet, is most commonly identified as the father of the European Community, which he helped along from his position as the founder of the European Coal and Steel Community.

European cooperation after World War II

The United States played a dominant role in assisting European unity. Before World War II had ended, it took the initiative in the Bretton-Woods Conference at which 50 nations met to seek ways to establish lower trade barriers, long-term development loans, and liquid short-term funds, all designed to permit world trade to grow. From this conference came the General Agreement on Tariffs and Trade (GATT), the International Monetary Fund (IMF), and the International Bank for Reconstruction and Development (IBRD) to perform those functions. After the war, America's Marshall Plan led to the the the development of the Organization for European Economic Cooperation (OEEC) in 1948. Through the OEEC, the United States channeled $12.5 billion to give tangible demonstration to the benefits of economic cooperation.

The European Coal and Steel Community, formed in 1951, is perhaps the most direct forerunner of the European Common Market. It provided the pattern for further development of the European Community. All the groups mentioned laid the foundation for the European Common Market with the Treaty of Rome. This was ratified in 1957 by six nations, but was initially rejected by Britain, one of its chief protagonists. After 13 years, the United Kingdom reassessed the question and along with Ireland and Denmark, joined the Community. Turkey and Greece were admitted to associate memberships in 1978; Greece became a full member in 1982, and Spain and Portugal are scheduled for full membership in 1984.

". . . COMMON MARKET, HELL! . . . THAT'S A SUPERMARKET . . ."

With permission of *The Denver Post* and Conrad.

The European Community today

It is easy to be confused in evaluating the progress of the European Community through information in the public press. Journalism seems to thrive on bad news, so many of the articles about the Community focus on its problems, limitations, disputes, lack of cohesiveness, and limited progress. The international marketer, however, must appreciate the real power of the Community. Despite problems, the Community does exist as a functional entity exerting a major force in commercial affairs. Its court system has overriding powers in many areas of litigation; common tariff walls protect the market against production outside its borders; internal tariffs among the countries have been reduced. The European Community negotiates as a single entity in matters of world trade and politics and has become the voice of Europe in international discussions. There can be no denying the importance of Community-wide policies in such broad areas as environment and energy where detailed programs have been developed.

Over the years, the Community has gained an increasing amount of authority over its member states. The Community's institutions (the Commission, the Council of Ministers, the European Parliament, and the Court of Justice) and their decision-making processes distinguish the EC from other international cooperative organizations. The institutions have legal status and extensive powers in fields covered by common policies. The institutions are the support structure of the integration process leading toward a federal system. Community institutions have the power to make decisions and execute policies in specific areas. They form a federal pattern with executive, parliament, and judicial branches.

The Commission, a 13 member body, initiates policy and supervises its observance by the member states. It proposes and supervises execution of laws and policies. It has a president and four vice presidents holding office for two-year, renewable terms.

The Council of Ministers, composed of a minister from each member country, passes laws based on Commission proposals. And the **European Parliament,** with 198 members appointed from and by the national legislatures, has limited but gradually increasing budgetary powers. It is mainly a consultative body which passes on most Community legislation.

The Court of Justice, consisting of nine judges, is the Community's "Supreme Court." Its decisions are final and cannot be appealed in national courts. The Court of Justice has increased its presence in the Community in the last decade and has become very important in enforcing Community laws and regulations.

The European Community was created as a result of three treaties, the European Coal and Steel Community (ECSC), the European Economic Community (EEC), and the European Atomic Energy Community (EURATOM). These three treaties are incorporated within the European Community and serve as the Community's "constitution." They provide a policy framework and empower the Commission and the Council of Ministers to pass laws to carry out Community policy. The Community uses three types of legal instruments: (1) regulations binding the member states directly and having the same strength as national laws; (2) directives also binding the member states but allowing them to choose the means of execution; and, (3) decisions addressed to a government, an enterprise, or an individual, binding the parties named.[7]

The strength in the European Community can be seen in the increased activity of the various Community branches involved in Community affairs. For example, the European Commission, EC's executive branch, has recently won the right to take part in consultations on EC foreign policy. This is a significant breakthrough in its battle to be taken seriously by the governments of the 10 member countries.[8] In addition, the European Commission has become much more active in exercising its powers of investigation over unfair trading practices by member countries.[9]

International marketers in Europe encounter the Community, its rules, its guidelines, and its supervision on a routine basis. The Commission promulgates and enforces rules of competition and organizational structure relating to mergers, antitrust, and taxation. Even pricing, advertising, and other day-to-day operations are scrutinized so the international marketer must not only be aware of the market policies of the government of the country in which operating, but those of the Community as well.

It may appear that the Community functions mainly in a restrictive capacity, but it also provides a broad range of specific services. The goal is to facilitate business operations rather than to limit them. The Community has standardized and upgraded data collection for member countries and established a basic uniform accounting procedure. A Community-wide incorporation system is being developed so that companies doing business in more than one country need only be incorporated once for the Community as a whole. On behalf of its consumers, it has developed a product liability program which holds producers, importers, or vendors responsible for product performance. Marketer's activities in every area are heavily influenced by the agencies of the European Community.

The European Community as a single market becomes, by a large margin, the largest market in the world. Its 10 member countries include some of the world's most developed nations, its population is huge and affluent, and additional countries have applied for admission. Questioning the strength and reality of the European Community is similar to denying the market potential of East Europe, or the existence of Latin America. There

---

[7] "European Community, the Facts" (Washington, D.C.: European Community Information Service, 1980), p. 32.

[8] "More Power to the Commission," *World Business Weekly*, September 21, 1981, p. 67.

[9] "European Community, Dawn Raid by Anti-trust Probers," *World Business Weekly*, April 20, 1981, p. 27.

is every reason to believe that the market will continue to grow and the Community will play an increasingly dominant role in European and world commercial and political affairs.

LA RAISON D'ETRE

Successful economic union requires favorable economic, political, social, and geographic factors as a basis for success. Major flaws in any one factor could destroy the union unless the other factors provide sufficient strength to overcome the weaknesses. In general, the advantages of economic union must be clear cut and significant and the benefits must greatly outweigh the disadvantages before nations will forego their sovereignty. Often a strong threat to the economic or political security of a nation is needed to provide the impetus for cooperation.

Economic factors

Every type of economic union shares the development and enlargement of market opportunities as a basic orientation; usually markets are enlarged through preferential tariff treatment for participating members or common tariff barriers against outsiders. Enlarged, protected markets stimulate internal economic development by providing assured outlets and preferential treatment for goods produced within the customs union. Consumers benefit from lower internal tariff barriers among the participating countries. In many cases, external as well as internal barriers are reduced because of the greater economic security afforded domestic producers by the enlarged market.

Nations with complementary economic bases are least likely to encounter frictions in the development and operation of a common market unit. The European Community includes countries with diverse agricultural bases, different industries, and different natural resources. It is significant that most of the problems the Common Market has encountered were concerned with agricultural products where several countries had significant productive capability and the national producers each desired protection. In fact, the problems still exist. For example, a flap arose between Britain, France, and Italy over poultry and wine. Reportedly to protect the British poultry industry from a poultry virus on the Continent, the British banned French poultry. In unrelated incidents, the French banned Italian wine and the Irish banned all poultry and eggs from other member countries. In each of the cases, the underlying reasons probably were more a desire to protect local markets than to protect health. The European Commission entered the dispute and charged all countries involved with violations of EC regulations.[10] With the recent addition of Greece and the eventual addition of Spain and Portugal,

---

[10] "European Community—Britain and France on the Mat," *World Business Weekly*, September 28, 1981.

economic issues arising from economic disparity among member nations will intensify. This probably will push the desired economic and monetary union further into the future.[11]

Similar productive incapabilities are likely to be a major stumbling block in the success of such nearly homogeneous markets as the Central American Common Market (CACM) countries. One advantage that Latin countries have is an economic base that is not yet highly developed. A major orientation of CACM, so far, has been to encourage different member countries to follow different industrial lines. Protecting markets from exploitation by foreign companies was a major factor in the development of the CACM and that has become an increasingly important element in Common Market developments.[12]

The demise of the Latin American Free Trade Association (LAFTA) in 1981 was caused, in part, by its economically stronger members not allowing for the needs of the weaker ones. The new Latin American Integration Association (LAIA) which replaces LAFTA permits more flexibility in bilateral agreements and less rigid operational rules.[13] Most attempts at common markets which do not work as well as expected can count economic incompatibility as the major reason.

Political factors

Political amenability among countries is another basic requisite for development of a supranational market arrangement. Participating countries must have comparable aspirations and general compatibility before they will give up any part of their national sovereignty. State sovereignty is one of the most cherished possessions of any nation and will be given up only for a promise of significant improvement of the national position through cooperation.

Economic considerations provide the basic catalyst for the formation of a customs union group, but political elements are equally important. The uniting of the original European Community countries was partially a response to the outside threat of Russia's great political and economic power; the countries of Western Europe were willing to settle their family squabbles to present a unified front to the Russian bear.

One of the chief arguments for the admission of Spain and Portugal to the EC is that participation will help stabilize their governments and stay the threat of Communism in those countries. The EC's united front is also evident from time to time in negotiations between the EC and USA. The

---

[11] "Key Questions on the Twelve," *World Business Weekly*, December 29, 1980, p. 7.

[12] For a detailed study of the economic problems of regional economic integration, see Germanico S. Penaherrera, "Viable Integrations and the Economic Co-operation Problems of the Developing World," *Journal of Common Market Studies*, part 1, September 1980, pp. 65–77 and part 2, December 1980, pp. 175–89.

[13] "A Replacement for LAFTA," *World Business Weekly*, April 6, 1981, p. 26.

United States has been concerned about developing an economic and political union to provide a lasting countervailing power in Europe. A basic
premise of the European Community is that it will gradually develop into
a political as well as economic union.

Geographic proximity

Although it is not absolutely imperative that cooperating members of
the customs union have geographical proximity, such closeness facilitates
the functioning of a common market. Transportation networks basic to any
marketing system, are likely to be interrelated and well developed when
countries are close together. Countries which are widely separated geographically have a major barrier to overcome in attempting economic fusion.

BOX 10–2: Marriage without power

"The first 20 years of the Common Market were really an engagement. Now it
has become a marriage: for better or worse. And in the future we will have to get
used to smaller growth for everybody in it, because of the disparities between the
various members.

"While the EEC is complex, it speaks with one voice in such matters as GATT
negotiations, international policies, and the North-South dialogue. On the matter of
fishing rights, the Soviet Union now has recognized the EEC as a political unity and
the same holds for talks about uranium safeguards and nonproliferation of atomic
reactors.

"And yet, internally the EEC has become somewhat dormant. It lacks economic
structure, monetary and political structure, sufficiently coherent to keep things moving.
Its diplomatic representations abroad are only for trade; politically the EEC is a double-
headed creature which next year will have a parliament without power, that cannot
act without approval of the population in the member states."

Michael Van den Abeele, a European
Community official

Source: "The EEC itself is Cool to Expansion," *Canadian Business*, August 1977, p. 18.

Social factors

Cultural similarity can ease the shock of economic cooperation with other
countries. The more similar the cultures, the more likely a market is to succeed
because members understand the outlook and viewpoints of their colleagues.
Although there is great cultural diversity in the European Community, key
member countries share a long-established Christian heritage. They are also
commonly aware of being "European."

Language, as a part of culture, did not create as much a barrier for
European Community countries as was expected. Initially there were seven
major languages, but such linguistic diversity did not impede trade because
European businesses historically have been multilingual. Nearly every edu-

cated European can converse and do business in at least two or three languages; thus, in every relationship, there is likely to be a linguistic common
ground. However, when the number of countries expanded beyond the
original seven, language difficulties began to complicate the process.

With the addition of Greece in 1982 and Spain and Portugal scheduled
for entry in 1984, language has become a definite problem in the European
Community. Common Market rules require that at all official meetings translation will be available for all languages of its members. This means that a
meeting including all members of the fully expanded European Community
in 1984 would require 30 interpreters. The number itself is not as crucial
as the problem of finding interpreters to translate among the 12 languages.
Greek poses a special problem since there are not many who speak Greek
fluently in combination with other European languages, even in Greece.
When asked about the additional complications with Turkey's entry into
the EC, one interpreter critically commented "impossible."[14]

In summary, the major components of a successful economic union are
complementary economies, combined large-sized market, and politically
amenable leaders willing to give up some sovereignty.

PATTERNS OF MULTINATIONAL COOPERATION

Multinational market groups take several forms varying significantly in
the degree of cooperation, dependence, and interrelationship among participating nations. In a sense, the United States may be thought of as a fully
operative, integrated, economic group of states. The Constitution requires
there be no tariff barriers between the regions or states. The United States
provides a common external trade barrier for all states and a free flow of
labor and capital from one state or region to another. These U.S. characteristics also represent the principal characteristics of a fully economically integrated union. The United States is both politically and economically integrated, but there are some economic unions which are not politically integrated and there are political unions which are not completely integrated
economically. In some nations, various regions or "states" have the power
to limit entry of products from other states through tariffs. There is, for example, a small amount of product exclusion in the United States, as in the
case of milk and some agricultural products; but internal tariffs are not tolerated by the Constitution.

This section examines five types of arrangements for regional economic
integration: regional cooperation for development plans, free-trade area arrangements, customs union programs, common market arrangements, and
semipolitical unions.

_____

[14] David Brand, "In Brussels Today, a Great Dane is One Who Knows Greek," _Wall Street
Journal,_ January 12, 1981, p. 1.

Regional cooperation groups

A new variety of multinational market group that developed in recent years is called Regional Cooperation for Development (RCD). In the RCD arrangement, several governments agree to participate jointly with business in developing basic industries beneficial to the economy. Each country makes an advance commitment to participate in the financing of new joint-venture projects and to purchase a specified share of the output of the production facilities developed.

In one RCD, Turkey, Pakistan, and Iran are cooperating with private industry in some 12 to 15 different projects. One, for example, established the Iranian Aluminum Company, in cooperation with Reynolds Metal Company who will provide technical assistance and manage the operation for 10 years. Reynolds has a 25 percent equity; Pakistan, 10 percent; and Iran, 65 percent. The group has a 50,000-metric-ton production facility. Pakistan agreed to buy 10,000 tons annually for five years at world market prices.

The ASEAN (Association of South East Asian Nations) group, activated in 1978, has established a program for complementary sectorial development of various industries. Indonesia and Malaya, for example, have been allocated urea production; Singapore, heavy diesel engines; the Philippines, superphosphates; and Thailand, soda ash. The economic ministry has developed an extensive list of future projects for intragroup cooperation. ASEAN falls somewhere between a regional cooperation group and a free-trade area because it also has a specific program for reducing tariffs and nontrade barriers within the group.[15]

Regional cooperation groups differ from common markets in that there is no elimination or lowering of tariffs or structuring of external tariffs. In a sense, they are simply joint ventures of various governments cooperating with private business to develop new facilities. Such cooperation, however, is likely to presage fuller multinational developments.

Free-trade area

The key function of a free-trade association is to provide a mass market without barriers impede the flow of goods and services among participating member countries.

Although a free-trade association does not establish common external barriers and does not provide for a free flow of labor and capital within countries, such a cooperative venture has important nontariff benefits. In general, the very act of association leads to increased communication and cooperation on economic matters. The centralized agency acts as a clearing-

---

[15] ASEAN Nations Sign Preferential Trade Pact: Implications for Firms, *Business International*, March 11, 1977, p. 76.

house when the countries decide to upgrade the area to greater cooperative efforts.

Until its major members joined the EC, the European Free Trade Association functioned effectively for over a decade as a second European market group. America has the Latin American Free Trade Association. Unfortunately, rivalries and political volatility LAFTA from coming anywhere near achieving its potential role and finally brought it down in 1981.

Full customs union

The customs union represents the next stage in the development of cooperation. This customs union enjoys the free-trade area's reduced or eliminated internal tariffs and in addition, a common external tariff on products imported from countries outside the union. The union is a logical stage of development in the transition from free-trade area to a common market. The Benelux nations have been participants in a customs union dating back to 1921. Other customs unions exist between France and Monaco, Italy and San Marino, and Switzerland and Leichtenstein.

Common Market

The common market builds on the reduction or elimination of internal tariffs and the development of a common external tariff structure characteristic of the preceding class of economic integration. It adds the further elements of free flow of capital and labor from country to country. Thus, a common market is a common marketplace, not only for goods, but for services (including labor), and for capital. It is *a unified economy* and lacks only political unity to become a nation. The common market may establish further objectives and additional devices to assure effective economic integration. Some idea of the scope of these activities may be gained by reviewing the provisions of the Treaty of Rome which established the EC, an outstanding example of regional market integration.

The treaty called for common external tariffs and the gradual elimination of intramarket tariffs, quotas, and other trade barriers—both now in effect. It also called for elimination of restrictions on the movement of services, labor, and capital; prohibition of cartels; coordinated monetary and fiscal policies; common agricultural policies; use of common investment funds for regional industrial development; and similar rules for wage and welfare payments.

The founders of the European Community intended it to be a truly common market; so much so that economic integration must eventually be supplemented by political integration to accomplish the objectives completely. In such an arrangement, members of the European Community will become truly interdependent members of a supranational community.

Latin America boasts two common markets, the Central American Common Market and the Andean Common Market. Both have roughly similar goals and seek eventual full economic integration. The CACM provides a successful example of cooperation in normally individualistic Latin America. It pioneered the unique feature called *sectorial development;* it's governing body formally allocates production authority for certain manufactured products to individual member countries. In this way, the group has encouraged development of a number of industries by guaranteeing the entire CACM market to a single producer.

Africa has had a wide variety of proposed economic unions including one common market, the Economic Community of West African States. Its 15 members have a population of some 130 million people. The record of economic integration efforts in Africa has been dismal; despite such experience, ECOWAS has scheduled full customs union integration by 1990 including elimination of internal duties and a common external tariff wall.

BOX 10–3: Oil money—Basis for new-type market group?

(You know OPEC, but do you know OAPEC? The latter is the Organization of *Arab* Petroleum Exporting Countries. OAPEC includes Saudi Arabia, Kuwait, Qatar, the United Arab Emirates, Iraq, Libya, and Algeria and excludes six OPEC members.)

"OAPEC is a think tank for the formulation of energy policies in Arab lands that produce a third of the world's oil. OAPEC promotes cooperation among Arab lands in petroleum and other economic fields. It launches multigovernment enterprises. It is involved in manpower training.

"OAPEC's Arab Petroleum Investments Corporation is headquartered at Damman, Saudi Arabia, only a few miles from that country's still-flowing first-discovery well. The investment concern, created in November 1975 with authorized capital of $1 billion, seeks to help finance economic projects, especially ones that are Arab and oil related. As of last June 30, it had managed or participated in loans totaling $900 million."

Source: Ray Vicker, "OAPEC, an Arab Group That Spends Big Money on Development Projects, is Expanding Rapidly." Reprinted with permission of *The Wall Street Journal,* © Dow Jones & Company, Inc. 1977. All rights reserved.

Political union

Political union of economic affairs may be voluntary or enforced; but regardless of the motivation, such union ultimately depends on economic logic for success.

The Commonwealth of Nations. *Time* magazine has commented that:

> the Commonwealth of Nations is clearly impossible. Except for the colonial past, its 18 member nations—five white, nine black, four brown—have nothing, not even wealth in common. They are divided by almost every possible denominator: color, geography, education, culture, nationalism, and economic interests. And so, before each meeting of the Commonwealth Prime Ministers in London, logical men quite logically predict its collapse. They are always wrong. The Commonwealth not only staggers through but it keeps growing.

Indeed, it is somewhat unbelievable that the British Commonwealth survives at all. Its completely voluntary organization provides for the loosest possible relationship which could still be classified as economic integration. Still, its membership covers one fourth of the earth's land mass, contains one fourth of the world's people, and carries on within its confines one third of the world's trade. Despite its size, the bonds holding together the Commonwealth are hard to visualize. One Whitehall official has commented that "I am not sure that all this scrutinizing is a good thing. The Commonwealth is something that may disappear if you stare at it too hard." Although it is technically neither a legal nor a political conglomeration, the Commonwealth can best be classified as a political union based on economic history and a sense of tradition. One authority comments that the real binding forces are the English language and parliamentary democracy. The Commonwealth does not even share the common internal tariff structure which characterizes even the weakest of the other forms of economic integration. Even the bilateral trade preferences between the United Kingdom and the individual commonwealths were largely dissipated when Britain entered the EC.

Despite its loose bonds and its informal relationship, the Commonwealth still exists as an example of one form of politically based economic integration and cooperation.

Enforced political union.   Reacting to the popularity and exceptional success of the Marshall Plan in Western Europe, Joseph Stalin in 1949 established the Council for Mutual Economic Assistance (COMECON). Although it is centrally controlled and more tightly organized than the Commonwealth, COMECON has not approached any of the other methods of economic integration in effectiveness. COMECON has been, in part, an agency for the exploitation of its member countries; because of the satellites' defensiveness, it has not been an effective union.

Complaints at the 30th COMECON summit (1976) indicated that member states were upset about intrablock pricing. In one year, COMECON policies had more than doubled the amount satellites had to pay for Soviet raw materials while increasing earnings from exports of industrial goods only marginally. Another major complaint was that joint investment projects wound up legally defined as the property of the Soviet Union.

For 20 years the controlling council had emphasized the development of international division of labor among members through central planning. No agreement was reached on establishing a central planning office so the subject was quietly dropped. This idea, like others promoted by the Soviets, failed to arouse enthusiasm because it meant suppression of national priorities in favor of intangible future benefits from long-range integration. By 1980, Eastern European countries had accumulated monumental trade deficits. COMECON did not succeed in accomplishing its goal of dealing with Western European countries without the intervention of the EC. In a five-year period COMECON's trade deficit with the United States, the EC, and Japan grew from $775 million to $5.5 billion (roughly 60 percent with the EC, 25 percent with the United States, and 15 percent with Japan). At that level of deficit, interest payments alone amounted to nearly 20 percent of the hard currency export receipts, several percentage points above the considered safe ceiling.

BOX 10–4: Let's have a little cooperation please

Cia Andina de Triconos (CATSA), a Bolivian joint venture of the U.S. Dresser Industries and local investors, which had based its investment on an allocation under the metalworking program, closed its doors after failing to penetrate the Andean market after more than two years in operation.

The prospect of duty-free access to the Andean market, plus protection provided by a 55 percent "ad valorem" common outer tariff on bits sourced from outside the bloc, made the sales outlook seem good.

However, CATSA's "monopoly" position in Ancom proved specious. Although the plant went on stream in 1974, the company was never able to export a single drill bit to the Andean market; and its local sales were confined to the state-owned petroleum company YPFB. This market was clearly insufficient, since the operation had been based on exporting the bulk of the plant's 200-unit-per-month capacity to the Andean area.

CATSA could not penetrate the Ancom market for several reasons:

Although Ancom has imposed a 55 percent common outer tariff on third-country imports, some Ancom countries had previously granted LAFTA tariff concessions, which take precedence over the Ancom tariffs.

Ancom members simply did not honor the spirit of the metalworking agreement. After the installation of the CATSA facility, plants producing tricone bits were set up in Peru and Venezuela. Under the metalworking program, participating member governments were committed to prohibiting new foreign investment in allocations of other Ancom countries. But on the question of new investment by local industry, the obligation was only *not to encourage it,* with no requirement to prevent it. In the case of Venezuela, it has no commitment to limit local production or to honor the outer tariff, because it was not yet a member of Ancom when the metalworking agreement was signed and was thus not a party to the pact.

Also, according to Bolivia, Colombia and Ecuador employed a series of obstacles to avoid applying the common outer tariff.

The withdrawal of Chile from Ancom cost Bolivia a lucrative potential market, too.

Source: "The Pullout of Dresser from Bolivian Operation Shows Problems of Ancom." Reprinted with permission from page 57 of the February 23, 1977 issue of *Business Latin America*, with permission of the publisher, Business International Corp. (New York).

Except for the political pressures involved, COMECON can be said to have failed as an agency for economic integration because its member countries do not meet the basic requisites for effective union and because it has failed to establish agencies which permit mutual benefit. The East European economies are not complementary; language and cultural barriers exist; and the satellite countries are unwilling to give up what sovereignty they do possess.

MULTINATIONAL MARKETS TODAY

The following pages summarize only basic information about the world's major market groups. Their names and compositions change frequently, but the very number of groups attests to the vitality of the multinational market group movement, which seems to be the dominant theme of international trade in the last half of the 20th century.

Europe

In a little over a decade, Europe has been transformed from a group of 30 small, segmented, and weak markets into a number of strong, coherent, multinational market groups (see Exhibit 10–1). Nearly every type of multinational market grouping is found in Europe and all have functioned with relatively high degrees of success. The progress of the EC has been punctuated by extremes of optimism and pessimism relative to its future potential. In the year of exuberant expansion from six to nine "locals," the market was plunged into depression by the infighting associated with the energy crisis and monetary devaluations. Nonetheless, one should not overlook

EXHIBIT 10–1:   European Market groups

Name of association	Members	Population (millions)	GDP (billions U.S. dollars)	National income per capita (U.S. dollars)	Imports (millions U.S. dollars)
European Community (EC)	Belgium	9.7	96.9	9,025	71,185
	Luxembourg	0.3	3.5	10,040	—
	Denmark	4.9	55.9	9,869	19,363
	France	52.7	471.6	7,918	134,912
	Germany	60.7	638.8	9,278	188,001
	Ireland	3.4	12.2	2,711	11,159
	Italy	53.8	260.1	4,118	99,452
	United Kingdom	55.5	309.5	4,955	120,095
	Netherlands	13.0	130.8	8,509	76,881
	Greece	8.8	31.6	3,209	10,531
European Free Trade Association (EFTA)	Austria	7.5	58.0	6,739	24,495
	Norway	3.9	39.9	7,949	16,957
	Portugal	8.6	17.8	1,577	9,410
	Sweden	8.2	87.3	9,274	33,441
	Switzerland	6.3	84.5	12,408	36,356
	Iceland	.2	2.2	8,392	1,000
EC and EFTA Associates	Finland	4.7	33.8	6,090	15,580
	Spain	34.0	147.1	3,625	34,080
	Turkey	40.3	50.0	873	4,946

Source: *Statistical Yearbook* 1979–1980 (New York: United Nations, 1981).

the solid gains of the market or the basic strengths which undergird its progress.

The name change alone from the European Economic Community to the European Community symbolizes the broadened concept the Community has of its role. Building on a host of specific achievements, the market group continues to plan increasing integration; the program for the early 1980s includes Community-wide charters for European companies, consolidation of accounts of EC portions of business done by individual companies, merger control and increasing antitrust emphasis, environmental regulation, consumer protection, and integrated energy legislation. These are all major subjects and reflect the underlying optimism of the Community. Certainly Western Europe has benefitted greatly from establishment of the various multinational market groups.

Africa

Africa's multinational market development activities can be characterized by a great deal of activity but little progress. Including bilateral agreements, an estimated 200 economic arrangements exist between African countries (see Exhibit 10–2). Despite the large numbers and assortment of paper organizations, there has been little progress in actual economic integration. This is understandable in light of the political instability which has characterized Africa in the last decades and the unstable economic base on which Africa has been required to build. The United Nations Economic Commission for Africa has held numerous conferences but has been hampered by governmental inexperience, undeveloped resources, manpower problems, and chronic product shortages. It has managed to sponsor an African Development Bank, which began making loans against a $250 million capital in 1967. ECA is also working to induce African members to develop modern

EXHIBIT 10–2: African Market groups

Name of association	Members	Population (millions)	GNP (billions U.S. dollars)	National income per capita (U.S. dollars)	Imports (millions U.S. dollars)
Afro-Malagasy Economic Union	Cameroon	7.0	3.0	361	1,271
	Central African Republic	1.8	.4	185	70
	Chad	3.2	.7	165	118
	Congo Brazzaville	—	—	—	—
	Dahomey	—	—	—	—
	Gabon	.4	2.2	887	804
	Ivory Coast	6.7	7.7	534	2,493
	Mali	6.0	.5	94	367
	Mauritania	1.5	.4	264	259
	Niger	2.5	.7	152	127

EXHIBIT 10–2 (concluded)

Name of association	Members	Population (millions)	GNP (billions U.S. dollars)	National income per capita (U.S. dollars)	Imports (millions U.S. dollars)
	Senegal	5.0	2.0	361	942
	Togo	2.0	.6	246	518
	Upper Volta	6.1	.8	84	593
East Africa Customs	Ethiopia	—	2.7	91	567
Union	Kenya	15.3	5.5	216	2,305
	Sudan	14.1	5.3	304	1,616
	Tanzania	15.2	4.4	159	1,258
	Uganda	9.5	2.6	208	167
	Zambia	4.0	2.8	394	755
Maghreb Economic	Algeria	17.4	19.7	803	8,537
Community	Libya	—	20.0	4,424	5,311
	Tunisia	5.6	6.0	728	2,830
	Morocco	15.4	12.4	517	3,678
Casablanca Group	Egypt	36.6	18.8	308	4,860
	Ghana	8.5	4.6	433	993
	Guinea	2.6	.7	155	—
	Morocco	15.4	12.4	517	3,678
Economic Community of	Benin	2.1	.6	401	267
West African States	Cape Verde	.3	—	—	44
(ECOWAS)	Gambia	.5	.1	225	126
	Ghana	8.6	4.6	433	993
	Guinea	2.6	.7	155	—
	Guinea-Bissau	.8	.2	318	32
	Ivory Coast	6.7	7.7	534	2,493
	Liberia	1.5	.7	392	487
	Mali	6.0	.5	94	367
	Mauritania	1.5	.5	264	259
	Niger	2.5	.7	152	127
	Nigeria	55.7	50.2	510	12,399
	Senegal	5.1	2.0	361	888
	Sierra Leone	2.7	.7	202	297
	Togo	2.0	.6	246	518
	Upper Volta	6.1	.8	84	593
West African Economic	Ivory Coast	6.7	7.7	534	2,493
Community (CEAO)	Mali	6.0	.5	94	367
	Mauritania	1.5	.5	664	259
	Niger	2.5	.7	152	127
	Senegal	5.1	2.0	361	942
	Upper Volta	6.1	.8	84	593
Customs and Economic	Central African				
Union of Central Africa	Republic	—	.4	185	70
(CEUCA)	Congo	1.3	.8	514	184
	Gaban	.4	2.2	3,287	804
	Cameroon	7.1	3.1	361	1,271

Source: *Statistical Yearbook* 1979–1980 (New York: United Nations, 1981).

customs services and to adopt the Brussels tariff nomenclature which is standard in the Western world.

Political sovereignty is a new enough phenomenon to most African nations that they are reluctant to relinquish any part of it without specific and tangible benefits in return. André Simmons cited a major problem in his study of economic integration of Africa. When the population and income factors are combined in a country 2 million inhabitants with an income of about $100 per capita per year, it has an aggregate purchasing power similar to that of a U.S. community of 50,000 people. He suggests that no one would consider an economic unit of that size economically viable. Somehow, sovereignty, history, and tribal pride maintain such nations.

Two approaches are being employed to integrate Africa. First are attempts to bring together a few (three or four) nations into close economic relationships emphasizing economic growth in the industrial sector. The second approach involves more grandiose schemes grouping a large number of nations (perhaps 12 to 15) and is designed to bring about cooperation in nearly all areas of economic activity, including transportation, education, manpower, natural resources, agriculture, and industrial development.

The Economic Community of West African States, ECOWAS, is the most recent and apparently most ambitious of the African regional cooperative groups. ECOWAS has an aggregate GNP of more than $28 million, and the 16-nation group hopes to achieve full economic integration by 1990. Experts suggest that the economic domination by Nigeria (64 percent of all the market's exports) may create internal strains that cannot be repaired. Yet, of all the attempts at economic integration among African states, ECOWAS seems to have the best chance of succeeding. There have been a number of African organizations including the East African Community which attempted to organize regional cooperative trading programs. The East African Community, established in 1967 and ended in 1977, was considered by many to have some reasonable chance of succeeding; however, a dispute between Kenya and Tanzania, two major member states, led to closing of their borders to one another and the eventual demise of the organization. Of the many economic groups organized, ECOWAS has been the only one to survive to date. It is safe to say that among all the world's regional integration schemes, African attempts have been the least successful.[16]

The Americas

The United States of America and the Economic Commission for Latin America have played major roles in the development of the various market groups in Latin America (see Exhibit 10–3). Progress has been slow because

---

[16] Arthur Hazlewood, "The End of the East African Community: What Are the Lessons for Regional Integration Schemes?" *Journal of Common Market Studies* September 1979, pp. 40–57.

EXHIBIT 10–3: Latin American groups

Name of association	Members	Population (millions)	GDP* (billions U.S. dollars)	National income per capita* (U.S. dollars)	Imports (millions U.S. dollars)
Andean Common	Bolivia	4.6	4.2	477	985
Market (ANCOM)	Colombia	22.6	22.8	803	3,233
	Ecuador	6.5	7.5	574	1,986
	Peru	13.5	11.2	586	2,090
	Venezuela	10.7	39.7	2,772	9,618
	Panama (Association)	1.4	2.3	1,116	1,187
Central Amerian	Guatemala	.5	6.2	749	1,504
Common Market	El Salvador	3.6	3.1	621	1,012
(CACM)	Costa Rica	1.9	3.5	1,378	1,397
	Nicaragua	1.9	2.1	896	360
	Honduras	2.7	1.8	426	830
Caribbean Community	Antigua	.1	.05	677	35
and Common Market	Barbados	.2	.5	1,586	424
(CARICOM)	Belize	.1	.1	639	79
	Pominica	.1	.03	354	28
	Grenada	.1	.04	389	45
	Guyana	.7	.4	603	425
	Jamaica	1.8	3.3	1,254	1,178
	Montserrat	.01	92.4	538	10
	St-Kitts-Neris-Anguilla	.1	.03	463	11
	St. Lucia	.1	.1	499	101
	St. Vincent	.1	.04	331	36
	Trinidad-Tobago	.1	3.9	2,059	3,178
Latin American Integra-	Argentina	23.4	36.7	677	6,713
tion Association	Bolivia	4.6	.4.2	477	985
(LAIA) (formerly	Brazil	92.3	188.7	1,523	19,804
LAFTA, Treaty of	Chile	8.9	11.5	421	4,219
Montevideo 80, Au-	Colombia	22.6	22.8	803	3,233
gust 1980)	Ecuador	6.5	7.5	574	1,986
	Mexico	48.2	92.4	1,244	11,829
	Paraguay	2.4	2.6	776	432
	Peru	13.5	11.2	586	2,090
	Uruguay	2.8	4.9	1,612	1,231
	Venezuela	10.7	39.7	2,772	9,618

* GDP and national income per capita from *Yearbook of National Account Statistics* 1979, vol. 2 (New York: United Nations, 1980); *GDP*—Table 1A, pp. 3–9, national income—Table 1B pp. 10–16.
Source: *Statistical Yearbook,* 1979–1980 (New York: United Nations, 1981).

of the low-level development and political instability which characterize Latin American nations. Nevertheless, there has been measurable progress; in fact, the miracle has been that the markets have functioned as well as they have.

The Latin America Free Trade Association (LAFTA) was the first and most ambitious, but it made less progress than other market groups. For years the Central American Common Market (CACM) was proof that union could work among underdeveloped countries.

Conflict in the early 1970s almost destroyed the market, but by 1977 the group was considering a new "treaty for a Central American economic and social community" to coordinate virtually all aspects of economic and social interchange. It was to build on existing free trade programs, include harmonization of tax and foreign investment rules, grant full free movement of labor and capital, and build common agricultural and social policies. The program would also have added a sectorial complementation program to provide access to the entire market for basic industries, but hostilities between El Salvador and Honduras eventually lead to Honduras' withdrawal in 1980. Because of a lack of cooperation, CACM has been less than effective.[17]

The Andean Common Market (sometimes referred to as the Andean Pact) continues to survive similar conflicts. Although considerable progress has been made in the Andean Common Market's internal economic aid and sectorial programs, excessive restrictions on foreign investments may mean Peru and perhaps Bolivia will leave the pact as Chili did in 1976. Problems center around the Andean Pact's strict regulation on foreign investments which has kept many foreign companies away from the region. A controversial rule called "Decision 24" stipulates that foreign companies must agree to convert to "mixed" or "national" status by taking on government partners before they are allowed to participate in the enlarged Andean market. Further, they are prohibited from repatriating more than 20 percent of the direct capital they invest and can only reinvest 70 percent of their profits every year. Most multinationals have refused to meet these requirements and are limiting their business to local markets. Pressures are mounting to ease these restrictions against foreign investments; Peru has threatened to quit the pact unless Decision 24 is revised to allow more liberal investment procedures.[18]

Similar economic disagreements among member nations led to the dismantling of LAFTA and the creation of the new Latin America Integration Association (LAIA). The original 11 members of LAFTA signed an accord to create the new organization in 1980. The long-term goal of LAIA (like LAFTA) will be the establishment, in a gradual and progressive manner,

---

[17] "A Continent at Odds With Itself," *World Business Weekly*, August 24, 1981, p. 29.

[18] "South America—Why The Andean Pact is Falling Apart," *Business Weekly*, September 21, 1981, pp. 49–50.

of a Latin American Common Market. In the initial stages, this will consist of an area of economic preferences and not a free trade area.

LAIA differs from LAFTA in several ways.

1. It encourages bilateral, subregional, and extraregional trade and tariff agreements. This elastic manner of promoting economic integration reflects the vastly different political and economic climates of member countries.

2. A distinguishing feature of LAIA is that no timetables for tariff reductions will be set. One major disagreement among members of LAFTA centered on the imposed timetable for tariff reductions which for many lesser developed countries proved to be uneconomical.

One of the more important aspects of the new treaty is the differential treatment of member countries according to their level of economic development. In order to avoid the big country bias for which LAFTA was criticized, there are three recognized levels under the LAIA framework: the more developed countries (MDCs) including Argentina, Brazil, and Mexico; the less developed countries (LDCs)—Chili, Colombia, Venezuela, Peru, Paraguay; and the least developed countries (LLDCs)—Bolivia, Equador, and Paraguay. The differential benefits are designated for the LLDCs and the LDCs by application of the "principle of nonreciprocal treatment" when they signed their bilateral trade arrangements with the MDCs. The LLDCs are to receive most favored nation treatment, thereby receiving the same rights other LAIA countries have obtained through their bilateral treaties. These changes in the new organization were designed to permit the less economically developed members of the group to participate more fully than under LAFTA rules.[19] Perhaps greater economic integration will be achieved among the LAIA members than ever occurred in LAFTA.

The Caribbean Free Trade Association tasted the fruits of success and opted for even stronger management, forming the Caribbean Community Market (CARICOM) which initially included the more developed countries and was expected to incorporate lesser developed members also. While there were high expectations for the success of CARICOM when it was developed in 1973, it has not lived up to expectations. It still survives, but the extent of its overall achievements and its current standing among the Caribbean nations is disappointing. The organization is weakened by the continued economic problems confronting its Caribbean members. Most of the Caribbean members have had a short history free of commonwealth status and thus they have been reluctant to give up any of their recently acquired political freedom to a regional organization.[20]

---

[19] "New Latin American Association Carries on Traditions of LAFTA, With Some Important Differences," *Business America*, April 6, 1981, p. 15; "LAIA Takes Hold as LAFTA Accords are Renegotiated," *Business Latin America*, January 21, 1981, pp. 23–24.

[20] Anthony Paine, "The Rise and Fall of Caribbean Regionalisation," *Journal of Common Market Studies*, March 1981, pp. 255–80.

BOX 10–5: North American Common Market?

A North American Common Market (NACM) does *not* exist, but for several years there have been some advocating the establishment of NACM. Most recently, a few prominent American publications and business executives have expressed the idea that the United States, Canada, and Mexico should be tied together in an "economic community" patterned after the European Community. Those who suggest such a union (mostly from the U.S.) see NACM as a means of increasing the flow of oil and natural gas from Canada and Mexico to the United States. The attraction for Mexico and Canada is supposed to be the vast U.S. market for those country's goods and a solution for Mexico's unemployed and underemployed labor problems. It is projected that these problems could be remedied by the increased industrial activity that would result from U.S. demand and the free movement of labor that would exist under NACM.

How would such an alliance compare with the European Community? A NACM would be a colossal, almost self-sufficient market with vast reserves of oil, gas, coal, and other minerals and a formidable world competitor.

But would the Canadians and Mexicans go for the idea? Probably not. They would not get much better trade advantage than they presently have; Mexico exports to the United States almost duty free as does Canada. So joining NACM would not significantly improve trade for them and, more importantly, both countries fear the U.S.'s economic dominance. They do not want to become "branch-plant economies" serving the United States with cheap goods and unlimited oil and gas.

However, don't underestimate U.S. desire for a dependable source of oil and gas.

Source: Adapted from Herbert E. Meyer, "Why a North American Common Market Won't Work—Yet," *Fortune*, September 10, 1979, pp. 118–24.

The major contribution of the Latin American market groups to international market theory is the concept of "sectorial" development. In this arrangement, different sectors of business, such as metalworking, are studied by the Sectorial Commissions and various segments of the industry are assigned to different countries for development. They then hold common-market monopolies on the goods they are producing. The result is a series of agreements which provide for marketing and sharing on a complementary basis among LAIA members.

Middle East

Less developed than Europe to begin with, the Middle East has been slower in the formation of successfully functioning multinational market groups. Some progress is now being made toward the development of freer trade. (See Exhibit 10–4.) Countries belonging to the Arab Common Market set a goal of free internal trade by 1974 but did not make it; they are planning to equalize external tariffs at some later date. A new variety of economic cooperation has been pioneered through the Regional Cooperation for Development, formed by Pakistan, Iran, and Turkey, which had made impressive strides in encouraging basic industrial production in those

EXHIBIT 10–4:   Middle and Far East Market groups

Name of association	Members	Population (millions)	GDP (billions U.S. dollars)	National income per capita (U.S. dollars)	Imports (millions U.S. dollars)
Arab Common Market	Iraq	12	19.2	1,561	4,213
	Kuwait	1	13.4	11,431	5,204
	Jordan	2	1.5	457	1,949
	Syria	7	6.5	702	3,329
	Egypt	37	18.8	308	4,860
Regional Cooperative	Pakistan	65	19.7	261	4,056
for Development	Iran	34	53.0	1,600	9,738
	Turkey	40	50.0	873	4,946
Association of	Indonesia	119	49.3	304	10,834
South East	Malaysia	10	15.5	714	7,844
Asian Nations	Singapore	2	7.7	2,279	24,008
(ASEAN)	Philippines	42	23.4	457	7,727
	Thailand	34	21.8	444	9,214

Source: *Statistical Yearbook* 1979–1980 (New York: United Nations, 1981).

countries until the revolution in Iran ended any economic activity. So far, the RCDs have not succeeded in lowering or eliminating tariffs or in building a common external tariff wall, but the degree of cooperation is encouraging.

The area's economic boom from crude oil price increases has kept the major producer countries busy on national economic development and spending and investing surplus income. Religious and ethenic bonds are strong among the Arabs, so increased activity in economic cooperation may be expected. Saudi Arabia has already taken the lead in assisting with economic development of other Arab countries.

Asia

About one third of the world's population (even excluding China) lives in Asia and the Far East, but this massive population produces less than 2 percent of the world's industrial output. The United Nations Economic Commission for Asia and the Far East (ECAFE) has worked diligently to strengthen the Asian market through development of multinational market groups. It also formed the Asian Industrial Development Council, dedicated to the development of trade and commercial arrangements and multicountry joint ventures to speed the industrialization of Asia. It has created the Asian Development Bank, which has been in full operation since 1966 and has an authorized capital of $1 billion (a third of which is subscribed to by European and North American countries). Despite the low volume of trade in the area, Asia has a heritage of international trading, and one third of its international trade has been on an interregional basis. This, coupled with the fact that many Asian nations are members of the Commonwealth and already have established working relationships, makes the future of multinational economic organizations promising.

The Association of Southeast Asian Nations is the primary multinational group in Asia. The first meetings were in 1967, but the group did not become operative until Vietnam was unified under Communist domination. In response, representatives of Indonesia, Malaysia, Singapore, the Philippines, and Thailand formalized arrangements in 1977 for an operational regional cooperation group that became operational in 1978. The goals of the group are: economic integration and cooperation through a complementary industry program; preferential trading including reduced tariff and nontariff barriers; guaranteed member access to markets throughout the community; and harmonized investment incentives. Like all multinational market groups, ASEAN has experienced many problems and false starts in attempting to unify their $90 billion combined economy. One problem is the small amount of interarea trade because of similar exports and similar national assets. All of nations except Singapore have an abundance of labor and an undeveloped economic infrastructure. Nevertheless, a long list of products are covered by preferential trading agreements and the group has weathered some extreme economic disagreements and disappointments when proposed sectorial investment projects did not materialize.[21]

SUMMARY

The experience of the multinational market groups developed since World War II points up both the possible successes and the hazards such groups encounter. The various attempts at economic cooperation represent varying degrees of success and failure, but, almost without regard to their degree of success, the economic market groups have created great excitement among marketers.

Economic benefits possible through cooperation relate to more efficient marketing and production: marketing efficiency is effected through the development of mass markets, encouragement of competition, the improvement of personal income, and various psychological market factors. Production efficiency derives from specialization, mass production for mass markets, and the free movement of the factors of production. Economic integration also tends to foster political harmony among the countries involved; such harmony leads to stability, which is beneficial to the marketer.

The marketing implications of multinational market groups may be studied from the standpoint of firms located inside the market or of firms located outside which wish to sell the markets. For each viewpoint the problems and opportunities are somewhat different; but regardless of the location of

---

[21] "ASEAN Revisited: Few Firms Using it; A New Wrinkle to Consider," *Business International,* May 8, 1981, pp. 147–48.

the marketer, multinational market groups do provide great opportunity for the creative marketer who wishes to expand volume. Market groupings make it economically feasible to enter new markets and to employ new marketing strategies which could not be applied to the smaller markets represented by individual countries.

The success of the European Community and the relative success of some of the other multinational market groups indicate that there will be continued development in this field. Such development will continue to challenge the international marketer by providing continually growing market opportunities.

QUESTIONS

1. Elaborate on the problems and benefits for international marketers from multinational market groups.

2. Explain the political role of multinational market groups. Identify the factors on which one may judge the potential success or failure of a multinational market group.

3. Explain the marketing implications of the factors contributing to the successful development of a multinational market group.

4. Imagine that the United States was composed of many separate countries with individual trade barriers. What marketing effects might one visualize?

5. Discuss the possible types of arrangements for regional economic integration.

6. Differentiate between a free-trade area and a common market. Explain the marketing implication of the differences.

7. It seems obvious that the founders of the European Community intended it to be a truly common market; so much so that economic integration must obviously be supplemented by political integration in order to accomplish these objectives completely. Discuss.

8. The Commission, the Council of Ministers, and the Court of Justice of the EC have gained power in the last decade. Comment.

9. Select any three countries which might have some logical basis for establishing a multinational market organization (such as Canada, the United States, and Mexico). Identify the various problems which would be encountered in forming multinational market groups of such countries.

10. U.S. exports to the European Community are expected to decline in future years. What marketing actions may a company take to counteract such changes?

11. "Because they are dynamic and because they have great growth possibilities, the multinational markets are likely to be especially rough and tumble for the external business." Discuss.

12. Differentiate between a full customs union and a political union.

13. Define:

OECD	COMECON	LLDC
Zollverein	Sectorial program	LAIA
Commonwealth	ECOWAS	

14. What actions must be taken by business to cope with limitations imposed by sectorial programs?

15. Why have African nations had such difficulty in forming effective economic unions?

16. Discuss the future of international market groups in light of increased world competition and protectionist pressures.

17. What is different about LAIA's organization and structure from LAFTA's that is expected to increase its chances of success?

18. How do LAFTA and LAIA differ?

Chapter 11

Developing markets and market behavior

Since the decade of the 1950s, few nations have been content with an economic status quo; instead, they seek economic growth, increased standards of living, lower poverty levels, and an opportunity for the "good life." The world's economies are on the move and, although not all at the same level or rate of development, most are experiencing some degree of industrialization, urbanization, rising productivity, higher personal incomes, and technological progress. There is rising demand for goods and services the world over from the most underdeveloped country to the most industrialized. Markets are dynamic, developing entities reflecting the changing life styles of a culture—they are becoming different, larger, more demanding. Instant tortilla meal is consumed in Guatemala, hotdogs and hamburgers in France; supermarkets are displacing specialty stores and market vendors in some countries; and, should present trends continue, Japan may be the world's most affluent nation by the end of this century. Old stereotypes, traditions, and habits are being cast aside or tempered, and new patterns of consumer behavior are emerging.

Continual and rapid changes are so much the rule in today's markets that change must be recognized and viewed in its proper perspective.[1] An important fact about the transformation of consumer behavior is that it is not occurring at a uniform rate throughout the world, nor is the character of the change necessarily the same. For example, a study of purchase patterns in Europe showed that while Europe's two major economic blocks have prospered during the decade of the 1970s, each had different ideas on what to do with the new affluence. Households in European Community countries spent their newfound wealth on labor-saving devices, while families in other European nations showed a distinct preference for products linked with leisure-time activities, affluence, or product innovations.

Opportunities for the marketer are afforded through continuous increases in demand in more industrialized countries and in emerging demand in less developed countries. If marketing efforts are made to coincide with the developmental goals of the host country, prime opportunities await marketers in the decades of the 1980s and 90s in the less-developed countries where three quarters of mankind lives. Further, in more advanced econo-

[1] Leslie M. Dawson, "Facing the New Realities of International Development," *Business*, January/February, 1981, pp. 29–35.

mies, consumer life-styles change as a country's economy moves from one level of economic development to another; the resultant impact on market characteristics is often sudden, causing rapid change in degree and/or kind. Failure to keep abreast of these changes and differences and their implications can end in costly disappointment. This chapter will explore economic development and marketing and changing market patterns around the world.

MARKETING AND ECONOMIC DEVELOPMENT

The economic level of the country is the single most important environmental element to which the foreign marketer must adjust the marketing task in a developing market. The stage of economic growth within a country affects attitudes toward foreign business activity, the demand for goods, distribution systems found within a country and, indeed, the entire marketing process. Growth forces successful marketing to achieve the zenith of the marketing concept. In static economies, consumption patterns become rigid and marketing is typically nothing more than a supply effort. In a dynamic economy, consumption patterns frequently change rapidly, marketing is constantly faced with the challenge of detecting and providing for new levels of consumption, and marketing efforts must be matched with ever-changing market needs and wants. Certainly a nation's economy and its dynamic nature must be paramount in the evaluation of any potential market, domestic or foreign.[2]

As part of the world marketing environment to which the marketer must become attuned, economic development presents a two-sided challenge. First, a study of the general aspects of economic development is necessary to gain empathy for the economic climate within developing countries. A country's economic goals, marketing's assigned role in such expectations, and marketing's actual role must be examined to appreciate the environment which faces a foreign marketer in a developing country.

Second, the state of economic development should be studied with respect to market potential, including the present level of economic achievement and the economy's growth potential. The current level of economic development dictates the kind and degree of market potential that exists, while a knowledge of the dynamism of the economy allows the marketer to prepare for dramatic economic shifts. To begin, a definition of economic development is in order.

Stages of economic development

Economic development is generally understood to mean an increase in national production that results in an increase in the average per capita

---

[2] Robert Bartels, *Global Development and Marketing* (Columbus, Ohio: Grid, 1981), 117 pp.

gross national product (GNP). An increase in average per capita GNP alone, however, is not sufficient to denote the implied or expected meaning of economic development. Besides an increase in average per capita GNP, most interpretations of the concept imply a widespread distribution of the increased income as well. Economic development, as commonly defined today, also tends to mean *rapid growth*—improvements achieved "in decades rather than centuries."

One frequently used model for classifying countries by stage of economic development is that presented by Rostow. He identifies five stages of development—growth is the movement from one stage to another, and countries in the first three stages are considered to be underdeveloped. Briefly, the stages are:

Stage 1:   *The traditional society.*   Countries in this stage lack the capability of significantly increasing the level of productivity. There is a marked absence of systematic application of the methods of modern science and technology. Literacy is low as well as other types of social overhead.

Stage 2:   *The preconditions for take-off.*   This second stage includes those societies which are in the process of transition to the take-off stage. During this period, the advances of modern science are beginning to be applied in agriculture and production. The development of transportation, communications, power, education, health, and other public undertakings are begun in a small but important way.

Stage 3:   *The take-off.*   At this stage, countries achieve a growth pattern which becomes a normal condition. Human resources and social overhead have been developed to sustain steady development. Agricultural and industrial modernization lead to rapid expansion in these areas.

Stage 4:   *The drive to maturity.*   After take-off, sustained progress is maintained and the economy seeks to extend modern technology to all fronts of economic activity. The economy takes on international involvement. In this stage, an economy demonstrates that it has the technological and entrepreneurial skills to produce not everything, but anything it chooses to produce.

Stage 5:   *The age of high mass consumption.*   The age of high mass consumption leads to shifts in the leading economic sectors toward durable consumers' goods and services. Real income per capita rises to the point where a very large number of people have significant amounts of discretionary income.

For purposes of this chapter, the terms *less-developed, underdeveloped,* and so forth, will refer to countries whose economies would fall in one of Rostow's first three categories. In order to quantify this degree of development, it is frequently the practice to arbitrarily place all those economies with less than $300 to $500 annual per capita income in the underdeveloped category. A range of this level classifies many of the nations of Asia, Africa, Latin America, and Southern and Eastern Europe as underdeveloped. Under the preceding conditions, the category of "developing country" will comprise those underdeveloped countries that are taking steps to move from a lower stage to a higher one with some degree of success. The author realizes, of course, that such an approach in identifying underdeveloped countries is not without its faults, but nevertheless, it will serve in the ensuing discussion.

Several developing countries have experienced relatively rapid industrial growth during the last two decades. They have grown more rapidly than most LDCs and have experienced improvement in their general economic well-being. These NICs (Newly Industrialized Countries)[3] do not fit the traditional mode of developing countries. Their GNP per capita generally exceeds $1,500 and, further, their rapid industrialization includes locally owned companies as well as several joint ventures with foreign MNCs. The majority of the manufactured products produced are exported and include items such as clothing, athletic and rubber footwear, and electronics. It is estimated that the exports of these countries have risen from $4.6 billion in 1965 to over $100 billion in 1980.[4]

Brazil is a good example of the growing importance of NICs in world trade. Five years ago Brazil's exports of technological goods and services were negligible. In 1981, such exports should reach $1.6 billion and include high-technology items such as high-performance pistons for U.S. lighter-than-air aircraft engine manufacturers, chassis for Washington, D.C. subway cars, and high-strength steel made by a Brazilian company, now being tested for use in the undercarriages of U.S. jumbo jets.[5]

Infrastructure and development

One indicator of economic development is the extent of social overhead capital or infrastructure within the economy. Infrastructure are those types of capital goods that serve the activities of many industries. Included in a country's infrastructure are support facilities, such as paved roads, railroads, seaports, communications networks, and energy supplies—all necessary to support production and marketing. The quality of infrastructure directly affects a country's economic growth potential and the ability of an enterprise to engage effectively in business.

---

[3] NICs include Brazil, Mexico, South Korea, Taiwan, Singapore, and Hong Kong.

[4] See L. H. Wortzel and H. Z. Wortzel, "Export Marketing Strategies for NIC LDC-based Firms," *Columbia Journal of World Business,* Spring 1981, pp. 51–60, for an interesting discussion of the strategies of NIC firms.

[5] "Brazil Raises Exports of High Technology, to Pace Third World," *The Wall Street Journal,* Tuesday, October 6, 1981, p. 18.

The infrastructure is a crucial component of the uncontrollable elements facing marketers. Without adequate transportation facilities, for example, a marketer's distribution costs can increase substantially, and the ability to reach certain segments of the market may be impaired. In fact, a market's full potential may never be realized because of an inadequate existing infrastructure. To a marketer, the key issues in evaluating the importance of infrastructure concern the types necessary for profitable trade and the impact on a firm's ability to market effectively if a country's infrastructure is underdeveloped. In addition to the social overhead capital type of infrastructure

---

BOX 11-1:   Infrastructure—LDC versus NIC

India (Less Developed Country):

Mrs. Indira Gandhi claimed that animals in India provided 30,000 MW of power, more than the 29,000 MW provided by electricity.

Since the slaughter of cattle is banned in almost all states in the country, India has the highest cattle population in the world—perhaps as many as 360m. Bullocks are used for ploughing fields, turning water-wheels, working crushers and threshers, and above all for hauling carts. The number of bullock carts has doubled to 15m since India's independence in 1947. Bullocks haul more tonnage than the entire railway system (though over a much shorter distance); in many parts of rural India they are the only practical means of moving things about.

As a bonus, India's cattle produce enormous quantities of dung, which is used both as farmyard manure and (in the form of dried cakes) as household fuel. Some studies suggest that these forms of energy are the equivalent of another 10,000 MW.*

Mexico† (Newly Industrialized Country):

Mexico's archaic transport system will grind to a halt if the economy continues to grow 7 percent–8 percent a year. Roads and seaports are inadequate, and the railroad system has hardly been modernized since the 1910 revolution.

Bottlenecks are already making it difficult to market goods and are raising consumer prices. Late delivery of raw materials is holding back corporate expansion plans. Mexico City suffers doubly: Imports must be shipped over long distances, and the city's internal transit system is a smog-filled nightmare. There is no direct link to Tampico; trains are routed via San Luis Potosi, which doubles the distance. The journey to Veracruz, another major port, takes 15 hours by train, though the distance is only 250 miles. By road the time is cut to seven hours.

Toward the end of last year railroad freight temporarily collapsed. The state-run *Ferrocarriles Nacionales de Mexico* imposed a two-month embargo on incoming freight from the United States, in order to clear a massive backlog of railroad cars. A U.S. official reported that every siding from Laredo to Oklahoma, a distance of 550 miles, was backed up with Mexican-bound freight. More than 32,000 American and Canadian rail cars were just waiting in line.

This not only caused industrial chaos; it also cost the government dearly. At the height of the logjam Mexico was paying an estimated $400,000 a day rental on stalled cars, as well as a 5¢-per-mile charge. Mexico is forced to rent a huge number of cars, because it lacks its own rolling stock.

* "Bullock Manure," *The Economist,* London, October 17, 1981, p. 88.

† "Arteriosclerosis Threatens Chaos and Raises Costs," *World Business Weekly,* October 5, 1981, p. 36. Reprinted by permission of the Financial Times, London.

EXHIBIT 11-1: Infrastructure—selected countries

Country	Highways (paved, km)	Railways (km)	Trucks and buses in use (000)	Electricity production (kwh billion)	Newspapers (circulation per 1,000 population)
United States	6,251,700	600,000	31,921	2,328	277
Brazil	1,384,400	30,645	1,919	89	45
China	880,000*	52,000	650	136	na
Colombia	65,161	3,421	177	13	50
Germany	479,658	31,692	1,617	353	42
Kenya	50,600	5,919	100	1	11
Mexico	212,400*	16,250	1,213	47	60
Spain	227,513	16,700	1,381	110	128

* Includes unpaved and paved.

Sources: *Business Latin America*, December 24, 1980, pp. 412–14. *Business Europe*, January 30, 1981, pp. 2–6; February 13, 1981, pp. 7–10; February 12, 1982, pp. 51–54; January 29, 1982, pp. 35–37; and Frank E. Bair, *International Marketing Handbook*, 1st ed. (Detroit: Gale Research Co., 1982).

described above, business efficiency is also affected by the presence of financial and commercial service infrastructure such as advertising agencies, warehousing/storage facilities, credit and banking facilities, marketing research agencies, and quality level specialized middlemen found within a country. Generally speaking, the less developed a country is, the less adequate the infrastructure is for conducting business.[6]

As trade develops, a country's infrastructure typically expands to meet the needs of an expanding economy. There is some question of whether effective marketing increases the pace of infrastructure development or whether an expanded infrastructure leads to more effective marketing. The issue is similar to the old question, "which came first, the chicken or the egg?" Most probably, infrastructure and effective economic development and marketing activity increase concurrently but never progressing at the same pace. Certainly companies still market when an inadequate infrastructure exists, but it is usually necessary to modify the offerings and approach to meet existing infrastructure levels. A significant portion of the capital spent by developing countries is on the expansion of their infrastructure.[7] (See Exhibit 11–1.)

When infrastructure does not develop with an expanding population and economy, countries begin to lose economic development ground. Conditions can develop where a country produces commodities for export but cannot export them because of inadequacies of the infrastructure. For example, in Zimbabwe, they expanded the agricultural sector of their economy

---

[6] Paul Mitchell, "Infrastructures and International Marketing Effectiveness," *Columbia Journal of World Business*, Spring 1979, pp. 91–101.

[7] "Working on Infrastructure," *The Asian Wall Street Journal Weekly*, August 24, 1981, p. 10.

to the point that they had excess agricultural products for export. However, of the 1.5 million tons of maize available for export, only a third could be moved to ports because the rolling stock for railroads was so inadequate. This added further economic hardships to an already weakened country.[8]

This problem is not unique to LDCs; even NICs must struggle with inadequate support services. Mexico's rapidly expanding economy has been throttled by its archaic transport system. Some observers estimate that the system will grind to a halt if the economy continues to grow at its present 7 to 8 percent a year. Roads and seaports are inadequate, and the railroad system has seen little modernization since the 1910 revolution. If it were not for Mexico's highway system (although it too is inadequate) the economy would have come to a halt already. In 1980, for example, the highways carried 300 million tons of freight compared to 73 million tons carried by the railroads.[9]

Objectives of developing countries

A thorough assessment of economic development and marketing should begin with a brief review of the basic facts and objective of economic development. To be capable of adjusting to a foreign economic environment an international marketer must be able to answer questions such as: (1) What are the objectives of the developing nations? (2) What role is marketing assigned, if any, in economic growth plans? (3) What contribution must marketing make, whether overtly planned or not, for a country to grow successfully? (4) What attitudes prevail which might hamper marketing strategies, development, and growth? and (5) How can the market potential, present and future, be assessed?

Industrialization is the fundamental objective of most developing countries, although for an appreciation of its impact on a nation's people, economic growth must be viewed as a means to an end rather than as the end itself. Certainly, most countries see in "economic growth" the achievement of social as well as economic goals. Better education, better and more effective government, eliminations of many social inequities, and improvements in moral and ethical responsibilities, are some of the expectations of developing countries. Thus, economic growth is not measured solely in economic goals but also in social achievements. An understanding of these objectives can help explain attitudes and behavior toward marketing which often exist within an underdeveloped country in the growth stage. The fact that most countries wish to determine their own economic, political, and cultural future goes far in explaining the potential vulnerability of a foreign marketer in these countries. Because foreign marketers are outsiders, it is

---

[8] "Question Marks Over Zimbabwe," *World Business Weekly*, October 19, 1981, p. 33.

[9] "Arteriosclerosis Threatens Chaos and Raises Costs," *World Business Weekly*, October 5, 1981, p. 36.

often assumed their presence is limiting the attainment of these objectives. This can result in political and governmental harassment and, sometimes, consumer boycott of goods. The widespread fear and resentment of foreign control of an economy commonly leads to the adoption of policies and actions which retard rather than facilitate economic progress. Though marketing's crucial role is often not appreciated, foreign enterprise and marketing can play a significant role in helping countries achieve their growth objectives.

Marketing's contribution neglected

How important is marketing to the achievement of the goals mentioned above? Unfortunately, marketing (or distribution) is not always considered meaningful to those responsible for planning. Economic planners frequently are more production than marketing oriented and tend to ignore or regard distribution as an inferior economic activity. Given such attitudes, economic plans generally are more concerned with the problems of production, investment, and finance than the problems of efficiency of distribution. An examination of agricultural development plans for 13 developing countries reveal that none assigned more than 6 percent of total planned agricultural investment to marketing the expected agricultural output. Yet agricultural exports were a major source of each country's income.[10]

There is a strongly held opinion (albeit wrong) that an economic system must first have the capacity to produce before the level of consumption and distribution becomes a problem. With this concept in mind, one developing nation invested $20 million in a fertilizer plant without making provisions for the sale and distribution of the product. After a few weeks of production, the plant accumulated a huge inventory it was unable to effectively distribute. Marketing problems had been ignored. The net result was that the plant had excess inventory and had stopped production while a severe shortage of fertilizer existed in a nearby area. The country had production capability, but the product was not being marketed.

Lack of concern for distribution and economic planning extends to the technical assistance offered by developed countries as well. The United States, for example, has ignored many of the problems of distribution or marketing in its technical assistance programs for underdeveloped countries. Of the several explanations for such an orientation, the first is that concern for production seems more practical than concern for consumption in an underdeveloped country. Second, many cultures view marketing as a wasteful activity and those engaged in marketing as parasites. The utility of advertising, product planning, and innovation is constantly questioned in even the most mature economic systems.

---

[10] Paul L. Oritt and Alfred J. Hagen, "Channels of Distribution and Economic Development," *Atlanta Economic Review*, July/August 1977, p. 40.

Third, the cultural or traditional rigidity found in the distribution structure of many countries has caused neglect of the distribution problem. The intangible nature of marketing fosters general neglect; it is difficult to quantify marketing benefits compared to production. Furthermore, of all the skills, those in marketing may be the most difficult to transfer from one economy to another. Machines can be built in the United States and used in Egypt, but a marketing plan or system adequate for the U.S. market usually will be inappropriate in another culture. One authority noted that production or technical know-how is about 100 percent transferable to Mexico from the United States, but marketing know-how is only about 20 percent transferable. Even if marketing skills were 100 percent transferable, they could not be applied efficiently in many of the developing countries because the distribution and *economic infrastructure* necessary to implement marketing programs is not available. Imagine marketing where there is production but no disposable income, no storage, the only transportation available is to the wrong markets, and no middlemen and facilitating agents exist to participate in the flow of goods from the manufacturer to the consumer. When such conditions exist in developing markets, marketing and economic progress are retarded.

Finally, low evaluation of the marketing function in many underdeveloped economies can be explained by the fact that effective marketing, unlike production, cannot develop without the general use of money. The use of money as a medium of exchange is a relatively new and unusual practice for many economic groups; therefore, an aura of mystery and sometimes distrust surrounds its use. Frequently only small segments of the population, often of different ethnic backgrounds, are the money users in these underdeveloped economies, adding to the suspicious attitude toward money and the distribution system on which it thrives. In spite of the many negative notions, marketing makes a positive contribution to the economic development of a country.

Walt Rostow notes that if the process of modernization is to continue in developing nations, distribution and the entire process of widening the market will lead the way. Marketing is an economy's arbitrator between productive capacity and consumer demand. The marketing process is the critical element in effectively utilizing production resulting from economic growth; it can create a balance between higher production and higher consumption. Effective marketing not only improves the lifestyle and well-being of people in a specific economy, it upgrades world markets; after all, a developed country's best customer is another developed country.

Although marketing may be considered a passive function, it is instrumental in laying the groundwork necessary for rapid development. A developed marketing system providing effective distribution for whatever a country produces is essential. Most underdeveloped countries have an inefficient, "outrageously" high-cost market structure in which those engaged in marketing barely manage to survive. Poor physical distribution, failure to match market needs to productive potential, and ineffective demand produce unbelievable waste. To eliminate some of the inefficiencies that sap economies of underdeveloped countries, the traditional "trader and merchant" system must be replaced by a fully developed distribution system with adequate financing of the distribution of goods and the means of matching production capacity and resources with consumer needs, wants, and purchasing power. In fact, marketing itself might go far toward changing the entire economic tone of an existing system—without any change in methods of production, distribution of population, or of income.

Marketing also helps increase existing markets. Although marketing cannot create purchasing power, it can uncover and direct what already exists. Increased economic activity leads to enlarged markets which set the stage for economies of scale in distribution and production that may not have existed before.

Another important contribution of marketing to very underdeveloped economies is the growth or spread of a money economy. Marketing requires a money system to be effective. Many underdeveloped economies have significant nonmonetized economic segments which stunt growth at a very low level. In rural India, for example, the barter system still prevails; goods

---

BOX 11–2: Junk, new measure of economic development

"For U.S. entrepreneurs going to strange foreign countries, junk studies can be very suggestive. Junk tends to be a leading economic indicator," said the professor.

According to Dr. Richard N. Farmer, "Most economic data is erroneous for reasons beyond the control of statisticians."

In quest of knowledge, Farmer has roamed the junkyards of at least 10 countries.

"Every country," he maintains, "is in at least one of five-level junk and trash development cycles," which he labels:

1. Nothing gets used. Mainly because the natives don't have the skill to make use of junk. Characteristic of primitive and remote tribes of desert nomads. Per capita income of less than $50 a year.
2. Everything gets used. Indicative of rudimentary skills in reusing old materials. Nothing is thrown away for good. Ingenuity develops. Autos are totally stripped. Per capita income up to $200.
3. Piling up phase. Low-grade materials show up in junkyards and about the countryside: broken bottles, cement fragments, occasional tires, leaking bottles, and autos almost, but not quite totally, stripped.

   "Labor, particularly skilled labor, is being drawn off into more productive pursuits, so cars begin to have bits and pieces of hard-to-get things left on them." The junkyard "comes into its own."
4. The Age of Affluence. Usable trash accumulates. Lots of bottles, cans, tires, occasional abandoned cars. Useful stuff appears such as copper piping, two-by-fours, wire. Per capita income up to $1,200. Influential people talk about ecology. Trash no longer an asset but a costly burden.
5. Total Affluence. Per capita income up to $2,500 or more. Trash becomes a major public issue. Abandoned cars, throw-away containers, piles of paper become problems.

Source: John Cunniff, "Junk Pile Analyzation Gives Clues to Economic Conditions of Countries" (New York: Associated Press).

are exchanged for other goods and services. Carpenters, goldsmiths, black-smiths, chauffeurs, weavers, and others, still provide their services in ex-change for food grains to farmers and others.[11]

With money instead of barter as a medium of trade, a society can develop a wider choice in consumption opportunity. Since the range of available products generally increases as marketing grows, people are exposed to a greater variety of goods. The possibility of acquiring these goods has a stimulating effect on the self-discipline and motivation of the people; instead of labor meaning subsistence living, as in many backward economies, it becomes the means of obtaining a more satisfying list of wants.

The growth and stimulation from increased desire for material possessions frequently lead to development of much needed managers and entrepre-neurs. For accelerated economic growth, a country needs a ready supply of entrepreneurs who can see and seize the opportunities for joining availa-ble capital with available resources in new combinations. Even with ample capital and opportunity, there must be indigenous entrepreneurs of vision willing to run the purposeful risk of taking the necessary action for develop-ment or rapid growth can be thwarted.

Finally, marketing contributes to the development of standards for eco-nomic behavior, integrity, and product and service reliability. A population struggling for survival tends to overlook the importance of private ownership of personal property; with such an attitude, the pattern for honesty in all parts of the society bears little relationship to the level of honesty accepted as normal in the United States. Business needs standards of integrity, honesty, workmanship, and quality if it is to expand. Thus, as business develops in scope and size, it fosters the development of these characteristics. As Drucker points out, the activity of Sears in Latin America resulted in making customers more cognizant of value; in forcing consumer credit; in changing attitudes toward the customer, store clerks, suppliers, and merchandise. Sears's growth has spawned the creation of new local businesses with higher stan-dards of workmanship, quality, and delivery to supply Sears with goods. The net result is that in a very few years, the science of management has been advanced at least a generation in these countries.

In short, marketing not only contributes to economic development, with humanitarian effect, but it is a good and profitable business with extraordi-nary growth potential.

MARKETING IN A DEVELOPING COUNTRY

In making a market appraisal, the economic level of a country must be reviewed to determine the limitations which exist in the marketplace and must be accounted for and adjusted to in marketing plans and strategies.

A marketer cannot superimpose a sophisticated marketing program on

---

[11] Y. S. Verma, "Marketing in Rural India," *Management International Review* 20, no. 4 (1980), p. 48.

an underdeveloped economy. Marketing effort must be keyed to each situation: it is a job of "custom tailoring" for each set of circumstances. A promotional program for a population 90 percent illiterate is vastly different from a program for a population that is 90 percent literate. Pricing in a subsistence market poses different problems than pricing in an "affluent society." The distribution structure should provide an efficient method of matching productive capacity with available demand. An efficient marketing program is one that provides for optimum utility at a single point in time, given a specific set of circumstances. In evaluating the potential in a developing country, the marketer must make an assessment of the existing level of marketing development within the country.

Level of marketing development

The level of the marketing function roughly parallels the stages of economic development. Exhibit 11–2 illustrates various stages of the marketing process as they develop in a growing economy. The table is a static model representing in some respects an idealized type of evolutionary process; economic cooperation and assistance, technological change, and political, social, and cultural factors can and do cause significant deviations in the evolutionary process. However, the table focuses on the logic and interdependence of marketing and economic development. The more developed an economy, the greater the variety of marketing functions demanded, and the more sophisticated and specialized the institutions become to perform marketing functions.

Perhaps the most strikingly obvious illustration of the relationship between marketing development and the stage of economic development of a country can be found in the evolution of the channel structure. One study found that with increasing economic development:

1. More developed countries have more levels of distribution, more specialty stores and supermarkets, more department stores, and more stores in rural areas.
2. The influence of the foreign import agent declines.
3. Manufacturer-wholesaler-retailer functions become separated.
4. Wholesaler functions approximate those in North America.
5. The financing function of wholesalers declines and wholesale markup increases.
6. The number of small stores declines and the size of the average store increases.
7. The role of the peddler and itinerant trader and the importance of the open-garden fair declines.
8. Retail margins improve.[12]

---

[12] George Wadinambiaratchi, "Channels of Distribution in Developing Economies," *The Business Quarterly*, Winter 1965, pp. 74–82. Reprints of this article in its entirety may be obtained from *The Business Quarterly*, School of Business Administration, The University of Western Ontario, London 72, Canada.

EXHIBIT 11-2: Evolution of the marketing process

Stage	Substage	Examples	Marketing functions	Marketing institutions	Channel control	Primary orientation	Resources employed	Comments
Agricultural and raw materials (Mk.(f) = prod.)*	Self-sufficient	Nomadic or hunting tribes	None	None	Traditional authority	Subsistence	Labor Land	Labor intensive No organized markets
	Surplus commodity producer	Agricultural economy—such as coffee, bananas	Exchange	Small-scale merchants, traders, fairs, export-import	Traditional authority	Entrepreneurial Commercial	Labor Land	Labor and land intensive Product specialization Local markets Import oriented
Manufacturing (Mk.(f) = prod.)	Small scale	Cottage industry	Exchange Physical distribution	Merchants, wholesalers, export-import	Middlemen	Entrepreneurial Financial	Labor Land Technology Transportation	Labor intensive Product standardization and grading Regional and export markets Import oriented
	Mass production	U.S. economy 1885–1914	Demand creation Physical distribution	Merchants, wholesalers, traders, and specialized institutions	Producer	Production and finance	Labor Land Technology Transportation Capital	Capital intensive Product differentiation National, regional, and export markets
Marketing (Prod.(f) = mk.)	Commercial— transition	U.S. economy 1915–1929	Demand creation Physical distribution Market information	Large-scale and chain retailers Increase in specialized middlemen	Producer	Entrepreneurial Commercial	Labor Land Technology Transportation Capital Communication	Capital intensive Changes in structure of distribution National, regional, and export markets
	Mass distribution	U.S. economy 1950 to present	Demand creation Physical distribution Market information Market and product planning, development	Integrated channels of distribution Increase in specialized middlemen	Producer Retailer	Marketing	Labor Land Technology Transportation Capital Communication	Capital and land intensive Rapid product innovation National, regional, and export markets

* Mk.(f) = prod.: Marketing is a function of production.

Advertising agencies, facilities for marketing research, repair services, specialized consumer financing agencies, and storage and warehousing facilities are supportive facilitating agencies created to serve the particular needs of expanded markets and economies. It is important to remember that these institutions do not come about automatically, nor does the necessary marketing institution simply appear. Part of the marketer's task, as an economy is studied, is to determine what in the foreign environment will be useful and how much adjustment will be necessary to carry out stated objectives. In some less developed countries, it may be up to the marketer to institute the foundations of a modern marketing system. As discussed in subsequent chapters, adequate research agencies and media are not available in many countries.

The limitation of Exhibit 11–2 in evaluating the market system of a particular country stems from the fact that the marketing system is in a constant state of flux. To expect neat, precise progression through each successive growth stage, as in the geological sciences, is to oversimplify the complex nature of marketing development.

One significant factor in evaluating a developing market is the influence of borrowed technology on the acceleration of market development. Examples can be found of countries or areas of countries that have been propelled from the 18th century to the 20th century in the span of two decades. In such cases, a country might spend a relatively short time in any given stage, bypass stages completely, or telescope several stages into one. In fact, the marketing structures within many developing countries are simultaneously at many stages; it would not be unusual to find traditional marketing retail outlets functioning side-by-side with advanced, modern markets. This is true especially in food retailing where a large segment of the population buys food from small specialty stores while the same economy supports modern supermarkets comparing favorably with any found in the United States.

Influence of import orientation

The source of manufactured goods can condition and influence the characteristics and development of a country's market system. A strong dependence on imported manufactured goods is reflected in the structure of the market and general business practices frequently found in developing countries.

Some of the differences between foreign-based market systems and domestic-based systems result from two factors. First, the foreign-based market system creates a "seller's market"; and second, the source of supply is limited and controlled by a few importers. The entire marketing system develops around the philosophy of selling a limited supply of goods at high prices to a small number of affluent consumers. Market penetration or a developed system of mass distribution is not necessary since demand exceeds supply and, in most cases, the customer seeks the supply. This, of course, is in contrast to the mass consumption-distribution philosophy of domestic-based systems which prevails in industrialized nations like the United States. In such cases, it is generally a "buyer's market," and supply can be increased or decreased within a given range. This creates a need to penetrate the market and push the goods out to the consumer, resulting in a highly developed system of intermediaries. One authority notes that an import-oriented market system usually works backwards:

> Consumers, retailers, and other intermediaries are always seeking goods. This results from the tendency of importers to throttle the flow of goods, and from this sporadic and uneven flow of imports, inventory hoarding as a means of checking the market can be achieved at relatively low cost, and is obviously justified because of its lucrative and speculative yields.[13]

This import-oriented philosophy manifests itself in much of the activity and behavior in marketing. An interesting anecdote told by an authority on Brazil concerned a bank which had ordered piggy banks for a local promotion. The promotion went better than expected so the banker placed a reorder of an amount three times the original. The local manufacturer immediately increased the price and, despite arguments that pointed out reduced production costs and other supply-cost factors involved, could not be dissuaded from this move. The entire notion of economies of scale in production and the use of price as a demand stimulus is contrary to the traditional beliefs in an import-oriented market. The manufacturers were going on the theory that with demand up the price also had to go up. A "one deal" mentality of pricing at the retail and wholesale levels exists because in an import-oriented market, goods come in at a landed price and pricing from there on is simply an assessment of demand and diminishing supply. Thus, variations in manufacturing costs are of little concern; each shipment is a deal, and when that is gone the merchant waits for another good deal, basing the price of each deal on the landed cost and assessment of demand and supply at that time.

An import-oriented philosophy also affects the development of intermediaries and the functions they perform. Most distribution systems are local in nature with national distribution being of little importance since it is contrary to the import-oriented philosophy. The relationship between the importer and any middleman in the marketplace is considerably different from that found in domestic-based manufacturing or mass marketing systems. The idea of a channel as a chain of intermediaries performing specific activities and each selling to a smaller unit beneath it until the chain reaches the ultimate consumer is relatively unknown. In an import-oriented economy, an intermediary may not sell to a specific link in the channel but to a range

---

[13] A. A. Sherbini, "Import-Oriented Marketing Mechanisms," *MSU Business Topics,* Spring 1968, p. 71. Reprinted by permission of the publisher, the Bureau of Business and Economic Research, Division of Research, Graduate School of Business Administration, Michigan State University.

of other intermediaries. Some simultaneously assume all the different functions—importing, wholesaling, semiwholesaling, and retailing—while other
middlemen are so specialized that a high degree of division of labor is
created. Such tasks as financing, storage, trucking, shipping, packaging,
and breaking bulk may each have to be performed by separate agencies,
thereby creating extremely high-cost distribution.

Besides different operating procedures, an import-oriented market dominated by an importer-wholesaler system may present special public relations
problems that obstruct the goals of a marketer attempting to substitute locally
manufactured products for imported ones or making a total market commitment in the country.[14] The major point of contention is the threat posed
by the foreign marketer who, with a mass-marketing philosophy, attempts
to control the distribution process to the point where consumption causes
shifts in the location and control of many marketing activities and functions.

> In an import-oriented marketing system, the locus (of market activities and
> functions) lies near the consumer end of the marketing channel. Many market-
> ing functions such as sorting and assorting, selling, storage and warehousing,
> advertising and promotion, and financing are performed by wholesale and
> retail intermediaries.
>
> But the establishment of domestic manufacturing of the import substitution
> type (or mass-marketers) invariably shifts the locus of marketing functions to
> the production end of the channel. This is particularly true of advertising and
> promotion, standardization and grading, and storage and warehousing.[15]

This shift is seen as altering the position of the local importer-wholesalers
from a dominant position in the marketplace to a secondary one. Since it
threatens their very existence, resistance to changes in the locus of marketing
functions is intense. Resistance may cause outright competitive warfare, bargaining, or eventual government intervention on behalf of the domestic
importer-wholesaler.

In addition to problems resulting from a country having an import-oriented
market system, developing nations seldom have a very large or significant
middle-income class—the market consists mainly of the very wealthy and
the very poor. This creates some interesting demand characteristics which
must be considered in planning and estimating market potential.

Demand in a less developed country

Estimating market potential in less developed countries involves myriad
problems. Apparently most difficulty stems from the economic dualism which

---

[14] The assumption here and throughout the book is that the foreign marketer enters a market
with the intent of making a full commitment, that is, establishing market objectives and maintaining a continuous market representation, with broad distribution and market penetration. This
approach is taken regardless of whether the products marketed are manufactured within the
political boundaries of the country or are imported.

[15] Sherbini, "Marketing Mechanisms," p. 72. Reprinted with permission.

exists, that is, the coexistence of modern and traditional sectors within the economy. The modern sector is centered in the capital city, and has jet airports, international hotels, new factories, and a small Westernized middle class. But along with every modern sector there is a traditional sector containing the remainder of the country's population. Although the traditional sector is only miles away geographically, it is centuries away in terms of production and consumerism. This dual economy obviously affects the size of the market and in many countries, creates two distinct marketing levels. In estimating potential under these conditions, the marketer must make an assessment for each sector. Because they are substantially different and require different approaches for marketing success, they cannot be combined into a single market estimate. The modern sector demands products and services similar to those found in any industrialized Western country while the traditional sector demands items more indigenous and basic to subsistence. As one authority on India's market observed, "a rural Indian can live a very sound life without many products. For example, toothpaste, sugar, coffee, washing soap, bathing soap, kerosene, are all bare necessities of life to those who live in semiurban and urban areas, but rural Indians have less to spend so they search out substitutes for the 'bare necessities.' "[16]

In an import-oriented economy, the modern sector presents a highly segmented, thin market and the importer tends to specialize in the unique needs of a relatively narrow range of customers.

> Thus the aggregate demand for a "given product" often consists of many thin and heterogeneous demand schedules that are not necessarily additive.
>
> The demand for even a simple product such as imported sardines sometimes reflects a high degree of consumer attachment to certain product attributes; for example, shape and type of tin, sauce packed or oil packed, flavor, and price. Foreign exporters who sell in worldwide markets generally find it economically feasible to cater to thin domestic market segments in the developing countries.[17]

For a company desirous of developing a long-term market commitment within a country, it may be economically impossible to serve all the thin market segments, and a single segment may be too small to warrant a substantial market investment.

The traditional sector may offer the greatest potential for a company that is willing to change from production orientation to marketing orientation. Briefly, this means that a company begins producing products geared to the investment, production, and distribution needs of the traditional sector rather than trying to sell what has already been accepted in a more modern market. This can require substantial changes in marketing strategies and tactics: penetration pricing as a means to market cultivation, new distribution

---

[16] Y. A. Verma, "Marketing in Rural India," *Management International Review* 20, no. 4 (1980), p. 47.

[17] Ibid.

practices devised to economically place products throughout the economy, redesigned products more fitting to the lifestyle of the traditional sector, and/or changes in promotional objectives. Products designed for industrialized Western markets may be unknown or unusable in the traditional sectors of a developing nation. Since product design must be geared to the basic wants of the population, promotion must create primary demand, acquainting the market with the attributes of a "new" product. Besides changes in market strategies, this market orientation approach could necessitate a longer investment period before profitability occurs.

Less developed countries and long-range potential

The growth of tomorrow's markets will include expansion in industrialized countries and the development of the traditional side of less developed nations, as well as continued expansion of the modern sectors of such countries. In fact, the greatest long-range potential is found in growth in the traditional sector, realizing that a profit may require not only a change in orientation but a willingness to invest time and effort for longer periods. The development of demand in a traditional market sector means higher marketing costs initially, compromises in marketing methods, and even the redesigning of products; in other words, market investment today is necessary to achieve profits tomorrow.

In some of the less developed countries, it may be up to the marketer to institute the very foundations of a modern marketing system, thereby gaining a foothold in an economy that will some day be highly profitable. *The price paid for entering in the early stages of development may be lower initial returns on investment, but the price paid for waiting until the*

BOX 11-3: Making do with what you have

Catastrophe and religion happen on a big scale in India. The monsoon rains wash away 500 villages; 1,000 people die in a railroad accident; 45,000 pilgrims climb the Himalayas to revere a stalagmite; 800,000 mothers offer yellow saris to the Ganges when one among them dreams of an epidemic.

But living proceeds on a small scale. Two to a narrow rope bed, three on a bicycle, cigarettes sold separately—20 sales to the pack. One indication of the small scale of life in India is what people do to earn a rupee, or even a paisa (1 rupee = 11 cents U.S. and there are 100 paisa per rupee). They sell drinking water on the street corners for a half cent a glass. They go door to door with charcoal-burning irons offering to press your shirts. A taxi driver, afraid of losing a fare, insists on waiting while you keep an appointment, eat your lunch, spend an evening with friends. Hours pass. His waiting charge is two rupees—22 cents—an hour. On the grounds surrounding the Taj Mahal, young women sit slicing off handfuls of grass with short kitchen blades. The grass clippings are then wrapped in burlap, balanced on heads or on the fenders of bicycles and taken home to feed the livestock.

Source: From "India Notebook: Life on a Small Scale Means Three on a Bike, Cabs That Wait," *The Wall Street Journal*, October 7, 1981, p. 26.

market becomes profitable may be a blocked market with no opportunity for entry. Once a country gains momentum in development, feelings of nationalism run high, and, if foreign companies are allowed to operate, there is a tendency to give preferential treatment to those that have helped in its development while closing doors to all others. The political price a company must be willing to pay for entry into a less-developed country market is one of entering when most of the benefits of the company's activities will be enjoyed by the host country. Once profitability is assured, many companies want into the market.

Some companies are currently designing products specifically for the needs of traditional sectors of less developed countries in the long-range hope of being established when these sectors gain greater affluence.

National Cash Register is a company pursuing a strategy for the future. With their Japanese subsidiary, they have developed a crank-operated cash register sold successfully in the Philippines, Latin America, the Orient, and Spain. With only half the parts of more advanced registers, the machine sells for about half the price of the cheapest models available in the United States. There is a demand for these low-cost machines, and the director is quoted as saying that the hope is for their customers to advance to more automatic machines as the country progresses, giving National Cash Register a foot in the door of a growth market.

SOCIALIST COUNTRIES—A SPECIAL CASE

The Socialist countries of Eastern Europe[18], Russia, and China constitute a market of increasing importance for non-Socialist nations. While Western Europe, Canada, and Japan have been trading with these countries for several decades, the easing of tensions among the USSR, People's Republic of China, and the United States has led to increased sales activity by U.S. firms in these developing markets. Contrasting political systems and economic philosophies account for major differences in the trade characteristics of Eastern and Western countries. For example, within a non-Socialist economy, supply and demand are the most important determinants of price. In Socialist countries, national goals for economic development are more crucial determinants for pricing policies than are market conditions. Further, because of centralized planning, most trade is conducted by state trading organizations rather than by individual profit-oriented end-users as in most Western economies. Suppliers never (or rarely) negotiate directly with the final user of a product. This arrangement requires different marketing strategies and tactics than those the U.S. marketer recognizes as traditional. Purchase patterns and demand estimations are different; promotion and adver-

---

[18] Bulgaria, Czechoslovakia, German Democratic Republic, Hungary, Poland, and Romania.

BOX 11-4

Marketing in a free enterprise society	**Marketing in a traditional socialist economy**
In order to compare Socialist marketing to our Western system, it is important to extract the essence of marketing as we practice it. There seem to be five fundamentals in Western marketing:	Marketing has a completely different starting point under traditional Socialism. The teachings of Marx, Engels, and Lenin offer some insight into the role of marketing. Their views seem to be in direct contrast with the give fundamentals of Western marketing:
1. The central organizing principle of production and distribution is consumer satisfaction (the marketing concept).	1. Supply creates its own demand (Say's Law).
2. Consumer satisfaction is derived from both goods and services.	2. Only goods have labor content value; services and other marketing activities add nothing (Labor Theory of Value).
3. The market is composed of different segments, each with its own needs and wants.	3. Consumer communes are viewed as uniform.
4. The profit motive brings forth new goods and services.	4. The output of society is distributed to its members not in relation to productivity, but according to needs.
5. The standard of living is uniquely determined according to the satisfaction of *his* needs and wants.	5. The standard of living is determined and administered centrally.

Source: Charles S. Mayer, "Marketing in Eastern European Socialist Countries." Reprinted by permission from the January 1976 issue of the *University of Michigan Business Review*, published by the Graduate School of Business Administration, The University of Michigan.

---

tising must be approached differently; and methods of payments and the demand for certain classes of goods are different. Potential demand for industrial goods and some consumer goods is so great and business practices are so different that the problems associated with marketing need special attention.

Estimating demand

With the initial step in appraising a potential market, estimating demand, a marketer encounters the first major problem in Socialist countries. Meaningful economic data is infrequently published and their economic plans, the most meaningful indicator of industrial goods demand, are considered state secrets. Thus, a marketer cannot engage in forecasting future market demand but must wait for a request for goods. Even if reliable economic statistics were available, they would be of little use in demand assessments since the basic buying decisions are not determined by marketing forces familiar to Western exporters. Buying decisions are determined by long-range economic plans (which are state secrets) and only products included in those plans are purchased. A further problem in estimating demand is the general lack of a profit motive in Communist countries. In planning export sales to Western countries, the marketer can promote sales to the decision maker on the basis of what the product will do for the decision maker's profits since it can be assumed the buyer is largely motivated by and evaluated on profits. For Socialist decision makers controlled by centralized economic plans, a marketer cannot be certain what besides profits affects demand and their purchase decisions. The situation is further complicated by the difficulty of describing products except in terms of cost savings, even though the potential buyer is not necessarily evaluating the product on that basis. Consequently, estimating demand involves conjecture and reliance on the meager data available. Even with little data, some insights into the characteristics of trade are possible. As would be expected in a country dedicated to rapid industrialization, industrial goods necessary for growth and development are in greatest demand. Increasingly, demand includes entire manufacturing plants delivered on a turn-key basis. As an example, Poland purchased from the West industrial plants valued at over $100 million to produce tractors, harvesting machines, electronics and data processing equipment, and chemicals.

In addition to the problems of estimating long-range demand, communications with potential buyers can also be troublesome.

Communications process

Aside from estimating potential demand for goods in Socialist countries, knowing who affects decisions regarding your products and getting your message to them can be a problem. Even though negotiations for a final sale may be conducted between the seller and a state-controlled buying organization, it cannot be assumed that the end-user has no say in such negotiations. The fact is that the degree of influence end-users have within the Socialist bloc varies among countries. In Russia, the end-user probably has the most control over products sought and finally agreed on. While centralized planning and control in Russia are substantial, a local decision is not precluded if the user demonstrates a specific product to be superior to its alternatives. Even when a Russian user selects a specific product, recommendations generally go through channels to the foreign trade organization responsible for making the purchase and the seller may never have any face-to-face meetings with the end-user. As a result, it is essential to try to communicate with others beyond those with whom the marketer is trading or negotiating because of the inaccessibility of the end-user in many

---

BOX 11–5: Future consumer markets in Russia

Next time you start worrying about the high cost of living, pause a moment—and thank your lucky stars you're not a Russian.

The average wage-earner works:

Nearly three times as long to buy a loaf of white bread as the American worker.

Three times as long to buy a cut of beef for dinner.

Six times as long to buy a bottle of vodka or gin.

Ten times as long to buy a dozen eggs.

If you're a housewife, you would have to do your washing with a machine that has a hand wringer. Seventy percent of all washing machines in the Soviet Union have hand wringers.

Apartment dwellers (including those on the fourth floor) must share their bathroom and kitchen facilities with their neighbors—and these rooms are usually on the ground floor. Even in the large Soviet cities, about 25 percent of new apartments are not equipped with running water. or other plumbing conveniences. And taking national averages, the Soviet family enjoys only one third the living area of an American family the same size.

The average American worker can buy a 19-inch TV, priced at about $400 with 165 hours of work. The Russian must work 1,169 hours to buy an equivalent set, which has a price tag of—hold your breath—$1,323.

Automobiles? "These are clearly out of the reach of the average person" in the Soviet Union. It costs a Russian 43.3 months of work—over 3½ years' salary even if he or she buys nothing else in that time—to acquire a Soviet version of the small Fiat car. An American wage-earner, however, could buy it with 4.4 months of work.

Source: "Economic Aspects of Life in the USSR," *North Atlantic Treaty Organization.*

---

countries and the uncertainty of when an end-user may be influential in a decision.[19]

Newspapers, outdoor advertising, industry-related magazines, and even direct mail are available in all of the Socialist-based countries and are a viable means of communicating product data. Russia probably has the most highly developed means of communications including readership of major American and foreign publications, an effective means of communication to industrial customers.

In several of the countries, consumer goods can be advertised via television, radio, and newspapers. In Russia, time can be purchased on television and in general magazines; in Poland, advertising on television and radio is available although all television and radio advertising is grouped together during the broadcasting day (commercials are short). Until the 1980s, the People's Republic of China was the least open to advertising. With the current Chinese attitude toward industrialization and more open trade with the West, comes a more liberal approach to advertising. Catalogs and advertising in U.S. journals distributed in China effectively get the message to

---

[19] For an interesting discussion of one company's approach to this problem see "Unique Marketing Enables Company to Expand PRC Sales," *Business Asia,* April 3, 1981, p. 106.

potential buyers and even consumer goods advertising is available. Posters advertising Coca-Cola can be seen in Beijing.

Negotiating a trade

In most instances, the selling process in Socialist-based economies is done through hard-driving negotiations between the seller and a trading company representative. Everything from price to delivery times, supplies, and so on is negotiated as a total package. A recurring problem for marketers in Socialist countries is the scarcity of hard currency for the buyer. Just as a planned economy affects the types of goods to be imported, the scarcity of hard currencies—usually available only for priority goods designated by the economic plan—affects price negotiations. This shortage of currency has resulted in heavy reliance on countertrade—the exchange of goods, either in part or totally, for other goods. Countertrade is a major factor in Socialist-bloc marketing. A study recently completed by the author indicated over 40 percent of trade with Eastern Europe is, in total or in part, paid for by other goods. It would be safe to say that anyone attempting to conduct business with Socialist countries should be prepared to deal with countertrade. Either early in negotiations or more frequently toward the end, the Socialist-bloc buyer will stipulate that the final price will be paid in part or in total with goods produced within those countries. U.S. marketers are usually at a disadvantage since few have experience in countertrading; nevertheless, the competition, notably Western Europe and Japan, are more than willing. The Japanese have been supplying the Soviets with equipment for mining and logging in trade for coal and timber. France, Germany, and Italy have built pipelines in Eastern European countries in return for future delivery of natural gas. Even Pepsi-Cola is sold in Russia on a countertrade arrangement—Pepsi-Cola concentrate is exchanged for Russian Vodka. A very large portion of trade with China has involved countertrade transactions; the Japanese have been especially adept at selling major installations of petrochemical manufacturing plants on a buy-back arrangement where Japan will receive some of the output of the plant as partial payment for the construction. The complete range of countertrade transactions[20] from straight barter to buy-back arrangements is utilized in trade with the Socialist-bloc countries, and they are the major factors in effectively competing in these countries.

CHANGING MARKET BEHAVIOR AND POTENTIAL

As a country develops, profound changes occur which affect its people. Incomes change, population concentrations shift, expectations for a better life adjust to higher levels, new infrastructures evolve, social capital invest-

---

[20] See Chapter 14 for a complete discussion of countertrading.

EXHIBIT 11–3: Items owned by Japanese and European homes

	Japan	Europe
Men's suits	8	4
Men's coats	6	4
Men's shirts	15	20
Women's Dresses and shoes	6	3
Women's skirts	19	8
Women's handbags	6	5
Chairs and sofas	for 8 people	for 23 people
Tablecloths	3	10
Napkins	7	26
Forks	9	24
Cup-saucer sets	17	17

Source: "Consumer Goods in Japanese Homes," *Focus Japan*, April 1981, p. 1.

ments are made, and foreign and domestic companies seek new markets or expand their positions in existing markets. All of this results in changes in market behavior and potential.

Markets are people with needs and wants and the means to satisfy those needs and wants. The needs and wants which exist and the economic ability to satisfy them are the result of the triune *interaction of the economy, the culture, and marketing efforts of businesses.* In other words, markets evolve from the interaction of the economy, the culture, and the marketing efforts of companies. Markets are different and are changing the world over, some more rapidly and dramatically than others. Increased wealth, accelerated economic development, and the efforts of MNCs are sparking changes to the extent that the "old ways" are quickly joined or replaced by new patterns.

There are universal similarities in markets; practically everyone desires "the good life" as characterized by consumer goods. Within these similarities, however, the marketer must recognize individual characteristics of nationality and levels of economic and industrial development to determine consumer behavior. Therefore, even though everyone seeks the good life, each group's interpretation of that concept as reflected in consumer behavior is embedded deeply in cultural heritage. Compare, for example, the differences in consumption and ownership patterns between Japanese and European homes as illustrated in Exhibit 11–3. Incomes are not too dissimilar but there are some interesting differences in ownership of the items listed. Interestingly enough, Japanese women, whose traditional dress one would not expect to include skirts, have more than twice as many skirts as European women. That the European own almost three times more forks than the Japanese is not as surprising.

Exhibit 11–4 presents some of the market differences which occur throughout the world. When examining Exhibit 11–4 carefully, the real meaning of less developed versus developed nations becomes apparent.

BOX 11-6

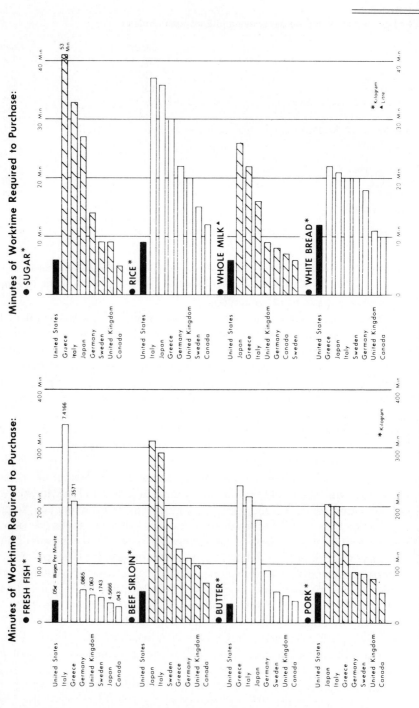

Minutes of Worktime Required to Purchase:

● FRESH FISH*

United States
Italy 7.4166
Greece 3571
Germany .0865
United Kingdom 2.063
Sweden 1743
Japan 4.5666
Canada .043

05¢ - Wages Per Minute

● BEEF SIRLOIN*

United States
Japan
Italy
Sweden
Greece
Germany
United Kingdom
Canada

● BUTTER*

United States
Greece
Italy
Japan
Germany
Sweden
United Kingdom
Canada

● PORK*

United States
Japan
Italy
Greece
Germany
Sweden
United Kingdom
Canada

* Kilogram

Minutes of Worktime Required to Purchase:

● SUGAR*

United States
Greece   53 Min
Italy
Japan
Germany
Sweden
United Kingdom
Canada

● RICE*

United States
Italy
Japan
Greece
Germany
United Kingdom
Sweden
Canada

● WHOLE MILK▲

United States
Japan
Greece
Italy
United Kingdom
Germany
Canada
Sweden

● WHITE BREAD*

United States
Greece
Japan
Italy
Sweden
Germany
United Kingdom
Canada

* Kilogram
▲ Litre

Source: National Industrial Conference Board, Inc., Road Maps of Industry No. 1645.

EXHIBIT 11–4: Market indicators for selected countries

Column	(A) Market growth percent change (1975–1980)	(B) GDP per capita (U.S. dollars)	(C) Passenger cars per 1,000 population	(D) TVs per 1,000 population	(E) Telephones per 100 population	(F) Energy consumption per capita (coal equivalent in kg)
Chile	9	1,578	30	112	4.95	1,006
Argentina	23	3,726	103	233	10.08	1,872
Paraguay	129	1,167	10	0.2	1.89	207
Colombia	41	1,027	19	67	5.64	706
Mexico	54	1,771	45	110	6.33	1,414
Brazil	82	1,664	62	94	4.8	767
All Latin America	47	1,681	47	97	5.22	1,081
Belgium	9	11,233	315	287	35.4	6,376
France	19	10,747	346	331	33.1	4,368
Greece	42	4,183	90	161	16.1	1,925
U.K.	6	7,025	260	349	34.9	5,212
Norway	17	11,293	290	277	27.7	5,571
Spain	19	5,324	190	227	22.7	2,405
All Europe	14	7,844	260	264	36.4	4,150
Egypt	46	600	7.9	31.7	1.2	463
Saudi Arabia	77	10,247	59.1	38.3	2.4	1,306
Algeria	56	1,623	24.6	27.3	1.8	687
Ghana	15	650	5.4	3.3	0.5	165
Nigeria	53	610	5.4	6.0	0.2	106
Kenya	19	392	8.0	3.9	1.0	139
Zimbabwe	–10	549	24.1	9.9	2.9	579
All Mid East and Africa	34	1,030	16.5	22.3	1.6	666
Czechoslovakia	17	5,671	53.0	257	20.2	7,531
Poland	22	4,263	59.8	203	9.2	5,596
USSR	23	3,836	26.5	303	8.5	5,500
Yugoslavia	32	2,846	103.4	159	8.7	2,035
All Eastern Europe	21	4,007	44.3	272	9.5	5,037
United States	—	10,650	463	623	77.3	—

* Market growth is an average of growth of various indicators (energy & steel consumption, cement and electricity production, passenger cars and trucks and buses in use) over a 5-year period.

Sources: *Business Latin America*, December 24, 1980, 411–14; *Business Europe*, January 30, 1981, pp. 1–10; and *The OECD Observer* No. 109, March 1981, 8 pp.

Consider, for example, the differences between France and Chile. Per capita GDP in France is almost seven times greater than in Chile and, with the exception of TVs, ownership of automobiles, telephones, and energy consumption range from four to over 10 times greater in France. While ownership of automobiles, TVs, and telephones may not necessarily be considered the good life by some, they are indicators of wealth and the figures in Exhibit 11–4 clearly illustrate the disparity which exists between countries.

In the midst of this growth are problems in the gaps that exist between the rich and the poor. In Mexico, for example, the difference between the haves and have-nots is substantial despite considerable improvement in that country's economy over the last two decades. Half of all Mexicans live in rural areas, and of these, one half have no reportable income, while the remainder earn about $400 per year compared with the national average in excess of $1,000. Regardless of this disparity, Mexico is a rapidly growing economy with great potential in the decades ahead for the marketer who can adjust to the peculiarities and differences of economically emerging nations.

Even though economic opulence or a lack of it varies from country to country, most world markets are continually expanding. Column A of Exhibit 11–4 is an indicator of market growth based on average percentage growth over a five-year period of various indicators such as the consumption of energy; steel; cement; trucks, buses, and automobiles. An interesting point is that countries with the highest market growth are the developing countries. For example, total Europe has a market growth percentage of 14, while all of Latin America has 47, the Mid-East and Africa have 34, and Eastern Europe has 21. This apparently greater growth is due partly to the fact that developing countries' economies are small and a small absolute change results in greater percentage changes.

The indicators in Exhibit 11–5 illustrate the growth and improved living

---

BOX 11–7: Just because it sells in Mexico doesn't mean it will sell elsewhere in Latin America

Gerber, the baby food company, is perplexed because their line of baby foods which have done well in other countries in Latin America, haven't done well in Brazil.

After eight years of trying, Gerber has not done well enough to justify continuing their Brazilian operation. They were never able to convince mothers to use baby food as an everyday feeding item. The Brazilian mother would use prepackaged baby food only when visiting or on a beach outing.

They failed in spite of an award-winning advertisement telling mothers they would have more time to show affection to their infants if they were not bent over a sink preparing food. The company underestimated a cultural factor: Brazilian mothers are not willing to accept the fact that prepared baby food is a good substitute for fresh food made by themselves or, more likely, by their live-in maids.

Source: From "Brazil: Gerber Abandons a Baby-Food Market," *Business Week*, February 8, 1982, p. 45.

EXHIBIT 11–5: **Living standards (selected countries)**

Country	Rooms per dwelling	Persons per room	Percent of piped water	Percent of flush toilet	Percent of electric lighting
Brazil	4.0	1.2	40	29	67
Chile	2.8	1.5	71	55	87
Costa Rica	4.5	1.5	86	55	70
El Salvador	1.7	3.3	31	26	39
Ethiopia	1.9	2.5	82	na	60
Guatemala	2.4	2.3	17	8	32
Hong Kong	2.9	1.8	98	75	85
Indonesia	3.3	1.4	9	19	33
Japan	4.1	0.9	99	49	98
Peru	2.0	2.1	30	33	42
Saudi Arabia	3.0	2.6	40	19	46
Singapore	2.1	2.9	92	77	96
Sri Lanka	2.2	2.6	11	12	18
United States	5.1	0.6	99	99	99

Sources: *International Marketing Data and Statistics*, 6th ed. (London: Euromonitor Publications Ltd. 1981); and *European Market Data and Statistics*, 17th ed. (London: Euromonitor Publications Ltd., 1981).

standards of world markets even though disparities between the rich and poor still exist in many countries (see Exhibit 11–3).[21]

As living standards improve, the demand for different types of products changes. In 1950, for example, the item most wanted by the Japanese was an electric iron. In 1980, a survey reported that Japanese families in a similar income class as those in 1950 wanted pleasure boats, second cars, and weekend homes. These changes in expectations and demand are apparent wherever economies are growing and they are the basis for changing trends in world marketing.[22]

TRENDS IN WORLD CONSUMER MARKETS

The various social and economic changes occurring in many countries have led to numerous trends in market characteristics which, if continued, will result in significant changes in world markets. Among the more pronounced trends are the development of mass merchandising, the changing role of women in the economy and society, and a willingness to use installment credit.

A rapid transition in "traditional retailing" is occurring in some countries because of the development and wholehearted acceptance of mass merchandising, including self-service, checkout counters, prepackaged and frozen foods, adequate parking, and big stores that stock as many as 20,000

---

[21] For a detailed discussion of living standards in Asia, see "Asian Living Standards are Improving, but Disparities Widen in Some Nations," *The Asian Wall Street Journal Weekly*, October 12, 1981, p. 2.

[22] "What Make the Consumers Tick?", *World Business Weekly*, February 23, 1981, p. 8.

different products. These innovations represent a significant departure from shops catering to a daily pattern of shopping for food at as many as six specialty shops. This is not to say that traditional retailing has disappeared, but in many countries, significant changes are taking place to the extent that one authority recommends two sales forces be established: one for discount houses and mailorder houses, the other for small traditional shops.

The growth of full-fledged supermarkets all over the world during the last 20 years has been spectacular. In Germany, over 70 percent of all food sales are made in supermarkets; in Holland, 32 percent in supermarkets and self-service stores, compared to less than 10 percent in 1950.

In Argentina supermarkets sell nearly 24 percent of all foods compared to only 10 percent 10 years ago. In fact, the Argentine government encourages the development of supermarkets by foreign chains, hoping that modern marketing, "particularly aggressive price competition, will help break traditional buying habits" and create consumer resistance to high prices and poor quality.[23]

The trend in self-service supermarkets is not limited to Western Europe and Latin America; in Hong Kong, there were 80 supermarkets in 1977, by 1980 more than 250 had been completed. Similar growth in mass merchandising is underway in Japan.

Changes in retailing are not only affecting supermarkets and discount houses; automatic vending has developed to help solve such problems as personnel shortages, higher pay, profits squeeze, and the restriction of business hours found in many parts of the world. In addition, there is substantial growth of shopping centers as an important method of distribution. Exhibit 11–6 illustrates a definite trend away from free-standing department stores to regional shopping centers in major metropolitan cities of Latin America. The importance of these retailing trends to marketing strategies is obvious. What confronts the international marketer is the need for strategies that permit efficient functioning in dual systems; the traditional small store with minimum inventories and minimum consumer services alongside modern, high-inventory retailing. If dual distribution systems are the only effective way to capitalize on the potential in developing markets, it is possible that the cost may be higher than a marketer cares to pay.

Another important fact about the consumer boom experienced in Europe and other parts of the world is the working woman who not only provides additional family income to purchase the ever-increasing list of consumer products, but who also helps fill a dire labor shortage. Currently about one third of all married women in Europe are employed, 3 million of whom are mothers, and the number of working women has increased to such an extent that there is a shortage of domestic help. The cultural impact from this phenomenon has produced an increase in demand for one-stop shop-

[23] "New Supermarkets for Argentina," *World Business Weekly,* June 29, 1981, p. 45.

EXHIBIT 11–6: Stages of retail development in major Latin American metropolitan areas: 1973–1983

Metropolitan area	Central business district	Free-standing department stores; Community shopping centers	Regional centers*		
			One anchor	Two anchor	Enclosed two anchors
Mexico City				⇒	➡
São Paulo			⇒	➡	
Caracas			⇒	➡	
Lima		⇒	➡		
Bogota		⇒	➡		
Panama City		⇒	➡		
Buenos Aires		⇒➡			

Note: Open arrow refers to the current stage of retail development in each metropolitan area. Dark arrow represents the projected stage of development in 1983.
* Anchored by full-line conventional department store.
Source: From Ross W. Campbell, "Stages of Shopping Center Development in Major Latin American Metropolitan Markets," *Land Economics*, February 1974, © 1974 by the Board of Regents of the University of Wisconsin System, p. 69.

ping in shopping centers, increased mail-order sales,[24] and a substantial increase in demand for labor-saving devices, convenience foods, and other means of extending time at home.

The rise of personal credit in Europe is a trend of significant importance to foreign marketing. There has been substantial growth since World War II and this personal credit trend is extending to other parts of the world as well.

Even for the Japanese, who save more of their household disposable income than do most Westerners (20.1 percent for Japanese to 13.9 percent for West Germany and 5.1 percent in the U.S.), the use of consumer credit is increasing. Household debt increased from 32.6 percent in 1976 to 40 percent in 1980.[25] Expanding use of credit is seen as important in increasing effective demand for household appliances, automobiles, and homes.

Another trend of considerable significance that develops as incomes grow is the extension of individual purchasing power with the use of installment credit (hire purchase). Compared to its U.S. development, installment credit is in its infancy in the rest of the world, but there are substantial growth factors in this area.

---

[24] "Italian Mail-Order Houses Grab Larger Slice of Market," *Business Europe*, April 10, 1981, p. 116.

[25] "Savings and Debts of Japanese Household," *Focus Japan*, December 1980, p. 1.

The parallel between the growth of these trends in many of the world's markets and the economic development of the respective countries is interesting. Perhaps a valid generalization is that as a country experiences higher personal incomes, rising productivity, urbanization, and all the other trappings of industrialization, a "consumer revolution" can be anticipated which will include the development and acceptance of such innovations as mass merchandising, increased employment of women, and the increased use of installment credit. The development of these trends in parts of Europe and Japan and other countries of the world can be compared to similar development in the United States after World War II.

SUMMARY

Since World War II, the scope and level of technical and economic growth have enabled some nations to advance their standards of living by two centuries. As a nation develops, its capacity to produce develops pressures, typically in the distribution structure. Emphasis by the marketer must be on developing marketing systems designed to utilize to the utmost the economic level of development. The impact of social and economic trends will continue to be felt in many countries during the next decade causing significant changes in distribution systems, personal shopping habits, and consumer demand. Easing of political tensions in the last decade has opened the Socialist-bloc nations to foreign marketing and, although there are special problems in these countries, they are promising markets for a broad range of products. The continued growth of these trends requires the foreign marketer to constantly evaluate the dynamic aspects of a market, since it is likely that many of today's market facts will be tomorrow's historical myths.

QUESTIONS

1. It is possible for an economy to experience economic growth as measured by total GNP without a commensurate rise in the standard of living. Discuss fully.

2. Why do technical assistance programs of more affluent nations typically ignore the distribution problem or relegate it to a minor role in development planning? Explain.

3. Discuss each of the stages of evolution in the marketing process. Illustrate each stage with a particular country.

4. As a country progresses from one economic stage to another, what in general are the marketing effects?

5. Locate a country in the agricultural and raw material stage of economic development and discuss what changes will occur in marketing when it passes to a manufacturing stage.

6. What are the consequences of each stage of marketing development on the potential for industrial goods within a country? For consumer goods?

7. Discuss the significance of economic development to international marketing. Why is the knowledge of economic development of importance in assessing the world marketing environment? Discuss.

8. Select one country in each of the five stages of economic development. For each country outline the basic existing marketing institutions and show how their stages of development differ. Explain why.

9. Select one country each in Asia, Western Europe, North America, and Latin America in the manufacturing stage of development. See Exhibit 11–2. Explain the differences and similarities among the countries in market potential for consumer goods.

10. Why should economic development be studied by a foreign marketer? Discuss.

11. The infrastructure is important to the economic growth of an economy. Comment.

12. What are the objectives of economically developing countries? How do these objectives relate to marketing? Comment.

13. What is marketing's role in economic development? Discuss marketing's contributions to economic development.

14. Define the following terms:
Underdeveloped
Economic development
NICs

15. Discuss the problems a marketer might encounter when considering the Socialist countries as a market.

16. Why do the Socialist countries demand countertrade when they buy? What problems do marketers face when confronted with a countertrade?

17. The needs and wants of a market and the ability to satisfy them are the result of the triune interaction of the economy, culture and the marketing efforts of businesses. Comment.

18. Discuss how the trend in shopping centers in developing countries will affect marketing strategies.

CASES—PART THREE

Case III-1

American baby foods—a preliminary report

As assistant to the vice president of marketing for American Baby Foods, you have been given the task of preparing a preliminary report on Japan as a possible market for one of the company's product lines.

The American Baby Food Company, located in Camden, New Jersey, is a well-established manufacturer of a wide line of baby products. Its motto "Babies are our business . . . our only business," aptly describes the parameters of the firm's activities. The product line is divided into food and nonfood items for the baby. Nonfood items include rubber pants, bibs, bottles, nipples, toys, and other accessory items. Food items are cereals, fruits and vegetables, and strained meat products which meet the dietary requirements for babies 2 to 18 months old. The products are widely used in the United States and Canada and compete to a moderate degree in Europe with the products of Kraft, Heinz, Carnation, and Gerber.

As part of long-range strategy the company is interested in accelerating its growth outside the U.S. market. The drop in the U.S. birth rate in the early 1960s and approaching zero population growth in the 1980s has caused the company substantial long-range concern. Japan is an appealing market because of their concern for their diet and, more specifically, their increasing population growth.

The product to be considered for marketing in Japan is the line of instant dry cereals which need only water or milk added to make them ready for eating. They can be used as the only food or as a supplement to other foods in a baby's diet until the infant is on a full, varied diet of table food at about 18 months. The cereals come in 1-ounce, 8-ounce, and 16-ounce packages. The 8-ounce size contains about two weeks' supply of cereal. American Baby Foods produces oatmeal, barley, rice, mixed cereal, and high protein cereals, all to be considered for marketing in Japan.

As is usually the case, the vice president of marketing "wants the report yesterday." What the vice president really wants to know is if there is reason to spend additional money to prepare a complete market analysis on Japan.

Since this is a "hurry up" job, about all you can be expected to do is the following:

1. Make a rough estimate of market demand, immediate and long term.
2. Outline the major marketing problems that will face American Baby Foods in successfully marketing the cereal.
3. Suggest steps that might be taken to overcome the problems.
4. Suggest to research the additional information necessary before a thorough market analysis and report can be made.

All the information research could dig up on such short notice is reproduced below. While there are some real holes in the data, there should be enough information to make a preliminary report. Remember, one of your main tasks is to advise research on what other data you will need.

Population facts.   In 1982, the total population of Japan was approximately 116 million persons and it is expected to be 123 million by 1990. Exhibit 1 shows 1982 population figures for the major urban areas of Japan. The birth rate for 1982 according to the Ministry of Welfare was 19.2 per 1,000 people. A steady but slow increase was predicted for the future. Exhibit 2 shows the average number of live births in the major urban areas of Japan for 1970–1982.

Diet.   By tradition, a Japanese starts the day with a bowl of mashed soybean soup, pickled horseradish, and seaweed. The rest of the day, a few bits of raw octopus or dried squid accompanied by gobs of the inevitable Asian staple—rice are the primary diet.

Now, as the Japanese grow in affluence and sophistication, such picturesque eating habits are changing. Today, a typical Japanese breakfast is likely to be toast and coffee. The Japanese diet is rapidly becoming internationalized, primarily westernized. And as it does, more and more U.S. and European food-processing companies are moving into Japan to take advantage of it. Among the American companies with established beachheads in Japan are Kellogg (cornflakes), H. J. Heinz (catsup), Del Monte Corporation (tomato juice), General Mills (cake mixes), Libby, McNeil & Libby Inc. (canned peaches), Corn Products (Knorr packaged soups), McDonald's (fast foods), General Foods (Maxwell House instant coffee), Coca-Cola, Pepsi-Cola, and Canada Dry. Switzerland's food giant, Nestlé, has scored big in Japan with its Nescafé instant coffee.

EXHIBIT 1

City	Population (millions)	Percent of total population
Tokyo	11.7	10.5
Osaka	8.5	7.4
Aichi	6.2	5.3
Kanagawa	6.8	5.8

EXHIBIT 2:   Live births (1970–1982)

County	Approximately annual average
Tokyo	209,240
Kanagawa	128,800
Toyama	18,650
Ichikawa	19,720
Fukui	12,950
Yamanashi	12,120
Nagano	34,150
Gifu	33,600
Shizuoka	61,060
Aichi	120,760
Mie	27,420
Shiga	18,300
Kyoto	43,440
Osaka	165,560
Hyogo	93,350
Total	987,000

Says an executive of one of the biggest U.S. food companies: "Japan should be one of the two fastest-growing food markets in the world this year." (The other is Mexico.) Beyond this, the Japanese are improving their diet as a matter of pride. They are a small people by U.S. standards and they want to become bigger. It's humiliating when a Japanese basketball team is matched against an American basketball team.

Year by year, the Japanese diet is changing. They now eat less rice and more animal and vegetable protein. A Health and Welfare Ministry survey just released finds the average Japanese intake of animal fat and protein exceeded vegetables for the first time ever. "We have become aware of the value of nutrition and a balanced diet," says the director of one of Japan's biggest cooking schools.

Japanese babies normally are fed milk only until the age of four months, at which time they are given supplemental soft foods prepared in the mother's kitchen. These soft foods are often a mashed mixture of rice, liver, spinach, or other highly nutritional foods saved from the adults' meal. As in many foreign countries, a mortar and pestle are used to grind the food for the babies and small children.

Market characteristics.   There are headaches at the processing level. Many Japanese industries are fragmented, but food is the most fragmented of all—there are almost 100,000 companies engaged in food processing in Japan. Japan has more than 5,000 makers of soy sauce and more than 500 flour milling concerns. U.S. companies would like to spend more on advertising and promotion but are limited by the Japanese government in the amount of money that can be pumped in by the foreign parent. Japanese companies are under no such restrictions, and, in some cases, a large manufacturer has almost a monopoly position in a market. Even so, Western food companies are pushing to get into Japan in several ways, and each has its limitations and advantages. Some companies, such as Campbell Soup Company, do a fair business in Japan through exports. But it's tough to turn a profit this way because of high freight costs and Japanese import duties that range from 15 to 50 percent. A few companies have tried licensing. Kellogg set up a subsidiary to provide technical and sales assistance to Ajinomoto Company, Japan's top maker of seasonings, which produces several varieties of Kellogg dry cereals. And Gerber Products Company licenses its baby food processes and labels to a Japanese group. But, again, profit potential is limited.

U.S. companies that would like to set up their own processing plants in Japan run into tough restrictions against foreigners *controlling* Japanese industry. Japan's Ministry of International Trade and Industry has relaxed restrictions a bit, allowing foreign companies to get a controlling interest in certain industries. But the food business categories included in the liberalization were few: beer (It would seem that no outsider could hope to compete against the three big Japanese breweries although Anheuser-Busch, Inc. announced they were going to try.); monosodium glutamate (Ajinomoto has an impregnable position); and ice (nobody is interested in making ice in Japan).

To be sure, a few of the more successful Western food operations are subsidiaries owned 100 percent outside Japan. Among them are Nestlé, Coca-Cola, and General Foods. But these were established years back when it was possible to set up subsidiaries capitalized in yen, not dollars; neither the capital nor profits could be repatriated. Few 100-percent ownership deals can be made now.

Most companies have sought out Japanese partners with which to form joint ventures. Through such ventures, Heinz is linked with Nichiro Fisheries; Corn Products with Ajinomoto; Unilever (the British-Dutch giant) with Hohnen Oil Company; General Mills with Morinaga Confectionery; Libby with Mitsubishi Shoji Kaisha; and Del Monte Corporation with Mitsui and Company and Kikkoman Shoyu Company; and Budweiser with Suntory. National Dairy Products is studying a deal to have its Kraft brand cheese made in Japan, and Corn Products and Ajinomoto introduced a new line of mayonnaise in Japan.

Company experiences.   Most Western companies' efforts to cash in on changing Japanese diets have been a mixed bag profitably. As well as differences in tastes and other problems, they are confronted with an excruciating array of restrictions imposed by the Japanese government on foreign companies doing business there. As a result, U.S. food companies have only a small share of the more than $25 billion that the Japanese spend annually for food and drink (although sales of American agricultural products to Japan—wheat, soybeans, and so forth—run to more than $2.5 billion a year). Food companies are persisting because of the obvious attractions of the Japanese market. Japan is big—over 116 million population—

and it is growing more Western in its tastes. More important, its fast economic growth rate in recent years has brought more disposable income for food. In 1985, Japan's gross national product is expected to rise to $1,239 billion. Per capita income is expected to top the $8,000 mark, but companies have had mixed results trying to sell processed foods in Japan.

Corn Products has done well with packaged dry soups. General Foods' Maxwell House is battling to hold its estimated 10 percent of the instant coffee market. (Nestlé, which spent heavily in creating a brand image at a time when the instant coffee idea was new to Japan, has 70 percent.) Among European companies, Unilever has run up sizable losses in its venture with Hohnen Oil Company. Heinz and Unilever ran into serious difficulties with their Japanese partners and have since been allowed to boost their equity to over 50 percent.

In addition, the American food companies have found scores of other problems. For instance, the Japanese government, to protect domestic manufacturers, restricts foreign companies to producing limited lines of products and imposes ceilings on volume. Foods often have to be adapted to the Japanese palate which may be getting way from traditional dishes but still hasn't accepted Western tastes exactly. Heinz's spaghetti sauce has to be blander than the U.S. product; Corn Products' mayonnaise isn't as sweet as the American. Largely because of the underdevelopment of Japan's milk industry, Kellogg's dry cereals generally are eaten right out of the box as a confection.

Indeed, Japan's limited agriculture poses problems in getting raw materials for foods. Heinz, Del Monte, and Libby are obligated to use domestic tomatoes in their catsup but can only get small quantities. Corn Products' concern over making mayonnaise is how to get a steady supply of fresh eggs.

Food imports. Japan is not self-sufficient in food production, and her ability to feed herself has declined since the end of World War II. In 1980, Japan imported over 40 percent of all food products consumed, and this trend is likely to continue as the population increases and the land suitable for food production diminishes. Exhibit 3 shows the substantial increases in food imports which have occurred between 1970 and 1980.

EXHIBIT 3: Imports of selected foods, 1970–1980 (1,000 metric tons)

	1970	1980	Percent of increase
Cereals	15,803	25,303	60
Vegetables	98	452	361
Fruits	1,182	1,610	36
Meat	220	791	260
Dairy products and milk	561	1,109	98

Source: Japan Institute for Social and Economic Affairs, 1981.

Distribution system.   Japan has 1.74 million retail and wholesale outlets which employ 8.5 million people. Over 85 percent of the retail outlets
are individually or small-family owned and only 5 percent of the retailers
have more than $30,000 (U.S. dollars) in sales. There are 292,000 wholesal-
ers, which amount to one wholesaler for every six retail units. There are
83,093 grocery stores serving households which spend about $450 per
month each on food.

Wholesaling in Japan is a major economic factor in distribution. A large
percentage of all consumer goods goes through three or more wholesalers
between manufacturer and ultimate consumer, with two middlemen being
the minimum.

Case III–2

A North American Common Market?*

An economically united Europe is a reality. The European Community
(EC) now numbers 10 nations with a population of over 262.8 million and
has become a formidable trading bloc and world market.

As Europe looks inward to itself as its own best market economists and
politicians—mostly from the United States—have begun to question the possibilities of a similar type of union in North America. It would be called the
North American Economic Union (NAEU), and its members would be Canada, the United States, and Mexico. This idea has been around for a number
of years and earlier versions included Central America. However, Central
America is not actively considered now because of the political instability
of that area. Further, the prospects of creating a NAEU among three nations
are difficult enough without adding the six countries of Central America.

The major questions are: (1) How would it work? (2) What would each
of the member nations gain or lose from the union? and (3) Will the three
nations each accept such a union?

---

* This case is based in part on Sandra Salmans, "A North American Economic Union,"
Mainliner Magazine, August 1973; Herbert E. Meyer, "Why a North American Common Market
Won't Work—Yet," *Fortune,* September 10, 1979, pp. 118–24; and Jon Stewart, "A North
American Common Market," Pacific News Service, October 7, 1980.

The European Common Market today

Before we discuss the proposed NAEU, let's examine the European Community. For all its growing pains, the EC, or Common Market, is the economic success story of the 20th century. Founded in 1958 by six nations—Belgium, Luxembourg, the Netherlands, France, West Germany, and Italy—the EC now numbers 10 with the recent addition of the United Kingdom, Ireland, Denmark, and the newest member, Greece. Spain and Portugal are waiting for expected entry by 1984.

The present EC (10 countries) has become the largest trading bloc in the world. Its share of world exports is approximately 30 percent, compared with approximately 17 percent for the United States. The EC's gross domestic product (GDP) exceeds that of the United States; $2.78 trillion for the EC compared to $2.55 trillion for the United States.

The EC has negotiated preferential trade agreements with a host of countries in the Mediterranean, the Middle East, and Africa. Under an agreement already worked out, the EC will, within the next few years, bring in Iceland, Finland, Norway, Sweden, Switzerland, and Austria to form a 16-nation industrial free trade zone.

The magnitude of an expanded EC as a trading bloc inevitably begins to dwarf the current economic giants, the United States and Japan. Total population of the 16 countries is over 300 million versus the United States' 221 million and Japan's 116 million.

Those nations that fall outside Europe's massive new free trade zone will be cut out of some profitable opportunities for international business. The United States, for example, worries that the EC will discriminate against American industrial and farm products. And, as Britain relinquishes its Commonwealth trade preference, Canada may lose one of its prime trading partners. Thus, there is a greater interest on the part of some in the United States and to a lesser extent in Canada and to a much lesser extent in Mexico, to look at the possibility of a North American Economic Union.

What would a North American Economic Union be like?

Imagine for a moment what an NAEU would look like today. By itself, the United States has a larger GDP ($2.55 trillion) than Japan ($785 billion) and almost equal to the 10-nation EC ($2.78 trillion). Moreover, the United States alone produces 19 percent of the world's grain. Join the United States with Canada and Mexico, and that combination creates an impressive colossus. With a population of 324 million, it would contain more people than the (260 million) European Community. GDP would approach $3 trillion and because of Canada's agricultural output, the market's share of world grain production would amount to 22 percent. And because of their vast proven reserves of oil, gas, and coal, the three nations would have the potential of becoming self-sufficient in energy. In other words, a North American Economic Union would become an economic force with substantial economic muscle.

The 1980s will almost certainly be marked by active competition among the industrialized countries for Third World markets and raw materials and an NAEU would guarantee its three members at least a fair share of the pie; a larger share at any rate, than each would be able to grab by itself. If an NAEU were formed, there would be free trade among the three countries, with a common external tariff on the goods of nonmember nations. Capital for investment in stocks and bonds, plants and equipment could move freely from country to country as could labor. Initially there would be a problem for the weak and inefficient industries in the three countries as free trade within the NAEU would expose them to stiff competition. Those that survived, however, could compete more effectively around the world.

These conditions would seem to provide some rather important economic opportunities for its three member countries. Manufacturers in the United States, Canada, and Mexico would have unrestricted access to one another's markets. U.S. capital and technology could move to Canada and Mexico and theoretically produce jobs in both countries. It is feasible that Mexico's backward agricultural sector would benefit from the technology of both the United States and Canada which would help Mexico's fast-growing, underfed population. In addition, open borders would serve to alleviate Mexico's critical population and unemployment problems by permitting a free and legal flow of workers into the United States, where a job market swelled by the larger North American consumer market could presumably absorb them.

Further, with Canada's and Mexico's oil and natural gas, and the United States' coal, energy needs of the three could be met and the constant flow of dollars to OPEC would be stopped. On balance, it appears that an NAEU makes economic sense to everyone.

What are the benefits of an NAEU?

The Canadians and Mexicans are not nearly so enthusiastic about the prospect of an NAEU as are the advocates in the United States. In fact, they are somewhat apprehensive of the prospect. Some of the cause of their apprehension is economic, some is nationalistic, and some stems from a fear of the strength of the United States and its possible domination of any union.

Mexicans often express their concern about the United States' heavy handed influence in Mexican affairs with a statement, loosely translated, "Poor Mexico—so far from God and so close to the United States." Some Canadians are even less kind when they insinuate that an NAEU is a U.S. effort to rewrite the Manifest Destiny; a reference to historical U.S. attempts to rationalize domination of the North American continent.

To understand the concern, look at the continent's lopsided trade pattern, which now favors Canadian and Mexican export to the United States. Under the new U.S.-Canada bilateral trade agreement, recently negotiated as part of the GATT Tokyo Round, 80 percent of all Canadian exports to the United States will be duty free. Another 15 percent will enter at tariffs of 5 percent or less. Mexican oil and coffee beans, which represent nearly 40 percent of that country's exports to the United States, are duty free. The average U.S. tariff on all other Mexican products, from machinery to cork, is 6.03 percent.

U.S. products are not nearly so welcome in Mexico or Canada. Under the new bilateral agreement, Canada will allow only 65 percent of U.S. exports to enter duty free. And Canada's average tariff on dutiable U.S. imports will be 8.5 percent, down from 14.8 percent under the old agreement but still more than double the average U.S. tariff on dutiable imports from Canada. Mexico uses a complex licensing system to bar many U.S. manufactured goods from that market. Those that do enter are hit with tariffs ranging from 35 to 100 percent. Initially then, the big winners in any NAEU would be U.S. manufacturers who could expand both north and south under a duty-free customs union and build or buy plants in Mexico and Canada.

One other possible advantage to the United States would be available sources of oil and gas. However, that prospect might be just an illusion. In no way does the formation of a common market give member nations the rights to each other's natural resources. Even in the European Community the U.K. sells most of its North Sea petroleum on the open market—much of it to the United States.

Regardless of the problems and obstacles to a union, from a purely economic standpoint, in the long run it makes sense for the United States, Canada, and Mexico to join forces to form a major world trading unit. Especially is this true as the industrialized world competes more fiercely for world markets and resources. Although the problems appear difficult and two of the proposed members are not too enthusiastic, remember that the European Common Market was first suggested by Napoleon and it didn't get started until 1958. Even then, there were many of the original members that would have rejected the plan had European economic conditions not left all other alternatives unworkable. And, which among the original six member countries that had fought two world wars in 20 years, were fiercely competitive, nationalistic, drastically different culturally and in languages and each with economic weaknesses that would suffer with any economic union, would have ever thought the Common Market would come as far as it has in so short a time?

QUESTIONS:

1. Compare and contrast the situation that exists with the proposed NAEU and that which existed with the original members of the European Common Market. Are there any clues that suggest an NAEU will work?

2. Will a North American Economic Union work?

3. Take either side of the proposition that there should be a North American Economic Union and support your position.

Case III–3

Nestlé in LDCs*

Henry Ciocca, as Vice-President of Nestlé, U.S.A., was given the task of analyzing and administering a massive external affairs program aimed at counteracting the increasingly successful worldwide boycott against Nestlé. He organized a team of four full-time experts with the option of supplementing their efforts with 10 additional members. The company also hired an external public relations firm to publicize the six-year old story which has led to the current turmoil. Mr. Ciocca was reviewing the situation in order to consider his next move.

The boycott, supported by a number of community organizations and church groups, was an attempt to exert pressure on infant formula producers (Nestlé, in particular) to drop their promotional activities in the Third World. The supporters lamented that these promotions induced mothers in the LDCs to switch from breast-feeding to the use of formula—however, many mothers lacked the knowledge to properly use formula and tended to underfeed their babies, leading to malnutrition.

Company background

Nestlé Alimentana S.A., a Swiss-based food complex, is a leading worldwide producer of goods ranging from powdered milk to pharmaceuticals. Under its processes or licensing agreements, more than 300 plants were operating in 52 countries with sales that amounted to $10.9 billion and $12 billion in 1978 and 1979 respectively. In 1976, 95 percent of Nestlé's sales came from its foreign markets. Its product lines had been diversified from milk products into other food areas such as coffee, cocoa, and frozen foods. Four main products: infant formula, condensed milk, powdered milk,

---

* Case written by J. Alex Murray, University of Windsor, Windsor, Ontario, Canada; Gregory M. Gazda and Mary J. Molenaar, San Diego State University.

and chocolate, accounted for about 35 percent of total sales in 1979. In 1978, infant formula sales were $250 million which gave Nestlé the largest share of the world infant formula market among the 16 companies involved.

Nestlé's policy in developing countries

Nestlé's entrance into developing countries was mainly a response to the economic needs and the strong desires of those countries to acquire their own production facilities. Whenever local demand warranted, or raw materials were available, Nestlé would take the risk of investing in order to substitute imports by indigeneous products. This investment helped the local economy with jobs and saved foreign exchange. They also made attempts to train and promote local people to replace Nestlé's international staffs—they had their own permanent training center (near Vevey) to train candidates from countries where it had industrial operations.

A major food and nutrition policy adopted by Nestlé was to improve quality control standards in the manufacture of local foodstuffs. In addition, a Nestlé research team was studying the problems of malnutrition in different developing countries, in order that their Vevey Research Center could develop highly nutritional products which would be tailored to the needs of particular areas.

Infant formula promotion in the Third World

Formulas sold in developed countries were usually in a liquid, ready-to-use form, but the products most commonly marketed in developing countries were in powder form. The powdered formulas must be mixed with sterile water.

Infant formulas were generally promoted in the Third World countries through mass media advertising, medical professions, and "mothercraft nurses." Mass media advertisements included media such as newspaper ads, radio, posters, and billboards. Promotion to physicians included the use of free samples, conferences, and regional educational seminars. Mothercraft nurses and nurses' aides were employed by companies to promote their products. These nurses wore uniforms to project a professional image and promoted the use of infant formula through other health professionals on the village's clinic staff.

Infant formula controversy

In the early 1970s, medical professionals had preached the danger of increasing promotion of infant formula in underdeveloped countries. The reason was that initial studies indicated that mothers in these developing countries were preparing the formula with contaminated water. Also, the high illiteracy rate among mothers exacerbated the problem; instructions went unread, resulting in improper mixing in unclean conditions. In many cases, the mixture was diluted to increase the yield of the powder concentrate.

Between the years 1973 and 1975 a series of developments caused Nestlé to rethink their strategy:

1. In 1973, the *New International* (British publication) publicized a story called "The Baby Food Tragedy," which was based on an interview with two tropical medical experts. The two medical experts expressed that in their opinion the marketing efforts of Western corporations in part contributed to the already confused infant nutrition situation in developing countries.

2. In February, 1974, the controversy was carried forward by a British charitable agency, "The War on Want," which published a report on the infant malnutrition problem entitled "The Baby Killer," criticizing the multinational firms in regard to their promotional activities of hard-selling products to people incapable of using them.

3. In May 1974, the Third World Action Group (TWAG) translated the report, with some changes and entitled the pamphlet "Nestlé Kills Babies." Nestlé sued for libel and won the case, but the court ruled that it must carry out a fundamental reconsideration of its promotion method.

4. In 1975, Peter Kreig, an independent filmmaker, produced a film entitled, "Bottle Babies." It was his intention to support those in Kenya who made charges against Nestlé's marketing of infant formula in the Third World. Unfortunately, most of the persons and groups in the United States who eventually came to support the Nestlé boycott were initially enlisted by viewing this film.

By November 1975, Nestlé had organized a group of large infant formula companies and formed the International Council of Infant Food Industries (ICIFI) to impose industry self-regulation. They subsequently published a "code of ethics" for members to follow.

The boycott

Although the ICIFI had initiated industry self-regulation, opponents to infant formula milk claimed that the code was vague and meaningless. Thus in 1977, the Infant Formula Action Coalition (INFACT) was formed in Minneapolis, Minnesota, and organized the Nestlé boycott. Supported by a number of church groups, organizations, and many volunteers, INFACT operated on an annual budget of contributions of approximately $30,000.

The boycott, although started in the United States, was intended to be international. INFACT and its supporting organization demanded that Nestlé halt all mass consumer promotion; distribution of free samples to hospitals, clinics and homes of newborns; and promotion through "mothercraft nurses."

Nestlé's response

Nestlé has steadily reduced its direct consumer advertising in Third World countries since the early 1970s, and a total termination was in effect by 1978. The company agreed that breast-feeding was best for babies but emphasized the fact that there is a need for a supplement to breast milk in these countries.

Nestlé noted that mortality rates in the developing countries had decreased sharply on all continents over the past decades. More specifically, UN statistics showed that, in most developing countries, mortality rates had dropped approximately 50 per cent since 1940. They also argued that there was no clear evidence that breast-feeding had declined in the Third World countries. For example, results of a survey carried out in Nigeria showed that in all social-economic groups studied virtually all mothers breast-fed. Yet Nigeria had the highest per capita consumption of infant formula.

In response to the boycott in the United States, Nestlé established an office of corporate responsibility in its New York headquarters.

World Health Organization conference

Senator Edward Kennedy requested the World Health Organization (WHO) to convene an international conference in Geneva in October, 1979 on infant formula promotion marketing and recommended use. WHO recommended the following:

> On advertising: "There should be no sales promotion, including promotional advertising to the public, of products to be used as breast milk substitutes or bottle-fed supplements and feeding bottles."
>
> On free samples: Advertising or promotional distribution of free samples of breast milk substitutes through health service channels should not be allowed. Artificial feeding should not be openly demonstrated in health facilities.
>
> On company personnel: "No personnel paid by companies producing or selling breast milk substitutes should be allowed to work in the health care system, even if they are assigned more general responsibilities that do not directly include the promotion of formulas, in order to avoid the risk of conflict of interest."

Nestlé promptly endorsed the guidelines and promised to work with the WHO and UNICEF on world marketing standards for infant formulas. However, the Interfaith Center on Corporate Responsibility (ICCR) together with INFACT claimed that the marketing practices of Nestlé still remained inconsistent with WHO's recommendations; and, in March, 1980, and February, 1981, they insisted that the boycott must be continued and intensified.

QUESTIONS

1. The major thrust of the campaign has been against Nestlé rather than other manufacturers, for example, Wyeth, American Home Products. Why? Does the fact that Nestlé is a foreign firm make it an easier target? Or is it simply easier to apply pressure by boycotting consumer products, such as Nestlé's, rather than chemical or pharmaceutical products, such as Wyeth's?

2. The companies marketing infant formula in the developing nations seem to have assumed that the pattern of development there would follow the same trends observed in the developed countries—that is, a process of urbanization and increased participation of women in the work force, thus prompting demand (and ability to pay) for formula. Cultural differences and specific economic problems do not appear to have been rigorously analyzed. Why?

3. Nestlé, in particular, seems to have been blind to cultural issues in the United States—and as a result, underestimated the strength of the antiformula movement. How can such things happen, and why?

4. There has been a tendency in recent years for a return to breast-feeding in North America. When combined with the decline in the birth rate, it appears that the overall market in western countries is not likely to grow, at least in the short run. Could this situation have impacted on the decision of the manufacturers to market their product in LDCs?

PART FOUR

INTERNATIONAL MARKETING MANAGEMENT I

CHAPTERS:

12. Strategic planning and organizing for international marketing
13. Planning and developing consumer products for foreign markets
14. Marketing industrial products and services
15. International promotion—Advertising and sales promotions
16. Personal selling and personnel management

CASES:

IV–1. Levi's—worldwide advertising strategy or localized campaigns?
IV–2. Developing a Kodak promotional program in Japan
IV–3. Rallysport International—promoting racquetball in Japan
IV–4. A job in Grenoble
IV–5. A policy for selection and compensation of overseas managers
IV–6. National office machines—motivating Japanese salespeople: Straight salary or commission?

Chapter 12

Strategic planning and organizing for international marketing

At this point, the reader must be wondering how all the information confronting an international marketer can be focused on the marketing of a product in a foreign country. The most effective approach to managing and utilizing all such information is careful planning and an organizational structure designed to facilitate the needs of international marketing.

Interestingly, not all international firms use strategic planning nor are all structured to reflect the special problems of international business. However, as involvement deepens and firms are faced with uncertainties caused by rapid environmental changes in markets, competition, resource availability, fluctuating foreign currencies, shifting political alignments, and/or the complexities of expansion into multiple markets, formal corporate-level strategic planning and organizational restructuring are generally adopted. Among U.S. multinationals, implementation of strategic planning is a major trend. A study of *Fortune 500* firms found 90 percent of the firms responding to the study indicated they engage to some degree in long-range planning. The most interesting finding was that two fifths had begun such activities only within the past five years.[1]

Strategic planning and the development of an organizational structure are interrelated. A specific organizational structure can shape and affect the planning and decision processes and, at the same time, the planning processes can affect the organizational structure. "The relationship between corporate organizational structure and strategic planning is both intimate and powerful."[2] There is a definite need to adapt a corporation's organization to the demands of multinational involvement. An MNC's market strategy tends to be three dimensional—based on products, customer group, and country. Frequent changes in structure occur as companies attempt to adjust their organization to facilitate the special needs of international marketing.

Reorganizing, reforming, restructuring, and regrouping are increasingly necessary as firms become aware of the needs for better organizational

---

[1] Noel Capon, John U. Farley, and James Hulbert, "International Diffusion of Corporate and Strategic Planning Practices," *Columbia Journal of World Business*, Fall 1980, pp. 5–6.

[2] "Global Strategic Planning—III: Organizational Issues can Stand in the Way," *Business International*, September 25, 1981, p. 305.

structures that will accommodate the complexities of international marketing operations. The domestic bias in an organizational structure quickly becomes apparent when a substantial portion of a firm's profits are generated offshore; then inadequate planning and lines of communication are highly visible.

This chapter discusses strategic planning for international marketing and attempts to isolate and identify the elements which contribute to effective international organization. The materials pertain specifically to the internal and overall corporate organizational arrangements used to facilitate decision making. The focus of this chapter is on the role of marketing in an international organization and it stresses strategic planning and organizing for effective international marketing.

STRATEGIC PLANNING

Strategic planning is a systematized way of relating to the future. It is an attempt to manage the effects of external, uncontrollable factors on the firm's strengths, weaknesses, objectives, and goals to attain a desired end. Further, it is a commitment of resources to a country market to achieve specific goals. In other words, planning is the job of making things happen that may not have otherwise occurred.[3]

The question that needs addressing is whether or not there is a difference between strategic planning for a domestic company and for an international company. The principles of planning are not in themselves different but the intricacies of the operating environments of the MNC (host country, home and corporate environments), its organizational structure, and the task of controlling a multicountry operation create differences in the complexity and process of international planning.[4]

Strategic planning allows for rapid growth of the international function, changing markets, increasing competition, and the ever varying challenges of different national markets. The plan must blend the changing parameters of external country environments with corporate objectives and capabilities to develop a sound, workable marketing program. A strategic plan is a program which commits corporate resources to products and markets to increase competitiveness and profits.[5]

Planning relates to the formulation of goals and methods of accomplishing them, so it is both a process and a philosophy. Structurally, planning may be viewed as corporate, strategic, and/or tactical. International planning at the corporate level is essentially long-term, incorporating generalized

---

[3] For a comprehensive report on planning, see David S. Hopkins, *The Marketing Plan*, Report No. 801 (New York: The Conference Board, Inc., 1981), 138 pp.

[4] For complete coverage of the process of MNC planning, see Derek S. Channon and Michael Jalland, *Multinational Strategic Planning* (New York: American Management Assoc., 1978), 344 pp.

[5] Gilbert D. Harrell and Richard O. Kiefer, "Multinational Strategic Market Portfolios," *MSU Business Topics*, Winter 1981, p. 5.

goals for the enterprise as a whole. Strategic planning is conducted at the highest levels of management and deals with long- and short-term goals of the company, while tactical planning or market planning pertains to specific actions and to the allocation of resources used to implement strategic planning goals in specific markets.

A major advantage to an MNC involved in strategic planning is the discipline imposed by the process. An international marketer who has gone through the planning process has a framework for analyzing marketing problems and opportunities and a basis for coordinating information from different country markets. The process of planning may be as important as the plan itself since it forces decision makers to examine all factors which can affect the success of a marketing program and involves those who will be responsible for its implementation. When Massey Ferguson, Canada's farm implement producer, completed their first strategic planning program for the 1980s, the final product represented the efforts of 200 managers worldwide, combining input from field operating managers and senior management alike.[6] Another key to successful planning is evaluating company objectives, including an assessment of management's commitment and philosophical orientation to international business.[7]

Company objectives and resources

Evaluation of a company's objectives and resources is crucial in all stages of planning for international operations. Each new market entered can require a complete evaluation relative to the parent company's objectives and resources. As markets grow increasingly competitive, as companies find new opportunities, and as the cost of entering foreign markets increases, companies need such planning.[8]

Defining objectives clarifies the orientation of the domestic and international divisions, thus permitting consistent policies. A lack of well-defined objectives has found companies rushing into promising foreign markets only to find activities that conflict with or detract from the companies' primary objectives.

Foreign market opportunities do not always parallel corporate objectives; it may be necessary to change the objectives, change the scale of international plans or abandon them. One market may offer immediate profit but have a poor long-run outlook while another may offer the reverse situation.

---

[6] "Move by Massey-Ferguson into Strategic Planning Should Benefit Its Business," *Business International,* December 12, 1980, pp. 393–94.

[7] For a report on the success of one firm which went from no planning to successful strategic planning, see "Cadbury Schweppes Ltd. or: How to Market Successfully Abroad," from *Marketing News,* reprinted in *International Marketing Strategy,* ed. Hans Thorelli and Helmut Becker, rev. ed. (New York: Pergamon Press, 1980), pp. 325–27.

[8] See Walter Kiechel III, "Playing The Global Game," *Fortune,* November 16, 1981, pp. 111–26.

One organizational arrangement may couple high returns and high investment, whereas another may permit cheaper entry but not provide market
strength. Only when corporate objectives are clear can such differences
be reconciled effectively.

International commitment and philosophical orientation

After company objectives have been identified, management needs to
determine whether they are prepared to make the level of commitment
required for successful international operations—commitment in terms of
dollars to be invested, personnel for managing the international organization,
and determination to stay in the market long enough to recognize a return
on these investments.

The degree of commitment to an international marketing cause can affect
considerably the extent of a company's involvement. If a company is uncertain of its prospects, it is likely to enter a market half-heartedly; use inefficient
marketing methods, channels, or organizational forms; thus setting the stage
for the failure of a venture which could have succeeded with full commitment
and support by the parent company. Occasionally casual market entry is
successful, but more often than not, market success requires long-term commitment.

Both the strategic planning and organizational approach taken by an
international firm are affected by the degree of internationalization to which
management is philosophically committed. Such commitment affects the specific international strategies and decisions of the firm. While it is difficult
to present a scheme to include all the various philosophical orientations a
firm may take, one scheme identifies four orientations toward internationalization which can also be associated with succesive stages in the evolution
of the international operations. This is the EPRG schema—ethnocentrism,
polycentrism, regiocentrism, or geocentrism.[9]

The authors of this schema state that "a key assumption underlining the
EPRG framework is that the degree of internationalization to which management is committed or willing to move towards affects the specific international
strategies and decision rules of the firm."

Ethnocentrism. The *ethnocentric firm* views international operations
as secondary to their domestic operation. The motivation behind their international operations is to dispose of excess domestic production. Typically,
firms with this orientation centralize most international marketing plans in
the home office and policies and procedures are most often identical to
those employed at home. Basically the firm is marketing the same products
they market at home in much the same manner as they market them in
the domestic market.

---

[9] Yoram Wind, Susan P. Douglas, and Howard Z. Pearlmutter, "Guidelines for Developing
International Marketing Strategy," *Journal of Marketing,* April 1973, pp. 14–23.

Polycentrism. Once a company recognizes the importance of differences that occur in overseas markets and the importance of off-shore business to their organization, they may adopt a polycentric attitude toward their business. Firms at this stage react to market differences by allowing subsidiaries to operate independently of one another in establishing their marketing objectives and plans. Marketing is organized on a country-by-country basis with each country having its own policies and programs. Some see the polycentric orientation as an overreaction to the recognition that country markets are vastly different and that success requires an almost independent program for each country.

Regiocentrism and geocentrism. When companies evolve into regiocentric and geocentric orientations, it is generally an indication of some maturity on their part. In these phases, companies view regions or the entire world as markets and seek to develop integrated regional or world market programs. While the ethnocentric company tends to be highly centralized and the polycentric company decentralized, the regiocentric and geocentric companies are more integrated in their approaches. Regiocentrism recognizes regional commonalities in markets and attempts are made to design regional strategies for these markets. Geocentrism deals with markets on a worldwide basis. Some consider that the regiocentric and geocentric orientations reflect a more sophisticated understanding of world marketing. In these stages, attempts are made to standardize on a worldwide basis as much of the marketing program as is practical. Some decisions are viewed as applicable on a worldwide basis while others that require consideration of local influences are localized. The issues of whether marketing programs are standardized or why they are localized are not as critical as the recognition at the geocentrism stage of orientation that marketing planning *processes* need to be standardized. It is generally at the regiocentrism and geocentrism stages of development that formal international strategic planning occurs. At these two stages companies frequently reorganize, adopting structures which reflect the implications of these orientations.

When a company operates on a worldwide basis and in a multitude of countries, planning on a country-by-country basis without some overall integrating process can result in spotty world marketing performance. The complexities encountered in multinational marketing make if difficult to coordinate worldwide product and marketing strategies concurrently without a planning process that focuses simultaneously on a broad range of environments.

The planning process

Whether a company is marketing in several countries or is entering a foreign market for the first time, planning is beneficial. The first-time foreign marketer must decide in the most effective way which products to develop, in which markets, and with what level of resource commitment. For the company already involved, the key decisions revolve around allocating effort and resources among countries and product; deciding which new markets to develop or old ones to withdraw from; and, what products to develop or drop. Guidelines and systematic procedures are essential for evaluating international opportunities and risks and for developing strategic plans to take advantage of such opportunities. The process illustrated in Exhibit 12–1 offers a systematic guide to planning for the multinational firm operating in several countries.

Phase 1—preliminary analysis and screening: matching company/country needs.   Whether a company is new to international marketing or heavily involved, an evaluation of potential markets must be the first step in the planning process. Of all the existing country markets, which one or ones should a company make a market investment in is a critical first question in the international marketing planning process. A company's strengths and weaknesses, products, philosophies, and objectives must be matched with a country's constraining factors as well as limitations and potential. In the first part of the planning process, countries are analyzed and screened to eliminate those countries that do not offer sufficient potential for further consideration.

The next step is to establish screening criteria against which prospective countries will be evaluated. These criteria are ascertained by an analysis of company objectives, resources, and other corporate capabilities and limitations. It is important to determine the reasons for a company entering a foreign market and the returns expected from such an investment. A company's commitment to international business and objectives for going international are important in establishing evaluation criteria. Minimum market potential, minimum profit, return on investment, acceptable competitive levels, standards of political stability, acceptable legal requirements, and other measures appropriate for the company's products are examples of the types of evaluation criteria to be established.

Once evaluation criteria are set, a complete analysis of the environment within which a company plans to operate is made. The environment consists of the uncontrollable elements discussed in earlier chapters and they include both home-country and host-country restraints, marketing objectives, and any other company limitations or strengths which exist at the beginning of each planning period. Although an understanding of uncontrollable environments is important in domestic market planning, the task is more complex in foreign marketing since each country under consideration presents the foreign marketer with a different set of unfamiliar environmental constraints. It is this stage in the planning process that more than anything else distinguishes international from domestic marketing planning.

The results of Phase 1 provide the marketer with the basic information necessary to: (1) evaluate the potential of a proposed country market; (2) identify problems that would eliminate the country from further consideration; (3) identify environmental elements which need further analysis; (4) deter-

EXHIBIT 12-1: International planning process

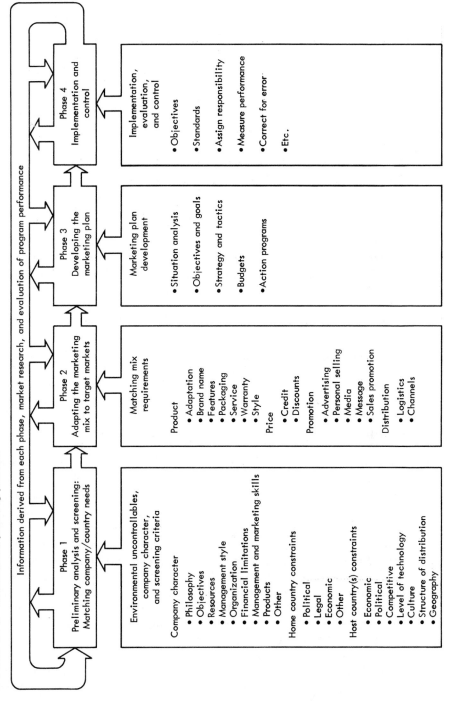

Information derived from each phase, market research, and evaluation of program performance

Phase 1
Preliminary analysis and screening:
Matching company/country needs

Environmental uncontrollables,
company character,
and screening criteria

Company character
• Philosophy
• Objectives
• Resources
• Management style
• Organization
• Financial limitations
• Management and marketing skills
• Products
• Other

Home country constraints
• Political
• Legal
• Economic
• Other

Host country(s) constraints
• Economic
• Political
• Competitive
• Level of technology
• Culture
• Structure of distribution
• Geography

Phase 2
Adapting the marketing
mix to target markets

Matching mix
requirements

Product
• Adaptation
• Brand name
• Features
• Packaging
• Service
• Warranty
• Style

Price
• Credit
• Discounts

Promotion
• Advertising
• Personal selling
• Media
• Message
• Sales promotion

Distribution
• Logistics
• Channels

Phase 3
Developing the
marketing plan

Marketing plan
development

• Situation analysis
• Objectives and goals
• Strategy and tactics
• Budgets
• Action programs

Phase 4
Implementation and
control

Implementation,
evaluation,
and control

• Objectives
• Standards
• Assign responsibility
• Measure performance
• Correct for error
• Etc.

BOX 12–1:   Standardized versus localized marketing plans

Many market conditions would preclude the standardization of marketing plans. Since national identity can influence buyers, many manufacturers understand the importance of having country identity both with the manufacture of a product and in advertising. For example, for certain kinds of products in certain parts of the United States, buy American is a very important issue. Conversely, some products associated with particular countries such as wine or fine cameras may have greater market demand when associated with the foreign home country rather than a local market. In addition, national taste preferences differ for some kinds of products from market to market. For example, in Britain, gelatin desserts are preferred in solid wafer or cake form while in the United States and other parts of the world, they are sold as a powder. Germans are accustomed to buying salad dressing in tubes.

While some market conditions prevent standardization, other conditions would certainly encourage standardizing worldwide marketing plans. Some products actually lend themselves to standardization. This is certainly true for cola beverages and gasoline, as well as many fast foods and hotel services. Most of these are standardized although there are some exceptions. Kentucky Fried Chicken is prepared differently in Malaysia than in other parts of the world. The parent company was opposed to any change since they have attempted to standardize their product line throughout their markets. However, after a comprehensive survey they succumbed to local cultural taste preferences. The change required that the chicken be cooked to a firm texture instead of the standard "soft" texture. The Malaysians considered a "firm" chicken to be "fresh" and a soft texture to have been frozen and not "fresh." Packaging, prices, and distribution methods may also be standardized across markets.*

* From David Zielenziger, "Fast-Food Chains Flocking to Malaysia to Tap Expanding Consumer Market," *Asian Wall Street Journal*, June 1, 1981, p. 15.

---

mine what parts of and how the marketing mix must be adapted to meet local market needs; and, (5) develop and implement a marketing action plan.

Information generated in Phase 1 helps a company avoid the kind of mistakes that plagued Radio Shack Corporation, a leading merchandiser of consumer electronic equipment in the United States, when they first went international. Radio Shack's early attempts at international marketing in Western Europe resulted in a series of costly mistakes that could have been avoided had they properly analyzed the uncontrollable elements of the countries targeted for their first attempt at multinational marketing. In Holland, for example, the company staged its first Christmas promotion for December 25, unaware that the Dutch celebrate St. Nicholas Day and gift giving on December 6. Legal problems in various countries interfered with some of their plans; they were unaware that most European countries have laws prohibiting the sale of citizen-band radios, one of the company's most lucrative U.S. products and one they expected to sell in Europe. A free flashlight promotion in German stores was promptly stopped by German courts because giveaways violate German sales laws. In Belgium, they overlooked a law requiring a government tax stamp on all window signs and poorly selected store sites resulted in many of the new stores closing shortly after opening.[10]

With the analysis in Phase 1 completed, the decision maker faces the more specific task of selecting country target markets, identifying problems and opportunities in these markets, and beginning the process of creating marketing programs.

Phase 2—adapting the marketing mix to target markets. A more detailed examination of the components of the marketing mix is the purpose of Phase 2. When target markets are selected, the market mix must be evaluated in light of the data generated in Phase 1. In what ways do product, promotion, price, and distribution need to be adapted to meet target market requirements? Incorrect decisions at this point can lead to costly mistakes such as improper pricing, advertising and promotional blunders, and/or products inappropriate for the intended market. The primary goal of Phase 2 is to decide on a marketing mix adapted to the cultural constraints imposed by the uncontrollable elements of the environment which will effectively achieve corporate objectives and goals.

One example of the type of analysis done in Phase 2 is the process followed by the Nestlé Company. Each product manager has a country fact book that includes much of the information suggested in Phase 1. In the country fact book, a variety of culturally related questions are analyzed in detail. As an example, in Germany the product manager for coffee must furnish answers to a number of questions: How does a German rank coffee in the hierarchy of consumer products? Is Germany a high or a low per capita consumption market? (These facts alone can be of enormous consequence. In Sweden, for instance, the annual per capita consumption of coffee is 18 pounds, while in Japan it's half a gram!) How is coffee used—in bean form, ground, or powdered? If it is ground, how is it brewed? Which coffee is preferred—Brazilian Santos blended with Colombian coffee, or robusta from the Ivory Coast? Is it roasted? Do the people prefer dark roasted or blond coffee? (The answer to this question is likewise important: the color of Nestlé's soluble coffee must resemble as closely as possible the color of the coffee consumed in the country.) Do the Germans drink coffee after lunch or with their breakfast? Do they take it black or with cream or milk? Do they drink coffee in the evening? Do they sweeten it? (In France, the answer is clear: in the morning, coffee with milk; at noon, black coffee—that is, two totally different coffees.) At what age do people begin drinking coffee? Is it a traditional beverage, as in France, or is it a form of rebellion, as in England and Japan, where the younger generation has taken up coffee drinking in order to defy their tea-drinking parents?[11]

---

[10] David Ricks, *Big Business Blunders: Mistakes in Multinational Marketing* (Homewood, Ill.: Richard D. Irwin, 1983) p. 36.

[11] P. d'Antin, "The Nestlé Product Manager as Demigod," *European Business* (Spring 1971) as reprinted in Thorelli and Becker *International Marketing Strategy*, 1980, p. 308.

With this and similar information, the product manager evaluates the marketing mix in terms of the information in the country fact book.

Frequently, the results from the analysis made in Phase 2 indicate that the marketing mix would require such drastic adaptation that a decision not to enter a particular market is made. For example, a company may find a product has to be reduced in physical size to fit the needs of the market but the additional manufacturing cost of a smaller size is too high to justify market entry. Also the price required to show a profit is too high for a majority of the market to afford. If there is no way to reduce the price, sales potential at the higher price may be too low to justify entry.

On the other hand, additional research in this phase may provide information that can suggest ways to standardize marketing programs among two or more country markets. This was the case for Nestlé when research revealed that young coffee drinkers in England and Japan had indentical motivations. As a result, Nestlé now uses principally the same message in both markets.

The answers to two major questions are generated in Phase 2: (1) what cultural/environmental adaptations are necessary for successful acceptance of the marketing mix, and (2) will adaptation costs allow for profitable market entry? Based on the results in Phase 2, a second screening of countries may take place with some countries dropped from further consideration. The next phase in the planning process is development of a marketing plan.

Phase 3—developing the marketing plan.   At this stage of the planning process, a marketing plan is developed for a specific country target market. It begins with a situation analysis and culminates in a specific action program for the market. The specific plan establishes what is to be done, by whom, how it is to be done, and when. Included are budgets and sales and profit expectations. Just as in Phase 2, a decision not to enter a specific market may be made if it is determined that company marketing objectives and goals cannot be met.

Phase 4—implementation and control.   A "go" decision in Phase 3 triggers implementation of specific plans and anticipation of successful marketing. However, the planning process does not end at this point. All marketing plans require coordination and control (Phase 4) during the period of implementation. Many businesses do not yet control marketing plans as thoroughly as they could even though they can increase their degree of success with continuous monitoring and control. An evaluation and control system requires a manager to have performance objectives for successive time intervals covering the duration of the plan: a means of measuring against predetermined standards, plus the flexibility to take corrective action, that is, bring the plan back on track should standards of performance fall short. As you will see in Chapter 22, coordinating and controlling an international marketing plan is a difficult but extremely important task. The complexities of operating internationally make coordination and control a critical part of management responsibility in international marketing.

As the model in Exhibit 12–1 illustrates, there is a flow of information from each phase in addition to information generated through marketing research and program evaluation. This flow of information is important for all future planning activities. One of the major contributions of the multinational marketing information system (MMIS) discussed in Chapter 9 is that information generated by an international marketing plan is stored for future use. Equally important is the fact that an MMIS provides a source of information which can be applied from one country to another. One of the weaknesses of current national marketing patterns is that companies frequently do not learn from past mistakes or successes. An effective MMIS can help correct this problem.[12]

BOX 12–2: Anheuser-Busch goes international but not with Budweiser

In 1980, Anheuser-Busch made a decision to begin distributing its beer in Europe's largest beer markets: Great Britain, Germany, and France. Distribution agreements were made with some of Europe's largest brewers but there was one hitch—they can't use the brand name Budweiser in Europe.

In 1911, Anheuser-Busch purchased American rights to the name and recipe for the beer from the brewers of Budweis in Czechoslovakia. The Czechs sold the United States rights but held on to all rights in Europe. Budweis' Budweiser brand beer is available in Europe so the U.S. beer will be sold under the brand name of *Anheuser-Busch*.

Source: From "Bitte, Herr Ober, ein Anheuser-Busch!" *World Business Weekly*, June 22, 1981, p. 42.

While the model is presented as a series of sequential phases, the reader should view the planning process as a dynamic, continuous set of interacting variables with information continuously building among phases. The phases outline a critical path to be followed for effective, systematic planning.[13]

Although the model depicts a large MNC operating in multiple countries, it is equally applicable for a small company interested in a single country. Phases 1 and 2 are completed for one country or for several and Phases 3 and 4 are developed individually for each country target market. Multinational companies use the same processes but integrate their planning and information to serve as many of their markets as feasible, concentrating on individual markets in Phases 3 and 4.

Utilizing a strategic planning process encourages the deicison maker to consider all variables that can affect the success of the company's plan. Furthermore, it provides the basis for viewing all market countries and their interrelationships as an integrated unit. When an MNC begins planning on a worldwide basis, one of the first issues to surface in Phase 1 is which

---

[12] See Chapter 9 for a discussion of an MMIS.

[13] Robert J. McMahon, *Marketing Planning* 3d ed. (Scotsdale, Ariz.: Thunderbird Press, 1981), p. 8.

products and markets should be expanded, contracted, or dropped. Product portfolio analysis is a strategic planning approach that suggests a solution for this problem.

Product portfolio analysis

Since multinational companies operate in a number of countries with a variety of products, it is possible for individual products to have different market shares, different market growth potentials, and different present and future profitability potentials in each country market. In addition, the U.S. multinational's products are, more frequently than not, in a dominate market position in the United States and, therefore, at a more advanced stage in the product life cycle than in most of the foreign markets under consideration. These inconsistencies confront the planner with the problems of how to be certain that the worldwide strategies developed will maximize profit and growth potential for all products in all country markets. There are several product portfolio models available to offer possible solutions to these problems and to guide the formulation of strategic plans. Among the more widely discussed are the various portfolio planning systems which the Boston Consulting Group (BCG) has popularized.[14]

A portfolio planning system recognizes that a company is comprised of a portfolio of businesses (businesses are defined as product lines or product categories), each of which contributes to the total profit pool of the company. Further, the system recognizes that to maximize potential opportunities each business or product market needs different degrees of management attention and effort. Some product markets should be expanded, others maintained at current levels of development, some phased down to a smaller size, and still others phased out entirely.

Traditionally, businesses have been managed from the perspective that all their products should be encouraged to grow; budgets have been allocated to all in ever-larger amounts so each could achieve greater sales and profits. Now, however, more precise management planning requires recognition of the differences in potential that exist among product country markets. Although the various product portfolio systems were developed primarily for U.S. firms operating with multiproduct lines in the U.S. market, these systems have application for MNCs. Many believe that product portfolio[15] analysis has greater application for MNCs than for strictly domestic companies.

In fact, these systems address the growing concern of many international

---

[14] For a concise but complete discussion of the BCG portfolio analysis system see Philip Kotler, *Marketing Management: Analysis, Planning, and Control,* 4th ed. (Englewood Cliffs, N.J.: Prentice-Hall, 1980), pp. 75–80.

[15] For a discussion of the application of this concept in foreign markets see, Gilbert D. Harrell and Richard O. Kiefer, "Multinational Strategic Market Portfolios," *MSU Business Topics,* Winter 1981, pp. 5–15.

marketing decision makers about their ability to identify the different characteristics of each of their country markets and plan the strategic future of
the total corporate effort. Further, product portfolio analysis permits management to take a rational account of "achieving a suitable geographic and
sociopolitical balance among its operations"[16] which is of particular importance to the MNC.

In using the product portfolio concept, the firm analyzes the cash flow
potential of each product. The concept recognizes that future profitability
is affected by the relationship of three factors: rate of market growth, relative
market share, and product unit cost. The cost of producing a product declines
predictably as output increases. When a product has a high market share,
unit cost will typically be low and profit will be greater. Further, if the market
is growing, it is less costly to acquire increased market share; those with
large market shares *in mature markets* can protect them with less cost than
it would take a low-market-share competitor to increase its share.

Conversely, a product with a low market share will most probably have
a relatively high unit cost and the profit generated by such a product will
be relatively low compared to a high-share, low-unit-cost product. However,
it is not reasonable to assume that a product with low share can capture a
large share of market at a profitable return on marketing investment. If
the product life cycle is at market maturity or if competition is strong with
a large market share, then capturing a significantly larger share of market
may be a costly venture. For those products in the growth stage of the

EXHIBIT 12-2:   Market share/growth matrix

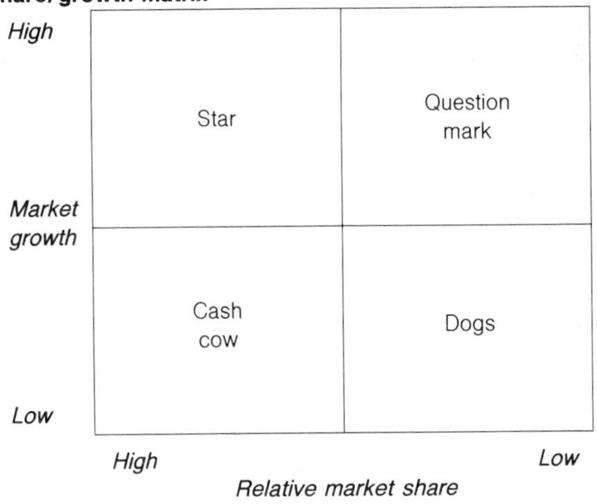

Relative market share

---

[16] For a discussion of the application of strategic portfolio planning systems to multinational firms see, Jean-Claude Larreche, "The International Product/Market Portfolio," 1978 AMA Educators' Proceedings, Subbash C. Jain, ed., AMA Series No. 73, 1978, pp. 276–80; and Derek Channon and Michael Jalland, *Multinational Strategic Planning* (New York: American Management Assoc., 1978), pp. 89–119.

product life cycle, there is a very real prospect that a product which gains share will have an increasingly lower unit cost and increasing profitability.

This relationship of market growth, unit cost, and market share is traditionally illustrated by the matrix in Exhibit 12–2. The vertical axis, market growth, reflects growth potential from low to high while the horizontal axis, relative market share, depicts market share for the product. Thus, products with high market share and in a high-growth market are positioned in the upper lefthand corner. These products, sometimes called "stars," have a high or dominate market share in a market with continued growth potential. The assumption is that as the market grows, the *stars'* sales will increase and unit costs will decline. Thus, as the market grows and market share remains high, cash flow and profit potential of *stars* increase.

In the upper righthand corner of the matrix in Exhibit 12–2 are products with low market share in a growing market. Products here, frequently referred to as "problem children" or "question marks," have potential if market share can be increased; for some reason, however, their market share has not increased with market growth. The mediocre performance of the *question mark* may be the result of inadequate market effort by the company or strong competitive pressures. *Question marks* should be evaluated carefully since some have the potential to be made into *stars* while others should be dropped from the product line.

Below the *question marks* in the bottom righthand quadrant of the matrix are those products classified as "dogs." They have a low share of market in a market that has very little market growth potential. While these products can generate some cash flow and profit, the possibility for improved profitability position is minimal. Certainly, a decision to make additional investment of marketing dollars must be made carefully and frequently is unwarranted.

The last quadrant of the matrix (bottom lefthand corner) is occupied by the "cash cows." As the name implies, these products are money machines. Although they have little potential for increased growth since they are in a low-growth market (they are generally in markets at the mature stage of the product life cycle), their large share position and implied lower product unit costs make them profitable items. These former *stars* are cash generators, providing the cash flow to be used in developing other products.

With proper product management, products can change positions; *question marks* can be cultivated to become *stars* and *stars* can be made into *cash cows.* The task of management is to achieve a balance in the company's portfolio of products by eliminating *dogs* and some *question marks* and taking the cash generated by *cash cows* to support the *stars* and those selected *question marks* that analysis indicates have a high probability of being transformed into *stars* and later *cash cows.*

Product portfolio analysis has gained general acceptance by U.S. firms in their planning, although there are some questions arising from its overly enthusiastic application by some.[17]

---

[17] See, for example, Walter Kiechel III, "Oh Where, Oh Where Has My Little Dog Gone? Or My Cash Cow? Or My Star?", *Fortune,* November 2, 1981, pp. 148–51.

Also, the process may have some negative impact on international product management if not properly applied on a global basis.[18] The BCG approach defines the market share/growth matrix in terms of products in single national markets. When applied to international markets the analysis becomes more involved. A product which might be designated a *cash cow* in one country market can conceivably be a *question mark*, a *dog*, or a *star* in another country, depending on the market share held by the product, rate of market growth, and competition in that particular market. When dealing with more than one country market, it may be more meaningful to define the portfolio entries as product/markets, treating each as a separate entity. In fact, the idea of the relative market share/market growth matrix suggests that entries be defined in terms of products and markets. Since the multinational company often has the same product in different markets, the approach may be more appropriately viewed for the MNC as a product/market portfolio analysis with each product/market treated as an entry.[19]

Problems can arise when a product is analyzed only in terms of the national market without thought of the consequences to the foreign market. For example, a *cash cow* in the domestic market may be "milked" on the basis of its position at home without concern that such a product is a *star* in a foreign market or markets. Thus, because of improper treatment, a product with potential for development into a *cash cow* is precluded from its full potential. Further, firms have been short sighted and milked their foreign market *stars* to satisfy cash needs in the home market. One observer suggests that this happened when Ford Motor Company took cash from its German subsidiary (a *star*) to cover increased domestic financial needs resulting from costly U.S. pollution and gas mileage standards. A *star* was milked to support a declining *cash cow* or perhaps a *dog*(?). As a result, in a growing market, Ford's West German operations decreased in four years from a 15 percent share to just over 9 percent. That slide in share can mean that the subsidiary may lose for good its earlier gains or, in other words, it may have reverted from a *star* to a *question mark* or *dog*.[20]

Another potential problem occurs when the product is a *dog* in the home market but could be a *star* or *question mark* in a foreign market. The tendency may be to phase out the *dog* without consideration of its *star* or *cash cow* potential in foreign markets. What the international market planner must do is analyze the product portfolio in each market or group of markets, including the domestic market, and manage the portfolio in such a way that each product market is treated as a *cash cow*, *star*, and so on.

Product market portfolio analysis may lead to other special benefits for the multinational marketer. As *cash cows* reach the decline stage of the product life cycle and begin to diminish in profitability, they may still be

---

[18] See, for example, William L. Shanklin and John K. Ryans, Jr., "Is the International Cash Cow Really a Prize Heifer?", *Business Horizons,* March 1981, pp. 10–16.

[19] Larreche, "The International Product/Market Portfolio," p. 276.

[20] Shanklin and Ryans, "Is the International Cash Cow Really a Prize Heifer?" p. 13.

profitable in other markets. For example, the technology could be transferred to a foreign market where the product might become a *star*. This may entail dismantling a production facility and moving it to the new market or if that is not feasible, licensing the technology. Companies have been success-ful with their *dogs* in other markets through licensing their technology, thus affording them a profit that would not be possible if capital investment was required.[21] As a company expands into larger numbers of foreign markets with several products, it becomes more difficult to manage efficiently all products across all markets. Strategic marketing planning helps the marketer focus on all the variables to be considered for successful worldwide market-ing and product/market portfolio analysis is an important tool in that planning process. As companies expand their global reach and become concerned with strategic planning, the issue of an effective organization surfaces.[22]

ORGANIZATIONAL STRATEGY

An international marketing plan should optimize the benefits of resources committed to stated company objectives. The organizational plan must in-clude the type of organizational arrangements to be used, the mode and timing of entry, and the scope and location of responsibility. The localization of decision-making authority and the degree of autonomy at each level of decision making are crucial decisions in the planning stage. Even though a planner spends time and effort developing a coordinated global marketing strategy, the plan will be no better than its implementation. Multinational headquarters must rely on subsidiaries throughout the world for implementa-tion of the plan. Many ambitious multinational plans meet less than full suc-cess because of confused lines of authority and poor communications be-tween headquarters and subsidiary organizations.[23]

Responsibility for each marketing function must be assigned or the com-pany could lose flexibility and decisiveness in the crucial early months in foreign markets. If lines of authority are clearly defined, then the equally important lines of communication will usually function smoothly.

Enough flexibility must be planned into an organization to account for the contingencies which inevitably arise. Companies in international partner-ships have sometimes found that their partners lacked the capital or the ability to cope with growing market potential, and were forced to buy out

---

[21] Farok J. Contractor, "The Profitability of Technology Licensing by U.S. Multinationals: A Framework for Analysis and an Empirical Study," *Journal of International Business Studies,* Fall 1980, pp. 40–64.

[22] For a discussion of growth and organizational change see Rodman L. Drake and Lee M. Caudill, "Management of the Large Multinational: Trends and Future Challenges," *Business Horizons,* May/June 1981, pp. 83–91.

[23] James M. Hulbert, William K. Brandt, and Raimar Richards, "Marketing Planning in the Multinational Subsidiary: Practices and Problems," *Journal of Marketing,* Summer 1980, pp. 7–15.

unsatisfactory partners at exorbitant prices or contend with an unsatisfactory operation. Because of the dynamic nature of international business, some executives tend to think in rather short-run terms even though long-range planning is crucial to continuing successful operations. In as short a period as five years, a business situation can change completely or a business relationship can undergo a total transformation. As companies expand their global reach, the issue of an effective organization surfaces.[24]

Basis for organization

Innumerable considerations must be reviewed when establishing an organization for doing business internationally. Five areas need careful consideration: production, ownership (financial), legal, control, and marketing. Production decisions and ownership structures are often forced by host country regulations governing international business operations while legal considerations within each country must be understood and carefully adhered to. Control and marketing are major concerns for a company but they can be dealt with effectively if the marketer has established a well-researched organizational structure.

BOX 12–3: Plan ahead!

"In Europe strategy is too often the product of intuition or even random events. A firm finds itself pursuing a given course of action without knowing why. There is little systematic search to generate strategic alternatives and there is little systematic thinking to optimize the corporate strategic posture" This statement by a French executive with extensive planning experience in a U.S. company synthesizes the rising awareness that strategic planning is still a relatively unknown phenomenon in the European community (EC).

A major firm reports that:

50 percent of its European clients have no strategic planning at all;

32 percent have "something which they believe is strategic planning but which, in fact, is useless, indeed misleading;"

18 percent have an appropriate strategic planning system.

Source: Renato Mazzolini, "European Corporate Strategies," *Columbia Journal of World Business,* Spring 1975, p. 98.

Corporate planners must also consider the countless elements complicating the task of organizing for international marketing. Each environmental parameter produces special circumstances contributing to the complexity of organizational patterns.[25]

---

[24] For a discussion of growth and organizational change, see Drake and Caudill, "Management of the Large Multinational: Trends and Future Challenges," pp. 83–91.

[25] "Tips to Consider before Restructuring Your World Operations," *Business International,* July 4, 1980, pp. 210–11.

Company growth and the dynamic nature of the market itself are likely to cause recurring organizational restructuring. World market conditions change rapidly, often requiring modifications in a company's organization. A company could need several variations of a marketing organization as its enters different countries.

Market opportunities and *increasing commitments* to worldwide business have caused large scale shifts into the arena of multinational business. Some companies have moved from the national to the transnational level of operation in less than a decade. As the scope of business changes, company philosophy and organization must keep pace.

BOX 12–4: Put Africa wherever there's room on the chart

The survey reveals that Africa often does not come under any existing organizational unit so is handled rather informally by whatever entities within the firm have sales there.

Typical of this situation is a chemical firm that has well-defined regional organizations for Europe, Latin America, Asia, and even the Middle East, and half jokingly refers to Africa as "all other." At this firm, occasional sales to Africa are managed by the export group at international division headquarters, and once or twice a year a marketing representative is dispatched from the United States to visit the firm's African sales agents.

Source: "Selling to Africa." Reprinted from p. 191 of the June 11, 1976 issue of *Business International*, with permission of the publisher, Business International Corporation (New York).

Geographical distance may cause a company to organize its business to minimize the time and expense of executive travel. Cultural and economic differences from country to country not only require special attention, but limit the flexibility of the organization in shifting management from one area to another. There is little problem in moving an employee from New York City to Chicago, but it may be nearly impossible to move an equally adaptable person from Paris to Berlin.

Governmental regulations strongly affect a marketing organization; some nations have local ownership requirements, some require a certain percentage of indigenous personnel, and others require production to be located locally.[26] Even giants like International Business Machines, old hands at planning, are sometimes taken by surprise. IBM simply abandoned the Indian market after a two-year dispute with the Indian government who demanded that IBM reduce its ownership of Indian operations from 100 percent to 40 percent. The company chose to leave the market rather than change its long-time ownership philosophy.[27]

---

[26] Jonathan Weeks, "Planning for Physical Distribution," *Long-Range Planning,* June 1977, p. 64.

[27] Hans J. Krijnen, "Formulating Corporate Objectives and Strategies," *Long-Range Planning,* August 1977, p. 78.

Structural basis

International marketing organizations are structured around considerations dealing with a product, a function, or the geographical location of activities. The *product*-oriented organization places responsibility for worldwide distribution on the product manager, who is in charge of all distribution anywhere in the world. Under the *functional* arrangement, each manager is responsible for the performance of a given function wherever it may take place. Following the *geographical* setup, a manager is responsible for all products and functions within a given geographical area; within that area, the manager runs the company and is responsible for all aspects of its operation.

Typically, organizations combine various approaches depending on geographic, market, and manpower factors. For one product they may use a geographic arrangement, for another, a product arrangement. Some functions are handled centrally for all countries, and others are decentralized. For a large firm, a combined approach is virtually mandatory because world conditions vary so widely.

Locus of decision

Considerations of where decisions will be made, by whom, and by what method constitute a major element of organizational strategy. Management policy must be explicit about which decisions are to be made at corporate headquarters, which at international headquarters, which at regional levels, and which at national or even local levels. Most companies also limit the amount of money to be spent at each level. Decision levels for determination of policy, strategy, and tactical decisions must be established. Tactical decisions normally should be made at the lowest level such decisions can be made at without country-by-country duplication. If a tactical decision applies to several countries, it probably should be made at the regional level, but, if it applies to only one country, it should be made at the national level.[28]

When U.S. expatriate managers and foreign national managers are working together either in a training or working capacity, it is especially important to delineate carefully the areas of decision-making responsibility for each party. Predetermination of the final decision-making authority among product managers, functional managers, and line managers also can lessen the possiblity of conflict.

When determining the locus of decision the method of decision making to be employed should also be considered. Europeans tend to have one fairly highly placed executive make decisions autonomously. Americans are more likely to delegate decision making to a lower level of management

---

[28] Y. L. Doz, "Strategic Management in Multinational Companies," *Sloan Management Reveiw*, Winter 1980, pp. 27–46.

and use various committee arrangements. Japanese are noted for their "ringi" type of decision making calling for consensus.[29]

Maintaining flexibility

In developing its organizational strategy, management must maintain as much flexibility as possible to allow for future reorganizations, mergers, and dissolutions. Sometimes organizational arrangement can be modified only with governmental consent. It took Saint-Gobain, Europe's largest glass-maker, two years of concerted effort and negotiations with the government to transform a branch operation into a subsidiary. Countries often have vested interests in a given type of organization, particularly if production facilities or extensive distribution facilities are included. Raytheon, a U.S. electronics components manufacturer, found itself in luck when it had to liquidate its Palermo, Sicily firm, Raytheon Elsi. Because this was a separate subsidiary organization rather than a branch of the parent company, Raytheon was able to disavow some $12 million worth of debts.

One of the conclusions of a business strategy conference sponsored by France's National Association of Doctors of Economics was that American companies are open minded and likely to shape their organizations to fit the markets in which they are dealing, whereas European companies tend to be locked into national molds. Such rigidity limits the effectiveness of many foreign companies.

The organizational process is facilitated by careful analysis of the functions to be performed, the control desired, corporate and market situations, and the available alternatives. Organizations must grow and change with the situation. The object is not to develop the perfect organization but to develop the one best suited to the moment and offering maximum flexibility for future modification.[30]

HEADQUARTERS ORGANIZATIONAL ALTERNATIVES

Organizational arrangements employed in international marketing are difficult to categorize. Nearly every company has its own modification of a standard organizational pattern. Some firms profess to have one kind of organization, but an analysis of their operations reveals an altogether different organizational setup.

In building an organization, it is important to consider level of policy decisions, length of chain of command, staff support, source of natural and personnel resources, degree of control, centralization, and the type or level

[29] For an interesting discussion of *ringi* see, "Japan's Risk-Taking Middle Managers," *World Business Weekly,* July 13, 1981, p. 52.

[30] See, for example, James R. Basche, Jr., "Shifting Patterns in International Organization: U.S. Experiences in the 1970s." *Information Bulletin,* No. 42, The Conference Board, September 1978, 19 pp.

of marketing involvement. Such considerations provide the general orientation for the international marketing organization which can be analyzed in terms of geography, function, and product.

A company may be organized by product lines but have geographical subdivisions under the product categories. Both may be supplemented by functional staff support. Exhibit 12–3 shows such a combination. Modifications of this basic combination arrangement are used by a majority of large companies doing business internationally.

Centralization, regionalization, and decentralization

An infinite number of organizational patterns for *headquarters activities* of multinational firms could be identified, but most can be fitted into one of three categories: centralized, regionalized, and decentralized organizations. The fact that all of the systems are used indicates that each has certain advantages and disadvantages. Chief advantages of centralization are the availability of experts at one location, the ability to exercise a high degree of control on both the planning and implementation phases, and the centralization of all records and information.

BOX 12–5: Call it ringi—It's still bureaucracy

This system is perplexing to Americans accustomed to a more dictatorial style of leadership from the top down in that it has given rise to the myth that the Japanese have a mysterious bottom to top form of leadership called the *ringi* system. The *ringi* system is the wide circulation of documents to which large numbers of persons affix their seals as a sign that they have seen the document and do not actively oppose what it says. It is analogous to the clearance system in American bureaucracies and to the distribution of memorandums for information. Some relatively routine matters can be settled in this way on the basis of documents originating at a relatively low level. But it is not a peculiar Japanese system for making important or difficult decisions.

If the Japanese have a special decision-making process, it is the system of careful and extensive consultations before a decision is arrived at by general consensus.*

That massive wave of Japanese foreign investment appears to be colored bright red. One third of all established Japanese overseas manufacturing ventures operate at a loss, according to Nomura Securities Company, Tokyo's largest brokerage house. Nomura blames Japan's diffused system of decision making, in which no executive wants to admit an investment failure that should be terminated.

* Edwin O. Reischauer, "The Japanese Way," *Across the Board*, December 1977, p. 39.

Companies often shift from one pattern to another to gain temporary advantages. Franklin Mint Corporation, for example, moved its international division from Philadelphia to London to facilitate expansion of the firm's overseas sales. Four years later, having succeeded in establishing its international base, the parent company moved its offices back to Philadelphia so marketing and planning personnel could be in closer contact with parent-

EXHIBIT 12–3: Schematic marketing organization plan combining product, geographic, and functional approaches

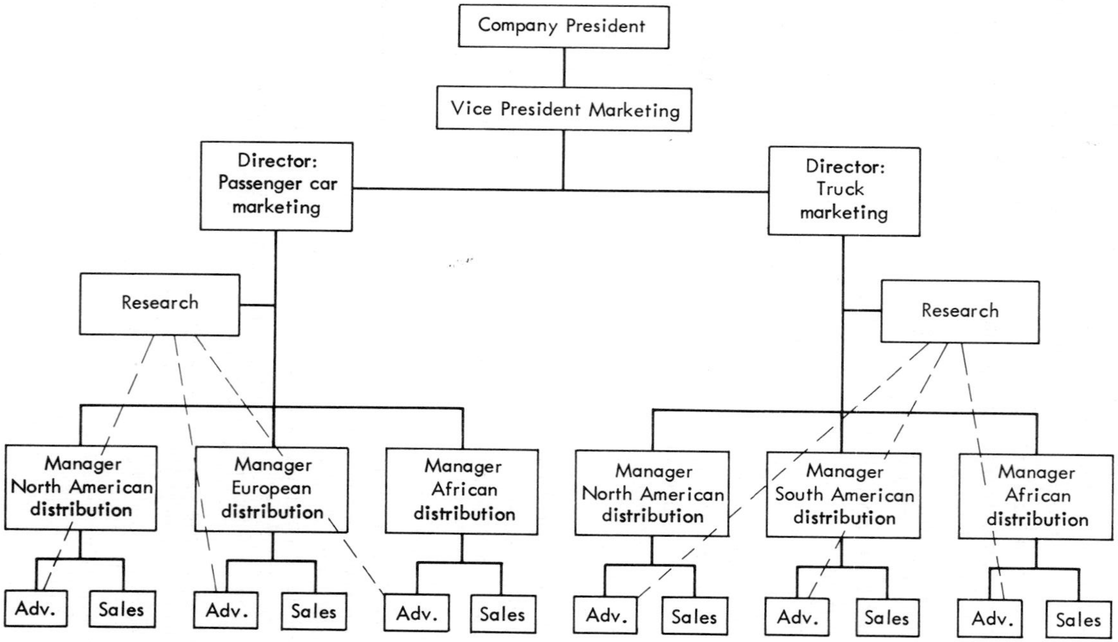

company management. Now the company uses what it calls a satellite organizational arrangement for its branches. Each established branch takes responsibility for new branches in adjacent countries until they are well established. This system allows support from experienced executives in a similar market during critical start-up periods.

Some companies effect extreme decentralization by selecting competent managers and giving them full responsibility for national or regional operations. These executives are in direct day-to-day contact with the market but lack a broad company view, which can mean partial loss of control for the parent company. Massey Ferguson has nine major market subsidiaries, each of which operates quasi-independently. All are run by nationals with the support of an "export" subsidiary in Toronto to provide staff support and maintain contact. Phillips Lamp, the fourth largest industrial company outside the United States, operated as a loosely run collection of national companies for 14 years after formation of the European Community. Its decentralized organizational approach is considered to have seriously hampered company growth before the organization was centralized and tightened up to take advantage of the mass market after the entry of Britain into the EC.

Volvo has developed an interesting combination approach. In the late 1970s, most of their sales growth was in well-established markets but they saw dynamic future potential in less developed markets. They set up a separate subsidiary, Volvo International Development Corporation, to be responsible for all the geographic areas outside major markets. That company has worldwide responsibility but specializes in developing markets.

For most large companies the trend seems to be toward regionalized and/or decentralized systems designed to combine the control and expertise of a central organization with the close contact of a decentralized organization.[31] Union Carbide, for example, has subsidiaries in Europe, the Middle East, the Far East, Latin America, and Africa. This company, with sales outside the United States of nearly $800 million, departed from a centralized organization because the operation was too large and growing too rapidly to be handled effectively from the central headquarters.

In many cases, whether or not a company's formal organizational system is centralized or decentralized, the informal organization reflects some aspect of all organizational systems. This is especially true relative to the locus of decision making. Studies show that while product decisions may be highly centralized, subsidiaries may have a substantial amount of local influence in pricing, advertising, and distribution decisions. If a product is culturally sensitive, the decisions are more apt to be decentralized.[32]

[31] "Corporate Organization: Where in the World Is It Going?," *Business International,* August 15, 1980, pp. 257–58.

[32] Jacques Picard, "Determinants of Centralization of Marketing Decision Making in Multinational Corporations," *Marketing in the 80s,* 1980 Educator's Conference Proceedings, No. 46, August 1980, pp. 259–61.

Exhibit 12–4 is a list of multinationals and their dominate organizational structure.

Patterns of responsibility

Whatever the approach to organization, someone in the parent company must be responsible for the international function. Even foreign operations that are almost completely autonomous must answer to the parent company at some point. Exhibit 12–5 shows some of the more basic relationships. The top grouping shows various arrangements which might be used at the parent company level. The group on the left shows alternate ways of handling foreign business through a company-owned marketing organization, while the group on the right lists alternate ways of handling foreign business through non-owned or external organizations. Each group is discussed below or in Chapter 19; keep in mind that corporate organizational arrangements frequently include *several* of the variations identified in the chart. For analytical purposes, however, the various sub-elements are considered separately.

EXHIBIT 12–4: Dominate organizational concept for selected multinationals

Company	Organization
American Cyanamid Company (U.S.)	Product divisions with global responsibility (*centralized*).
General Electric Company (U.S.)	Product-oriented strategic business units on a worldwide basis (*centralized*).
Rhone-Poulenc S.A. (France)	Product divisions with global responsibility, but major country organizations retain special status (*regional*).
N.V. Phillips' Gloeilampen-fabrieken (The Netherlands)	Product divisions with global responsibility, but gradual strengthening of geographic organizations; U.S. company financially and legally separate from parent (*regional*).
CIBA-GEIGY Limited (Switzerland)	Product divisions with global responsibility, but gradual strengthening of key regional organizations (*regional*).
The Dow Chemical Company (U.S.)	Decentralized geographically into six regional companies; central coordination through World Headquarters Group (*decentralized*).
Nestlé S.A. (Switzerland)	Decentralized regional and country organizations (*decentralized*).
Imperial Chemical Industries Limited (U.K.)	Product divisions with global responsibility, but gradual strengthening of regional organizations (*decentralized*).
Solvay and Cie S.A. (Belgium)	Product divisions with global responsibility, but national and subsidiary organizations allowed to exercise a reasonable degree of autonomy (*decentralized*).

Adapted from Rodman Drake and Lee M. Caudill, "Management of the Large Multinational: Trends and Future Challenges," *Business Horizons*, May/June 1981, pp. 88–90.

EXHIBIT 12–5:   Alternative organizational patterns

Corporate management of international marketing

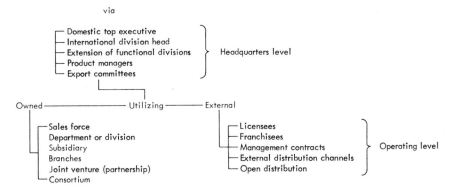

Top executive. The foreign operations of such companies as Colgate-Palmolive Co. and Ford Motor Company are closely integrated with overall company operations and dominated by a domestic company president or marketing vice president. The strong executive approach breaks down sharp separation of domestic and foreign operations. If a separate international division remains, it merely coordinates day-by-day operations.

Division head. The subsidiary or division head arrangement may be controlled by a domestically located division head or by the president of a subsidiary foreign trading company. Such organization is common because it permits delegation of authority but still permits close liaison between the foreign and domestic operations.

Extension of functional divisions. Functional area management is undertaken by individuals responsible for functional areas in the parent company. Functional organization offers flexibility and control of functional components. Some activities may be controlled by the home office, some may be controlled by the foreign branch office, and others may be controlled directly by a product manager. Such a breakdown might identify the following functional areas: (1) managerial functions (pricing, product development, and overall marketing strategy); (2) sales functions; (3) advertising functions; (4) marketing research functions; (5) physical handling; and (6) customer services.

Product management. Product specialization, direct responsibility, and fast action characterize organizations utilizing product managers or product line managers. The domestic product manager may be responsible for foreign sales of the product, or an international marketer may be assigned so each type of product may be marketed using the most suitable methods.

The Celanese Corporation of America has organized its diverse product lines into three groups: chemicals, plastics, and synthetic fibers because products in these three groups are marketed quite differently from products in the other two groups.

Export committees.   Group management is popular in companies new to international business. Export marketing committees typically include representation of marketing, production, and finance. This approach allegedly offers the advantage of balanced home office supervision, but is most likely to work satisfactorily in a company that does not highly prize aggressive international marketing.

OWNED INTERNATIONAL AFFILIATES

A company may be active in a market through its own organization by establishing a sales force, branch, or a subsidiary, or by participating in a joint venture or a consortium. In addition to starting its own branches or subsidiaries, companies may acquire existing companies through purchase of stock from existent stockholders, purchase of new issues of stock from the company, purchase of assets, or some type of merger. However, there is increased resistance by governments to the acquisition of local companies by foreign firms.

The U.S. Justice Department also takes a hard line on acquisitions of U.S. businesses by foreign firms in the same general product area. The Federal Trade Commission has taken a similar position when such acquisitions constitute a reduction in competition; they are as suspect as a local takeover of a competing company. Cases challenged in the late 1970s included purchase of 35 percent interest in Airco By British Oxygen Corporation, BIC Corporation's anticipated acquisition of Philip Morris Incorporated's safety razor division, and the acquisition of Stouffer Foods by Nestlé's Alimentana of Switzerland. Takeovers are also accomplished quite unnoticed. Standard Brands, Incorporated, of the United States, simply announced to the Dutch food company, De Erven de Wed. J. van Nelle, that it had acquired some 60 percent of that food marketer's stock (300 million in sales). It had possessed ownership for some half dozen years without even notifying the Rotterdam company to that effect.

Branches and subsidiaries

The branch is simply an outpost or detachment of a company placed in a given location to accomplish designated goals on a local level. Like their domestic counterparts, branches are an integral part of a company. Organizationally, the branch in São Paulo may differ little from the branch in Salt Lake City. Operationally, of course, the branches may be quite dissimilar; even within a country, branches may differ widely in their assignment, function, and operation. Often a branch is responsible only for the selling function, but, it can have broader responsibilities including full management of production and marketing for the assigned areas.

Subsidiaries differ from branches chiefly in that they are separate companies which have been organized to perform functions assigned or delegated by the parent company. A subsidiary is controlled, but not always wholly owned, by the parent. Ownership may be shared for financial reasons, to satisfy foreign governmental requirements, to permit management equity participation, or for other reasons related to the parent company's goals. Many subsidiaries are full-scale companies covering major regions of the world outside the parent country, undertaking full-scale operations, and having dollar sales volume in tens of millions. On the other hand, subsidiaries are often small local operations. The range of operating methods is nearly as wide; subsidiaries may be completely autonomous, independently financed enterprises or be totally dependent on the parent in nearly all respects.

Joint ventures

Joint-venture fever has been sweeping the world. Nearly all companies that are very active in world trade participate in at least one joint venture somewhere; many number their joint ventures in the dozens. A recent Conference Board study indicates the 40 percent of Fortune 500 companies with more than $100 million in sales were engaged in one or more international joint ventures.[33]

There is no one reason for the increase in joint ventures. Commitment to joint venture depends on the type of market, the country in which the company plans to do business, and the basis for the business. The Conference Board study revealed a variety of reasons for companies to try a joint venture. Among the more important reasons listed were:

1. Attractive new markets for companies in mature home markets.

2. The need to deal with rising economic nationalism, especially important in Third World countries where many require local participation for any investment.

3. The need for new raw materials, important for politically sensitive extractive industries seeking new sources of raw materials and a means of passing along the heightened economic risk of new business ventures. (In the face of worldwide inflation, political instability, terrorism, and other uncertainties, many companies believe a local partner will lessen such risks.)

4. Provide an exporting base from a region; when a partner is in a common market association, a joint venture with a partner in one country eases the task of exporting to all other common market members. (For example, a joint venture with a partner in a Central American country would probably make it easier to export to member countries in the Latin American

---

[33] Allen R. Janger, *Organization of International Joint Ventures* (New York: The Conference Board, Inc., 1980), Report No. 787, p. 1.

EXHIBIT 12–6: Why joint venture?

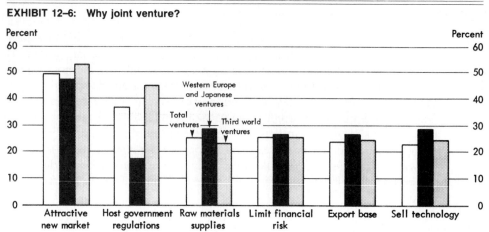

Source: Allen R. Janger, *Organization of International Joint Ventures* (New York: The Conference Board, Inc., 1980), Report No. 787, p. 3.

Integration Association [formerly Latin American Free Trade Area] than if exports were made from a non-LAIA member country.)

5.   To sell technology; of the five reasons for joining joint ventures, selling technology is the least important, but, in many countries, a joint venture with a local partner is necessary to sell or license technology.

Exhibit 12–6 illustrates the varied components that make up joint ventures in Western Europe and Japan and Third World countries. Attractive new markets are important for both Western Europe and Third World countries; however, the next most important reason for joint ventures is to overcome host country regulations. (This, of course, is most predominant in the Third World.) There are numerous legal methods of joining companies together, but the joint-venture form is essentially a merger or partnership of two or more participating companies which have joined forces for marketing, financing, and/or managerial reasons.

Joint ventures should be differentiated from minority holdings by an MNC in a local firm. Three very definite attributes are associated with joint ventures: (1) There is an acknowledged intent by the partners to share in the management of the joint venture; (2) Joint ventures are partnerships between legally incorporated entities such as companies, chartered organizations, or governments and not between individuals; (3) Equity positions are held by each of the partners.

Joint-venture patterns have changed significantly since the early 1970s. Foreign government restriction of ownership of joint ventures has intensified in recent years. For example, Venezuela publishes a list of companies in which foreign partners cannot have over 20 percent interest; India specifies maximum foreign participation at 40 percent in many industries; Nigeria has a long list of business enterprises reserved exclusively for Nigerian ownership, plus a second list in which foreign equity is limited to 40 percent;

BOX 12–6:   **Ten ways to control a 50–50 joint venture abroad**

1. Issue two kinds of stock—voting and nonvoting—that will divide the profits evenly but give a majority vote to the U.S. side.
2. Arrange the deal 49–49 with 2 percent in the hands of a third party friendly to the U.S. side.
3. Provide in the by-laws that the U.S. side will have a majority of directors.
4. Have the by-laws stipulate that the U.S. directors (even though equal in number with the partner's directors) will appoint the management.
5. Have the by-laws provide that in the case of a tie vote, the position of the U.S. side will prevail.
6. Arrange a 50–50 deal, but with a management contract awarded to the U.S. investor.
7. Arrange a contract for the entire output of the jointly owned producing facility to be sold to a U.S.-controlled marketing company. The marketing company should get what it wants from the producing company.
8. A modification of number 7: give 51 percent of the producing company to the local partner in exchange for 51 percent of the selling company.
9. Satisfy the pressure for 50 percent local ownership by putting the local 50 percent in the hands of a local insurance company that has no interest in management.
10. Better yet, spread the local 50 percent over a multitude of shareholders. Union Carbide in India and Kaiser in Brazil have thousands of local shareholders.

Source: Reprinted from ''75 Management Checklists for Foreign Operations'' with permission of the publisher, Business International Corporation (New York).

Japan still severely limits foreign ownership, but increasingly, foreign firms are permitted to own a majority of Japanese firms. Companies have found they do not necessarily need majority interest to control joint ventures.[34]

Joint-venture patterns vary considerably from country to country. U.S. companies prefer complete ownership when possible and tend to avoid joint ventures with governments. European companies are more likely to go into joint ventures with smaller ownership and to participate in government- or union-owned joint ventures. Some interesting patterns emerge; only slightly more than one third of U.S. businesses abroad are joint ventures, whereas over 60 percent of European foreign businesses are joint ventures. Some 15–18 percent of European joint ventures are with foreign governments whereas only about 1 percent of U.S. joint ventures involve government participation. The Japanese have changed their attitudes; at one time they were very reluctant to join ventures with non-Japanese companies, but in recent years have been turning increasingly to international joint ventures.

Marketing motives.   Market access is the chief marketing reason for joint ventures; nearly all of the developing countries, and many developed countries, require at least some degree of local participation of firms operating in their country. Foreign automobile makers for years were completely

---

[34] Janger, *"Organization of International Joint Ventures,* p. 1.

closed out of Japan, but finally were able to enter the market through joint ventures.

Mergers with companies which have well-established local distribution may provide rapid market entry. When American companies first entered Europe, they found inadequate distribution facilities and insufficient local capital for expansion, so American firms formed partnerships and provided needed funds to strengthen the local middlemen. Local firms possessed market information and marketing know-how which would have taken years for a foreign company to acquire. Such participation minimizes the risk of market failure and speeds the marketing effort.

Financial and personnel advantages.   Merger through joint venture may provide tax advantages, funds, or access to local capital markets and combine the resources and fund-raising capabilities of the companies. As a low-cost method of keeping up with the growing requirements of their international clients, advertising agencies have employed the joint-venture method of expansion extensively in the last decade.

The worldwide shortage of capable management personnel has been another reason for mergers. Numerous joint ventures have been worked out so that nationals with managerial ability could be acquired. In some countries it is almost impossible to gain effective distribution without joining forces with firms which have already developed large sales forces.

Unique skills.   One purpose of a joint venture may be to capitalize on the unique skills of a joint-venture partner. This is often the case in major construction projects. One of the largest U.S. joint-venture projects ever structured involves Union Pacific of the United States, ICI (a British chemical firm), and Volvay et Cie of Belgium and was undertaken for two purposes: (1) to provide the $6 million capital required to build a petrochemical plant and (2) to take advantage of the specialized abilities of each of the three companies. A subsidiary of U.P. (Champlin Petroleum Company) built and operates the plant. A subsidiary of ICI (ICI-U.S.) is responsible for marketing and is a major customer for the output. Solvay's subsidiary (Soltex) handles pipeline operations. The company, called Corpus Christi Petrochemical Company, is managed by an executive committee consisting of one member from each of the three parent companies. Interestingly, all three must agree on major policy or investment questions but two of the three will control operational and routine management issues.[35]

Consortia

The consortium and syndicate are similar to the joint venture and could be classified as such except for two unique characteristics: (1) they typically involve a rather large number of participants; and (2) they frequently operate

[35] "How Two European Firms Will use Joint Venture Route Into U.S. Market," *Business International*, January 7, 1977, p. 4.

in a country or market in which none of the participants is currently active. Consortia are developed for pooling financial and managerial resources and to lessen risks. Often, huge construction projects are built under a consortium arrangement in which major contractors with different specialties form a separate company specifically to negotiate for and produce one job. One firm usually acts as the lead firm, or the newly formed corporation may exist quite independently.

EXTERNAL ARRANGEMENTS

A company may turn over the task of international marketing to an external group or organization in which it has no ownership. Because it lacks equity, the producer company can seldom exert extensive control over the external organization. In some instances, the external group may represent little more than an element in the channel of distribution; in others, it substitutes for the parent company's own international organization. *It is often difficult to determine when corporate organization ends and the channel of distribution begins.*

Beside the channel middlemen, the chief types of external arrangements are: (1) licensing, (2) franchising, (3) management contracts, and (4) open distribution.

International licensing

Licensing in international business may take several forms; licenses may be granted for production processes, for the use of a trade name, or for the distribution of imported products. In some circumstances, licensing provides an ideal entry into foreign countries that might otherwise block non-domestic enterprises. Licenses may be closely controlled or autonomous and permit expansion without great capital or personnel commitment if licensees have the requisite capabilities. Not all licensing experiences are successful because of the burden of finding, supervising, and inspiring licensees. Licensing, however, does provide the basis for many success stories in various kinds of businesses.

A measure of licensing's importance may be seen in the example of a Detroit materials handling firm, Jervis B. Webb Company. They found they did not have sufficient capital or personnel to cover many world markets so they turned to licensing. Licensee sales constitute about one third of the company's total worldwide sales of $150 million. West Germany has incurred a deficit of nearly a quarter billion Deutsch marks when comparing payments for patent licenses to receipts from German patent and licenses used in other countries. U.S. companies received over half of the German license revenues but contributed only 16 percent of the license fees paid in Germany. Licensing also supplies the means by which Eastern European markets may be tapped.

Franchising

Franchising is a rapidly growing form of licensing in which the franchiser provides a standard package of products, systems, and management services, and the franchisee provides market knowledge, capital, and personal involvement in management. The combination of skills permits flexibility to deal with local market conditions and yet provides the parent firm with a reasonable degree of control. The franchiser can follow through on marketing of the products all the way to the point of final sale. It is thus an important form of vertical market integration. Potentially, the franchise system provides an effective blending of skill centralization and operational decentralization, and has become an increasingly important form of international marketing.

Prior to 1970, international franchising was not a major activity. The survey of the International Franchising Association revealed that only 14 percent of its member firms had franchises out of the United States and the majority of those were in Canada only. By 1980, more than 15,000 franchises of U.S. firms were located in countries throughout the world. These franchises included such fields as soft drinks, motels, retailing, fast foods, car rentals, automotive services, and recreational services.[36]

Management contract

Quite a different kind of arrangement is the management contract where the management company agrees to manage some or all functions of another company's operations in return for management fees, a share of the profits, and sometimes an option to purchase stock in the company at a given price. The management contract can assure operating control in joint ventures or consortia or be used when the company wishes to gain an immediate return for services rendered. A company that has been expropriated or "purchased" by a local government may be able to maintain a profitable position by consenting to operate the enterprise through a management contract. It often permits participation in a foreign venture without capital risk or investment and is a major tool for maintaining managerial control in situations where governments require nationals to own a majority of stock interest.

Open distribution

An explicit policy usually chosen as a course of least resistance, open distribution means simply that the company is willing to sell products to overseas or domestic customers or middlemen for overseas consumption. Open distribution requires virtually no effort; it gives the company no control

---

[36] Donald W. Hackett, "The International Expansion of U.S. Franchise Systems: Status and Strategies," *Journal of International Business Studies,* 1977.

and often results in no sales. In a sense, one could say it is an absence of an organization rather than an organizational method.

SUMMARY

Market-oriented firms build their organizations around company objectives, structure of the market, and the competitive environment. Because of varying objectives or needs, the organization that suits one company in a given market situation will not be satisfactory for another. Similarly, the company organization which meets corporate objectives may be suitable for one market but not another. Organizing for marketing may be complicated even for one country, but, when a company is doing business internationally, the problems are multiplied. Company objectives may vary from market to market and from time to time; the structure of international markets also changes periodically and from country to country, and the competitive, governmental, and economic parameters affecting organization are in a constant state of flux. These variations require the international marketing executive to be especially flexible and creative in orientation to organization for international marketing.

Level, type, and extent of control are relevant organizational determinants given prime consideration in the marketing approach to international organization. This chapter considers international organization first from the viewpoint of the parent company arrangements which are used in directing the world marketing operation. Second, it considers the various arrangements which may be used in the actual operations of the worldwide marketing activity, including a variety of alternatives of owned or external organizations which may be subject to tight or loose control, depending on the wishes of management. Many international marketers utilize several different organizational structures, and may be classed as having a conglomerate organizational pattern.

Change, adaptation, and restructuring are ever-present needs within growing companies operating in constantly changing markets, so organization for international marketing should be built around dynamic elements of the marketplace.

QUESTIONS

1. Define:

Cash cows	Managing agent
Product portfolio	EPRG framework
analysis	Joint venture
Polycentrism	Open distribution

2. Define strategic planning. How is strategic planning different for international marketing than domestic marketing?

3. The relationship between corporate organization structure and strategic planning is both intimate and powerful. Discuss.

4. Discuss the differences that might exist in the planning in a firm that is ethocentric versus geocentric.

5. In Phases 1 and 2 of the international planning process, countries may be dropped from further consideration as potential markets. Discuss some of the conditions in each phase that may exist in a country that would lead a marketer to exclude a country.

6. Assume that you are the Director of International Marketing for a company producing refrigerators. Select one country in Latin America and one in Europe and develop screening criteria to use in evaluating the two countries. Make any additional assumptions about your company that are necessary.

7. In the Market Share/Growth Matrix (Exhibit 12–2), differentiate among *stars, cash cows, question marks, and dogs.*

8. Discuss some of the problems that can arise when a company does not include international markets when applying product portfolio analysis.

9. "The dichotomy typically drawn between export marketing and overseas marketing is partly fictional; from a marketing standpoint, they are but alternative methods of capitalizing on foreign market opportunities." Discuss.

10. Review the parameters complicating international marketing organization.

11. How will entry into a developed foreign market differ from entry into a relatively untapped market?

12. What is the value of the marketing approach to international organization?

13. Explain the "Schematic Marketing Organization Plan Combining Product, Geographic, and Functional Approaches." (Exhibit 12–3)

14. Explain the five headquarters-level managerial arrangements. Cite an instance when each might be used.

15. How do governments influence the organizational pattern of companies in international business?

16. Formulate a general rule for deciding where international business decisions should be made.

17. Explain the popularity of joint ventures.

18. Discuss the impact of U.S. and foreign antitrust legislation on organizational patterns.

19. Compare the organizational implications of joint ventures versus licensing.

READING

Multinational strategic market portfolios (Ford Tractor has developed an analytical approach to planning designed for use in environments outside the United States.)
Gilbert D. Harrell and
Richard O. Kiefer*

Multinational business executives are facing complex strategic planning decisions at a time when rapid shifts in world markets are causing broad fluctuations in potential profitability. Planning on a country-by-country or even regional basis can result in spotty worldwide market performance. The problem of international strategic planning is particularly salient for industries in which major corporations are competing on a global scale—automotives, steel, energy, heavy construction equipment, and agricultural equipment.

Planning processes that focus simultaneously across a broad range of markets provide multinational businesses with tools to help balance risks, capital requirements, competitive economies of scale, and profitability to gain stronger long-term market positions. For example, by systematically choosing well-balanced product and market strategic combinations, Japanese auto companies have reached world prominence in a few short years.

Strategic planning, in the broadest sense, seeks to match markets with products and other corporate resources in order to strengthen a firm's competitive stance. It requires the involvement of a broad range of executives—marketing, research and development, production, and finance—to name a few. Together, these executives can focus their attention on both products and markets. However, there is a strong tendency to plan around either products or markets, but not both. The problem is one of perspective: The complexity of world business makes it difficult to comprehend either product strategies or market strategies, much less both at the same time.

To aid international strategic planning, several domestic planning tools can be used, but most lose effectiveness when applied to international settings. They tend to focus on *products* as the principal unit of strategic endeavor. Yet, the great variations in market conditions around the world suggest that it is more appropriate to make decisions about *market* portfolios. For example, although Ford Tractor operations have experienced varying profitability, cash flow, and market share by product type (such as light versus heavy tractors), some of their greatest opportunities were due to broad potential profit variations across market areas.

The purpose of this article is to describe an analytical approach to strategic planning that is useful in sorting international market environments so that market portfolios will be emphasized. The case of International Tractor Operations of Ford Motor Company will be used to describe key aspects of the process.

Several major corporations, including General Electric Co., Westinghouse, Shell, and Borg-Warner Corp., use product portfolio analysis in their domestic planning. Bruce Henderson of the Boston Consulting Group first demonstrated the importance

---

* Gilbert D. Harrell is associate professor of marketing, Graduate School of Business Administration, Michigan State University. Richard O. Kiefer is marketing manager, Ford Tractor Operations.

of analyzing product portfolios according to business growth and market share matrices.[1]

Business or product portfolio analysis can be viewed as an effort to sort opportunities according to a few strategic variables. Much of the work is the outgrowth of observations by the Boston Consulting Group concerning the *experience curve*. They observed that the cost of producing a product declines predictably as output increases. Because companies with a high market share produce more than their competitors, their costs are less and their profit greater. In addition, market growth has much to do with the degree of difficulty in securing market share, that is, it is easier to secure increased share while the market is growing. Furthermore, those firms that enjoy large market shares in mature markets are likely to maintain them. Thus, market share and market growth can be used as coordinates to plot a company's products in four categories—high share/slow growth (cash cows), high share/rapid growth (stars), low share/rapid growth (sweepstakes), and low share/slow growth (dogs), as indicated in Exhibit 1.

EXHIBIT 1: A company's product array

Market share

	High	Low
Market growth (High)	Star products	Sweepstakes products
Market growth (Low)	Cash cow products	Dog products

George Steiner and others have extended the procedures by replacing business growth with a more elaborate market attractiveness index and market share with a competitive strength index.[2] Their scheme uses the findings of PIMS (Profit Impact Market Strategy Group) and others regarding the characteristics that produce strong returns on investment.[3] In addition, many corporations have related the product portfolio to the product life cycle concept. Sweepstake products are in the introduction

---

[1] Bruce D. Henderson, *Henderson on Corporate Strategy* (Cambridge, Mass.: ABT Books, 1979).

[2] George Steiner, *Strategic Planning* (New York: Free Press, 1979); George S. Day, "Diagnosing the Product Portfolio," *Journal of Marketing* 41, April 1977, pp. 29–38; and Derek F. Abell and John S. Hammond, *Strategic Marketing Planning* (Englewood Cliffs, N.J.: Prentice-Hall, 1979).

[3] Sidney Schoeffler, Robert D. Buzzell, and Donald F. Heany, "Impact of Strategic Planning on Profit Performance," *Harvard Business Review* 52 March/April 1974, pp. 137–45.

phase of the life cycle; stars are in the growth phase; cash cows are in the maturity phase; and dogs are in the decline phase. In this way, companies' domestic operational programs can be altered depending on the amount of growth or decline in product sales. But, again, the focus is on product elements, and while domestic life cycles may tend to follow a pattern, international life cycles are more complex. For example, one of the many international patterns has been: (1) invention in, for example, the United States; (2) heavy domestic production and sales of the product; (3) export to foreign countries; (4) stimulation of foreign production based on the U.S. version; (5) foreign economies of scale and lower labor rates in other nations' own markets; and (6) export from the foreign manufacturer back into the U.S. market. Again, while the product life cycle is helpful, a more functional picture of the international pattern can be drawn by looking at market development stages.

Market portfolios

The conceptual simplicity of presenting the combinations of competitive strengths and market attractiveness provide a two-dimensional matrix useful for plotting products. More important to the international planner, each axis is a linear combination of factors that together can be used to define a country's attractiveness from a market view and determine the company's competitive strength in that country, as shown in Exhibit 2.

EXHIBIT 2:   Matrix for plotting products

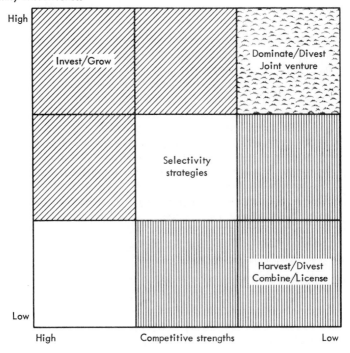

Data on international markets, although much improved in recent years, are difficult to obtain for elaborate measures of country attractiveness. However, Ford Tractor is extensively exploring four basic elements—market size, market growth rate, government regulation, and economic and political stability.

Also, competitive strength must be defined within an international context. Unfortunately, no quantitative models exist. Ford Tractor executives suggested the following factors for this scale: market share, product fit, contribution margin, and market representation and market support.

The country attractiveness and competitive strength scales are plotted to form a 3 × 3 matrix, as indicated in Exhibit 2. Those countries that fall in the upper left generally should receive funding for growth, while those in the lower right are prime areas to harvest or divest—or to ignore if no operations have been started. Those countries falling on the lower left to upper right diagonal will require selective funding strategies. The reasons for these generalizations will be clearer after a more complete discussion of the content of the two scales.

Country attractiveness scale development

Market size is measured according to projected average annual sales in units. Ford selected a three-year average to avoid anomalies resulting from short-term economic shifts and strike effects among major companies. This measure provides a good base on which to build growth projections, the second element of the scale.

Market size, obviously, is critical because minimum volumes are required to achieve the economies of scale necessary for entry, including technical assistance, training, and product and service information. Large volumes provide support for permanent local organizations and affiliated companies as well as justification for on-site manufacturing.

Market rate of growth is estimated as the ten-year annual compound percentage increase in sales. This is longer than most domestic time frames; however, the long time frame is warranted.

Government regulation includes three subfactors: price control and regulations, homologation requirements, and regulations covering local content and compensatory exports. Homologation relates to nontariff barriers, for example, local safety and product requirements and, in many cases, simple red tape designed to restrict foreign market entry. Local content and compensatory export laws require that end products contain components manufactured locally or that exports of products be made from the receiving country to offset imports. Governments play a significant role in determining the ease of market entry through safety and environmental regulations, price regulation and incentives, and protection of local industry against foreign competition.

Economic and political factors include the inflation rate and trade balance. Ford has used sophisticated measures of political stability developed in conjunction with consulting groups and government agencies.

A single linear scale comprised of the four factors was computed as follows:

Country attractiveness = Market size + 2 × Market growth + (.5 × Price control/ Regulation + .25 × Homologation requirements + .25 × Local content and Compensatory export requirements) + (.35 × Inflation + .35 × Trade balance + .3 × Political factors).

TABLE 1: Country attractiveness scale weights

1. Market size		2. Market growth	
Units	Rating	Amount (percent)	Rating
25,000	10	5+	10
22,500–24,999	9	4–4.9	9
20,000–22,499	8	3–3.9	8
—	—	—	—
—	—	—	—
—	—	—	—
5,000	1	Under 3	1

3. Government regulation

a. Price control		b. Homologation		c. Local content/ compensatory exports	
Type	Rating	Type	Rating	Type	Rating
None	10	None	10	None	10
Easy to comply	6	Easy	6	Easy to comply	6
Moderately easy to comply	4	Moderate	4	Moderately easy to comply	4
Rigid controls	2	Tough	2	Tough	2

4. Economic and political stability

a. Inflation		b. Trade balance		c. Political stability	
Amount (percent)	Rating	Amount (percent)	Rating	Type	Rating
7 and under	10	5 and over	10	Stable market	10
—	—	0–4.9	9	Moderate	5
—	—	−5–0	8	Unstable	1
40 and over	1	—	—		
		—	—		
		—	—		
		−36	1		

Note: These measurements are indicative of what might be done, rather than concrete examples.

The weights represent the relative importance of each variable to Ford's strategic planning efforts.[4] In order to standardize each of the analysis units, all estimates are transposed to 10-point scales, as Table 1 demonstrates. The above formula is then applied to provide a single number that falls on the linear country attractiveness scale. This number is then transformed to conform to another 10-point index for plotting.

---

[4] To protect the confidentiality of information proprietary to Ford, we have used simplified measures and changed some of the data. Therefore, the article presents findings that are only suggestive of the way Ford rates various countries. Actual ratings may vary.

Competitive strength scale development

Market share, critical in domestic profitability, is likely to be the most important characteristic in international business because of experience curve volumes and costs. Because market share tends to vary considerably from country to country, this is a good discriminating factor. In domestic markets, many stable industries have only three or four major competitors. In international markets, they may have many more. In some cases, certain national manufacturers have strong market shares and brand loyalty, and are protected by nontariff barriers. Thus, two market share factors are relevant to Ford in this case, the number of major competitors in the market and Ford's total market share.

Product fit represents an estimate of how closely the product fits a particular market need. In the tractor industry, Ford defines this broadly in terms of horsepower classes and more specifically in terms of unique product features that may or may not match country needs. The broad range of environmental differences and buyer tastes and preferences makes product fit a key strategic factor. If the product is tailored closely to unique national needs, the firm may be able to forfeit economies of scale.

Contribution margin is a measure of profit per unit and profit as a percentage of net dealer cost. Low contribution margins often reflect limited price scope because of competition or government controls. They may also reflect an inefficiently operated local group. While this measure should be reflected in the other three elements, it does serve as a measure of ability to gain profit, an important competitive strength. Again, relatively broad fluctuations do exist across countries.

Market support includes the quantity and quality of company personnel located in the country, parts and technical service support, and advertising and sales promotion capability within the country; that is, it represents the general company image in a local environment. This is difficult to quantify, which is a major drawback.

Ford used all these factors to compute a single linear scale reflecting its competitive strength as follows:

Competitive strength = (.5 × Absolute market share + .5 Industry position) × 2 + Product fit + (.5 × Profit per unit + .5 × Profit percentage of Net dealer cost) + Market support

Again, the weights reflect Ford executives' subjective estimates of the relative importance of each variable in defining the competitive strength required to excel in international markets. Table 2 provides examples of the 10-point scales used for this measure.

Strategic situations

In Exhibits 3 and 4, each European country and key countries from the rest of the world are located on the market matrices based on the ratings assigned for country attractiveness and competitive strength. These examples show one way Ford can look at the world. Obviously, the picture is incomplete for all parts of the strategic plan, but it does offer strong implications for finance, production, research and development, and marketing, as well as for the overall corporate objective for each country.

Invest/Grow countries call for corporate commitment to a strong market position. A dominant share in a rapidly growing market will require substantial financial invest-

TABLE 2: Competitive strength weights

1. Market share

a. Percentage of market		b. Position	
Share	Rating	Rank	Rating
30+	10	1	10
27–21	9	2	8
—	—	3	6
—	—	4	4
—	—	5	2
4	1		

2. Product fit

Because this scale suggests Ford's competitive product strategy, we decided not to publish it. In general, a 10-point subjective index was created to match product characteristics with key local product needs.

3. Contribution margin

Again, this is proprietary, but it reflects two factors.

a. Profit per unit		b. Profit percentage of net dealer cost	
Amount	Rating	Amount (percent)	Rating
$5,000	10	40+	10
(example)	—	—	—
—	—	—	—
—	—	—	—
1–400	1	5–	1

4. Market support

a. Market representation		b. Market support	
Evaluation	Rating	Evaluation	Rating
Quantity and quality of Ford distributors and service are clearly "best in country"	10	Ford market support in advertising promotion is clearly "best in country"	10
Ford representation is equal to leading competitor's	8	Ford support is equal to leading competitor's	8
Ford representation is behind several leading competitors'	2	Ford support is behind several leading competitors'	2

Note: These measurements are indicative of what might be done, rather than concrete examples.

ments. Equally important are the investments in people at the country level to sustain a strong competitive position.

Research and development will be important to match products closely with specific market requirements. This will involve both the addition of new models and the expansion of options for more applications. The growth in models should be, where practical, in directions that will capitalize on the company's experience curve in mature markets. However, action is required so that unique product demands in these growth areas are not excluded. This is particularly important for firms from countries such as the United States, in which the domestic market has lost its innovative posture.

EXHIBIT 3: European matrix

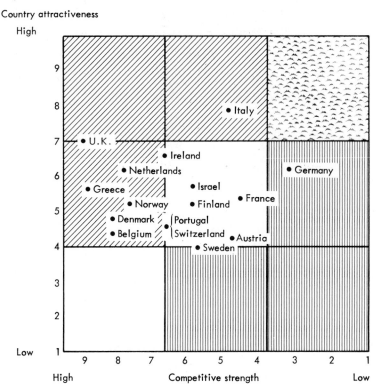

Country attractiveness

Local production often is required for the sake of rapid delivery and service. Major competitors usually will be producing close to the market in these countries. Export strategies are likely to fail because of cost problems, or government pressure when balance of trade considerations are involved.

Marketing supports of all kinds should be expansive—number of personnel, advertising, quality of trade services, and support. All of these investments will support growth. Personnel selection should foucs on increasing realistic risk taking and the cutting of red tape. Doers are a must in these markets.

Harvest/Divest/License/Combine countries often call for strategies to harvest profits or sell the business. Generally, any cash they generate will be required to maintain share; therefore, share generally is given up for profit. Cash flow timing becomes critical. Since the corporation's market share and competitive position are probably low, and the market is relatively small and the growth low, strategic plans should focus on harvesting near-term profits until the day the business is sold or abandoned.

Finance should concentrate on frequent cash flow calculations to ensure that variable costs are covered. Pricing policy will be keyed to short-term considerations. By increasing price and reducing the marketing costs, the firm generally can produce cash from those sales that do occur. Thus, market share will be sold off in the interest of maintaining margins.

EXHIBIT 4: Key-country matrix

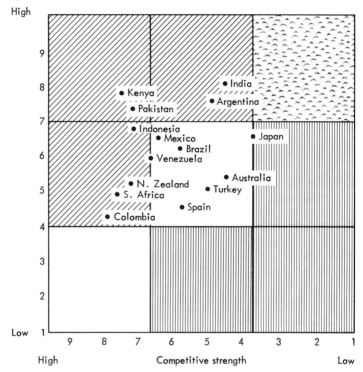

Country attractiveness

Exceptions to abandonment occur when several of these countries can be combined to give enough volume for a sizable export or subsidiary business. In addition, licensing arrangements can be beneficial to the licensor as well as the local licensee.

Dominate/Divest/Joint venture countries (the upper right in Exhibits 3 and 4) present a particularly difficult strategic choice because the firm is competitively weak but the market appealing. Movement toward dominance requires long-term cash flow deficits; divestiture requires the presence of a buyer and cuts the company off from cash and profit opportunities.

The decision demands a careful analysis of cash requirements and cash availability, as well as most of the other factors pertinent to entering a new venture. This is a particularly good time to enter into joint ventures with firms that complement the organization. It would be wise, for example, to match a corporation with product design strength with one possessing distribution and marketing strength.

Selectivity countries (center and lower left in Exhibits 3 and 4) present another problem. In domestic situations, products falling into these two sections on the grid generally are perfect candidates for milking. They produce strong cash flows. This is only partially the case in international environments. In general, in these countries market share will be difficult to maintain even if the corporation is in a second- or third-ranking competitive position. Competition is extreme. Yet, these markets clearly suggest maintenance strategies that build cash flow or, if technological and other advantages can be transferred from Star environments, strategies that build share. (The share building domestic strategy generally is avoided because it can be destructive to the industry.) Unfortunately, many international markets fail to reach the mature stability of traditional U.S. markets, and such strategies are necessary.

The finance department should do frequent analyses to ensure that strategies are properly focused. Often, strategies require transfer of excess funds to other countries. Full product costing usually is required.

Manufacturing usually will involve plants in or near the market. They will be maintained efficiently rather than expanded drastically. Profit can come from capacity utilization, thus marketing will be important here. Marketing will concentrate on strong reliability and adequate but not excessive margins. Much of the focus will be on current customers.

Research and development will be primarily interested in maintaining an efficient, full line of products. Therefore, modular units and many options will make good use of inventory availability, in contrast to building many unique models.

In this area, any of the three primary strategies mentioned before might also apply. For example, Ford in Mexico might set its share objective to move from 30 percent to 50 percent, that is, seek market dominance. For example, if Ford's current price is at a premium, it might drop down to the market leader and strengthen its dealership network. At the same time, a fuller product line would provide a larger potential customer base.

In contrast, Ford in Japan might require the same or a completely different strategy, depending on management risk preferences and company condition.

Conclusions

Ford has been taking a close look at international market portfolios. Although Ford has been strong in product strategy, it is finding new opportunities based on variances among countries. The strategic planning tool presented in this article is one step toward dealing simultaneously with world markets.

Several suggestions are in order when applying such a tool. First, because the implications extend across several business functions, it is important to involve finance, production, research and development, and marketing in development of the strategic options for each type of country as well as in measuring country attractiveness and competitive strength. Second, the approach should be recognized as only a tool and not a set of hard and fast rules. Once in a while, the dynamics of international markets warrant special attention that runs counter to the strategies that match a particular portfolio category. Thus, the market portfolio provides only a part of the total picture. Also, although many of the calculations require subjective information, rigorous development of scales is useful. The better the information, whether objective or subjective, the closer the market portfolio plots will match actual conditions.

Finally, the process can aid executives in the analysis of current world market positions. It can be used to plot the movement of markets over time, thus keeping track of environmental and competitive shifts for future projections. To the degree that patterns begin to emerge, the strategic planning organization can better track its successes and failures and learn about its capabilities in diverse international markets.

Chapter 13

Planning and developing consumer products for foreign markets

Implicit in the development of any marketing program is the question, "What products should we sell?" For many international firms the answer is almost always the same, "Whatever we are selling in the United States." For some, this policy proves to be a successful and profitable approach to the product question. For others, it has led to marketing poorly conceived products in incorrectly defined markets with inappropriate marketing effort resulting in costly and sometimes ruinous returns. As a firm's involvement in a foreign market increases, competition from U.S. and non-U.S. multinational firms intensifies; and, as markets are penetrated to lower and lower income strata, "Whatever we are selling in the United States" becomes less and less adequate as a product planning policy.

Product planning, the continuous job of developing products and product lines to satisfy the constantly changing desires and needs of customers, is a concept on which all marketing plans and strategies should be based. Unfortunately, product planning for many international firms consists of adapting domestically successful products to the needs of a foreign consumer; i.e., selling what is produced for the domestic market in the same manner it is sold at home, disregarding all but the most obvious differences in market requirements. Journals are replete with the sad histories of companies which have followed this naïve policy.

One of the most difficult obstacles a decision-maker must overcome with product development decisions is the self-reference criterion (SRC); that is, assuming that a product successful in the domestic market will be successful in any other market. The best way to avoid the pitfalls inherent in the SRC is to accept that there are alternatives worthy of consideration and to establish a process for decision making that will include an evaluation of all relevant issues and problems.

The purpose of this chapter is to explore some of the relevant issues facing an international marketer when planning and developing consumer product lines for foreign markets. There are many questions to be answered about product planning and development; they range from the obvious—what products to sell—to the more complex—when and how products should be adapted for different markets, if at all.

407

STANDARDIZED VERSUS DIFFERENTIATED PRODUCTS

A recurring debate exists relative to product planning. It focuses on the question of standardized products marketed worldwide versus differentiated products adapted and even redesigned for each culturally unique market. Those with a strong production and unit cost orientation advocate standardization and others, perhaps more culturally sensitive, propose the policy of a different product for each market. The issue cannot be resolved with a simple either/or decision. Cost-revenue analyses need to be done and decisions made in the hard, cold light of profitability. There is no question that significant cost savings can be realized from standardized products, packages, brand names, and promotional messages; but this makes sense only if there is adequate demand for the standardized product: costs must be balanced with demand. On the other hand, if the cost of an individualized product when evaluated against price/demand characteristics within a market exceeds potential profit, then other alternatives, including not marketing the product at all, must be considered.

To differentiate for the sake of differentiation is not a solution; realistic business practice requires a company to strive for uniformity in its marketing mix whenever and wherever possible. Economies of production, better planning, more effective control, and better use of creative managerial personnel are all advantages of standardization.[1] The continual conflict between differentiation to accommodate small market segments and standardization to reduce unit costs can be settled only when the marketer's evaluation identifies "when there are market differences sufficient to justify the loss of standardization,"[2] and when sufficient demand exists to offset increases in cost. The issue of standardized worldwide product and marketing programs versus programs tailored to accommodate unique cultural differences can be resolved with a sound marketing analysis and a profitability study of both approaches.

PRODUCT LINE ALTERNATIVES

When a company plans to enter the market in another country, careful consideration must be given to whether or not the present product lines will prove adequate in a new culture—will they sell in quantities large enough and at prices high enough to be profitable? If not, what other alternatives are available? The marketer has at least three viable alternatives when entering a new market: (1) sell the same product presently sold elsewhere, (2) individualize the existing product to the tastes and specific needs of the new country, or (3) develop a totally new product. These three alternatives,

[1] R. Buzzell, "Can You Standardize Marketing?" *Harvard Business Review*, November/December 1968, p. 102.

[2] S. H. Robock, K. Simmonds, and Jack Zwick, *International Business and Multinational Enterprises*, rev. ed. (Homewood, Ill.: Richard D. Irwin, 1977), p. 453.

when combined with promotional effort, can be developed into five different product strategies available to the international marketer.

First, a company can sell the same product using the same promotional message worldwide as the Pepsi-Cola and Coca-Cola companies do. A second version is to sell the same product but with promotions featuring different use patterns—for example, garden power equipment designed for United States home use is sold as agricultural equipment in underdeveloped countries. A third strategy involves altering the basic physical features of the product to meet local environmental needs but promoting the product

---

BOX 13–1: Exporting the Big Mac

With all the fervor of the Pilgrims returned, McDonald's set out to introduce Europe to the joys of the *real* American hamburger. Most people assumed that golden arches, like blue jeans and Coke, would sprout up overnight across the Continent. McDonald's set a goal of 300 European stores by 1977. So far, there are 38. After four years, the company has lost none of its zeal, but it has learned the hard way about doing business with the natives. The qualities that made McDonald's so successful in North America may be nibbling at its margins abroad. Fast service gives McDonald's much higher labor costs than Kentucky Fried Chicken or Britain's Wimpy International and quality control is another high cost factor. McDonald's is fanatical about quality. A Big Mac tastes the same in Des Moines as in London or in Amsterdam. The company adheres to strict specifications for meat, buns, apple pies, and most everything else, specifications that may differ from those of European suppliers. So it must either import long distances (French fries from Canada, pies from Tulsa) or place special and more costly orders locally.

Wimpy hamburger bars, by contrast, don't worry so much about consistency, and most franchises solve their supply problems by buying from Wimpy's giant parent food company. It takes under $25,000 to open a Wimpy or KFC store in Britain. A McDonald's costs over $200,000.

It is conceded that McDonald's made mistakes. It thought it should put its first European store—Amsterdam—in the suburbs, just as it had started up in suburban Chicago. But as they soon learned, the suburbs are not where it's at in Europe. Most people still live in cities, and they are less mobile than Americans. The shopping centers that sprang up all over the United States and provided good sites for fast-fooders have not caught on in much of Europe. The original Amsterdam store was moved into town.

McDonald's says that, as in the States, it is aiming to get the whole family in. McDonald's contrasts its relaxed approach to the more refined European restaurant, where the waiter may look askance at messy, noisy children. But, "The Germans and Swiss are still quite traditional, and we are more gastronomically minded. Even if the wife works, dinner means a home-cooked meal. And once the family is home at the end of the day, it is not likely to go out again." So the real promise seems to lie with the lunchtime and Saturday shopping crowds.

McDonald's has made a few changes in its menu to accommodate European tastes: tea in Britain, beer and—to head off Kentucky Fried—chicken on the Continent. A *New York Times* columnist recently lamented that McDonald's was luring Swedes away from their good old smoked herring. His worry may prove to have been a bit premature. Even missionaries have to adapt.

Source: Adapted from "Not for Export?" *Forbes*, October 15, 1975, pp. 23–24.

to fill the same use patterns as in the domestic market. Detergents redesigned to function in cold water but still promoted to get clothes clean is an example of this strategy. The fourth strategy requires both a change in the product to meet different use patterns and change in the promotional message accompanying it. For example, in some parts of the world, the verse in greeting cards is deleted and the card is sold for any "special occasion" rather than a special event. The fifth strategy is one of investing or developing a totally new product rather than adapting an existing one. This is less frequently done, but as companies move into less developed markets and seek greater economic penetration into these markets, it becomes more prevalent. For example, food companies such as Pillsbury, Swift, and Coca-Cola have developed high protein foods to sell in foreign countries as diet supplements. These dietary products appear to be reasonably successful, but other attempts at developing specific products for a market have not worked.

Both Ford and General Motors Corporation developed a "bare bones" Model T-type vehicle to sell in developing countries; both products failed. The General Motor's product, a truck designed for the Far East, lost out to low-priced, used passenger cars converted to utility vehicles. The local market felt the General Motor's product was too sophisticated and costly. On the other hand, Ford Motor's attempt to develop an "Asian People's Car" failed for just the opposite reason; the demand was for more sophisticated and more expensive Japanese vehicles.[3]

The success of these strategies depends on the product and the fundamental need it fulfills, its characteristics and their perception within the culture, and the associated costs of each program.[4] To know that foreign markets are different and that different product strategies may be needed is one thing; to know when adaptation of your product line and marketing program is necessary is another and more complicated problem. However, there are some logical steps to help clarify the process.

PRODUCT LINE ADAPTATION

To understand fully the concept of a product one needs to appreciate how interwoven the aspects of culture are with the perceptions of the many facets of a product. Whether a company is doing business at home or in a foreign market, the concept of a product as used in marketing should be the same, that is, a product is more than just a physical item, it is a "bundle of satisfactions" (or utility) that the buyer receives.

The benefits or bundle of satisfactions received, as Exhibit 13–1 shows,

---

[3] Hill, Roy "Are Multinationals Aliens in the Third World?", *International Management,* January 1981, p. 14.

[4] W. J. Keegan, "Multinational Product Planning: Strategic Alternatives," *Journal of Marketing,* January 1969, p. 58.

EXHIBIT 13–1: Product components

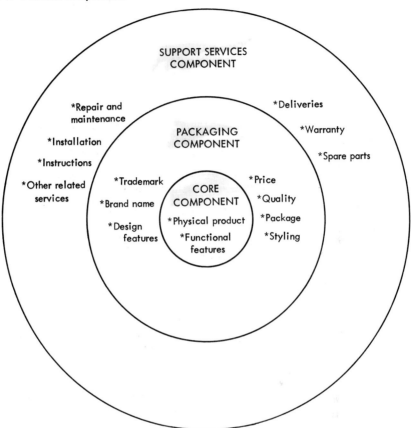

includes three major components. At the center is the core, the physical product and all its functional features. This part of the product along with the other two components, provides the bundle of utilities that the market derives from use of the product. Surrounding the core component is the packaging component that includes the physical package in which the product is presented as well as the brand name, trademark, styling and design features, price, and quality levels. The support services component completes the product buyers receive and from which the bundle of satisfactions received are derived. This support services component includes repair and maintenance services, installation, delivery, warranty, spare parts, training and instructions, credit, and any other services related to the use and purchase of the product.[5]

---

[5] See Philip Kotler, *Marketing Management: Analysis, Planning, and Control,* 4th ed. (Englewood Cliffs, N.J.: Prentice Hall, 1980), pp. 351–53.

The importance of each component as well as the perceived component attributes are functions of culture. What may be desirable in one culture may be unimportant in another, or a color acceptable in one country may be undesirable or even offensive in another. In short, what a product *is,* is, in large part, a cultural phenomenon; that is, culture determines the individual's perception of what a product is and what satisfaction that product provides. Thus, in developing products for international markets, adaptation of that "bundle of utilities or satisfactions received" may be necessary to bring the product in line with a culture's needs. Such adaptation may require changes of any one or all of the product components as defined earlier.

Except in instances when a product is developed specifically for a new market, most products are transposed from one market to another; thus, product components are a reflection of the needs of the market for which the product was originally developed.

When analyzing a product for a second market, the extent of adaptation required will depend on cultural differences in product use and perception between the market the product was originally developed for and the new market. The greater these cultural differences between the two markets, the greater the extent of adaptation necessary. However, even in markets with few cultural differences, substantial adaptation can be necessary if the product is in a different stage of it's life cycle in each market.

A product in a mature stage of its life cycle in one market can have unwanted or unknown attributes in a market where the product is perceived as new and, thus, in its introductory stage. Marketing history is replete with examples of mature products in one market being introduced in another and failing. An example is Campbell Soup's introduction of condensed soups in England; they were rejected until the market "learned" that condensed soups were as good as "full-strength" soups. After 20 years of success with the instant camera, Polaroid introduced the Model 20 "Swinger" Land Camera to a mature United States market in 1965. The Swinger was designed to place Polaroid, for the first time, in the mass market for inexpensive cameras. The Swinger capitalized on the established reputation of Polaroid and its concept of instant photography and was very successful.

In 1966, after a phenomenally successful introduction in the United States, Polaroid introduced the Swinger into the French market using its "successful" U.S. marketing program. The Swinger was Polaroid's first product in France and a spectacular failure. Polaroid withdrew the product, changed the marketing approach, and successfully reintroduced it.

What happened? As far as the French market was concerned, the Swinger and its concept of instant photography were unknown. In short, the product was in the introductory stage of its life cycle and the marketing effort required adaptation of the marketing program which had been designed for the mature U.S. market. The major problem was a lack of awareness of the concept of instant photography. A company study done after the poor showing in the initial introduction found that only 5 percent of the French market was familiar with instant photography whereas, in the United States, over 85 percent were knowledgeable about the concept. What Polaroid failed to appreciate was the 20 years of development and use of instant photography that was lacking in France. The French consumer did not perceive any "bundle of satisfaction" from this new product. Certainly an important approach in analyzing products for foreign markets is determining the stage of the product's life cycle. All subsequent marketing plans must then include all adaptations necessary to correspond to the stage of the product life cycle in the new market.[6]

Physical adaptation

There are a variety of ways a product may need changing to meet the market requirements of a new culture. They range from simple package changes to total redesign of the physical core product. Some changes are obvious with relatively little analysis. For example, a cursory examination of a country will uncover the need to rewire electrical goods if they use a different voltage system, to simplify a product when the local level of technology is not high, or to change a color if the present color violates local taboos.

Superficial changes can be spotted by looking at product use patterns, the economy, and other related cultural elements. Other necessary changes, however, are recognized only after careful study of the product in terms of the prospective market. The changes can run from the simple to the complex. One international scholar categorized these changes into 9 environmental factors and the design changes necessary.[7]

Environmental factor	Design change
Level of technical skills.	Product simplification.
Level of labor cost.	Automation or manualization of product.
Level of literacy.	Remarking and simplification of product.
Level of income.	Quality and price change.
Level of interest rates.	Quality and price change (investment in high quality might not be financially desirable).
Level of maintenance.	Change in tolerances.
Climatic differences.	Product adaptation.
Isolation (heavy repair difficult and expensive).	Product simplification and reliability improvement.
Differences in standards.	Recalibration of product and resizing.

The suggested changes are primarily concerned with price and physical or mechanical properties of a product. These product characteristics can

[6] Jose de la Torre, "Product Life Cycle as a Determinant of Global Marketing Strategies," in Subhash C. Jain and Lewis R. Tucker, Jr., *International Marketing: Managerial Perspectives* (Boston: CBI Publishing Co., Inc., 1979) pp. 278–79.

[7] Richard Robinson, *International Business Policy* (New York: Holt, Rinehart & Winston, 1964), p. 42.

and do impede effective use and acceptance of a product within another culture; however, subtle differences within a culture often require other changes that must be resolved before a product gains acceptance.

Cultural adaptation

Internal cultural variations can require product adaptation that hinges more on the product's conflict with norms, values, and behavior patterns than on its physical or mechanical aspects. For example, introduction of a new product into a culture that does not perceive a need for such an item can conflict with established norms; locally accepted values can be upset by introducing personal care items into a culture that prefers body functions remain private; assuming too high a level of sophistication in product usage may overlook local behavior patterns. As one authority states:

> In short, it is not just lack of money, nor even differences in the natural environment, that constitutes major barriers to the acceptance of new products and new ways of behaving. A novelty always comes up against a closely-integrated cultural pattern, and it is primarily this that determines whether, when, how, and in what form it gets adopted. Insurance has been difficult to introduce into Moslem countries, because the pious could claim that it partook of both usury and gambling, which are explicitly vetoed in the Koran. The Japanese have always found all body jewelry repugnant. The Scots have a decided resistance to pork and all its associated products, apparently from days long ago when such taboos were decided by fundamentalist interpretations of the Bible.
>
> The French, equally, proved unexpectedly hostile to frozen foods—to the extent that Unilever was at first forced out of this market altogether. Filter cigarettes have failed in at least one Asian country because the local life expectancy of 29 years hardly places many people in the age-bracket most prone to fears of lung cancer—even supposing that they shared the Western attitudes to death.[8]

A thorough cultural analysis would have alerted the marketer to these risks, but, as the same author notes, "perhaps they are warned but refused to acknowledge the strength of the factors."

When dealing with a culturally familiar item, it is difficult for marketers to sense the absolute newness of a product in a foreign market. The time and effort originally expended on domestic market acceptance of a product is often forgotten. In other words, the marketer uses the self-reference criterion to assess a culturally unique market, and overlooks the obvious.

An example of this involves an undisputed American leader in cake mixes which tacitly admitted failure in the English market by closing down operations after five unsuccessful years. Taking its most successful mixes

---

[8] D. E. Allen, "Anthropological Insights into Customer Behavior," *European Journal of Marketing,* vol. 5, no. 3, p. 54.

in the U.S. market, the company introduced them into the British market. A considerable amount of time, money, and effort was expended to introduce its variety of cake mixes to this new market. With benefit of hindsight several probable causes can be seen for the company's failure. Traditionalism was certainly among the most important. The British eat most of their cake with tea instead of dinner and have always preferred dry sponge cake, which is easy to handle; the fancy, iced cakes favored in the United States were the type introduced. Fancy, iced cakes are accepted in Britain, but they are generally considered extra special and purchased from a bakery or made with much effort and care at home. The company introduced what they thought to be an "easy" cake mix. This easy cake mix was considered a slight to housewifely duties. Housewives felt guilty about not even cracking an egg, and there was suspicion that dried eggs and milk were just not as good as fresh ones. Therefore, when the occasion called for a fancy cake, an easy cake mix was simply not good enough. Ironically, this same company had faced almost identical problems, which they eventually overcame, when introducing "new" easy cake mixes on the U.S. market. There was initial concern about the quality of mixes and the resulting effect on the housewife's reputation as a baker. Even today there remains the feeling that "scratch" cakes are of special quality and significance and should be made for extra-important occasions. This, in spite of the fact that the uniform quality of results from almost all mixes and the wide variety of flavors certainly equal, if not exceed, the ability of most to bake from scratch.

BOX 13–2: McDonald's cheeseburger—a diet food?

One key to success in international marketing is to adapt your marketing program and product to the needs of the market. McDonald's sells hamburgers in Australia to one segment of the market as a low-calorie food. Here is an excerpt from a McDonald's advertisement appearing in a leading women's magazine in Australia.

"Low Calorie Counter

If you are counting calories (or kilojoules) come to our counter. Here's a meal that will fit into your diet and it's food you can really enjoy.

Cheeseburger, french fries (reg. serv.), black coffee—527 calories—less than a third of what the average woman uses each day.

Above is a well-balanced, low-calorie (kilojoule), nutritious meal. We believe any McDonald's menu combination makes a significant contribution to your nutritional requirements. We want you to enjoy good food and enjoy it in good health. *Come to our counter and see how our figures can help your figure.*"

Source: *The Australian Women's Weekly*, August 5, 1981, p. 44.

The problems of adapting a product to sell abroad are similar to those associated with the introduction of a new product at home. Products are not measured solely in terms of their physical specifications; the nature of the new is in what it does to and for the customer—"to his habits, his tastes, and his patterns of life."[9] The problems illustrated in the cake mix example have little to do with the physical product or the user's ability to make effective use of it, but more with the fact that acceptance and use of the cake mixes would have required upsetting behavior patterns considered correct or ideal.

What significance, outside the intended use, might a product have in a different culture? When product acceptance requires changes in patterns of life, habits, tastes, the understanding of new ideas, acceptance of the difficult to believe, or the acquisition of completely new tastes or habits, special emphasis must be used to overcome natural resistance to change.

PRODUCT DIFFUSION

Unless the newness of a product to a foreign consumer is fully appreciated, a marketer cannot take the necessary steps to assure successful operations. How people react to newness and how *new* a product is to a market must be understood. An important first step in adapting a product to a foreign market is to determine the degree of newness perceived by the intended market.

In evaluating the newness of a product, the international marketer must be aware that many products successful in the United States and which have reached the maturity or even decline stage in their life cycle may be perceived as new in another country or culture and, thus, must be treated as innovations. From a sociological viewpoint, any idea perceived as new by a group of people is an innovation. Whether or not a group accepts an innovation and the time it takes depend on its characteristics. Products new to a social system are innovations, and knowledge about the diffusion (i.e., the process by which innovation spreads) of innovations is helpful in developing a successful product strategy. Marketing strategies can guide and control to a considerable extent the rate and extent of new product diffusion since successful new product diffusion is dependent on the ability to communicate relevant product information and new product attributes.

A critical factor in the newness of a product is its effect on established patterns of consumption and behavior. In the cake mix example above, the fancy, iced cake mix was a product that required acceptance of the "difficult to believe," i.e., that dried eggs and milk are as good in cake as the fresh products; and the "acquisition of new ideas" i.e., that easy-to-bake fancy cakes are not a slight to one's housewifely integrity. In this case, two important aspects of consumer behavior were directly affected by the product and the product innovation met with sufficient resistance to convince the company to leave the market. Had the company studied their target market before introducing their product, perhaps they could

---

[9] Chester Wason, "What is New About a New Product?" *Journal of Marketing,* July 1960, pp. 52–56.

have avoided the failure. Another U.S. cake mix company did enter the British market but carefully eliminated most of the newness of their product. Instead of introducing the most popular American cake mixes, the company asked 500 British housewives to bake their favorite cake. Since the majority baked a simple, very popular dry sponge cake, the company brought to the market a similar "easy" mix and gained 30 to 35 percent of the British cake-mix market.

The second cake mix represented more familiar tastes and habits that could be translated into a convenience item, and it did not infringe on the emotional aspects of preparing a fancy product for special occasions. Consequently, after a short period of time the second company's product gained acceptance.

Generally, the goal of a foreign marketer is to gain product acceptance by the largest number of consumers in the market in the shortest span of time. However, as discussed in Chapter 4 and as many of the examples cited have illustrated, new products are not always readily accepted by a culture; indeed, they are more apt to meet resistance. Although they may ultimately be accepted, the time it takes for a culture to learn new ways, to learn to accept a new product, is of critical importance to the marketer since planning reflects a time frame for investment and profitability. If a marketer invests with the expectation that a venture will break even in three years and it takes seven to gain profitable volume, the efforts may have to be prematurely abandoned. The question comes to mind whether or not the probable rate of acceptance can be predicted before committing resources and, more critically, if the probable rate of acceptance is too slow, whether it can be accelerated. In both cases, the answer is a qualified *yes*. Answers to these questions come from examining the work done in diffusion research—research on the process by which "innovations spread to the members of a social system."[10]

One authority notes that "crucial elements in the diffusion of new ideas are (1) an innovation (2) which is communicated through certain channels (3) over time (4) among the members of a social system."[11] The author continues with the statement that it is the element of time which differentiates diffusion from other types of communications research. The goals of the diffusion researcher and the marketer are to shorten the time lag between introduction of an idea or product and its widespread adoption.

There is ample evidence of the fact that product innovations have a varying rate of acceptance. Some diffuse from introduction to widespread use in a few years, others take decades. Microwave ovens, introduced in the United States initially in the 1950s, have only recently reached widespread acceptance; whereas the contraceptive pill was introduced during

---

[10] Everett M. Rogers and F. Floyd Shoemaker, *Communications of Innovations* (New York: Free Press, 1971), p. 12.

[11] Ibid., p. 18.

BOX 13–3:   Four in a package has got to be better than three

A leading U.S. golf ball manufacturer targeted Japan as an important new market by virtue of the expanding popularity of golf in that nation. Special packaging in sets of four was developed for export although golf balls are generally packaged in sets of 3, 6, or 12 for domestic consumption. The company's sales were well below anticipated volume. Research eventually targeted packaging in fours as a primary factor for lagging sales. *Four is the number of death in Japan.*

---

that same period and gained acceptance in a few years. In the field of education, modern math took only five years to diffuse through U.S. schools while the idea of kindergartens took nearly 50 years to gain total acceptance.[12] There is also a growing body of evidence that the understanding of diffusion theory may provide ways in which the process of diffusion can be accelerated. Knowledge of the process of diffusion may provide the foreign marketer with the ability to assess the time it will take for a product to diffuse before it is necessary to make a financial commitment. It also focuses the marketer's attention on features of a product which provoke resistance, thereby providing an opportunity to minimize resistance and hasten product acceptance.[13] There are at least three extraneous variables which affect the rate of diffusion of an object: (1) the degree of perceived newness, (2) the perceived attributes of the innovation, and (3) the method used to communicate the idea. Each variable has a bearing on consumer reaction to a new product and the time needed for acceptance of different, new products. An understanding of these variables can produce better product strategies for the international marketer.

Degree of newness

As perceived by the market, there are varied degrees of newness which categorize all new products. To each category there are myriad reactions all affecting the rate of diffusion. In giving a name to these categories one might think in terms of (1) congruent innovations, (2) continuous innovations, (3) dynamically continuous innovations, and (4) discontinuous innovations.

1.   A *congruent* innovation is actually no innovation at all because it causes absolutely no disruption of established consumption patterns. The product concept is accepted by the culture and the innovativeness is typically one of introducing variety and quality or functional features, style, or perhaps an exact duplicate of an already existing product—exact in the sense that the market perceives no newness, such as cane sugar *versus* beet sugar.

2.   A *continuous* innovation has the least disruptive influence on estab-

---

[12] Ibid., p. 60, Figure 2–2.

[13] For an interesting study of diffusion, see J. F. Ryan and S. A. Murray, "The Diffusion of a Pharmaceutical Innovation in Ireland," *European Journal of Marketing,* vol. 2, November/October 1977, p. 3.

lished consumption patterns. Alteration of a product is almost always involved rather than the creation of a new product. Generally the alterations result in better use patterns—perceived improvement in the satisfaction derived from its use. In some segments of the market, a continuous innovation may be more disruptive than in others. Examples include: fluoride toothpaste, menthol cigarettes, and annual new-model automobile changeovers.

3.　A *dynamically continuous* innovation has more disruptive effects than a continuous innovation, although it still generally does not involve new consumption patterns. It may mean the creation of a new product or considerable alteration of an existing one designed to fulfill new needs arising from changes in lifestyles or new expectations brought about by change. It is generally disruptive and therefore resisted because old patterns of behavior must change if consumers are to fully accept and perceive the value of the dynamically continuous innovation. Examples include: electric toothbrushes, electric haircurlers, central air conditioning, and frozen dinners.

4.　A *discontinuous* innovation involves the establishment of new consumption patterns and the creation of previously unknown products. It introduces an idea or behavior pattern where there was none before. Examples include: television, the computer, the automobile, and microwave ovens.[14]

Most innovation in the U.S. economy is of a continuous nature. However, a product that could be described as a continuous innovation in the U.S. market would be a dynamically continuous innovation, if not a discontinuous innovation, in many industrialized nations of the world. For example, when the cake mix was first introduced into the American economy, it was a dynamically continuous innovation. However, with time it overcame resistances, consumption and behavior patterns changed, and it was accepted in the U.S. market. Indeed, there are many continuous innovations involving the cake mix itself, such as the introduction of new flavors, changes in package size, elimination of dried eggs in favor of fresh eggs, and so on. That same cake mix, now a part of U.S. eating habits, is a congruent innovation when a new brand is offered on the U.S. market. If it is offered in a new, unique flavor, it is a continuous innovation; if it is introduced at the same time into a market unfamiliar with cake mixes, it is a dynamically continuous innovation. That same product also could be classified as a discontinuous innovation in a market which had no previous knowledge of cakes. In all cases, we are dealing basically with a cake mix, but in terms of acceptance and marketing success we are dealing with people, their feelings, and their perception of the product.

Continuing with the previous example, the second U.S. cake mix company which entered the British market with a sponge cake had, in fact, changed the product innovation from a dynamically continuous innovation to a contin-

---

[14] Thomas S. Robertson, "The New Product Diffusion Process," in *American Marketing Association Proceedings*, ed. Bernard A. Marvin (Chicago: American Marketing Association, June 1969), p. 81.

BOX 13–4: Deja vu or we will get it right someday

In 1978, Campbell entered a joint venture with a Brazilian company to produce and market soups. In 1980, after fiscal losses of $1.2 million the Campbell Soup Company announced it would stop producing and selling canned soup in Brazil.

What went wrong for Campbell in soup-conscious Brazil? Campbell's offerings—mostly vegetable and beef combinations in extra-large cans—failed to catch on. Brazilian housewives seemed to prefer the dehydrated products of competitors such as Knorr and Maggi which they used as a soup starter adding their own flair and extra ingredients. If one bought Campbell's soup, it was usually to put aside for an emergency, "like when she was late coming home from a tea party."

A comprehensive, in-depth study revealed that the Brazilian housewife felt she was not fulfilling her role as homemaker if she served her family a soup she could not call her own.

This was the second failure for the Campbell Soup Company. Fifteen years earlier, they introduced canned soup into another soup-eating market. The introduction in England was also a loser for a number of years. One of the problems then was the difference between the condensed soup which Campbell introduced and was unknown to the English market and the more familiar "full-strength," ready-to-eat soup to which the English market was accustomed. The company failed to appreciate the market's lack of familiarity with the preparation of condensed soups. The English housewife opened a can of condensed Campbell soup and heated it without the necessary can of water. No wonder it tasted too strong and spicy.

In each case, the company failed to appreciate the need to adapt the marketing program to the market. For Brazil, behavior patterns and attitudes about roles had to be changed or accounted for in the marketing program; and for the English, market knowledge, that is, the consumers' ability to properly prepare the product, had to be developed.

Sources: "The $30 Million Lesson," *Sales Management,* March 1, 1967, pp. 31–38; and "Brazil: Campbell Soup Fails to Make It to the Table," *Business Week,* October 12, 1981, p. 66.

---

uous innovation by simply altering the cake in the mix from a fancy cake to an already accepted dry sponge cake. Thus, one advantage of analyzing a product in terms of its degree of innovativeness is to determine what may alter the degree of newness to gain quicker acceptance. Even a tractor must be modified to meet local needs and uses if it is to be accepted in place of an ox-drawn plow.

The time the diffusion process takes, i.e., the time it takes for an innovation to be adopted by a majority in the marketplace, is of prime importance to a marketer. Generally speaking, the more disruptive the innovation the longer the diffusion process takes.

The extent of a product's diffusion and its rate of diffusion are partly a function of the particular product's attributes. Each innovation has characteristics by which it can be described, and each person's perception of these characteristics can be utilized in explaining the differences in perceived newness of an innovation. These attributes can also be utilized in predicting the rate of adoption, and the adjustment of these attributes by a marketer can lead to changes in consumer perception and thus to altered rates of diffusion. Emphasis given particular attributes, and the overall brand image created, are critical marketing decision areas.[15]

Characteristics of innovations

One study of the diffusion of innovations proposes a set of five characteristics which are relevant in accounting for differential diffusion rates. These characteristics are (1) relative advantage, (2) compatibility, (3) complexity, (4) trialability, and (5) observability.[16]

BOX 13–5: Super Limonada—changing traditional beliefs

Mothers of young Nicaraguan children are learning to combat diarrhea which causes one out of four deaths among Nicaraguan children under five. Marketing methods are being designed to combine traditional folk remedies with a new soft drink quickly prepared from normal household ingredients. An old medical prescription under a new name, Super Limonada, will hopefully provide a solution to the problem. Super Limonada is made from a liter of water, two tablespoons of sugar, a half teaspoon of salt, and lemon juice. The physiological action of the formula replenishes lost fluids while providing salt to promote fluid retention.

The question is how to overcome traditional beliefs about feeding sick children and get the mother to accept Super Limonada as proper medication. Traditional beliefs that a baby with diarrhea should be given a purgative "to clean out the system" and that no food be given while the baby has diarrhea have been handed down from generation to generation and are recommended by the older mother or grandmother. Conflict between the "old and right" and a "new way" prevents acceptance of the new. The solution calls for a sensitive psychological approach to win the mother's acceptance rather than an assault on tradition, which would inevitably arouse resistance to change and a subsequent rejection of the "new ideas."

The approach used was to present a series of sketches on radio broadcast in the local Spanish idiom which varied from village to village. Each sketch confirmed the original validity of the audiences' earlier belief while presenting and promoting new information to justify a change. It is important not to reject old customs outright as new information and change are more readily accepted if presented as an improvement on the familiar.

In three messages, a mother and a doctor speak, and in three others, traditional authority, Doña Carmen, an older woman, appears. In one message the doctor or Doña Carmen urges: "Don't let diarrhea kill your children. Kill diarrhea with Super Limonada." In another message, the mother tells the doctor or Doña Carmen that she gives the baby a purgative, as a neighbor suggested. The doctor or Doña Carmen asks, "Did she also advise you to stop giving your baby food while she has diarrhea?" When the mother says, "Yes," the doctor or Doña Carmen tells her, "We used to believe that way. Now we have discovered such treatment is wrong," and explains why. The third message urges mothers to continue breast-feeding their children and to feed them soft foods after the first day of illness.

Source: Adapted from "U.S. Marketers Aid Nicaraguan Effort to Overcome Children's Alimentary Ailments by Promoting Super Limonada from Original Household Items," *Marketing News*, November 5, 1976, p. 4.

---

[15] Ibid., p. 84.

[16] Rogers and Shoemaker, *Communication of Innovations*, pp. 22–23.

Relative advantage. Relative advantage is the degree to which an innovation is better than the product it replaces or with which it competes, i.e., an innovation with relative advantage has additional value as perceived by the consumer. The more relative advantage perceived by the consumer, the quicker the adoption process; conversely, the less relative advantage perceived, the slower the adoption process.

Compatibility. Compatibility is concerned with how consistent a product is with existing value and behavior patterns. The diffusion process will take longer for a product not compatible with current behavior because it requires the restructuring of thinking or necessitates engaging in different modes of behavior.

Complexity. Complexity refers to how difficult it is to understand and use the new product. The more complex the product, the longer the rate of diffusion; and conversely, the less complex, the quicker the adoption process.

Trialability. Trialability is the degree to which a product may be tried on a limited basis without complete commitment to it. If the product is a take-it-or-leave-it proposition and the consumer cannot easily sample it or purchase it in limited quantity, the risk involved in adoption of the innovation will be greater and the adoption process will be slower.

Observability. Observability refers to the ease with which the results of an innovation may be observed by others. Some innovations or product results are easily observed while others are difficult to describe. An integral part of the adoption process of an innovation is that others be aware of the advantages of accepting the new product. The easier it is to communicate the advantages of the innovation through print media, by word of mouth, or by observation, the more rapid the diffusion rate will be.

In general, it can be postulated that the rate of diffusion is positively related to relative advantage, compatibility, trialability, and observability, but negatively related to complexity.[17] Thus an innovation which would take the longest time to diffuse through a market would be a product with low perceived relative advantage, noncompatibility, extreme complexity, nontrialability, and difficult observability; an innovation taking the least amount of time for diffusion would be a product where the consumer could perceive maximum advantage, extreme compatibility, no complexity, high trialability, and easy observability. Such innovation characteristics provide a product profile which can be extremely useful as a model for planning a product's strategy. By analyzing those attributes which contribute to its newness (or innovativeness), the marketer's attention is focused on factors which give rise to resistance; thus, the marketer can estimate the possible rate of adoption. The adoption rate then can be adjusted by changing characteristics through physical modifications, advertising, and/or sales promotion efforts. Although this appears simple, a word of warning is in order.

---

[17] Ibid., p. 85.

The evaluator must remember it is the perception of an innovation's characteristics by the potential adopter, not the marketer, that is crucial to the evaluation. A market analyst's SRC (self-reference criterion) may cause a perceptual bias when interpreting the characteristics of an innovation. Thus, instead of evaluating product characteristics from the foreign user's frame of reference, the innovation is analyzed from the marketer's frame of reference, leading to a misinterpretation of their cultural importance.

Once the innovative analysis has been made, some of the perceived newness or cause for resistance can be minimized through adroit marketing. The more congruent with current cultural values perceptions of the product can be, the less the probable resistance and the more rapid the diffusion. A product frequently can be modified physically to improve its relative advantage over competing products, enhance its compatibility with cultural values, and even minimize its complexity. Its relative advantage and compatibility also can be enhanced and some degree of complexity lessened through advertising efforts. Small sizes, samples, packaging, and product demonstrations are all sales promotion efforts which can be used to alter the characteristics of an innovation and accelerate its rate of adoption.

The marketer must recognize not only the degree of innovativeness a product possesses in relation to each culture, but marketing efforts must reflect an understanding of the importance of innovativeness to product acceptance and adoption.[18]

Communication of innovations

The final step in the process of diffusion is communication of the idea. Until the innovation or idea becomes known, acceptance or rejection cannot take place. An idea may become known slowly via word of mouth or more rapidly if communicated through mass media. The use of a variety of media to communicate an idea is no stranger to the marketer. However, a vital question is what to communicate? The value of an *attributes of an innovation analysis* is that it focuses the efforts of the communicator on those issues which can influence diffusion of the idea. It is possible to accentuate the positive attributes of an innovation, thus changing the market's perception to a more positive and, therefore, acceptable attitude.

The potential of communication in terms of product innovations can be illustrated with some hypothetical questions about the cake mix example; would the company have had the same results if it had analyzed the cake mix as an innovation and then set out to make the idea a more acceptable one? What would have been the result, for example, if their introduction had been the traditional sponge cake which would have required no commu-

---

[18] For an interesting study see G. Hayward, D. H. Allen, and J. Masterson, "Innovation Profiles: A New Tool for Capital Equipment Manufacturers," *European Journal of Marketing* 11, no. 4 (1977), p. 299.

nication to gain acceptance? Or, in offering the market a fancy cake mix, they had set out to convince the market of the advantages of that type of cake over the traditional, thus enhancing its relative advantage? They could also have set out to promote advantages of the "new" cake mix over the old tradition so that it would have seemed more compatible with present behavior. There are many "what ifs" to be asked; "what if they had communicated the product's ease of trialability and observability to allay fears as to quality, taste, flavor, and ease of preparation?" In retrospect, the answers to these questions are of little value to the cake mix company but they

---

BOX 13–6: The diffusion of five innovations

A study of 137 flouring mills in the United Kingdom and Eire was done to determine the rate of diffusion within that industry of five innovations. The respondents were asked to rate each of the innovations on the five characteristics of an innovation, that is, relative advantage, compatibility, and so forth. Each of the characteristics was rated on an arbitrary scale of 1 to 5, a (1) *one* being the best score, i.e., most favorable and a (5) *five* being the worst. For example, a score of (1) on relative advantage means a very high perceived relative advantage of the innovation and a score of (5) on relative advantage would mean a very low perceived relative advantage.

It will be seen in the table that pneumatic conveying has taken 19 years from its introduction to adoption by 50 percent of the respondents. The total number of points received by pneumatics on the innovative scale is 15 against a best possible score of 5. The innovation of pneumatics is particularly lacking in trialability (d) since the system should be adopted full scale to achieve maximum benefits.

Rate of adoption in relation to the characteristics of the innovations under study

Characteristics*	a	b	c	d	e	Total points (a, b, c, d, e)	Time for 50 percent to adopt
Innovations							
Pneumatics	2	3	3	4	3	15	19 years
Bulk outloading	1	2	2	5	2	12	15 years
Flour silo	2	3	3	3	2	13	16 years
Short surface	3	2	2	5	3	15	No figure
Reverse jet	1	1	1	1	1	5	8 years

* Key: (a) relative advantage; (b) compatibility; (c) complexity; (d) trialability; (e) observability.

Bulk outloading bins took 15 years for adoption by 50 percent of respondents and have a total of 12 points on the innovative scale. Trialability again has a poor score. The reverse jet filter dust collector was adopted by 50 percent of respondents in eight years and gained the best rating of 5 on the innovative scale.

Further work is required in this area, but it would appear that the lower the reading on the innovative scale the shorter is the diffustion time for the innovation.

Source: "Diffusion of Innovation in the Flour Milling Industry," *European Journal of Marketing*, vol. 6, no. 3, p. 199.

can prove to the marketer the value of viewing a product in terms of innovation and characteristic analysis and then communicating a positive product picture to the new market. Frequently, the cause of failure for a U.S. marketer abroad is not poor marketing practices but failure to employ the right marketing practices against the correct problems.

As discussed in Chapter 4, the foreign marketer can function as a change agent and design a strategy to change certain aspects of a culture in order to overcome resistance to an innovative product. If a strategy of planned change is implemented, the marketer has some responsibility to determine the consequences of such action.

Consequences of an innovation

When product diffusion occurs a process of social change may also occur. One issue infrequently addressed concerns the consequences of the changes which happen within a social system as a result of adoption of an innovation. The marketer seeking product acceptance and diffusion may inadvertently bring about change which affects the very fabric of a social system. Consequences of diffusion of an innovation may be *functional or dysfunctional depending on whether the effects on the social system are desirable* or *undesirable*. In most instances, the marketer's concern is with perceived functional consequences—the positive benefits of product use. It would be difficult to determine any dysfunctional consequences of the acceptance of the cake mix described previously. Indeed, in most situations, new innovative products for which the marketer purposely sets out to gain cultural acceptance will have minimal if any dysfunctional consequences but that cannot be taken for granted. On the surface, it would appear that the introduction of condensed milk into the diet of babies in underdeveloped countries where protein deficiency is a health problem would have all the functional consequences of better nutrition and health, stronger and faster growth, etc.

There is evidence, however, that in at least one situation, the dysfunctional consequences far exceeded the benefits. In Nicaragua, as the result of the introduction of condensed milk, a significant number of babies annually are changed from breast-feeding to bottle feeding before the age of six months. In the United States, with appropriate refrigeration and sanitation standards, a similar pattern exists with no apparent negative consequences; but, in Nicaragua, where sanitation methods are inadequate, a substantial increase in dysentery, diarrhea, and a higher infant mortality rate have resulted. A change from breast-feeding to bottle feeding at an early age without complete understanding of purification by the user has caused dysfunctional consequences. This was the result of two factors: the impurity of the water used with the condensed milk and loss of the natural immunity to childhood disease a mother's milk provides. To counteract this phenomenon, the Nicaraguan Ministry of Public Health and a U.S. agency have launched a program to deal with the control of dysentery and diarrhea in children. Milk marketers have responded positively to this and similar situations by altering their marketing programs substantially in an attempt to offset the dysfunctional consequences of using condensed milk as a substitute for breast-feeding. Additional studies have revealed other situations where introduction of an innovation has produced dysfunctional consequences that far exceeded the positive results of the innovation.

Some may question their responsibility beyond product safety as far as the consequences of being change agents are concerned. The author's position is that the marketer has some responsibility for the results of marketing efforts whether intentional or not. Foreign marketers may cause cultural change which can create dysfunctional consequences. If proper analysis indicates negative results can be anticipated from the acceptance of an innovation, then it is the responsibility of the marketer to design programs not only to gain acceptance for a product but to eliminate any negative cultural effects as well.

WORLDWIDE CONSUMERISM

Consumerism is a social movement spreading throughout the world. It involves the actions of individuals and organizations responding to consumers' complaints and concern about product safety, quality, and information.[19] Consumerism is not necessarily a new movement. Consumer organizations existed in Denmark well before 1935, and consumer protection laws have been enforced in the United States since the 1920s. However, the trend in the last decade is toward greater effort on the part of consumers to seek from the business community and government agencies protection from what the consumer perceives to be a business community out of control. Many governments are taking legislative initiative to protect consumers; in some countries, consumers are banding together to force legislation. In some cases, the consumer movement, both in concerted consumer action and government legislation, is substantially behind the United States but, in other cases, substantially ahead. For example, it was 1974 before Sweden had laws to control deceptive advertising, the same laws enforced in the United States for over 40 years. At the same time, legislation passed in 1971 created a Swedish national consumer agency and established a consumer ombudsman to whom any disgruntled consumer could appeal directly. This reflected Swedish government consumer policy and went well beyond anything existing in the United States at the time. Most of Europe was well behind the rest of the world until the Commission of European Communities enacted laws to deal specifically with consumer protection

---

[19] For a comprehensive study of consumerism issues see E. Patrick McGuire, ed., *Consumer Protection: Implications for International Trade,* (New York: The Conference Board, Report No. 789, 1980), p. 63.

and the problems of harmful products, consumer credit, and misleading advertising.[20]

More important than the legislation is the growing concern on the part of consumers and their willingness to take action against perceived injustices. In the last decade, stronger consumer laws have been effectively enforced through the actions of consumer groups. In Japan, for example, consumers have acted in unison, achieving spectacular results. The Japanese consumer movement has successfully dealt with dual pricing systems of color televisions and fraudulent encyclopedia sales methods and brought the government's attention to environmental, educational, and social welfare issues. Consumers have reacted with boycott movements and lawsuits.[21] The Japan Consumer Association, Housewives Association, and National Council for Regional Women's Organizations are well organized grass-root associations with effective national organizations.[22]

In Europe, the influence of consumerism activity is also being felt. A Business International study found major trends in Europe included a growing movement to strengthen product liability laws, a move to block multi-branding, (i.e., using a different brand name for the same product in different European countries), more product[23] information on running costs (including probable repair and spare parts costs over a product's life, and the expected life span of the product itself), and improved product quality and durability with special concern for "planned obsolescence."[24] While not on a par with activities in the United States, Japan, and Europe, there is growing concern for consumer protection in less developed countries as well.[25]

One of the more noteworthy attacks on a product was that launched against the advertising and marketing of canned baby formula in Third World countries.[26] Several worldwide consumer groups were successful in getting the World Health Organization to issue a code regulating worldwide advertising and marketing of baby formula. In addition, several of these organizations have led a worldwide boycott against products of the Nestlè Corporation, considered to be one of the major baby formula marketers. While they have not been successful in getting Nestlè to cease the production

[20] "Consumer Groups are Adding Muscle and Becoming Feistier," *Business International,* November 21, 1980, pp. 369–70.

[21] Maurine A. Kirkpatrick, "Consumerism and Japan's New Citizen Politics," *Asian Survey,* March 1975, pp. 234–46.

[22] "Consumers Speak Out," *Focus Japan,* August 1980, pp. 3–4.

[23] "Marketing Strategies of Companies in Europe Coming Under Fire," *Business International,* February 27, 1981, pp. 65–69.

[24] "Consumerism Issues: How Companies Will Feel the Pinch," *Business Europe,* August 22, 1980, pp. 265–66.

[25] "Consumer Protection is Underdeveloped in the Third World," *The Wall Street Journal,* April 8, 1980, p. 1.

[26] H. Anton Keller, "Behind WHO's Ban on Baby Formula Ads," *The Wall Street Journal,* June 29, 1981.

and marketing of baby formula, they have had some minor effect on Nestlé's sales in some parts of the world.[27]

Although the consumerism movement is only just beginning in many countries, the long-range trend is for consumers to become more involved. International businesses should be acutely aware of the potential impact of the consumerism movement.[28] Most U.S. firms have had some experience dealing with the movement and that experience should not be forgotten when moving abroad.[29]

SUMMARY

Evidence supports the premise that for most firms moving from U.S. to foreign markets, product development consists primarily of adapting present lines to the peculiarities of foreign markets rather than the creation of totally new products. However, what is acceptable and comfortable within one group may be radically new and resisted within others depending on the experiences and perceptions of each group. Understanding that an established product in one culture may be considered an innovation in another is critical in planning and developing consumer products for foreign markets. Analyzing a product as an innovation may provide the marketer with important insights into this difference. With the growing importance of consumer protection groups around the world, a product must meet increasingly stringent standards of quality and its effect within a market.

QUESTIONS

1. Terms: Define and show the significance to international marketing:

Market saturation	Trialability
Product diffusion	Dynamically continuous innovation
Innovation	Functional innovation
Relative advantage	Dysfunctional innovation

2. Debate the issue of standardized versus differentiated products for the international marketer.

3. Discuss the different promotional/product strategies available to an international marketer.

4. Assume you are deciding to "go international," and outline the steps you would take to help you decide on a product line.

5. Products can be adapted physically and culturally for foreign markets. Discuss.

---

[27] "Nestlé Boycott Expands Worldwide," *Infact Newsletter*, February 1979, p. 1.

[28] "U.S. Exporters are Bracing," *Sales and Marketing Management*, March 17, 1980, p. 72.

[29] Dianne McKaig, "Consumer-Issue Strategies can be Shared on a Worldwide Basis," *International Advertiser*, July/August, 1981, pp. 20–49.

6. What are the three major components of a product? Discuss their importance to product adaptation.

7. How can a knowledge of the diffusion of innovations help a product manager plan his international investments?

8. Old products (that is, old in the U.S. market) may be innovations in a foreign market. Discuss fully.

9. ". . . If the product sells in Dallas, it will sell in Tokyo or Berlin." Comment.

10. How can a country with a per capita GNP of $100 be a potential market for consumer goods? What kinds of goods would probably be in demand? Discuss.

11. Discuss the four types of innovations. Give examples of a product which would be considered by the U.S. market as one type of innovation but a different type in another market. Support your choice.

12. Discuss the characteristics of an innovation which can account for differential diffusion rates.

13. Give an example of how a foreign marketer can use knowledge of the characteristics of innovations in product adaptation decisions.

14. Innovations are described as being either functional or dysfunctional. Explain and give examples of each.

15. Defend the proposition that a MNC has no responsibility for the consequences of an innovation beyond the direct effects of the innovation such as the product's safety, performance, and so forth.

16. Define consumerism. Discuss its importance to an international marketer.

17. Find a product whose introduction into a foreign culture may cause dysfunctional consequences and describe how the consequences might be eliminated and the product still profitably introduced.

Chapter 14

Marketing industrial products and services

Marketing texts frequently discuss the significant differences between industrial goods markets and consumer goods markets. The differences are basic and result from two fundamental factors: (1) the inherent characteristics in the nature of the products (industrial products are those goods and services used in the process of creating other goods and services, while consumer goods are in their final form and are consumed by individuals) and (2) the motive or intent of the user (industrial consumers are seeking a profit, while the ultimate consumer is seeking self-satisfaction). These differences manifest themselves in buying patterns, demand characteristics, and selling techniques.

The committee on definitions of the National Association of Marketing Teachers in a statement on the fundamental differences between industrial and consumer marketing reported four important differences between these two markets requiring major diversity in marketing practices. The differences are:

1. Differences owing to the nature of the market or the buyer.
2. Differences arising from organizational or operational setup.
3. Differences arising from the characteristics of the product.
4. Miscellaneous differences including such points as the need for a highly skilled sales force and speed and dependability of delivery.

In marketing both types of goods, the fundamental marketing concepts and principles are the same; however, there is considerable diversity in the tactics used to implement the marketing programs and in the degree of emphasis applied to the various components of the marketing mix. Whether a company is marketing at home or abroad, the differences between industrial and consumer markets merit special consideration.

Foreign marketing requires a clear-cut distinction between the two kinds of goods. The basic differences become more pronounced because of the additional and oftentimes unique emphasis demanded by changing environments. For example, a fundamental characteristic of industrial marketing true the world over is that goods are purchased on a performance basis. However, in countries where the culture of prospective users has not equipped them with the basic rudiments of technical skills, extraordinary steps must be taken to ensure such simple tasks as adequate maintenance. Otherwise, a company runs the risk of sullying the reputation of its products through no fault of the product but because of improper use or poor maintenance. After all, there are millions of people in the world who put gas in an automobile to make it go but do not bother about adding oil. It is still common practice to run a machine until it breaks down before thinking about repairs. Preventive maintenance seems to be a concept related to more advanced levels of technology.

Aside from problems created by environmental differences between countries, there are two significant trends to consider in the marketing of industrial goods: (1) a rapidly growing demand and (2) sharply increasing competition from long-time producers of industrial goods like Western Europe and Japan and from a new list of developing countries such as Brazil, Mexico and Argentina. For example, there has been a substantial growth of Third World multinationals during the last decade; in 1979, 34 of *Fortune*'s "overseas 500" companies were headquartered in such developing countries as Brazil, Taiwan, Korea, and the Philippines.[1]

To remain competitive in today's foreign markets requires a reevaluation of marketing programs in light of current trends. The successful industrial goods manufacturing firm cannot expect to be sought out to have its goods *bought;* instead, the firm must effectively compete with the many eager and relatively new competitors actively *selling* to increasingly demanding customers. In addition, restricted competition has to be dealt with in some areas.

Home countries are very protective of their "infant" industries and frequently close their borders to foreign competition. To protect Embraer (a manufacturer of a commuter airliner flown by small airlines in 24 countries including the United States), the Brazilian government stopped imports of private airplanes after 1974. In that year, Brazil imported 600 planes, but, since that date, fewer than 20 planes have been allowed to enter; a sizable market has vanished.[2]

Growth is occurring not only in the sale of tangible industrial goods but also in the sale of intangibles or services. Rapid economic growth, active competition, and a lack in many developing countries of a ready pool of highly skilled technicians and experts have created a steadily growing international market for services ranging from marketing research to engineering assistance.

The objective of this chapter is to discuss the special problems in marketing industrial goods internationally, the increased competition and demand for industrial goods, and their implications for the foreign marketer.

[1] David A. Heenan and Warren J. Keegan, "The Rise of Third World Multinationals," *Harvard Business Review,* January/February, 1979, p. 102.

[2] "Brazil Raises Exports of High Technology, to Pace Third World," *The Wall Street Journal,* October 6, 1981, p. 1.

THE INDUSTRIAL PRODUCT

Since an industrial product is purchased for business use and thus sought, not as an entity in itself, but as part of a total process, the buyer places stress on such features as service, dependability, quality, performance, and costs. In foreign markets these features are complicated for the marketer by the differences that exist between countries. Such cultural and environmental variations place different emphasis on service, dependability, performance, and costs. One such complicating factor is the degree of industrial development reached by each country.

Stage of economic development

Perhaps the most significant environmental factor affecting the market for industrial products is the degree of industrialization. Although generalizing about countries is a dangerous practice, the degree of economic development in a country can be used as a rough gauge of market characteristics for industrial goods. Regardless of the degree, demand for industrial products exists, but different levels of development typically result in changes in demand and kinds or quality of industrial goods sought.

Since industrial goods are products for industry, it is only logical for there to be a relationship between the degree of economic development and the character of demand for industrial goods found within a country. One authority suggests that nations can be classified into one of five stages of development. This classification is essentially a production-oriented approach to economic development in contrast to the marketing-oriented approach used in Chapter 11. Although the development of productive facilities parallels the evolution of the marketing process, emphasis in this section is on the development of manufacturing as a basis for the demand for industrial products rather than development of the marketing process. A production orientation is helpful since at each stage some broad generalizations can be made about the level of development and the industrial market within the country.

The first phase of development is really a preindustrial or commercial stage with little or no manufacturing and an economy almost wholly based on the exploitation of raw materials and agricultural products. The demand for industrial products is confined to a limited range of goods used in the simple production of the country's resources, i.e. the industrial machinery, equipment, and goods required in the production of these resources. During this stage a transportation system develops which creates a market for highly specialized and expensive construction equipment that must be imported. Take, for example, what is happening in the Mideast where the revenues from oil are being used, in part, to build the infrastructure for a developing country. Included are railroads linking the Mideast with Western Europe, "project packages" such as new schools or fully equipped hospitals and highways. Such projects are expected to cost several billion dollars when completed.[3]

The second stage reflects the development of primary manufacturing concerned with the partial processing of raw materials and resources which in stage one were shipped in raw form. At this level there is a demand for the machinery and other industrial goods necessary for processing raw materials prior to exportation. For example, in Kenya, a trade mission reports the need for empty jute bags, sulphur in lumps, bleaching powder and alum for a sugar factory, and fertilizers for a plantation.

The third stage of development is characterized by the growth of manufacturing facilities for nondurable and semidurable consumer goods. Generally, the industries are small local manufacturers of consumer goods having relative mass appeal. In such cases, the demand for industrial products extends to entire factories and the supplies necessary to support manufacturing. Liberia is a country at this stage of development, and the Liberian Development Corporation has been focusing attention on developing small- and medium-size industries such as shoe factories and battery and nail manufacturing. Such a degree of industrialization requires machinery and equipment to build and equip the factories and the supplies to keep them operating. Liberia's chief imports from the United States are construction and mining equipment, motor vehicles and parts, metal structures and parts, and manufactured rubber goods. In some cases, countries at the third stage are good markets for used plants; that is, plants deemed obsolete in more economically advanced countries but adequate in size and modest enough in cost to meet the needs of a developing country. For example, a used alkaline plant was dismantled in Canada, shipped to India, and set up for a total cost of $4 million; a new plant was estimated at a cost of more than $10 million. A cement plant sent to Venezuela from Pennsylvania cost $30 million against $50 to $60 million for a new one.[4]

A country at stage four is a well-industrialized economy. This stage reflects the production of capital goods as well as consumer goods, including products such as automobiles, refrigerators, and machinery. Even though there is production of industrial goods within the country, there is still a need to import industrial goods for the more specialized and heavy capital equipment not yet produced in the country but necessary for domestic industry. This stage is often accompanied by a rapid growth of consumer demand which in turn creates an increase in demand for industrial goods. In Italy, for example, a U.S. Department of Commerce study revealed that, as a result of a fairly rapid increase in auto ownership in Italy, there is a sizable increase in the need for diagnostic and testing apparatus. Presently about

---

[3] "Concentrate on Seven Major Markets," *World Business Weekly,* February 23, 1981, p. 19; and "Railroad Boom on the Horizon," *World Business Weekly,* June 8, 1981, p. 19.

[4] "Used Factories are Being Exported to Developing Countries," *The Wall Street Journal,* February 26, 1981, p. 1.

2,000 shops have this equipment, but there is need for approximately 23,000 repair shops with such modern equipment as wheel alignment indicators and motor analyzers. It is this kind of equipment which will be produced within the country as it moves from the fourth to the fifth stage of development, complete industrialization.

A country in stage five has reached a point of complete industrialization generally denoting world leadership in the production of a large variety of goods. Countries that have achieved this level typically compete the world over for markets for both their consumer and industrial goods. Even though a country is completely industrialized, a demand still exists within it for industrial goods from other countries. Characteristic of a high degree of industrialization is a tendency to specialize in the production of certain goods which could not include everything such an industrialized nation would need. Such specialization creates intense competition with domestic industries as well as with foreign industries.

Japan has achieved the fifth stage of industrial development, and although it is an industrialized economy, there is still the need to import products such as automated industrial equipment, large electronic computers, bookkeeping and accounting machines, and scientific controlling and measuring equipment. Just a few years ago, a widely held impression of trade with Japan was that the market consisted mainly of raw materials. Although there is a vast market for raw materials in resource-poor Japan, there is an equally vast market for industrial goods. In fact, the leading U.S. export to Japan is machinery. The mushrooming industrial growth in the various countries is not a threat to demand, but a widening market for more advanced and highly engineered products.

Although each stage of industrial development appears to be clear cut, most countries are actually in a state of economic and industrial flux striving for greater and more rapid economic growth. As one observer noted: "Don't expect to sell an automation feature in places where people till their fields by hand. On the other hand, don't underestimate the newly awakening nations. The term *underdeveloped* can be very deceiving." India, (along with most other less developed countries), has, or is seeking, the latest nuclear technology as well as the latest computer technology.

Further, regardless of the level of industrialization, there is a fascination for the latest technology in many Third World countries whether or not the technology can be used effectively.[5] One of the challenges facing the international marketer selling to developing countries is how to deal with a country seeking the most up-to-date technology when there is reason to doubt their ability to absorb the high technology. The marketer is faced

---

[5] For a complete and extensive article on the importance of newness in the exportability of products see Norman W. McGuinness and Blair Little, "The Influence of Product Characteristics on the Export Performance of New Industrial Products," *Journal of Marketing*, Spring 1981, pp. 110–22.

BOX 14–1: Japan's remarkable machine

How do you compete with a country that seems able to take over the market for just about any product it aims at—in Europe, Latin America, Southeast Asia, or the United States? Since the early 1950s, Japan, like a relentless juggernaut, has forced its way to a commanding position in one industry after another. The first triumphs were synthetic yarns, textiles, and clothing in the early postwar period. In the late 1950s, Japan quickly out-distanced Germany and the United States to become the world's largest exporter of radios, phonographs, and small household appliances. The early 1960s saw the Japanese beginning to win huge orders for ships. Their new yards were capable of building the largest tankers in the world and attracted delegations of shipbuilders from the United States and Europe.

Meanwhile, Japan, which has practically no raw materials for making steel, developed one of the most efficient and innovative steel industries in the world and rapidly carved out a major share of the world market. After ships and steel came black and white television sets, then color TVs. The Japanese have sought and got a voluntary agreement to limit TV shipments from Japan. Ironically, the Japanese now own TV plants in the United States.

In the late 1960s, Japan went after more formidable prey, the car industry, characterized by rapid change, high volume, and heavy capital investments. Today, Japan exports more autos than any other country. Toyota has become the third largest producer in the world, and Nissan is the fourth. Three out of five foreign-made automobiles sold in the United States are Japanese.

The early 1970s saw Japanese producers taking world leadership in 35-millimeter cameras and related equipment, a market in which the Germans had been preeminent. After that, Japan grabbed the major role in the manufacturing and export of small hand-held calculators that American companies had pioneered. The office copy machine, developed by America's Xerox Company into a necessary accessory in almost every modern office of substantial size, is the latest example of Japanese conquest. The Japanese company Richo, using an American license, makes more copiers than any other firm in the world. What's next?The Japanese have made it clear that they aim to be a major manufacturer in the computer industry: their goal is to win 18 percent of the computer business in the U.S. and a 30 percent share of global sales by 1990. Further, Japan's plans call for world leadership in fifth-generation computers, word processing, biotechnology, and industrial robots.

Why are the Japanese such formidable competitors? Much can be attributed to attitude: An American executive asks, "What have we got that we can sell abroad?"; the Japanese ask, "What will that country need? What will it buy and what can we make?" Then they concentrate on making that product or a whole string of products specifically for that market, concentrating on goods of top quality.

Source: Adapted from "Key to Japan's Success," *U.S. News & World Report,* September 26, 1977, p. 44; "Worry for World Business: How to Compete with Japan," *U.S. News & World Report,* September 26, 1977, p. 43; and "Japan's Strategy for the '80s," *Business Week* (Special Report), December 14, 1981, pp. 39–120.

---

with the dilemma of losing a sale if the company refuses the order because the buyer cannot effectively use the technology, or making the sale and being blamed for failures when the technology cannot be properly utilized. One international authority suggests that the marketer assess the level of technology needed, and "sell" the proper technology with appropriate service support systems including necessary training in product use and maintenance.[6]

The rate of industrialization in many Third World nations is occurring rapidly although there are gaps within the economy. Not all segments of a nation's economy will be at the same stage of development. An economy may operate at several levels of industrial development at once, but one degree of development will be more prominent than another.

Political and national implications

The political and national implications affecting the demand for industrial goods must also be kept in mind when studying industrial markets. Industrialization is typically a national issue, and industrial goods are the fodder for industrial growth; consequently, purchasing motives and patterns can have political overtones both internally and internationally. Industrial goods frequently are counted among the implements of economic warfare, and a market may be turned into a battlefield of international political aspirations of foreign powers. The stage of economic development achieved often reflects significant internal political changes in addition to increased demand for industrial goods. In fact, at certain stages of development, the government is, in reality, the customer for most industrial goods.

Product design

Besides the effect economic development has on the demand for kinds of goods, it also affects product development. Each stage of industrial advancement requires a greater degree of sophistication in necessary equipment since the general technological proficiency of a country is tied closely to its economic development. For example, a country in the third stage of industrialization does not have an adequate pool of trained technicians, nor has the general level of technical abilities reached a significant degree of achievement. Therefore, the adequacy of a product must be considered in relation to the general environment within which it will be operated rather than solely on the basis of technical efficiency. Equipment that requires a high degree of technical skill to operate, maintain, or repair can be inadequate in a country that lacks a pool of technically skilled labor.

Industrial marketers must not forget that industrial goods are ultimately evaluated on the basis of their contribution to profit or the improvement of the production process of the buyer. Consequently, products designed to meet the needs of individual industrial users are critical for competitive advantage. Certainly this is more the case today when there is competition from industrial goods producers such as Germany, France, and Japan. When

---

[6] A. Coskun Samli, "Five Steps can Help Industrial Marketer Transfer Technology to Third World," *Marketing News,* May 1, 1981, p. 6.

there was little competition, a U.S. manufacturer could sell a machine designed for a 40,000-unit production run to a foreign company that needed a machine with only one quarter that capacity. But, if competitors from other countries are willing to offer a machine with the desired capacity at competitive prices, how can U.S. companies compete? Ironically, U.S. companies in the domestic market are very consumer oriented, producing what the market wants, yet in foreign marketing, they are highly production oriented.

An example of this attitude is reflected in a statement reportedly made by a manufacturer of agricultural equipment commenting on the lack of cooperation of Thailand farmers to combine their plots into larger farms. Thai farmers often grow different crops on their small, adjacent plots and thus, large equipment cannot effectively be utilized. The U.S. company wants to sell combines for harvesting rice and corn; if the farmers could be persuaded to plant similar crops adjacent to each other, this equipment could be sold. But, as the executive commented, "Until the farmers agree to cooperate, there aren't going to be opportunities in Thailand to sell the large grain combines that we and other major companies manufacture."[7] As competition increases on the international level, U.S. companies must become more marketing oriented to survive.

In light of today's competition, a company must consider the nature of its market along with the possibility of designs adapted to such markets if it is to remain competitive. More and more companies have concluded that to effectively compete internationally they must put aside designs appropriate for industrialized countries and develop new ones aimed at the differing needs of markets at various stages of economic development. Success in many foreign markets depends on giving each market the kind of products it needs and wants, not products designed for industrially developed markets. Certainly one of the marketing strengths of the Japanese as world competitors is their willingness to adapt products to the needs of the target market.[8]

Concept of quality. Industrial marketers frequently misinterpret the concepts of quality. Good quality as interpreted by a highly industrialized market may be inadequate when interpreted by standards of less industrialized nations. For example, an African government had been buying hand-operated dusters for use in distributing pesticides in cotton fields; the dusters were loaned to individual farmers. The duster supplied was a finely machined device requiring regular oiling and good care. But the fact that this duster turned more easily than any other on the market was relatively unimportant to the farmers. Furthermore, the requirement for careful oiling

---

[7] Steve Galante, "Thai Officials Court U.S. Agribusinesses," *Asian Wall Street Journal,* October 12, 1981, p. 8.

[8] Alan L. Otten, "Pilot Plant Tests and Trains Aiding Third-World Industry," *The Wall Street Journal,* February 27, 1981, p. 21.

and care simply meant that in a relatively short time the machines froze up and broke. The result? The local government went back to an older type of French duster which was heavy, turned with difficulty, and gave a poorer distribution of dust, but which lasted longer because it required less care and lubrication. In this situation, the French machine possessed more relevant quality features and, therefore, in marketing terms, possessed the higher quality.

It must be kept in mind that the concept of quality is not an absolute measure but one relative to use patterns and/or predetermined standards. Best quality is best because the product adheres exactly to specified standards which have been determined by expected use of the product. Since use patterns are frequently different from one economy to another, standards will vary so that superior quality in one country falls short of superior quality as determined by needs in another country.

Variations in product features.   The design and quality of a product should be viewed from many points. Extreme variations in climate create problems in designing equipment that is universally operable. Products that function effectively in the United States may require major design changes in order to operate as well in the hot, dry Sahara region or the humid, tropical rain forests of Latin America. Trucks designed to travel the superhighways of the United States almost surely will experience operational difficulties in the mountainous regions of Latin America on roads that closely resemble jeep trails. There are many variations to be considered if a manufacturer is to make a product that is functional for far-flung markets.

Service, replacement parts, and standards

Effective competition abroad not only requires proper product design but prompt deliveries and the ability to furnish spare and replacement parts without delay. In the highly competitive European Community, for example, it is imperative to be in a position to give the same kind of service a domestic company or EC company can give. One U.S. export management firm warned that U.S. business may be too apathetic about Europe, treating it as a subsidiary market not worthy of "spending time to develop." It cites the case "of an American firm with a 3 million dollar potential sale in Europe which did not even give engineering support to its representatives when the same sale in the States would have brought out all the troops."

A recent study of international users of heavy construction equipment revealed that, next to the manufacturer's reputation, quick delivery of replacement parts was of major importance in purchasing construction equipment. Furthermore, 70 percent of those questioned indicated they bought parts not made by the original manufacturer of the equipment because of the difficulty of getting original parts. Smaller importers complain of U.S. exporting firms not responding to orders or responding only after extensive delay. It sometimes appears the importance of timely availability of spare

---

BOX 14–2: Now this is what you call service!

Maschinenfabrik Augsburg-Nuernberg, (MAN) the West German commercial vehicle and machinery group, has won a $109 million, two-year contract to provide trucks and backup services to the Iraqi-Jordanian Overland Transport Company. The order is for 400 60-metric-ton trucks to operate along the highways linking the Jordanian port of Aqaba with Iraq.

MAN won the deal against competition from most of the major European commercial vehicle manufacturers. Company executives attribute their success to the firm's offer of extensive backup services. While most of the bidders could provide drivers for their trucks, few could match MAN's promise of mobile repair workshops, water supply facilities, and a drivers' camp complete with butcher shop and dispensary.

Source: "MAN Lands an Iraqi-Jordanian Deal," *World Business Weekly,* August 24, 1981, p. 19. Reprinted by permission of the Financial Times, London.

---

parts to sustain a market is forgotten by American exporters; frequently, orders for replacement parts are ignored. When companies are responsive, the rewards are significant. U.S. chemical production equipment manufacturers dominate sales in Mexico because, according to the U.S. Bureau of International Commerce, they deliver quickly. The ready availability of parts and services provided by U.S. marketers gives them a competitive edge over other manufacturers.

The foreign marketer also may be foregoing the opportunity of participating in a lucrative after market. Since some kinds of machine tools use up five times their original value in replacement parts during an average lifetime and thus represent an even greater market, one international machine tool company has capitalized on the need for direct service and available parts

---

BOX 14–3: Japan eyes the auto-service market

As the Mideast automobile market expands, so too does demand for spare parts, gas station equipment, tires, repair-shop tools, and mechanical services. Japanese motor vehicle manufacturers have been quick to see the potential of this market and have begun training auto mechanics all over the region in the art of auto repair. In the latest such venture, *Toyota, Nissan,* and *Honda* have announced plans to help Libya set up service shops in 44 towns and cities.

Toyota will soon send three experts to Libya to give technical advice on building a repair shop in Tripoli, and five Libyans will go to Japan in August for training in motor-servicing techniques. Honda will also send auto experts to Libya, while Nissan will train Libyan mechanics at its service center in Athens as well as in Japan.

The auto makers are counting on the service market not only to provide a lucrative sidelight to the main business of selling cars but also to boost Mideast demand for Japanese vehicles. The region is now Japan's second-largest market for automobile sales, but it is way behind the No. 1 market—the United States. If Mideast mechanics are trained to service Japanese cars, the reasoning goes, people in the market for a new car are more likely to choose a brand they know they can have repaired locally.

Source: "Japan Eyes the Auto-Service Market," *World Business Weekly,* June 22, 1981, p. 19. Reprinted by permission of the Financial Times, London.

by changing its distribution system from the "normal" to one of stressing rapid service and readily available parts. Instead of selling through independent distributors as most machine tool manufacturers in foreign markets do, this company has established a series of company stores and service centers similar to those found in the United States. As a result of the change, the company stands ready to render service through its system of local stores, while most competitors dispatch service people from their home-based factories. Service people are kept on tap for rapid service calls in each of its network of local stores, and each store keeps a large stock of standard parts available for immediate delivery. The net result of meeting industrial needs quickly is keeping the company among the top suppliers in foreign sales of machine tools.

Universal standards

A lack of universal standards is another problem faced by manufacturers of industrial products for foreign trade. In the United States there are two major areas of concern to the industrial exporter. One is a lack of common standards for highly specialized equipment manufacturing, such as machine tools, and the other problem area is in the use of the inch-pound[9] or English system of measurement. Domestically, the use of the inch-pound and the lack of a universal manufacturing standard are not much of a problem, but it has serious consequences when affected products are scheduled for export. Conflicting standards are encountered in test methods for materials and equipment, quality control systems, and machine specifications. Most countries except England and its former colonies use the metric system, and the difficulty and complexity of change or adjustment from the inch-pound system to the metric system and vice versa creates many costly problems. Major steps are being taken to alleviate the problem.

Efforts at universal standardization are being made through international organizations dedicated to the creation of international standards; e.g., the IEC (International Electrotechnical Commission) is concerned with standard specifications for electrical equipment of machine tools. Another international organization interested in the development of world standards is the ISO (International Organization of Standardization). In the United States, conversion to the metric system and acceptance of international standards have been slow.[10] Congress and industry have dragged their feet for fear that conversion would be too costly. General Electric Co. estimated that changing to metric would cost $200 million and Ford Motor Company estimates that a switch would take up to 25 percent of their capital investment. But, as American industry sales are accounted for more and more by foreign custom-

---

[9] Also referred to as the *foot* or *yard-pound* system.

[10] Arlen J. Large, "The Slow March to Metric," *The Wall Street Journal,* November 16, 1977, p. 12.

ers who are on the metric system, it becomes increasingly evident that the United States must change or be left behind.

In 1965, Great Britain created a Metrication Board designed as an advisory body to establish the metric system in Great Britain by 1975; by 1980, Great Britain still had not achieved complete conversion. Critics of the metric system feel that it may take much longer for Britain to convert to the metric system because there is no cut-off date in the Metrication Board Act for complete conversion to the metric system. Similarly, in 1975, the United States created the Metric Conversion Act which declared "a national policy coordinating the increasing use of the metric system in the United States to bring about conversion from the inch-pound system to the metric system." Critics maintain that the U.S. system will not be any more successful than Great Britain's since there is no specific cut-off date nor any penalties for not converting by a specific date. Many observers believe that unless there is a specific cut-off date or economic penalties, U.S. industry will not change quickly. International market positions can be lost if we remain on the inch-pound system and, with the remainder of the world on the metric system, it would be foolish for U.S. industry not to convert.

BOX 14–4:   Nigeria now enforcing metric import markings

All imports into Nigeria must now carry metric labeling exclusively. The same rule will apply to invoices, bills of lading, and other import documents. Nigeria, which enacted legislation in 1974 to recognize the metric system as the official system of weights and measures, had heretofore permitted dual markings on imported goods.

The Nigerian authorities have stated that goods arriving with markings contrary to the new provisions will be excluded from entry to Nigeria or may be confiscated.

Source: "Nigeria Now Enforcing Metric Import Markings," *Commerce America*, January 2, 1978, p. 18

The marketing of industrial goods in the domestic market requires service, available replacement parts, and uniform standards to be successful in competitive marketing. When a company goes abroad, these problems are magnified because of distribution problems, inadequate service facilities, and differing standards that lead to incompatibility of machinery and equipment. These problems must receive extra emphasis if the company intends to assign itself to a long-range complete commitment in foreign markets. Product is only one decision area affected by the environment of the nation. The industrial marketer operating in foreign countries must also consider channels of distribution and their availability.

CHANNEL STRATEGY FOR INDUSTRIAL PRODUCTS

There are a multitude of channel alternatives available to the foreign marketer of industrial goods. American firms distribute in three distinct ways:[11] through American-based export middlemen; through foreign-based middlemen; and through company-managed and organized sales forces. Companies can use any combination of these three distribution systems or only one, depending on the extent of their involvement in foreign marketing, their organization, production facilities, and financial status. In each category, several kinds of institutions are available for use, or several kinds of company-owned sales organizations are utilized.

The type of distribution employed depends on several factors. The use of domestic-based exporters is probably adequate for small companies without extensive acumen in foreign operations or for a firm that prefers a minimum of involvement in foreign sales. Those companies that intend to become truly international in scope and are totally committed to foreign marketing need the more direct methods available. The decision to deal with an agent or distributor or to set up an independent sales organization is influenced by many factors—availability of adequate middlemen, finances, desired control of sales, character of the product. The successful use of entirely different methods of distribution by two large companies serves as an illustration. A leading manufacturer of machine tools established its own sales distribution points throughout Europe. The decision was based on the need to provide rapid service for its equipment to remain competitive and on a desire to participate in the lucrative parts market associated with the use of its products. It was found that this method of distribution was the most suitable for the company's circumstances.

On the other hand, a leading manufacturer of farm and earth-moving equipment recently changed from direct distribution through company-owned sales subsidiaries to the use of independent local distributors. It was decided that independent local distributors would provide this company with a stronger organization that was more economical and far more stable since its products are sensitive to economic shifts. Particularly in smaller markets, a local distributor would be better able to weather economic ups and downs by carrying complementary products. Furthermore, the manufacturer felt that a local distributor would be more effective than its own sales organization because the former would have better market knowledge and would eliminate the normal break-in period required by company-owned operations. A final point—through the use of local distributors, the company could exploit markets that were too small to support a company sales organization but needed the services available from locally based distribution points.

In today's buyer's market, unless a company can provide after-sales service, including prompt delivery, repair, and adequate supplies of replacement parts, a direct sales force may not be effective. The representative or agent who handles many lines from a small office is slowly losing ground to the engineering firm which can prepare technical bids and stock spare

---

[11] For a complete discussion see Chapters 18 and 19.

BOX 14–5: Super salesperson

Virtually all Russian women of child-bearing age work—some 90 percent between the ages of 18 and 45. Lacking extra bedrooms, Pampers, and plentiful commercial baby food, they have repeatedly let down the birthrate planners. But hold your ears for the baby boom. Dutch-born deal maker Bettina Parker has sold a plant to Russia to make Similac, an infant formula.

The deal, which she negotiated for Abbott Laboratories, is her latest in a 10-year series between Russia and the United States. Starting with her first large sale—an amusement park—she has steadily expanded her list of U.S. corporate clients to 12—as widely varied as Esmark, Pitney-Bowes, and Babcock & Wilcox—whose world sales exceed $28 billion.

Of her Similac sale, Ms. Parker says bluntly, "I did the whole deal, start to finish," and she argues its political and sociological significance in meeting the needs of Russian women. Until quite recently, Ms. Parker hired only women for the Moscow, London, and New York offices of Parker Associates because, she says, "they work harder. But I have just become an equal-opportunity employer. I hired my first man."

That man is Ken Ho, 34, who this month will complete a deal to import beer from the People's Republic of China. Ms. Parker sees no conflict of interest in trading with the Soviet Union's political enemy No. 1.

Source: "Businessmen in the News, 'Goo,' " Reprinted from the January 1977 issue of *Fortune Magazine* by special permission; © 1976 Time, Inc.

---

parts. The evolving market pattern indicates that the company which plans a long-range program abroad and wishes to remain competitive will have to select full-service distributors or organize its own sales unit to include a complete stock of parts and full service facilities. Since agents do not normally provide much in the way of extra services, a company which utilizes agents in its distribution system must arrange for additional services through other channels.

International trade fairs and trade centers found throughout major market areas of the world may also be considered methods of distribution. Although these fairs do provide a means for the introduction of new products or an introduction into new markets, thereby helping to establish trade relations, they are primarily classified as promotional activities and will be discussed in the following section on promotion.

PROMOTIONAL PROBLEMS ABROAD

The promotional problems encountered by foreign industrial marketers are little different from the problems faced by domestic marketers. Until recently, there was a paucity of specialized advertising media in many countries; but, in the last decade, especially in Western Europe and to some extent in Eastern Europe, Russia, and China, specialized industrial media have developed to provide the industrial marketer with a means of communicating with potential customers. In addition to the advertising that would normally take place in print media, many industrial markets can also be reached through catalogs, direct mail, and trade fairs which are important promotional media in international industrial marketing.

Industrial trade fairs and trade centers

Trade fairs date back in history to the time when most trade was centered at markets or fairs. Today's international fairs are generally government-sponsored attempts to facilitate foreign trade. Governments, among them the U.S. government, often sponsor international trade fairs within their own countries which are open to domestic and foreign exhibitors. They also sponsor fairs and trade centers in other countries to facilitate foreign trade for their domestic industries in these countries.

Fairs provide the facilities for a manufacturer to exhibit and demonstrate products to potential users. They are an opportunity to create sales and establish relationships with agents and distributors which can lead to more permanent distribution channels in foreign markets.[12] Thirty-nine American firms participated in a seven-day electronics production equipment exhibition in Osaka, Japan, and came home with $1.6 million in confirmed orders and estimates for the coming year of $10.1 million. Five of the companies were seeking Far Eastern agent/distributors through the show and each was able to sign a representative before the show closed. Trade fairs are scheduled periodically and any interested manufacturer can reserve space to exhibit goods.

The American government has also established permanent trade centers where products from various American industries are exhibited for specific time periods. There are 17 permanent U.S. trade centers in industrial centers such as London, Frankfurt, Milan, Bangkok, Stockholm, Tokyo, and Rome. The trade center functions in the same manner as a trade fair except that the former is permanent and operates the year round with an average of 8 to 10 shows a year. In conjunction with the trade centers, the Commerce Department began in 1977 to offer another meaningful service to industrial buyers. Rather than attend all annual trade show circuits, manufacturers seeking business overseas can have their products presented to potential buyers on a videotape and thus gain greater exposure of their goods.[13]

Proper emphasis in promotional mix

Although international trade fairs are generally a successful means of promotion, they should not be expected to serve as the primary means of promotion since they lack the range of promotional coverage necessary

---

[12] John M. Geddes, "Small U.S. Firms use European Trade Fairs as an Inexpensive Way to Tap New Markets," *The Wall Street Journal*, November 11, 1981, p. 18.

[13] For a complete description of the steps in conducting a trade show, see Stuart C. Rogers, "How Kodak Breathes Fire into International Trade Shows, *International Advertiser*, September/October, 1981, pp. 26–35.

for industrial goods.[14] A combination of promotional devices is required for an adequate promotional mix. A survey in England indicated that the entire promotional mix in at least one industry may need some overhauling. The survey included both the buyers and sellers of machine tools. Sellers were asked to give the percentage of their promotional dollar spent on various media, and the buyers were asked to list in order of importance the channels of information they regarded as important in hearing about industrial goods. The results of the study indicated that the sellers were spending over 60 percent of their funds on display advertising and exhibitions at trade fairs, whereas 84 percent of the buyers surveyed indicated that although they encouraged their technical staffs to attend trade fairs, they considered them inadequate for disseminating industrial product information. They relied most heavily on technical journal ads and manufacturers' catalogs.

While exhibitions and trade fairs help promote products, an industrial marketer must keep in mind that promotional problems abroad are similar to those in the United States. The product and the company must be known to potential buyers. One of the major weaknesses of international advertising of industrial goods is the relatively small amount of money spent to create the product and corporate image necessary to support exhibitions and other selling methods.[15] While the company's name may be familiar in markets in the United States, insufficient money is spent making potential buyers abroad aware of the company, its products, and its sales force. Since specialized media are increasingly more available, especially in Europe, it should become part of a promotional mix similar to that utilized in the United States.

It should be remembered that the survey discussed above was limited to a particular industry and country and therefore would not be generally applicable; however, the apparently misplaced emphasis brought to light by the study suggests that other promotional mixes may be as out of phase as the English machine tool manufacturers in question. A foreign marketer unsure of a proposed promotional mix and with no substantial evidence of what the proper mix should be, would be well advised to conduct research on market and industry characteristics before obligating promotional funds to any "obvious or normal" promotional pattern.

Promoting to Socialist countries

With increasing trade taking place between Western industrialized nations and Communist Eastern European countries, the People's Republic of China, and Russia, a critical question arises on the means of promoting to these

---

[14] International Direct Mail—the Most Misunderstood International Medium," *Industrial Marketing,* January 1982, pp. 88–92.

[15] Michael J. Porcaro, "The Promotion of Capital Goods in Latin America," *International Advertiser,* January/February, 1981, pp. 21–24.

potential customers. Surprisingly enough, advertising is a viable institution in most of the Socialist nations, including China and Russia. In China, for example, not only are there advertising media available but also advertising agencies. In Eastern European countries, the agencies provide services similar to those provided by capitalist countries, i.e., media selection; copy and art; production for television, radio, and cinema; direct mail, and publicity. In many of these countries, catalogs and advertisements that can be circulated are as important in reaching potential customers as trade shows and trade fairs.

Establishing contact in China

Dramatic developments have taken place in the People's Republic of China (PRC) since the death of Chairman Mao. China has embarked on a course toward rapid economic growth and various commercial practices, unacceptable just a few years ago, are now standard practice. For example, foreign companies may advertise in Chinese media, China accepts foreign credits and loans from private and government agencies, contract manufacturing to foreign buyer's specifications is possible and, further, joint ventures between Chinese and foreign capitalist firms have been approved. Even capitalist management techniques are actively sought—U.S. business professors are now teaching business and management to Chinese managers.[16]

These changes are quite a departure from the restrictive atmosphere that existed under Chairman Mao. Although the attitude of China toward trade with the capitalist world has improved substantially, the process of successfully doing business in China is still sufficiently different from most of the rest of the world that it deserves special attention.[17]

The secrets of success in marketing to the PRC are still linked to the "Three Ps"—patience, persistence, and product.[18] A high-quality product including technical know-how on the part of the foreign salespeople involved in Chinese negotiations and services is a must since one of China's goals is to improve the level of their industrial technology. Patience and persistence are needed from the first attempts to establish contact with a potential customer through the sometimes long negotiation periods to the final stages of shipping and installing goods. For those who follow the three Ps of marketing to China, the rewards can be substantial since a satisfied Chinese buyer is a demanding but loyal customer.

During Chairman Mao's period, all importing and exporting by the PRC

---

[16] "China's Managers get U.S. Lessons," *The Wall Street Journal*, January 1, 1981, p. 17.

[17] Bob Donath, "China Trade Growth: Will the Cookie Crumble?" *Industrial Marketing*, November 1980, pp. 52–65.

[18] For a comprehensive report on trading in China from which this section draws extensively see *Business Strategies for the People's Republic of China* (New York: Business International Asia/Pacific, Ltd., November 1980), 360 pp.

was handled through seven Foreign Trading Companies (FTC), each having responsibility for specific product groups. Product sales generally took place at the Canton (now called Guangzhou) trade fair, and the sale of capital equipment took place in Peking (now Beijing) by executives who were invited for a stay of one to six weeks.[19] Representatives from the appropriate FTC negotiated the contract rather than the end-user. A seller rarely dealt directly with end-users nor could they send literature or samples to them without the specific permission of the relevant FTC. In fact, attempts to cir- cumvent "proper channels" could lead to breaking off of negotiations. To- day, such restrictions have eased considerably.[20]

BOX 14–6: Tips for visitors to China

Don't discuss politics, and never, never speak lightly of political leaders. The West- ern custom of joking about politics and political leaders has not yet reached China.

Try not to show annoyance at the incessant slogans and political songs emanating from public loudspeakers.

Do not try to hand out tips for any service. It is considered an insult to the very proud Chinese. However, the visitor is expected to express his thanks profusely, to his personal host and the hotel staff.

Do not try to bargain in the shops. This practice, commonplace in other parts of the Orient, is strictly forbidden in China.

Do not touch any part of your acquaintance's anatomy—particularly the head. This would be considered a sign of disrespect. Shaking hands is the exception to the rule, but shoulder-slapping, button-holing, and arm-gripping are in extremely bad taste.

Flirting with Chinese women, even in the mildest and most innocent way, is definitely out. The Chinese code for conduct between the sexes is ultra-Puritan.

Absolutely no horseplay. One visiting European businessman who playfully flipped a piece of ice from his drink at a companion was sent home when it accidentally landed on a nearby official. So was another visitor who playfully patted a waitress.

Source: Reprinted from p. 115 of "Doing Business with the People's Republic of China," with permission of the publisher, Business International Corporation, New York.

The number of FTCs has increased to 12 and while the FTC is ultimately responsible for any final contract, negotiations and contact now can be made with end-users. Provinces and municipalities can pursue and handle direct trade and business transactions with foreign firms; and, factories and other state enterprises are permitted to procure supplies where they choose. Advertising in technical journals and other Chinese media, as well as some U.S. media which circulate in China, is not only permitted but encouraged. With their hunger for technical data, the Chinese are avid technical journal

---

[19] The customary names of China's provinces and their capitals have been changed by the Chinese to reflect a more correct spelling. For example, Canton is now Guangzhou, Taipei is Taibei, Szechwan is Sichuan, and Peking is Beijing.

[20] For a complete description of how one firm sells to China, see Robert D. Langer, "How Borden Tapped the China Market," *International Advertiser,* September/October 1981, pp. 36–48.

readers. In addition to technical journals, local and national television carry commercials for consumer and industrial products—industrial films even have been aired as regular programming. Radio is available in major markets, as are newspapers and magazines.[21]

These changes have made it somewhat easier to reach potential customers and end-users although the process can still be lengthy. Business International (BI) suggests a multifaceted approach to making contact in China. Included in any promotion should be the appropite FTC; but, in addition, BI suggests a marketer use media advertising, direct-mail contact, trade fairs, direct invitations to Chinese officials to visit manufacturing plants in the United States, and the China Phone Book as a source of potential customers. Once contact is made, the next step in the process is to secure an invitation to visit China. Business representatives must be specifically invited to China for negotiations; those who have traveled there on tourist visas without appointments have mostly been unsuccessful in arranging them on the spot. To obtain an invitation, contact should be made with the appropriate ministry, FTC, or industrial corporation with a specific proposal.

The new openness allows for some creativeness in reaching potential customers. One English firm, Gestetner International, producer of rephotographic equipment, rented two railway cars from the Ministry of Railways to conduct a series of promotional symposiums in 17 Chinese cities. One of the cars was converted to a 60-seat theater for visual presentations and the other to a display case for their products. More than 10,000 end-users were expected to visit the exhibit along its train route.[22]

To get an invitation, *Business International* recommends extensive mailings of at least 15 copies each of a complete brochure on the company and its products to the proper trading companies, another 15 copies each to two catalog libraries in Beijing, 10 copies to the Hong Kong agents of the trading companies, and finally, copies to all branches of the trading corporation in China's main cities. If the product is of interest, the trading corporation may write for more information which, in turn, could lead to an invitation to China for further discussion of matters or an invitation to the Guangzhou Trade Fair to meet with representatives. Even if there is no immediate response, the mailings should continue so the trading companies will be aware of the product and be kept abreast of any changes or improvements.

The Guangzhou Fair is an important vehicle for China trade. Representation at the Fair gives a company an opportunity to interest the Chinese in its product, and provides an important means of contact with end-users. Attendance at the Fair is by invitation only and may come directly from

---

[21] Bob Donath, "Peddling to the PRC," *Industrial Marketing*, November 1980, p. 77.

[22] "Unique Marketing Enables Company to Expand PRC Sales," *Business Asia*, April 3, 1981, p. 106.

interested trading corporations; also, it is not out of order for a firm to request an invitation from the Secretary of the Chinese Export Commodities Fair. Accompanying such a request three or four months before the Fair should be a mailing campaign as described.

The key to catching the interest of a trading company in a product is the brochure: full information about the selling company and its products is necessary. Ideally, it should be in Chinese, although English, German, or French with a Chinese introduction are acceptable; no prices should be quoted or proposals for actual transactions made at this stage. Since this promotional piece may be the only opportunity a company has to establish contact, specific and thorough detail must be included in its production. The smallest detail must not be overlooked, and special concern for Chinese sensitivities should be shown. The sensitivity of PRC officials toward political terminology is shown by the example of a Swedish firm which had to amend an English-language catalog because it referred to "North Korea." Avoid referring to "North Vietnam" also; both should be referred to as the People's Republic of Korea or Vietnam. Be especially careful of referring to Taiwan and, if you do, the country should be referred to as *Taiwan Province* and not *The Republic of China.* Further, the PRC considers Hong Kong a colony and not a country and never refer to *mainland China* or *Red China*—use either PRC or simply China.[23]

BOX 14–7: Now that's a "classy" turn down

The Chinese are very polite and frequently their responses reflect the traditional exaggerated courtesy and honorific behavior of the academic Chinese. A rejection slip from a Beijing (Peking) economic journal, received recently by a British writer, was couched in these flowing terms:

"We have read your manuscript with boundless delight. If we were to publish your paper it would be impossible for us to publish any work of a lower standard. And as it is unthinkable that, in the next thousand years, we shall see its equal, we are, to our regret, compelled to return your divine composition, and beg you a thousand times to overlook our short sight and timidity."

Source: "Atlantic Monthly, Please Take Note," *World Business Weekly*, December 15, 1981, p. 43.

In dealing with the Chinese market, cultural empathy is not only good business sense but mandatory if a company is to get an opportunity to introduce its product. One further caveat: if the Chinese language is used, utmost attention must be given to its complexities. The PRC has officially adopted simplified Chinese characters. These generally are not used outside the PRC, but they should be employed in the interests of accurate translation.

---

[23] "Doing Business in China: Initiating a Marketing Campaign," *Business America*, September 8, 1980, pp. 7–9.

PRICING AND COMPETITION

One of the outgrowths of rapidly growing world markets for industrial goods is the considerable price competition among those vying for this expanding market. The problem is compounded by aggressive competition from suppliers and by the political involvement of governments of some manufacturers. As mentioned earlier, industrial goods are often the cannon fodder of economic wars being waged to win the political allegiance of underdeveloped countries. As a result, foreign marketers are sometimes confronted with impossible price competition because prices are shaded by a foreign government for political rather than economic reasons. Today, India, Brazil, or any underdeveloped and industrializing nation can buy Russian-made machinery and equipment at prices at least 50 percent lower than those charged by American manufacturers for similar goods. Such political price competition cannot be overcome by private industry.

American manufacturers also face other kinds of price problems abroad. It has been charged that they are pricing themselves out of the market and they follow too conservative a policy with regard to price and credit. Reports from India indicate that while there is a booming market there for machine tools, selling American products is difficult, if not impossible, because of the manufacturer's insistence on payment in dollars. Soviet bloc nations and our West European competitors are not making this mistake.

Although European concerns offer liberal credit terms and payment in almost any of the world's currency, U.S. manufacturers are hesitant about granting credit and usually demand payment in dollars. Price alone is not always the sole determinant in purchasing decisions. In fact, some Venezuelan firms reportedly have indicated a willingness to pay 30 to 40 percent more for U.S. industrial products than for European products if adequate credit was available: presumably this is because of the better quality image of U.S. products. However, U.S. industrial goods are also being challenged on this front now by other competitors. One Department of Commerce study revealed that the demand for U.S. goods in Ecuador was extremely high, however, the trend was for Ecuadorians to buy from suppliers who offered the best payment terms rather than the lowest price.[24]

Equally important in industrial sales are such other factors as dependability, service, and parts replacement.

Price-quality relationship

A price-quality relationship plagues the U.S. manufacturer. Standard quality requirements of industrial products sold in the American market that require commensurately higher prices may be completely out of line for the needs of many of the underdeveloped growth markets of the world.

---

[24] "Ecuador's Market can Absorb Greater Volume of Products; Financing Remains Important," *Commerce America*, April 25, 1977, p. 30.

BOX 14–8: Selling machinery to the Arabs

Arab markets do not welcome all foreign companies indiscriminately. Some are more selective than others. Generally, Arab markets are not fruitful for the speculative— and only rarely for the highly innovative service or product, unless the latter already is fully developed, proven in other markets, and actually chaper in the short run than comparable products or processes.

Arab markets are extremely price conscious and, although they want to buy the highest quality they can get for their money, they will not choose quality at the expense of cost in most instances. If any consideration is overriding, it is price.

A foreign company's belief that its product or service is superior will convince no one in Arab markets. Even scientific evidence may not be convincing, since there will be few decision makers with the technical competence to understand it.

High technology machinery or services which require a large labor input in installation or maintenance may not be suitable or welcome. Labor at all levels must be imported in all Gulf countries. That which is available in overpopulated areas, such as Egypt, is not readily trainable in high technology work, especially since skilled supervisory personnel also are lacking.

For the Gulf, capital and, possibly, energy-intensive projects are most suitable. In Egypt, labor-intensive projects requiring minimal training and producing goods or services for a poverty-stricken mass market or for export are the most appropriate manufacturing ventures.

Lack of skilled supervisory and middle-management personnel in Gulf states makes them chary of purchasing high-technology products and processes unless a training program for locals is available and feasible.

Source: Nancy A. Shilling, "Arab Market: The Opportunities and Obstacles," *Marketing in the Middle East* (Editors: *Advertising Age* and *Industrial Marketing*, 1977).

Rather than question if American manufacturers are pricing themselves out of world markets, it may be more appropriate to ask whether or not they are advancing themselves out of some world markets with products of extremely high quality. When you pay labor $15 or more per hour, labor-saving features in a product make sense, but not when the going rate of pay is $1.50 per day as in India. One Indian observer commented that the purchase of modern equipment in the West is often justified purely in labor-saving terms. But with an adult population of 326 million and an official urban unemployment rate of 15 million, the last thing India needs is labor-saving equipment.[25] In fact, India is having serious reservations about highly automated industry. The country has embarked on a program to scale down many industries that could be labor intensive. The Labor Minister suggested that by converting to a cottage industry, a highly automated match company currently employing 15,000 workers, could create 250,000 new jobs immediately.[26]

Labor-saving features in a product have little value when time is not worth much and labor is plentiful. Also of little value is the ability of machinery

---

[25] Rex Winsbury, "India's Technology Dilemma," *World Press Review*, February 1981, p. 60.

[26] "India, a Return to Rural Capitalism," *Business Week*, June 11, 1979, p. 48.

BOX 14–9:   That cheap Japanese labor—look again at that Japanese technology

Inland Steel Company's giant new blast furnace, rising above its Indiana Harbor Works, illuminates the competitive dilemma facing the sagging American iron and steel industry.

When completed in 1979, the new "superfurnace" could reduce Inland's iron-making costs by at least $3 a ton, and thus boost the company's efficiency and profitability. But to build it, Inland had to turn for help to the world's leading innovators in blast-furnace technology (and the American steel industry's nemesis): the Japanese.

"We simply didn't have the experience to design a furnace that will eventually produce 10,000 tons of iron a day," an Inland official explained. So several years ago the company signed a technical-assistance agreement with Nippon Kokan K.K., Japan's second-largest steelmaker; the pact brought Japanese consultants to the shores of Lake Michigan and sent Inlanders to Japan.

Inland's decision to purchase what the company's magazine termed "Japanese expertise" illustrates a problem that the American steel industry would probably rather ignore in its current campaign to restrict "unfair" import competition: the Japanese, thanks to rapid, debt-financed expansion, have become probably the most-advanced and lowest-cost steel producers in the world. . . .

Although Inland is among the most profitable American steel producers, its new furnace is its first built since World War II. In the same period, Nippon Kokan has built 13 furnaces, with progressively greater capacity and productivity. Indeed, Nippon Kokan's oldest operating blast furnace dates back to 1962.

Source: David Ignatius, "U.S. Steelmakers Fail to Modernize Quickly, Fall Behind Japanese," *The Wall Street Journal*, August 3, 1977, p. 1.

---

to hold close tolerances where people are not quality-control conscious, where production runs in the American volume sense do not exist, and where skillful workers cost so little it is affordable to let them take their time to do what amounts to selective fits in assembly and repair work.[27] This does not mean there is no interest in quality or cost in developing countries like India, but that the achievement of low costs and good quality in these countries is not through high-production, high-precision equipment, and minimum labor cost but through the use of skillful labor under close supervision with a minimum of the most versatile low-cost equipment adequate for the job. Hence, for the company that wants to market its industrial goods in some countries, it may be necessary to design products for the export market with fewer functional features in order to lower the price and thereby compete effectively on price.

In addition to the price-quality relationship discussed, the issue of quality image of industrial products is becoming more of a competitive factor in industrial goods. When the United States was dominant in the marketing of industrial goods with minimum competition from other countries, some of the competitive factors in industrial marketing (such as price, service,

---

[27] For an interesting article which includes interviews from industrial customers in several countries see "Why Uncle Sam Gets a Bad Trade Report Card," *Industrial Marketing*, January 1982, pp. 50–84.

and quality) were moot issues. But today, when U.S. businesses are in competition with Germany, France, Japan, and even less developed countries such as Brazil, many of the competitive factors become more critical. For example, one interesting study done of U.S. purchasing agents on quality perceptions of industrial goods sold by the United States, West Germany, Japan, Brazil, East Germany, France, Italy, and England found that on a product quality dimension both East Germany and West Germany were perceived to have a better quality relationship than the United States, and further, that the United States, England, and Japan shared the same level of quality perception. On the dimension of marketing characteristics, which included such items as service, delivery performance, and advertising support, the United States ranked the highest, but Japan was very close in ratings. And on a third dimension, the product price factor, the United States shared the same image with West Germany, France, Brazil, England, and East Germany as being among the highest priced, whereas Japan was considered the lowest priced. Looking at Japan as a direct competitor with the United States in industrial goods, the results indicated that Japan ranked the same as the United States on quality and was just slightly below the United States on marketing characteristics. On price, the United States was the highest, and Japan was the lowest with eight other countries in between. The job of selling industrial goods requires careful attention on all fronts in order to remain competitive.[28]

Leasing in international markets

An increasingly important selling technique that helps alleviate high prices and capital shortages for capital equipment is the leasing system. The concept of equipment leasing has become increasingly important as a means of selling capital equipment in overseas markets. In fact, it is estimated that $30 billion worth (in original cost) of U.S.- and foreign-made equipment was on lease in Western Europe in 1975.[29]

The system of leasing used by industrial exporters is similar to the typical lease contracts used in the United States. Terms of the leases usually run one to five years, with payment made monthly or annually; included in the rental fee is servicing, repairs, and spare parts. Just as contracts for domestic and overseas leasing arrangements are similar, so are the basic motivations and the shortcomings. For example:

1. Leasing opens the door for a large segment of nominally financed foreign firms which can be sold on a lease but might be unable to buy for cash.

[28] Phillip D. White, "Attitudes of U.S. Purchasing Managers Toward Industrial Products Manufactured in Selected Western European Nations," *Journal of International Business Studies*, Spring/Summer 1979, p. 81.

[29] "Spotlight on U.S. Service Industries in World Markets," *Commerce America*, April 11, 1977, p. 11.

2. Leasing can ease the problems of selling new experimental equipment, since less risk is involved for the users.
3. Leasing helps guarantee better maintenance and service on overseas equipment.
4. Equipment leased and in use helps to sell other companies in that country.
5. Lease revenue tends to be more stable over a period of time than direct sales would be.

The disadvantages or shortcomings, however, take on a more international flavor. Besides the inherent disadvantages of leasing, there are some problems compounded by international relationships. In a country beset with inflation, lease contracts that include maintenance and supply parts, as most do, can lead to heavy losses toward the end of the contract period. Further, countries where leasing is most attractive are also those where spiraling inflation is most likely to occur. The added problems of currency devaluation, expropriation, or other political risks are operative longer than if the sale of the same equipment is made outright. In the light of these perils, there is greater risk in leasing than outright sale. However, there is a definite trend toward increased use of this method of selling internationally.

COUNTERTRADES[30]

Of growing importance to sales in Eastern European countries, Russia, People's Republic of China, and many less developed countries, is a sale that is paid for with something other than convertible currencies. *Countertrade* is the inclusive term used to describe transactions where all or partial payment is made in kind rather than cash. There was a significant increase in countertrade transactions during the late 1960s through the 1970s. This is primarily the result of shortages of hard currencies available to industrializing nations. For Communist countries, purchases from non-Communist suppliers must be made with monies earned from Western nations; and the less developed countries' (LDCs') inflation-ridden or weak currencies are insufficient to meet all the demands of industrialization. In all situations, hard currencies are reserved for top priority purchases while goods of less importance, as well as top priority needs, are being purchased with some form of countertrade.

Barter, the basic type of countertrade, has been used in foreign trade since the beginning of economic history. After World War I, economically devastated countries resorted to barter to cope with financial crises in the aftermath of the war. During the worldwide depression of the 1930s, barter was again revived as a means of trade, and Germany proved a most effective

---

[30] There are a variety of terms used to describe the transactions that the author classifies as *countertrades*. In order not to further confuse the issue and to help standardize terminology, I have used the terms developed by Business International Corporation.

user of barter in rebuilding after World War II. Again, in the 1980s, the use of barter is on the upswing apparently as a result of inflation.

Types of countertrade

Countertrade includes four distinct types of transactions: *barter, compensation deals, counterpurchase, and buy-back.*[31]

Barter is the direct exchange of goods between two parties in a transaction. One of the largest barter deals made to date involved Occidental Petroleum Corporation's agreement to ship superphosphoric acid to the Soviet Union for ammonia urea and potash under a 20-year, $20 billion deal. No money changed hands nor were any third parties involved. Obviously, in a barter transaction, the seller (Occidental Petroleum) must be able to dispose of the goods at a net price equal to the expected selling price in a regular, for-cash, transaction. Further, during the negotiation stage of a barter deal, the seller must have some knowledge of the market and the price for the items offered in trade. In the Russian barter trade example, the price and a market for the ammonia urea and potash were established since Occidental could use the products in its operations. But, bartered goods can range from hams to iron pellets, mineral water, furniture, or olive oil—all somewhat more difficult to establish a price and market for when customers are needed.[32] Because of the almost limitless range of goods and quality grades possible, and a lack of expertise or information necessary, sellers rely on barter houses to provide information and find potential buyers for the goods received. Another possibility is the use of a switch trader, an outsider who will "switch" the traded goods to a third country where a market exists.

Compensation deals involve payment in goods and in cash. A seller delivers lathes to a buyer in Venezuela and receives 70 percent of the payment in convertible currency and 30 percent in tanned hides and wool. In an actual deal, General Motors Corporation sold $12 million worth of locomotives and diesel engines to Yugoslavia and took cash and $4 million in Yugoslavian cutting tools as payment.[33]

An advantage of a compensation deal over barter is the immediate cash settlement of a portion of the bill; the remainder of the cash is generated after successful sale of the goods received. If the company has a use for the goods received, the process is relatively simple and uncomplicated. On the other hand, if the seller has to rely on a third party to find a buyer, the cost involved must be anticipated in the original compensation negotiation if the net proceeds to the seller are to be equal to the market price.

---

[31] *Switch trading, parallel trades, offset trades,* and *clearing agreements* are other terms used to describe countertrade but they are only variations of the four types mentioned here.

[32] Thomas M. Chesser, "Barter Becomes Big Business in World Trade," *The New York Times,* July 26, 1981, p. 15.

[33] "Accepting Imports now Exporter's Job," *Associated Press,* June 7, 1981.

BOX 14–10: Let's trade!

It goes this way: a British manufacturer undertakes an export contract for cash settlement then, under a separate deal, agrees to buy goods from the importing country either to the full value of the contract or just part of it. Then a customer for these exchanged goods must be found elsewhere in order to receive payment. The attraction for the importing country with this type of arrangement is that it effectively reduces their currency outflow. Ford provides a good example of this in practice. They swapped a consignment of Cortinas to Ecuador in return for fish manure which they then sold for cash to Norway. Other examples of counterpurchase: one company made a deal for 400 cars and accepted jam in exchange. Ford Motor Company agreed to export 500 knocked-down Escorts a year to Uruguay in exchange for thousands of sheepskin seat covers; Ford has been on the receiving end of such improbable items as school furniture, azalea plants, and even lavatory seats.

Source: "The Barter Business," *Industrial Management,* January 1976, pp. 18–19.

Counterpurchase is probably the most frequently used type of countertrade. For this trade, two contracts are negotiated. The seller agrees to sell a product at a set price to a buyer and receives payment in cash. However, the first contract is contingent on a second contract which is an agreement by the original seller to buy goods from the buyer for the total monetary amount involved in the first contract or for a set percentage of that amount. This arrangement provides the seller with more flexibility than the compensation deal since there is generally a time period (perhaps 6 to 12 months or longer) during which the second contract has to be completed. During the time that markets are sought for the goods in the second contract, the seller has received full payment for the original sale. Further, the goods to be purchased in the second contract are generally of greater variety than those offered in a compensation deal. Even greater flexibility is offered when the second contract is nonspecific, that is, the books on sales and purchases need to be cleared only at certain intervals. The seller is obligated to generate enough purchases to keep the "books balanced" or clear between purchases and sales. For example, McDonnell Douglas sold 22 DC-9s worth $100 million to Yugoslavia and, in turn, agreed to sell or buy $25 million in Yugoslavian goods. Some of McDonnell Douglas's commitment to Yugoslavia was settled by Douglas buying Yugoslavian equipment for their own use, but they also sold to others such items as hams, iron castings, rubber bumper guards, and transmission towers. They held showings for department-store buyers to sell glassware and leather goods to fulfill their counterpurchase agreement. Twice a year, Douglas officials meet to claim credits for sales and clear the books in fulfillment of their counterpurchase agreement.[34]

Product buy-back agreement is the last of the four types of countertrade transactions. This type of agreement is made when the sale involves goods

---

[34] Falko Schuster, "Barter Arrangements With Money: The Modern Form of Compensation Trading," *The Columbia Journal of World Business,* Fall 1980, pp. 61–66.

or services which produce other goods and services, i.e., production plant, production equipment, or technology. The buy-back agreement usually involves one of two situations: the seller agrees to accept as partial payment a certain portion of the output or the seller receives full price initially but agrees to buy back a certain portion of the output. For example, one U.S. firm, a farm equipment manufacturer, sold a tractor plant to Poland and was paid part in hard currency and the balance in Polish-built tractors. In another situation, General Motors Corporation bought autos from Brazil in partial payment for building an automobile manufacturing plant there. Levi Strauss and Company is taking Hungarian blue jeans, which it will sell abroad, in exchange for setting up a jeans factory near Budapest.[35] A major drawback to product buy-back agreements comes when the seller finds that the products bought back are in competition with their own similarly produced goods. On the other hand, some have found that a product buy-back agreement provides them with a supplemental source in an area of the world where there is demand but where they have no available supply.

U.S. firms hesitant to countertrade

Countertrade transactions are definitely on the increase in world trade. It is estimated that 20 percent of all international trade now involves some type of countertrade transaction and it has been predicted that this percentage will increase substantially in the near future. Much of the increase will come in trading with Third World countries; in fact, some require countertrades of some sort with all foreign trade. Indonesia requires all foreign companies awarded major government contracts to export Indonesian products equivalent to the amount of the contract. In an estimated 50 percent or more of all international trade with Communist-bloc countries, countertrade arrangements are involved.[36]

Western European and Japanese firms have the longest history of countertrade because of their trading experience with Eastern Europe. U.S. firms have been slow to accept countertrade, preferring to lose a sale rather than become involved in an unfamiliar situation. In fact, a recent survey of several hundred U.S. firms involved in international trade indicated that a majority would refuse a countertrade offer. This attitude seems to stem from inexperience and, as one respondent candidly replied, "We don't need the hassle. We have enough business without it." Regardless of prevailing U.S. attitudes, demands for countertrade probably will increase and many firms will find they have little choice but to cope with the hassles or problems of countertrade.[37]

---

[35] Roger Lowenstein, "U.S. Firms Move to 'Countertrading,'" *The Wall Street Journal,* November 4, 1981, p. 29.

[36] Joseph P. Manguno, "Jakarta to Require Foreign Firms Given Major Contracts to Export Local Goods," *Asian Wall Street Journal,* December 14, 1981, p. 8.

[37] Louis Kraar, "Having Set Up a Canton Container Plant, CIT can Hardly Help but Profit— Especially if China Ever Uses Containers," *Fortune,* March 23, 1981, p. 95.

While many U.S. firms shun barter or countertrade arrangements, others are profitably involved. Certainly one of the more interesting trades involves Pepsi-Cola which has barter arrangements with Russia and Romania. Pepsi-Cola sells Russia and Romania cola concentrate to produce Pepsi-Cola and receives vodka (sold under the brand name *Stolichnaya*) from Russia and bottled wines (sold under the brand name *Premiat*) from Romania as full payment. From all indications, this has been a very profitable arrangement for Russia, Romania, and Pepsi-Cola.[38]

Problems of countertrading

The crucial problem confronting a seller in a countertrade negotiation is determining the value and potential demand of the goods offered. Frequently there is inadequate time to conduct a market analysis; in fact, it is not unusual to have sale negotiations almost completed before countertrade is introduced as a requirement in the transaction.

Although such problems can be difficult to deal with, they can be minimized with some preparation. In most cases where losses have occurred in countertrades, the seller has been unprepared to negotiate in anything other than cash. Some preliminary research should be done in anticipation of being confronted with a countertrade proposal. Countries with a history of countertrading are easily identified and the products most likely to be offered in a countertrade can be quickly ascertained. For a company trading with Third World countries or Communist countries, these facts and some background on handling countertrades should be a part of every "pricing tool kit."[39] Once goods are acquired, they can be passed along to institutions that assist companies in selling barter goods.

Barter houses specialize in trading goods acquired through barter arrangements and are the primary outside source of aid for companies beset by the uncertainty of a countertrade. Barter houses, most of which are found in Europe, can find a market for bartered goods but the time it may require can put a financial strain on a company because its capital is tied up longer than for normal transactions. A solution to this problem would be for a company to seek loans to tide them over until sales are completed.

In the United States, there is at least one company organized to assist companies with bartered goods and their financing, and Citibank has created a countertrade department to allow the bank to act as a consultant as well as to provide financing for countertrades.

Barter houses serve a vital role in countertrade but for companies with a large percentage of their business involving barter, a third party is not

[38] Robert E. Weigand, "Apricots for Ammonia," *California Management Review,* as reprinted in *Annual Editions Marketing 81/82,* ed., Richard Windel (Guilford, Conn.: *Dushkin Publishing Group, Inc.,* 1981), pp. 204–11.

[39] "Coping With Soviet Countertrade Demands," *Business Eastern Europe,* March 27, 1981, pp. 99–100.

always the answer. Some companies have organized their own inhouse trading groups to privide the assistance needed to effectively deal in counter-trades. One such inside group, perhaps a forerunner of many to come, is Motors Trading Company, a wholly-owned subsidiary of General Motors Corporation. It is designed to develop markets for GM products in countries where cash deals or capital investments are not practical. General Motors has countertrade deals with 20 countries which account for more than 50 percent of all the business it does with Eastern-bloc nations. General Electric Co., McDonnell Douglas, and several other major U.S. corporations have recently established their own special departments to help dispose of coun-tertraded goods. In many situations, these companies have been able to deal with countertrades when the competition has been less flexible, thus enabling them to consummate a transaction not possible for the competitor to handle successfully.

There are many examples of companies losing sales to competitors who were willing to enter into countertrade agreements. For example, a U.S. oil-field equipment manufacturer claims they submitted the lowest dollar bid in an Egyptian offer but lost the sale to a bidder who offered a counterpur-chase arrangement. Incidentally, the successful company was Japanese with a sizable trading company established to dispose of the Egyptian goods received in the counterpurchase arrangement.

One experienced countertrader suggests the following be considered before entering into a countertrade agreement. (1) Is it the only way the order can be secured? (2) Is there a ready market for the goods bartered? (3) Can the countertrade portion be kept to a minimum? (4) Can the exporter handle the negotiations alone or are experts needed? (5) Has the exporter increased the contract price to cover the cost of barter? (6) Has the would-be barterer considered exchange-control regulations which require payment for exports to places outside scheduled territories? (7) Are the goods offered in exchange subject to import control? It is advisable to check this first with the trade department. Despite the U.S. government's muted objections to compensation trading it nevertheless offers the use of the usual range of services to companies undertaking such deals.[40]

SERVICE AS A PRODUCT

When thinking of exporting or foreign marketing, the image of some tangible product (a consumer durable, a piece of machinery, or clothing) generally comes to mind. The intangible product or business service (legal services, computer data services, advertising, consulting, contracting ser-vices, accounting services) is frequently overlooked as a subject of study. Accompanying the growth of multinational manufacturing and extractive

---

[40] Robert E. Weigand, "Barter and Buy-Backs—Problems for the Marketing Channel," in *Marketing In The 80s,* ed. Richard P. Bagozzi et. al., 1980 Educators' Conference Proceedings, Series No. 46, American Marketing Association, 1980, pp. 256–58.

industries is an increase in the number of service companies which have entered multinational markets.

Services is the fastest growing sector of international trade; it is estimated that services account for about one-fourth of the value of all international trade.[41] Further, in 1980, estimates put the annual rate of world growth above 15 percent compared to an estimated annual average of less than 7 percent for merchandise exports. The U.S. dominates in international services, accounting for 20.8 percent of the total, followed by the United Kingdom (9.2%), and France (8.9%). Services exported from the United States, excluding return on investment, were valued at $50.7 billion in 1980, 23 percent of all U.S. exports.[42]

BOX 14–11:   No credit limit?—but the charge is $2 million

The international credit card battle is about to spread to the Mideast where credit card holders are steadily increasing in number. Visa, American Express, Diners Club, and MasterCard currently are competing for a share of the Mideast credit business; however, the problems may differ somewhat from those in the United States.

A story reported by one credit card company demonstrated some of the problems that may arise. "One of our clients recently received a card and charged $2 million worth of jewelry in London in one week," a senior executive reported. "We pride ourselves on not having a credit limit, but we had no idea whether he could actually pay such a large amount. On the other hand, if we refused to okay the credit, we ran the risk that he would spread the word throughout Saudi Arabia and possibly do grave damage to our reputation."

As a result, the company reluctantly approved all of the purchases and, in the meantime, dispatched two executives to Riyadh with a copy of the bill. The company, however, need not have worried. The client was somewhat perplexed by the arrival of the two employees but he paid the bill at once—*in cash.*

Source: "The Mideast Credit Card Competition," *World Business Weekly*, July 13, 1981, p. 19. Reprinted by permission of the Financial Times, London.

Of the different types of services, financial and consulting are among the fastest growing.[43] U.S. consultants' billings are running about $1 billion annually and have been growing about 15 percent annually. Some of the more important U.S. based consultants derive a major portion of their earnings from international sales (see Exhibit 14–1).[44]

The growth of international services has been so rapid during the last decade it has drawn the attention of domestic companies. As a result, direct and indirect trade barriers have been imposed to restrict foreign companies

---

[41] Albert N. Alexander, "Services Exports: Brightening the '80s," *Business America*, October 20, 1980, pp. 25.

[42] Laura Wallace, "Global Trade Skirmish Looms as Restrictions on Services Multiply," *The Wall Street Journal*, October 5, 1981, p. 1.

[43] Louis Kraar, "Our Small-Loan Companies Invade Japan," *Fortune*, September 22, 1980, pp. 146–50.

[44] "International Consultants: Worldly Wisdom for Hire," *World Business Weekly*, December 15, 1980, p. 20.

EXHIBIT 14–1: U.S.-based multinational consultants

Firm	Non-U.S. billings (1979)*	Total billings (1979)*	Foreign as percent of total	Number of consultants outside the United States	Areas of expertise
McKinsey and Company	60	100	60	314	Counseling and corporate planning
Price Waterhouse	45	98	46	785	Accounting and financial management
Booz Allen and Hamilton, Incorporated	40	160	25	160	Large-scale industrial and development projects
Hay Associates	37	64	58	360	Human resource management
Arthur D. Little	33.5	140	24	226	Applied science and technology
Lester B. Knight	15	20	75	220	Productivity and manufacturing and engineering systems

* In millions of dollars.
Source: "International Consultants: Worldly Wisdom for Hire," *World Business Weekly*, December 15, 1980, p. 21.

from domestic markets. Every reason, from the protection of infant industries to national security, has been used to justify some of the restrictive practices. U.S. officials compiled a 210-page list of more than 2,000 instances of barriers to the free flow of services among nations.

The following are a sample of some of the listings. Australia will not allow foreign banks to open branches or subsidiaries; Sweden bars local offices of foreign companies from processing payrolls abroad; Argentina requires car importers to insure shipments with domestic insurance companies; and, if a U.S. company uses American models for an advertisement that will appear in a West German magazine, it has to hire the models through a German agency—even if the ad is being photographed in Manhattan.[45]

One of the more potentially damaging restrictions to both the service industry and other MNCs who rely on data transfer across borders to conduct their business are the efforts of some nations to control data in computers and the transfer of those data from one computer to another across borders. Some countries impose tariffs on the transmission of data and many nations are passing laws which would force companies to open their computer files to inspection by government agencies.[46]

Attempts to solve some of these problems are underway but, to date, they are not considered very effective. The major effort comes from the United States government which is attempting to get an agreement through the General Agreement on Trade and Tariffs (GATT) for multilateral talks on curtailing restrictive barriers to the importation of services; there appears to be little chance that anything effective will occur.[47]

The risks of going international with a business service are the same as for any other business: political risks such as currency inconvertibility, cancellation of import or export licenses, war, revolution, expropriation, and commercial credit risks involving insolvent customers or failure to pay. All of these and other risks can now be covered by FCIA (Foreign Credit Insurance Association) insurance. The only qualifications for FCIA coverage is that "a service contract must call for payment to be made in U.S. dollars and involve services performed by U.S.-based personnel.[48]

SUMMARY

Adaptability is the key to the industrial markets of the world. Industrial users must buy on a profit basis; therefore, products which fulfill their needs exactly, not more nor less than they need, are the products which will be

---

[45] Wallace, "Global Trade Skirmish Looms as Restrictions on Services Multiply, p. 1.

[46] "The Global Data War," *World Press Review,* November 1981, p. 54.

[47] "International Trade: Efforts Begin Against Barriers to Services," *Business International,* July 25, 1980, pp. 233–34.

[48] Richard Barovick, "International Services: A Major New Government Policy Issue," *Business America,* January 25, 1982, pp. 6–9.

in demand. Companies which adapt their products to the variety of differing needs are the ones that should be the most effective in the marketplace. Industrial markets are lucrative and continue to grow as more countries strive for at least a semblance of industrial self-sufficiency.

Furthermore, although a particular country's state of economic and industrial development may not provide the industrial marketer with profitable demands for products at a particular point in time, the future potential should be examined thoroughly with the thought of gaining market position. It must be remembered that the economic development of a country can pass through several stages in a short period of time. A company which establishes itself in a market and assists in this growth before it is profitable may find itself in an unparalleled competitive position once the market has developed.

As the market grows, however, so does competition from the world's industrial nations. Success will most probably be enjoyed by those companies which are user oriented and produce for the specific needs of their industrial customers.

QUESTIONS

1. Define the following terms and show the significance to international marketing:

   Inch-pound system   Universal standards
   Trade centers   Service
   Trade fairs   Compensation deals
   Price-quality relationship Countertrades
   Buy-back agreements

2. Outline the steps a manufacturer desiring to sell to the PRC would follow in order to establish contact.

3. Why does Japan's history of buying and selling through trading companies give her an advantage when trading with China?

4. Discuss why countertrading is on the increase.

5. What are the differences between consumer and industrial goods and what are the implications for international marketing? Discuss.

6. Discuss how the various stages of economic development affect the demand for industrial goods.

7. "Industrialization is typically a national issue, and industrial goods are the fodder for industrial growth." Comment.

8. ". . . the adequacy of a product must be considered in relation to the general environment within which it will be operated rather than solely on the basis of technical efficiency." Discuss the implications of this statement.

9. Why hasn't the United States been more helpful in setting universal standards for industrial equipment? Do you feel that the argument is economically sound? Discuss.

10. What role do service, replacement parts, and standards play in competition in foreign marketing? Illustrate.

11. Discuss the part industrial trade fairs and trade centers play in international marketing of industrial goods. What is the difference between industrial trade fairs and trade centers?

12. Discuss some of the more pertinent problems in pricing industrial goods.

13. What is the price-quality relationship? How does this affect a U.S. firm's comparative position in world markets?

14. Discuss leasing of industrial goods in foreign markets. Why is leasing used by the seller? By the buyer?

15. Select several countries, each at a different stage of economic development, and illustrate how the stage affects demand for industrial goods.

16. England has recently indicated it will shift from the inch-pound system to the metric system. What effect do you think this will have on the traditional U.S. relutance to such a change? Discuss the economic implications of such a move.

17. Discuss the major problems facing a company which is countertrading?

18. The "Three Ps"—patience, persistence, and product are the secrets to success in China. Comment.

Chapter 15

International promotion—
Advertising and sales promotions

International promotion is a fundamental activity in an international company's marketing mix. Once a product is developed to meet consumer needs and is properly priced and distributed, the intended consumers must be informed of the product's availability and value. International promotion consists of those activities used by marketers to inform and persuade consumers to buy. A well-designed promotion mix includes advertising, sales promotions, personal selling, and public relations which are mutually reinforcing and focused on a common objective.[1]

Developing an international promotional strategy involves five steps: (1) determining the promotional mix (the blend of advertising, personal selling, and sales promotions) by national markets; (2) determining the extent of worldwide standardization; (3) developing the most effective message(s); (4) selecting effective media; and (5) establishing the necessary controls to assist in achieving worldwide marketing objectives. The basic framework and concepts of international promotion are essentially those employed in the United States.[2] Promotion is the side of international marketing with the greatest similarities around the world. Paradoxically, it may also have the distinction of involving the greatest number of unique, culturally related problems. Adapting promotional strategy to the cultural peculiarities in the world's markets is the challenge confronting the international marketer. Promotional activities most likely to require adaptation to reflect the diversity of cultures will be stressed in this and Chapter 16. Besides an analysis of the scope and scale of world advertising, this chapter reviews some of the problems and challenges for international marketers, including organizational arrangements, basic creative strategy, international advertising media planning and selection, sales promotions, and the communications process. Chapter 16 will conclude the international promotion presentation with a discussion of personal selling and personnel management.

---

[1] Because of the strong focus public relations has on the political environment, it is discussed in Chapter 6.

[2] Those unfamiliar with the fundamentals of promotion should read a basic marketing text. See, for example, William J. Stanton, *Fundamentals of Marketing,* 6th ed. (New York: McGraw-Hill 1981), chaps. 18–20.

ROLE OF ADVERTISING

The strategic role of advertising in marketing programs varies by time, place, and company. Advertising is but one element of the promotional mix, and promotion is but one element of the marketing mix. The potential cost and accomplishment of advertising must be weighed against the cost and benefits to be gained by focusing on other elements of the promotional or marketing program. Advertising can be most effective in a nation with well-developed advertising facilities and a market that responds to such stimulation. Like any other strategic weapon, advertising should be used only when it can contribute economically and effectively to the attainment of corporate goals.

The increasing sophistication of foreign consumers and the presence of competition from *many* countries place great emphasis on the role of advertising. Advertisers from all countries have picked up American know-how and have become formidable competitors.

VOLUME OF WORLD ADVERTISING

A review of world advertising activities is somewhat like a history of advertising in the United States. Currently, advertising in underdeveloped countries resembles American advertising at the end of the 19th century. In more highly developed countries, advertising activities closely parallel American advertising of recent decades. This analogy does not hold exactly true because nearly all countries are further advanced (through imported techniques) than was the United States at a similar stage of growth. The quality of international advertising is amazingly high. In fact, some consider European ad agencies as good as, if not better for Europe than, many from the United States. In certain kinds of advertising such as cinema and poster, advertisers other than those from the United States are preeminent.

Figures developed by the International Advertising Association, the American Association of Advertising Agencies, and *Advertising Age* magazine seem to indicate that advertising expenditures throughout the world are growing at the rate of approximately 10 percent per year. In the case of Japan, the growth has been little short of phenomenal. The United States is still ahead of all other countries in terms of aggregate dollar expenditures for advertising, both as a percentage of gross national product and in dollar expenditures per capita. Because expenditures by countries outside the United States amount to an excess of $48 billion there is intense interest in international advertising on the part of American agencies.

The magnitude of dollar expenditures for advertising throughout the world does not reflect advertising's ever-greater social impact. Advertising is changing communication customs and habits in nearly all countries. (See Exhibit 15–1.) In localities where television and other commercial media are not available, there is continuing demand for the development of such

EXHIBIT 15–1:   Ad volumes in selected nations*

	Population (millions)	Total advertising expenditures (millions of U.S. dollars)	Per capita advertising expenditures (in U.S. dollars)	Percent of GNP
North America:				
United States	221.6	49,720.0	224.37	2.02
Canada	23.7	2,892.3	122.04	1.32
Mexico	66.6	489.5	7.35	0.55
Europe:				
West Germany	61.4	6,271.1	102.14	1.00
France	53.5	4,350.1	81.31	0.91
Italy	57.0	1,077.9	18.91	0.46
Spain	37.8	1,259.3	33.31	0.89
Turkey	44.3	172.0	3.88	0.31
Pacific basin:				
Japan	115.9	8,851.0	76.37	0.92
Taiwan	17.6	310.4	17.64	1.15
Thailand	44.9	92.4	2.06	0.39
Australia	14.3	1,647.0	115.17	1.37
Central and South America:				
Argentina	26.7	674.1	25.25	1.27
Brazil	125.8	1,650.0	13.12	0.80
Chile	10.9	115.0	10.55	0.75
Venezuela	15.3	378.2	24.72	0.88
Guatemala	6.8	58.9	8.66	0.92
Mideast and Africa:				
Israel	3.8	125.7	33.08	0.90
Saudi Arabia	9.6	60.8†	6.33	0.08
Ghana	11.4	7.8	0.68	0.20
South Africa	28.5	515.5	18.09	1.20
Egypt	40.6	169.4	4.17	1.02
Iran	37.1	71.4	1.92	0.08
Iraq	12.5	41.8	3.34	0.17

* All figures are for 1979.
† Radio and television not available for advertising.
Source: *World Advertising Expenditures 1980 Edition,* Starch INRA Hooper, International Advertising Association, Tables I and II, pp. 8–13.

media. The development of mass communications broadens local concepts of the world and of political affairs and may prove to be of major importance in influencing and speeding cultural, political, and economic integration. Even in Russia there is a need for advertising. It is estimated that Russians spend more than $500 million annually on broadcast and print space to help create demand for new products. The development of mass advertising media is also important in the development of international markets. In many areas of the world, people have income with which to buy products, but these potential consumers are not a part of world markets because they lack information about available products.

Although mass communications have improved markedly in the past decade, advertisers are still without adequate media alternatives in many parts of the world. A UNESCO study shows that some 2 billion persons residing in 100 countries lack adequate communications facilities. Nineteen African countries have no daily press, and newspaper circulation is only one per hundred persons compared to 50 per hundred in the United Kingdom. On the basis of per capita advertising expenditures and recent growth patterns, it is apparent that nearly all nations can anticipate continued advertising expansion.

ORGANIZATIONAL AND AGENCY ARRANGEMENTS

Almost all large firms use advertising agencies; but, whether or not an agency is used, the alternative types of organization are relevant. Under one organizational framework, the parent company maintains central control of advertising policy and implements advertising campaigns from a central firm. A second alternative calls for central policy control but local implementation in the countries in question. A third possible structure uses local policy control and local implementation.

Innumerable variations of these basic patterns have been tried by international advertisers, but basically the question comes down to one of centralization versus decentralization. The chief arguments for centralization relate to the use of high-level talent in managerial skills in the home office, to the economy inherent in running a centralized campaign, and to corporate control. These arguments relate to managerial *efficiency* but such efficiency in advertising operations may be detrimental to market development and market effectiveness. Such limitations constitute the primary argument for decentralization; proponents of this concept argue that diverse cultures require local expertise, as do the problems of language translation and understanding the media requirements and availabilities in various markets.

Agency arrangements

Whatever system is utilized, it is probable that the advertiser will employ the services of advertising agencies using (1) a domestic agency, (2) a company-owned agency in each country, (3) one of the large international agencies with branches in various countries, or (4) a coordinating agency dealing with independents in various countries. In this last arrangement, the coordinating agency provides overall direction, and the independent agencies provide local expertise.

Advertising agencies exist in nearly every commercially significant country in the world. Admittedly, the development of the agency field is still spotty. Numerous countries offer only one agency, while others permit a choice among only a few marginal agencies. The ideal of having a choice among competent agencies may soon be possible if the world rate of agency formation continues.

Agency operations

American agencies operating abroad have followed five patterns in developing their international operations. Some of the largest, such as Young and Rubicam, J. Walter Thompson Company and McCann-Erickson, have set up their own wholly-owned agencies. Others, such as Fred Bates and BBDO, have purchased existing major overseas agencies. Still others buy an interest (majority, half, or minority) in foreign agencies, thus combining expertise from both agencies. Another system was used by D'Arcy Advertising; they joined forces with agencies in other countries to set up third companies which they jointly own. The most common setup has been the development of corresponding agency relationships; these are foreign agencies which handle advertising in that country for American agencies. Regardless of the agency arrangement, great discrepancies in the level and caliber of service provided exist.

Compensation arrangements for advertising agencies throughout the world are based on the U.S. system of 15 percent commissions. However, agency commission patterns throughout the world are not as consistently uniform as they are in the United States; in some countries, agency commissions vary from medium to medium. Services provided by advertising agencies also vary greatly but few foreign agencies offer full services.

Even such a sophisticated business function as advertising may find it is involved in primitive practices. In some parts of the world, advertisers often pay for the promotion with the product advertised rather than with cash. Kickbacks on agency commissions are prevalent in some parts of the world and account in part for the low profitability of international advertising agencies. In some countries such as Mexico, India, and Greece, the advertiser returns half the media commissions to the agencies. In many of the developing countries, long-term credit is used to attract clients. Venezuela, for example, has a rather highly developed advertising agency system, yet 120 days is the *average* time between the agency's payment to the media and the client's payment. Some agencies actually negotiate agency contracts on the size of the kickback and the duration of the credit extension. Such policies are bound to result in less-effective selection and, therefore, less-effective advertising effort than choosing an agency on merit alone.

The task of selecting and maintaining international advertising agencies is not easy. The comprehensive services of American agencies may be one reason so many firms seek branch offices of these agencies.

CREATIVE CHALLENGES

The growing intensity of international competition coupled with the complexity of marketing multinationally demand that the international advertiser function at the absolute highest creative level. Advertisers from around the world have developed their skills and abilities to the point that advertisements from different countries reveal basic similarities and a growing level of sophistication. To complicate matters further, boundaries are placed on creativity by company policy and legal, language, cultural, media, production, and cost limitations.

Standardization versus modification

A multinational advertiser establishes an environment for creativity through basic advertising policies. Every area of advertising activity needs basic policies covering centralized or decentralized authority, use of single or multiple foreign or domestic agencies, appropriation and allocation procedures, copy, media, and research. All other areas covered by policy statements in domestic advertising should be governed by policy statements in foreign operations. One of the most widely debated areas of policy pertains to the degree of advertising variation from country to country. One view sees advertising customized for each individual country or region because every country is a special problem. Executives in such companies argue that the only way to achieve adequate and relevant advertising is to develop separate campaigns for each country. At the other extreme are those who suggest that advertising can be standardized for all markets of the world. Fortunately, neither extreme prevails today.[3]

The mature and experienced international advertiser realizes that the question of standardization or modification depends more on motivational patterns than geography. Advertising must relate to motivation; if people in different markets buy similar products for significantly different reasons, the advertising campaigns should be reoriented to these reasons. When various markets react best to similar stimuli, it would be unwise to vary the stimulus just for the sake of variation. In those instances when purchase motivations are similar for a given product, many companies follow a strategy of "pattern" standardization of advertising, that is, a strategy designed for standardized worldwide application but allowing some degree of modification to meet local situations.[4] In this way, some economies of standardization can be achieved at the same time important specific cultural differences between countries are accommodated. Royal Dutch Shell has been successful in carrying its "Come to Shell for Answers" campaign developed in

---

[3] Jacob Hornik, "Comparative Evaluation of International vs. National Advertising Strategies," *Columbia Journal of World Business,* Spring 1980, pp. 36–46.

[4] Michael Colvin, Roger Heeler, and Jim Thorpe, "Developing International Advertising Strategy," *Journal of Marketing,* Fall 1980, pp. 73–79.

the United States to 12 countries. The basic theme, to create a positive public image for Shell, was carried through in each country with some minor modifications to meet country needs.[5]

BOX 15–1: Selling Levi's around the world

Levi's are sold in more than 70 countries with different cultural and political aspects affecting advertising appeals. The company is evaluating its present advertising strategy to determine whether to apply a worldwide strategy to all advertising or settle on localized campaigns in each country. Currently, the company creates campaigns locally or regionally. Here are some of the appeals used:

In Europe, TV commercials have a super-sexy appeal.

In the United Kingdom, ads emphasize that Levi's are an American brand and star an all-American hero, the cowboy, in fantasy wild West settings.

In Japan, local jeans companies had already positioned themselves as American. To differentiate Levi's, the company positioned themselves as *legendary* American jeans with commercials themed "Heroes Wear Levi's" featuring clips of cult figures like James Dean. The Japanese responded—awareness of Levi's in Japan went from 35 percent to 95 percent as a result of this campaign.

In Brazil, the market is strongly influenced by fashion trends emanating from the Continent rather than America. Thus, the ads for Brazil are filmed in Paris featuring young people, cool amidst a wild Parisian traffic scene.

In Australia, commercials were designed to build brand awareness with product benefits. The lines "fit looks tight, doesn't feel tight, can feel comfortable all night" and "a legend doesn't come apart at the seams" highlighted Levi's quality image and "since 1850 Levi jeans have handled everything from bucking broncos . . ." stressed Levi's unique positioning.

Source: Adapted from "Exporting a Legend," *International Advertiser*, November/December 1981, pp. 2–3.

The Levi company has recently changed from all localized ads to a pattern advertising strategy "where the broad outlines of the campaign are given but the details are not."[6] Another example of pattern advertising is the successful Esso "Tiger in the Tank" campaign which was translated and exported intact. Record sales have been rung up because of the slogans *Pack'den Tiger in den Tank* (West Germany), *Stop 'n Tijger in uw Tank* (Netherlands), *Mettez un tigre dans votre moteur* (France), and *Metti un tigre nel motore* (Italy). (In France and Italy "motor" was used because there is no directly translatable word for *tank*.)[7] Seven-Up advertises in dozens of countries, yet its policy allows variation in specific detail to suit local market conditions. Certain elements of Seven-Up advertising remain constant, whether in Africa, Europe, or South America: the Seven-Up logo-

[5] Roger W. Fox, "Can an International Campaign get Much Better?", *International Advertiser*, July/August 1981, pp. 16–18.

[6] Dennis Chase and Eugene Bacot, "Levi Zipping up World Image," *Advertising Age*, September 14, 1981, p. 34.

[7] James Killough, "Improved Payoffs From Transnational Advertising," *Harvard Business Review*, July/August 1978, p. 107.

type; the basic color combination; the Seven-Up bottle crown; and fundamental point-of-purchase units such as illuminated plastic signs, metal tackers,
and brand signs. Libby is another company which has successfully standardized creativity from country to country through effective techniques. The
Libby commercial, used by subsidiaries throughout the world, features a
clown, pantomime, and the simple story of the clown enjoying Libby food
products.[8]

While attempts to control costs and to control worldwide promotional
programs place emphasis on standardization, there is strong evidence that
basic national differences between countries require adaptation in many
situations. The consensus among multinational companies is that it is beneficial to standardize from a cost and control point and most strive for high
standardization. In order to achieve a high degree of standardization, most
firms develop a prototype advertising campaign at headquarters and disseminate it to subsidiaries; each subsidiary is expected to adopt the basic
theme but is left with a great deal of autonomy in varying the creative
expression of that theme. Thus, some attempt at control of the advertising
theme worldwide is achieved, but where necessary, it is possible to include
the peculiarities of the local marketplace. Successful standardization of international advertising depends on good intracompany communications to
ensure coordination and control.[9]

In reflecting on what a marketer is trying to achieve through advertising,
i.e., communicate with the market, inform consumers about a product, and
persuade them to buy, the issue of standardization or local modification is
the wrong question. The question must be: Does our advertisement communicate to the market what is relevant to that market? If a standardized promotion
can effectively communicate in all markets, then standardize; otherwise, modify. It is the message received that generates sales whether it is standardized
or modified.[10]

Legal and tax considerations

In some countries, advertising is more closely regulated than in others
which requires modification of the creative approach from country to country.
Laws pertaining to advertising may restrict the amount spent on advertising,
media used, the type of product advertised, manner in which price may
be advertised, the type of copy and illustration material used, and other
aspects of the advertising program. In Germany, for example, it is against

---

[8] S. Watson Dunn, "Effect of National Identity on Multinational Promotional Strategy in
Europe," *Journal of Marketing,* October 1976, p. 55.

[9] For a discussion on ways to ensure intracompany communications see Robert F. Roth,
"Intra-Company Communications," *International Advertiser,* September/October 1981, pp.
21–25.

[10] Dean M. Peebles, John K. Ryans, Jr., and Ivan R. Vernon, "Coordinating International
Advertising," *Journal of Marketing,* January 1978, p. 28.

the law to use comparative terminology. An advertiser cannot say that one soap gets clothes cleaner than another because the statement implies that other products do not get clothes clean. Advertisers live under the threat of immediate lawsuit from competitors if they claim their brand is best. Similar restrictions exist in most European countries; in Italy, even common words like deodorant and perspiration are banned from television.[11]

In Kuwait, the government-controlled TV network allows only 32 minutes of advertising per day and this in the evenings. Commercials are controlled to exclude superlative descriptions, indecent words, fearful or shocking shots, indecent clothing or dancing, contests, hatred or revenge shots, or attacks on competition. It is also illegal to advertise cigarettes, lighters, pharmaceuticals, alcohol, airlines, chocolates and candy.[12]

Some countries have special taxes which apply to advertising and which might restrict creative freedom in media selection. The tax structure in Austria probably best illustrates how advertising taxation can distort media choice by changing the cost ratios of various media. In federal states, with the exception of Bergenland and Tyrol, there is a 10 percent ad tax on ad insertions. For posters there is a 10–30 percent tax, according to state and municipality. Radio advertising carries a 10 percent tax, except in Tyrol where it is 20 percent. In Salzburg, Steiermark, Karnten, and Voralbert, there is no tax. There is a uniform ad tax of 10 percent throughout the country on television. Cinema advertising has a 10 percent tax in Vienna, 20 percent tax in Bergenland, and 30 percent tax in Steiermark. There is no cinema tax in the other federal states.

The Monopolies Commission in England has accused The Procter & Gamble Co. and Unilever of creating a monopoly (duopoly?) situation by spending nearly one fourth of their revenues on advertising. The companies were also criticized for earning too much. Legislation for new taxes and restrictions on advertising has been introduced and some passed nearly every year in countries which have traditionally imposed minimal restrictions on advertising and free competition. The variations between countries in interpreting what constitutes acceptable, honest advertising causes most problems. What is acceptable in one country may be deemed false and misleading in another. Legal and tax considerations comprise a major deterrent to complete standardization of advertising.

Language limitations

Language is one of the major barriers to effective communication through advertising. The problem involves the different languages in different coun-

---

[11] See, for example, J. J. Boddewyn, "The Global Spread of Advertising Regulation," *MSU Business Topics,* Spring 1981, pp. 5–13.

[12] "Familiarity Breeds Success in the Middle East," *International Advertiser,* November/ December 1980, pp. 11–12.

tries, different languages within one country, and the subtler problems of linguistic nuance and vernacular.

Incautious handling of language has created problems for companies in nearly every country. Some automotive examples suffice. Chrysler Corporation was nearly laughed out of Spain when it translated the U.S. theme advertising, "Dart is Power." To the Spanish, the phrase implied that buyers lacked but sought sexual vigor. Ford floundered on the linguistic problems of number; in many languages the word *company* is plural rather than singular, as in English. "Ford Have Something for It" trumpeted one headline in English. Ford goofed again when it named its low-cost "Third World" truck *Fiera,* which means "ugly old woman" in Spanish. American Motors has had its problems too. Market research showed that AMC's *Matador* name meant virility and excitement, but when the car was introduced in Puerto Rico it was discovered that the word meant "killer"—"an unfortunate choice for Puerto Rico, which has an unusually high traffic fatality rate." The advertising manager for Honeywell in Germany wrote of a Rambler ad, I've been reading the copy over and over again—it does not make sense. Rambler ran into the same trap most U.S. companies run into when they think of using translated U.S. copy. Instead of translating, it needs rewriting in the new language.[13]

Low literacy in many countries seriously impedes communications and calls for greater creativity and use of verbal media. Turkey, for example, has a literacy rate of approximately 25 percent; an advertiser attempting to reach a large segment of the population must use radio advertising. Multiple languages within a country or advertising area provide another problem for the advertiser. Even a tiny country like Switzerland has three separate languages. The melting-pot character of the Israeli population accounts for some 50 languages. A Jerusalem commentator says that even though Hebrew "has become a negotiable instrument of daily speech, this has yet to be converted into advertising idiom."

Language translation encounters innumerable barriers which impede effective, idiomatic translation and thereby hampers communication. This is especially apparent in advertising materials. Abstraction, terse writing, and word economy, the most effective tools of the advertiser, pose problems for translators. Communication is impeded by the great diversity of cultural heritage and education which exists within countries and which causes varying interpretations of even single sentences and simple concepts. Some companies have tried to solve the translation problem by hiring foreign translators who live in the United States, but this usually is not satisfactory; both the language and the translator change so the expatriate in the United States is out of touch after a few years. Everyday words have different mean-

---

[13] See David A Ricks, Jeffrey S. Arpan, and Marilyn Y. Fu, "Pitfalls in Advertising Overseas," *Journal of Advertising Research,* reprinted in *International Advertising and Marketing,* ed. S. Watson Dunn and E. S. Lorimer (Columbus, Ohio: Grid, 1979) pp. 87–93.

ings in different cultures. The advertising manager of Ampex commented, "We can't do our French translations in Geneva any more; the French insisted that the *patois* used by the Genevese was closer to Pawnee or Swahili than the language of their customers. And any day now I expect our man in Marseilles will ask to change our Paris ads for the Marseilles market." Even pronunciation causes problems; Wm. Wrigley Jr. Company had trouble selling Spearmint gum in Germany until it changed the spelling to Speermint. Seeking universally pronounceable brand names, that company selected the brand YUSI for an inexpensive gum to market in low-income countries.[14]

BOX 15–2: A European consumer?

"The day you find a product labeled 'Made in Europe,' send it to me and I'll frame it as an historic document." So speaks the head of a French advertising agency.

"Europe?" questions another. "It's a concept, no more. Certainly we advertise all over the continent, but it's a lot more difficult than it is in the United States. Do you know how many languages there are here?" (In the Common Market alone, there are six languages: English, French, German, Italian, Danish, and Dutch, not counting Flemish, Luxembourgois, Gaelic, or the various—and numerous—regional dialects.)

"A Europroduct?" asks another ad agency man. "What's that? The only one I know of that's acceptable anywhere is a Eurocheque. Money is one of the few things that can be internationalized."

Source: Barbara Farnsworth, "Advertising in Europe," © European Community. Reprinted with permission. All rights reserved.

Cultural diversity

Overcoming the problems of communicating to people in diverse cultures is one of the great creative challenges in advertising. In moving from one culture to another, communication is more difficult because cultural factors largely determine the way various phenomena will be perceived. If the perceptual framework is different, perception of the message itself will differ.

International marketers are becoming accustomed to the problems of adapting from culture to culture. Knowledge of differing symbolisms of colors is a basic part of the international marketer's encyclopedia. An astute marketer knows that white in Europe is associated with purity but in Asia it is commonly associated with death. The marketer must also be sophisticated enough to know that the presence of black in the West or white in Eastern countries does not automatically connote death. Color is a small part of the communications package, but if the symbolism is understood in each culture, the marketer will have an educated choice of using or not using various colors.

---

[14] For an excellent discussion of language and marketing, see Vern Terpstra, *The Cultural Environment of International Business* (Cincinnati: South-Western Publishing, 1978), chap. 1.

Knowledge of cultural diversity must include the total advertising project. General Mills had two problems with one product. When they introduced instant cake mixes in the United States and England, they had the problem of overcoming the housewife's guilt feelings. When they introduced instant cake mixes in Japan, their problem changed; cakes were not commonly eaten in Japan. There was no guilt feeling associated with the instant cakes, but the housewife was concerned about failing. She wanted the cake mix as complete as possible. In testing TV commercials promoting the notion that making cake is as easy as making rice, they learned they were offending the Japanese housewife who believes the preparation of rice requires great skill.

Existing perceptions based on tradition and heritage are often hard to overcome. Marketing researchers in Hong Kong found that cheese is associated with Yeung-Yen (foreigners) and rejected by the Chinese. The concept of cooling and heating the body is important in Chinese thinking; malted milk is considered heating, while fresh milk is cooling; brandy is sustaining, whiskey harmful. Even marketers in their home countries often have to deal with problems of traditional conceptions. French drivers were so accustomed to buying gasoline refined in foreign countries that when gas was refined locally they assumed the French product was inferior.

As though it were not enough for advertisers to be concerned with differences among nations, they find subcultures within a country require attention as well. In Hong Kong, for example, there are 10 different patterns of breakfast eating. The youth of a country almost always constitutes a different consuming culture from the older people, and urban dwellers differ significantly from rural dwellers. Besides these differences, there is the problem of changing traditions. In all countries, people of all ages, urban or rural,

---

BOX 15–3:   Where the commercial is the program

There are around 775 radio stations in Mexico, 57 of these in Mexico City (30 AM, 27 FM). Radio covers 83 percent of Mexico; 95 percent of Mexico City. There are close to 9 million radio households in the country and 2,715,000 in Mexico City.

Mexicans consider radio an excellent medium because of the high market penetration. But program ratings are low. In order to make an impact, the advertiser has to buy a large number of stations and spots. It is not unusual for a liquor advertiser to buy 40 spots per day on 32 stations in Mexico City alone—a total of 200 spots per week per station.

There are only two stations in Mexico that carry continuous programming for 15 to 25 minutes. On most stations, there are 24 minutes of commercial time per hour, and two commercial minutes per break with approximately 11 breaks per hour. As such, the entertainment on Mexican radio is so fragmented that listeners change stations constantly and never become attached to one program, announcer, or station.

Needless to say advertising clutter is tremendous. The usual commercial length is 30 seconds; the longest is 60 and the shortest, 10.

Source: Adapted from Erika Engels Levine, "Commercial Radio in Latin America," *International Advertiser*, January/February 1982, p. 27.

cling to their heritage to a certain degree but are willing to change some areas of behavior. A few years back, it was unthinkable to try to market coffee in Japan, but recently it has become the fashionable drink for younger people and urban dwellers who like to think of themselves as very European and sophisticated. Coffee drinking in Japan was introduced with instant coffee and there is virtually no market for anything else. As shown by the examples in this section, cultural diversity requires the advertiser to be constantly alert to cultural variation because it constitutes one of the greatest creative challenges in international business.

Media limitations

Media are discussed at length later, so mention of the limitations on creative strategy imposed by media will note only that media limitations may diminish the role of advertising in the promotional program and may force marketers to emphasize other elements of the marketing mix.

A marketer's creativity is certainly challenged when a television commercial is limited to 10 showings a year with no two exposures closer than 10 days, as is the case in Italy. Creative advertisers in some countries have even developed their own media for overcoming media limitations. In some African countries, advertisers run boats up and down the rivers playing popular music and broadcasting commercials into the bush as they travel.

Production and cost limitations

Creativity is especially important when a budget is small or where there are severe production limitations; limitations which exist in nearly every advertising medium. Poor quality printing and the lack of high-grade paper are simple examples. The necessity for low-cost reproduction in small markets poses another problem in many countries. For example, hand-painted billboards must be used instead of printed sheets because the limited number of billboards does not warrant the production of printed sheets.

The cost of reaching different market segments can become almost prohibitive in some instances. In Hong Kong, for example, it is imperative that ads run in both English and Chinese. Even if the market being sought is Chinese, English must be used so Orientals will know the product is not inferior and being advertised only to Asians. To continue the Far Eastern example, advertisers in Bangkok must use English, Chinese, and Thai languages. In Singapore, besides English and Chinese, Malay and Tamil are necessary if the market is to be reached. All these factors, even translations alone, impose significant cost and production burdens for the advertiser.

Credibility of advertising

Consumer criticisms of advertising are not just a phenomenon of the U.S. market. Consumer concern with the standards and believability of ad-

---

BOX 15–4:   Underbudgeting or over-fragmenting your international advertising budget

When a company launches a new product or opens a new sales territory in its domestic market, it takes certain steps to assure the success of that venture. It should do no less abroad. But inadequate international budgets are one of the most common errors of international advertising.

There is simply no way to inform and persuade prospects in international markets at as low a cost-per-thousand as can be done in the homogeneous domestic market. And don't let anyone tell you differently. Much of the current literature on this subject is bogus. Recently, an advertising journal reported on an interview with the international buyer of a major advertising agency. The buyer was quoted as saying how surprised clients are to find they can do the same thing in international markets for a quarter of a million dollars which would cost $2 million to do in the United States. That's nonsense. If the buyer is really talking about doing *the same thing*.

Take the following real-world example: the universe of materials handling and physical distribution buying influences is about 200,000 in both the United States and Western Europe. You can reach the U.S. universe with three magazines in one language, 7-by-10-inch size, all printed offset, same screen. To reach the universe in Western Europe it takes 21 magazines, published in nine languages, in widely different page sizes. In one country alone, the U.K., in one language, English, the sizes of the magazines vary from a standard page to a 5-by-15-inch page. What's more, screens and printing processes vary.

You can imagine the additional make-ready costs involved in preparing the European program. And even when specialized media are available, the *cost-per-thousand is often as much as twice as high in Europe as it is in the United States*. Often precise media aren't available, so advertisers are forced to buy more waste circulation. Obviously economies of scale are missing in nonhomogeneous areas of the world.

Don't think your money will go as far in international advertising as it does in domestic. It won't.

Source: "Another Deadly Sin: Underbudgeting or Over-Fragmenting Your International Advertising Budget," *International Marketing Report*, July 1977, pp. 1–2.

---

vertising may have jumped the Atlantic to Europe more swiftly than having many marketing techniques. A study of a representative sample of European consumers indicated that only half believe advertisements give consumers any useful information, six out of ten believe that advertising means higher prices (if a product is heavily advertised, it will often sell for more than brands that are seldom or never advertised), and nearly eight out of ten believe advertising often makes them buy things they do not really need or that ads are often deceptive about product quality. The advertising industry is sufficiently concerned with the negative attitudes of consumers and governments and with the poor practices of some advertisers that the International Advertising Association and other national and international industry groups have developed a variety of self-regulating codes.[15] Sponsors of these codes feel that unless the advertisers themselves come up with an effective framework for control, governments will intervene. This threat of

---

[15] James P. Neelankavil and Albert B. Stridsberg, *Advertising Self-Regulation* (New York: Hastings House Publishers, 1980) 211 pp.

government intervention has spurred interested groups in Europe to develop codes to ensure the majority of ads conform to standards set for "honesty, truth, and decency."[16] In those countries where the credibility of advertising is questioned and in those where the consumerism movement exists (as discussed in Chapter 13), the creativity of the advertiser will be challenged.

MEDIA PLANNING AND ANALYSIS

Tactical considerations

Although nearly every sizable nation essentially has the same kinds of media, there are a number of specific considerations, problems, and differences encountered from one nation to another. The primary areas an advertiser must consider in international advertising are the availability, cost, and coverage of the media. Local variations and lack of market data provide fertile areas for additional attention.

Imagine the ingenuity required of advertisers who confront the following situations:

1. TV commercials are sandwiched together in a string of 10 to 50 commercials within one station break in Brazil.
2. In many countries, national coverage means using as many as 40 to 50 different media.
3. Specialized media which reach small segments of the market only. In the Netherlands, there are Catholic, Protestant, Socialist, neutral, and other specialized broadcasting systems.
4. In Germany, TV scheduling for an entire year must be arranged by August 30 of the preceding year, and there is no guarantee that commercials intended for summer viewing will not be run in the middle of winter.

Availability. One of the contrasts of international advertising is that some countries have too few advertising media and others have too many. In some countries, certain advertising media are forbidden by government edict to accept some advertising materials. Such restrictions are most prevalent in radio and television broadcasting. In numerous countries, there are just too few magazines and newspapers to run all the advertising offered to them. Conversely, some nations segment the market with so many newspapers that the advertiser cannot gain effective coverage at a reasonable cost. Gilberto Sozzani, head of an Italian advertising agency, comments about his country: "One fundamental rule. You cannot buy what you want." Additional information on availability is discussed in the section on specific media below.

---

[16] Elizabeth Guider, "Venice Session: Ad Self-Rule Still Alive in Europe," *Advertising Age*, December 7, 1981, p. 70.

Cost.   Media prices are susceptible to negotiation in most countries. Agency space discounts are often split with the client in order to bring down the cost of media. The advertiser may find the cost of reaching a prospect through advertising is dependent on the agent's bargaining ability. The per-contract cost will vary widely from country to country. One study showed the cost of reaching a thousand readers in 11 different European countries ranged from $1.58 in Belgium to $5.91 in Italy; in women's service magazines, the page cost per thousand circulation ranged from $2.51 in Denmark to $10.87 in West Germany.

BOX 15–5:   The wash bucket they understand!!

One noted advertising executive in Mexico comments that ads that are successful in Mexico might be considered too simple or unsophisticated in the United States or Europe but they do work well in Mexico.

He offers an example to illustrate his point. Ariel, the largest-selling detergent in Mexico, successfully used a campaign which put the detergent into a washtub. In the TV ad, the suds rotate in a washtub which turns into a washing machine. Following the promotional dialogue, the clothes are taken out spanking clean.

He stresses that to the Mexican viewer the bucket is the washer. "We deal with people who still do their daily wash in a washtub. But they can relate to the luxury of a washing machine. What the ad says is that no matter what you wash your clothes in, Ariel gets them clean."

Source: Adapted from Laurie M. Kassman, "Ed Noble's Mexican Mastery," *International Advertiser*, November/December 1980, p. 35.

A recent five-year study of advertising costs in nine major foreign markets indicated that advertising costs were increasing at a rate of 10 to 15 percent each year; a rate considerably higher than the cost increases in U.S. media. In some markets, because of the shortage of advertising time on commercial television, prices have increased substantially more.

Coverage.   Closely akin to the cost dilemma is the problem of coverage. Two points are particularly important: one pertains to the difficulty of reaching certain sectors of the population with advertising; the other relates to the lack of information on coverage. In many world marketplaces, a wide variety of media must be used to reach the majority of the market. In some countries, large numbers of separate media have divided markets into uneconomical advertising segments. A majority of the native population of less developed countries cannot be reached readily through the medium of advertising.

Verification of circulation or coverage figures is a difficult task; even though many countries have organizations like the Audit Bureau of Circulation, it does not assure accurate circulation and audience data. For example, the president of the Mexican National Advertisers Association charged that newspaper circulation figures are "grossly exaggerated." He suggested that "As a rule agencies divide these figures in two and take the result with a grain of salt."[17] Radio and television audiences are always difficult to measure, but at least in most countries, geographic coverage is known. Not so in Brazil where privately owned transmitters are under contract to broadcasting stations. When the transcription contracts are shifted from station to station, a station may advise agencies of its increased audience resulting from a new pact with the owner of a transmitter while the station with the old contract does not mention the shift, thus giving rise to a ghost audience. Private companies gather and disseminate audience and cost data but do not guarantee accuracy.

Lack of market data. Even where advertising coverage can be measured with some accuracy, there are still questions about the composition of the market reached. Lack of available market data seems to characterize most international markets; advertisers shoud have information on income, age, and geographic distribution, but even such basic data seems chronically illusive. If adequate market data were available, they would show great variation in the audiences of different periodicals and broadcast media. They would also show the great diversity and variations which exist from country to country. Often even a small nation will have half a dozen or more subcultures within its borders. The advertiser is confounded with the problem of selecting media which can provide coverage for an entire market.

Media patterns

Perhaps the dominant pattern in the arena of world advertising is the proliferation of advertising media. Some countries have more media than their economy or population can adequately support. However, many countries have been long underdeveloped in terms of commercial mass communication media. The addition of other magazines, newspapers, and radio and television stations will be a boon to many advertisers.

In most countries, the introduction of television as an advertising medium greatly distorts traditional media patterns. The pattern in the United States is roughly paralleled in other countries. After the introduction of television, the initial impact is to sharply reduce advertising on radio and cause significant reductions in newspaper and magazine advertising. Within about five years of the introduction of television, there is a gradual shift back to radio and print media. Once established, television generally keeps a strong share of the market.

Exhibit 15–2 illustrates the variety of local media expenditure patterns found throughout the world. Variation in dollar expenditures by different kinds of media reflects rather directly the effectiveness of those different media in communicating with local audiences.

---

[17] For a comprehensive review of major audits in Europe see Rosemarie Grieb, "What the Audits Tell," *International Advertiser,* May/June 1981, pp. 45–47.

EXHIBIT 15–2:   Media expenditures (millions of U.S. dollars)*

Region	Print†	Television	Radio	Total
U.S. and Canada	$20,410.1	$10,645.3	$3,685.9	$34,741.3
Europe	14,797.6	3,162.2	927.7	18,887.5
Asia	3,920.6	3,565.6	601.1	8,087.3
Latin America	1,170.2	1,602.7	671.6	3,444.5
Australia and New Zealand	952.4	566.8	177.5	1,696.7
Mideast and Africa	558.5	159.0	88.6	806.1
Total world 59 countries	$41,809.4	$19,701.6	$6,152.4	$67,663.4

* All figures are for 1979.
† Print includes newspapers, consumer magazines, and trade and technical magazines.
Source: *World Advertising Expenditures 1980 Edition*, Starch INRA Hooper, International Advertising Assoc., pp. 16–17.

Specific media information

An attempt to evaluate specific characteristics of each medium is beyond the scope of this discussion. Furthermore, such information would quickly become outdated because of the rapid changes in the international advertising media field. It may be interesting, however, to examine some of the particularly unique international characteristics of various advertising media. In most instances, the major implications of each variation may be discerned from the data presented.

Newspapers.   The newspaper industry is suffering in some countries from lack of competition and choking in others because of it. In the United States, most cities have just two major daily newspapers. In many countries, the opposite is true with so many newspapers an advertiser has trouble reaching even partial market coverage. Tiny Lebanon, for example, with a population of only 1.5 million, has 210 daily or weekly newspapers; only four have a circulation of over 10,000, with the average circulation being 3,500. Imagine the complexity of trying to reach 200,000 households through the newspaper medium in Lebanon. In Turkey, in addition to the problem of selecting from some 380 newspapers, the advertiser must also be concerned with the political position of the newspapers used so the product's reputation is not harmed through affiliations with unpopular positions.

Contrast the foregoing examples with Japan where there are five national daily newspapers; the largest, *Asahi*, has a circulation of almost 7 million, reaching 85 percent of all politicians and government officials, 81 percent of all business people, 44 percent of the nation's college graduates, and nearly 40 percent of households with incomes in the upper-middle range. Unfortunately, the complications of producing a Japanese-language newspaper are such that the newspaper contains just 16 to 20 pages. Connections are necessary to buy advertising space; Asahi has been known to turn down over a million dollars a month in advertising revenue.

Newspapers customarily list timeliness and short lead time for advertisements as one of their major advantages, yet in an international context that, too, changes. In many countries there is a long time lag before an advertisement can be run in a newspaper. In India, paper shortages require ads be booked up to six months before their desired publication. An advertising executive describes a similar condition in Indonesia: "The situation at the newspapers is almost indescribable. Because of a lack of paper, the bigger newspapers are constantly short of advertising space and this means that you have to bribe the administration every time you want to run an ad." Furthermore, newspapers simply cannot be made larger to accommodate the increase in advertising demand. One newspaper publisher indicated that because of equipment limitations it is impossible to print more than 12 pages daily; thus, when advertising demand exceeds the space allocated for advertising, some must be postponed.[18]

Policies regarding separation between editorial and advertising content in newspapers provide another basis for contrast on the international scene. In some countries, it is possible to buy editorial space for advertising and promotional purposes. "The news columns are for sale not only to the government but to anyone who has the price." Since there is no indication that the space is paid for, it is impossible to tell exactly how much advertising appears in a given newspaper. The government, along with private industry, helps publishers pay reporters by handing out a monthly stipend to reporters on a given beat. Foreign newspapers cannot be considered as homogeneous advertising entities, so the advertiser must exert considerable judgment in spending international advertising dollars in newspapers.

Magazines. The use of foreign national consumer magazines by international advertisers has been notably low because of the many problems involved. Few magazines have large circulations or provide dependable circulation figures. Technical magazines are used rather extensively to promote export goods; but, as in the case of newspapers, paper shortages cause placement problems. One British agency manager says, "Can you imagine what it feels like to be a media planner here when the largest magazine accepts up to twice as many advertisements as it has space to run them in? Then they decide what advertisements will go in just before going to press by means of a raffle." Local practices such as these may be key items favoring the growth of so-called international media which attempt to serve many nations. There is such a shortage of business and technical journals in underdeveloped nations that in countries like India it is not unusual to find complicated technical advertising being run in daily newspapers, even though only 1 or 2 percent of the newspaper's readers are likely to be potential customers.

Advertisers accustomed to the broad assortment of magazines published

---

[18] "Ads Limited by Newspapers in Marketing in the Middle East," *Industrial Marketing*, 1978, p. 48.

in economically advanced countries may have to reassess media strategies involving magazines as they shift their attention from country to country. The media void not only may shift media usage but could force the company to change its entire promotion mix and could affect distribution channels and market coverage.

Radio and television. Possibly because of their inherent entertainment value, radio and television have become major communications media in most nations. (See Exhibit 15–3.) Most populous areas have television broadcasting facilities. In some markets, such as Japan, television has become almost a national obsession and thus finds tremendous audiences for its advertisers. Radio has been relegated to a subordinate position in the media race in countries where television facilities are well developed. In many countries, however, radio is a particularly important and vital advertising medium because it is the only one which reaches large segments of the population.

Television and radio advertising availability varies between countries. Three patterns are discernible; competitive commercial broadcasting, commercial monopolies, and noncommercial broadcasting. Countries with free competitive commercial radio and television normally encourage competition and have minimal broadcast regulations. Local or national monopolies are granted by the government in other countries; individual stations or networks may then accept radio commercials according to rules established by the government. In some countries, the commercial monopolies may accept all the advertising they wish; in others, only spot advertising is permissible and programs may not be sponsored. In some countries, live commercials are not permitted; in others, commercial stations must compete for audiences against the government's noncommercial broadcasting network.

In some countries, no commercial radio or television is permitted, but several of the traditional noncommercial countries have changed their policies in recent years because television production is so expensive. The argument over commercial television in the Netherlands toppled the government and forced the cabinet to resign. As the Prime Minister handed his resignation to the Queen, he said "I never knew that television was such a difficult business." Countries with limited commercial television cause availability problems for advertisers.[19] Germany, for example, permits only 20 minutes a day for commercials and runs them bunched together between 6 and 8 p.m. daily, except Sundays and holidays. Not only is the time segment for commercials controlled, so are content and audience. For example, the Quebec, Canada, government passed a bill completely banning television advertising directed toward children and all commercials that urge people to borrow money; further, the beer/liquor industry has been told that advertising can no longer imply people will enjoy themselves if they drink.

---

[19] "Where Advertisers Will It, There's a Way," *World Business Weekly,* February 16, 1981, p. 12.

EXHIBIT 15–3: Radio and television ownership in selected countries*

Country	Radios (thousands)	Televisions (thousands)
Europe:		
Austria	2,280	2,114
W. Germany	22,770	20,760
Hungary†	2,577	2,557
Netherlands†	4,500	4,000
Portugal	1,950	1,660
Sweden†	3,500	3,000
United Kingdom†	50,600	19,000
North America:		
Canada†	23,677	9,900
Cuba†	1,895	800
Mexico	9,000	7,500
United States	450,000	127,421
South America:		
Argentina	6,107	4,629
Chile†	2,519	1,610
Colombia†	5,300	1,627
Venezuela†	5,273	1,530
Asia:		
India†	19,980	677
Iran‡	7,000	2,000
Israel	1,500	900
South Korea	13,000	6,000
Saudi Arabia	N.A.	1,200
Oceania:		
Australia†	12,500	5,500
New Zealand	3,092	860
Africa:		
Kenya§	600	30
Nigeria†	7,000	300
South Africa	17,000	1,300

* All data for 1979 unless otherwise indicated.
† 1977 data.
‡ 1976 data.
§ 1978 data.
Sources: *World Advertising Expenditures 1980 Edition,* Starch INRA Hooper, International Advertising Assoc., Tables 8 and 9, pp. 37–38; *Statistical Yearbook, 1980* (England: UNESCO, 1980), Table 10.2, pp. 1210–17; *Business Latin America,* December 24, 1980, p. 414.

Although commercial programming is limited, people in most countries have an opportunity to hear or view commercial radio and television. Entrepreneurs in the radio-television field have discovered audiences in commercially restricted countries are hungry for commercial television and radio and that marketers are eager to bring their messages into these countries. Because of both business and public demand for more programming, countries that have not allowed private broadcast media have changed their laws in recent years to allow privately-owned broadcasting stations. Italy, which had no private/local radio or TV until 1976, currently has some 300 privately owned stations.[20] In countries where advertising has not been permitted on government-owned stations, there has been some softening of restrictions, allowing limited amounts of airtime for commercials. In Belgium, for example, advertising now will be allowed on state-controlled radio and television, but television advertising will be concentrated in time slots at the beginning and end of evening programs.[21]

Despite such limitations, television as a major medium for advertising is growing in most countries. In England, for example, there are three TV channels and two are reserved for the BBC which carries no advertising. The commercial channel had revenues of $1.3 billion in 1980—three times the figure for 1975.[22]

BOX 15–6:   Worldwide television by satellite

Worldwide television is a reality in Latin America. On October 11, 1981, over 270 million Spanish-speaking viewers in 20 countries tuned in to the premiere of Univision, a joint venture of SIN, Mexico's Televisa, and Spain's Radio-Television Espanola. Companies such as Colgate-Palmolive Co., Coca-Cola, Kimberly-Clark, and Bacardi paid $140,000 for a minute on the total network. Spots could be bought locally as well.

Dealing with different accents and intonations is perhaps the first question a multinational advertiser might raise. The network recommended that commercials be developed with neutral Spanish; the analogy in the United States is Midwest English.

Crossing eight time zones, these countries were reached by Univision: Argentina, Bolivia, Colombia, Costa Rica, Chile, Dominican Republic, Ecuador, El Salvador, Guatemala, Honduras, Mexico, Nicaragua, Panama, Paraguay, Peru, Spain, United States, Uruguay, and Venezuela.

Source: Adapted from "Univision Unites the Spanish-Speaking World," *International Advertiser,* January/February 1982, p. 30.

Of increasing importance in TV advertising is the growth and development of satellite TV broadcasting. Although not now in place, by 1983 there are plans to have two satellites over Europe. These two satellites will cover most of Europe and broadcast over six channels. The ability to reach all of Europe with a single message will challenge the creativity of advertisers and put greater emphasis on standardized messages.

Both advertisers and governments are concerned about the impact of satellite TV. Governments are concerned because they see satellite TV as losing control of their airways. As discussed earlier, commercials in many

---

[20] "Italy's Private TV Networks Prove Strong Magnet for MNC Advertising," *Business Europe,* December 5, 1980, pp. 385–86.

[21] "Commercial TV and Radio Come to Belgium," *International Advertiser,* November/December 1981, p. 4.

[22] "The Fight Over Commercial TV," *World Business Weekly,* November 17, 1980, p. 32.

countries are severely restricted and programming is frequently restricted as well.[23]

Advertisers must face the problems of developing advertising campaigns that will be effective across European borders. One such problem has already arisen with Renault. When Renault Auto introduced the new "World Car," Renault 9, for all Europe, many distributors throughout Europe did not like the name and wanted to modify it to fit local markets. The brand name *Renault 9* had been selected, in part, as a pan-European brand name that could be advertised via satellite to all of Europe.[24]

The reality of satellite TV raises the issue of standardization (which satellite TV would necessitate) versus locally developed ads. Problems such as different languages and laws raise doubts about the effectiveness of pan-European ads. There are strong feelings that any ad designed for all of Europe would be so bland that the universal TV commercial would be "no more than a video billboard."[25]

Lack of reliable audience data is another major problem in international marketing via radio and television. Measurement of radio and television audiences is always a precarious business even where techniques are as highly developed as they are in the United States. In most countries, audience measurement is either unaudited, or auditing associations have no effective power. Despite the lack of data on audience, many advertisers use radio and television extensively. They justify their inclusion in the media schedule on the inherent logic favoring the use of these media or defend its use on a basis of sales results.

Other media.   Restrictions on the major media in performing the advertising communication function adequately causes advertisers in various parts of the world to call on lesser media for the solution of particular local problems. Cinema plays a large advertising role in many countries.

The dearth of trade and industrial magazines in most countries places great emphasis on direct mail. As is often the case in international marketing, however, even such a basic medium is subject to some odd and novel quirks. For example, in Chile, direct mail is virtually eliminated as an effective medium because the sender pays only part of the mailing fee; the letter carrier must collect additional postage for every item delivered. Obviously, advertisers cannot afford to alienate customers by forcing them to pay for unsolicited advertisements. Despite some similar limitations with direct mail, many companies have found it a meaningful way to reach their markets. For example, *Reader's Digest* has used direct mail advertising in Mexico quite successfully in marketing their magazines; and, in Socialist countries,

---

[23] Jasper Becker and Wellington Long," Belgium, RTL in TV Clash," *Advertising Age,* July 13, 1981, p. 28.

[24] Carolyn Pfaff, "Renault 9 Sparks Debate," *Advertising Age,* November 2, 1981, p. 38.

[25] Dennis Chase, "Exec has Doubts on Europe Satellite TV," *Advertising Age,* December 7, 1981, p. 60.

direct mail is considered one of the most effective ways to reach those responsible for making industrial goods purchases. Industrial advertisers are heavy mail users and rely on catalogs and sales sheets to generate large volumes of international business.

Billboards are regulated in many countries in addition to their natural limitations. In Switzerland, small signs and posters are permitted in urban areas, but billboards as such are unknown. Billboards are also useful in countries with high illiteracy rates because messages can be conveyed pictorially.

In Haiti, sound trucks equipped with powerful loudspeakers provide an effective and widespread advertising medium. Private contractors own the equipment and sell advertising space much as a radio station would. This medium effectively combats the problems of illiteracy, lack of radio and television set ownership, and limited print media circulation.

For industrial advertisers one of the most powerful international media is the trade show or trade fair. Products and product demonstrations almost automatically surmount all communications barriers. As part of the U.S. Department of Commerce's international promotion activities, the U.S. government sponsors trade fair centers in a variety of cities around the world, including London, Frankfurt, Milan, Bangkok, Tokyo, and Stockholm.

In addition to trade fairs sponsored by governments, a number of private firms sponsor their own, including a flying fair using converted jet airliners as exhibition halls, a floating fair using ships as showrooms, and fairs sponsored by international trade and professional associations.

SALES PROMOTION

All marketing activities other than advertising, personal selling, and publicity, that stimulate consumer purchases and improve retailer or middleman effectiveness and cooperation are sales promotions. Cents-off, in-store demonstrations, samples, coupons, product tie-ins, contests, sweepstakes, sponsorship of special events such as concerts and fairs, and point-of-purchase displays are types of sales promotion devices designed to supplement advertising and personal selling in the promotional mix.

Sales promotions are short-term efforts directed to the consumer and/or retailer to achieve such specific objectives as: (1) consumer-product trial and/or immediate purchase, (2) consumer introduction to the store, (3) gaining retail point-of-purchase displays, (4) encouraging stores to stock the product, and (5) supporting and augmenting advertising and personal sales efforts. An example of sales promotion is the African cigarette manufacturer who, in addition to regular advertising, sponsored musical groups, river explorations, and participated in local fairs in attempts to make the public aware of the product.[26] In a similar vein, R. J. Reynolds Tobacco entered

---

[26] "Marketing in Africa: How BAT Promotes Locally-Made Products," *Business Europe,* September 23, 1977, p. 300.

into an agreement with a European clothing manufacturer to carry a silhouette of their camel on a designer collection of clothing as a sales promotion effort for both.

In markets where the consumer is hard to reach because of media limitations, the percentage of the promotional budget allocated to sales promotions may have to be increased. In some less developed countries, sales promotions constitute the major portion of the promotional effort in rural and less-accessible parts of the market. For example, in parts of Latin America, a portion of the advertising-sales budget for both Pepsi-Cola and Coca-Cola Companies is spent on "carnival trucks" which make frequent trips to outlying villages to promote their products. When a carnival truck makes a stop in a village, it may show a movie or provide some other kind of entertainment and an unopened bottle of the product purchased from the local retailer is the price of admission. The unopened bottle is to be exchanged for a cold bottle plus a coupon for another bottle. This promotional effort tends to stimulate sales and encourages local retailers, who are given prior notice of the carnival truck's arrival, to stock the product. Nearly 100 percent coverage of retailers in the village is achieved with this type of promotion. In other situations, village stores may be given free samples, have the outsides of their stores painted, or receive clock signs in attempts to promote sales.

As is the case in advertising, the success of the promotion may depend on local adaptation. Major constraints are imposed by local laws which may not permit premiums or free gifts to be given. Some countries' laws control the amount of discount given at retail, others require permits for all sales promotions, and, in at least one country, no competitor is permitted to spend more on a sales promotion than any other company selling the product. Effective sales promotions can enhance the advertising and personal selling efforts and, in some instances, may be an effective substitute when environmental constraints prevent full utilization of advertising.

INTERNATIONAL ADVERTISING AND THE COMMUNICATIONS PROCESS

Promotional activities (advertising, personal selling, sales promotions, and public relations) are basically a communications process. All the attendant problems of developing an effective promotional strategy in domestic marketing plus all the cultural problems discussed above must be overcome to have a successful international promotional program. A major consideration for foreign marketers is to ascertain that all constraints (cultural diversity, media limitations, legal problems, etc.) are controlled so that the right message is communicated and is the same message received by prospective consumers. International communications may fail for a variety of reasons: a message may not get through because of media inadequacy; the message may be received by the intended audience but not be understood because of different cultural interpretations; or the message may reach the intended audience and be understood but have no effect because the marketer did not correctly assess the needs and wants of the target market.

The effectiveness of promotional strategy can be jeopardized by so many different influences that a marketer must be certain no influences are overlooked. Those international executives who understand the communications process will be better equipped to manage the diversity they face in developing an international promotional program.

In the communications process each of the seven identifiable segments can ultimately affect the accuracy of the process. As illustrated in Exhibit 15–4, the process consists of (1) an information source—an international marketing executive with a product message to communicate; (2) encoding—the message from the source converted into effective symbolism for transmission to a receiver; (3) a message channel—the sales force and/or advertising media which will convey the encoded message to the intended receiver; (4) decoding—the interpretation by the receiver of the symbolism transmitted from the information source; (5) receiver—consumer action by those who receive the message and are the target for the thought transmitted; (6) feedback—information about the effectiveness of the message which flows from the receiver (the intended target) back to the information source for evaluation of the effectiveness of the process; and, to complete the pro-

EXHIBIT 15–4:   The international communications process

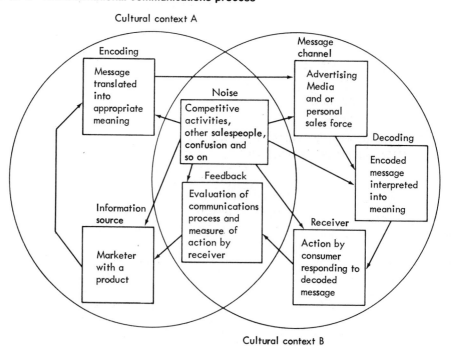

cess, (7) noise—uncontrollable and unpredictable influences such as competitive activities and confusion which detract from the process and can affect any or all of the other six steps. Unfortunately, the process is not as simple as just sending a message via a medium to a receiver and being certain that the intended message sent is the same one perceived by the receiver. In Exhibit 15-4, the communications-process steps are encased in Cultural Context A and Cultural Context B to illustrate the influences complicating the process when the message is encoded in one culture and decoded in another. If not properly considered, the different cultural contexts can increase the probability of misunderstanding.

Most promotional misfires or mistakes in international marketing are attributable to one or several of these steps not proprerly reflecting cultural influences and/or a general lack of knowledge about the target market. A review of some of the points discussed in this chapter will serve to illustrate this point. The information source is a marketer with a product to sell to a specific target market. The product message to be conveyed should reflect the needs and wants of the target market; however, as many previous examples have illustrated, the marketer's perception of market needs and actual market needs do not always coincide. This is especially true when the marketer relies more on the SRC (self-reference criterion) than on effective research. It can never be assumed that "if it sells well in one country, it will sell in another!" For example, bicycles designed and sold in the United States to consumers fulfilling recreational-exercise needs cannot be sold for the same reasons in a market where the primary use of the bicycle is transportation. Cavity reducing fluoride toothpastes sell well the United States where healthy teeth are perceived as important, but they have limited appeal in markets such as Great Britain and the French areas of Canada where the reason for buying toothpaste is breath control.[27]

Thus, from the onset of the communications process, if basic needs are incorrectly defined, communications will fail even though the remaining steps in the process are executed properly because an incorrect or meaningless message is received.

The encoding step in the system can cause problems even with a proper message. At this step such factors as color, values, beliefs, and tastes can cause the international marketer to incorrectly symbolize the message. For example, the marketer wants the product to convey coolness so the color green is used; however, people in the tropics might decode green as dangerous or associate it with disease. Another example of the encoding process causing failure is General Motors' use of "Body by Fisher" to symbolize craftsmanship, a necessary factor for successfully selling their automobiles in Europe. The message decoded into a meaningless, if not negative, "Corpse by Fisher."

---

[27] James Killough, "Improved Payoffs From Transnational Advertising," *Harvard Business Review*, July/August 1981, p. 106.

In the United States, the Marlboro man sells a lot of cigarettes but in Hong Kong, the appeal failed. The Hong Kong consumers are increasingly affluent buyers and very urbane, so they saw little charm in riding around in the hot sun all day. The basic need or want can be correctly identified but the encoding step in the communications process may render the result ineffective.

BOX 15–7:   What's in a name?

If you are going to do business in Europe, you should become familiar with *Firenze, 's Gravenhage, Hellas, Helsingfors, Kobenhavn, Koln, Moskva, Munchen, Norge, Osterreich, Polska, Praha, Sverige,* and *Warszawa.* They are countries and cities we know as Florence, The Hague, Greece, Helsinki, Copenhagen, Cologne, Moscow, Munich, Norway, Austria, Poland, Prague, Sweden, and Warsaw.

You can imagine how those same names have been converted into other languages! In French, just as one example, Austria is *l'Autriche,* Belgium is *la Belgique,* England *l'Angleterre,* Germany *l'Allemagne,* London *Londres,* The Netherlands *Les Pays-Bas,* and Spain *l'Espagne.*

Source: Howard G. Sawyer, "If It's Mardi, This Must Be la Belgique, or, What We Do to Each Other's Names." Reprinted from *Industrial Marketing,* July 1977, p. 133, by Crain Communications, Inc., Chicago.

Message channels must be carefully selected if an encoded message is to reach the consumer. Media problems are generally thought of in terms of the difficulty in getting a message to the intended market. Problems of literacy, media availability, and types of media create problems in the communications process at this step. Errors such as using television as a medium when only a small percentage of an intended market are exposed to TV or using print media for a channel of communications when the majority of the intended users cannot read are examples of ineffective media channel selection in the communications process.

Decoding problems are generally created by improper encoding, causing such errors as Pepsi's "Come Alive" slogan which decoded as "Come out of the grave," and Chevrolet's brand name for the NOVA model which decoded into Spanish as No Va!—meaning it "doesn't go." Decoding errors may also occur accidently. Such was the case with Colgate-Palmolive's selection of the brand name CUE for their toothpaste. The brand name was not intended to have any symbolism; nevertheless, it was decoded by the French into a pornographic word. In some cases, the intended symbolism has no meaning to the decoder. One soft drink manufacturer's advertisement promised a thirst-quenching reward based on the concepts "Glacier Fresh" or "Avalanche of Taste" in a part of the world where wintery mountain temperatures are an unknown experience. Errors at the receiver end of the process generally result from a combination of factors: an improper message resulting from incorrect knowledge of use patterns, poor encoding producing a meaningless message, poor media selection that does not get the message to the receiver, or inaccurate decoding by the receiver so that the message is garbled or incorrect.

Finally, the feedback step of the communications process is important as a check on the effectiveness of the other steps. Companies that do not measure their communications efforts are apt to allow errors of source, encoding, media selection, decoding, or receiver to continue longer than necessary. In fact, a proper feedback system would allow a company to correct errors before substantial damage could occur.

In addition to the problems inherent in the steps outlined, the communications process's effectiveness can be impaired by *noise*. Noise is all other external influences such as competitive advertising, other sales personnel, and confusion at the receiving end which can detract from the ultimate effectiveness of the communications process. Noise is a disruptive force interfering with the process at any step and is frequently beyond the control of the sender or the receiver. The significance is that at one or all steps in the process, cultural factors, or the marketer's SRC can affect the ultimate success of the communications. For example, the message, encoding, media,

---

BOX 15–8: Some advertising misses and near-misses

Fortunately some culturally incorrect ads are caught before they get into print. Here are some that were stopped in time:

An American cleansing-product manufacturer developed some commercials that showed people tossing hats around in jest. One advertisement had a green hat landing on a male model's head. It was pointed out to the advertiser that among the Chinese a green hat signifies that the male in question has an unfaithful wife.*

A U.S. luggage manufacturer came up with the idea of designing a Middle East advertising campaign around an illustration showing its suitcases being flown aloft by a magic carpet. A pretest showed that the Arab audience thought it was an advertisement for Samsonite *Carpets.†*

The foregoing ads were caught in time, this one wasn't. Parker Pen Company translated a counter display card for their brand of ink which had been very successful in the United States. The card said, "Avoid Embarrassment—use Quink." The Spanish translation, "Evite embarazos—use Quink," unfortunately meant idiomatically "avoid pregnancy—use Quink."‡

A British ad agency thought the Fiat 127 Palio (a sporty automobile) was a nice bit of goods with a shapely rear end and, for the English audience, coined the slogan: "If it were a lady, it would get its bottom pinched." There were 21 individual complaints about the ad along with one letter with 34 indignant feminist signatures. The ad was considered "offensive" and "tantamount to inciting sexual molestation." The agency disagreed saying it thought the advertisement would "generally be interpreted as a humorous allusion to the Italian origin of the car." Shows you how wrong you can be.§

* "Be Sure Not to Wear a Green Hat if You Visit in Hong Kong," *The Wall Street Journal*, May 10, 1979, p. 1.
† "How to Sell Success in the Middle East," *International Management*, October 1981, p. 61.
‡ "Oscar S. Cornejo, "Avoid Embarrassments in Latin America," *International Advertiser*, May/June 1981, p. 12.
§ "An Ad With a (humorous) Italian Accent," *World Business Weekly*, April 21, 1980, p. 39.

and the intended receiver can be designed perfectly but the inability of
the receiver to decode may render the final message inoperative. In designing an international promotional strategy, the international marketer can
effectively use this model as a guide to help assure all potential constraints
and problems are considered so that the final communication received and
the action taken corresponds with the intent of the source.

ADVERTISING AND ECONOMIC DEVELOPMENT

Advertising is both potentially and actually a force enhancing economic
development. Newspapers, magazines, television, and radio have all developed and flourished in large part because of the great sums of money
supplied to these media through advertising expenditures. The growing
economic health of the media, and the freedom from central control which
advertising funds make possible, greatly enhance communications throughout the world; and effective communication is a basic requirement of economic development.

Most analyses of the economic aspects of advertising concentrate on
the contributions of advertising in helping to develop mass markets, which
in turn foster mass production and facilitate mass distribution.

It is axiomatic that when consumers are exposed to products which are
new and attractive to them, they raise their own personal goals and consumption aspirations and are motivated to work harder to earn the new products
they want. Authorities who have studied motivational patterns in underdeveloped countries attribute slow economic development to low levels of personal aspiration and motivation. People who have become apathetic because
they are habituated to poverty may be motivated to increased efforts simply
through exposure to a wide variety of desirable goods.

Advertising's function is not to rob sales from competitors or to gull the
unsophisticated, but to teach new need-satisfying consumption patterns in
developing countries. As one authority notes, "The role of the mass media
in developing countries is often to spur primary demand instead of building
brand preference as in industrialized countries."[28] Advertising has demonstrated its effectiveness as a teacher of new ways of living. It shows people
how to use products and gives them confidence to try better foods, new
ways of keeping clean, use of tools, and a whole host of improved ways
of living. Advertising also explains the use of money to purchase alternatives,
to save for the future and for future purchases. In effect, advertising helps
to change expectations for the material future as well as aid economic and
social change.

Once mass markets have been developed, mass production inevitably
follows, bringing the consequent economies of large-scale operation. Then

---

[28] Paul Michell, "Infrastructures and International Marketing Effectiveness," *Columbia Journal of World Business,* Spring 1979, p. 94.

advertising enters the picture again to facilitate mass distribution by helping to establish brand names, product preferences, and product information and by performing other consumer-assistance functions. Perhaps the most eloquent testimonial to the economic relevance of advertising is the extensive use of advertising in communist countries which deny the efficacy of advertising in their economic doctrine but employ it in their distribution systems. Mass markets, mass production, and mass distribution are enhanced by advertising, so despite its many shortcomings, advertising does contribute significantly to economic development.

BOX 15–9: First, you have to sell them on the idea of shaving or what do you do when a Coca-Cola bottle is your biggest competitor?

Gillette is trying to sell razor blades all around the world, but in many lands the company first has to sell people on the idea of shaving. Competition to Gillette razors ranges from pairs of coins used as tweezers to honed edges on broken soda bottles.

The firm has been developing overseas markets since it first sold razor blades to the British 75 years ago. Today its international division sells toiletries in 22 countries and operates 29 foreign plants. Gillette is now in the Third World, laying the groundwork for what could be a thriving market when developing nations develop a need for razor blades and deodorant.

One of Gillette's more popular marketing devices in Africa and Asia is a giant shaving brush. The brush is carried from village to village in vans equipped with wash basins, towels, and razors. When the native hucksters who travel in the van attract a crowd, the big brush is produced and used to paste a volunteer with a faceful of shaving cream. He is then shaved, and, in an atmosphere of great hilarity, other villagers are invited into the van to try their hand at lather and blade. "It's a long process, developing a market," commented the assistant general manager of Gillette International.

Source: News report by *Associated Press*, August 1980.

The power of advertising in changing expectations is not always received with a positive reaction in some countries. Indonesia, for example, has banned all TV advertising on the country's only TV channel which is state owned. The ban was imposed to placate those who feared that advertising would stir materialist wants and lead the predominantly rural population (80% rural) to envy those in the cities. A random survey of the content of 30 minutes of TV commercials seems to support the idea that most advertised products were out of the reach of most of the rural viewers. Of the 38 commercials in the 30-minute sample, 19 offered goods that catered to the wealthy—among the 19 were 5 commercials for cars and motor bikes, 3 for color TV sets, and 5 for cosmetics. Most of the commercials were set in an atmosphere of luxury living, far removed from the modest realities of people who have an annual per capita income under $400. Further, a survey found that in one village on the most populous island of Java, people bought large quantities of pills that promised quick relief from colds. Asked why, "the villagers replied they believed the tablets can make the user strong like the karate expert in the commercial."[29] In many countries, there is a feeling that advertising and especially TV advertising is too powerful and persuades consumers to buy what they do not need. Certainly this is an issue that has been debated in the United States for many years.

SUMMARY

Similarities in advertising from country to country are more apparent than real. Though it is true that advertisers can adapt their basic skills to any environment, it is equally true that much of their information base will be irrelevant. International advertisers face unique legal, language, media, and production limitations. The nature and extent of these limitations varies largely with the stage of economic and marketing development of the countries in which they are doing business. In the more highly developed countries, advertisers have a wider range of media, production capability, and skilled personnel at their disposal, but they still must cope with cultural, legal, and language problems.

Basic considerations in international advertising relate to organizational questions of centralization of responsibility and a standardized approach for all countries. The most logical conclusion seems to be that, when buying motives and company objectives are the same for various countries, the advertising orientation can be the same. When they vary from nation to nation, the advertising effort will have to reflect these variations. In any case, variety in media availability, coverage, and effectiveness will have to be taken into consideration in the advertiser's plans. Therefore, even if common appeals are used, they may have to be presented by a radio broadcast in one country, by cinema in another, and by television in still a third.

A skilled advertising practitioner must be sensitive to the environment and alert to new facts about the market. It is also essential for success in international advertising endeavors to pay close attention to the communications process and the steps involved.

Questions

1. Define:

International media	Noise
Pirate radio	Sales promotion
Promotion mix	Communications process
	Encoding

---

[29] Wasief Djajanto, "Indonesia Government Expands Ad Ban," *Advertising Age,* March 16, 1981, p. 22.

2. "Perhaps advertising is the side of international marketing with the greatest similarities from country to country throughout the world. Paradoxically, despite its many similarities, it may also be credited with the greatest number of unique problems in international marketing." Discuss.

3. Someone once commented that advertising is America's greatest export. Discuss.

4. Select three dissimilar countries from Exhibit 15–1 and explain differences in advertising per capita as best you can.

5. "Advertising is changing communication customs and habits in nearly all countries." Explain.

6. Outline some of the major problems confronting an international advertiser.

7. Defend either side of the proposition that advertising can be standardized for all countries.

8. Review the basic areas of advertising regulation. Are such regulations purely foreign phenomena?

9. How can advertisers overcome the problems of low literacy in their markets?

10. What special media problems confront the international advertiser?

11. Discuss the reason for "pattern" advertising.

12. Discuss the advantages and problems in using satellite TV advertising in Europe or any other group of countries.

13. Will the ability to broadcast advertisements over TV satellites increase or decrease the need for standardization of advertisements? What are the problems associated with satellite broadcasting? Comment.

14. "In many of the world's marketplaces, a broad variety of media must be utilized to reach the majority of the market." Explain.

15. Cinema advertising is unimportant in the United States but a major medium in such countries as Austria. Why?

16. Identify some of the major differences in media usage patterns from the information in Exhibit 15–2. Explain each variation.

17. "Foreign newspapers obviously cannot be considered as homogeneous advertising entities." Elaborate. *Literacy , Dialects, gov't.*

18. Borrow a foreign magazine from the library. Compare the foreign advertising to that in an American magazine.

19. What is sales promotion and how is it used in international marketing?

20. Show how the communications process can help an international marketer avoid problems in international advertising.

21. Take each of the steps of the communications process and give an example of how cultural differences can affect the final message received.

22. Discuss the problems created because the communications process is initiated in one cultural context and ends in another.

23. What is the importance of feedback in the communications process? of noise?

Chapter 16

Personal selling and personnel management

As international business becomes increasingly competitive, companies find they must take direct responsibility for marketing personnel in foreign markets to attain marketing objectives. What kinds of marketing personnel are involved? Those who have direct and continuing responsibility for international marketing activities including those in the home office organization. This chapter is concerned with personnel who have marketing management responsibility and direct field assignments; specifically, personnel who make up the international sales force and their managers. The sales force comprises the numerical bulk of people employed in foreign positions and deals most directly with middlemen and the public in foreign markets.

"What is an international sales force?" Such a force is composed of personnel from the parent company, foreign nationals directed by a foreign sales or domestic sales manager operating abroad, or a group of individuals from *both* the parent country and the country in which business is being sought. To think only in terms of an international sales force doing business in one foreign country is also misleading; in many instances, the international salesperson does business in a number of countries.

International organization, international distribution channels, and international personnel management are three interrelated aspects of international distribution arrangements yet each is distinctly separate.

The personnel-needs requirements and organizational structure of the international marketing function present some interesting variations. The tasks of building, training, compensating, and motivating an international marketing group generate unique problems at every stage of development and management. Although the conceptual orientation of marketing personnel management is similar for domestic and foreign operations, international marketing personnel management presents a variety of unique problems. The material in this chapter illustrates some of the alternatives and problems a firm attempting to manage its own marketing/sales operations must deal with.

BOX 16–1: It's still work

"In my judgment foreign service is not exciting *per se.* I really don't find much in the way of added stimulation coming to work in the morning in Brussels than I did in California, New York, or any other place."

Source: An American executive.

ANALYSIS OF PERSONNEL NEEDS

Study after study of problems in international business focuses specifically on the need for qualified personnel and the chronic shortage of it. As markets develop in size and wealth and as they attract an increasing number of competitors, there is likely to be a continuing shortage of qualified marketing personnel.

Four categories of personnel requirements can be identified in the international marketing effort: (1) home-office personnel, (2) temporary personnel, (3) marketing managers abroad, and (4) foreign sales forces.

Home-office staff directly concerned with international marketing efforts should be considered international personnel; besides those directly responsible, it can also include people involved with advertising, packaging, distribution systems, and product development. Some companies have found their efforts to extend operations internationally hampered because they do not have experienced, qualified, home-office personnel to provide the informed home-office guidance and support necessary for the success of such an effort.

Temporary personnel are troubleshooters and start-up teams transferable to any location where new operations are being initiated or where existing operations have lost key personnel or are experiencing managerial difficulties. General Motors Corporation has a team of professional expatriates called HOSP (Home Office Status Personnel) who are shuffled from assignment to assignment around the world. GM's operations provide an interesting perspective: in addition to the 300 HOSP, the company has about 2,000 U.S.-based personnel assigned to the overseas division, and some 162,000 personnel (mostly nationals) in overseas assignments.

The number of marketing management personnel actually assigned in foreign countries varies according to the operation, but generally it is not large. For a given country it may include only the marketing manager for that country; or for a larger operation, it may include a marketing manager, an advertising manager, a sales manager, and someone in charge of middleman relations. Such personnel are either foreign nationals or expatriates, but most companies utilize foreign nationals in as many management positions as possible.

The sales force itself is by far the largest market personnel requirement abroad for most companies, and includes three types of sales personnel: (1) the *expatriate* salesperson, who is working in a foreign country; (2)

BOX 16–2:   Coca-Cola and American Standards, Inc., truly multinational?

When U.S. companies become more involved in foreign markets, will their managements take on an international character? Well they certainly have at the Coca-Cola
Company and American Standard, Inc.

When J. Paul Austin retired as Chairman and Chief Executive Officer, he was
replaced by Roberto Goizueta, a refugee from Castro's Cuba. The other members
of Goizueta's new management team include his chief financial officer, an Egyptian;
and, as president of Coca-Cola U.S.A., an Argentine; and his marketing vice-president,
a Mexican. There is one Iowan among the top five officers, the President of Coca-
Cola Company. Once, when all five were making a presentation, the Iowan followed
the other four and in his perfect Midwestern diction commented, "I'd like to apologize
for my accent. I hope it doesn't detract from the international flavor of the company."

At American Standard, Inc., eight out of 28 vice-presidential posts at corporate
headquarters are filled by foreign-born personnel, many of whom were recruited from
the company's European operations. The company's U.S. railway products division
is headed by a German manager, plumbing products operations are run by an Englishman, and a Greek manages the international and exporting operations for the company's building division.

Sources: Adapted from "New Top Executives Shake up Old Order at Soft-Drink Giant," *The
Wall Street Journal,* November 6, 1981, p. 1 and "American Standard's Executive Melting Pot,"
Business Week, July 2, 1979, pp. 92–93.

---

the *foreign* salesperson, who is working at home for a foreign company;
and (3) the *cosmopolitan* salesperson, a special sort of expatriate who works
in various countries. These types are indentified for analytical purposes and
refer to individuals, but a given company may employ all three types in a
single foreign operation.

SOURCES OF MARKETING AND SALES PERSONNEL

Any level of marketing personnel may be derived from one of three
sources: (1) the home country of the hiring firm, (2) the country in which
the firm is doing business, and (3) a third country. Actual employment practices place heavy reliance on expatriates for top- and middle-management
positions. However, changes in attitudes in many host countries plus the
need for larger numbers of personnel have caused many companies to
increase their dependency on foreign nationals. When international business
functioned at the level of one salesperson per foreign country or per several
foreign countries, expatriate sales people made sense. Now with hundreds
of sales personnel in some markets, it is prohibitively expensive and virtually
impossible to field an expatriate sales force.

Expatriates

Expatriates working in a country or countries other than their own, are
declining in importance as the volume of world trade increases and as
more companies find they can secure foreign nationals to fill marketing

positions. However, when products are highly technical, or where selling requires an extensive background of information and applications, an expatriate sales force may be the better choice.

BOX 16–3: Model Latin American manager

Although selecting a manager to head a Latin American operation depends on a firm's specific needs at a particular time, most companies have a good idea of the characteristics they would most like to find in an ideal candidate. Firms say the four leading traits, in order of importance, are flexibility, empathy with the environment (defined by one company as the ability to understand and operate in a Latin environment and enjoy it), the desire to take on change, and self-confidence.

The list includes many other desirable attributes. Knowing the language—Spanish in the bulk of Latin America or Portuguese in Brazil—is considered very important by almost all companies, although a strong minority believes this skill can be mastered after the person gets to the country. Next in line come such traits as the ability to recognize and develop the skills of others, generate enthusiasm and achieve results within budget limits. Other companies stress the need for an individual who can deal with local regulatory bodies, can think in a disciplined and logical manner, and is energetic and persistent.

Other corporate checklists cite an aggressive person with a feel for strategic thinking and the high moral standards necessary to withstand the temptation of corruption in many Latin American countries. Other sought-after traits include the ability to confront conflicts, take action without being asked, and identify key issues in a disagreement.

All companies want strong managers who can lead and influence people—staff, clients, government officials, and shareholders. The ideal choice should also be endowed with strong entrepreneurial drive, be efficiency oriented and strive for high performance. Companies also agree that personality definitely gets the edge over technical skill. One MNC explains: **"In Europe, our top requirement would be strategic planning abilities; in Latin America we need a person who can fit in the environment."**

"Companies Offer Tips on how to Select Managers for Latin American Subs." Reprinted from page 266 of the August 29, 1981 issue of *Business Latin America* (BL), with the permission of the publisher, Business International Corporation (New York).

The expatriate salesperson may have the advantages of greater technical training, better knowledge of the company and its product line, and proven dependability and effectiveness. Because they are not natives, expatriates sometime add to the prestige of the product line in the eyes of foreign customers.

Chief disadvantages of an expatriate sales force are high cost, cultural and legal barriers, and the limited numbers of high-caliber personnel willing to live abroad for extended periods. U.S. companies are finding it difficult to persuade outstanding employees to take overseas posts at a time when the companies are relying more heavily on their experience. There are many reasons for the reluctance of experienced personnel to go abroad. Some find it difficult to up-root their families for the two- or three-year assignment; with an increasingly larger number of dual-career couples, a suitable job often must be found for the spouse. Another reason executives are not anxious to go abroad is that many feel such an assignment will impede their subsequent promotions at home. In companies that have well-planned career development programs there is less difficulty than in companies with poorly defined programs. The problem stems from the participants' feelings that out of sight is out of mind and thus, they fear the loss of their corporate visibility.

Expatriates are committed to foreign assignments for varying lengths of time, from a few weeks or months to a lifetime. Some expatriates have one-time assignments (which may last for years) after which they are returned to the parent company, while others are essentially professional expatriates working abroad in country after country. Still another expatriate assignment is a career-long assignment to a given country or region; this is likely to lead to assimilation of the expatriate into the foreign culture to such an extent that the person may more closely resemble a foreign national than an expatriate. Marketing personnel on expatriate status are likely to cost a company a great deal more than foreign nationals, so the company must be certain that their effectiveness is commensurate with the added expense.

Foreign nationals

The historical preference for using expatriate managers from the home-office country is gradually giving way to a preference for foreign nationals. At the sales level, the picture is clearly biased in favor of the foreign national. Most companies with sales forces abroad use foreign nationals because they transcend both cultural and legal barriers. Furthermore, companies are finding more qualified foreign personnel available and that salary and selling expenses for foreign salespeople less than for expatriates. One study estimated the percentage of executive and technical positions held overseas by U.S. citizens shrank to 37 percent in 1980 from about 84 percent in 1972. National Cash Register Company, which pioneered the development of foreign sales forces, has developed its intraining process to the point that it is almost as efficient at training in foreign markets as it is domestically. Selection and training do remain problems, however, for companies without such experience.

Cosmopolitan personnel

The growing internationalization of business breeds a cosmopolitan expatriate from country A working for a company headquartered in country B, in country C, or in countries C, D, E, and so on. Such third-country arrangements are most likely found at management levels and infrequently at the sales level. Development of cosmopolitan executives reflects not only a growing internationalization of business but acknowledges that personnel skills and motivations are not the exclusive property of one nation. At one time, Burroughs Corporation's Italian company was run by a Frenchman, their Swiss company by a Dane, their German company by an Englishman, their

French company by a Swiss, their Venezuelan company by an Argentinian, and their Danish company by a Dutchman.

Host country restrictions

The flexibility of selecting expatriate U.S. nationals, cosmopolitan nationals, or local nationals has been complicated in recent years by changes in attitude toward foreign workers by many governments. As discussed in earlier chapters, many countries are exhibiting concern with foreign corporate domination by tightening investment controls, limiting foreign companies to specific industries, and a variety of other controls over the influence of the foreign investor. In seeking ways to maximize benefits from foreign investment, many countries insist on increasingly more locals being hired at the management level. Over the last few decades this has consistently reduced the opportunities for sending personnel from the home country to management positions in a foreign country.

Many countries have specific laws limiting work permits for foreigners to those positions that cannot be filled by a national. Further, if the permit is issued, the law usually requires it be limited to a period just long enough to train a local for that specific position. Thus, MNCs must staff more positions with locals and be more selective about the home-country nationals sent abroad. This fundamental change in the attitude of host countries toward foreign employees has had a profound effect on the entire personnel management process. For example, in many situations where they have been forced to hire a local, the title may be similar (e.g., a foreign country national comptroller versus a U.S. comptroller), but the skill level is quite dissimilar.[1] This requires shifts in supervisory and control methods as well as organizational responsibility to accommodate personnel with limited skills. The most profound effect has been felt among U.S. citizens; in earlier years, many lower-management positions abroad could be staffed with less-experienced personnel who gained the necessary training to eventually assume top level positions in these countries. Now U.S. companies find they can no longer use foreign assignments for training experience but must send only the more-experienced personnel abroad.

In addition to government restrictions regarding foreign nationals, an international marketer must keep in mind the differences in managing personnel with varied cultural backgrounds.

MANAGING INTERNATIONAL MARKETING AND SALES PERSONNEL

There are several vital questions that arise when attempting to manage in other cultures. How much effect does culture have on the effectiveness

---

[1] "How Companies Cope With Portugal's Dearth of Managers," *Business Europe,* January 9, 1981, p. 12.

of management practices, processes, and concepts used in the United States? Will those practices that work well in the United States be equally effective when customs, values, and lifestyles differ? The transference of management practices to other cultures without concern for their exportability is no more effective than assuming a successful U.S. product will be successful elsewhere. The success of management concepts is influenced by cultural diversity and must be evaluated in terms of local norms; whether or not any single management practice needs adapting depends on the culture.[2]

Since diversity among cultures in values, attitudes, and beliefs which affect management practice are unlimited, only those fundamental premises on which U.S. management practices are based are presented here for comparison. International managers must analyze the management practices normally used in terms of their transferability to another culture. The purpose of this section is to heighten the reader's awareness of the need for adaptation of management rather than to present a complete discussion of U.S. culture and management behavior.

There are many divergent views on the most important ideas on which normative U.S. cultural concepts are based. Those that occur most frequently in discussions of cross-cultural evaluations are represented by the following: (1) "master of destiny" viewpoint, (2) independent enterprise—the instrument of social action, (3) personnel selection on merit, (4) decisions based on objective analysis, (5) wide sharing in decision making, (6) never-ending quest for improvement.[3]

The *master of destiny* philosophy underlies much of U.S. management thought and is a belief held by many in our culture. Simply stated: people can substantially influence the future, we are in control of our own destiny. This viewpoint also reflects the attitude that while luck may have some influence on an individual's future, on balance, persistence, hard work, a commitment to fulfill expectations, and effective use of time give people control of their destinies. Many cultures have a fatalistic approach to life—*individual* destiny is determined by a higher order and what happens cannot be controlled.[4]

In the United States, approaches to planning, control, supervision, commitment, motivation, scheduling, and deadlines are all influenced by the concept that individuals can control their future. In cultures with more fatalistic beliefs, these "good" business practices may be followed but concern for the final outcome is different. After all, if one believes the future is determined

---

[2] Lane Kelley and Reginald Worthley, "The Role of Culture in Comparative Management: A Cross-Cultural Perspective," *Academy of Management Journal,* March 1981, pp. 164–73.

[3] Also see Paul E. Illman, *Developing Overseas Managers—and Managers Overseas* (New York: American Management Association, AMACOM, 1980), 298 pp.

[4] For a more detailed discussion of the material on which this section is based, see William H. Newman and Warren E. Kirby, *The Process of Management* (Englewood Cliffs, N.J.: Prentice-Hall, 1981), 735 pp.

BOX 16–4: Now this is salesmanship

In 1975, G. and J. Greenhall Distillers of Warrington and the *Export Times* of London sponsored the Vladivar Vodka Incredible Export Award to honor British capitalistic ingenuity. Here are some of the winners.

1. *Tom-toms to Nigeria:*
The Premier Drum Company of Leicester won first prize with their sale of four shipments of tom-toms to Nigeria, including complete kits for the Nigerian Police Band and the country's top band (Dr. Victor Oliyia and his all-star orchestra). Premier also sold maracas to South America and xylophones to Cuba.

2. *Oil to the Arabs:*
Second place went to Permaflex Ltd. of Stoke-on-Trent, which exports £50,000 of petroleum a year to the Arab states in the form of lighter fluid.

3. *Sand to Abu Dhabi:*
Eastern Sands and Refractories of Cambridge shipped 1,800 tons of sand to sand-rich Abu Dhabi, which needed sand grains of a special shape for water filtration.

4. *Snowplow to Arabia:*
The defense force of the Arab sheikhdom of Dubai purchased from Bunce Ltd. of Ashbury, Wiltshire, one snowplow. It is to be used to clear sand from remote roads.

5. *Coals to Newcastle:*
Timothy Dexter (1747–1806), an American merchant prince and eccentric who once published a book without punctuation actually sent a shipload of coal to Newcastle, known as a center for shipping coal *out*. The coal arrived just as Newcastle was paralyzed by a coal strike and there was a shortage of fuel for the citizenry. Dexter came away with enormous profits.

6. *Peking ducks to China:*
Cherry Valley Duck Farms signed in Canton a 10-year contract to sell British-bred Peking ducks to a farm at Tai Ling Shan, China.

Sources: *Export Times*, London, 1975; and "China Gives British Firm Order for Peking Ducks," *The Wall Street Journal*, January 29, 1981, p. 27.

---

by an uncontrollable "higher order" then what difference does effort really make?

The acceptance of the idea that *independent enterprise* is an *instrument for social action* is the fundamental concept of U.S. corporations. A corporation is recognized as an entity that has rules, continuity of existence, and is a separate and vital social institution. This recognition of the corporation as an entity can result in strong feelings of obligation to serve the company. In fact, the enterprise can take priority over personal preferences and social obligations since it is viewed as an entity that must be protected and developed. This concept ties into the master of destiny concept in that for a company to work and for individuals to control their destinies, they must feel a strong obligation to fulfill the requirements necessary to the success of the enterprise. Indeed, the company may take precedence over family, friends, or other activities which might detract from what is best for the company. "American management theory rests on the assumption that each member of an organization will give primary efforts to performing assigned tasks in the interests of that organization." Thus, in the United States an enterprise takes precedence and receives loyalty and the willingness to conform to its managerial systems. Contrast such attitudes with those held by Latin Americans who feel strongly that personal relationships are more important in daily life than the corporation.

BOX 16–5: Managing locals

An American tin mining company operating in Bolivia was competing with a French mining firm for the limited local labor. Reasoning that what attracts labor stateside would attract labor in the Andes, management erected a movie theater, provided modern housing, and doubled the customary wages. But still, few takers. Most of the available manpower went to the French despite minimal housing, long cafeteria lines, and low pay. After many months and numerous visits from top brass, American management discovered why: during their months of feasibility studies, they'd overlooked a basic human factor. Freedom of time was the prime consideration for the local Indians, and because the French paid by the hour in contrast to the American's weekly wage, they were able to take time off for fiestas in their village without questions, criticism, or docked paychecks. As a lesson in effective management abroad, this one came at a high price.

Linda Edwards, "Present Shock, and How to Avoid it Abroad," *Across the Board*, published by The Conference Board, February 1978, p. 36.

Consistent with the view that individuals control their own destiny is the belief that *personnel selection is made on merit.* The selection, promotion, motivation, or dismissal of personnel by U.S. managers emphasizes the need to select the best qualified persons for jobs, retaining them as long as their performance meets standards of expectations, and continuing the opportunity for upward mobility as long as those standards are met. Indeed, the belief that anyone can become the corporate president prevails among management personnel within the United States. Such presumptions lead to the belief that striving and making accomplishments will be rewarded, and conversely, the failure to do so will be penalized. The penalty for poor performance could be, and often is, dismissal. The reward and penalty scheme is a major basis for motivating U.S. personnel. In other cultures where friendship or family ties may be more important than the vitality of the organization, the criteria for selection, organization, and motivation are substantially different than those found in U.S. companies. In some cultures, organizations expand to accommodate the maximum number of friends and relatives. Further, if one knows that promotions are made on the basis of personal ties and friendships rather than on merit, a fundamental motivating lever is lost.[5]

The very strong belief in the United States that business *decisions are based on objective analysis* and that managers strive to be more scientific has a profound affect on the U.S. manager's attitudes toward objectivity

---

[5] Regina Ordonez, "Asians Favor Family-Style Management," *Asian Wall Street Journal,* April 13, 1981, p. 11.

in decision making and accuracy of data. While judgment and intuition are important criteria for making decisions, most U.S. managers believe decisions must be supported and based on accurate and relevant information. This "scientific approach" is not necessarily the premise on which foreign executives base decisions. In fact, the infallibility of the judgment of a key executive in many foreign cultures may be more important in the decision process than any other single factor. If one accepts "scientific management" as a fundamental basis for decision making, then attitudes toward accuracy and promptness in reporting data, availability and openness of data to all levels within the corporation, and the willingness to express even unpopular judgments become important characteristics of the business process. Thus, in U.S. business, great emphasis is placed on the collection and free flow of information to all levels within the organization and on frankness of expression in the evaluation of business opinions or decisions. In other cultures, such high value on factual and rational support for decisions is not important; the accuracy of data and even the proper reporting of data is not a prime prerequisite. Further, existing data frequently are for the eyes of a select few. The frankness of expression and openness in dealing with data characteristic of U.S. businesses does not fit easily in some cultures.

Compatible with views of controlling one's own destiny and that advancement is based on merit is the prevailing idea of *wide sharing in decision making*. Although decision making is not truly a democratic process in U.S. businesses, there is a strong belief that personnel in an organization require and, indeed, need the responsibility of making decisions for continued development. Thus, decision making is frequently decentralized and the ability as well as the responsibility of making decisions is pushed down to lower ranks of management. In this way, employees have an opportunity to grow with responsibility and to prove their ability. In many cultures, decisions are highly centralized, in part, because of the belief that only a few in the company have the right or the ability to make decisions. In the MidEast for Example, only the top executive makes decisions.[6]

Finally, all of these concepts culminate in a *never-ending quest for improvement*. The United States has always been a relatively activist society; in many walks of life the prevailing question is: "Can it be done better?" Thus, management concepts reflect the belief that change is not only normal but necessary, that no aspects are sacred or above improvement. In fact, the merit on which one achieves advancement is frequently tied to one's ability to make improvements. In line with this quest for improvement, results are what count and if practices must change to achieve results, then change is in order. Present practices are constantly evaluated in the hope this will result in continuing improvement of the system. In other cultures, the strength and power of those in command frequently rests not on change but on

---

[6] M. K. Badawy, "Styles of Mideastern Managers," *California Management Review,* Spring 1980, p. 57.

the premise that the status quo demands stable structure. To suggest improvement implies that those in power have failed; for someone in a lower position to suggest change would be viewed as a threat to another's private domain rather than the suggestion of an alert and dynamic individual.

The views expressed here pervade much of what is considered U.S. management technique. They affect our management attitudes, and must be considered by the international marketer when developing and managing an international marketing force.

DEVELOPING INTERNATIONAL SALES PERSONNEL

Several types of personnel are needed to undertake the international marketing function on a large scale: (1) managerial personnel, (2) staff functionaries, and (3) field sales representatives. Each requires different handling, but for all groups it is necessary to recruit, train, motivate, and compensate. With all these tasks accomplished, an international marketing force has been initiated although it needs continuing supervision and control. Cost factors alone demand effective performance in international personnel management; regardless of the organizational arrangements utilized, it is costly to maintain an international marketing operation.[7]

Although the stages in the development of an overseas sales force are the same as those in domestic marketing, there are vast differences in the approaches used and the problems encountered in accomplishing these steps in the world market. Motivation is especially complicated because the firm is dealing with different cultures, different sources, different philosophies—and always dealing with individuals. To simplify analysis, marketers are divided into managers and sales people. This section is not a handbook for performing personnel functions but is designed to offer insights into the complexities associated with developing an international marketing force.

Recruiting

To recruit and select personnel for international positions effectively, management must define precisely what it expects of its people. A formal job description can aid management in expressing those desires; such a description must consider the long-range needs of the company as well as current needs. In addition to descriptions for each marketing position, the criteria should include special requirements indigenous to various countries. With the continuing shortage of marketing personnel at both management and sales levels, it is imperative for companies to develop comprehensive recruiting procedures. Virtually all techniques used in domestic personnel recruit-

---

[7] "MNC Reveals Strategy for Building Strong Staff in Latin America," *Business Latin America,* September 30, 1981, pp. 312–13.

ing are effective in world markets. Some additional sources include: (1) recruitment of foreign students while they are on domestic campuses (such students combine a knowledge of both cultures, so need only be trained in the company aspects of the job); (2) raiding other companies for executive personnel; (3) recruitment of foreign nationals not living in their home country who wish to return home; (4) acquisition of foreign companies or development of joint ventures to tap existing personnel pools.[8]

Recruiting expatriate personnel from within the company can be a delicate subject. The advantages of foreign assignments should be explained, but the disadvantages must also be pointed out. In most companies there are many people interested in overseas assignments to prime (North European) locations but fewer takers for less-desirable assignments in Latin America or the poorer African and Middle Eastern countries.

Selecting

Personnel requirements for each position vary considerably, but there are some requisite skills, attitudes, and personal characteristics considered important to the ultimate adjustment and success of those selected for foreign assignment. Personnel operating in the home country need only the attributes of an effective salesperson while a transnational manager can require skills and attitudes that would challenge a diplomat. Despite the range of difference, some basic requisites leading to effective performance should be considered because effective executives and salespeople, regardless of where they are operating, share certain characteristics. International operations, however, demand special attention in terms of personal characteristics, skills, and orientations.

Maturity is a prime requisite for expatriate and cosmopolitan personnel. Managers and sales personnel working abroad typically must work more independently than their domestic counterparts; all are serving as company representatives in countries where the company reputation still may be in the formative stage. Personnel working overseas are often called on to make decisions and offer services for which their domestic counterpart could seek staff support. The company must have confidence in the ability of its personnel to make decisions and commitments without constant recourse to the home office or they cannot be individually effective.

International personnel require a kind of *emotional stability* not demanded in domestic positions. Regardless of location, they are living in cultures dissimilar to their own, to some extent always under scrutiny, and always aware that they are official representatives of the company abroad. They need a sensitivity to behavioral variations in different countries but cannot be so hypersensitive that their behavior is affected adversely. Finally, manag-

---

[8] Hsin-Min Tong and Beheruz N. Sethna, "U.S.-Educated Foreign Students: An Untapped Resource for Multinational Corporations," *Personnel Journal*, September 1980, pp. 769–71.

ers or sales personnel operating in foreign countries need *considerable breadth* and knowledge of many subjects, both on and off the job. The ability to handle several languages is always preferable.[9]

BOX 16–6:   Choosing the right person for overseas

Several years ago a U.S. engineering company ran into trouble while working on a steel mill in Italy. The crisis stemmed neither from inexperienced Italian personnel nor from volatile Italian politics but from the inability of an American executive's wife to adapt to Italy. Frustrated by language, schooling, and shopping problems, she complained incessantly to other company wives, who began to feel that they, too, suffered hardships and started complaining to their husbands. Morale became so bad the company missed deadlines and, eventually, replaced almost every American on the job.

Source: Quoted from the April 16, 1979 issue of *Business Week* by special permission. © 1979 by McGraw-Hill, Inc., New York, N.Y. 10020. All rights reserved.

In addition to the intangible skills international marketers must have in handling interpersonal relationships, they must also be effective salespeople. It would seem apparent that every marketing person in a foreign position is directly involved in the selling effort and must possess a "sales sense" that cuts through personal, cultural, and language differences and deals effectively with the selling situation.

The marketer who expects to be effective in the international marketplace needs to have a *favorable outlook on an international assignment.* People that do not genuinely like what they are doing and where they are doing it stand little chance of success. Failures usually are the result of overselling the assignment, showing the bright side of the picture and not warning about the bleak side.

An international salesperson must have a high level of adaptability whether working in a foreign country or at home. Expatriates working in a foreign country must be particularly sensitive to the habits of the market; those working at home for a foreign company must adapt to the requirements and ways of the parent company.

Successful adaptation in international affairs is based on a combination of attitude and effort. The best of intentions can backfire unless a careful study of the customs of the market country is made. Such a study should be initiated before the marketer arrives in a country, and should continue as long as there are facets of the culture that are not clear. One useful approach is to listen to the advice of national and foreign business people operating in that country. Cultural empathy is clearly a part of basic orientation because it is unlikely that anyone can be effective if antagonistic or confused about the environment.

---

[9] "The Language Barrier to Trade," *World Business Weekly*, December 8, 1980, p. 43.

The personal characteristics, skills, and orientation which identify the potentially effective person have been identified and labeled in many different ways. Each person studying the field has a preferred list of characteristics, yet rising above all the characteristics there is an intangible something which some people have referred to as "factor X," or a "sixth sense." This implies that regardless of the individual attributes, there is a certain blend of personal characteristics, skills, and orientation which is hard to pinpoint and which may differ from individual to individual but which produces the most effective overseas personnel.

Getting the right person to handle the job is a primary function of personnel management. It becomes especially important in the selection of home-country nationals to work for foreign companies within their home country. The multinational company does not have the freedom to hire and fire at will without relatively high costs. Most less developed countries and many European countries have stringent laws protecting workers' rights. These laws usually are specific as to penalties for the dismissal of employees. Venezuela has the most stringent dismissal legislation: with more than three months of service in the same firm, a worker gets severance pay amounting to one month's pay at severance notice plus 15 days' pay for every month of service exceeding eight months plus an additional 15 days' pay for each year employed. Further, after an employee is dismissed, the law requires that that person be replaced within 30 days at the same salary. Colombia and Brazil have similar laws that make employee dismissal a high-cost proposition.[10]

The most important reasons a growing number of companies are including an evaluation of an *employee's family* among selection criteria are: (1) the high cost of sending an expatriate abroad[11] and (2) increasing evidence that unsuccessful family adjustment is the single most important reason for expatriate dissatisfaction and the resultant request for return home. In fact, a study of personnel directors of over 300 international firms found that the inability of the manager's spouse to adjust to a different physical or cultural environment was the most important reason for an expatriate's failure to function effectively in a foreign assignment.[12] A new culture requires a family to adjust to a new household lifestyle, new schools, new friends, a new status in a new community, restrictions on freedom, lack of basic conveniences, new food, new climate, and new social value systems. The employee is immediately thrust into a familiar business routine during most of the day regardless of the country, but the family is left to establish completely new living patterns. Frequently, family members cannot be employed and

---

[10] "Dismissing Workers Becomes More Costly in Latin America," *Business International,* January 2, 1976, p. 2.

[11] As one indication of the high cost, see "Residential Rents are Rising Sharply in Asia's Expatriate Housing Market," *Asian Wall Street Journal,* June 15, 1981, p. 17.

[12] Rosalie L. Tung, "Selection and Training of Personnel for Overseas Assignments," *Columbia Journal of World Business,* Spring 1981, p. 76.

in many cultures, female members of the family face severe social restrictions. In Saudi Arabia, for example, the female's role is strictly dictated. In one situation, a woman's hemline offended a religious official who, in protest, sprayed black paint on her legs. In short, the family has the greater problems of cultural shock; it is understandable that many companies include an evaluation of the family's ability to adjust. Although it may be difficult for a family to adjust, proper preparations can make it easier and more successful. Preparing a family for the foreign assignment will be discussed in this section.

Developing cultural awareness

Throughout the text, the need to adapt to the local culture has been stressed over and over again. Developing cultural sensitivity is a necessary attribute for all international marketers. Personnel can be selected with great care, but, if they do not possess or are not given the opportunity to develop some understanding of the culture to which they are being assigned, there is every chance they will develop cultural shock, inadvertently alienate those with whom they come in contact in the new culture, and/or make all the cultural mistakes discussed in this text. As the world becomes more interdependent and as companies become more dependent on foreign earnings, there is a growing concern within many companies for developing cultural awareness.

Just as we remark that someone has achieved good "social skills," that is, an ability to remain poised and be in control under all social situations, so good "cultural skills," can be developed also. These skills serve a similar function in varying cultural situations, that is, they provide the individual with the ability to relate to a different culture even when the individual is unfamiliar with the details of that particular culture. Cultural skills can be learned just as social skills can be learned. Someone with cultural skills can (1) communicate respect and convey verbally and nonverbally a positive regard and sincere interest in people and their culture; (2) tolerate ambiguity and cope with cultural differences and the frustration that frequently develops when things are different and circumstances change; (3) display empathy by understanding other people's needs and differences from *their* point of view rather than their own; (4) be nonjudgmental, avoid judging the behavior of others on their own value standards; (5) recognize and control the SRC, that is, recognize their own culture and values as an influence on their perceptions, evaluations, and judgment in a situation; (6) laugh things off, a good sense of humor helps when frustration levels rise and things do not work out as planned.[13]

Anyone being sent into another culture should receive training to develop

---

[13] Philip R. Harris, "Cultural Awareness Training for Human Resource Development," *Training and Development Journal*, March 1979, p. 66.; L. Robert Kohls, *Survival Kit For Overseas Living* (Chicago: Intercultural Press, Inc., 1979) p. 72.

the cultural skills discussed. In addition, they should receive specific schooling on the customs, values, and social and political institutions of the host country. There are a variety of organizations involved in intercultural training and many companies are doing "in-house" training as well.[14]

Training

The nature of a training program depends largely on whether it is expatriate or foreign personnel being trained for overseas positions. The former will focus on the customs and special foreign sales problems that will be encountered. Foreign national personnel require more emphasis on the company, its products, technical information, and the selling methods to be utilized. In training either type of personnel, the sales training activity will be burdened with problems because the trainer will be dealing with long-established behavior and attitudes. Foreign nationals cling to habits continually reinforced by local culture; expatriates, too, are captives of their habits and patterns. Americans, particularly, may think there is little to be learned from the foreign culture or from the way things are done in a foreign country. Before any training can be effective, open-minded attitudes must be established.

Continuation training may be more important in foreign markets than in domestic ones because of the lack of routine contact with the parent company and its marketing personnel. One aspect of training is frequently overlooked; home office personnel dealing with international marketing operations need training designed to make them responsive to the needs of the foreign operations. In most companies, the requisite sensitivities are expected to be developed by osmosis in the process of dealing with foreign affairs; a few companies send home-office personnel abroad periodically to increase their awareness of the problems of the foreign operations.

Motivating

Marketing is a business function requiring high motivation regardless of the location of the practitioner. Marketing managers and sales managers typically work hard, travel extensively, and have day-to-day challenges and measures of performance. Selling is hard, competitive work wherever undertaken and a constant flow of inspiration is needed to keep personnel functioning at their optimal level. Consideration of national differences must always be kept in mind in motivating the marketing force. One company found its sales people were losing respect and had low motivation because they did not have girls in the Japanese branch offices to pour tea for customers.

---

[14] For specific information about cultural training programs consult *International Resource Directory*, IFTDO, P.O. Box 5307, Madison, Wis.; and James B. Stull and John W. Baird, "Cross-Cultural Marketing: A Classroom Simulation," *Journal of Marketing Education*, April 1980, pp. 11–18.

The company learned that when male personnel served tea, they felt they lost face; tea girls were authorized for all branches.

Communications are also important in maintaining high levels of motivation; foreign managers need to know the home office is interested in their operations, and, in turn, they want to know what is happening in the parent country. Everyone performs better when well informed. Some companies use the "college football" approach in "controlling the emotional swings of sales personnel from peak to depth and back to peak again."

Promotion and the opportunity to improve status are important motivators so a company needs to make the opportunities for growth within the firm clear. One of the greatest fears of expatriate managers is that they will be forgotten by the home office, but such fears can be easily allayed.

Since the cultural differences reviewed in earlier chapters affect the motivational patterns of a sales force, a manager must be extremely sensitive to the personal behavior patterns of employees. Individual incentives which work effectively in the United States can fail completely in other cultures. For example, with Japan's emphasis on paternalism and collectivism and the system of lifetime employment and seniority, motivation through individual incentive does not work because the Japanese employee seems to derive the greatest satisfaction from being a comfortable member of a group. Thus, an offer of financial reward for outstanding work could be turned down because the employee would prefer not to appear different from peers and possibly attract their resentment.[15] Blending company sales objectives and the personal objectives of the salespeople and other employees is a task worthy of the most skilled manager. The U.S. manager must be constantly aware that many of the techniques used to motivate U.S. personnel and their response to these techniques are based on six basic cultural premises discussed earlier. Therefore, each method used to motivate a foreigner should be examined for cultural compatibility.

Compensating

Developing an equitable and functional compensation plan that combines balance, consistent motivation, and flexibility is extremely challenging in international operations. This is especially true when a company operates in a number of countries, when it has individuals who work in a number of countries, or when the force is composed of expatriate and foreign personnel. Fringe benefits play a major role in many countries. Those working in high-tax countries prefer liberal expense accounts and fringe benefits which are nontaxable instead of direct income subject to high taxes. Fringe-benefit costs are high in Europe; in Belgium, fringe benefits add about

---

[15] Yoshimatsu Anonuma, "A Japanese Explains Japan's Business Style," *Across the Board,* February 1981, pp. 41–50.

35 percent of salary costs, in Germany, 40 percent, and in France, nearly 60 percent.[16]

Pay can be a significant factor in making it difficult for a person to be repatriated. Often, those returning home realize they have been making considerably more money with a lower cost of living in the overseas market and that returning to the home country means a cut in pay and a cut in their standard of living.

Conglomerate operations that include domestic and foreign personnel cause the greatest problems in compensation planning. Expatriates tend to compare their compensation with what they would have received at the home office; at the same time, foreign personnel and expatriate personnel are likely to compare notes on salary. Although any differences in the compensation level may easily and logically be explained, the group receiving the lower amount almost always feels aggrieved and mistreated.

Short-term assignments for expatriates further complicate the compensation issue, particularly when the short-term assignments extends into a longer time. In general, short-term assignments involve payments of overseas premiums (sometimes called *separation allowances* if the family does not go along), all excess expenses, and allowances for tax differentials. Longer assignments can include home-leave benefits or travel allowances for the spouse. Many companies estimate that these expenses will approximately equal the base compensation of the employee.

Besides rewarding an individual's contribution to the firm, a compensation program can be used effectively to recruit, develop, motivate, or retain personnel. Most recommendations for developing a compensation program suggest that a program focus on whichever one of these purposes fits the needs in the particular situation. In international compensation, most plans try to accomplish all four purposes resulting in unwieldy programs that have become completely unmanageable for many. International compensation programs also provide additional payments for hardship locations and special inducements to entice reluctant personnel to accept overseas employment and to remain in the position. See Exhibit 16–1 for an idea of the kinds of inducements offered expatriate executives by MNCs. Such fringe benefits have resulted in a continuing escalation of overseas compensation packages. Exhibit 16–1 shows the effects of fringe benefit costs for a base salary of $40,000 in four different locations for a three-year period. The range from $138,300 in Canada to $427,800 in Nigeria explains why multinational companies are seeking ways to reduce the multinational executive compensation package.[17]

---

[16] For an interesting article on executive compensation see: "Is any Executive Worth his Weight in Gold?" *International Management,* June 1981, pp. 20–24.

[17] "Executive Opportunities at Home and Abroad," *World Business Weekly,* January 26, 1981, pp. 20–22.

BOX 16–7: Incentives for expatriate executives

A breakdown by country	Australia	Hong Kong	Brazil	Venezuela	Mexico	Saudi Arabia	Bahrain	Abu Dhabi	Oman	Nigeria	New Guinea	Ghana	Ivory Coast
Are American executives still as enthusiastic about working in this country as they were five years ago?	No	Yes	No	No	Yes	No	Yes	Yes	Yes	No	Yes	Yes	No
Is the standard of living for US executives working in this country higher, about equal, or lower than that in the United States?	Somewhat lower	Somewhat lower	Far lower	Far lower	Equal	Lower	Lower	Lower	Lower	Lower	Lower	Lower	Lower
What perquisites should the American executive working in this country expect?	Car, pension, clubs, travel	Car, pension, health care, house, clubs	Car, pension, clubs, travel	Car, house, clubs, travel	Car, pension, health care, clubs, travel	Free housing, car, school for children, ample vacation, leaves, bonuses, health care, relocation							
Can an American working for an American multinational company based in this country expect to be compensated for income lost because of double taxation?	Yes	Yes	Yes	Yes	Yes	Yes, and can expect to make substantial profit							
Are opportunities for American executives to improve their financial worth by working in this country better, the same, or worse than those in the United States?	Better	Worse	Better	Better	Same	Far better	Far better	Far better	Far better	Far better	Far better	Far better	Far better
Are women executives gaining acceptance in this country?	No	Yes	No	Yes, but at low level and slowly	No	No	No	No	No	No	No	No	No
What industries in this country are currently most in need of executives?	Merchant banking, mining, manufacturing	Electronics, banking, consumer products	Chemicals, high technology	Petrochemicals, aluminum, steel, banking, financial services	Chemicals, automotive, metals	Construction, energy, heavy industry	Same	Same	Same	Construction, packaged goods, food services	Same	Same	Same
What executive job functions are companies in this country interested in?	Finance, engineering	Marketing, banking	Engineering, finance	Finance, administration, marketing	Finance, managing director, industrial relations	Chief engineer, project engineer, project manager	Same	Same	Same	Sales and marketing	Research and development, distribution	Sales and marketing	Sales and marketing

Data compiled by Boyden Associates Inc.
Source: "Executive Opportunities at Home and Abroad," *World Business Weekly*, January 26, 1981, pp. 20–21. Reprinted by permission of the Financial Times, London.

EXHIBIT 16–1: Typical expatriate allowance packages by country

	Canada	Belgium	Japan	Nigeria
Salary	$ 40,000	$ 40,000	$ 40,000	$ 40,000
Allowances	3,200	39,300	59,900	75,900
Foreign taxes	2,900	13,400	12,800	26,700
Employers annual cost	46,100	92,700	112,700	142,600
Employers three-year cost	138,300	278,100	368,100	427,800

Note: Based on total additional expatriate costs for a married expatriate with two school-aged children, who earns a base salary of $40,000 and who works overseas for three years.

Source: Based on "Tax and Total Cost of U.S. Citizens Abroad," a study by Ernst and Whinney as reported in "The High Cost of Overseas Staff," *World Business Weekly,* April 27, 1981, p. 48.

Many companies are examining their compensation packages with the thought of reducing them substantially. Some are questioning the need to continue to pay premium salaries to attract and retain capable people. A few companies are changing their philosophies toward international business to include the international commitment as an integral part of an individual's future with the firm. Those companies could then reduce the compensation normally paid to expatriates as an inducement to go and as a bonus for the hardship of a foreign assignment. A more important trend seems to be one which questions the need for expatriates to fill foreign positions. Many companies feel that the increase in the number and quality of managers in other countries means that many positions now being filled by expatriates could be filled by nationals and/or third-country nationals who would require lower compensation packages.[18] With more emphasis being placed on the development of third-country nationals and locals for managerial positions, companies find they can reduce compensation packages. The original premise of compensation packages for U.S. international executives, that of increased income benefits, was jeopardized by the 1976 Tax Reform Act.

The 1976 Tax Reform Act reduced considerably the tax advantages a U.S. expatriate had when remaining abroad for periods longer than 18 months. Because of the higher taxes imposed, many executives found overseas assignments unattractive and business found the law increased its costs of sending an executive abroad (to get an executive to accept foreign assignments, many companies had to pay the additional employee taxes). The law had the effect of making it more difficult to attract the caliber of executive necessary in the increasingly competitive international market.[19]

A subsequent tax law that became effective in 1982 eased the tax burden considerably. The congressional bill provided an exclusion of $75,000 in foreign-earned income from taxes (the 1976 law allowed only $25,000);

---

[18] "U.S. Concerns are Hiring More Foreigners Abroad," *Wall Street Journal,* May 29, 1981, p. 31.

[19] Stephen Grover, "Employees Start Looking Again at Jobs Abroad," *The Wall Street Journal,* October 28, 1981, p. 25.

this will increase to $95,000 in 1986. Virtually all extra benefits are also exempt from taxable personal income. In addition, the time that must be spent abroad before the exclusion becomes effective has been reduced from 18 months to 12 months. International marketers expect the change in the law to make it easier to attract qualified personnel to foreign assignments and thus enhance companies' competitiveness abroad.[20]

PLANNING THE FOREIGN ASSIGNMENT

Estimates of the annual cost of sending and supporting a manager and the family in a foreign assignment range from 150 to 475 percent of base salary. The costs in money as well as morale increase substantially if the expatriate requests a return home before completing the normal tour of duty (a normal stay ranges from two to four years). In addition, if repatriation into domestic operations is not successful and the employee leaves the company, an indeterminately high cost in low morale and loss of experienced personnel results. To ameliorate these problems, international personnel management has increased planning for expatriate personnel to move abroad, remain abroad, and then return to the home country.[21] The planning process must begin prior to the selection of those who go abroad and extend to their specific assignments after returning home. Selection, training, compensation, and career development policies (including repatriation) should reflect the unique problems of managing the expatriate.

Besides the job-related criteria for a specific position, the typical candidate for an international assignment is married, has two school-age children, is expected to stay overseas three years, and has the potential for promotion into higher management levels. These characteristics of the typical selectee are the basis of most of the difficulties associated with getting the best of the qualified to go overseas, keeping them there, and assimilating them on their return.

Overcoming reluctance to accept a foreign assignment

Concerns for career and family are the most frequently mentioned reasons for a manager to refuse a foreign assignment. The most important career-related reservation is the fear that a two- or three-year absence will adversely affect opportunities for advancement. This "out of sight, out of mind" fear is closely linked to the problems of repatriation. Without evidence of advance planning to protect career development, better qualified and ambitious personnel may decline the offer to go abroad. However, if candidates for expatriate assignments are picked thoughtfully and returned to the home office

---

[20] "Easing Tax Burdens Overseas," *Business Week,* April 6, 1981, p. 70, and "Reagan's Tax Package: What's in it for International Business?" *World Business Weekly,* August 31, 1981, pp. 20–21.

[21] Kenneth F. Misa and Joseph M Fabricatore, "Return on Investment of Overseas Personnel," *Financial Executive,* April 1979, pp. 42–46.

at the right moment and rewarded for good performance with subsequent promotions at home, companies find the recruiting of executives for international assignments eased.

Even though the career development question may be adequately answered with proper planning, concern for one's family may interfere with many accepting an assignment abroad. Initially, most potential candidates are concerned with the problems of uprooting a family and taking them into a strange environment. Such questions as the education of the children, isolation from family and friends, proper medical and health care, and, in some countries, the potential for violence reflect the misgivings a family may have about relocating in a foreign country. Special compensation packages have been the typical way to deal with this problem. A hardship allowance, allowances to cover special educational requirements that frequently include private schools, housing allowances, and extended all expense-paid vacations are part of compensation packages designed to overcome family-related problems with an overseas assignment. Ironically, the solution to one problem creates a later problem when that family returns to the United States and must give up those extra compensation benefits used to induce them to accept the position.

Reducing the rate of early returns

Once the employee and family accept the assignment abroad, the next critical problem is keeping them there for the assigned time. The attrition rate of those selected for overseas positions can be very high. One firm with a hospital management contract experienced an annualized failure rate of 120 percent which does not seem high when compared with the construction contractor who started out in Saudia Arabia with 155 Americans and was down to 65 after only two months (annualized, that is an attrition rate of 368 percent).[22]

There is no question that the single most important reason for expatriates requesting early return to the United States is directly related to the dissatisfaction of the family. Dissatisfaction is caused by the stress and trauma of adjusting to new and often strange cultures. Rarely does the employee have trouble adjusting; the expatriate moves in a familiar environment even abroad and frequently is isolated from the cultural differences which create problems for the rest of the family. Family members have far greater daily exposure to the new culture but are seldom given assistance in adjusting. The solution to this problem involves better selection and preparation for the assignment abroad. Certainly any recruiting and selection procedure should include an evaluation of the family's ability to adjust.[23]

---

[22] Linda Edwards, "Present Shock, and How to Avoid it Abroad," *Across the Board,* February 1978, p. 42.

[23] "Guaging a Family's Suitability for a Stint Overseas," *Business Week,* April 16, 1979, pp. 127–28.

Families that have the potential and personality traits that would enable them to adjust to a different environment may still become dissatisfied with living abroad if they are not properly prepared for the new assignment. More and more companies are realizing the need for cross-cultural training to prepare families for their new homes. One- to two-day briefings to two- to three-week intensive programs that include all members of the family are provided to help in assimilation into new cultures. Language training, films, discussions, and lectures on cultural differences, potential problems, and stress areas in adjusting to a new way of life are provided to minimize the frustration of the initial cultural shock. This cultural training helps a family anticipate problems and eases their adjustment. Once the family is abroad, some companies even provide a local ombudsman (someone experienced in the country) to whom they can take their problems and get immediate assistance. Companies that have used ombudsman programs have found this procedure most effective in eliminating some of the frustration before it develops into a major problem. Although the cost of preparing a family for an overseas assignment may appear high, consider that one company "estimates that the measurable cost of one prematurely returned family could cover cross-cultural training for 300 to 500 families."[24] Companies that do not prepare employees and their families for the cultural shock have the highest incidence of premature return to the United States. For those assignments abroad which are successful, the next hurdle confronting the expatriate and family is coming home or repatriation.

Successful expatriate repatriation

A Conference Board study reported that many firms have sophisticated plans for executives going overseas but few have comprehensive programs to deal with those returning home.

Low morale among returning expatriates and a growing amount of attrition among returnees have many reasons. Some complaints and problems are family related, others are career related. The family-related problems generally deal with financial and lifestyle readjustments. For example, some expatriates find that in spite of higher compensation programs, their net worths have not increased. Many have found on returning home that the inflation of intervening years makes it impossible to buy a home comparable to the one they sold on leaving.[25] The hardship compensation programs used to induce the executive to go abroad create readjustment problems on the return home. Such compensation benefits permitted the family to live at a much higher level abroad than at home (for example, yard boys, chauffeurs, domestic help, etc.). Since most compensation benefits are withdrawn

---

[24] Edwards, "Present Shock and How to Avoid it Abroad," p. 37.

[25] Lawrence Rout, "Try to Hold on to the House if You're Transferred Overseas," *The Wall Street Journal,* May 27, 1981, p. 27.

when employees return to the home country, their standard of living decreases and they must readjust. Another objection to returning to the United States is the location of the new assignment; frequently, the new location is not viewed as desirable as the location before the foreign tour. Unfortunately, little can be done to ameliorate these kinds of problems short of transferring the managers to other foreign locations. It is being repeatedly suggested that the problem of dissatisfaction with compensation and benefits can be reduced by reducing benefits. Rather than provide the family abroad with hardship payments, some companies are considering reducing payments on the premise that the assignment abroad is an integral requirement for growth, development, and advancement within the firm. While family dissatisfaction may cause stress within the family on returning home, the problem is not as severe as career-related complaints.[26]

A returning expatriate's dissatisfaction with the perceived future is usually the reason many resign their positions after returning to the United States. The problem is not unique to U.S. citizens, Japanese companies have similar difficulties with their personnel.[27] The most frequently heard complaint involves the lack of a detailed plan for the expatriate's career when returning home. New home-country assignments are frequently mundane and do not reflect the experience gained or the challenges met during foreign assignment. Some feel their time out of the mainstream of corporate affairs has made them technically obsolete and thus ineffective in competing immediately on return. Finally, there is some loss of status requiring ego adjustment when an executive returns home. As discussed earlier, overseas assignments are most successfully filled by independent, mature, self-starters. The expatriate executive enjoyed a certain degree of autonomy, independence, and power with all the prerequisites of office not generally afforded in comparable positions domestically. On returning home many find it difficult to adjust to being just another middle manager. In short, returning expatriates have a series of personal and career-related questions to anticipate with anxiety back at corporate headquarters. Companies with the least amount of returnee attrition differ from those with the highest attrition in one significant way—personal career planning for the expatriate.

Expatriate career planning begins with the decision to send the person abroad. The initial transfer abroad should be made in the context of a long-term company career plan. Under these circumstances, the individual knows not only the importance of the foreign assignment but when to expect to return and at what level. Near the end of the foreign assignment, the process for repatriation is begun.

The critical aspect of the return home is to keep the executive completely informed: proposed return time, new assignment and whether it is interim

---

[26] "How to Ease Reentry After Overseas Duty," *Business Week,* June 11, 1979, pp. 82–83.

[27] Merry I. White, "The Rites of Return: The Re-entry and Reintegration of the Japanese International Businessman," *Japan Society Newsletter,* October 1979, pp. 7–9.

BOX 16–8: International personnel repatriation

Will I be able to use the number of skills that I have acquired? Will the family have the same living standards as before? Will the type of acceptance I have at corporate office equal the total acceptance I enjoyed from my foreign colleagues? Will the loss of the foreign assignment be detrimental to my total financial package? Will this move be a lateral shift or an upward move in the organization hierarchy? Will I lose my freedom to make decisions without being intangled in the bureaucratic red tape? In general, will the job give me the same standards (measured on many personal scales) as my foreign assignment? All these questions if not answered to the satisfaction of the expatriate can result in decisions to leave the firm.

J. Alex Murray, "International Personnel Repatriation: Cultural Shock in Reverse," p. 63, *MSU Business Topics,* Summer 1973. Reprinted by permission of the publisher, Division of Research, Graduate School of Business Administration, Michigan State University.

---

or permanent, new responsibilities, and future prospects. In short, the returnees should know where they are going and what they will be doing next month and several years ahead. To provide such a program requires considerable preparation prior to the assignment. The most effective solution to handling international personnel management is probably reflected in corporate attitudes toward the long-term importance of foreign assignments. If it is understood that foreign corporate experience is a necessary prerequisite for growth and promotion within the company, many of the problems faced today with foreign assignments will be eliminated. As all employees— management, office staff, blue-collar workers—develop a multinational outlook, as the company effectively prepares employees for overseas assignments, and if expectations for management jobs are high, most of the problems discussed will be substantially eased. Although this discussion has been directed primarily toward U.S. personnel, it is equally applicable and important for the assignment of third-country nationals.[28]

SUMMARY

An effective international personnel force constitutes one of the international marketer's greatest concerns. The company sales force represents the major alternate method of organizing a company for foreign distribution and, as such, is on the front line of a marketing organization.

The role of marketers in both domestic and foreign markets is rapidly changing, along with the composition of international managerial and sales forces. Such forces have many unique requirements which are being filled by expatriates, foreign nationals, cosmopolitan personnel, or a combination of the three. In recent years, the pattern of development has been to place more emphasis on the foreign personnel operating in their own land. This,

---

[28] Yoram Zeira and Ehud Harari, "Managing Third-Country Nationals in Multinational Corporations," *Business Horizons,* October 1977, p. 83.

in turn, has highlighted the importance of adapting U.S. managerial techniques to local needs.

The development of an effective marketing organization calls for careful recruiting, selecting, training, motivating, and compensating of expatriate personnel and their families to insure maximization of a company's return on its personnel expenditures. The most practical method of maintaining an efficient international marketing force is careful, concerned planning at all stages of career development.

QUESTIONS

1. Define:
   Expatriate
   Cosmopolitan personnel
   Line and staff organization
   "Master of destiny" viewpoint
   "Cultural skills"

2. Why may it be difficult to adhere to set job criteria in selecting foreign personnel? What compensating actions might be necessary?

3. Why does the conglomerate sales force cause special compensation problems? Suggest some alternative solutions.

4. Under what circumstances should expatriate salespeople be utilized?

5. Discuss the problems which might be encountered in having an expatriate sales manager supervising foreign salespeople.

6. "To some extent, the exigencies of the personnel situation will dictate the approach to overseas sales organization." Discuss.

7. How do legal factors affect international sales management?

8. How does the sales force relate to company organization? To channels of distribution?

9. "It is costly to maintain an international sales force." Comment.

10. Adaptability and maturity are traits needed by all salespeople. Why should they be singled out as especially important for international salespeople?

11. Can a person develop good cultural skills? Discuss.

12. Describe the six attributes of a person with good cultural skills.

13. Interview a local company that has a foreign sales operation. Draw an organization chart for the sales function and explain why that particular structure was used by that company.

14. Evaluate the three major sources of multinational personnel.

15. What factors complicate the task of motivating the foreign sales force?

16. Discuss how the "master of destiny" viewpoint would affect attitudes of an American and a Mexican toward job promotion. Give an example.

17. Discuss the basic ideas on which U.S. management practices are based.

18. Why do companies include an evaluation of an employee's family among selection criteria?

19. Discuss how a family can affect the entire process of selecting personnel for foreign assignment.

20. "Concern for career and family is the most frequently mentioned reason for a manager to refuse a foreign assignment." Why?

21. Discuss and give examples of why returning U.S. expatriates are dissatisfied. How can these problems be overcome?

CASES—PART FOUR

CASE IV–1

Levi's—worldwide advertising strategy or localized campaigns?*

The Levi Strauss Company, manufacturer of the famous LEVI'S jeans and other wearing apparel, markets its products in 70 countries. The company owns and operates plants in 25 countries and has licensees, distributors, and joint ventures in others.

The company is now in the process of evaluating its advertising policy to determine whether to apply a worldwide strategy to all advertising or settle on localized campaigns for each country in which it sells its products.

You have been asked to evaluate their present programs and to make recommendations that will assist management in deciding whether it is better (1) to create advertising campaigns locally or regionally but with a good deal of input and influence from headquarters as they presently do, (2) to allow campaigns to be created independently by local advertising companies or (3) to centralize at national headquarters all advertising and develop a consistent worldwide advertising campaign.

You are asked to do the following:

1. Prepare a report listing the pros and cons of each of the three approaches listed.
2. Make a recommendation as to the direction the company should take.
3. Support your recommendation and outline major objectives for whichever approach you recommend.

The following information should be of assistance in completing this assignment.

---

*Information for this case was taken in part from the following sources: Levi Strauss and Company, Annual Report, 1980, "Exporting a Legend," *International Advertising,* November/December 1981, pp. 2–3, and "Levi Zipping up World Image," *Advertising Age,* September 14, 1981, pp. 35–36.

Company objectives

In a recent Annual Report, the following statement of objectives of Levi Strauss International was made:

> "In addition to posting record sales, Levi Strauss International continued to advance toward two long-term objectives.
>
> The first is to develop a solid and continuing base of regular jeans business in markets throughout the world, thus providing a foundation for product diversification into women's-fit jeans, youthwear, menswear, and related tops.
>
> The second objective is to attain the greatest possible self-sufficiency in each of the major geographic areas where Levi Strauss International markets: Europe, Canada, Latin America, and Asia/Pacific. This requires the development of raw material resources and manufacturing in areas where the products are marketed thus reducing exposure to long supply lines and shipping products across national borders.
>
> Unlike some competitors, Levi Strauss International does not, in its normal markets, seek "targets of opportunity," that is, large one-time shipments to customers it may never serve again. Rather, the goal is to develop sustainable and growing shipment levels to long-term customers."

Self sufficient
long term markets x

198– Sales/profits
(millions)

	Total	U.S.	Europe	Other International
Sales	$2,840	$1,888	$526	$426
Profits	468	314	92	62
Assets	1,375	882	240	253

Organization

Western European group. The company's European operations began in 1959 with a small export business, and, in 1965, an office was opened in Brussels. The company now has 15 European manufacturing plants and marketing organizations in 12 countries. This group includes all Western Europe served by the Continental and Northern European divisions.

The Continental European Division is headquartered in Brussels and is responsible for operations in Germany, France, Switzerland, the Benelux countries, Spain and Italy. *The Northern European Division* is headquartered in London and is responsible for all marketing and production in the United Kingdom and the Scandinavian nations.

Other international group. The divisions in this group report directly to the president of Levi Strauss International. They are Canada, Latin America, and Asia/Pacific.

The Canadian Division consists of two separate operating units: Levi Strauss of Canada and GWG. Levi Strauss and Company is sole owner of GWG which manufactures and markets casual and work garments under the GWG brand.

The Latin American Division traces it origins to 1966 when operations began in Mexico. In the early 1970s, the business was expanded to Argentina, Brazil, and Puerto Rico. In addition to these countries, the division now serves Chile, Venezuela, Uruguay, Paraguay, Peru, Colombia, and Central America. Plans call for the division to explore new markets in Central America and the Andean Region.

The Asia/Pacific Division had its beginning in the 1940s when jeans reached this market through U.S. military exchanges. In 1965, a sales facility was established in Hong Kong. Markets now served include Australia and Japan, the two largest, as well as, Hong Kong, the Philippines, Singapore/Malaysia, and New Zealand. Business in Indonesia and Thailand is handled through licensees. The markets served by this division present opportunity for growth in jeanswear. However, diversification potential in Asia/Pacific is centered in Japan and Australia.

Other operating units.   One other unit, EXIMCO, not aligned with either Levi Strauss USA or Levi Strauss International, reports directly to the president.

EXIMCO has two major responsibilities; market development and joint ventures in Eastern Europe, the USSR, and the People's Republic of China, and directing offshore contract production for the company's divisions.

Comments

The director of advertising and communications for International shares with you the following thoughts about advertising:

The success of Levi Strauss International's advertising is derived principally from their judging it consistently against three criteria: (1) Is the proposition meaningful to the consumer? (2) Is the message believable? and (3) Is it exclusive to the brand?

A set of core values underlies their advertising wherever it is produced and regardless of strategy: honesty/integrity, consistency/reliability, relevance, social responsibility, credibility, excellence, and style. The question remains whether a centralized advertising campaign can be based on this core of values.

Levi Strauss' marketing plans must include 70 countries and recognize the cultural and political differences affecting advertising appeals.

Uniform advertising (i.e., standardized) could ignore local customs and unique product uses, while locally prepared advertising risks uneven creative work, is likely to waste time and money on preparation, and might blur the corporate image.

Consistency in product image is a priority.

International advertising now appears in 25 countries. Levi currently uses
seven different agencies outside the United States, although one agency
handles 80 percent of the business worldwide. In Latin America, they
use four different agencies, and still a different agency in Hong Kong.

Levi is not satisfied with some of the creative work in parts of Latin America.
The company wants consistency in Latin American strategy rather than
appearing to be a different company in different countries. They are
not satisfied with production costs and casting of commercials, and
the fact that local agencies are often resistant to outside suggestions
to change. They feel there is a knee-jerk reaction in Latin America
that results in the attitude that everything must be developed locally.

The risks of too closely controlling a campaign result in uninteresting
ads compared with decentralizing all marketing which produces uneven creative quality.

Competition

At the same time that Levi is looking at more centralized control of its
advertising, another jeans maker is going in the opposite direction. Blue
Bell International's Wrangler jeans company has just ended a six-month
review of its international advertising and decided against coordinating its
advertising more closely in Europe.

The concept of one idea which will work effectively in all markets is
attractive to Wrangler. Yet the disadvantages are just as clear; the individual
needs of each market can not be met, resistance from local managers could
be an obstacle, and the management of a centralized advertising campaign
would require an organizational structure different from their present one.

To add to the confusion, a leading European jean manufacturer, the
Spanish textile company Y Confecciones Europeas, makers of "Louis" jeans,
recently centralized its marketing through one single advertising agency.
Louis, fourth largest jeans maker after Levi, Lee Cooper, and Wrangler, is
intent on developing a worldwide international image for its Louis brand.

Review of current ads

A review of a selection of Levi advertisements from around the world
provided the following notes:

European television commercials for Levi's were super-sexy in appeal,
projecting, in the minds of some at headquarters, an objectionable
personality for the brand. These commercials were the result of allowing
complete autonomy to a sales region.

Levi's commercials prepared in Latin America projected a far different
image than those in Europe. Latin American ads addressed a family
oriented, Catholic market. However, the quality of the creative work
was far below the standards set by the company.

Ads for the United Kingdom, emphasizing that Levi's are an American brand, star an all-American hero, the cowboy, in fantasy wild West settings. In Northern Europe, both Scandinavia and the U.K., they are buying a slice of America when they buy Levi's.

In Japan, where an attitude similar to that in the U.K. prevails, a problem confronted Levi's. Local jeans companies had already established themselves as very American. To overcome this, Levi's positioned themselves against these brands as legendary American jeans with commercials themed "Heroes Wear Levi's," featuring clips of cult figures like James Dean. These commercials were very effective and carried Levi's from a 35 percent to a 95 percent awareness level in Japan.

In Brazil, unlike the United Kingdom, consumers are more strongly influenced by fashion trends emanating from the European Continent rather than from America. Thus, the Brazilian-made commercial filmed in Paris featured young people, cool amidst a wild traffic scene—very French. This commercial was intended to project the impression that Levi's are the favored brand among young, trend-setting Europeans.

Australian commercials showed that creating brand awareness is important in that market. The lines "fit looks tight, doesn't feel tight, can feel comfortable all night" and "a legend doesn't come apart at the seams" highlighted Levi's quality image, and "since 1850 Levi jeans have handled everything from bucking broncos . . ." amplified Levi's unique positioning. This campaign resulted in a 99 percent brand awareness among Australians.

Case IV–2

Developing a Kodak promotional program in Japan*

Eastman Kodak Company is the largest manufacturer of cameras and other photographic equipment in the United States. Film sales constitute nearly 65 percent of the firm's total sales. For over 20 years Kodak has been selling film in Japan where its sales are lower than in any other nation

---

* Based on a case written by Martin R. Walsh.

of its size. This is so because of tough competition from both Fugi and Sakura, who presently dominate the majority of the market.

Until 1978 there had been a sharp rise in the sales volume of Kodak color film in contrast to that of Kodak black and white in Japan. However, in 1979 the film shipment to Japan showed a slight decrease for the first time. Color and black-and-white film sales combined for a total decrease of 10 percent, with black and white alone decreasing 16 percent. In terms of yen value, the contrast between the color and the black-and-white volume decrease is more dramatic: Color accounted for 50 percent of all film in volume terms, but 78 percent of all film in yen terms.

The company decided in January of 1980 that something had to be done regarding their sales in Japan. Walter A. Fallon, President and Chief Executive Officer, directed Wiley P. Robson, head of the international Photographic Division, to have his marketing department assess the current problems and opportunities and offer alternative solutions which could be put into action within three months. The International Marketing Division began immediately and, on January 29, 1980, presented Mr. Robson with their evaluation. The most important idea they presented him was that all the marketing effort should be aimed at color film, which is more vital to sales than black and white. Also, the following problems were singled out: the price gap which exists between Kodak color film and the competition, the huge inferiority to Fuji in terms of retail shelf space, the lack of brand awareness, the fear of trial use, and the fact that, in many cases, consumers do not purchase Kodak color film unless it is recommended by the clerk in the shop.

The marketing objective of this project was to somehow get the dealers to promote Kodak color film more positively, thus increasing brand awareness and ultimately sales. The marketing strategies that they would use in their promotion were: to narrow the price gap through price reduction, to alter the price-value relationship, to encourage trial use, and to make those with little or no brand loyalty switch to Kodak. The company felt these strategies were conducive to the effort because of the importance of the retailer in the project.

With all the preceding facts in mind, the marketing department produced two alternative solutions to the problem.

The first was a large price reduction to take effect on March 1, 1980, and last for three months. This reduction was to be much larger than originally suggested and would be offered to the retailer only, in exchange for a greater share of shelf space and personal promotion on the retailer's part. It was felt that by doing this the retailer would increase brand awareness of Kodak color film among consumers and alter the price-value relationship by pointing out its superiority. The estimated cost of this solution was $5.2 million.

The other alternative was to initiate a large advertising campaign for the same time period of March to May, 1980. The idea of a premium promo-

EXHIBIT 1

tion campaign was decided upon with the title of "Kitten Poster Present Campaign." (See Exhibit 1.) The campaign would feature the giving away of a free poster with each roll of film purchased. The poster would be a color picture of five kittens. These kittens were selected because of a Japanese superstition that associates this type of kitten with good luck. On the back of the poster would be a character reading with which the consumer could have a lot of fun. Kodak would send to the dealer numerous merchandising setups for store display. Also, a 15-second television commercial was conceptualized along with newspaper and magazine ads that would be run nationally. The total cost of this alternative was estimated at $9.6 million.

On February 6, 1980, a meeting was held with Mr. Fallon and his staff to decide on a method of promotion to begin the following month. After both ideas were explained in full, one of the top international executives voiced the opinion that the idea of the ad campaign was sound but that Japan was an almost hopeless market. Any three-month promotional effort carried out in a market where Kodak possesses only a 7 percent share could not justify spending such a large amount. Also, he stated that since many of the Japanese listen to the advice of the shop clerk, an incentive such as a wholesale price reduction would be more than enough initiative to the retailer for personal promotion.

Kodak's head of marketing in Japan spoke on the merits of the campaign.

He stated that the Japanese retailer would be delighted with the posters and the colorful merchandising displays because of the attraction they add to the store, whereas a simple price reduction would draw no new customers. The association with picture-taking that the poster would have could significantly increase brand awareness, also. In addition, he stressed that Kodak has the highest quality color film on the market and that a price reduction could cause some consumers, both at home and abroad, to begin to doubt this if the price was reduced as drastically as planned. Mr. Hartman also pointed out that the Japanese are an extremely aesthetically inclined race; consequently, the retailer would be proud to display and give away the kitten poster. This could very possibly capture those consumers who have no brand loyalty, they being one of the major targets.

QUESTIONS

1. Based on the preceding information, which course of action do you recommend Kodak initiate and why?

2. Would a price reduction along with the advertising campaign be a solid idea or not?

Case IV–3

Rallysport International—promoting racquetball in Japan

In 10 years, racquetball grew from an obscure sport played in just a few cities in the United States to the fastest growing participation sport on the American scene. In 1970 there were fewer than 30 private court clubs in the entire nation featuring racquetball. By 1980, every major city had a number of clubs devoted exclusively to racquetball or to racquetball and squash. San Diego, California, provides an excellent example of the game's growth. In 1970, the first club was still under construction. By 1980, over 16 clubs were in operation. Rallysport International was started in 1975 by Dana Edwards to capitalize on the trend. It was his expressed intention that Rallysport International would become "the McDonald's of the racquetball world." To do so, Rallysport developed several sets of plans, a packaged marketing and promotional program, an entire management and management control system, and subsidiaries devoted to court construction and supervisory management. The company's plans called for a three-stage expansion: the first in prime markets throughout the United States; the second into less-desirable but substantial markets in the United States; the third into developed countries outside the United States.

Three five-year plans were developed; 1975 to 1980—Phase I, 1980 to 1985—Phase II, 1985 to 1990—Phase III (International). During the first five-year plan, however, Mr. Edwards observed that competition in the United States was growing so quickly that the company would not have enough time to establish its primacy in domestic market categories so decided to enter the international markets before they became saturated. Tobby Lewis, the company's development manager, was given responsibility for determining whether first to enter Japan or Germany, the company's two target markets. His research led him to the conclusion that the character of the game was ideally fitted to the Japanese who, he said, "are competitive, fast, sports oriented, and tuned into American athletics". He also pointed out that expensive land costs and relative lack of urban land made the racquetball business ideal for Japan because it took so little space. A few squash courts exist in Japan and are considered very exclusive. This is because they are fully enclosed heavy construction which is expensive and unusual in Japan.

I. A. Savant and Company was hired to conduct a market study of the Japanese market and make general recommendations concerning market entry. The company discovered that there are some 115 million Japanese spread among some 40 million households, 90 percent of whom classified themselves as middle class. Sixty percent of the national population inhabit an area adjacent to three major cities, Tokyo, Nagoya, and Osaka, which essentially constitute one major metropolitan area. Savant's conclusion was that the metro market alone could support at least 24 racquet clubs, averaging 10 courts each. That would represent only one club per 1 million households. Their report pointed out that the average per capita income in 1981 was 520,000 yen per year ($1.00 = 220 yen), two thirds of which came from the male head of household's regular monthly income, 20 percent from a semiannual bonus, 6 percent from wives, 3 percent from other family members, and 3 percent from other sources. Although those figures are considerably lower than the per capita income in the United States, Savant pointed out that Japanese like new things, are particularly addicted to U.S. products and activities (although that followership may have eroded somewhat in recent years), and that Japanese had shown consistent ability to spend on products which were meaningful to them while saving in other areas. Approximately 20 percent of the population is in the 20-to-35-year age bracket which is considered to be a prime market for racquetball in the United States. The consultant saw no reason to question the acceptance of the game in Japan. Volleyball is extremely popular with housewives who have formed many large leagues.

Tobby Lewis developed an overall plan for invading the Japanese market. He first recommended that at least four clubs be built simultaneously for the following reasons. (1) The market is segmented, and should be tested thoroughly. Therefore one club would be built in a purely business location, one in a business-residential combination area, and two in residential areas—one close in, and one further out. One of the locations was to be in the Kanto region where the head offices of most major Japanese companies are located. (2) Advertising expenditures must be heavy enough to make strong initial impact—one club alone could not support heavy advertising in such a high cost market. (3) Rallysport's Japanese joint venture partners are prepared to finance four clubs. (4) By building four clubs a market presence will be established which will make market entry difficult for other firms. (5) Because of the immense demand potential, each of the four clubs should be immediately profitable.

Savant did foresee some problems. One is that many industrial companies have extensive recreational programs for their employees so that those employees might not be in the market for private recreation. The second problem was that the clubs need to be operated 10 to 11 hours per day in order to function profitably. Clubs in the United States often operate above that range, but Savant suggested that there were some cultural questions to be considered. Counteracting these issues, the consultant suggested, was a recent survey showing that the target youth market had four primary interests—music, sports, fashion, and travel. The same study pointed out that youth were particularly concerned with health and environmental problems and that the nation's general shift to a five-day week had placed more emphasis on sports and recreation.

The primary contributions of Rallysport International were to be promotional programs, developmental activities, managerial systems, and construction advice. Among other activities, Mr. Edwards and Mr. Lewis structured an advertising and promotional campaign plan for review by their Japanese joint venture partner, a major financial institution with extensive experience in industrial goods but limited involvement in the consumer arena. Because the international expansion is of such importance to the company, the board of directors was asked to review the total development program before showing it to the Japanese partner. At the board meeting when it was reviewed, Dave Irwin raised several questions; specifically he mentioned his concern about the cultural fit of the game. He also suggested that the promotional program made basic assumptions about the way the Japanese market would react. He personally questioned, although he admitted he did not know the answers, whether the promotional program was appropriate for the Japanese market or whether it reflected U.S. thinking patterns. He therefore recommended that someone thoroughly familiar with the Japanese culture be asked to review the promotion plan to try to identify problem areas and inconsistencies. He was particularly concerned that Rallysport not present a program which would cause the company to "lose face" when it was presented to the Japanese partner.

Following are the main items included in the advertising and promotional plan devised by Dana Edwards and Tobby Lewis:

Rallysport - International

Promotion

1. All clubs will tie into the Rallysport name: Rallysport-Tokyo, Rallysport-Kanto, and so forth.
2. Club use will be restricted to members only. (In the United States, some have restricted and some have open-member policies.)
3. Members will be charged a flat monthly fee rather than hourly rate (both systems are used in the United States.)
4. Primary target market will be white-collar workers, 25- to 35-year age range, upper-middle income.
5. Secondary target market will be Japanese housewives and female office employees.
6. Low cost one-month trial memberships will be widely used.
7. Celebrities will be widely used in promotion. A championship U.S. racquetball player may be utilized, or we may tie-in with someone such as Sadeharu Oh and the Myomuri Giants (leading baseball player and team in Japan, presently endorse Sogo department stores, Toshiba watches, Nichiban plastic bandages, Kyo-Komachi rice cakes, and Pepsi-Cola. Mr. Oh and the Giants would be very expensive, perhaps as much as 2 million yen per year for full tie-in).

Advertising

1. *Themes:* Three types of advertising are widely used in Japan—follow-the-leader advertising, celebrity tie-ins, and mood advertising. Rally will use the celebrity mode.

2. *Multiple themes:* Different themes will be used for each market segment, but all will tie to some general themes. The three major market segments to be appealed to will be middle-management executives, clerical workers, and housewives.
3. *Overall theme:* "Economical Fun and Health with America's Fastest Growing Sport."
4. Subthemes: Exclusive Clubs; a New Sport; Health and Fitness—stressing cardiovascular benefits; "You Don't Have to Leave the City to Have Fun"; "Easy to Learn, After Just One Hour You Can Have Fun."
5. Campaign will utilize heavy copy and active photography which will explain the game, its benefits, and popularity in the United States. Above all, stress fun.

Media policy and timing

1. *Timing:* A significant segment of the budget will be devoted to a long build-up, teaser type campaign to establish interest and familiarity and, hopefully, encourage membership presales.
2. *Budget allocation:* Twenty percent of the total budget will be used for endorsements and for exhibitions by endorsers of the new clubs. Forty percent of the budget will be devoted to television commercials utilizing 60-second spots rather than the more typical 15-second spots. The 60-second spots will give time to show plenty of action and explain the game and benefits of club membership. Twenty-five percent of the budget will be devoted to newspapers, spread between the nationwide dailies, which reach some 90 percent of all the households, or local dailies, which reach over 40 percent of the market, and sports newspapers such as those owned by Chunichi Shimbum. Ten percent of the budget will be allocated to develop publicity in television, newspapers, and magazines. Overall media expenditures in Japan are as follows: 35 percent television, 31 percent newspapers, 6 percent magazines, 6 percent direct mail, 5 percent radio, 17 percent outdoor and all other.

Graphics

Graphics will emphasize racquetball play. They will focus on (1) celebrities who are sponsored by the company, (2) American players in tournament competition, and (3) playing women or husband and wife combinations showing the game's broad appeal.

QUESTIONS

1. You have been appointed promotional consultant. Analyze the general promotion policy, the budget, advertising themes, and the graphics approach.

2. What other areas or activities should be included in the promotional advertising program?

3. Evaluate other aspects of the proposal.

4. Who else should review this proposal before it is presented to the joint venture partner?

Case IV-4

A job in Grenoble*

Mr. Pete Atherton has a difficult decision to make. He is 42 years old and has been with Sentrics, an electronics firm, for 18 years. He has advanced to his present position of sales manager for the Southern California region. He is married with three children—a daughter, 17 years old, who is editor of a high school newspaper and active in many clubs and organizations; a son, 15, who is on the school tennis team; and another son who is just starting junior high school. His wife, Cathy, is working as a real estate saleswoman in an active real estate market.

Pete has been offered a job as the sales manager for Sentrics in France in conjunction with a new plant which is being built in Grenoble, France, not far from Geneva, Switzerland. Although Sentrics has plants in Scotland, England, and West Germany, this will be their first plant in France. They need Pete's managerial expertise to assure that the French sales force effectively sells the product to industrial users in France. This is especially important since Sentrics is entering the French market with a direct investment rather than a joint venture, which is a common entry strategy of many of their competitors.

While the company does not require its managers to work abroad in order to be eligible for promotion to top executive positions, the foreign assignment would provide Pete with more visibility than in his present position, since the French venture would be closely watched. The job itself would be primarily a lateral transfer rather than a promotion, with no increase in salary. However, the company pays the costs for comparable housing and living expenses. They would also pay for English language schooling for their children.

---

* Case written by Gregory M. Gazda and Mary J. Molenaar, San Diego State

The foreign assignment in Grenoble would be for at least two years, but probably not more than three years. Although the company has no formal training program for people going abroad, an individual is encouraged to set up an overseas learning experience (i.e., language training, cultural schooling, etc.) which Sentrics would pay for.

Pete is having a hard time making a decision because of conflicting factors. On the one hand, he would like to go abroad for a few years since he has never been to Europe. He and his entire family have recently become skiers, a sport which they all enjoy, and the country around Grenoble is noted for some of the best skiing in the world. Also, his wife is quite supportive of this new job opportunity.

However, the children do not want to leave their friends and social activities. Also, it would probably be necessary to send the children to an English-speaking school in Switzerland for them to get a comparable education. What also worries Pete is that he likes Southern California and has made many close friends in the area where he lives. There would be no guarantee that he could return to a job in Southern California after his work in Grenoble. Pete has been putting a decision off, but needs to decide this week about whether to take the French sales manager position.

QUESTIONS

1. What would you do if you were in Pete's situation?

2. What factors do you think are the most important ones to consider in making the decision?

3. Is there anything the company could have done to make the job decision easier for Pete?

Case IV-5

A policy for selection and compensation of overseas managers

Assume you have been given the task of formulating a policy for the selection and compensation of overseas managers for a multinational firm operating in several Latin American countries and Europe. Your company is a major manufacturer of heavy industrial equipment that has been operating in foreign markets for over 40 years. Like many early export-oriented companies, most of the international business was export with no manufacturing abroad. In recent years, the company orientation and attitudes toward foreign operations have shifted drastically; they now have manufacturing in six countries and the international portion of their business accounts for well over 50 percent of their annual profits. The company philosophy toward International has been shifting away from viewing the international portion as export only and trying to organize into a multinational company. This shift in philosophy and the importance of the international division has placed greater emphasis on the type and function of the international manager sent abroad. While the company has effectively utilized the typical "expatriate freewheeler" to represent them abroad (although mavericks in their management style, they have proved to be extremely effective for the company), it is now becoming more evident that there is need for a different type of person to spend a shorter period of time abroad. Most host countries have changed their policies toward foreigners working in their countries from relatively liberal permission to operate at many levels to increasingly more restrictive policies. For example, many Latin American countries will not permit foreign personnel when there are qualified nationals. The only exception is that a U.S. citizen will be given a work permit for three or four years to train a national replacement. Even in Europe, it is becoming more and more politically astute to hire nationals. For the company this has meant sending fewer people to represent their worldwide operations abroad, and further, those who are sent abroad must be extremely capable, understand the total operation, and be effective teachers. The "right person" to go abroad is the same person with the same qualifications who would be in demand in the domestic operation as well.

The company has, historically, provided the typical inducements for moving abroad: cost of living allowances, depending on the country, from 20 percent to 30 percent of the base salary; paid vacations on an annual basis back to the United States; schooling allowances for children back in the States or in private schools; and all moving expenses including complete household furnishings. Despite such inducements there have been some real problems with prospective people you have wanted to send abroad. Many of them center around the family. Over the years, the personnel director has kept a record of some typical complaints and questions raised when executives have been asked to go abroad. For example, "Will you keep us supplied with baby food in Colombia? You mean you pay only 20 percent premium for the sacrifice of leaving the United States? My daughter could live at home while she attends college; will you bring her back to the States and pay her living expenses? Will you pay my way back to see my own doctor if it's necessary? Will you move my new outboard cruiser? Will you move my mother-in-law, who lives with us, to Buenos Aires too?" While these questions may not seem relevant to an outsider, to the individual raising the questions they are important. It has been felt that these kinds of issues are critical in the initial decision to go abroad and are also quite important as reasons why executives return ahead of schedule. A recent study of 245 multinationals concludes that the adjustment problems of U.S. citizens abroad are severe. The inability to completely adjust to their new environment was found to be costly in terms of operations efficiency, client relations, management performance, and personal effectiveness.

The premature return rate on foreign assignments ranges from 25 to 40 percent of those sent abroad. It currently costs an average of $55,000 per family to return prematurely from an overseas assignment. This is the actual out-of-pocket cost for the company. It does not include the personal and emotional impact of an overseas failure or a period of poor work performance and low morale which may precede the actual decision to return.

Culture shock is the term used to describe most of the problems expatriates have in adjusting overseas. Wives of expatriate managers often play a crucial role in determining whether or not an expatriate will continue an assignment or opt for an early return. While the manager has had perhaps some orientation and language training, the wife frequently has not; and yet, she must deal with the foreign culture in the most immediate, everyday fashion.

You have heard of an expatriate support system (ESS) that some companies have used to prevent early return. Some companies have had the experience of reducing their return rate to only 10 percent with the use of effective support systems. A typical ESS is a comprehensive effort beginning with straightforward recruitment information, careful employee and family screening, cross-cultural and language training for managers and families, special workshops for wives, stress management training for effective cultural adjustment, and on-site support and intervention. The system is designed to weed out those who see their assignment as a glamorous trip, as a means to solve already existing family problems (they hope going overseas will give them a "fresh start"), and similar indications that a family is predisposed to an early return.[1]

Today, serving a hitch overseas for the company is required of almost anyone wanting company advancement. Many problems arise in sending executives overseas, but one of the most critical is compensation. Some feel the overseas executive or expatriate is overcompensated; others feel that, considering the sacrifice, he is undercompensated.

On the plus side, a man of 28 to 45 (the usual age range of overseas appointees) generally gets a boost in his career, higher pay, and broader responsibilities. Major companies are sending their top-ranking younger men abroad not employees they want to "bury."

[1] For an interesting article on the problems of the cost of overseas personnel see, Kenneth F. Misa, "Return on Investment of Overseas Personnel," *Financial Executive*, April 1979, pp. 42–46.

Says a Chase Manhattan Bank executive: "A man is smart to have some overseas time if he really wants to move up the ladder." About 80 percent of those Chase sends abroad are sent for career development. The same holds for a growing number of big and medium-size international outfits. The usual hitch lasts from two to five years, and the persons most apt to benefit from it are middle managers. They probably will control a whole local operation which lets them prove their general managerial ability. If successful, they return home with higher status. A younger person is smart to go for experience—even without more pay.

A far less attractive deal involves going overseas for an indeterminate period to train a national for a job in their home country. This missionary may return home to discover a former equal has stepped above him or her. Usually, of course, a person over 50 goes abroad only to fill a high-ranking spot. Some big companies now provide an added incentive; they allow foreign-service people to retire early (often at 60) with varying retirement benefits.

The cost of sending an employee overseas can be staggering.[2] For example, a $40,000-a-year married employee with one child could cost your company a total of $142,600 in Nigeria. If you send them to Sweden it will be $120,400 and for that same $40,000 employee, Japan will cost $112,700 and Saudi Arabia $108,100. The escalation is caused by the extra allowances for housing, schooling, and so on that it takes to get someone to make the move, plus the additional foreign taxes the company generally pays for the employee.

An extensive survey by the Conference Board of 267 of the largest U.S.-based international corporations showed the following: 84 percent paid their American officials abroad a premium for foreign service; 81 percent paid cost-of-living allowances for what was perceived as the higher cost of maintaining an American standard of living abroad; and 72 percent gave housing subsidies. Allowances can range from over 100 percent to 30 percent of a person's base pay. For example, in the case of Nigeria, the allowance on a $40,000 salary is $75,900. With the new tax bill passed in 1981 allowing for a $75,000 exclusion from U.S. income taxes and increasing to $95,000 by 1986, the compensation package will be somewhat better for the employee as well as the company than it was when the maximum exclusion was only $15,000.

Your compensation program is not too different from the ones discussed. You also have had several executives return from foreign assignments within six to eight months, and, in most cases, after returning they have left the company. Some were not considered a loss, but there were at least one or two whom you did not want to lose. While this has not been a major problem, certainly your immediate superior feels that part of the reason

---

[2] For more detail on costs of overseas staff see, "The High Cost of Overseas Staff," *World Business Weekly,* April 27, 1981, p. 48.

some executives have returned before their assignments were up was the arm twisting done to get them to accept the assignment. They were not really enthusiastic about going abroad in the first place but felt obligated, and further, they were not properly prepared to face the cultural shock involved. There is more to recruiting for a foreign assignment than just getting someone willing to go. Rarely does a U.S. manager abroad fail because of technical incompetence. It is fairly easy for us to evaluate whether or not the individual knows the job. Failure stems far more frequently from behavioral traits and an inability to adjust to the foreign way of life.

Another problem many companies are having and your company faces as you expand is how to deal effectively with the returning executive. In the past, you have been able to absorb all of your returning personnel in meaningful positions at headquarters. However, as policies and changes mentioned above lead to a larger turnover in your foreign executive personnel, you need to consider the effective integration of these executives in meaningful positions when they return to the U.S. The cultural shock experienced by returning executives worries you since you can see this as a possible problem for your company.

A recent study of repatriated executives from 25 international companies suggests some of the problems of integrating returning executives into regular company operations. Those interviewed were between the ages of 30 and 45, married, with an average of 3 children, and had spent from two to six years abroad. Many left their jobs for positions with other companies shortly after returning from abroad. The principal reason given for leaving was dissatisfaction with their new domestic assignments.

In general, most of the executives were alienated from their companies and the reasons cited were: (1) the nature of the new domestic assignment was too disagreeable; (2) the location of the domestic assignment was unacceptable to the returnee; (3) salary and fringe benefits to which the individual and the family had become accustomed while on foreign assignment were lost; (4) the skills and experience acquired could be marketed more to the individual's advantage either domestically or internationally through another company; and finally, several individuals complained of unfair discriminatory practice by the company in dealing with their objections and grievances.

The findings of this study were supported by a recent incident involving a financial officer of your company who had been stationed in Western Europe. The Browns lived in Paris where Mr. Brown was responsible for overseeing the financial operations of your company in six European countries. He and his family had enjoyed their five-year stay in Paris and had become accustomed to French culture and the higher level of living there. Their children had been enrolled in private schools outside Paris and liked the more relaxed pace of European life. The company ordered him back to the United States since it wanted to provide foreign experience for another executive. A new company policy of calling back executives after a four-year assignment had rencently been initiated. This policy was considered necessary to provide foreign experience for as many key personnel as possible. Brown was the first to be affected.

Brown was ordered back to Chicago as assistant to the Vice President of Finance. In this position he had much less responsibility and authority than he had had in the European post where he reported directly to the President of European operations. As a consequence, he found his new job strange and certainly less challenging. Even though his salary had not been reduced, he was not happy in Chicago. In his European job, he had operated in a number of different capacities and become very familiar with the entire European operation. He felt that the company did not appreciate him and was not effectively using his experience gained as a key European financial officer. In addition to his job dissatisfaction, the lifestyle in Chicago was substantially different than that in Paris, and his whole family was upset about having to move back to the States. In fact, one daughter stayed in Europe to complete her education since she had received most of her education there and didn't want to transfer to U.S. schools. After about six months in Chicago, Brown quit and went to work with a competitor.

There is no simple solution to repatriating executives, and you must also deal with the negative aspects of sending people abroad because of the hardships of moving and the cost of maintaining an American style of living standard abroad at today's prices.

Further, when you read about the kidnappings of U.S. business executives in South America, Italy, and elsewhere, it is hard to believe it will not create more resistance to moving abroad. Additional resistance is likely when the outstanding person you want to assign abroad can see there is as much opportunity in the States as there would be in a foreign assignment. There is no doubt, however, that the trend is to keep the number of Americans overseas as low as possible and to eventually reduce the number in relation to business volume as rapidly as possible, while at the same time giving as many as possible international experience. Thus those assigned to foreign operations almost always are picked for special knowledge and are expected to train nationals to replace them; this means you must send your best.

Part of your task is to determine if the new policy of rotating key personnel in foreign assignments should be continued, and if so, how to avoid losing men like Brown. There is no doubt that top management was upset about losing Brown whom they considered to have been a definite asset to the organization. You must also devise a policy to help solve the immediate problems as well as those you can anticipate in the future. This policy may entail recommendations for specific changes in organization and methods of control. The new policy should help motivate your executives to go overseas and provide you with the best possible talent abroad, talent you will be able to effectively utilize once they return to the United States.

Case IV–6

National office machines—motivating Japanese salespeople: Straight salary or commission?

National Office Machines of Dayton, Ohio, manufacturers of cash registers, EDP equipment, adding machines, and other small office equipment, has recently entered into a joint venture with Nippon Cash Machines of Tokyo, Japan. Last year, National Office Machines (N.O.M.) had domestic sales of over $220 million and foreign sales of nearly $100 million. Besides the United States, they operate in most of Western Europe, the Mideast, and some parts of the Far East. In the past, they have had no significant sales or sales force in Japan although they were represented there by a small trading company until a few years ago. In the United States, they are one of the leaders in their field and considered to have one of the most successful and aggressive sales forces found in this highly competitive industry.

Nippon Cash Machines (N.C.M.) is an old-line cash register manufacturing company organized in 1872. At one time, they were the major manufacturer of cash register equipment in Japan but they have been losing ground since 1960 even though they produce perhaps the best cash register in Japan. Last year's sales were 9 billion yen (220 yen = $1 U.S.), a 15 percent decrease over sales the prior year. The fact that they produce only cash registers is one of their major problems; the merger with N.O.M. will give them much-needed breadth in their product offerings. Another hoped-for strength to be gained from the joint venture is managerial leadership which they sorely need.

There are 14 Japanese companies with products that compete with Nippon, plus several foreign giants such as IBM, National Cash Register, Burroughs of the United States, and Sweda Machines of Sweden. Nippon has a small sales force of 21 men, most of whom have been with the company since shortly after World War II. These salesmen have been responsible for selling to Japanese trading companies and to a few large purchasers of equipment.

Part of the joint venture agreement included doubling the sales force within a year, with N.O.M. responsible for hiring and training the new salesmen who must all be young, college-trained Japanese nationals. The agreement also allowed for U.S. personnel in supervisory positions for an indeterminate period of time and retaining the current Nippon sales force.

One of the many sales management problems facing the Nippon/American Business Machines Corporation (N.A.B.M.C.—the name of the new joint venture) was what sales compensation plan to use, i.e., should they follow the Japanese tradition of straight salary and guaranteed employment until death with no incentive program, or the U.S. method (very successful for N.O.M. in the United States) of commissions and various incentives based on sales performance, with the ultimate threat of being fired if sales quotas continuously go unfilled?

The immediate response to the problem might well be one of using the tried and true U.S. compensation methods since they have worked so well in the United States and are perhaps the kind of changes needed and expected from U.S. management. N.O.M. management is convinced that salespeople selling their kinds of products in a competitive market must have strong incentives in order to produce. In fact, N.O.M. had experimented on a limited basis in the United States with straight salary about 10 years ago and it was a "bomb." Unfortunately the problem is considerably more complex than it appears on the surface.

One of the facts to be faced by N.O.M. management is the traditional labor-management relations and employment systems which exist in Japan. The roots of the system go back to Japan's feudal era when a serf promised a lifetime of service to his lord in exchange for a lifetime of protection. By the start of Japan's industrial revolution in the 1880s, an unskilled worker pledged to remain with a company all his useful life if the employer would teach him the new mechanical arts. The tradition of spending a lifetime with a single employer survives today mainly because most workers like it that way. There is little chance of being fired, pay raises are regular, and there is a strict order of job-protecting seniority.

Japanese workers at larger companies still are protected from outright dismissal by union contracts and an industrial tradition that some personnel specialists believe has the force of law. Under this tradition, a worker can be dismissed after an initial trial period only for gross cause, such as theft or some other major infraction. As long as the company remains in business the worker isn't discharged, or even furloughed, simply because there isn't enough work to be done.

Besides the guarantee of employment for life, the typical Japanese worker receives many fringe benefits from the company. Just how paternalistic the typical Japanese firm can be is illustrated by a statement from the Japanese Ministry of Foreign Affairs which gives the example of "A," a male worker who is employed in a fairly representative company in Tokyo:

> To begin with, A lives in a house provided by his company, and the rent he pays is amazingly low when compared with average city rents. His daily trips between home and factory are paid by the company. A's working hours are from 9 a.m. to 5 p.m. with a break for lunch which he usually takes in the company restaurant at a very cheap price. He often brings food, clothing, and other miscellaneous articles he has bought at the company store at a

discount ranging from 10 percent to 30 percent below city prices back to his wife. The company store even supplies furniture, refrigerators, and television sets on an installment basis, for which, if necessary, A can obtain a loan from the company almost free of interest.

In case of illness, A is given free medical treatment in the company hospital, and if his indisposition extends over a number of years, the company will continue paying almost his full salary. The company maintains lodges at seaside or mountain resorts where A can spend the holidays or an occasional weekend with the family at moderate prices. . . . It must also be remembered that when A reaches retirement age (usually 55) he will receive a lump sum retirement allowance or a pension, either of which will assure him a relatively stable living for the rest of his life.

Even though "A" is only an example of a typical employee, a salesperson can expect the same treatment. Job security is such an expected part of everyday life that no attempt is made to motivate the Japanese salesperson in the same manner as in the United States; as a consequence, selling traditionally has been primarily an order-taking job. Except for the fact that sales work offers some travel, entry to outside executive offices, the opportunity to entertain, and similar side benefits, it provides a young person with little other incentive to surpass basic quotas and drum up new business. The traditional Japanese bonuses (which normally amount to about two or four months' salary over the year) are no larger for salespeople than any other functional job in the company.

As a key executive in a Mitsui-affiliated engineering firm put it recently: "The typical salesman in Japan isn't required to have any particular talent." In return for meeting sales quotas, most Japanese salespeople draw a modest monthly salary, sweetened about twice a year by bonuses. Manufacturers of industrial products generally pay no commission or other incentives to boost their businesses.

Besides the problem of motivation, a foreign company faces other strange customs when trying to put together and manage a sales force. Class systems and the Japanese distribution system with its penchant for reciprocity put strain on the creative talents of the best sales managers, as Simmons, the U.S. bedding manufacturer, was quick to learn. One Simmons executive explained he had no idea of the workings of the class system. Hiring a good person from the lower classes, for instance could be a disaster. If that person called on a client of a higher class, there was a good chance the client would be insulted. There is also a major difference in lánguage among the classes.

In the field, Simmons found itself stymied by the bewildering realities of Japanese marketing, especially the traditional distribution system which operates on a philosophy of reciprocity that goes beyond mere business to the core of the Japanese character. It's involved with "on," the notion that regards a favor of any kind as a debt that must be repaid. To "wear" another's "on" in business and then turn against that person is to lose face,

Who you know, important

abhorrent to most Japanese. Thus, the owner of large Western-style apartments, hotels, or developments will buy his beds from the supplier to whom he owes a favor, no matter what the competition offers.

In small department and other retail stores, where most items are handled on consignment, the bond with the supplier is even stronger. Consequently, all sales outlets are connected in a complicated web that runs from the largest supplier, with a huge national force to the smallest local distributor, with a handful of door-to-door salespeople. The system is self-perpetuating and all but impossible to crack from the outside.

However, there is some change in attitude taking place as both workers and companies start discarding traditions for the job mobility common in the United States. Skilled workers are willing to bargain on the strength of their experience in an open labor market in an effort to get higher wages or better job opportunities; in the United States it's called "shopping around." And a few companies are showing a willingness to lure workers away from other concerns. A number of companies are also plotting on how to rid themselves of some of the "deadwood" workers accumulated as a result of promotions by strict seniority.

Toyo Rayon Company, Japan's largest producer of synthetic fibers, says it will start reevaluating all its senior employees every five years with the implied threat that those who don't measure up to the company's expectations will have to accept reassignment and possibly demotion; some may even be asked to resign. A chemical engineering and construction firm is planning to ask all its employees over 42 to negotiate a new contract with the company every two years. Pay raises and promotions will go to those the company wants to keep. For those who think they are worth more than the company is willing to pay, the company will offer "retirement" with something less than the $15,000 lump-sum payment the average Japanese worker receives at age 55.

A few U.S. companies operating in Japan are also experimenting with incentive plans. Marco and Company, a belting manufacturer and Japanese distributor for Power Packing and Seal Company, was persuaded by Power Company to set up a travel plan incentive for salespeople who topped their regular sales quotas. Unorthodox as the idea was for Japan, Marco went along, and, the first year, special one-week trips to Far East holiday spots like Hong Kong, Taiwan, Manila, and Macaco were inaugurated. Marco's sales of products jumped 212 percent, and the next year sales were up an additional 60 percent.

Last April, Marco took the full step toward an American-style sales program. Under Power's guidance, the company eliminated bonuses and initiated a sales commission plan.

When the first quarterly commission checks were mailed last June, the top salespeople found they had earned an average of $550 per month each, compared to original basic salaries of about $100 a month.

At first, Marco's management had resisted any form of incentive program for its personnel, arguing that to do so would "disrupt" all normal business operations of the company. The virtually instantaneous success of the travel incentives in motivating previously plodding sales performances into an enthusiastic burst of initiative has prompted Marco to consider installing some form of incentive and/or commission sales plan for its extensive non-Power operations. The company is one of the largest manufacturers of industrial belting in Japan.

IBM also has made a move toward chucking the traditional Japanese sales system (salary plus a bonus but no incentives). For about a year it has been working with a combination which retains the semiannual bonus while adding commission payments on sales over pre-set quotas.

"It's difficult to apply a straight commission system in selling computers because of the complexities of the product," an IBM-Japan official said. "Our salesmen don't get big commissions because other employees would be jealous." To head off possible ill-feeling, therefore, some nonselling IBM employees receive monetary incentives.

Most Japanese companies seem reluctant to follow IBM's and Marco's example because they have doubts about directing older salesmen to go beyond their usual order-taking role. High-pressure tactics are not well accepted here, and sales channels are often pretty well set by custom and long practice (e.g., a manufacturer normally deals with one trading company, which in turn sells only to customers A, B, C, and D). A salesman or trading company, for that matter, is not often encouraged to go after customer Z and get him away from a rival supplier.

Japanese companies also consider nonsales employees a tough problem to handle. With salesmen deprived of the "glamour" status often accorded by many top managements in the United States, even Marco executives admit they have a ticklish problem in explaining how salesmen—who are considered to be just another key working group in the company with no special status—rate incentive pay and special earning opportunities.

The Japanese market is becoming more competitive and there is real fear on the part of N.O.M. executives that the traditional system just won't work in a competitive market. On the other hand, the proponents of the incentive system agree that the system really has not been tested over long periods or even very adequately in the short term since it has been applied only in a growing market. In other words, was it the incentive system which caused the successes achieved by the companies or was it market growth? Especially there is doubt since other companies following the traditional method of compensation and employee relations also have had sales increases during the same period.

The problem is further complicated for Nippon/American because they will have both new and old salespeople. The young Japanese seem eager to accept the incentive method but older ones are hesitant. How do you satisfy both since you must, by agreement, retain all the sales staff?[1]

---

[1] "A U.S. Turn to Native Talent in Japan," *Business Week* December 8, 1980, pp. 56–57.

EXHIBIT 1: Life goals

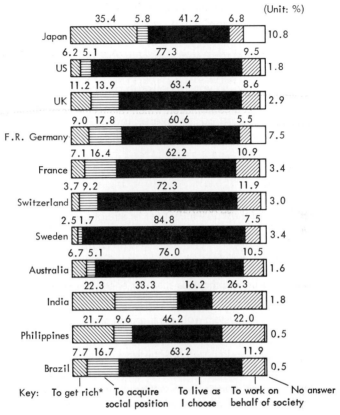

Key: To get rich*   To acquire   To live as   To work on   No answer
                      social position   I choose   behalf of society

Note: The respondents were asked to choose one answer.
  * The literal translation of the question asked the Japanese pollees is closer to
"to be well-off economically." Had the Japanese respondents been asked the more
blunt "to get rich," probably fewer of them would have chosen this alternative.
  Source: Prime Minister's Office; "How Youth See Life," *Focus Japan* December
1978, p. 9.

A recent study done by the Japanese government on attitudes of youth around the world suggests that younger Japanese may be more receptive to U.S. incentive methods than one would anticipate. In a study done by the Prime Minister's Office of Japan there were some surprising results when Japanese responses are compared with responses of similar aged youths from other countries. Exhibit 1 summarizes some of the information gathered on life goals. One point that may be of importance in shedding light on the decision N.O.M. has to make is a comparison of Japanese attitudes with young people in 11 other countries—the Japanese young people are less satisfied with their home life, school, and working situations, and are more passive in their attitude toward social and political problems. Further, almost a third of those employed said they were dissatisfied with their present jobs primarily because of low income and short vacations. Asked if they had to choose between a difficult job with responsibility and authority, or an easy job without responsibility and authority, 64 percent of the Japanese picked the former, somewhat less than the 70–80 percent average in other countries.[2]

Another critical problem lies with the nonsales employees; trditionally, all employees on the same level are treated equally whether sales, production, or staff. How do you encourage competitive, aggressive salesmanship in a market unfamiliar to such tactics, and how do you compensate salespeople to promote more aggressive selling in the face of tradition-bound practices of paternalistic company behavior?

QUESTIONS

1. What should they do—incentives or straight salary? Suppport your answer.

2. If incentives are out, how do you motivate salespeople and get them to aggressively compete?

3. Design a U.S.-type program for motivation and compensation of salespeople. Point out where difficulties may be encountered with your plan and how the problems are to be overcome.

4. Design a pay system you think would work, satisfying old salespeople, new salespeople, and other employees.

5. Discuss the idea that perhaps the kind of motivation and aggressiveness found in the United States is not necessary in the Japanese market.

6. Develop some principles in motivation which could be applied by an international marketer in other countries.

---

[2] "How Youth See Life," *Focus Japan,* December 1978, pp. 9–10.

PART FIVE

INTERNATIONAL MARKETING MANAGEMENT II

CHAPTERS:

CASES:

Chapter 17

Pricing in international markets

In recent years, the intensification of competition in the world marketplace has focused increasing attention on the role of pricing as a competitive weapon. Price determination has consistently baffled both practitioners and theoreticians and the addition of an international parameter certainly does not simplify the process. Nevertheless, a student who understands price theory and is aware of the pricing methods of industry can comprehend the pricing problems of international business.

Whether exporting or managing overseas operations, the international marketing manager is ultimately responsible for establishing price policies for the company's international operations. Within the range of prices permitted by the market, competition, and various government regulations, the manager may also be responsible for setting and attempting to control the actual prices for goods as they are traded in different markets.[1] Operating in different markets adds new problems and market variables to be considered and governmental attitudes vary significantly from country to country. Differing tariffs, costs, attitudes, and methods of price quotation all contribute to confounding the marketing executive.

Three basic situations prevail relative to pricing. In one, the market sets the price absolutely and the producer has little control over the level of prices; this is the situation in markets for wheat, raw plastic, standard steel shapes, cement flour, and other standardized or relatively undifferentiated products. In the second, the market situation offers genuine alternatives for setting prices; this condition exists with an oligopoly when products are differentiated, as with most manufactured goods sold in nonregulated markets. In the third circumstance, the market becomes secondary to political considerations. Sometimes a product may be admitted to a market only through governmental permission with the purchasing government acting as the price setter, for example, armaments or nuclear reactors.

Business executives from different countries view the strategic role of pricing differently. In general, American marketers tend to regard price as an important variable in marketing decision making while in other

---

[1] The decision process in price setting is discussed in John U. Farley, J. M. Hulbert, and D. Weinstein, "Price Setting and Volume Planning by Two European Industrial Companies: A Study and Comparison of Decision Processes," *Journal of Marketing*, Winter 1980, pp. 46–54.

countries, attitudes vary widely toward the importance of pricing. In many countries, including most of Europe, managers do not generally employ pricing as a major competitive element; however, this situation is changing. Companies such as Ford Motor, General Motors, and Sony, seemingly above price competition, are placing increasing emphasis on pricing. Target pricing and fixed list prices are no longer the rule as excess production capacity around the world forces flexible pricing policies. One commentator suggests that "if excess capacity in the United States has contributed to the new price strategy, excess capacity abroad is making it vital to survival."

In this chapter, the focus is on pricing considerations of particular significance in the international marketplace. Basic policy questions related to the special cost, market, and competitive factors in foreign markets are reviewed. Consideration is given to price escalation and its control as well as the problems and policies associated with price fixing on business, governmental, and international levels, and mention is made of some of the mechanics of international price quotation. The considerations in this chapter are relevant to all firms doing business internationally.

PRICING POLICY

Active marketing in a number of countries compounds the number of pricing problems and the number of variables relating to price policy. Unless the firm has a clearly thought-out, explicitly defined price policy, it will establish prices by expediency rather than design. Pricing activity will be affected by the country in which business is being conducted, the type of product, variations in competitive conditions, and other strategic factors. In any case, price and terms cannot be based on domestic criteria alone.

Who is to set the price? As pricing becomes increasingly complex because of national laws, intracompany competition, and monopsonistic purchasers, emphasis on market considerations declines. Ultimately, the marketing executive lacks adequate control to function effectively in international competition.

It must be recognized that the marketplace ultimately through interplay of supply and demand, prevails as the final determinant of prices; even governments and strong monopsonists can not repeal that law. Major industries such as steel, paper, glass, chemicals, aluminum, and automobiles have learned that lesson to their discomfort.

Pricing objectives

Two choices are available to a compnay in setting its price policy. Pricing can be viewed as an active instrument for the accomplishment of marketing objectives, or considered as a static element in business decisions. If the former viewpoint is adhered to, the company will utilize prices to accomplish certain objectives relative to a target return or profit from overseas operations or for the accomplishment of a target volume of market share. If the second approach is followed, the company will likely be content to sell what it can in overseas markets and look on this as bonus volume. Obviously, the second alternative is hardly adequate for enterprises with operations in foreign countries. It is more likely to be the viewpoint of a firm which exports only and which places a low priority on foreign business. Profit is by far the most important of the pricing objectives. When U.S. and Canadian international businesses were asked to rate, on a scale of one to five, several factors important in price setting, total profits received an average rating of 4.7, followed by return on investment (4.41), market share (4.13), total sales volume (4.06), and liquidity ranking the lowest (2.19)[2]

BOX 17–1: Who sets prices?

Pricing problems in international operations are a source of concern to executives with varying and diverse management responsibilities. The international division vice president is concerned with the effect of pricing on divisional profits; the regional manager is concerned with the impact that policies on intercorporate and local market pricing will have in his geographic area; the subsidiary manager tries to operate on a profitable basis within the policy limitations on intercorporate transfer, export, and local market pricing imposed on him. The director of international marketing wants a price that will be competitive in the marketplace; the controller and the treasurer want prices that will be profitable; and the manufacturing director wants prices that will give longer production runs with evenly distributed plant loads for more efficient operations. The tax manager looks at the implications of pricing policy on the total tax burden to the corporation and tax-deferral opportunities; and the lawyer is concerned with pricing policies and practices that may lead to antitrust or restriction-of-trade violations. Even domestic product managers have an interest in transfer prices to the international division or to overseas units.

Source: *Solving International Pricing Problems*, p. 3. Reprinted with permission of the publisher, Business International Corp. (New York).

A company's policies may emphasize control over final prices or the net price received by the business. In the latter case, the producer may not attempt to control the price at which the product is ultimately sold; in the former, price is considered an important strategic element of the marketing mix so the company will want to retain all possible control over the end price. Firms, however, that follow a price control policy in their domestic business found they were unable to control end prices in foreign markets, and therefore have reoriented their thinking to "mill net pricing," i.e., prices received for goods when shipped from the plant.

Price control is a many-faceted activity. End prices charged to consumers must be controlled if a marketer is to reach the desired level of market penetration. Profits and profit margins must be maintained and controlled country by country, product by product, and for every type of transaction.

---

[2] "Factors That Influence Pricing Decisions," *International Management*, June 1981, p. 3.

Competition within a company must be controlled so that different divisions subsidiaries, or branches of a company are not undercutting each other, thus depriving the company as a whole of profits.

One of the complicated areas of pricing policy relates to the objectives sought in intracompany sales, i.e., sales between a parent company and a subsidiary, from one subsidiary to another, or from a foreign subsidiary to a parent company. Intracorporate pricing objectives may be related to minimization of tax burdens and duties, repatriation of profits, profit balancing among units, and, of course, maximizing profit. The continuing growth and proliferation of marketing activities and organizational arrangements make it imperative to establish corporate policies and procedures for handling intracompany pricing that meet these requirements. Intracorporate pricing policy and strategy are discussed later in this chapter.

Approaches to international pricing

Whether the orientation is toward control over end prices or over net prices, the company will have a policy relative to net prices that must be received. Both cost and market considerations are important; the company will not sell goods below cost of production and cannot sell goods at a price not acceptable in the marketplace. Firms unfamiliar with overseas marketing and many firms producing industrial goods orient their pricing solely on a cost basis. Firms which employ pricing as part of the strategic mix, however, will be aware of such alternatives as market segmentation from country to country or market to market, competitive pricing in the marketplace, and other market-oriented pricing factors.

Firms which orient their price thinking around cost must determine whether to use variable cost pricing or full cost pricing in costing their goods. In variable cost pricing, the firm is concerned only with the marginal or incremental cost of producing goods to be sold in overseas markets. Such firms regard foreign sales as bonus sales and assume any return over their variable cost makes a contribution to net profit. These firms may be able to price most competitively in foreign markets; but, because they are selling products abroad at lower net prices than they are selling them in the domestic market, they may be subject to charges of dumping. In that case, they open themselves to antidumping tariffs or penalties which take away their competitive advantage. Companies which follow the full-cost pricing philosophy insist that no unit of a similar product is different from any other unit in terms of cost and that each unit bears its full share of the total fixed and variable cost.

In domestic marketing, both variable cost and full cost policies are followed. An international firm that uses variable cost pricing must ultimately decided if they are a marketer exporting from one country into another or a world marketer. If the firm regards itself as a world marketer, it is more likely to think in terms of full cost pricing for all markets. There remains the question of whether pricing should be below full costs if it increases profits and there is no other access to certain markets. These are all policy questions to be resolved by the firm.

COST FACTORS

Regardless of the strategic factors involved and the company's orientation to market pricing, every price must be set with cost considerations in mind. At a minimum, prices over a long run must cover full costs for a business to survive. Full costs do not have to be covered in every market so long as total company sales cover all costs in international marketing. In the case of intracorporate transfers, such transfers may be based solely on direct production costs (variable costs only) or may include profit plus general administrative costs, research and development costs, and so forth. In determining producer company overhead, management must not include factors which would raise foreign prices to the point that sales volume is reduced. Sometimes domestic marketing sales and advertising costs are included in the base price of the goods, but because such costs are re-incurred in the foreign markets, they should not be included in basic cost determination.

Widely fluctuating costs of raw materials and supplies and equally widely fluctuating exchange rates have become especially important in recent years and have forced increasing emphasis on pricing.

A number of other costs unique to international marketing or exaggerated in international marketing should be borne in mind by the pricing executive. Some of the major categories considered below are taxes and tariffs, inflation, exchange rate fluctuations, and middlemen and transportation costs.

Taxes and tariffs

"Nothing is surer than death and taxes" has a particularly familiar ring to the ears of the international trader because taxes include tariffs, and tariffs are one of the most pervasive features of international trading. Taxes and tariffs affect the ultimate consumer price for a product, and, in most instances, the consumer bears the burden of both. Sometimes, however, the consumer benefits when manufacturers selling goods into foreign countries reduce their net return to gain access on a competitive footing to a foreign market. Absorbed or passed on, taxes and tariffs must be considered by the international business person.

A tariff, or duty, is a special form of taxation, and, like other forms of taxes, may be levied for the purpose of protecting a market or for increasing government revenue. A tariff is a fee charged when goods are brought into a country from another country. The level of tariff is typically expressed as the rate of duty and may be levied as specific, ad valorem, or a combination. A *specific* duty is a flat charge per physical unit imported, such as 15 cents per bushel of rye. *Ad valorem* duties are levied as a percentage of the value of the goods imported, such as 20 percent of the value of imported watches. *Combination* tariffs include both a specific and an ad valorem charge, such as $1 per camera plus 10 percent of its value.

Tariffs and other forms of import taxes serve to discriminate against all foreign goods. Fees for import certificates or for other administrative processing can assume such levels that they are, in fact, import taxes. Many countries have purchase or excise taxes which apply to various categories of goods, value added or turnover taxes which apply as the product goes through a channel of distribution, and retail sales taxes. Such taxes increase the end price of goods, but, in general, do not discriminate against foreign goods. Tariffs are the primary discriminatory tax which must be taken into account in reckoning with foreign competition.

Inflation

The effect of inflation on cost must be accounted for. In countries with rapid inflation or exchange variation, selling price must be related to the cost of goods sold and the cost of replacing the items. Goods are often sold below their cost of replacement plus overhead and sometimes are sold even below replacement cost. In these instances, the company would be better off not to sell the products at all. When payment is likely to be delayed for several months or is worked out on a long-term contract, inflationary change must be figured into the price.

Exchange-rate fluctuations

At one time, world trade contracts could be easily written and payment was specified in a relatively stable currency. The American dollar was the standard and all transactions could be related to the dollar. Now that all major currencies are floating freely relative to one another, no one is quite sure of the value of *any* currency in the future. Increasingly, companies are insisting that transactions be written in terms of the vendor company's national currency, and forward hedging is becoming more common. Companies active in international business are more aware of currency fluctuations but have yet to find a better method of protecting themselves against currency fluctuations. If exchange rates are not carefully considered in long-term contracts, companies can find themselves unwittingly giving 15 to 20 percent discounts. The added cost incurred as exchange rates fluctuate on a day-to-day basis must be taken into account, especially when there is a significant time lapse between signing the order and delivery of the goods. Exchange-rate differentials mount up. Hewlett-Packard gained nearly half a million dollars additional profit through exchange-rate fluctuations in one year, Nestlé lost a million dollars in six years, while other companies have lost and gained even larger amounts.[3]

---

[3] Methods used to minimize exchange rate risks is discussed in detail in Chapter 21.

Innumerable other cost variables could be identified depending on the market, the product, and the situation. The cost, for example, of reaching a market with relatively small potential may be high. Intense competition in certain world markets raises the cost or lowers margins available to world business. Even such small things as payoffs to local officials can introduce unexpected cost to the unwary entrepreneur. Only experience in a given marketplace will provide the basis for compensating for cost differences in different markets. With experience, a firm that prices on a cost basis operates in a realm of reasonably measurable factors.

Middleman and transportation costs

Channel length and marketing patterns vary widely, but, in most countries, channels are longer and middleman margins larger than is customary in the United States. The diversity of channels used to reach markets and the lack of standardized middleman markups leave many producers not knowing the ultimate price of a product.

Besides channel diversity, the fully integrated marketer operating abroad faces various unanticipated costs because marketing and distribution channel infrastructures are undeveloped in so many countries. In addition, the marketer can incur added expenses for warehousing and handling of small shipments, and may have to bear increased financing costs when dealing with underfinanced middlemen.

Since no convenient source of data on middleman costs is available, the international marketer must rely on experience and marketing research to discover what middleman costs will be. For example, the Campbell Soup Company found their middleman and physical distribution costs in the United Kingdom to be 30 percent higher than in the United States. Extra costs were incurred because soup was purchased in such small quantities— English grocers typically purchase 24-can cases of *assorted* soups (each case being hand-packed for shipment). In the United States, typical purchase units are 48-can cases of one soup purchased by dozens, hundreds, or carloads. The purchase habits in Europe forced the company to an extra wholesale level in its channel to facilitate handling small orders. Purchase frequency patterns also run up billing and order costs; both wholesalers and retailers purchase two to three times as often as their U.S. counterparts. Sales-call costs become virtually prohibitive. These and other distribution cost factors not only caused the company to change its price and price patterns but also forced a complete restructuring of the channel system.

Exporting also incurrs increased transportation costs when moving goods from one country to another. If the goods go over water, there are additional costs for insurance, packing, and handling not generally added to locally produced goods. Such costs add yet another burden since import tariffs in many countries are based on the landed cost which would include transportation, insurance, and shipping charges.

Long distribution channels, tariffs, transportation costs and other costs associated with international marketing combine to escalate the final price to a level considerably higher than charged in the domestic market. A case in point is the pacemaker for heart patients that sells for $2,100 in the United States. The Japanese distribution system plus extra tariffs add substantially to the final price. As one executive of a U.S. pacemaker manufacturer realized, "the ailing Japanese wouldn't be able to get the product cheap. If and when the devices entered Japan," he was told, "they would first have to go through an importer, then to the company with primary responsibility for sales and service, then to a secondary and even a tertiary local distributor, and finally to the hospital."[4] Markups at each of these levels result in the $2,100 pacemaker selling for over $4,000 in Japan. The cost inflation fueled by such costs results in one of the major pricing obstacles facing the multinational marketer—price escalation.

PRICE ESCALATION

Business people or others traveling abroad are often surprised to find goods that are relatively inexpensive in their home country are priced "outrageously" in other countries. Because of the natural tendency to assume such prices are a result of profiteering, manufacturers often resolve to begin exporting to "crack" these new foreign markets.

BOX 17–2: It all adds up to price escalation

Even though the volume and profit are often good, exporting can be an endless battle with red tape and hassle. One exporter to Mexico comments about endless forms to fill out, wrong-color paper holding up shipments, letters of credit lost in the mail, payoffs to border officials, bank drafts disappearing for months, and a 2 percent to 3 percent "shrinkage" at the border. On top of that, there is always the possibility that the market will be suddenly closed to your products. In June 1981, the Mexican government imposed import restrictions on 240 products, and later in January 1982, it raised import duties on 330 products.

Source: Adapted from "In Mexico Operations, Foreign Concerns Face Reams of Red Tape," *The Wall Street Journal*, February 16, 1982, p. 1.

Excess profits may, in fact, exist, but more often the added costs discussed here are the cause of the disproportionate difference in price, here termed *price escalation*. Specifically the term relates to situations where ultimate prices are raised by shipping cost, tariffs, longer channels of distribution, larger middlemen margins, special taxes, and exchange rate fluctuations.

Sample effects of price escalation

Exhibit 17–1 illustrates some of the possible effects these factors may have on the end price of a consumer item. Because costs and tariffs vary

---

[4] Pamela Sherrid, "Learning the Tricks of the Japanese Trade," *Fortune,* November 20, 1978, p. 63.

EXHIBIT 17–1: Sample causes and effects of price escalation

	Domestic example	Foreign example 1: assuming the same channels with wholesaler importing directly	Foreign example 2: importer and same margins and channels	Foreign example 3: same as 2 but with 10 percent cumulative turnover tax
Manufacturing net	$ 5.00	$ 5.00	$ 5.00	$ 5.00
Transport, c.i.f.	n.a.	1.10	1.10	1.10
Tariff (20 percent c.i.f. value)	n.a.	1.22	1.22	1.22
Importer pays	n.a.	n.a.	7.32	7.32
Importer margin when sold to wholesaler				1.83
(25 percent) on cost	n.a.	n.a.	1.83	+ 0.73 turnover tax
				2.56
Wholesaler pays landed cost	5.00	7.32	9.15	= 9.88
				3.29
				+ 0.99 turnover tax
Wholesaler margin (33⅓ on cost)	1.67	2.44	3.05	= 4.28
Retailer pays	6.67	9.76	12.20	14.16
				7.08
				+ 1.42 turnover tax
Retail margin (50 percent on cost)	3.34	4.88	6.10	= 8.50
Retail price	10.01	14.64	18.30	22.66

Notes: a. All figures in U.S. dollars.
b. The exhibit assumes that all domestic transportation costs are absorbed by the middleman.
c. Transportation, tariffs, and middleman margins vary from country to country, but for purposes of comparison, only a few of the possible variations are shown.

so widely from country to country, a hypothetical but realistic example is used: it assumes: (1) that a constant net price is received by the manufacturer; (2) that all domestic transportation costs are absorbed by the various middlemen and reflected in their margins; and (3) that the foreign middlemen have the same margins as the domestic middlemen. In some instances, foreign middleman margins will be lower, but it is equally probable that foreign middleman margins will be greater. In fact, in many instances, middlemen will use higher wholesale and retail margins for foreign goods than for similar domestic goods.

Notice that the retail prices in Exhibit 17–1 range widely, illustrating the difficulty of price control by manufacturers in overseas retail markets. No matter how much the manufacturer may wish to market a product in a foreign country for a price equivalent to $10 U.S., there is little opportunity for such control. Even assuming the most optimistic conditions of Foreign Example 1, the producer would need to cut net by nearly one third to absorb freight plus tariff so that the goods could be priced the same in foreign and domestic markets.[5] Price escalation is everywhere; a man's dress shirt that sells for $25 in the United States retails for $55 in Caracas, and a bottle of Cutty Sark Scotch whiskey that retails for $18 in the United States sells for almost $50 in Japan. One study of European housewares provides numerous examples of price escalation. A $10 (U.S.) electric can opener is priced in Milan at $24; a $15 (U.S.) automatic toaster is priced at $22 in France.

Strategic approaches to price escalation

The manufacturer may employ several strategic approaches to counteract the problem of price differentials. Here are some of the more frequently used:

1. Tariffs and transportation charges which can be offset by lowering the net price for goods sold in foreign markets. This is not always an acceptable alternative because it can be viewed by the importing country as dumping and is then offset by countervailing tariffs which nullify the intended price advantage.
2. Tariff differentials can sometimes be partially overcome by modifying the product in a way that brings it into a different rate category by shipping components and assembling them in the foreign country where they are to be sold.

    Tariffs are frequently lower for unassembled or partially manufactured goods. One of the more important uses for foreign trade zones (FTZs) is to receive large quantities of unassembled goods which are then

---

[5] To compute, work backward from the retail price. Retail price minus retail margin, wholesaler margin, transportation and tariffs equals manufacturers' net.

assembled with local and frequently lower-priced labor.[6] This permits a lower tariff and perhaps a lower total cost for the finished product.

3. The manufacturer may go into overseas production to remain competitive in the foreign market. One of the more important reasons for manufacturing in a third country is an attempt to lower the effects of price escalation.

    Volkswagenwerk started producing the "Rabbit" in the United States in 1978 to increase the dollar content of the car so it would be price competitive in the American marketplace. The decision was made after considering the company's nearly third of a billion dollar loss in 1974. The profit problems and loss of dominant position in the U.S. market were attributed to high wages in Germany, increasing shipping costs, and unfavorable exchange rates. Continuous deterioration of the dollar relative to the mark was a day-to-day pressure on V.W.'s ability to compete in the American market. Honda of Japan and many other companies have moved some of their manufacturing to the United States in an attempt to lessen the higher costs of exporting and thus remain competitive in the U.S. market.

4. Shorter channels may keep prices under control. The process of eliminating middlemen is as costly in international markets as in domestic markets, and although channels may be shortened, marketing functions are not eliminated so marketing costs are not necessarily lowered. Many countries levy a *value added tax* on goods as they pass through channels; each time goods change hands they are taxed. The tax may be cumulative or noncumulative. The cumulative value added tax is based on total selling price and is assessed each time the goods change hands. Obviously, in countries where value added tax is cumulative, tax alone provides a special incentive for developing short distribution channels. In the latter case, tax is paid only on the difference between the middleman's cost and selling price.

5. Eliminating costly functional features or even lowering overall product quality is another method of minimizing price escalation. For U.S. manufactured products, the quality and additional features required for the more-developed market may not be necessary in countries which have not attained the same level of development or consumer demand. Elimination of such features or changing the quality may lower manufacturing costs and thus lessen escalation of costs when the product is exported.

MARKET PRICING

Without ignoring the realities of cost, many marketers find the market provides the most satisfactory basis for pricing. Market pricing recognizes the real value of a product and may vary significantly from one country

---

[6] See Chapter 20 for a complete discussion of foreign trade zones.

to another, or from one time to another. Considered in the context of demand and supply, the needs of the market and the state of competition are the primary determinants of such price variation.

From an economic point of view, market pricing is efficient at price levels that will clear markets. From the standpoint of the firm, however, the marketplace is cruel. Mighty Volkswagen lost $310 million in 1974, Singer Company lost $451 million in 1975; the inability to compete with market prices was the villain in both instances.

Demand

Demand conditions set the range of prices which will be paid for goods. On the demand side, the price range is largely a function of the level of need or desire for a product coupled with the customers' ability to pay. In negotiated pricing situations, the skills of the negotiating parties become a major factor determining the final price. If the buyer knows more about world demand conditions than the seller, the buyer will be at a considerable advantage.

Logically, demand should be assessed market by market; but, when selling goods in many markets, it must be decided if prices are to be uniform or variable across countries. Identical or similar prices may be necessary to minimize country-to-country arbitrage through companies outside the control of the company. If identical prices are selected, it must be decided which market or markets will be used in setting those prices. Typically, prices are established on a basis of demand in the producing country; however, demand in the consuming countries would probably be more relevant. For goods with high price sensitivity, prices must be based on a careful interpretation of demand conditions.

Competition

Competition is another critical element affecting the price level in a free marketplace. In any country, competition may be direct or indirect; competition of either type will affect price. Direct competition relates to products similar to one's own sold by competitors. In the case of direct competition, price may be an important, perhaps the sole, determinant of where a product is purchased. In the directly competitive situation, prices may be affected most by the level of competitive prices rather than by the market itself.

The chief competitive weapon of some businesses is price cutting, but where competition is particularly intense there is a tendency to try to limit price competition through various forms of agreement such as cartels. In many countries, discounting is considered to be a predatory practice even at the retail level. In other countries, price bargaining is not only accepted but assumed.

Regardless of a company or country's philosophy, price discounting has become a way of corporate life in the increasingly competitive world market-place. Competition for most products increases as the world becomes one large international marketplace with suppliers from many countries with different price philosophies competing directly. Companies may respond to competition by lowering prices or attempting to maintain list prices but offering price incentives in other guises. The steel industry, for example, often eliminates inventory or freight charges or reduces "extra charges" typically imposed for special cutting or treating of steel products. The chemical industry has consistently maintained prices established by price leadership policies, but overcapacity often forces temporary allowances or special discounts.

Indirect competition may be of special importance when attempting to sell a product from one culture to another. *Indirect competition* is defined as prospective customers satisfying their needs or desires with a completely different product than the one being offered. Industrial equipment makers promote their products as cost saving or efficient. These manufacturers have found that in the developing countries their main competition for laborsaving devices is not other laborsaving devices but labor itself. Indirect competition is also significant for consumer goods. Laborsaving products such as washing machines and prepared foods have little appeal for householders with servants. Even when servants are not available, the householder's pride or prejudices may cause products to be rejected in favor of indirect competitors. Cloth, for example, may compete with ready-made clothing. In some countries, ready-made clothing is considered a mark of poverty.

Dumping

A logical outgrowth of a market policy in international business is goods priced at widely differing prices in various markets. The market and economic logic of such policy can hardly be disputed, but the practice itself is often classified as dumping; as such, it is likely to be the subject of strong legislation. *Dumping* is defined differently by various economists. One approach classifies international shipments as "dumped" if the products are sold below their cost of production. The other characterizes dumping as selling goods in a foreign market below the price of the same goods in the home market. Even rate cutting on cargo shipping has been called dumping. Laws may invoke both definitions to plug all possible loopholes. The *Exporters' Encyclopedia* summarizes dumping legislation in most countries. Its description of the situation in Norway reflects the scope of provisions used to make the laws as inclusive as possible. Note especially the provisions for calculating subsidies in determining prices.

> Dumping and Countervailing Duty: The law authorizes the imposition of a dumping duty when goods are sold at a price lower than the normal export price or less than the cost in the country of origin increased by a reasonable amount for the cost of sales and profits; and when this is likely to be prejudicial

to the economic activity of the country. A countervailing duty may be imposed on foreign goods benefiting from subsidies in production, export, or transport.[7]

Before antidumping laws can be invoked, it must be shown not only that prices are lower in the importing country than in the producing country, but also that producers in the importing country are being *directly* harmed by the dumping.

Rigidly interpreted, the concepts of dumping or reverse dumping include any form of price differentiation in different markets. Dumping implies a lower price in the foreign market; reverse dumping indicates a lower price in the domestic market. On the basis of price theory, many economists have argued that the whole concept of dumping is fallacious and should be considered simply as differential pricing used to meet market demand. Three questions occur to the theoretician. (1) Should the world be considered one free market? (2) Should prices be established on a full-cost basis? (3) Is variable pricing acceptable? For business people and politicians, however, the question will continue to be viewed in terms of patriotism and protection of cherished home markets from "cheap foreign goods."[8]

In the 1960s and 1970s, dumping was hardly an issue because world markets were strong. As the decade of the 80s begins, dumping has become a major issue for a large number of industries. Excess production capacity relative to home-country demand causes many companies to price their goods on a marginal costing basis figuring that any contribution above variable cost is beneficial to company profits. In a classic case of dumping, prices are maintained in the home-country market and reduced in foreign markets.

Tighter government enforcement of dumping legislation is causing international marketers to seek new routes around such legislation. Some of the strategies include subsidies by government to exporting companies, kickbacks to purchasers, and model-year changes to permit discounting. The European Community provides an example of changing attitudes. It has maintained antidumping legislation from its inception, but the first antidumping duties ever imposed were on Taiwanese bicycle chains in 1976. Since that time, the Department of Trade has investigated ballbearings from Japan (and imposed antidumping duties) and reached agreements raising prices on horticultural glass, shoes, and suits from Eastern Europe, steel reinforcing bars from South Africa and Spain, socket-wrench sets from Japan, printed circuit board drills from the United States, fertilizer from Rumania, and wood paneling and sisal twine from Brazil.[9]

---

[7] From "Norway," in *Exporter's Encyclopedia*, published annually by Dun & Bradstreet, New York.

[8] For an interesting discussion on dumping and its many effects, see Steven E. Plaut, "Why Dumping is Good for us," *Fortune*, May 5, 1980, reprinted in *Annual Editions Marketing 81/82*, ed. Richard Windel (Guilford, Conn.: Dushking Publishing Group, Inc., 1981), pp. 212–14.

[9] "Antidumping Levies Assessed on Imports From Three Nations," *The Wall Street Journal*, March 7, 1980, p. 14.

Dumping has become a major strategy of Eastern European countries due to overproduction and hard-currency shortages; both cause pressure for price cutting to move volumes of merchandise abroad. The United Kingdom, United States, France, and West Germany have lodged complaints against Eastern European products ranging from childrens' shoes, to electric motors, to fiber insulating board.

Subsidies have long been an unacceptable device used by governments to aid exporters. Increasingly protectionist attitudes have caused the United States to add countervailing duties when government subsidies are involved. For example, the United States imposed countervailing duties of 19.6 percent for cotton yarn and 15.8 percent for scissors imported from Brazil. Exported scissors had recieved exemption from Brazilian industrial products tax, value-added tax, and income tax. Cotton yarn had benefitted from preferential government financing and regional investment incentives provided for building plants in remote areas of northeastern Brazil. The pressure of higher duties eventually forced Brazil to eliminate the subsidies and the U.S. government correspondingly reduced the countervailing duties.[10]

Kickbacks are another device used to get around antidumping legislation. In the case of Japanese television tubes imported into the United States, the export price matched the Japanese price (thus counteracting any possible notion of dumping), but the producer provided under-the-table payments to the importer. Zenith officials charged that nearly every television set brought into the United States in the late 1970s benefitted from such kickbacks, much to the detriment of Zenith and other domestic companies.

BOX 17–3: Dirt bikes run around dumping laws

Harley-Davidson Motor Company charged last week that its major Japanese competitors are using the auto market "model-year" concept as a ploy to evade U.S. antidumping laws. . . .

"Our information shows that there were more than 1 million excess Japanese motorcycle inventories here . . ." "To sell these, the Japanese cut prices even further than their already low U.S. prices," he said. "This practice of predatory price cutting was not followed in Japan or other such major markets as France, Italy, and West Germany."

. . . Harley-Davidson, the last American company with a niche in the motorcycle market, said motorcycle makers don't have "model years" like the auto industry. Japanese makers, it charged, copied the auto industry's practice of discounting prior year model prices simply as a means of moving inventories once demand for motorcycles turned soft.

According to Harley-Davidson estimates, the Japanese makers charge as much as 139 percent for the same motorcycle in Japan and some European countries than they do in the United States.

Source: "Harley-Davidson Cities Japanese Pricing Ploys." Reprinted with permission, from the June 1977 issue of *Advertising Age*. Copyright 1977 by Crain Communications Inc.

---

[10] "U.S. Tentatively Finds Japan's Typewriters Sold at Unfair Prices," *The Wall Street Journal,* January 7, 1980, p. 1.

Model-year discounts make possible price variation from country to country but have also come to the attention of antidumping authorities. The model-year device works this way: an exported item is designated as the previous year's model and discounted in the foreign country but still sold at the current model-year prices in the home country. These dumping devices are cheerfully winked at in times of soft world competition, but most all become transparent when competition is intense and antidumping commissions take a hard line against subterfuge.

ADMINISTERED PRICING

The terms *administered prices* and *administered pricing* relate to attempts to administer prices for an entire market. Such prices may be arranged through the cooperation of competitors; through national, state, or local governments; or by international agreement. The legality of administered pricing arrangements of various kinds differs from country to country and from time to time. A country may condone price fixing for foreign markets but condemn it for the domestic market.

In general, the end goal of all administered pricing activities is to reduce the impact of price competition or eliminate it. Price fixing by business is not viewed as acceptable procedure (at least in the domestic market), but, when governments enter the field of price administration, they presume to do it for the general welfare to lessen the effects of "destructive" competition.

The point when competition becomes destructive depends largely on the country in question. To the Japanese, excessive competition is *any* competition in the home market that disturbs the existing balance of trade or gives rise to market disruptions. Few countries apply more rigorous standards in judging competition as excessive, but no country favors or permits totally free competition. Even economists, the traditional champions of pure competition, acknowledge that perfect competition is unlikely and agree that some form of "workable" competition must be developed.

Countertrades

Today an international company must include in its market pricing tool kit some understanding of countertrading. Although cash is the preferred method of payment, more and more, countertrades[11] are becoming an important part of trade with Eastern Europe, China, and to a varying degree some Latin American and African nations. The key problems in successfully consummating countertrade transactions are (1) accurately establishing the market value of the goods being offered and (2) disposing of the bartered goods once they are received. Most countertrades judged unsuccessful are the result of one or both of the problems cited not being solved properly.

---

[11] For a complete discussion of countertrades, see Chapter 14.

Certainly it is possible for an international marketer to have some knowledge of the types of countertrade transactions that a particular customer might suggest and generally the type of products likely to be offered in a trade can be determined to some extent prior to negotiations. If a company anticipates the possibility of a countertrade, it can estimate product values and potential disposal channels for the goods before being confronted with an offer of a countertrade.[12] Most U.S. firms prefer to avoid countertrading and therefore ignore the subject. This strategy generally results in less than successful negotiations when countertrades arise.[13]

BOX 17–4: Beware of the "old" double trap door trick

Failure to raise questions about countertrade plays directly into the hands of willful Eastern European negotiators. One common tactic of Foreign Trade Offices (FTOs) is to volunteer cash payment and to ask for the "final" selling price of the Western product. A few days—or hours—after obtaining this quotation, the FTO team informs the Western side "with profound regret" that their overly rigid and insensitive government ministers have demanded that a certain percentage of countertrade must be accepted if the deal is to be signed. Trapped, the Western firm finds it almost impossible to raise its stated "final" price to cover the costs of disposing of the Eastern European countertrade items. Profit margins are thus quickly liquidated.

MNCs that do not want to confront the problem of countertrade also set themselves up for the "double trapdoor trick." After the FTO obtains the Western firm's quote for a no-countertrade cash sale, it then makes the mournful claim that higher officials have insisted on a substantial countertrade percentage. If the Western company finally agrees in an effort to preserve the sale, the "double trapdoor" is snapped: when the countertrade contract is just about to be signed, the FTO negotiators cheerfully announce that they have pressured their superiors into accepting a cash payment. However, there is one condition: since the Western seller will not be forced to take countertrade goods, it must grant a price discount.

Source: "Selling to Eastern Europe? Keep in Mind Tricks of the (Counter) Trade." Reprinted from p. 380 of the November 28, 1980 issue of *Business International* (BI), with the permission of the publisher, Business International Corporation (New York).

Price setting by business groups

The pervasiveness of price-fixing attempts in business is reflected by the diversity of the language of administered prices; pricing arrangements are known as agreements, arrangements, combines, conspiracies, cartels, communities of profit, profit pools, patent licensing, trade associations, price leadership, customary pricing, or informal interfirm agreements. The arrangements themselves range from completely informal arrangements with no spoken or acknowledged agreement to highly formalized and structured arrangements. Any type of price-fixing arrangement can be adapted to

---

[12] "U.S. Firm Puts CT First, Then Seeks EE Sales," *Business Eastern Europe,* July 10, 1981, p. 221.

[13] "Selling to Eastern Europe? Keep in Mind Tricks of the (Counter) Trade," *Business International,* November 28, 1980, p. 380.

international business; but of all the forms mentioned, the three most directly associated with international marketing are patent licensing, cartels, and trade associations.

Patent licensing agreements. In industries where technological innovation is especially important, patent or process agreements are the most common type of international combination. In most countries, patent licensing agreements are legally acceptable because the owner of the patent is granting an exclusive license to someone in another country to produce the product. By contractual definition, the patent holder can control territorial boundaries and, because of the monopoly, can control pricing. Often such arrangements go beyond a specific licensing agreement to include a gentlemen's agreement to give their foreign counterparts first rights on patents and new developments. Such arrangements can lead to national monopolies which significantly restrict competition and thereby raise product prices. Like so many other agreements related to restricting competition, the legality of patent licensing agreements is difficult to discuss outside the context of a specific situation. Patent licensing arrangements have been an important factor in international marketing in the past and continue to be important despite numerous restrictions.

Cartels. A cartel exists when various companies producing similar products work together to control markets for the types of goods they produce. Generally, a cartel involves more than a patent licensing agreement and endows the participants with greater power. The cartel association may use formal agreements to set prices, establish levels of production and sales for the participating companies, allocate market territories, and even redistribute profits. In some instances, the cartel organization itself takes over the entire selling function, sells the goods of all the producers, and distributes the profits.

The economic role of cartels is highly debatable, but their proponents argue that they eliminate cut-throat competition and "rationalize" business, permitting greater technical progress and lower prices to consumers. However, in the view of most experts, it is doubtful that the consumer benefits very often from cartels.

BOX 17–5: Shh! Cartel at work

For organizations that are wholly legal, international cartels are remarkably secretive. They never publish their agreements. They avoid the press. Their offices are hard to find. Members frequently deny their existence, and indeed are often bound to secrecy by their cartel agreement. A major reason is that publicity about their activities would cause protest in countries—often developing nations poorly equipped to handle the situation—whose markets they carve up. Sometimes there are other good reasons for secrecy. European antitrust officials are certain—although they can't always prove it—that firms grouped in overseas cartels sometimes use these legal contacts secretly to cartelize domestic markets.

Source: "The Flourishing Cartels." Reprinted with the special permission of *Dun's Review*, August 1976. Copyright, 1976, Dun & Bradstreet Publications Corporation.

Cartels are often thought of as peculiar to Europe, but U.S. companies have participated in international cartels as have producers from nearly every country at one time or another. Country cartels seem to exhibit a marked tenacity for survival despite attempts to regulate them.

World cartels currently exist in steel, glass, chemicals, and many other industries. The Netherlands provides an excellent example; in 1950 it had some 450 registered cartels of national scope. Between 1950 and 1956 the number rose to 850. A national anticartel policy was established in 1956; but in 1970, some 800 national cartels still functioned.

Japanese companies may participate in cartels called *recession cartels* with the explicit permission of the Trade Ministry (MITI). These confer all cartel benefits and are considered essential to survival for industries with highly leveraged debt financing and in which surplus workers cannot easily be terminated. They are used when market prices are below the average cost of production, a term which leaves considerable room for interpretation. Recession cartels create dilemmas for foreign producers; they almost must join recession cartels to participate in the market but may violate home-country laws in the process.

Although American companies are usually embarrassed by their participation in cartels, companies from other countries are not particularly concerned; perhaps because it pays so well. A worldwide uranium cartel drove world prices from $6 a pound to more than $40 a pound within a three-year period. Gulf Oil was a major participant in that cartel; the company representatives presumably helped draw up the cartel's rules. U.S. congressional hearings into that cartel had such severe repercussions that the Canadian finance minister urged President Carter to terminate the investigations. The Canadian government itself had helped set up the cartel to protect Canadian miners from "predatory tactics of American uranium producers."

The legality of cartels at present is not clearly delineated. Domestic cartelization is illegal in the United States, and the European Community has provisions for controlling cartels. The United States, however, does permit firms to take cartel-like actions in foreign, but not domestic, markets. The European Community's Rome Treaty is patterned after the old German cartel laws which technically forbade cartels. In reality, the treaty may permit them within the EC and generally approves export cartels that don't affect the home country. Increasingly, it has become apparent that many governments have concluded they cannot ignore or destroy cartels completely, so they have chosen to establish ground rules and regulatory agencies to oversee the cartel-like activities of businesses within their jurisdiction.

Trade associations. The very term *trade association* is so broad it is almost meaningless. Trade associations may exist as hard, tight cartels or merely informal trade organizations having nothing to do with pricing, market share, or levels of production. In many countries, trade associations gather information about prices and transactions within a given industry. Such associations have the general goal of protecting and maintaining the pricing structure most generally acceptable to industry members. In the early 1930s,

the National Industrial Recovery Act gave broad powers to U.S. trade associations for this type of activity. The act was declared unconstitutional and
trade associations in the United States since have been enjoined by antitrust
laws from playing a significant role in pricing. This is not the case in other
industrial nations; manufacturers' associations frequently represent 90 to
100 percent of an industry. The association is a club one must join for
access to customers and suppliers. It may handle industrywide labor negotiations and is often capable of influencing government decisions relating to
the industry.

The boycott is a chief weapon of the trade association. Two kinds of
boycotts are identified in Europe. The *boycottage-sanction* is directed
against a member or members of an association by other members as a
penalty for the former's failure to fulfill obligations to the group. Such a
boycott is appropriately regarded as lawful. *Boycottage d'aggression* is
directed against an outsider. The lawfulness of a boycott depends exclusively
on whether the collective refusal to deal is motivated by "a legitimate interest" of the boycotters or simply by a desire to eliminate a competitor.

Government-influenced pricing

Companies doing business in foreign countries will encounter a number
of different types of government price setting. To control prices, governments
may establish margins, set prices and floors or ceilings, restrict price changes,
compete in the market, grant subsidies, and act as a purchasing monopsony
or selling monopoly. The government may also influence prices by permitting, or even encouraging, business to collude in setting manipulative prices.

Establish margins. Middlemen sometimes are required to mark up
their goods by a government-dictated margin and may not be permitted
to deviate significantly from that margin. Even manufacturers may be subject
to dictated margins, with the government specifying the amount goods may
be marked up over cost. Both types of margin setting are encountered in
Norway, for example, where the government sets maximum ranges but permits some price cutting.

Set price floors and ceiling or actual prices. Numerous methods
of setting price floors and ceilings are employed in different countries. Some
have laws dictating that goods cannot be sold below their cost plus a govern-
ment-stipulated markup. Price ceilings imposed by government also are
not uncommon in the world marketplace. Bread, rice, milk, and other food
staples are often subject to price ceilings.

Some governments use rather innovative ways to set price floors and
ceilings. Argentina established a temporary price freeze in 1977 to help
restrain inflation. Rather than remove the freeze, the government took steps
to encourage competition but maintained price control on monopolistic or
oligopolistic industries. Tariffs on some products were lowered to help set
a ceiling price. On cigarettes, for example, the tariff was reduced to 5

percent, the logic being that cigarettes are particularly price sensitive and a lower price in foreign brands would keep domestic brand prices from rising. Usually government policy is not so explicitly aimed at controlling domestic prices.

Fixed prices in centrally planned economies do not permit the price mechanism to regulate the market; therefore, in the absence of perfect planning, supply and demand are equalized by rationing or the market is characterized by gluts and surpluses.

Restrict price changes. Regardless of the level of economic development of the country they are in, international marketers are likely to find they cannot change prices without government permission or at least giving official notification. In some countries, such as India and Spain, price changes for a wide range of products are regulated. American business may chafe at such regulation, but a clsoe look will remind marketers that the U.S. marketplace is not completely free of price change restrictions.

Although not designed primarily to limit freedom in changing prices, tax laws of various nations sometimes affect prices charged on final products and tend to restrict price changing. This is particularly true in the case of intercorporate transfers where changeovers from one pricing system to another can bring on retroactive tax penalties or higher taxes because of excessive profits.

Compete in the market. Governments frequently compete directly in the marketplace in order to control prices. For example, three U.S. companies raised aluminum ingot prices by one half cent a pound; within days, the U.S. government announced it would release two or three hundred thousand tons of aluminum from its strategic stockpile. Shortly afterward, the companies reevaluated the situation and rolled back prices to their original level. The continuing activity of the U.S. government in wheat and other commodities also has the effect of regulating prices through direct government competition.

In countries where the government owns a large share of productive assets, the government is a major competitor in the market. Some government-owned businesses, such as Italy's ENI, compete not only in the domestic market but in international markets as well.

Subsidies. Governmental subsidies may permit companies to lower prices of their goods in world competition, but they also involve government in the pricing picture. Subsidies may be direct or indirect. To encourage the development of an industry, a nation may pay a producer of shoes a direct subsidy of 50 cents per pair. That industry then may be able to compete more effectively in the local market against imported shoes because it can sell its shoes 50 cents cheaper than it normally would. It also can compete more effectively in foreign markets because of its subsidy.

An indirect subsidy is created when a nonexported component is subsidized and the component then becomes part of an exported product. A tentmaker, for example, may buy canvas made of subsidized cotton. GATT

agreements tend to outlaw direct export subsidies but do not normally prohibit indirect subsidies.

Government monopolies.   Government agencies in socialized countries may act as sole sellers for certain products at the domestic and import-
export levels. The Soviet Union, for example, handles its international sales
through Amtorg, a government trading agency.

Like a private monopolist, the government has price authority when acting
as a monopoly. Sometimes a government steps into a chaotic market situation
and attempts to bring order by purchasing and selling the entire output
of an industry. The Brazilian government, for example, sponsors the Brazilian
Coffee Institute (IBC), a clearinghouse that handles all Brazil's international
sales of raw coffee beans. Like other monopolies, the IBC has learned that
falsely inflated prices invite competition. As a result of monopoly-induced
price increases, the coffee market has been so favorable that production
was encouraged in French West Africa, Mexico, Guatemala, Indonesia,
and other countries not historically important as producers. A few decades
ago Brazil supplied approximately 80 percent of the world's coffee; at present it sells less than 40 percent of the coffee in the world marketplace.

Negotiating with monopsonies.   The word *monopsony* implies that
there is only one buyer in a given market. In a monopsonistic situation,
the buyer has great bargaining power and may play off a variety of suppliers
in order to secure the most advantageous price and terms.

Monopsonistic purchasing by the government can be especially troublesome for international marketers. They not only have to compete with firms
from many countries but also play by rules designed by the customers.
For example, a company will be unable to vary prices on the open market
to meet local situations because some countries will pay only the *lowest
price offered to any customer anywhere.* Cutting of margins in any area
may require cutting margins on all government sales to those countries.

East European countries have become particularly adept at taking advantage of their monopsonistic position by tying purchases to forced sale of
their own goods. One way is to insist on countertrade purchases requiring
a vendor to accept a certain amount of goods produced in the East European
country in payment. Countertrade lessens the pressure on the balance of
payments position but may leave the vendor with unwanted goods to dispose
of elsewhere. The volume of countertrade depends directly on the bargaining power of each party. Trade ratios range from 10 to 30 percent of the
value of the imported goods but sometimes have matched or even exceeded
the total value of the imports.

International agreements

Governments of producing and consuming countries seem to play an
ever-increasing role in the establishment of international prices for certain
basic commodities. There is, for example, an international coffee agreement,

an international cocoa agreement, and an international sugar agreement. The world price of wheat has long been at least partially determined by negotiations between national governments.

The success of OPEC (Organization of Petroleum Exporting Countries) has driven up world petroleum prices by concerted action. Producers of scarce commodities in other countries are now alerted to the possibility of worldwide price manipulation. The copper-producing organization CIPEC has sought to increase world prices since its inception in 1967, but so far its four member countries who supply 80 percent of the world's exported copper have failed to agree on tactics.

Despite the pressures of business, government, and international price agreements, most marketers still have wide latitude in their pricing decisions for most products and markets.

INTRACOMPANY PRICING STRATEGY

As companies increase the number of worldwide subsidiaries, joint ventures, company-owned distributing systems, and other marketing arrangements, the price charged to different affiliates becomes a preeminent question. Prices of goods transferred from operations or sales units in one country to a company's units elsewhere may be adjusted to enhance the ultimate profit of the company as a whole. The benefits are:

1. Lowering duty costs by shipping goods into high-tariff countries at minimal transfer prices so duty base and duty will be low.
2. Reduction of income taxes in high-tax countries by overpricing goods transferred to units in such countries; profits are eliminated and shifted to low-tax countries. Such profit shifting may also be used for "dressing up" financial statements by increasing reported profits in countries where borrowing and other financing are undertaken.
3. Facilitation of dividend repatriation. When dividend repatriation is curtailed by government policy, invisible income may be taken out in the form of high prices for products or components shipped to units in that country.

The tax and financial manipulation possibilities of transfer pricing have not been overlooked by government authorities. As multinational firms gain increasing prominence on the world marketing scene, national governments are becoming increasingly restrictive and paying special attention to transfer pricing in tax audits. The overall objectives of the intracompany pricing system include: (1) maximizing profits for the corporation as a whole, (2) facilitating parent-company control, and (3) offering management at all levels, both in the product divisions and in the international divisions, an adequate basis for maintaining, developing, and receiving credit for their own profitability. Transfer prices that are too low will be unsatisfactory to the product divisions because their overall results will look poor; prices that are too high make the international operations look bad and limit the effectiveness of foreign managers.

Part of an effective pricing system is recognition of the complexity of pricing and an awareness of variations in local conditions. Pricing policies of the parent company should be such that the international divisions maintain ultimate market initiative and have final profit responsibility for their operations. One recent study of intracorporate pricing showed conclusively that "setting up transfer prices remains the absolute prerogative of the parent company executives regardless of the firm's nationality." The systems should be simple enough so that all participants in the decision and transfer can understand how prices were established. Finally, the intracorporate pricing system should employ sound accounting techniques and be defensible to the tax authorities of the countries involved. All of these factors argue against a single uniform price or even a uniform pricing system for all international operations.

Four arrangements for pricing goods for intracompany transfer are:

1. Sales at the local manufacturing cost plus a standard markup.
2. Sales at the cost of the most efficient producer in the company plus a standard markup.
3. Sales at negotiated prices.
4. Arm's length sales using the same prices as quoted to independent customers.

Of the four, the arm's length transfer is most acceptable to tax authorities and most likely to be acceptable to foreign divisions, but the appropriate basis for intracompany transfers depends on the nature of the subsidiaries and market conditions. Sometimes inappropriate pricing policies can completely knock a product out of the market even though it might contribute significantly to the profitability of the company as a whole. For example, an item with a factory cost of $100 is transferred to the international division at $120 with an additional cost of $10 involved in the export; assume competition limits the international selling price to $135. The sale might be rejected because a $5 profit reflects only a 3.7 percent return on sales. The total profit to the corporation, however, will be $25, or 18.5 percent *if all* the profit to the corporation were taken into account. Thus what appears to be an unprofitable sale becomes a highly profitable one when viewed from the overall corporate perspective.

PRICE QUOTATIONS

In quoting the price of goods for international sale, a contract may include specific price elements affecting the price, such as credit, sales terms, and transportation. Parties to the transaction must be certain that the quotation settled on appropriately locates responsibility for the goods during transportation and spells out who pays transportation charges and from what point.

Price quotation must also specify the currency to be used, credit terms, and the type of documentation required.[14] Finally, the price quotation and contract should define quantity and quality. A quantity definition might be necessary because different countries use different units of measurement. In specifying a ton, for example, the contract should identify it as a metric or an English ton, and as a long or short ton. Furthermore, there should be complete agreement on quality standards to be used in evaluating the product. The international trader must review all terms of the contract; failure to do so may have the effect of modifying prices even though such a change is not intended.

SUMMARY

Pricing is one of the most complicated decision areas encountered by international marketers. Rather than deal with one set of market conditions, one group of competitors, one set of cost factors, and one set of government regulations, international marketers must take all these factors into account, not only for each country in which they are operating, but sometimes for each market within a country. Market prices at the consumer level are much more difficult to control in international than in domestic marketing, but the international marketer must still approach the pricing task on a basis of objectives and policy, leaving enough flexibility for tactical price movements. Pricing in the international marketplace requires a combination of intimate knowledge of market costs and regulations, infinite patience for detail, and a shrewd sense of market strategy.

QUESTIONS

1. Define:
    Dumping   Administered pricing S68
    Countervailing duty   Agreement
    Full cost   Cartel S70
    Subsidy   Monopsony
    Value added Tax

2. Why is it so difficult to control consumer prices when selling overseas?

3. Explain the concept of "price escalation" and tell why it can mislead an international marketer.

4. What are the causes of price escalation? Do they differ for exports and goods produced and sold in a foreign country?

5. Why is it seldom feasible for a company to absorb the high cost of international transportation and reduce the net price received?

---

[14] For a complete discussion of the details of price quotations see Chapter 20.

6. Price escalation is a major pricing problem for the international marketer. How can this problem be counteracted? Discuss.

7. "Regardless of the strategic factors involved and the company's orientation to market pricing, every price must be set with cost considerations in mind." Discuss.

8. "Price fixing by business is not generally viewed as an acceptable procedure (at least in the domestic market); but when governments enter the field of price administration, they presume to do it for the general welfare to lessen the effects of 'destructive' competition." Discuss.

9. Do value added taxes discriminate against imported goods?

10. Explain specific tariffs, ad valorem tariffs, and combination tariffs.

11. Suggest an approach a marketer may follow in adjusting prices to accommodate exchange-rate fluctuations.

12. Explain the effects of indirect competition and how they may be overcome.

13. Why has dumping become such an issue in recent years?

14. Cartels seem to rise phoenixlike after they have been destroyed. Why are they so appealing to business?

15. Develop a cartel policy for the United States.

16. Discuss the various ways in which governments set prices. Why do they engage in such activities?

17. Discuss the alternative objectives possible in setting prices for intracompany sales.

18. Why do governments so carefully scrutinize intracompany pricing arrangements?

19. Why are costs so difficult to assess in marketing internationally?

Chapter 18

The international distribution system

In every country, communist or capitalist, and in every market, urban or rural, rich or poor, all consumer and industrial products eventually go through the distribution process. The process includes not only the physical handling and distribution of goods but also relates to the passage of ownership and, most important from the standpoint of marketing strategy, to the buying and selling negotiations between middlemen, producers, and consumers. The concerns of this chapter are the types and characteristics of both domestic and foreign middlemen as well as distribution through a company's own marketing system. A thorough understanding of these middlemen and agencies is essential for establishing policies that will lead to the development of effective distribution systems. Chapter 19 emphasizes policies and strategies pertaining to the channel of distribution and addresses the questions of distribution channel management.

This chapter identifies the basic structural alternatives for both consumer and industrial goods. The latter typically employ shorter channels but the functional alternatives are the same. Actual structures available in a given country depend directly on its stage of economic develoment; but, in more advanced economies, all major types of middlemen are represented. In nearly all countries, the marketer has a variety of distribution methods.

STRUCTURAL ANALYSIS

Astute marketers with an adequate understanding of distribution channels in their own country have a basic understanding of the channel types available in international activities. The uniqueness of international distribution derives less from the structural alternatives than from the infinite operational and market variables which affect channel decisions.

Whether or not export is involved, marketers must meet the challenge of getting goods through the channels of distribution into the consumer's hands, and must choose between handling all distribution or turning part or all of it over to various middlemen. A manufacturer will vary distribution methods depending on market size, competition, and available distribution structures.

Key elements in a marketer's distribution decisions include: (1) availability of middlemen, (2) cost of their services, (3) functions performed (and the effectiveness with which each is performed), and (4) extent of control which

579

the manufacturer can exert over middlemen activities. Knowledge of the structural alternatives permits the marketing manager to select middlemen who will provide the optimum pattern of function, cost, and control for each market.

Exhibit 18–1 shows some of the many possible channel-of-distribution alternatives. The arrows show those to whom the producer and each of the middlemen may sell. The reader is reminded that the channel process includes all activities beginning with the manufacturer and ending with the final consumer. Further, the ultimate goal of the marketer is to insure that target markets receive the product in a manner that leads to customer satisfaction. This means the seller must exert influence over two sets of channels, one in the home country and the other in the country market. In the home country, the seller must have an organization (generally the international marketing division of the company) to relate to the channel members necessary to get the goods between countries. In the foreign country, the seller must also supervise the channels that supply the product to the end-user. Ideally, the company will control or be involved in the process all the way through the various channels to the final user. To do otherwise may result in unsatisfactory distribution and failure in reaching marketing objectives in the target market.

In all instances involving middlemen external to the company, only two basic types of middlemen are available: merchant middlemen who take title to the goods and buy and sell on their own account, and agent middlemen who directly represent the principal rather than themselves. The framework for analysis of both domestic and foreign middlemen hinges on whether the middlemen are agents or merchants.

EXHIBIT 18–1:   International channel-of-distribution alternatives

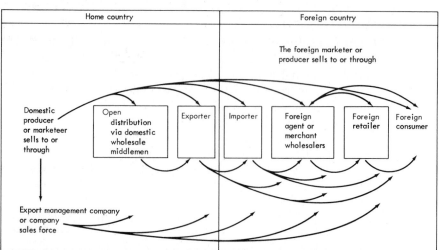

The reader is cautioned that international channels of distribution are not clear-cut, precise, easily defined entities. It is exceptional to find a firm which represents one of the pure types identified here. Thus, intimate knowledge of middlemen functions is especially important in international activity because misleading titles can easily fool a marketer who is not able to look beyond mere names. What functions, for example, are performed by the British middleman called a *stockist* or, for that matter, an exporter or importer? One exporter may, in fact, be an agent middleman, whereas another is a merchant. Many, perhaps most, international middlemen wear several hats and can be clearly identified only in the context of their relationship with a specific firm. One company, for example, engages in both importing and exporting; acts both as an agent and a merchant middleman; operates from offices in the United States, Germany, and Great Britain; provides financial services; and acts as a freight forwarder. It would be difficult to put this company into an appropriate pigeonhole. Many firms work in a single capacity, but the conglomerate type of middleman described here is a major force in some parts of international business. In Japan the *zaibatsu* (financial and trading combines) represent a high state of development of the conglomerate international financial, manufacturing, and trading company. Only by analyzing middlemen functions in skeletal simplicity can the nature of the channels be determined.

Three alternatives are considered in this chapter: first, middlemen physically located in the manufacturer's home country; next, middlemen located in the foreign countries one desires to sell in; and finally, the company's own personnel.

DOMESTIC MIDDLEMEN

Domestic middlemen are located in the same country as the producing firm and provide marketing services from the domestic base. Although they are closer to the manufacturer and may be more convenient to use, domestic middlemen are removed from their markets and may not be able to provide market information or overseas representation as well as foreign middlemen. Domestic middlemen are most likely to be used when the producer is not prepared or able to justify direct overseas contact in many markets. Like the other middlemen, they carry different names; but the classes described in the following sections represent types of operations and services offered.

Exhibit 18–2, summarizes information pertaining to the major kinds of domestic middlemen operating in foreign markets. No attempt is made to generalize about rates of commission, markup, or pay because so many factors influence compensation. Services offered or demanded, market structure, volume, and product type are some of the key determinants. The data represent the predominant patterns of operations; however, individual middlemen of a given type may vary in their operations.

EXHIBIT 18–2:   Characteristics of domestic middlemen serving overseas markets

	Agents				
Type of duties	EMC	MEA	Broker	Buying offices	Selling groups
Take title	No	No	No	No	No
Take possession . . .	Yes	Yes	No	Yes	Yes
Continuing relationship	Yes	Yes	No	Yes	Yes
Share of foreign output	All	All	Any	Small	All
Degree of control by principal	Fair	Fair	Nil	Nil	Good
Price authority	Advisory	Advisory	Yes (at market level)	Yes (to buy)	Advisory
Represent buyer or seller	Seller	Seller	Either	Buyer	Seller
Number of principals	Few—many	Few—many	Many	Small	Few
Arrange shipping . . .	Yes	Yes	Not usually	Yes	Yes
Type of goods	Manufactured goods and commodities	Staples and commodities	Staples and commodities	Staples and commodities	Complementary to their own lines
Breadth of line	Specialty—wide	All types of staples	All types of staples	Retail goods	Narrow
Handle competitive lines	No	No	Yes	Yes—utilizes many sources	No
Extent of promotion and selling effort	Good	Good	One shot	n.a.	Good
principal	Occasionally	Occasionally	Seldom	Seldom	Seldom
Market information	Fair	Fair	Price and market conditions	For principal not for manufacturer	Good

Note: n.a. = not available.

Domestic agent middlemen

One author calls the use of agent middlemen "domestic exporting." Export agents are known by many titles which leads to no end of confusion; to compound the confusion, agents may call themselves by one title but function in another capacity or function in several different agent-middleman capacities. Furthermore, every country has different titles for middlemen. For example, a broker in Belgium is called a *courtier,* in Germany, a *handel-*

Norazi	Merchants				
	Export merchant	Export jobber	Export buyers	Importers and trading companies	Complementary marketers
No	Yes	Yes	Yes	Yes	Yes
Yes	Yes	No	Yes	Yes	Yes
No	No	Yes	No	Yes	Yes
Small	Any	Small	Small	Any	Most
Nil	None	None	None	Nil	Fair
Yes	Yes	Yes	Yes	No	Some
Both	Self	Self	Self	Self	Self
Several per transaction	Many sources	Many sources	Many sources	Many sources	One per product
Yes Contraband	Yes Manufactured goods	Yes Bulky and raw materials	Yes All types	Yes Manufactured goods	Yes Complementary to line
n.a.	Broad	Broad	Broad	Broad	Narrow
Yes	Yes	Yes	Yes	Yes	No
Nil	Nil	Nil	Nil	Good	Good
No	Occasionally	Seldom	Seldom	Seldom	Seldom
No	Nil	Nil	Nil	Fair	Good

smakler, in Italy, a *mediatore,* in the Netherlands, a *makelaar.* Regardless of title, some basic types of domestic agent middlemen may be identified: export management company (EMC), manufacturer's export agent (MEA), broker, buying office, selling groups, intermerchant and Norazi agent.

A company can establish policy guidelines and prices and require its agent to provide sales records and customer information. Manufacturers may undertake their own advertising or have an agent handle it. In some

---

BOX 18–1:   All in the family

Japan's major corporate groups—descendants from the prewar *zaibatsu* (large business combines based on monopoly capital with a family-like organization)—put their best face forward through the regular friendship meetings of group company presidents.

Five *zaibatsu*-originated groups are particularly prominent, with presidents of a total 132 businesses regularly attending group get-togethers—Mitsubishi, with 27 firms; Mitsui, 23; Suminoto, 16; Sanwa, 36; and Fuyo 29. Those 132 companies hold a 17 percent slice of Japan's total corporate equity capital and 18 percent of corporate sales, according to the *Toyo Keizai,* one of the nation's leading economic weeklies. Intragroup financial ties are fairly strong: the average stock ownership and loan offer by group members stands at 16 percent and 22 percent, respectively, for the Mitsui group; 25 percent and 29 percent for Mitsubishi; 25 percent and 31 percent for Sumitomo; 15 percent and 21 percent for Sanwa, and 14 percent and 23 percent for Fuyo.

Source: "The New *Zaibatsu?*" *Focus Japan,* January 1977, p. 5.

---

cases, an agent middleman works from the company office, resulting in a very close working relationship.

Domestic agent middlemen work on a commission basis and arrange for sales in the foreign country, but do not take title to the merchandise.

Export management company.[1]   The export management company (EMC) is a particularly important agent middleman for firms with relatively small international volume or for those that do not want to involve their own personnel in the international function. EMC firms range in size from one person upward to a 100 and handle about 10 percent of the manufactured goods exported. Whether handling 5 clients or 100, the stock in trade of the EMC is personalized service.[2] Typically, the EMC becomes an integral part of the marketing operations of the client companies. Working under the name of the manufacturers, the EMC functions as a low-cost, independent marketing department with direct responsibility to the parent firm. The working relationship is so close that customers seldom realize they are not dealing directly with the export department of the company. (See Exhibit 18–3.)

The EMC firm provides many services for the manufacturer, but, in all instances, the main functions are contact with foreign customers (sometimes through an EMC's own foreign branches) and negotiations for sales. An EMC's specialization in a given field often makes it possible to offer a level of service which could not be attained by the manufacturer without years of ground work.

The EMC may take full or partial responsibility for promotion of the goods, credit arrangements, physical handling, market research, and information

---

[1] Formerly known as *Combination Export Manager* (CEM).

[2] For a comprehensive discussion of EMCs see John J. Brasch, "Using Export Specialists to Develop Overseas Sales," *Harvard Business Review,* May/June 1981, pp. 6–8.

EXHIBIT 18–3: How does an EMC operate?

Most export management companies offer a wide range of services and assistance, including:

Researching foreign markets for a client's products.

Traveling overseas to determine the best method of distributing the product.

Appointing distributors or commission representatives as needed in individual foreign countries, frequently within an already existing overseas network created for similar goods.

Exhibiting the client's products at international trade shows, such as U.S. Department of Commerce-sponsored commercial exhibitions at trade fairs and U.S. Export Development Offices around the world.

Handling the routine details in getting the product to the foreign customer—export declarations, shipping and customs documentation, insurance, banking, and instructions for special export packing and marking.

Granting the customary finance terms to the trade abroad and assuring payment to the manufacturer of the product.

Preparing advertising and sales literature in cooperation with the manufacturer and adapting it to overseas requirements for use in personal contacts with foreign buyers.

Corresponding in the necessary foreign languages.

Making sure that goods being shipped are suitable for local conditions, and meet overseas legal and trade norms, including labeling, packaging, purity, and electrical characteristics.

Advising on overseas patent and trademark protection requirements.

Source: "The Export Management Company" U.S. Dept. of Commerce, Washington, D.C., Revised October 1980.

---

on financial, patent and licensing matters. The EMC depends on commissions for compensation, but may also receive a retainer and various other fees. The services vary too greatly to pinpoint commission rates, but they usually range between 10 percent and 20 percent of the selling price of the goods.

Two of the chief advantages of using EMCs are (1) minimum investment on the part of the company to get into international markets, and (2) no company personnel or major expenditure of managerial effort. The result, in effect, is an extension of the market for the firm with negligible financial or personnel commitments.

The major disadvantage is that EMCs can seldom afford to make the kind of market investment needed to establish deep distribution for their products because they must have immediate payout for their sales efforts if they are to survive. Such a situation does not offer the market advantages gained by a company which can afford to build itself into a market. Carefully selected EMCs can do an excellent job, but the manufacturer must remember the EMC is dependent on sales volume for compensation and probably will not push the manufacturer's line if it is spread too thinly, generates too small a volume from a given principal, or cannot operate profitably in the short run. Then the EMC becomes an ordertaker and not the desired substitute for an international marketing department.

Manufacturer's export agent.   The manufacturer's export agent (MEA) is an individual agent middleman or an agent middleman firm providing a selling service for manufacturers. Unlike the EMC, the MEA does not serve as the producer's export department but has a short-term relationship, covers only one or two markets, and operates on a straight commission basis. Thus, a manufacturer would be likely to deal with only one EMC, but numerous MEAs. Another principal difference is that MEAs do business in their own names rather than in the name of the client.

Within a limited scope of operation, the MEAs provide services similar to those of the EMC, but for an internationally-minded firm their chief shortcoming is the lack of wide market coverage and an ongoing market relationship.

Broker.   The term *broker* is a catch-all for a variety of middlemen performing low-cost agent services. The term is typically applied to importexport brokers who provide the intermediary function of bringing buyers and sellers together, and who do not have a continuing relationship with their clients. Most brokers operate in bulky goods of the commodity field and specialize in one or more commodity types for which they maintain contact with major producers and purchasers throughout the world.

Other brokers specialize in individual countries rather than in commodities, and offer specialized knowledge of trading regulations and markets of the countries in which they deal. Satra Corporation in New York, for example, has exceeded $50 million yearly volume in its specialty of dealing with the Soviet Union and Eastern European countries.

Buying offices.   A variety of agent middlemen may be classified simply as buyers or buyers for export. Their common denominator is a primary function of seeking and purchasing merchandise on request from the principals; as such, they do not provide a selling service. In fact, their chief emphasis is on flexibility and the ability to find merchandise from any source. They do not often become involved in continuing relationships with domestic suppliers and do not provide a continuing source of representation. The buyer, however, is a good avenue for sales, and as long as the price, merchandise, and terms are right, may continue to buy from one firm over a period of years. Unfortunately, from a distribution control standpoint, the supplier firm's role is essentially passive.

The resident buyer, the most important form of buyer, specializes in a particular line of goods. In a typical transaction, the resident buyer is notified of the merchandise the client wants and the dollar amount or number of units to be purchased. The supplier firms are then contacted, merchandise is selected, a contract is executed on behalf of the principal, arrangements for payment are made, and then responsibility for the physical handling and shipment of the goods is assumed.

A special form of buyer called the *export commission house* or *commissionaire,* operates in a manner similar to the resident buyer but works only on commission and typically handles a broader range of merchandise than the resident buyer and operates on a transaction-by-transaction basis.

Selling groups.   Several types of arrangements have been developed in which various manufacturers or producers cooperate in a joint attempt to sell their merchandise abroad. This may take the form of complementary exporting or of selling to a business combine such as a Webb-Pomerene export association. Both are considered agency arrangements when the exporting is done on a fee or commission basis.

When business firms have unused marketing or export capacity, they sometimes share their facilities with companies having complementary but non-competing lines. Complementary exporting or piggybacking is covered at length in the Domestic Merchant Middlemen section of this chapter.

Webb-Pomerene Export Associations (WPEA) constitute another major form of group exporting. The Webb-Pomerene Act of 1918 made it possible for American business firms to join forces in export activities without being subject to the Sherman Antitrust Act. WPEAs cannot participate in cartels or other international agreements which would reduce competition in the United States, but can offer four major benefits: (1) reduction of export costs, (2) demand expansion through promotion, (3) trade barrier reductions, and (4) improvement of trade terms through bilateral bargaining. Additionally, WPEAs set prices, standardize products, and arrange for disposal of surplus products.

The mode of operation of the WPEA determines its place in the corporate organization. The association may: (1) limit itself to publicity, advertising, and information dissemination; (2) handle export procedures for its members but perform only an order-filling function; (3) act as a selling agent, promoting merchandise, negotiating sales, dividing orders among association members, and arranging for shipment; or (4) purchase products from corporate members under terms and proportional allotments agreed on by the membership, then act as a merchant wholesaler to market the products in foreign countries.

Although they account for less than 5 percent of U.S. exports, WPEAs include some of America's blue-chip companies in fields such as agricultural products, chemical and raw materials, forest products, pulp and paper, textiles, rubber products, motion pictures, and television.

Norazi agent.   Norazi agents are unique middlemen who specialize in shady or difficult transactions. They deal in contraband materials, such as radioactive products or war materials, and in providing strategic goods to countries that are closed to normal trading channels. The Norazi is also likely to be engaged in black market currency operations as well as trade in untaxed liquor, narcotics, industrial espionage, and other illicit traffic.[3]

Although they are called agents, the Norazi is not limited to an agent-type transaction. If the profit picture is exceptionally large, the Norazi will change from merchant to agent or agent to merchant, whichever is most advantageous. Despite the unsavory trade of Norazi agents, they have a

---

[3] "Industrial Espionage: U.S. Companies are 'Soft Targets,' " *World Business Weekly,* September 28, 1981, pp. 20–21.

reputation for dealing ethically with their clients. This is mandatory since neither client nor agent works on the basis of written contracts or has recourse to justice through the court system.

Norazi exist because tariffs, import taxes, and excise taxes make illegal movements of goods more profitable than legal movements. In Uruguay, for example, the legal cost of a package of U.S. cigarettes is $1.40 (U.S.), but it sells for $0.50 on the black market. Argentina estimates that it loses over $43 million (U.S.) a year in cigarette taxes alone because of smuggling from Uruguay. In Argentina, a smuggled Japanese camera can be bought for about half the price of the camera coming through official channels. As a top-ranking official commented, "Contrabanding has a major impact on the economies of Latin nations."

The volume of business transacted by Norazi is unknown but their activities have reached such a proportion that a counterforce called Inter-Respol has been organized to combat contrabanding on an international basis. Respol of Chile, for example, recently confiscated $100,000 worth of Japanese radio and television sets which were being flown into Chile from Panama. The Norazi is not without representation in the halls of government, however, and in Bolivia, a group called the Union of Minority Businessmen speaks openly in favor of the smuggling trade. It has communicated its story so well that one government official says, "Smuggling is a social and economic necessity since it allows people to buy goods at lower prices."

That most manufacturers do not need nor desire the services of Norazi agents is indeed fortunate; they are difficult to contact and their fees or markups are extremely high.

Domestic merchant middlemen

Merchant middlemen provide a variety of import and export wholesaling functions involving purchasing for their own account and selling in other countries. The merchant middleman bears the majority of trading risks for all products handled, and profit comes from the gross margin spread. Because merchant middlemen are primarily concerned with sales and profit margins on their merchandise, they cannot be depended on to represent the best interests of a given manufacturer. Unless they have a franchise on a strong and profitable brand, middlemen seek goods from any source and are likely to have low brand loyalty. Because they actually take title to the goods, merchant middlemen are less controllable than agent middlemen.

To a manufacturer, the advantages of using domestic merchant middlemen is the ease of contact, minimized credit risk, and elimination of all merchandise handling outside the United States. Major export middlemen considered in the following section include: export merchants and export jobbers, export buyers and domestic offices of foreign importers, trading companies, and complementary marketers.

Export merchants. Export merchants are essentially domestic whole-salers operating in foreign markets. As such they operate much like the domestic wholesaler. Specifically, they purchase goods from a large number of manufacturers, ship them to foreign countries, and take full responsibility for their marketing; sometimes they utilize their own organization, but, more commonly, they sell through other middlemen. They deal in either consumer or industrial goods and some merchants handle both. Export merchants carry competing lines if it suits their requirements, have full control over prices, and maintain little loyalty to suppliers although they will continue to handle their products as long as they are profitable. Most tend to specialize in a given field and offer a reasonable amount of foreign market information.

Export jobbers. Export jobbers are similar to domestic drop shippers or desk jobbers; they are, in fact, often called *export drop shippers.* Variations of the export drop shippers include cable merchants and export speculators. Typically these middlemen deal with bulky goods or raw materials. They do not take physical possession of the goods but assume responsibility for arranging transportation. Export jobbers represent only themselves and typically buy or sell goods only when they have arranged to complete both sides of the transaction. Export speculators, however, do purchase for their own account whenever they find an opportunity to buy or sell goods at a particularly favorable price. Obviously, all of these middlemen depend heavily on their knowledge of market conditions. Because they work on a job-lot basis, they do not provide a particularly attractive distribution alternative for most producers.

BOX 18–2: Norazi at work?

Every day of the year 15 trucks loaded with products disappear into thin air after they have crossed into Italy from neighboring countries. That's about 5,500 trucks a year. And that's not the worst of it. Physical distribution managers who complain about their losses get slapped with a bill for the full custom duties on the products the trucks carried. The police argue that the goods will be sold in Italy by somebody who isn't going to pay taxes on them, so how else can they collect.

Source: "Those Crooks!" Reprinted from *Industrial Marketing,* June 14, 1976 issue: Copyright 1976 by Crain Communications, Inc., Chicago, Ill.

Export buyers and foreign importers. Export buyers are bargain hunters, seeking distressed merchandise, overproduction, obsolete products, or other goods that can be bought cheaply and resold in foreign markets.

Domestic offices of importers provide a major source of direct distribution for the firm wishing to engage in international business without becoming involved in actual foreign distribution. Contact with the import companies can be made in the home country of the manufacturer; the sale is essentially domestic and the middlemen take the responsibility for all credit, shipment, and foreign marketing of the products.

Trading companies. Trading companies have a long and honorable history as important intermediaries in the development of trade between nations. Trading companies accumulate, transport, and distribute goods from many countries. In concept, the trading company has changed little in thousands of years.

Trading companies were important in the colonial movement and continue to be important in trade with developing countries. The English Hudson's Bay Company and East India Company were trading vehicles of the 16th, 17th, and 18th centuries. The United Africa Company (now a subsidiary of Unilever), formed in 1929 by joining several existing trading companies, has a series of department stores, retail grocery stores, and automobile agencies throughout the African continent.

BOX 18–3: Sogo shoshas: B I G business

The Japanese *sogo shosha*, general trading companies, are a breed of their own. Giants that stand astride the Japanese economy, the top 10 *sogo shoshas* in 1975 accounted for $155 billion in total revenues, representing 56 percent of total import-export and a whopping 30 percent of the country's gross national product.

An estimated 90 percent of the revenues of the top 10 *sogos* is in the export and import of nonconsumer products, both raw materials and industrial goods.

. . . Nissho-Iwai Company, Ltd., sixth largest of the great *sogo shosha*, with total revenues estimated at $20.8 billion (based on 250 yen per dollar) for the 12 months ending March 31, 1978, has created more than 100 subsidiaries around the world, manufacturing products ranging from auto transmissions and springs to chemical fertilizers and synthetic resins. In Japan, a subsidiary of the parent company is the largest seller of condominium apartments in the country, having first built the buildings and supplied the materials thru other Nissho-Iwai operations.

With so much attention focused on the U.S. trade deficit with Japan, it is worth noting that the trading companies actually export more from the United States to Japan than they import. Nissho-Iwai American Corporation, which accounts for 19 percent of total revenue, exported products valued at an estimated $1.69 billion to Japan from the United States during 1977 and imported to the United States from Japan a total of $1.31 billion.

Source: "Ten Sogo Shoshas: Trade Monarchs," *Marketing in Japan*, undated supplement to *Industrial Marketing*, pages unnumbered.

The French also were active in building trading companies. Two founded in Africa at the turn of the century are CFAO (Cie Française de l'Afrique Occidentale) and SCOA (Ste. Commerciale de l'Quest Africain). CFAO operates in 18 African states. In addition to a large chain of supermarkets and small country stores, CFAO has a capital goods division, manufacturing facilities, and a brewery. The type of goods handled indicates something about the state of the consumer market; simple iron utensils such as hoes and pots and pans and other implements account for some three fourths of the company's consumer goods sales. SCOA had sales of around $200 million (U.S.) and handles imports of foods, iron utensils, textiles, furniture, capital goods, and motor vehicles.

The rise of Middle Eastern countries as consumer markets emphasizes the importance of trading companies in reaching unique markets. Patterns vary widely; many local companies are built around families who have been merchants in the Middle East for generations. Others have been formed by new entrepeneurs armed with MBAs from the United States. Numerous British companies exist; Gray MacKenzie & Company has some 70 salespersons and handles consumer products ranging from toiletries to Mercury outboard motors and Scotch Whiskey. The key advantage of this type of trading company is that it covers the entire Middle East. Some companies prefer to deal with the strongest trading company it can find in each individual country.

The companies discussed represent a trading company located in a developed country selling manufactured goods to developing countries and buying back their raw materials and unprocessed goods. Quite a different pattern is encountered with Japanese trading companies, which were formed about 1700 to facilitate distribution of goods *within* the country. They later developed into companies emphasizing importing of goods into Japan. Their current role is that of merchant importers and exporters with widespread operations around the world. Some 300 are engaged in foreign and domestic trade through 2,000 branch offices outside Japan, and handle over $240 billion (U.S.) in trading volume annually. They perform five major functions: the importing and exporting functions per se, financing, development of joint ventures, technical assistance and advice, and production of goods.

For companies seeking entrance to the complicated Japanese distribution system, the Japanese trading company offers one of the easiest routes to success. The omnipresent trading companies virtually control distribution through all levels of channels in Japan. Many companies have experienced greater success selling consumer goods through trading companies than through other types of middlemen. Since trading companies may control many of the distributors and maintain broad distribution channels, they provide the best means for intensive coverage of the market.

An increasingly important part of trading company business consists of sales to markets in countries other than Japan. "Third Nation" or "offshore" deals make up a growing part of trading company business. Mitsui and Company, for example, helps export American grain to Europe. Nissho-Iwai Corporation arranges for athletic shoes to be manufactured in South Korea and Taiwan for Nike Incorporated of Beaverton, Oregon. The nine largest trading companies had a combined 52 percent increase in 1980 in Third Nation volume, sales of $287 billion or 10.6 percent of their combined sales compared with 3.8 percent just 10 years earlier. Do not think of Japanese trading companies as a means only to Japanese markets.[4]

Because they are efficient in foreign marketing, and because they some-

---

[4] "Japan's Big and Evolving Trading Firms: Can the U.S. use Something Like Them?" *The Wall Street Journal,* December 17, 1980, p. 48.

BOX 18–4: Mitsubishi–a giant Japanese industrial, trading, and banking conglomerate

Fiscal 1980 sales in billions of dollars

Trading
Mitsubishi Corp. . . $68.3

Oil
Mitsubishi Oil $6.5

Autos
Mitsubishi Motors . . $5.4

Foods
Kirin Brewery $4.2

Cement, glass, paper
Asahi Glass	$2.3
Mitsubishi Mining & Cement	1.2
Mitsubishi Paper Mills	0.7

Metals
Mitsubishi Metal	$1.6
Mitsubishi Steel	0.4
Mitsubishi Aluminum	0.4

Transport
Nippon Yusen Kaisha	$2.8
Mitsubishi Warehouse & Transportation	0.3

Banking
Mitsubishi Bank	$84.1 (assets)
Mitsubishi Trust & Banking	18.9 (assets)

Electrical and optical equipment
Mitsubishi Electric	$6.0
Nippon Kogaku	0.6

Machinery, ships, arms
Mitsubishi Heavy Industries	$6.5
Mitsubishi Kakoki Kaisha	0.2

Real estate and construction
Mitsubishi Estate	$0.7
Mitsubishi Construction	0.4

Banking
Mitsubishi Bank—branches	$4,000 (assets)
Mitsubishi Trust & Banking	600 (assets)
Mitsubishi Bank of California . .	500 (assets)

Chemicals, fibers
Mitsubishi Chemical Industries	$3.9
Mitsubishi Petrochemical	2.0
Mitsubishi Gas Chemical	0.9
Mitsubishi Rayon	0.9
Mitsubishi Monsanto Chemical	0.7
Mitsubishi Plastic Industries	0.4

Insurance
Meiji Mutual Life Insurance	$3.5 (premium income)
Tokio Marine & Fire Insurance . .	2.5 (premium income)

Trading
Mitsubishi International	$13,900
Koppel Inc.—grain elevators and shipping	465
RJM Co.—steel wholesaler, 2/3-owned	11

Marketing
Mitsubishi cars and trucks	$743
(imported by Chrysler)	
Nikon cameras, optical equipment	156
(imported by Nippon Kogaku subsidiary)	
Semiconductors and computers	18
(imported by Mitsubishi Electronics America)	
Kirin beer	3
(imported by wholly-owned distributor)	

Manufacturing, other investments
Amorient Petroleum—50% owned	$257
Filling stations	
Fletcher Oil & Refining—20% owned	200
Oil refining	
Mitsubishi Electric Sales America	130
TV sets, video equipment	
Chino mine—1/3 owned	130
Copper mining	
Mitsubishi Aircraft International	90
Corporate aircraft	
Palmco	59
Coconut and palm oil refining	
Bonaventure Hotel—Los Angeles—50% owned . . .	48
ATR Wire & Cable—20% owned	25
Steel tire cord	
MHI Corrugating Machinery—50% owned	10
Dosanko Foods—40% owned	2
Fast food chain	
MIC Petroleum	0
Oil exploration	

times encourage small producers to enter international markets, foreign trading companies are generally favored by their governments. Brazil, for example, passed a law in the early 1970s giving trading companies a variety of tax advantages. By 1978, 40 trading companies had been formed. One of the chief advantages of the Brazilian arrangement is the loans trading companies receive to purchase local products which the trading company then markets abroad. These companies have been a major factor in facilitating and enlarging Brazilian exports of manufactured goods.

The use of merchant importers and trading companies provides possible adequate coverage, market access, or political acceptability.

Complementary marketers. Companies with marketing facilities or contacts in different countries with excess marketing capacity or a desire for a broader product line sometimes take on additional lines for international distribution. The generic name for such activities is complementary marketing, but is commonly called *piggybacking*. General Electric Co. has been distributing merchandise for other suppliers for many years. They accept products that are noncompetitive but complementary and that add to the basic distribution strength of the company itself.[5] Singer Sewing Machine Company emphasizes products closely allied to its own. They piggyback fabrics, patterns, notions, and thread.

Most piggyback arrangements are undertaken when a firm wants to fill out its product line or keep its distribution channels for seasonal items functioning throughout the year. Companies may work either on an agency or merchant basis, but by far the greatest volume of piggyback business is handled on an ownership (merchant) purchase-resale arrangement.

The selection process for new products for piggyback distribution must answer the following questions. (1) Is the product related to the product line, and does it contribute to it? (2) Does the product fit the sales and distribution channel presently employed? (3) Is there an adequate margin to make the undertaking worthwhile? (4) Will the product find market acceptance and profitable volume? If these requirements are met, piggybacking could be a logical way of increasing volume and profit for both the carrier and the piggybacker.

There are other types of cooperative marketing ventures with two or more companies, but they are difficult to characterize under a single heading. In most cases, they work through joint ventures or cost-sharing distribution arrangements.

MIDDLEMEN IN FOREIGN MARKETS

Because manufacturers have little control over most domestic export middlemen, and know so little about their foreign operations, they may prefer

---

[5] For an interesting example of a company that engages in complementary or piggybacking, see Art Detman Jr., "TRW Datacom: A Better Idea of Overseas Distribution," as reprinted in Subhash C. Jain and Louis R. Tucker, Jr.'s, *International Marketing: Managerial Perspectives* (Boston: C.B.I. Publishing Company Inc., 1979), pp. 321–27.

to deal with middlemen in the customer countries. In doing so, they gain the advantage of shorter channels and can deal directly with middlemen who are in constant contact with the market.

Such involvement moves the manufacturers closer to the market and involves them more closely with problems of language, physical distribution, communications, and financing. Foreign middlemen may be agents or merchants; they may be associated with the parent company to varying degrees or may be temporarily hired for special purposes. Exhibit 18–4 reviews the basic characteristics of leading types of foreign middlemen.

Agents in customer countries

Agent middlemen work under a wide variety of names, but none take title to the goods with which they deal. Since names are particularly confusing in this field and are not necessarily descriptive, one must investigate the actual functions and activities undertaken by a given type of agent middleman in a foreign country. In general, the range of functions of foreign agents is similar to those of domestic agent middlemen.

BOX 18–5:   Who needs an agent?

If the Middle East's intermediaries didn't exist, they would have to be invented. For the Western business executive, the intermediaries:

Overcome the formidible language barrier.

Penetrate the orbit of Moslem power. "Foreign firms entering the market," explains Robert E. Bernard, executive vice president of Kaiser Engineers in charge of international operations, "have a difficulty getting to the handful of key people who make key decisions." The intermediary, however, knows who among the palace courtiers has the ruler's ear and which ministers truly hold the levers of decision.

Sandpaper the typical American business abrasiveness into acceptable Arab diplomatic verbage—an important consideration in a culture that places a high value on the "spoken" word.

Provide "thinking time" for the parties to consider all the implications invoked in the proposed transaction. By the same token, if, on reflection, it seems desirable for one of the parties to withdraw from negotiations, the presence of the intermediary allows this to be accomplished without a loss of face.

Short-circuit the Arab passion for verbosity and lyrical hyperbole.

Perform the contract haggling—a ritualized form of "horse trading" in the Middle East (and in other regions of the world) with which most U.S. executives are not psychologically attuned.

Bear the brunt of the interminable talk sessions, which are at odds with the Western-structured time frame.

Obtain from each side the concessions that enable the parties to strike a bargain.

Play down the U.S. business person's obsession with a written contract, which to the traditional Arab mind is an affront to the honor of a commitment conveyed by the spoken word and sealed with a handclasp.

Source: Peter Nehemkis, "Business Projects Abroad: Rhetoric and Reality," *Management Review*, Winter 1975, p. 16.

Brokers. Like the export broker discussed in an earlier section, brokers operating in a foreign country deal largely in commodities and food products. The foreign brokers are typically part of small brokerage firms operating in one country or in a few contiguous countries. Their strength is having good continuing relationships with customers and providing speedy market coverage at a low cost.

There are relatively few brokers in most countries, but they account for a large volume of merchandise because of the standard nature of the products and commodities in which they deal.

One major difficulty in dealing with brokers is finding competent individuals to provide adequate market coverage. The agents themselves have recognized this problem, and a German company of 22 regional sales agents has been formed. They constitute a brokerage consortium offering manufacturers full coverage of the nation's food trade. By contacting this one company, a producer can reach some 150 key accounts, 200 regional wholesalers, and 2,100 important major retailers.[6]

Factors. Because of the importance and complexity of international credit, agents called factors are rapidly growing in significance as international middlemen. Factors perform all of the normal brokerage functions but also finance the sales transactions. Factors may also take responsibility for financing goods while they are in various stages of manufacture, remanufacture, or assembly. The chief advantage of dealing with factors is that they relieve the selling company, and usually the buying company, of credit risk. The *del credere* agent is often considered to be a broker but is actually a special type of factor.

Manufacturer's representatives. Manufacturer's representatives may take responsibility for a producer's goods in a city, regional market area, entire country, or several adjacent countries. When responsible for an entire country, the middleman is often called a *sole agent.* As in the United States, the well-chosen, well-motivated, well-controlled manufacturer's representative can provide excellent market coverage for the manufacturer in certain circumstances. The manufacturer's representative is widely used in distribution of industrial goods overseas and is an excellent representative for any type of manufactured consumer goods.

Foreign manufacturers' representatives have a variety of titles, including sales agent, resident sales agent, exclusive agent, commission agent, and indent agent. They take no credit, exchange, or market risk but deal strictly as field sales representatives. They do not arrange for shipping or for handling and usually do not take physical possession. Manufacturers who wish the type of control and intensive market coverage which their own sales force would afford but who cannot field such a force may find the manufacturer's representative a satisfactory choice.

Managing agents and compradors. A managing agent conducts

---

[6] "A Shared Sales Force Cuts Company's Cost," *Business Europe,* February 20, 1976.

EXHIBIT 18–4: Characteristics of middlemen in foreign countries

Type of duties	Agents			
	Broker	Factor	Manufacturer's representative	Managing agent
Take title	No	No	No	No
Take possession	No	No	Seldom	Seldom
Continuing relationship	No	Sometimes	Often	With buyer, not seller
Share of foreign output	Small	Small	All or part for one area	n.a.
Degree of control by principal	Low	Low	Fair	None
Price authority	Nil	Nil	Nil	Nil
Represent buyer or seller	Either	Either	Seller	Buyer
Number of principals	Many	Many	Few	Many
Arrange shipping	No	No	No	No
Type of goods	Commodity and food	Commodity and food	Manufactured goods	All types manufactured goods
Breadth of line	Broad	Broad (often specialized)	Allied lines	Broad
Handle competitive lines	Yes	Yes	No	Yes
Extent of promotion and selling effort	Nil	Nil	Fair	Nil
Extend credit to principal	No	Yes	No	No
Market information	Nil	Fair	Good	Nil

Note: n.a. = not available.

business within a foreign nation under an exclusive contract arrangement with the parent company. The managing agent in some cases invests in the operation and in most instances operates under a contract with the managed company. Compensation is usually on the basis of cost plus a specified percentage of the profits of the managed company.

In Far Eastern countries, the managing agent is likely to be called a *comprador,* and is used because of his/her intimate knowledge of the obscure and enigmatic customs and languages of the importing country. Few of the true general-manager type of compradors are still in operation, but there is a tendency for other kinds of foreign middlemen to expand their functions to accommodate small manufacturers.

Foreign merchant middlemen

Merchant middlemen take title and, normally, possession of the goods. Although they are known by many titles, merchant middlemen in other

| Comprador | Merchants | | | |
	Distributor	Dealer	Import jobber	Wholesaler and retailer
No	Yes	Yes	Yes	Yes
Yes	Yes	Yes	Yes	Yes
Yes	Yes	Yes	No	Usually not
All one area	All, for certain countries	Assignment area	Small	Very small
Fair	High	High	Low	Nil
Partial	Partial	Partial	Full	Full
Seller	Seller	Seller	Self	Self
Few	Small	Few major	Many	Many
No	No	No	No	No
Manufactured goods	Manufactured goods	Manufactured goods	Manufactured goods	Manufactured consumer
	Narrow to broad	Narrow	Narrow to broad	Narrow to broad
No	No	No	Yes	Yes
Fair	Fair	Good	Nil	Nil usually
Sometimes	Sometimes	No	No	No
Good	Fair	Good	Nil	Nil

countries may be classified in four ways: distributors, dealers, import jobbers, and wholesalers and retailers. The titles imply functions basically the same as those associated with similar merchant middlemen in domestic channels. The advantages and disadvantages of using merchant middlemen in foreign and domestic situations are also similar. They provide time and place utility by purchasing and holding the goods at locations which are relatively convenient to customers; they provide credit service, take the risk of price fluctuations, and provide varying degrees of sales services. Merchant middlemen select their own selling prices and may have little manufacturer loyalty because they handle large numbers of goods. Since they also are more likely to favor high profit, high turnover items, it is unwise to place full reliance on merchant middlemen to promote and sell a product aggressively. As with all middlemen, particularly those working at a distance, effectiveness is directly dependent on the selection of the middleman and on the degree of control the manufacturer is willing and able to exert.

Distributors. A foreign distributor often has exclusive sales rights in a specific country and works in close cooperation with the manufacturer. The distributor has a relatively high degree of dependence on the supplier companies, and arrangements are likely to be on a long-run, continuous basis. Often distributor-manufacturer relationships are formalized through franchises or ownership arrangements. Working through distributors permits the manufacturer a reasonable degree of control over prices, promotional effort, inventory, servicing, and other distribution functions. If a line is profitable for distributors, they can be depended on to handle it in a manner closely approximating the desires of the manufacturer.

Dealers.   Generally speaking, anyone who has a continuing relationship with a supplier in buying and selling goods is considered a dealer. More specifically, dealers are middlemen selling industrial goods or durable consumer goods direct to customers; dealers are the last step in the channel of distribution. Dealers have continuing, close working relationships with their suppliers and exclusive selling rights for their producer's products within a given geographic area. Finally, they derive a large portion of their sales volume from the products of a single supplier firm. Usually the dealer is an independent merchant middleman, but sometimes the supplier company has an equity in its dealers.

Some of the best examples of dealer-type operations are found in the farm equipment, earth-moving, and automotive industries. These categories include such companies as Massey Ferguson, with a vast, worldwide network of dealers; Caterpillar Tractor Company, with dealers in every major city of the world; and the various automobile companies.

Import jobbers.   Import jobbers purchase goods directly from the manufacturer. They sell to wholesalers and retailers and to industrial customers. The import jobber is also known as an import house or an import merchant. Import jobbers differ from distributors mainly in that they do not have exclusive territorial rights. In a given port or country, one manufacturer may sell to several import jobbers.

Wholesalers and retailers.   Large and small wholesalers and retailers alike engage in direct importing both for their own outlets and for further redistribution to smaller middlemen. The combination retailer-wholesaler is more important in foreign countries than in the United States; it is not at all uncommon to find most of the larger retailers in any city wholesaling their goods to local shops and dealers.

COMPANY DISTRIBUTION ABROAD

Although the company's own selling force is not considered part of a channel of distribution *per se*, it should be, because the foreign marketing arm of the company is sufficiently independent that it often must be dealt with as if it were an independent channel. It also substitutes for or supplements independent channels of distribution. Companies undertake development of their own overseas marketing organizations for two reasons: (1) to increase volume of sales and (2) to increase control over the distribution system. The two activities should combine to give the company greater profitability and stability but sometimes the company finds it loses volume when it gives up established distribution channels and encounters intense competition from former distributors and middlemen. Though it may take two to five years before a new operation reaches the break-even point, many companies have found that establishing their own internal distribution channel has been the most satisfactory way of reaching certain major markets.

Increasingly, companies which are serious about the long-term relationship in a market tend to develop their own distribution system whenever it is economically possible.

Companies that want to establish their own marketing structures abroad may employ salespeople to report directly to the home office or establish sales branches or subsidiaries abroad. Some have utilized the joint-venture plan, or have merged with or purchased former middlemen in order to develop their own foreign marketing systems.

Rather than set up new sales offices or branches, some companies have chosen to utilize their own missionary sales force which, like its domestic counterpart, has the responsibility for making customer contact and sales presentations and for providing follow-up service. The actual physical distribution of the product is handled through an assortment of wholesalers or other middlemen.

GOVERNMENT AFFILIATED MIDDLEMEN

In every country of the world marketers must deal with governments. Products, services, and commodities for the government's own use are always procured through government purchasing offices at federal, regional, and local levels.[7] As more and more social services are undertaken by governments, the level of government purchasing activity is escalating. In the Netherlands, for example, the annual turnover of the state's purchasing office increased some 80 percent in five years. That office deals with more than 10,000 suppliers in 20 countries. About one third of the products purchased by that agency are produced outside the Netherlands; 90 percent of foreign purchases are handled through Dutch representatives. The other 10 percent are purchased directly from producing companies. In planned economies such as Eastern Europe, most import-export activity is handled by government agencies. In the Soviet Union, for example, 50 foreign trading organizations are part of the Ministry of Foreign Trade. Each has its own organization and is responsible for an exclusive product specialty. These organizations, in turn, are represented by government-owned foreign trading

---

[7] Louis T. Wells, Jr., Negotiating with Third World Governments, *Harvard Business Review*, January/February 1977, p. 72.

companies. The Amtorg Trading Corporation is responsible for handling exports and imports between the United States and the Soviet Union. Most countries have specialized trading organizations handling one specific type· of product (such as electrical machinery) and some deal direct without any Amtorg-type clearing agency.

BOX 18–6:   Avon calling—Asian style

The Avon lady travels by pedicab in Hong Kong, by minibus in Manila and Kuala Lumpur, or by boat along Bangkok's canals. Many of the cosmetics in her bag have been reworked to suit Asian tastes and she does not go door-to-door, for many Asians are wary of strangers.

In Japan, strong fragrances had to be toned down, because the Japanese are easily offended by them. Packaging had to be changed too. Since the Japanese like beautiful packaging, the normally-used cheaper plastic packaging had to be up-graded to crystalline glass.

Asian representatives don't knock on strangers' doors in Japan and Hong Kong because they wouldn't be welcome. They knock only on doors of friends and relatives. Kinship patterns in Asia extend through several generations on both paternal and maternal lines so an Avon representative usually is assured of an adequate market.

In Thailand, Malaysia, and the Philippines, an Avon lady can knock on a door if it belongs to a business acquaintance or to the friend of a friend. Neighborhood parties sponsored by Avon also are popular. One other difference. Once a sale is made, the Avon lady asks the customer to pick up the products from the nearest warehouse rather than wait for home delivery.

Source: From "Avon Lady in Asia Uses a Soft Sell," *New York Times*, August 26, 1981.

Various patterns of representation are employed in dealing with government-affiliated middlemen—the company may deal directly with the government agency or may use an agent middleman. Only rarely are merchant middlemen employed to handle goods for sale to or through government agencies. In some countries, a foreign company or agent may deal only with the foreign trading organization; in turn, it attempts to represent the interests of the company to customers in that country. Such arrangements generally offer little control over selling effort and are unsatisfactory. In an East-West trade seminar in West Berlin, only three of 25 West German companies indicated satisfaction with the performance of state trading agencies with which they dealt. In other countries, such as Poland, Czechoslovakia, Hungary, and Bulgaria, companies may hire an exclusive agent who not only deals with the foreign trading organization but also may represent the product to the foreign consumer or user. In this arrangement, the foreign trading organization is merely involved in handling the permits and paperwork, while the marketing is left to the agents.

FACILITATING AGENCIES

In addition to channel middlemen and physical distribution agencies, the process of selling and delivering goods calls into play a series of middlemen who play a distinct role in facilitating basic marketing functions. These middlemen provide various services to assist and protect the flow of goods in their journey to the consumer. Such middlemen provide communication, management services, financing, and insurance. Communications depend heavily on international mail and telephone service as well as cablegram, telex, and facsimile transmission services which, combined with translators, greatly aid the communication process. Management services include advertising agencies, marketing research firms, as well as such special services as international law, accounting, taxation, and management consulting services.

One seldom mentions finance, insurance, and credit institutions in the same breath with marketing channels, but all three have a particular bearing on the movements of goods and the development of distribution channels.

BOX 18–7: There was a woman from Poznan, who represented those whom she can, she . . .

According to information published in *Prawo i Zycie*, the journal of the Polish lawyers' association, an unnamed "attractive lady from Poznan" was sentenced to two years in prison and fined Z400,000 for "replacing foreign trade organizations" and "acting as a business representative" without Foreign Trade Ministry permission.

The woman allegedly established contacts in Poznan in 1972 with the Swiss citizen Rudolf Marti, representing the Maag textile equipment enterprise, and proceeded to sell Maag textile machinery to several Polish foreign trade organizations, including FTO Varimex.

Source: "Poles Jail Illegal Agent." Reprinted from page 267 of the August 26, 1977 issue of *Business Eastern Europe*, with permission of the publisher, Business International Corp. (New York).

SUMMARY

From the foregoing discussion, it is evident that the international marketer has a broad range of alternatives for developing an economical, efficient, high-volume international distribution system. To the uninitiated, however, the variety may be overwhelming.

Careful analysis of the functions performed suggests more similarity than difference between international and domestic distribution systems; in both cases there are three primary alternatives of using agent middlemen, merchant middlemen, or a company's own sales and distribution system. In many instances, all three types of middlemen will be employed on the international scene, and channel structure may vary from nation to nation or from continent to continent. The neophyte company in international marketing can gain strength from the knowledge that information and advice are available relative to the structuring of international distribution systems and that many well-developed and capable middleman firms exist for the international distribution of goods. Within the past decade, international middlemen have become more numerous, more reliable, more sophisticated, and more readily available to marketers in all countries. Such growth and development offer an ever-wider range of possibilities for entering foreign markets, but the international business person should remember that it is just as easy for competitors.

The next chapter deals with patterns of distribution and the development and implementation of international distribution strategy.

QUESTIONS

1. Define:
    Distribution structure   EMC
    Distribution channel   Factor
    Facilitating agency   Confirming house
    Zaibatsu   Barter broker

2. "Many, perhaps most, international middlemen wear several hats and can be clearly identified only in the context of their relationship with a specific firm." Discuss.

3. To what extent, and in what ways, do the functions of domestic middlemen differ from their foreign counterparts?

4. Why is the EMC sometimes called an independent export department?

5. Differentiate between a wholesaler and a distributor.

6. Can facilitating agencies be called a part of the channel of distribution? Explain.

7. Discuss how physical distribution relates to channel policy and how they affect one another.

8. Why should a company-owned sales organization be considered part of the channel structure?

9. Explain how and why distribution channels are affected as they are when the stage of development of an economy improves.

10. In what circumstances is the use of an EMC logical?

11. Predict whether the Norazi agent is likely to grow or decline in importance.

12. Discuss the possible antitrust ramification of WPEAs.

13. In what circumstances are trading companies likely to be used?

14. How is distribution-channel structure affected by increasing emphasis on the government as a customer and by the existence of state trading agencies?

READING
Demystifying Japanese distribution
Mitsuaki Shimaguchi and Larry J. Rosenberg*

Japan's consumer market poses a dilemma for American marketers. Opportunities have tempted them for over a decade as the Japanese economy has blossomed into the world's third richest. Japan's mass market of 113 million people—mainly affluent, urban, middle class, and of a single ethnic group speaking a single language—is receptive to most Western-made products. With the yen's rising value, imports especially from the United States have become cheaper. However, this market has long been considered impenetrable to Western products. Government-imposed trade barriers have largely protected it from foreign competition. But in response to huge trade surpluses with Western nations, the government has committed itself to *yunyu sokushin* (import promotion) through fewer tariffs, enlarged quotas, reduced bureaucratic red tape, relaxed foreign-exchange controls, and the like. While many restrictions still remain, the door is open for foreign consumer goods.

At this point, Occidental firms may feel like rushing into this lucrative market. But between easier entry and willing consumers lies a jungle—the Japanese distribution system. Accused of being a major nontariff barrier to foreign products, it is different enough from its Western counterparts to completely bewilder foreign firms and to bestow an advantage on domestic competitors. One Japanese distribution authority declares that "many failures of foreign firms in the Japanese market can be attributed to the lack of knowledge about our distribution system."[1]

This paper aims first to interpret Japan's distribution system for Western marketing practitioners. As shown in Exhibit 1, Japanese distribution may be characterized as having three layers. We shall examine: (1) the *structure* dominated by many small wholesalers dealing with many small retailers; (2) the *behavior* expressed in several baffling trade customs which reinforce the structure; and (3) the *philosophy* shaped by a unique culture, which underlies both the structure and behavior. Second, we shall spell out the steps for planning an effective distribution strategy. These are based on Western corporate experiences in navigating these often tortuous distribution channels.

Facing a complicated structure

From the Western point of view, Japan's distribution system appears outmoded, complex, cumbersome and inefficient. Looking at this maze, two features stand out: (1) distribution channels are typically long, and (2) they are full of many small firms.

In this multitier distribution, it is not unusual for goods to flow from producer to primary wholesaler to secondary wholesaler to regional or local wholesaler to retailer to consumer. Most of these intermediaries perform narrow and highly specialized

* Larry J. Rosenberg is Associate Professor of Marketing at New York University, and has consulted for many Japanese trade associations, retailers, and broadcasters; and Mitsuaki Shimaguchi is Associate Professor Marketing at Keio University in Tokyo, and is a consultant to government and business in Japan.
Source: *Columbia Journal of World Business,* Spring 1979.

[1] Yoshihiro Tajima, "Preface," *Outline of Japanese Distribution Structures* (Tokyo: The Distribution Economics Institute of Japan, 1973), p. x.

functions. In general, the smaller the producers or retailers, the more middlemen get involved, and the greater the wholesaler's power. Because many retailers and wholesalers carry only a single or narrow line of merchandise, a manufacturer, even of similar products, must deal with different sets of intermediaries.

The ratio of Japan's wholesale to retail sales is 5 to 1, in contrast to the United States's 1.3 to 1. In 1974, Japanese wholesalers sold 38 percent of their goods to other wholesalers, compared to 22 percent to retailers and 28 percent to industrial users.[2]

Compared to the modern production sector, the distribution services sector has been slow in concentrating and increasing productivity. Most of the Japanese firms engaging in distribution are small. Many neighborhood shops still exist to sell a single product line, such as tea or rice. Serving the Japanese population are 1.6 million retailers and 340,000 wholesalers. This represents about one retailer for over 69 persons and one wholesaler for every 323 persons—double the U.S.'s figures. From 1970–76, the number of retailers jumped 10 percent and the number of wholesalers 33 percent. Furthermore, 47 percent of wholesalers and 85 percent of retailers have fewer than four employees.

Dominance of the traditional structure

From the beginning of Japan's modernization in 1868 to the 1950s four sets of historical forces have shaped the conventional distribution structure.

Historical environment.   Japan's geography of four main islands, full of mountains and rivers, blocked the mobility of people and products. Therefore, suppliers had to rely on local intermediaries in remote areas. Furthermore, the government's industrial policy concentrated on building an efficient production sector, neglecting until recently the distribution sector.

Partly constraining mass retailing even today is the limited number of automobiles used for shopping. Inadequate parking, freeways, and shopping-center development hinder the expansion of large, wide variety retailing. The Japanese government still maintains a policy geared toward preserving small-scale retailers. Under the *Daiten-Ho* (Large-Scale Retailing Establishment Law), a large store can be erected only when the neighboring small merchants approve its size, days open, and business hours. While it is difficult enough for Japanese retailers to overcome this, foreign-owned retailers would encounter even more resistance.

Economic conditions.   Because the Japanese economy long suffered from heavy unemployment, low-skilled distribution jobs were easiest to find. For those retired and let go in time of economic slow-downs, these jobs provided a sponge and an alternative to welfare. Also, opening a store even today fulfills a deep cultural desire to be one's own boss. The debt of numerous wholesalers and retailers typically exceeds their equity capital. For them and manufacturers, relating to many partners spreads the risk. Given this serious shortage of financing, small-scale operations can rarely modernize and expand. While the lengthy distribution channel raises the final price for all products, foreign goods can end up with prohibitively high prices because of intermediary costs.

Traditional consumer patterns.   Until recently, Japan's per capita income was

---

[2] *Wagakuni-no-Shōgyō* [*Commerce in Japan,* 1977], (Tokyo: The Ministry of International Trade and Industry, 1978).

EXHIBIT 1: Japanese distribution in three layers

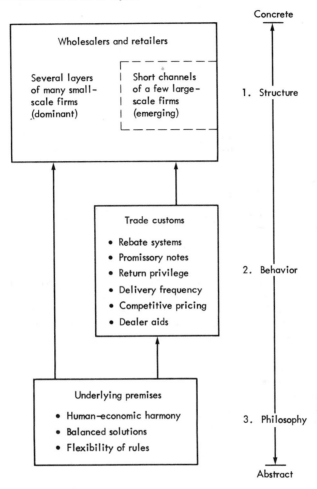

too low to permit buying large quantities at one time. In addition, consumers have believed in saving—giving them the world's highest rate. Most Japanese housewives lack storage space in their compact homes and prefer to shop several times weekly in neighborhood stores. Besides the sociability of these shops, their owners perform services that supermarkets cannot afford, such as suggesting seasonal recipes.

Supply constraints. Traditionally, Japanese manufacturers were small and local. To market their products widely, they required multiple levels of many middlemen, who often performed the marketing functions. Also, long distribution channels encouraged Japanese manufacturers to export. Instead of incurring the large intermediary cost in the domestic market, some manufacturers prefer to pay the same amount to the simpler export distribution channel, especially to the giant Japanese trading companies.

Emergence of large-scale enterprises

Signs exist that the distribution system is evolving with more large retailers, more self-service stores, more chain operations, consolidations of small wholesalers, and manufacturers' efforts to establish shorter, more efficient channels. Of all retail sales in 1976, department stores accounted for 8.2 percent and supermarkets 12.1 percent. The growth in selling space, 1966–76, for department stores has been 117 percent and for supermarkets 549 percent.[3] This expansion can be explained by several recent developments.

Contemporary environment.   The post-war modernization of transportation and communications has facilitated large-scale, centralized retailing. Also, the government is committed to making the nation's distribution system more efficient. For example, it helps small retailers form voluntary chains and wholesalers build large distribution centers.

Contemporary consumer patterns.   Along with unprecedented prosperity have come some of the world's highest commodity prices. The inflation subsequent to 1973's "oil shock" and consumer education campaigns have made consumers very price conscious. They are beginning to realize that inefficient small-scale distribution is one of the major culprits and have found large stores' lower prices appealing. They are relying more on brand names (national or private) rather than on retail personnel's advice.

Modern manufacturing.   In the decade preceding 1973, most Japanese manufacturers enjoyed impressive growth rates of over 10 percent annually. They expanded and invested in the most modern facilities to prepare for the next decade's growth. Meanwhile, high fixed costs and interest rates have compelled them to produce at full capacity. To dispose of this large volume, they have supported the spread of large retailers.

Financing ploy.   Because small-scale intermediaries lack the finances, they usually pay suppliers with 60-to-120-day promissory notes instead of cash. Although large retailers' high turnover generates more revenue than their small competitors, they cling to the custom of delayed payment to suppliers. As a result, they accumulate a sizable amount of interest-free trade credit, which permits them to expand further. Other traditional trade customs such as manufacturers' rebate systems and return goods privileges play a similar role.

The future structure

Because of these trends, a small number of large middlemen is challenging the dominance of a large number of small firms. Large-scale retailers benefit from small retailers' low operating efficiency, lack of systematization, and reluctance to innovate. Furthermore, a British executive of Johnson & Johnson Far East Inc. has observed that the major supermarket chains' share of the retail market will take off when they gain enough control so more manufacturers can deal directly with them, without endangering their traditional wholesaling channels.[4] But currently, Japanese retailing practices, with few exceptions, lag the United States by several years—especially in chain

---

[3] "Industry Report: Department Stores," *Fuji Bank Bulletin,* February 1978, pp. 30–31.

[4] Kneale H. Ashwell and Sueaki Takaoka, "Foreign and Japanese Managers Discuss Distribution," *Dentsu's Japan Marketing/Advertising,* 1977, p. 24.

stores, self-service, and mail order. A scarcity of management talent to operate multi-unit and vertically-integrated retail systems is also a problem.

For the foreseeable future, small-scale and large-scale distribution will coexist. Although several of Japan's large manufacturers have organized more efficient distribution routes, most still depend on the conventional arrangements. On balance, modernization of Japanese distribution should stimulate inflow of foreign capital and imported products.

Dealing with different trade customs

A prime reason that foreign firms cannot assume that Japanese distribution will become more Western in the near future is that several special trade customs are proving quite resistant to change. Six practices merit attention.

Rebate system. Understanding the intricacy of rebates as incentives to intermediaries is widely regarded as the mark of an expert on Japanese distribution. Originally given to resellers to induce buying, the rebate eventually became institutionalized. Over 500 names of rebates exist, varying by type, purpose, and function. For example, they can provide for sales promotion to motivate a middleman's purchases, rewards for extra display space, and control of price maintenance.

Offering rebates on a case-by-case basis makes this system unique. The confidentiality of rebates prevents one intermediary from knowing what others are receiving, although the rebator usually pretends he is extending the best offer to each. The rebatee, while demonstrating his loyalty, still attempts to negotiate a larger rebate. To avert a middleman's distrust, many manufacturers have initiated fixed rebate formulas, but their efforts have been in vain so far.

Promissory notes. As mentioned before, Japanese trade credit is based on a deferred payment system of promissory notes or IOUs to alleviate capital shortages among small retailers. Wholesalers accept long-term promissory notes and then ask their suppliers for equal or even longer credit terms. Payment periods range from 60 to 120 days, and even longer in some industries and special cases—180 to 210 days.

This system persists because it spreads the financial risk among more firms. It is so entrenched that even financially-strong retailers demand deferred payment and sometimes bargain for more favorable terms. Even with the system's great flexibility, credit largely depends on the buyer's financial position, with the strength of buyer-seller loyalty often influencing the terms.

Return privilege. Relatively liberal returning of goods exists throughout Japanese distribution. Many suppliers automatically expect a certain proportion of goods to be returned not because of damages but because they did not sell. The return privilege exists mainly to help small merchants who cannot afford to keep unsold products in limited space for long. Liberal returns also help attract large-volume retailers. Wholesalers transfer the returned goods burden to their manufacturers, who demand this privilege from their suppliers.

In highly competitive industries, manufacturers with excess production capacity often ship their products to wholesalers on a judgment basis rather than on specific orders. Wholesalers grudgingly accept these shipments and aggressively push them, assured that the manufacturer will accept the return of overshipments. In addition, many manufacturers with strong brand images protect list prices and avoid price cutting by favoring free returns.

Delivery frequency. A Polaroid Corporation of Japan executive contrasted the expectation of California outlets to be contacted—twice a year for small dealers and twice a month for large dealers—with the custom in Japan (itself the size of California)—daily or weekly for small dealers and a half-hour after a phone call from large dealers.[5] Again, this is a result of limited financial resources, vigorous competition in numerous industries, and the closeness of personal relationships. In highly competitive industries such as drugs, processed foods, and home appliances, wholesalers commonly ship daily to retailers.

Japanese government hearings on the delivery situation in 15 industries concluded that no rules or contracts established the minimum order in most industries.[6] Although wholesalers and retailers consider delivery an additional service, and therefore a cost, they still like quick service.

Competitive pricing. Active price competition pervades Japan's distribution system. Partly because of the Japanese firm's commitment to lifetime employment, prices are used to generate enough immediate revenue. This leads to price cutting which at least covers unavoidable costs.

Competition among thousands of financially-weak middlemen fosters it. They sometimes are pressured to set prices according to a "volume approach" rather than a "profit approach." Volume provides the basis for receiving larger rebates. For marginal firms, reducing prices may be their only effective way to boost sales. Family-run firms especially can afford to lower prices because they regard labor and some operating costs as zero.

Dealers aids. Intermediaries receive generous dealer aids from their suppliers. Some of these are called "dealer incentive plans" which include resort vacations, theater tickets, and membership in golf clubs. They encourage a closeness among business associates. The more conventional variety from manufacturers entails store display kits, managerial information, management education programs, and some types of financing. Manufacturers may assign detailmen who obtain orders from retailers yet pass them along to the wholesaler. Manufacturer-paid demonstrators in retail outlets strengthen the relationship with dealers.

Future practices. Most of these trade customs have been criticized by economists, consumer advocates, and government officials as vicious cycles and grossly inefficient. Nonetheless, large and small intermediaries alike continue to welcome the financial benefits, and most suppliers relish them as strategic tools. Decisive support comes from large middlemen who use them as weapons for bargaining with suppliers and for battling smaller rivals. In the long run, as Japan's distribution structure becomes more similar to the Western model, suppliers may dilute or even discontinue these six practices. In the predictable future, however, it is unlikely that they will be substantially curtailed.

Probing a unique philosophy

Japanese philosophy lies at the root of the distribution structure and trade customs, which persist in the face of market, production, and political changes. This philosophy

---

[5] Jack J. Schmuckli and Yoshihiro Tajima, "Archaic Distribution System Has its Use," *Dentsu's Japan Marketing/Advertising*, 1973/74, p. 102.

[6] *Torihiki Jōken no Tekseika* [*Toward a Justification of Trade Condition*], (Tokyo: Tusansyo Kigho-Kyoku, 1973), p. 118.

springs from an ancient, distinct, and enduring culture of a racially homogeneous society. Appreciating it enables foreign marketers to view distribution with more clarity and to improve the prospects of successful entry. Three underlying premises govern much of distribution behavior.

Human-economic harmony.   Great emphasis is always put on such ideals as harmony, traditional associations, mutual cooperation, and loyalty. Nevertheless, rational economic calculations play a paramount role—as evidenced by a manufacturer's system to determine margins and rebates for its wholesalers. The personal bonds used to be much stronger, but competitive, social, and international forces have compelled industry to assert the economic factors. As a result, companies weak in negotiating power tend to stress the human dimension, while stronger firms rely on the economic rationale. In effect, this means that the stronger a middleman is, the stronger he will become.

This pro-economic tendency appears to conflict with the harmony orientation of the Japanese people. Although Japan is a group-oriented society, the individual still believes that he must finally stand alone.[7] The emphasis on economic criteria can also be traced to the Japanese seniority and lifetime employment system. Because a business failure deprives one of valued status (or "face"), and job mobility remains relatively low, the individual dares not jeopardize his position in an organization. Therefore, suppliers who exercise wide discretion in negotiating with intermediaries find it easier to base a consensus on economic grounds.

Balanced solutions.   As a preference for moderation pervades the Japanese culture, distribution executives abhor extreme solutions. When the human and economic rationales clash, the firm strives to balance them. The economic dominates in the long run, while human considerations affect immediate goals. Harmony, loyalty, and friendship are cultivated to achieve economic ends more smoothly.

This ample latitude permits manufacturers to support small wholesalers who undershoot contracted sales targets (if the gap is reasonable). Although this situation creates the "structure of dependence" of Japanese society and some inefficiency, it also builds loyalty in wholesalers.

Channel members behave benevolently toward one another only so long as they perceive some future economic advantages in the partnership. While suppliers seldom terminate a traditionally-related customer, they will withhold additional trade incentives. The partner responds by leaving voluntarily or the supplier waits until the intermediary's chief executive officer retires before he severs the relationship.

Flexibility of rules.   Although industry-wide and business customs exist and individual firms specify policies, executives are often left with considerable discretion in trade relations. This free-style approach makes Japanese distribution quite adaptive to changing business conditions, and gives an "insider's advantage" to domestic industry, insulating it further from overseas competition. However, executives can lose sight of overall strategy through such an individualized approach.

Discretionary rules encourage channel members to seek benefits through negotiation, as when wholesalers fight for more concessions than their competitors. But without specific rules, multiple alternatives can inflate expectations. The resulting fierce competition can even undermine an industry's self-regulatory efforts.

---

[7] Tamotsu Sengoku and Atsuko Tohyama, *Hikaku Nihonjin Ron* [*Comparative Study of Japan*], (Tokyo: Shogaku-Kan, 1973).

Mastering a distribution strategy

Although the Japanese distribution system is a puzzle, numerous Western firms have cracked the code. This should dispel the notion that distribution poses an insurmountable hurdle to entry. The cases of Occidental consumer-goods marketers succeeding in Japan are varied—soft drinks, instant coffee, electrical appliances, razors and blades, headache remedies, fast-foods, and apparel.

At the outset, Western companies must realize that Japan is culturally a light-year away from the West. To develop an effective distribution strategy, foreign executives must acquire direct and wide experience with the market and the distribution scene. These six steps can help.

Find a Japanese partner.   Selecting a solid Japanese business partner is usually indispensable. As long as trade practices and thinking patterns remain mysterious, it is safer for foreign executives to rely on local experts. Several Japanese firms lately have become especially eager to forge partnerships with foreign importers to thwart protectionist efforts against their products overseas.

The most common Japanese partners are *import agents*—ranging from small local distributors to *sōgō-shōsha* (large trading companies). Of the 6,000 trading companies in existence, 10 giant ones dominate the market. To implement the marketing plan, a typical Japanese agent must be offered financial incentives—low purchase price, allowances for advertising and sales expenses, and a year-end bonus.

Another type of partnership is the *joint venture*. This opens up the Japanese partner's distribution network to the foreign company. It works well when selling a large quantity of goods, when benefiting from both companies' brand images, and when a sizable capital outlay is needed. A variation of the joint venture is franchising. Many Japanese firms welcome the franchisor's management and sales know-how.

Before going into a joint venture, the Japanese partner should be thoroughly evaluated. One American specialty vehicle producer, enjoying high sales at home, found its partner quite inept at attracting a profitable share of a potentially large market. Eventually it discovered that the Japanese firm had transferred its inefficient employees to this subsidiary, from which low profits were expected, as an alternative to violating lifetime employment by firing them.

The Occidental firm and its Japanese partner must agree about management philosophies. American clothing retailer Joseph Magnin sought an independent chain operation in Japan, but was overruled by its majority partner Dai-Ei, a top supermarket chain, which opened the shops within its own supermarkets. In addition, a joint venture is threatened when the Japanese partner wants to limit the imports it will sell to guard its own market share.

A Western firm can establish its own *marketing operation* after hiring seasoned Japanese executives. To form its own distribution network, it must invest heavily in information and support a large long-term financial burden. Most foreign companies, however, will find it difficult to circumvent some type of Japanese agent. Retailers possess such strong loyalty to certain suppliers that rather than offend them, they may refuse to sell or push the products of direct-dealing Occidental firms. Having a Japanese partner reduces the intermediaries' suspicion that a foreign supplier would prove unreliable in a crisis.

Seek a distinctive market position.   For a foreign company's products, the distribution strategy can only be as effective as the product's attractiveness to the Japanese market. Japanese consumers will embrace typically Western products—

such as Coca-Cola, McDonald's Big Macs, and St. Laurent fashions. In other cases, they will be selective in what they accept. Therefore, the product may have to be adapted to Japanese consumers and the way they live. To fit the compact Japanese home, Sears, Roebuck's refrigerators were redesigned to be smaller while retaining their original capacity.

The product should be competitive, or at least equivalent, to its Japanese competition. Because Japanese consumers tend to be conscious of a product's real value, the foreign company must offer superior quality or a better price. As Japanese firms often price competitively, the preferred strategy for Western firms would be in the product's quality and image, especially one with a Western origin or character.

Japanese consumer expectations often exceed those of Occidental consumers for product safety, quality, durability, design, packaging, cleanliness, and after-sale service. For example, in three years the U.S.'s Gayla Industries plastic kite, engineered to reach amazing heights, took an 80 percent share of a market it helped double in size. Because Japanese consumers have a favorable image of American goods, the Japanese producer of Bell & Howell photographic equipment vigorously promotes the Bell & Howell name and never its made-in-Japan origin. High-priced Western products often can be related to high quality. Wilson's set of golf clubs at $1,000 and Dior originals sell well.

To counteract the complexity of distribution, concentrating on a single product line stretches resources and increases impact on the market. Because of the Japanese consumer's fondness for novelty and the imitativeness of domestic competition, the foreign marketer must improve its product regularly.

Identify available distribution routes. The foreign company must determine the alternative distribution arrangements in Japan and the relative importance of each. Besides channels in use, other possible paths should be explored. These days more choices can be made between long and short distribution channels, and between small and large retail outlets.

Particular distribution patterns actually depend on the product and whether Japanese firms have built short, efficient channels. While 57.6 percent of fresh fish involves three wholesalers, 87.4 percent of furniture and 89.5 percent of shoes use only one wholesaler.[8] Small neighborhood stores are important for fresh produce and beer. In contrast, most major clothing purchases occur at department stores and specialty shops, and growing quantities of processed foods are sold at superstores (large supermarkets selling consumer durables).

Organize specific distribution alliances. A concentration strategy in territory and type of distribution channel is often advisable. It is inefficient to try to dominate the entire national market at once. Since the Tokyo and Osaka areas contain almost two thirds of Japan's population, the foreign firm can mass its resources there. In addition, these areas have more large stores and more sophisticated consumers. Relying on a limited number of large-scale middlemen can generate important benefits. They know domestic trade practices, sell large quantities through their chain operations, and may eventually create some of the special loyalty found among Japanese firms.

Direct distribution to department stores, supermarket chains, and voluntary chains is becoming more feasible for Occidental producers. For example, Western stationery

---

[8] "Japan's Consumer Goods Distribution System can Work for U.S. Exporters," *Commerce America,* March 14, 1977, p. 24.

and furniture would be unsuitable for neighborhood retailers dealing in traditional Japanese items, but right for larger-scale outlets. It may be possible to segment the market by contracting with a few specialized retailers. One European designer-clothing house selected a limited number of dealers, granting each an exclusive territory.

If the retailers that count are many in number and small in size, wholesalers may be the logical route. S. C. Johnson & Son, Inc.'s Japanese subsidiary demonstrates how wholesalers can pay off. Most foreign toiletry producers concentrate on the 8,000 mass merchandising firms with 40 percent of the market. However, Johnson linked up only with wholesalers to reach the 300,000 individually-operated retailers with 60 percent of the market and terminated its direct dealings with all large retailers. The company achieved a phenomenal penetration rate because many wholesalers sold to the mass merchandisers as well.

Caution must be observed when depending on a trading company's distribution channel to sell to a limited luxury market. This high-margin, low-volume strategy may foreclose future market expansion as domestic competitors preempt most of the market. This was averted by Britain's Twinings Tea, which began distribution in big-city department stores, positioning its black tea as an expensive gift. When sales growth slackened, the company added large food wholesalers and supermarket chains, carving out 20 percent of the black tea market.

Some Occidental companies have successfully forged their own distribution networks. Philips Industries in Japan even devised a way to market its shavers and coffee makers to both large and small outlets. First, it reached the large discount and department stores directly. As all appliance sales in these outlets have prospered, more and more of the 55,000 mom-and-pop shops have dropped their allegiance to a single producer. Thus, the Philips brand among others has been taken on by these retailers.

Accept long-term and small-sized returns.   It requires a long time and a sizable investment to pull off distribution in Japan. Western firms' expectations of fast and high profits rarely materialize. A European appliance executive in Japan eventually became satisfied with a fraction of 1 percent profit margin. Low profits result from the preference of most intermediaries for the mass distribution approach of a small margin on a large turnover.

A reason wide distribution takes time is that most import agents lack the capability to accomplish it rapidly. Thus, a long timetable for expanding distribution must be accepted. For example: first year, sell to downtown Tokyo and Osaka department stores; second year, to Tokyo suburban department stores and major specialty stores; and third year, to Tokyo and Osaka wholesalers and other large cities' department stores.

Occidental firms must be ready to incur large financial outlays. To match the large inventories kept by Japanese companies near their customers to ensure quick deliveries, some foreign producers have invested heavily in storage facilities and stockpiles in Japan. Also, spending for marketing research and distribution information should surpass what would be normal for entering other industrial nations. Furthermore, foreign companies must overcome a financial handicap because most Japanese middlemen find it easy to borrow substantially from local banks and to cooperate closely with domestic business allies. This can force Western marketers to provide low-interest credit.

Cultivate personal relationships in distribution.   Occidental executives must realize that a Japanese intermediary wants to know as much about their company's background and its representatives as it does about their products and prices. Developing a relationship must be done slowly and carefully. Besides honoring all the normal trade practices, aspects of loyalty and trust must be emphasized.

American business persons especially tend to rush in offering a better deal. The Japanese middleman views his distribution partner as his lifeblood. He feels that if the relationship with an American supplier rests mainly on financial grounds, he risks being abandoned for an even better deal.

Part of the promotional efforts of a Western supplier to its Japanese distribution participants must consist of human relations. These gestures can mean visiting the wholesaler to extend condolences on a death in his family, or stopping in on a retailer when he is on summer vacation.

Conclusion

For the typical Western consumer-goods company, successfully distributing to Japan's market poses one challenge after another. Executives must size up the many players in the game. Then, they have to grasp the unusual rules. Finally, they should become attuned to the cultural principles behind the system's behavior. Learning and practicing what it takes to win at Japanese distribution will be tough going. But the prize is worth the striving.

Long term large market share w/ low profit achieved by personal relationships, unusual credit arrangements will foster strong trusting relationships between a foreign co. and a Japanese expert.

Chapter 19

Developing and managing distribution channels

In preceding chapters, product development, pricing, and promotion issues have been discussed. To complete the components of the marketing mix and to get the product to the target market, channels of distribution must be developed. Every country or target market area presents the international marketer with unique middlemen and distribution patterns. The challenge for the international marketer is to forge channels from available middlemen which will be effective in meeting the needs of the target market within the constraints imposed by company policies and resources.

The first step in developing a channel program is to prepare an overall strategy that includes basic decisions on the degree of commitment to distribution and the amount of control the company wants to maintain over worldwide distribution. Once a channel program is constructed, the channel commander retains responsibility for motivating all middlemen to attain peak performance. The commander attempts to control channel factors to assure maximum volume, adequate market coverage, appropriate servicing, and proper selling effort and prices. These factors affect the results and the total distribution costs which, in turn, make the marketing enterprise profitable or unprofitable. These are the primary considerations of this chapter on developing and managing distribution channels.

CHANNEL STRATEGIES AND POLICIES

A host of policy and strategy questions confronts the international marketing manager. The policies and problems are not in themselves very different from those encountered in domestic distribution, but the solutions differ because of different market patterns and channel alternatives.

Target market needs must be the focal point of any marketing planning. As discussed in earlier chapters, price, promotion, and product decisions begin with an analysis of target market characteristics and needs relative to company policies and strategies reflecting these market characteristics. The marketer should extend this process to channel decisions as well. Frequently though, the marketer leaves control of distribution processes to middlemen in the channel with only minimal interest in the outcome. In this situation, middlemen are being treated as the final customer for a product rather than a means of delivery to a target market. To be fully involved in the marketing effort, the international marketer should approach the task of channel development with a detailed examination of the preferences of the target market, that is, what is the most competitively effective way to deliver the product to the customer? Based on such established criteria, a marketer must select the "best" retailer and other middlemen necessary to profitably and effectively get the product to the designated retailer. In an ideal sense, the international marketer views middlemen as means to achieving specific goals in the distribution process. However, the ideal cannot always be achieved because, the "best" middlemen may not be available. In some markets, the level of sophistication and the necessary services are not found in existing middlemen; or if found, they are not able or willing, because of their size, to accept a product. Also, because of prior commitments, middlemen do not necessarily see themselves as pawns in a marketer's channel strategy but as "customers" of the producers and as channel captains to those to whom they sell. Thus, their motives and goals are frequently contradictory to the strategy plans of the international marketer. Nevertheless, the international marketer needs a clear understanding of market characteristics and desires and must have established operating policies before beginning to select channel middlemen. The foundation for selection should rest on the following factors: (1) Questions of control, size of margins, length of channels, terms of sale, and channel ownership must be decided. (2) The company must establish basic policies, explicitly detailing the money and personnel commitment it is willing to make in developing international distribution, keeping profit goals in a foremost position. (3) Within those general guidelines, specific marketing goals, expressed in terms of volume, market share, and margin requirements, must be established. (4) Because of the difficulty of laying down precise operating policies, the international marketer may find it necessary to couch policies in terms of return on investment, sales volume, long-run potential, and other general guidelines and must acknowledge that lesser problems should be solved on the strategic level. (5) Policy must further delineate the relationship between long- and short-term goals and should specify the company's level of involvement in the distribution system and the extent of its ownership of middlemen.

Channel length and *multiple channel* questions must also be answered. In one country, a short channel may provide excellent results, whereas another market demands longer channels. Similarly, a company may prefer a nice clean channel arrangement utilizing only one major type of distribution, but, in order to achieve coverage, it may have to use all available channels. A decision made in New York to use the same types of channels in different countries may look logical on paper but may not work in practice. A company, therefore, may have to use nonparallel channels: its own sales force in one country; manufacturers' agent channels in another; and merchant wholesalers in still another. Differing circumstances impose a series of local, tactical policy decisions in each market.

The *level of selectivity* is clearly affected by local company conditions. It may be comfortable to think in terms of exclusive dealers or a highly selective distribution network, but, if such a system fails to cover certain markets adequately or does not produce the requisite sales volume, it may be necessary to seek more intensive distribution systems. Companies must learn that operating management decisions of the variety mentioned here are best made at the local level if international channels are to operate with optimum efficiency.

Regardless of the policies, the company must provide adequate flexibility for meeting local conditions and leave opportunity for the marketing strategists to ply their skills. Companies which have forgotten the basic lessons of flexibility and adaptability or lost sight of the primary policy objectives have not generally fared well in the international marketplace. Frigidaire and Whirlpool, two major U.S. producers of electrical appliances, were routed from the French refrigerator market after years of market involvement when aggressive Italian competitors moved in. German companies did no better against the intensive competition in either France or their own country. Marketers were hampered by corporate policy restrictions requiring that they refuse to supply discount and mail-order firms. German companies lost 20 percent of the German refrigerator market within two years to Italians who were marketing through mail-order and discount channels.

All established policies must be broad and flexible enough to permit adaptation to existing distribution patterns from country to country.[1] The firm operating in several countries cannot content itself with one set of solutions; there must be a solution for each marketplace. In the dynamic situation of world marketing, policies must not only be flexible and adaptable, they must also be open to review on relatively short notice.

ADAPTING TO DISTRIBUTION PATTERNS

It is important for international marketers to have a general awareness of the patterns of distribution with which they are confronted in the world marketplace. Nearly every international trading firm is *forced* by the structure of the market to use at least some middlemen in the distribution arrangement. It is all too easy to conclude that because the structural arrangements of foreign and domestic distribution seem alike, foreign channels are the same as domestic channels of the same name or they are similar to one another, but this is misleading. Only when the varied intricacies of actual distribution patterns are understood can the complexity of the distribution task be appreciated. Hopefully, the following material will dispel false notions or at least convey a sense of the variety of world distribution patterns.

---

[1] J. M. Ferre-Trenzano, "Spanish Distribution Channels: Their Current State and Consequent Implication in Marketing Mix Strategies, *European Journal of Marketing* 14, no. 4 (1980), pp. 211–22.

General patterns

Generalizing about internal distribution channel patterns of various countries throughout the world is almost as difficult as generalizing about behavior patterns of people throughout the world. There are certain patterns of similarity among distribution channels, and an understanding of the basic distribution alternatives lends a skeletal understanding of choices in all countries. Although this text has clearly differentiated types of middlemen, the segmentation is less valid in reality where most middlemen undertake activities reflecting the characteristics of several different kinds of middlemen. The conglomerate middleman pattern prevails in *all* countries, regardless of their level of market development.

Despite the similarities, marketing channels and methods are not the same throughout the world. Marketing methods taken for granted in the United States are rare in many countries. One pattern that recurs in studies of various countries is that in most countries middlemen are predominantly very large or very small. The middle-sized wholesalers and retailers seen in the United States are unable to survive at either the wholesale or retail level in many economies.

In the following sections, some generalizations relating to wholesalers and retailers are given, followed by discussion of patterns unique to wholesaling or retailing.

Social acceptance. The social status of tradesmen or middlemen reflects to some extent the level of productivity of the nation. In underdeveloped countries where the emphasis is directed to production, wholesalers and retailers are generally considered to be unproductive. Countries like England, which have long depended on trade for their prosperity, give the middleman a considerably higher place in the economy than India and Africa where traders are considered to impoverish both producers and consumers without adding any utility to the products. In some parts of the world, there is such a repugnance toward trading that it is left to foreigners. West African firms are owned by Levantines, while in East Africa the tradespeople are of Arab, Pakistani, or Indian origin. Much of the large-scale wholesaling and retailing is in the hands of Europeans. The Chinese have played a similar role in the Philippines and Indonesia, but the prosperity they have generated has resulted in considerable animosity and jealousy among the natives. This has led to government restrictions to close trading opportunities to foreigners. Acceptance of tradespeople is usually related to an economy's stage of development and the extent of its dependence on trade for prosperity.

Middleman services. The service attitudes of tradespeople vary sharply at both the retail and wholesale levels from country to country. In Egypt, for example, there is virtually no consumer orientation; the primary purpose of the simple trading system is to handle the physical distribution of available goods. On the other hand, because there are so many tradespeople in India, margins are low and there is a continuing battle for customer preference. Both wholesalers and retailers try to offer extra services to make their goods attractive to consumers.

All dimensions of distribution have been greatly affected by American marketing methods and the world trend toward internationalization of business. In Israel, most small retail establishments have traditionally closed for several hours during the noon period. There and in other countries with similar customs, the advent of self-service stores which are open throughout the day (and some into the evening hours) is causing shopkeeepers to rethink their policies on hours. High wage rates associated with industrialization cause curtailment of many traditional retail services. Even highly tradition-oriented countries have embraced infrequent deliveries, self-service, and discounting.

BOX 19–1:   Channels of distribution in India

Only 22 percent of India's 684 million people live in cities and 30 percent are literate. Fourteen major languages are spoken, and few shopkeepers speak English; a majority do not even speak Hindi. A poor road and railway system, and the lack of a well-developed telephone system compound the problems of reaching the millions of tiny retail outlets.

There are several distribution systems to choose from, but the most common and successful is the agent system. A network of agents, located throughout the country, handles a wide range of products from several noncompeting companies. The agents distribute the product to a large number of "stockists" who operate as wholesalers in specified territories. Agents often handle the entire distribution process—from arranging the transportation of goods to collecting the money from the "stockists" after the sale. The agent holds stock on consignment from the company which records a sale only when the goods are invoiced to the "stockist."

A cash collection system, based on mutual trust, is extremely efficient. The "stockist" gives signed, blank checks to the agent and as soon as the invoice for goods ordered by the "stockist" is prepared, the agent fills in the amount on the signed check, ships the goods, and deposits the check.

Source: "India's Sales Networks: Reaching the Inaccessible at a Reasonable Cost," *Business Asia*, May 8, 1981, p. 145.

Line breadth.   Every nation has a distinct pattern relative to the breadth of line carried by wholesalers and retailers. The distribution system of some countries seems to be characterized by middlemen who carry or can get everything. In others, every middleman seems to be a specialist dealing only in extremely narrow lines. In the United States, a specialization appears to increase with firm size; in other countries, there is an inverse relationship.

Government regulations in some countries limit the breadth of line that can be carried by middlemen. Norway has specific licensing requirements for middlemen, and in Italy, there is municipal discretion over the lines to be handled. In the city of Milan, a dairy store may sell boiled eggs or boiled rice with oil but may not sell boiled eggs with butter or boiled rice with tomato sauce. (Contrast this practice with the more modern outlook in some states in the United States, where for years grocery stores have been able to sell warm, but not cold, beer.) In selling a wide variety of products in many countries, Proctor & Gamble has encountered a host of restrictions which require continuous adaptation on its part. In Italy, for example, stores need a license for every product category they sell; therefore, some sell only soaps and others sell only detergents. Imagine the effect on distribution costs when specific merchandising ordinances vary considerably from city to city. The end result has been a general stifling of progress in the distributive trades, discouragement of more advanced merchandising techniques, and the granting of a premium to inefficient practices.

Cost and margins. Cost levels and middleman margins vary widely from country to country depending on the level of competition, the services offered, the efficiencies or inefficiencies of scale, and the geographic and turnover factors related to market size, purchasing power, tradition, and other basic determinants. In Italy, the political potency of small middlemen has kept direct competition to a minimum and costs high. In India, competition in large cities is so great that costs are low and margins thin; but, in rural areas, a lack of capital has permitted the few traders who have capital to gain monopolies with consequent high prices and wide margins. In most developing countries, manufacturers do not bear much of the marketing burden but shift such functions as credit, storage, shipping, market development, and even research directly to the channel of distribution.

Channel length. Some correlation may be found in the stage of economic development and the length of marketing channels. In every country, of course, channels are likely to be shorter for industrial goods and for high-priced consumer goods than for low-priced products. In general, there is an inverse relationship between channel length and the size of the purchase. Even Korea and Japan, which have notoriously long distribution channels, have found that market development has had a major impact on shortening distribution channels. Such flattening of the distribution system eventually eliminates middlemen and therefore some markups; the consumer eventually benefits from the greater efficiencies created by larger markets.

Combination wholesaler-retailer or semiwholesalers exist in many countries, adding one or two links to the length of the distribution chain. Channels in the United States and in Russia are shorter than in most countries. In the United States, length is shortened by efficiencies of scale and, in Russia, channels are shortened by administrative edict. This shortening often results in distribution inefficiencies because goods may not be available when or where needed.

With the internationalization of business, merchandising ideas and systems are being picked up and transferred from one country to another with ever-increasing speed. One of the results of this intelligence interchange is that channels throughout the world appear to be growing somewhat shorter.

An astute observer of the marketing scene can trace some of the channel-length differences back to the underlying factors causing such variation. One can make such an analysis if knowledgeable of differences in factors such as aggregate market potential, population and income distribution patterns, shopping habits, product preference, dealer inventory, supply sources, and so forth. Consideration of these factors helps explain many of the apparent differences, can help the marketer in planning, and may show the way to channel innovation.

Distribution intensity.   When international marketers enter a new or developing market for the first time, they usually have little concern for market penetration; the more affluent or more obvious market segments are dealt with first. When middlemen are chosen, those with strong or obvious market positions are selected whenever possible. Only as markets begin to mature, as in the case of Western Europe, or exhibit explosive tendencies, as in the Middle East, do marketers hone their distribution policies. At this point they become concerned with decisions about selective or intensive distribution, whether markets previously considered marginal should be exploited, and whether national or key market distribution should be attempted. As volume grows, marketers may encounter national laws affecting restrictive selective distribution policies and price controlling.

EXHIBIT 19–1:   Typical Japanese toy distribution system

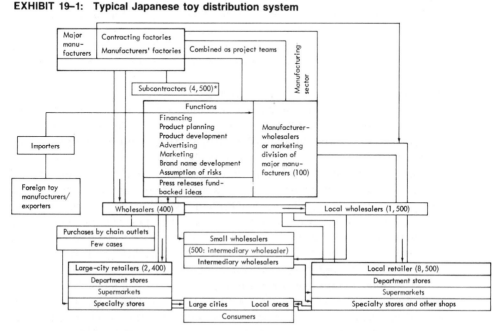

* Number of establishments.
Source: "Selling in Japan: Market Perspectives," *The Agoro*. Special edition, February 1977, p. 92.

Nonexistent channels. One of the first things companies discover about international channel-of-distribution patterns is that in most countries it is nearly impossible to gain adequate market coverage through a simple channel of distribution. In many instances, appropriate channels just do not exist; in others, parts of a channel system are available but other parts are not. Several distinct distribution channels must be established to reach different segments of a market; channels that are suitable for distribution in urban areas seldom provide adequate rural coverage. Companies may have to depart from their customary channel patterns to gain distribution. For example, Proctor & Gamble, well known for its mass merchandising in the United States and a mass merchandising pioneer in Europe, sells soap and other products through door-to-door salespeople in the Philippines, Iran, and other developing countries. It is interesting to note that, in earlier stages of economic development, the same company began operations by selling door-to-door in the United States.

Japanese and American ingenuity have triumphed again. Bristol Meyers, marketers of Bufferin, and its Japanese joint-venture partner have created a unique door-to-door program. One of their efforts has been a combination door-to-door and consignment scheme. The Japanese householder is induced to accept, on consignment, a box including a variety of dentrifices, analgesics, and other home remedies. About every six months a salesperson returns to replenish the collection and collect for the products which have been used. Who says there are no new marketing ideas under the sun?

Blocked channels. International marketers are often blocked from using the channel of their choice. Blockage may result because competitors have already established their lines in the various channels, because trade associations or cartels have closed up certain channels, or because customary marketing patterns preclude market acceptance of still another middleman. Finally, a major reason for blockage is politics.

Competition for the few available middlemen in most of the world marketplaces creates extreme difficulties for the marketer seeking an outlet for its product. Blockages are intensified in international business because the number of middlemen available is small and the number of potential suppliers is large relative to the market size in most countries. Companies suffer through spotty distribution for extended periods of time because they simply cannot gain entry through existing channels and cannot afford to establish new ones. One manufacturer found he was absolutely prevented from entering European markets because every middleman who logically could handle his product was either financially tied to a competitor or had long-term relationships or commitments to competitors.

Sometimes competition for distribution has been so intense that businessmen have established trade associations, cartels, or other regulatory groups to divide the market and eliminate new competition. General Tire Company was finally forced out of Europe because the tire cartel would not tolerate its presence and used duress to render its channels of distribution ineffective.

BOX 19–2: Selling do-it-yourself lumber and hardware stores to the Europeans

Wickes Corporation, the home improvement materials retailer, has 45 home-improvement centers in Belgium, Holland, England, and West Germany. It is considered to be one of the most successful retailing ventures ever launched in foreign markets by a U.S. company. It is also one of the corporation's most profitable divisions, earning 30 percent on assets. However, it was not all that easy at first. They had to overcome:

Tradition.	Until Wickes entered Europe in 1970, "Supermarkets of hardware and lumber" for do-it-yourselfers were unknown. Most such supplies were sold to professionals in "trade-only stores." Europeans didn't "do-it-themselves."
Competition resistance.	In several cities, local sellers of building materials persuaded their friendly burgomasters or relatives on town councils to reject or stall the company's applications for permission to open stores.
Bureaucracy delays.	There was confusion over the company's designation as a retailer of building materials rather than the more normal wholesaler. At one point, they were authorized to sell hammers to the public but not nails.
Supplier cartels.	Manufacturer's cartels were reluctant to supply Wickes for fear that the "traditional" stores would retaliate against the cartels.

They managed to overcome all the obstacles and things are more normal, that is, competition from European imitators is now their main problem. In Holland, the locally owned Gamma chain has 58 stores to Wickes 18; in Belgium, Grand Bazaar has 35 to Wickes nine; in Germany, OBI chain has 56 stores to 10 and so on.

Source: Adapted from: John Quirt, "Wickes Corp.'s Retailing Triumph in Europe," *Fortune,* August 13, 1979, pp. 178–84.

Associations of middlemen sometimes restrict the number of distribution alternatives available to a producer. Druggists in many countries, for example, have inhibited distribution of a wide range of goods through any retail outlets except drugstores. The drugstores, in turn, have been supplied by a relatively small number of wholesalers who have long-established relationships with their suppliers. Thus, through a combination of competition and association, a producer may be completely kept out of the market.

Government has been a major nonmarket force in blocking channels, particularly to foreign interlopers. Japan is notorious for its activities to protect local business. The Japan Soft Drink Bottlers Association staged an anti-Coca-Cola campaign in which they charged unfair marketing tactics. Then, when the Coca-Cola Company applied to introduce Fresca, the association put so much pressure on various Japanese ministries that the company withdrew the application. When it achieved "too much success," General Foods' Japanese subsidiary was required to cut down its promotional effort and limit sales of curry products; it earlier had had the same experience with instant coffee. Japan is by no means the only country to use strong political measures to limit competition in distribution.

Blocked channels can be opened. Sometimes the company hoping to enter a market can buy equity in middlemen and assure itself of market entry. United Fruit Company, for example, found that the only way it could adequately gain satisfactory distribution in Europe was to purchase distributors. A blocked company may simply "buy distribution" by offering extremely wide margins, contract bonuses, or other forms of cash settlement to middlemen who take on their line. In some instances, when distribution through normal channels is not available, companies may seek completely different types of channels; such changes in the past have been responsible for causing virtual distribution revolutions when the new channel caught on with the public.

Companies also may be forced to build their own channels. Although the most expensive method of gaining entry, it may be the only method; at least the marketer is then assured that someone else will not be able to buy out their channel.

Stocking and servicing. The high cost of credit, danger of loss through inflation, lack of capital, and other concerns cause foreign middlemen in many countries to carry inadequate inventories, resulting in out-of-stock conditions and loss of sales to competitors. Physical distribution lags intensify this problem, so that in many cases the manufacturer must provide local warehousing or extend long credit to encourage middlemen to carry large inventories. Considerable ingenuity, assistance and, perhaps, pressure are required to induce middlemen in most countries to carry adequate or even minimal inventories.

The services required or desired by manufacturers may be quite dissimilar from those the middlemen are willing or able to furnish. Since middlemen are unable to extend adequate credit to their customers, the selling company itself may have to take on the credit burden. In most nations, middlemen are notoriously disinterested in promoting or selling individual items of merchandise; the manufacturer, then, must provide adequate inducement to the middlemen or undertake much of the promotion and selling effort himself.

Wholesale patterns

Wholesalers sell to retailers or industrial users. Their main functions are negotiating, buying, selling, and storing; but they also offer a host of other services. A study of the wholesaling sector of an economy may provide some important clues to the stage of a nation's economic development (see Exhibit 19–2)

Power and competition. The structure of wholesaling, a cluster of extremely large middlemen at one end of a scale and a mass of small middlemen at the other end, provides the basis for an interesting study in contrasts. Large-small patterns seem to simplify wholesaling in many countries. In Malaysia, for example, fewer than a dozen (European) merchant houses handle over half the import trade, while hundreds of local trading companies handle the balance. In Israel, there are some 1,500 wholesalers, most are small except Hamashbir Hamerkazi, the giant Israeli wholesaler.

EXHIBIT 19–2: Wholesale patterns in selected countries

	Number of wholesalers (thousands)	Employees per wholesaler	Retailers per wholesaler	Population per wholesaler
United States	370	11	4	549
Japan	369	10	5	303
Brazil	45	6	13	2,052
Belgium	56	3	4	172
Turkey	23	1.3	8	1,754
Republic of Korea	20	5	18	1,734
Philippines	12	9	27	3,486
Sweden	21	9	3	391
New Zealand	6	9	4	489
Puerto Rico	2	12	14	1,232
USSR	1	120	481	174,922
Kenya	1	11	3.5	10,944
Yugoslavia	1	115	77	18,657
Panama	6	18	2	2,559

Source: *Statistical Yearbook 1979/1980*, (New York: United Nations, 1981) Table 134, pp. 404–20.

This firm handles all kinds of products and has full or partial ownership in 12 major industrial firms; they reportedly handle approximately one fifth of all the wholesaling volume of Israel. Such giant wholesalers are major factors in the political and competitive life of their countries. Their power lies in their financial, wholesaling, and manufacturing interest within the country.

There appears to be a worldwide trend toward more vertical integration from the wholesale or retail level back to manufacturing. Such a development is of great concern to marketers who have been dependent on a wholesaler to handle their products because they often find the channel is blocked by the wholesaler handling its own custom-manufactured products. In India, outside companies have a hard time gaining distribution because the large wholesalers have such an entrenched position that by providing the financial and marketing services they obtain monopsonistic power (the market condition which exists when there is one *buyer*).

Another development in the wholesale market which tends to concentrate distribution power in the hands of a relatively small number of wholesalers is the development of voluntary chains sponsored by wholesalers. According to a government study in Britain, one third of the soft goods wholesalers had set up voluntary retail chains which handle nearly three fourths of the volume in those goods.

The financial power of large wholesalers affects the geographic distribution patterns they undertake. In Japan, Israel, and Australia, nearly all major wholesalers operate on a nationwide basis. In sharp contrast are countries like Italy, Turkey, and Egypt, where government regulations, scattered markets, and poor transportation facilities have limited the growth of national wholesalers. A marketer must contact many middlemen to establish distribution.

Services and efficiency. A wholesaler is never considered a strong, hard-selling middleman, but in some countries, wholesalers and some distributors perform minimal selling functions. The oft-repeated complaint that wholesalers do an inadequate job of selling merchandise does have exceptions. In some countries where there are strong national distributors, there is usually a high level of selling; in fact, wholesalers in some such countries utilize their position in pressure selling; in production-oriented socialistic states such as Yugoslavia, wholesalers have taken over the selling function from manufacturers.

Most wholesalers offer credit, but the high cost of money in many countries keeps inventories at minimal levels, and reorder service is slow. Inflation may serve as a countervailing force when wholesalers (or retailers) purchase in larger-than-normal quantities to establish a supply of merchandise before price increases.

The wholesaler's efficiency varies with size, financial ability, market density, communications facilities, and a host of other things.

Retail patterns

Retailing shows even greater diversity in its structure than does wholesaling. In some countries, such as Italy and Morocco, retailing is composed largely of speciality houses carrying narrow lines. In other countries, such as Finland, most retailers carry a more general line of merchandise. Retail size is represented at one end by Japan's giant Mitsukoshi Ltd., which reportedly enjoys the patronage of more than 100,000 customers every day. The other extreme is represented in the market of Ibadan, Nigeria, where there are some 3,000 one- or two-person stalls and not many more customers.

Size patterns. The extremes in size in retailing are similar to those that predominate in the wholesaling field. Exhibit 19–3 dramatically illustrates some of the basic retailing relationships. Effective interpretation requires analysis of per capita consumption expenditures, average total sales per retail store, and number of customers per retail store. The statistics alone do not tell the whole story, but imagine how much wider the spread would be if other less developed countries of the world were considered. Imagine, too, the impact of such variation on wholesale structure and channel policy. The retail structure and the problems it engenders cause real difficulties for the international marketing firm selling consumer goods. Large dominant middlemen are approachable, but there is no adequate channel of distribution through which to make an effective marketing presentation to small retailers who, in the aggregate, handle a great volume of sales.

Change. Retailing around the world has been in a state of active ferment

EXHIBIT 19–3: Retail patterns in 16 countries

Country	Population (millions)	GDP per capita	Consumption per capita	Number of Retailers
Belgium	10	$4,725	$3,257	128,989
Colombia	23	1,117	845	547,000
France	53	4,692	2,883	569,000
West Germany	61	4,741	2,512	344,752
Hungary	10	2,741	1,729	35,346
India	548	383	260	3,760,000
Iran	34	1,762	1,008	214,063
Italy	54	2,950	2,060	927,372
Japan	112	3,960	2,248	1,548,000
Kenya	15	383	262	4,756
Republic of Korea	35	921	633	320,471
Malaysia	10	1,233	748	7,036
Netherlands	13	4,282	2,569	n.a.
Philippines	42	738	535	320,400
United Kingdom	56	3,789	2,632	262,501
United States	203	6,205	4,288	1,855,018

Source: *Statistical Yearbook 1979/1980*, (New York: United Nations, 1981), Table 165, pp. 705–06; Table 18, pp. 69–74; Table 134, pp. 404–15.

for some years.[2] The rate of change appears to be directly related to the stage and speed of economic development in the countries concerned, but even the least developed countries are experiencing dramatic changes. Self-service retailing has grown at an overwhelming rate throughout the world. Supermarkets of one variety or another are blossoming in developed and underdeveloped countries alike. Discount houses have taken increasing shares of the market in countries where such activity is legal. Automatic vending and mail-order trends are being set around the world, and, in both fields, the United States has been eclipsed by fast-moving business people in other countries. The mail-order business is booming internationally. In the United States, mail order accounts for about 1 percent of all retail sales, but in the United Kingdom, the figure is now closer to 5 percent. Franchising of fast-food is also expanding rapidly in countries from Latin America to Asia. Most of the major U.S. fast-food companies such as McDonalds, Pizza Hut, and Kentucky Fried Chicken have investments offshore. Some are having a profound effect on traditional businesses. In England, for example, it is estimated that annual franchised sales of fast-foods is nearly $2 billion which accounts for 30 percent of all foods Britons eat outside the home.[3]

The food industry is marked by highly developed voluntary chains, multi-

---

[2] For a discussion of change in the Japanese distribution system see Clifford Elliott and Jang H. Yoo, "Innovations in the Japanese Distributive System: Are the Barriers to Entry Being Lifted?" *Akron Business and Economic Review*, Spring 1980, pp. 28–33.

[3] "Business Briefs," *World Press Review*, February 1981, p. 55.

ple chain stores, consumer co-ops, supermarkets, convenience stores, and mail-order houses.[4] Franchising is not limited to fast-foods, but also includes soft drinks (Pepsi-Cola is in Russia and Coca-Cola is in China), automotive services, automobile rentals, hotels and motels as major franchisors.[5]

Self-service.   Started in the United States in 1930, self-service had only a few early imitators in other parts of the world. Sweden and Germany, for example, opened self-service stores in 1938. Since the end of World War II, however, self-service has been a major element in world retailing. Because of the larger unit size, their share of sales has grown even more rapidly. The effect on a manufacturer's marketing policy has been little short of revolutionary. Just a few years ago, a company selling in the food field had to have literally hundreds of salespeople; now many companies have cut back their sales force to the small number required to deal with wholesalers and self-service chains. The small grocers are never visited by these salespeople and must now seek out merchandise themselves through wholesalers. Some companies, such as Britain's Beechams, have developed different sales forces to deal with the different types of outlets: one force for grocery chains, one for large supermarkets, one for wholesalers, and one for the small retailers.

BOX 19–3: Shoppers' delight

MOSCOW—A decree published Tuesday in the official Soviet Communist newspaper called for new steps to deal with "serious deficiencies" at stores, restaurants, and other service establishments.

"The quality of service does not respond to the growing demands of the population," *Pravda* said, quoting the decree from the Communist Party Central Committee and the government's council of ministers.

The document reflected high-level dissatisfaction with Soviet retail trade, whose growing attention to the consumer still irks shoppers with shortages, crowded stores, long lines, surly service, and waiting lists for scarce items.

Although the government is trying to boost meat production, residents of some northern Russian towns tell travelers that for several months of the year the only meat available may be fatty sausage. In Novosibirsk, Siberia's largest city, a visiting foreigner last month found no meat at all in the city's Western-style supermarket.

Residents of some cities near Moscow frequently undertake all-day bus rides to the capital to obtain eggs, canned milk, and fruit because they are unavailable locally. Other items in chronically short supply include quality refrigerators and other appliances, better-grade women's shoes and underwear, good men's suits, and tape recorders.

Source: *Associated Press*, July 20, 1977.

---

[4] Nancy Ukai, "Convenience-Hungry Japanese Quick to Devour the Seven-Eleven Concept," *Asian Wall Street Journal*, November 30, 1981, p. 3.

[5] Donald W. Hackett, "The International Expansion of U.S. Franchise Systems: Status and Strategies," as reprinted in *International Marketing: Managerial Perspectives*, ed. Subbash C. Jain and Lewis R. Tucker, Jr. (Boston: CBI Publishing, Inc., 1979), pp. 303–15.

Discounting chains and groups.   The advent of national brands (and international brands) and heavy advertising to develop consumer awareness and brand preference has helped discounting become a major factor in most affluent nations. The strong antitrust provisions of the various common markets and free-trade areas and the general rejection of retail price maintenance laws have speeded up the trend of discount merchandising.

Germany provides a good case study of the rapid growth in discounting. In 1953 the first discount houses were opened; in 1957, there were still only 27, but, in 1963 there were over 300 and, by 1970, well over 1,000. By 1980 the number had doubled again to some 2,000 stores. More importantly, stores grow rapidly in size and volume and account for even larger proportions of the nation's retail sales.

The marketing task has become much easier in the United Kingdom; in 1978, well over half the retail grocery sales volume was garnered by chains, superstores (25–50,000 square feet) and hypermarkets (over 50,000 square feet). Interestingly enough, food manufacturers and processors who a few years ago were complaining because food distribution was highly segmented in the United Kingdom are now complaining about the buying power which the large-scale retailers wield and about private labeling which threatens manufacturers' brands. From 1950 through 1980 the number of retail stores declined significantly. In 1950 there were approximately 600,000 retail outlets but by 1980 there were about 400,000.

Even the numbers do not tell the story, however, for until the late 1960s nearly all of the discount stores were small and offered a limited assortment of merchandise. The new discount firms, called *consumer markets* are large self-service department stores with the same wide range of merchandise

---

BOX 19–4: Efficiency Is hard to stop

PARIS–Over the last four years, Europe's supermarket industry has been hit with everything from national legislation, restricting expansion in France and Belgium, to striking bread truck drivers in the UK. A powerful lobby appears to be holding the industry at bay in Germany, while in Italy a scant 500 supermarkets serve a population of 55 million, as shoppers stubbornly refuse to abandon small, traditional outlets, ranging from neighborhood *alimentari* (groceries) to *ambulanti* (pushcarts).

But above the battle that has pitted supermarkets against national regulatory commissions, local shopkeepers, town planners, skyrocketing labor costs, and an overcrowded, fiercely competitive retail market, there hovers one telling fact, the retail grocery industry definitely is big business.

The figures are clear: In Sweden, supermarkets and "superettes" account for 79.8 percent of food retailing (compared with 94.7 percent in the United States); in France the share is 71 percent, with 70.6 percent in Belguim and Holland, and 65 percent in Germany. Closer statistical analysis reveals that, for example, 60 percent of Belgian food retailing is handled by only 6 percent of the country's outlets.

Source: "Food Retailing Expands in Spite of Obstacles." Reprinted with permission from the September 1977 issue of *Advertising Age*. Copyright 1977 by Crain Communications Inc.

as traditional department stores. Integration of buying activities has been a dominant pattern in European retailing for many years. Consumer cooperatives have had minimal success in the United States but are tremendously important in most European countries.

In Switzerland, co-ops account for one fifth of retail food stores and over one fourth of retail food sales. Each of the two leading co-ops boasts memberships exceeding one third of the households in Switzerland. Despite the presence of these giants, however, two thirds of the retail business of Switzerland is carried out by small independent stores.

Sweden's giant KF Co-op introduced both supermarkets and hypermarkets to Scandanavia. Leased-space co-op department stores are popular in Scandinavia. In some ways these resemble the old farmers' markets where dozens of independent merchants lease space in a single building or department store. Small businesses are conducted in each space, with overall coordination in advertising, personnel training, and display.

BOX 19–5: Followers aren't always faster

In 1940, about 10 years following the supermarket introduction, there were an estimated 8,175 supermarkets in the United States with about 20 percent of total food sales.

In 1965, nine years after supermarket introduction in France, there were 504 freestanding supermarkets with a market share of approximately 2.5 percent.

In 1946, after 16 years of supermarket operations, there were 10,057 supermarkets with a market share of 27 percent in the United States.

In 1972, 16 years after the first supermarket opened, there were 1.830 supermarkets in France accounting for 12 percent of food sales.

Source: Eric Langeard and Robert A. Peterson, "Diffusion of Large-Scale Food Retailing in France: Supermarché et Hypermarché," *Journal of Retailing*, Fall 1975, p. 48.

Direct marketing. Selling directly to the consumer through the mail, by telephone, or door-to-door is certainly most highly developed in the United States. In 1980, about $110 billion in sales were generated that way, almost doubling the $60 billion in 1975. Although some countries are just beginning, there is a decided trend toward direct sales almost everywhere. Direct marketing sales totalled $10 billion in West Germany, over $3 billion each in France and the United Kingdom, and $2.4 billion in Japan.[6]

Products sold through direct marketing include books, insurance, general merchandise, electronic gear, home furnishings, housewares, and cosmetics. Avon, the cosmetics firm, has an Asian sales force of 10,000 and in 1981, its door-to-door sales were more than $200 million.[7] Changing lifestyles,

---

[6] "Direct Marketing is Gaining Impetus for a Number of Reasons," *Business International*, July 17, 1981, pp. 225–28.

[7] "Business Briefs," *World Press Review*, February 1981, p. 55.

acceptance of credit cards, improved postal and telephone services in many countries all assist in the growing trend of direct marketing.

Resistance to change.   Such developments as consolidation of middlemen, larger store size, self-service, and discounting have not gone unnoticed by small merchants; distribution is enmeshed in a battle between politically powerful independent retailers and wholesalers and economically powerful chain discount and department stores. In many cases, it is the manufacturers who get caught in the middle of this battle. If they avoid the large-volume retailers, these retailers turn to other sources, and the manufacturers have lost a portion of the market. If they move to the large-volume outlets, they are likely to be scorned by small-scale middlemen and lose that market segment.

In some countries, small but numerous independent merchants seem to be waging an effective delaying battle against discounting. In Italy, a new retail outlet must obtain a license from a municipal board composed of well-entrenched local tradespeople who hardly welcome new competition. In a two-year period some 200 applicants seeking to establish supermarkets in Milan were able to secure only 10 new licenses. In Belgium, national legislation does not permit new department stores to be opened in towns of less than 50,000, and any store that employs as few as five persons is considered a department store. In Norway and Sweden, potential entrepreneurs must serve a long apprenticeship in the business before they are considered for licensing.

Even in a progressive country like Japan, supermarkets and chains have run into formidable opposition. Summit Stores, Incorporation, is a chain of medium-sized supermarkets. In 1977, it completed construction on a new supermarket building. Six months later the store was still unable to open because of local opposition using a national "large retail store law" which forces chains to negotiate with local merchants about days, hours, and store size. In the case of that particular store, local retailers had pushed for a prefectural local government law and had it passed while the store was being built. Nevertheless, by 1978, Japanese supermarkets numbered over 5,000 and accounted for 12–14 percent of retail grocery sales.[8]

It appears in many cases that governments have placed a premium on retailing inefficiency to support politically powerful merchants. Taxes are a favorite restrictive tool of the small retailer groups to penalize the discounter or self-service store. Even health and sanitary regulations are called into play to hamper large-scale retailing. Milk in Switzerland, for example, may not be sold with other merchandise; supermarkets, therefore, cannot handle this product so small dairy product retailers flourish.

Giant Sears Roebuck & Company was defeated by Belgian "Davids." The company was in the midst of developing its recently acquired *Galeries*

---

[8] For an interesting article discussing the changing retailing institutions in Japan see Frank Meissner's, "Americans Must Practice the Marketing They Preach to Succeed in Japan's Mass Market," *Marketing News,* October 17, 1980, p. 5.

BOX 19–6:   As much as things change, the more they remain the same

The rapid and pervading Westernization of Japan has led to the emergence of new types of large-scale retail establishments to supplement both the small outlets and the traditional department stores.

Yet, the small family-run neighborhood stores persist, and continue to dominate the retailing sector in Japan. These small "Mom and Pop" stores account for over 80 percent of all stores in Japan, and a good 70 percent of these are independent retail outlets.

The shopkeeper often contributes to the relationship he has with his regular customers through extra, personalized service, called *omake. Omake* can take the form of a few extra grams of the item being purchased, an unexpected discount, assistance in finding the top quality item; there are many ways which this feeling of solidarity and good will for the customer can be manifested.

Of course, there are other considerations for the success of the neighborhood store, among them such things as the basic size of most Japanese refrigerators and kitchens, which are far smaller than their U.S. counterparts. Being so small, the consumer must purchase most perishables on a daily basis, and they appreciate the presence of a friendly neighborhood outlet for their needed items. Also, the small stores tailor their hours for the convenience of the area residents, with a good 70 percent of these stores doing business after 7 p.m., when commuters are returning from work. Quality of the product is also a prime consideration, and often-times, the store proprietor will take a personal interest in his customers' selections.

Source: Adapted from "The Small Neighborhood Store: Still a Major Element in Japanese Retailing," *Japanese Insights* (Los Angeles: Japan Trade Center, Winter 1980), p. 3.

Anspach retail chain. A national ban called *Loi Cadenas* was passed limiting retail chain expansion. Sears was caught with two thirds of its outlets in slow-growing city center stores. Excluded from its target market, the rapidly growing suburbs, Sears sold out at a considerable loss and abandoned the nation.

Nationalism has been a major force limiting the introduction of mass merchandising techniques by foreign firms. Unilever, for example, found consumers in Turkey were chafing under the exorbitant prices charged by monopolistic local tradesmen, so it purchased a fleet of van-type trucks and introduced mobile supermarkets to the countryside. The reaction was swift and certain; local merchants found their monopolies evaporating, contacted the government, and, within a matter of months, Unilever was out of the Turkish retailing picture. Through a joint venture, Safeway attempted to introduce a series of supermarkets in Japan, but, as soon as plans were announced, nationalistic groups seized on this as a major "cause." The resulting furor caused parliamentary debate on the subject and Safeway discreetly withdrew.

Opposition to retail innovation prevails everywhere, yet in the face of all the restrictions and hindrances, self-service, discount merchandising, and large-scale chains continue to grow because they offer the consumer a broad range of quality branded products at advantageous prices. Ultimately the consumer does prevail.

FACTORS AFFECTING CHOICE OF CHANNELS

While the overall marketing strategy of the firm must embody the company's goals of healthy profits in the short and the long run, the channel strategy itself may be considered to have six very specific strategic goals. These may be characterized as the *six Cs of channel strategy*—cost, capital, control, coverage, character, and continuity.

Cost

Two kinds of channel cost are encountered: the capital or investment cost of developing the channel and the continuing cost of maintaining it. The latter may be in the form of direct expenditure for the maintenance of the company's selling force or it may be in the form of the margins, markup, or commission of various middlemen who handle the goods. Marketing costs (the bulk of which is channel cost) must be considered to be the entire difference between the factory price of the goods and the price the customer ultimately pays for the merchandise. The costs of middlemen include transporting and storing the goods, breaking bulk, handling the paperwork, handling credit, and local advertising, sales representation, and negotiations.

The marketing decision maker may have a difficult time predicting the costs for these functions. Many companies have thought they could perform distribution miracles at low cost by assuming middleman functions but they have been forced to rethink or restructure their channels of distribution when their cost-saving dreams were not realized.

One study found that of five different channels, including selling to its own affiliate, consumer goods firms selling directly to a distributor in a country which has its own marketing channels was the most profitable. The least profitable was exporting directly to the retailers in the country. This was true even though the company provided extensive dealer training and support.[9]

High distribution costs have serious effects on a producer's ability to open new markets. The entire distribution strategy is based on balancing the desirable goals of minimizing distribution costs and maximizing the advantages of the other five Cs. Despite the old truism that you can eliminate middlemen but you can't eliminate their functions or cost, creative marketing does permit channel cost to be reduced in many circumstances. Various marketers have found, in fact, that they can reduce cost by using shorter channels. The Majestic Group, Mexico's largest producer of radio and television sets, has built a $36 million per year sales volume on its ability to sell goods at a low price because it eliminated middlemen, established its

---

[9] Warren J. Bilkey, "Variables Associated With Export Profitability," presented at the 1980 Annual Conference of the Academy of International Business, New Orleans, October 23, 1980.

own wholesalers, and kept margins low. Conversely, many firms accustomed to using their own sales force in large-volume domestic markets have found they must lengthen channels of distribution to keep costs in line in foreign markets.

BOX 19–7: Corner store—on every corner

MILAN—Via Padova is an ordinary busy street near the outskirts of Milan. In a six-block area, from Piazza Loreto to Via Mamiani, there are two PAM supermarkets and 41 other food stores.

Of these small stores, seven are *alimentari* or *drougherie*—i.e., traditional grocery stores. The others are bakeries, fruit and vegetable stores, milk stores; delicatessens, and butchers. But because of the complex licensing laws and a natural love of variety, a customer can buy vermouth from the milk store, canned goods from the fruit and vegetable store, fresh meat from the delicatessen, and eggs from the butcher.

The average number of clients for each retail food outlet in Italy is 130. The official figures dip as low as 82 in Sardegna and climb to 174 in Lombardy.

Supermarkets must be seen against this background. The law is weighted for the protection of thousands of small food outlets, and Italian supermarket operators run into inexorable difficulties.

"It is the nature of a supermarket to be part of a chain," says Dr. Alessandro Borrini, "but it is prohibitively difficult to get building permits."

Dr. Borrini, who is advertising manager for UPIM and SMA, both part of the Rinascente network, points out that these figures become even lower when the government method for reaching them—dividing population, including the newborn, by outlets—is considered.

"It is closer to reality to say there are, as a high average, 30 families per food outlet. There are perhaps less, since they don't count *ambulanti* (pushcarts), of which there are thousands, as outlets or small markets."

Source: Elspeth Durie, Italian Supers: "Up against the Little Guy." Reprinted with permission from the September 1977 issue of *Advertising Age*. © 1977 by Crain Communications, Inc.

Capital requirement

Financial ramifications of distribution policy are often overlooked. Two critical elements are capital requirement and cash-flow pattern associated with using a particular type of middleman. Maximum investment is usually required when a company establishes its own internal channels, its own sales force. Use of distributors or dealers may lessen the cash investment, but manufacturers often provide initial inventories on a consignment, loan, floor plan, or other arrangement. Agent middlemen may require no investment but are sometimes subsidized by the company during an introductory period. Agents, of course, do not provide any cash flow to the producer until transactions with the ultimate buyers are consummated. Distributors and dealers may provide immediate cash flow when they purchase the products but before the products reach users or consumers. Unless a company is expanding rapidly, capital investment and cash-flow factors are not likely to be crucial channel determinants. Channels must perform their distribution functions effectively, so the other Cs usually dominate the distribution decision.

Control

Companies involve themselves deeply in the distribution of their own goods to better control their marketing destinies. It is generally conceded that the company's own sales force permits maximum control even though it imposes additional cost burdens. Each type of channel arrangement, indeed each specific middleman, has a different level of susceptibility to control. As channels of distribution grow longer, the ability to control price, volume, promotion methods, and type of outlets is diminished. Some companies give up any attempt to control the end destiny of their products and are satisfied to place the goods in the hands of a middleman who passes them on for international distribution. Such a company cannot know where its product is going, what volume of sales can be expected, or the future of the international portion of its business.

On the other hand, growing levels of international involvement can contribute to greater sales volume, more market familiarity, and a better understanding of distribution channels, thus contributing to more effective control. Certainly marketers with full commitment and major investments in various markets will pay more attention to control. Firms marketing industrial goods on a large scale are particularly effective because they typically deal with relatively few customers, short channels of distribution, and large dollar volume.

Coverage

A third major goal is full market coverage, thereby (1) gaining the optimum volume of sales obtainable in each market, (2) securing a reasonable market share, and (3) attaining satisfactory market penetration. Coverage may be assessed on geographic or other market segments. Adequate market coverage may require changes in distribution systems from country to country or time to time. Coverage is difficult to develop both in highly developed areas and in sparse markets. The one because of heavy competition and the other because of inadequate channels.

Many companies do not attempt full market coverage but seek significant penetration in major population centers. In some countries, two or three cities constitute the majority of the national buying power. Sixty percent of the Japanese population lives in the Tokyo-Nagoya-Osaka market area, which essentially functions as one massive city.

Coverage also includes the concept of full representation for all lines a company wishes to sell within a given market. Sometimes middlemen will take on more lucrative parts of a line but neglect or refuse to handle other products which the manufacturer wants to emphasize. Without full-line coverage, a manufacturer can be seriously crippled in attempts to build profitable distribution.

Character

The channel-of-distribution system selected must fit the character of the company and the markets in which it is doing business. Some obvious product requirements relate to perishability or bulk of the product, complexity of sale, sales service required, and value of the product. These factors are often the first considered. Matching the character of the producer and middleman may be more difficult; sometimes meshing the two characters is so impossible companies have given up markets rather than compromise company standards. In other instances, company standards have been adhered to and local channel characteristics ignored with resulting distribution disasters.

Channel commanders must be aware that channel patterns change; they cannot assume that once a channel has been developed to fit the character of both company and market that no more needs to be done. Great Britain, for example, has epitomized distribution through specialty-type middlemen; distributors, wholesalers, and retailers, in fact, all middlemen have traditionally worked within narrow product specialty areas. Within the past few years, however, there has been a trend toward broader lines, conglomerate merchandising, and mass marketing. The firm that neglects the growth of self-service, scrambled merchandising, or discounting may find it has lost large segments of its market because its channels no longer reflect the character of the market.

Continuity

Channels of distribution often pose longevity problems. Most agent middlemen firms tend to be small institutions. When one individual retires or moves out of a line of business, the company may find it has lost its distribution in that area. Wholesalers and especially retailers are not noted for their continuity in business either. Most middlemen have little loyalty to their vendors. They handle brands in good times when the line is making money, but quickly reject such products within a season or a year if they fail to produce during that period. Distributors and dealers are probably the most loyal middlemen, but even with them, manufacturers must attempt to build brand loyalty downstream in a channel lest middlemen shift allegiance to other companies, or other inducements.

If a channel is to perform consistently well, it must have continuity, and this reason alone has prompted some companies to develop their own company-controlled distribution organizations. One American company in a highly competitive field of producers from Germany, England, and the Netherlands lost middlemen accounting for nearly 50 percent of its volume in

Latin America within a year. The reason for the loss was more readily discovered than remedied. Two major competitors had simultaneously hit on methods of squeezing the U.S. firm out of the market. One, marketing a broad product line, forced distributors to drop the U.S. company's narrow line if they wished to continue as distributors of the broader line. The other company purchased an interest in several large distributors who carried the U.S. company's products. Much to its chagrin, the U.S. company found that within a year it had lost over one quarter of its foreign distribution system. Continuity is important.

In building the overall channel-of-distribution strategy, *the six Cs of channels must be matched, balanced, and harmonized* with one another to build an economical, effective, distribution organization. This must be done within the long-range channel-of-distribution policies of the company, which in turn must fit the firm's overall marketing program. Building channels, as any international marketer will testify, is one of the most difficult tasks in international business.

LOCATING, SELECTING, AND MOTIVATING CHANNEL MEMBERS

The actual process of building channels for international distribution is seldom easy and many companies have been stopped in their efforts to develop international markets by their inability to construct a satisfactory system of channels.

Despite the chaotic condition of international distribution channels, international marketers can follow a logical procedure in developing channels. After general policy guides are established, marketers need to develop general criteria for the selection of specific middlemen. Construction of the middleman network includes seeking out potential middlemen, selecting those who fit the company's requirements, and establishing working relationships with them.

In international marketing, the channel-building process is hardly routine. The closer the company wants to get to the consumer in its channel contact the larger the sales force required. If a company is content with finding an exclusive importer or selling agent for a given country, channel building may not be too difficult, but if it goes down to the level of the subwholesaler or the retailer, it is taking on a tremendous task and must have an internal staff capable of such an effort.

Locating middlemen

The search for prospective middlemen should begin with study of the market and determination of criteria used for evaluation of middlemen servicing that market. The company's broad general policy guidelines should be followed, but expect expediency to override policy at times. The checklist of criteria will differ according to the type of middlemen being used and the nature of their relationship with the company. Basically, such lists are built around four subject areas: (1) productivity or volume, (2) financial strength, (3) managerial stability and capability, and (4) the nature and reputation of the business. Emphasis is usually placed on either the actual or potential productivity of the middleman.

Setting policies and making checklists is easy; the real task is implementation. The major problems will be locating information to aid in the selection and choice of specific middlemen and discovering middlemen available to handle one's merchandise. Firms seeking overseas representation should compile a list of middlemen from such sources as: (1) The U.S. Department of Commerce; (2) commercially published directories; (3) foreign consulates; (4) chamber of commerce groups located abroad; (5) other manufacturers producing similar but noncompetitive goods; (6) middlemen associations; (7) business publications; (8) management consultants; and (9) carriers—particularly airlines.

Selecting middlemen

Finding prospective middlemen is less a problem than discovering which of them can perform adequately. Most prospects will be hampered by low volume or low potential volume, many will be underfinanced, and some simply cannot be trusted. In many cases, when a manufacturer is not well known abroad, the reputation of the middleman becomes the reputation of the manufacturer, so poor choice at this point can be devastating.

Screening. The screening and selection process itself should follow this sequence: (1) a letter including product information and distributor requirements, in the native language, to each prospective middleman; (2) a follow-up to the best respondents for more specific information concerning lines handled, territory covered, size of firm, number of sales force, and other background information; (3) check of credit and references from other clients and customers of the prospective middleman; and (4) if possible, a personal check of the most promising firms.

One source suggests the only way to select middlemen is to go personally to the country and talk to ultimate users of your product to find whom they consider to be the best distributors. Visit each one before selecting the one to represent you; look for one with a key man who will "take the new line of equipment to his heart and make it his personal objective to make the sale of that line a success . . ."[10] Further, this exporter stresses that if you cannot sign one of the two or three customer recommended distributors, it might be better not to have a distributor in that country because, "having a worthless one will cost you time and money every year" and may cut you out when you finally find a good one.

---

[10] G. Beeth, "Distributors—Finding and Keeping the Good Ones," in *International Marketing Strategy,* ed. Hans Thorelli and Helmut Becker (New York: Pergamon Press, 1980), p. 261.

The agreement. Once a potential middleman has been found and evaluated, there remains the task of detailing the arrangements with that middleman. So far the company has been in a buying position; now it must shift into a selling and negotiating position to convince the middleman to handle the goods and accept a distribution agreement that is workable for the company. All agreements must spell out specific responsibilities of the manufacturer and the middleman including an annual sales minimum. The sales minimum serves as a basis for evaluation of the distributor and failure to meet sales minimums gives the exporter the right of termination.[11]

Some experienced exporters recommend that initial contracts be signed for one year only. They then should be reviewed for renewal for a longer period if the first year's performance is satisfactory. This permits easier termination and, more importantly, after a year of working together in the market, a more workable arrangement generally can be agreed on. At this point, success will depend on a good product and company reputation; a skilled negotiator or salesperson; and an intimate knowledge of the market, the middleman, and the environment within which they work.

Motivating middlemen

Once middlemen are selected, a promotional program must be started to maintain high-level interest in the manufacturer's products. A larger proportion of the advertising budget must be devoted to channel communications than in the United States because there are so many small middlemen to be contacted. Consumer advertising is of no avail unless the goods are actually available. Furthermore, few companies operating in international business have the strong brand image in foreign environments that they have in their own country. In most countries, retailers and wholesalers are only minimally brand conscious and yet to a large degree they control the success or failure of products in their countries. Witness the phenomenal acceptance of *Produits libres* (generic products) introduced by *Carrefour*, France's large *hypermarche* and *supermarche* operator.

The level of distribution and the importance of the individual middleman to the company will determine the activities undertaken to keep the middleman alert. On all levels, there is a clear correlation between the middleman's motivation and sales volume. The hundreds of motivational techniques that can be employed to maintain middleman interest and support for the product may be grouped into five categories: financial rewards, psychological rewards, communications, company support, and corporate rapport.

Obviously, financial rewards must be adequate for any middleman to carry and promote a company's product. Margins or commissions must be set to meet the needs of the middleman and may vary according to

---

[11] Jeffrey L. Brown, "Guidelines for an International Distribution Contract," *World Marketing*, Dun and Bradstreet International, October 31, 1979, p. 2.

the volume of sales and the level of services offered. Without a combination of adequate margin and adequate volume, a middleman cannot afford to give much attention to a product.

Being human, middlemen and their salespeople also need psychological rewards and recognition for the job they are doing. For most business people throughout the world, a trip to the United States or to the parent company's home or regional office is a great honor. The American company has been pictured as the business with all the answers so foreign associates are likely to be particularly flattered if it seeks their advice. Publicity in company media and local newspapers also builds esteem and involvement among foreign middlemen.

In all instances, the company should maintain a continuing flow of communication in the form of letters, newsletters, and periodicals to all its middlemen. The more personal these are, the better. One study of exporters indicated that the more intense the contact between the manufacturer and the distributor, the better the performance from the distributor. More and better contact naturally leads to less conflict and a smoother working relationship.[12] One factor that was partly responsible for the success of Smith, Kline, and French in building their own channels for Contac was a monthly periodical specifically published for the 1,200 wholesale salespeople dealing in their product.

A company can support its middlemen by offering advantageous credit terms, adequate product information, technical assistance, and product service. Such support helps build the distributors' confidence in the product and in their own ability to produce results.

Finally, considerable attention must be paid to the establishment of close rapport between the company and its middlemen. In addition to methods noted above, a company should be certain that conflicts that arise are handled skillfully and diplomatically. The American businessman is often preceived abroad as insensitive and impersonal, but this image can be overcome if the people representing the company make special efforts at diplomacy. It should be borne in mind that all over the world, business is a personal and vital thing to the people involved.

Terminating middlemen

When middlemen do not perform up to standards or when market situations change, requiring a company to structure its distribution differently, it may be necessary to terminate relationships with certain middlemen or certain types of middlemen. In the United States, it is usually a simple action regardless of the type of middlemen—agent, merchant, or employee; they

---

[12] Philip J. Rosson and I. David Ford, "Manufacturer—Overseas Distribution Relations and Export Performance," a paper presented at the Annual Academy of International Business Conference, New Orleans, October 1980, p. 10.

are simply dismissed. However, in other parts of the world, the middleman typically has some legal protection which makes it difficult to terminate relationships. In Norway, for example, manufacturers must usually have evidence of negligence on the part of the agents they seek to replace. Even if they succeed in dismissing an agent, they are likely to have to repay the agent for his investments in establishing customer contacts and creating goodwill. Recent court decisions have confirmed the customary practice of giving the dismissed agent indemnity equal to one year's commissions. Such restrictions may destroy a company's marketing plans and may make distribution difficult for firms that have merged. In some countries, an agent cannot be dismissed without going through an arbitration board to determine whether the relationship should be ended. Some companies make all middlemen contracts for one year, but, in a few instances, termination under these contracts has been contested. Competent local legal advice is a vital prerequisite to writing contracts with middlemen in any country. But as many experienced international marketers know, the best rule is to avoid the need to terminate distributors by screening all prospective middlemen carefully. "A poorly chosen distributor may not only fail to live up to expectations but, in addition, may adversely affect future business and prospects in the country."[13]

CHANNEL CONTROL

The extreme length of channels typically used in international distribution makes control of middlemen particularly difficult. Some companies solve this problem by establishing their own distribution systems; others issue franchises or exclusive distributorships in an effort to maintain control through the first stages of the channels. Until the various world markets are more highly developed, most international marketers cannot expect to exert a high degree of control over their international distribution operations. Although control is difficult, a company should attempt to control distribution. Companies that succeed in controlling distribution channels are most likely to be successful international marketers. Indeed, the desire for control is a major reason companies initiate their own distribution systems in domestic as well as in international business.

All control systems, of course, originate in corporate plans and goals. Marketing objectives must be spelled out both internally and to middlemen as explicitly as possible. Standards of performance should include: sales volume objective, market share in each market, inventory turnover ratio, number of accounts per area, growth objective, price stability objective, and quality of publicity. Obviously the more specific the standards of performance, the easier they are to administer. Ease of administration, however, should not be confused with control.

---

[13] Brown, "Guidelines for an International Distribution Contract," p. 4.

Control over the system and control over middlemen are necessary in international business. The first relates to control over the distribution channel *system* per se. This implies overall controls for the entire system to be certain operations are within the cost and market coverage objectives. The specifics of distribution must also be controlled since pricing margins, transshipping, and other specific elements affect the overall system. Some manufacturers have lost control through "secondary wholesaling" when rebuffed discounters have secured their products through unauthorized outlets. A company's goods intended for one country are sometimes diverted through distributors to another country where they compete with existing retail or wholesale organizations. A manufacturer may find some of the toughest competition from its own products diverted through other countries or manufactured by subsidiaries and exported or bootlegged into markets the parent would prefer to preserve. Such action can directly conflict with exclusive arrangements made with distributors in other countries and may undermine the entire distribution system by harming relationships between manufacturers and their channels.

The second type of control is at the middleman level. When possible, the parent company should know (and to a certain degree control) the activities of middlemen in respect to their volume of sales, market coverage, services offered, prices, advertising, payment of bills, and even profit. All levels of the distribution system cannot be controlled to the same degree or by the same methods, but quotas, reports, and personal visits by company representatives can be effective in managing middleman activities at any level of the channel.

When control fails and the best interests of the company are not being met, the middleman must be terminated. As mentioned earlier, middleman separations can be painful and expensive in other countries. American business is free to hire and fire middlemen with relative abandon unless specific contractual relationships to the contrary exist. In most other countries of the world, however, there is an implied obligation to middlemen who have incurred expenses or helped build distribution.[14]

SUMMARY

An ineffective distribution system can invalidate the most carefully developed marketing program. The international marketer must be thoroughly familiar with all the methods of organizing for international distribution. Distribution decisions hinge on middlemen availability, cost, controllability, functions performed, and effectiveness. If company plans call for the use of middlemen external to the company's own sales organization, management

---

[14] See Ahmed Ahmed, "Channel Control in International Markets," *European Journal of Marketing*, November 4, 1977, p. 327. Ahmed reviews controls of 12 companies exporting automobiles into the United States. Seven of the companies limit their distributor contracts to one year, mainly so that they can maintain a high degree of control over the operations.

may choose to use domestic middlemen to serve overseas markets or they may elect to use foreign middlemen. In either case, the further alternative of using agent or merchant middlemen is available. Finally, specific kinds of middlemen must be chosen, and specific middlemen must be selected and induced to handle the company's product or line.

International distribution facilities have developed rapidly in recent years to accommodate the increasing flow of goods and the development of new markets. As markets and economies grow and develop, the marketing system inevitably grows and develops along with them. Since developing nations are quick to capitalize on the marketing knowledge of the highly industrialized economies, the next few years will see an even greater growth in international channels of distribution which will provide manufacturers more ready access to world markets.

QUESTIONS

1. Define:
    Secondary wholesaling
    Hypermarket

2. Review the key variables which affect the marketer's choice of distribution channels.

3. Account, as best you can, for the differences in channel patterns which might be encountered in a highly developed country and an underdeveloped country.

4. Identify some of the underlying factors affecting channel-of-distribution patterns. Explain the role of each.

5. "Acceptance of tradespeople may be somewhat related to an economy's stage of economic development and the extent of its dependence on trade for prosperity." Discuss.

6. Explain why middleman margins vary so much from country to country.

7. Review the implications of the variations in sales volume and number of customers shown in Exhibit 19–3.

8. One of the first things companies discover about international channel-of-distribution patterns is that in most countries it is nearly impossible to gain adequate market coverage through a simple channel-of-distribution plan. Discuss.

9. Relate capital availability to channel-of-distribution structure.

10. Discuss the various methods of overcoming blocked channels.

11. Review the six Cs of channel strategy and show their interrelationships.

12. What strategy might be employed to distribute goods effectively in the dichotomous small-large middleman pattern which characterizes merchant middlemen in most countries?

13. Explain the wide variation and erratic pattern in population per wholesaler in Exhibit 19–2.

14. Review the underlying forces which create the trend to ever-larger retail stores in most nations.

15. Discuss the economic implications of charging termination penalties or restricting the termination of middlemen. Do you foresee such restriction in the United States?

16. "Nonbranded" products were a major success in Europe two years before "generic" products were widely used in the United States. Why?

Chapter 20

Export trade mechanics and logistics

A large majority of American companies actively engaged in foreign marketing manufacture products in the United States and export them to foreign customers. Although some of these companies maintain elaborate foreign-based marketing departments responsible for the sale of products, others maintain no foreign sales staff and rely exclusively on export middlemen to market their products in the foreign country. These middlemen are, in essence, their customers for the products. Increasingly common are companies engaged in manufacturing activities in several countries, a situation which involves them in worldwide exporting instead of the traditional exporting from home country to foreign destinations.

Whether a foreign marketer maintains marketing control over a product until it reaches the intended customer or sells to an intermediary early in the distribution chain, the marketing program is basically the same. A target market must be studied, a product designed, a price established, a promotional program planned, and a distribution channel developed to reflect country market requirements and uncontrollable environmental elements. (See Chapter 1.) Essential requirements unique to export marketing which must be considered relate to required documents, means of payment, requirements of tariff systems, and other impediments to the free flow of goods between independent sovereigns.[1] The mechanics of export marketing are the special concern of this chapter. Sometimes the mechanics are considered the essence of foreign marketing and their importance cannot be minimized, but they must not be viewed as the major task of foreign marketing.[2]

REGULATIONS AND RESTRICTIONS OF EXPORTING

All countries impose some form of regulation and restriction on the exporting and importing of goods; restrictions are placed on the movement of

---

[1] H. Ralph Jones, "Clearing the Way for Exporters," *Business Horizons,* October 1980, pp. 26–32; and "A Professional Approach to Exporting," *Business America,* August 24, 1981, pp. 11–12.

[2] The steps in an export transaction are covered in detail in Ellen M. Kleinberg, "Exporting Isn't That Tough, Even for the Little Guy," *Industrial Marketing,* February 1982, pp. 95–98.

goods in foreign markets for many reasons. Export regulations can be designed to conserve scarce goods for home consumption or to control the flow of strategic goods to actual or potential enemies. Import regulations may be imposed to protect health, conserve foreign exchange, serve as economic reprisals, protect home industry, or provide revenue in the form of tariffs. To comply with various regulations, the exporter may have to acquire licenses or permits from the home country and ascertain that the potential customer has the necessary permits for importing goods.

U.S. export restrictions

Although no formal or special license to engage in an export business from the United States is required, permission or a license to export is necessary for most goods. Most items requiring special permission or license for exportation are under the control of the Department of Commerce. Other departments responsible for various goods include: (1) arms and implements of war, Department of State; (2) atomic and fissionable energy material, Atomic Energy Commission; (3) gold and U.S. silver coins, U.S. Department of Treasury; (4) narcotic drugs, Department of Justice; (5) natural gas and electric energy, U.S. Federal Power Commission; and, (8) endangered wildlife, Department of the Interior.[3]

Unless an exporter's products are classified as one of these exceptions, the exporter must consult the Department of Commerce to determine whether a specific license to export a product is required. The export licensing controls administered by the Department of Commerce apply to (1) exports of commodities and technical data from the United States, (2) re-exports of U.S.-origin commodities and technical data from a foreign destination to another foreign destination, (3) U.S.-origin parts and components used in foreign countries to manufacture foreign products for exports; and, (4) in some instances, the foreign-produced direct product of U.S.-origin technical data.

All regulations imposed by the Department of Commerce are published in the *Export Administration Regulations* which is periodically revised and supplemented by the *Current Export Bulletin*. The respective department or bureau should be contacted for current control regulations since the specific products controlled change frequently.

Types of licenses.   There are two types of licenses for exporting from the United States: a general license and a validated license.

1.   A general license is a privilege permitting exportation within limits without requiring that an application be filed or that a license document be issued.

---

[3] A Summary of U.S. Export Control Regulations (Washington, D.C.: U.S. Department of Commerce, October 1981), p. 1.

2.   A validated license is a document authorizing exportation within the specific limitations it sets forth; it is issued only on formal application.[4]

Application must be made in accordance with procedures set forth in the *Export Administration Regulations*. Most commodities can be exported from the United States to free-world countries under a general license, but a validated license is required when exporting strategic goods and when exporting to unfriendly countries. Two points—the country of destination and the type of commodity—determine the type of export license requiring authorization by the Department of Commerce.

Country classification.   All the countries of the world, except Canada, are classified into eight groups designated by the symbols *P, Q, S, T, V, W, Y, Z*, depending on the degree of export restriction. The most stringent license requirements are set for Group Z (North Korea, Vietnam, Cuba, and Cambodia) with validated licenses being required for almost all commodities.

Commodity control list.   In the United States, commodities are classified according to their availability for export. Exporting scarce or strategic goods to foreign countries is either prohibited altogether or restricted in quantity. All commodities under the Department of Commerce export control and all country classifications are found in the *Commodity Control List* and *Country Groups Supplement* of the *Export Administration Regulations*. By consulting these lists, an exporter can determine whether a validated or general license is required for shipment of a particular commodity to a specific country. If a validated license is required the exporter must obtain the appropriate license before export shipment will be allowed. For shipments not requiring a validated license, the exporter must supply a specific notation in the "Shipper's Export Declaration" as to what kind of general license is applicable.[5]

Import restrictions

In any analysis of the feasibility of exporting to a foreign country, it is necessary to examine not only the export restrictions of the home country but the import restrictions and regulations of the foreign country. Although the responsibility of import restrictions would rest with the importer in the foreign country, they are an important consideration to the exporter in terms of the feasibility of conducting business with a particular foreign customer.

While the import tariff imposed by the foreign country is the major impediment to trade, there are many types of trade restrictions. Some examples

---

[4] A summary of U.S. Export Control Regulations (Washington, D.C.: U.S. Department of Commerce, October 1981), pp. 12–13.

[5] For a complete discussion of exports controls, consult the *Export Administration Regulations,* International Trade Administration, Office of Export Administration, U.S. Department of Commerce, Washington, D.C.

BOX 20–1:   Company fined for exporting goods to Iran

A New York firm was fined $40,000 for violating a presidential ban against exporting goods to Iran during the American hostage crisis.

The firm admitted that as a distributor for Onan-Global Limited, it arranged to export 250 welding machines worth $425,000 to Iran via a West German import firm that routed the shipment through the Soviet Union. When the shipment was stopped by Customs Service officials in Jersey City, the firm induced the West German firm to telegraph false assurances that the equipment was not destined for Iran.

In addition to the fine, the firm had to pay a $10,000 civil penalty.

Source: United Press International, News Release, "Company Fined for Exporting Goods to Iran," April 2, 1981.

---

of the 30 basic barriers to exporting considered important by *Business International* include: (1) import licenses, quotas, and other quantitative restrictions; (2) currency restrictions and allocation of exchange at unfavorable rates on payments for imports; (3) devaluation; (4) prohibitive prior import deposits, prohibition of collection-basis sales, and insistence on cash letters of credit; (5) arbitrarily short periods in which to apply for import licenses; and (6) delays resulting from pressure on overworked officials or from competitors' influence on susceptible officials.[6] Of all the trade restrictions, the most frequently encountered are tariffs, exchange permits, quotas, and import licenses.

Tariffs.   Tariffs are the taxes or customs duties levied against goods imported from another country. All countries have tariffs for the purpose of raising revenue or protecting home industries from the competition of foreign-produced goods. Tariff rates are based on value or quantity, or a combination of both. In the United States, for example, the types of custom duties used are classified as (1) ad valorem duties, based on a percentage of the determined value of the imported goods; (2) specific duties, a stipulated amount per unit weight or some other measure of quantity; and (3) a compound duty which combines both specific and ad valorem taxes on a particular item, that is, a tax per pound plus a percentage of value (ad valorem). Since tariffs are subject to frequent change, published tariff schedules for every country are available to the exporter on a current basis.

Exchange Permits.   Especially important to exporters are exchange restrictions placed on the flow of currency by some foreign countries. To conserve scarce foreign exchange and alleviate balance-of-payment difficulties, many countries impose restrictions on the amount of their currency they will exchange for the currency of another country. In effect, they ration the amount of currency available to pay for imports. Exchange controls may be applied in general to all commodities, or as is frequently the case, a country may employ a system of multiple exchange rates based on the

---

[6] "Potholes in the Export Highway: 30 Ways to Stumble," *201 Checklists: Decision-Making in International Operations* (New York: Business International, 1980), p. 31.

type of import. Essential products might have a very favorable exchange rate while nonessentials or luxuries would have a less favorable rate of exchange. In some cases, no exchange permits would be issued for certain classes of commodities.

In countries that utilize exchange controls, the typical procedure is for the importer to apply to the control agency of the importing country for an import permit; if the control agency approves the request, an import license is issued. Then, upon presentation to the proper government agency, the import license can be used to have local currency exchanged for the currency of the seller.

Receiving an import license or even an exchange permit does not guarantee a seller will be able to exchange local currency for the currency of the seller. If local currency is in short supply, a chronic problem in some countries, other means of acquiring home-country currency are necessary. For example, in a transaction between the government of Colombia and a U.S. truck manufacturer, there was a scarcity of U.S. currency to exchange for the 1,000 vehicles Colombia wanted to purchase. The problem was solved through a series of exchanges. Colombia had a surplus of coffee which the truck manufacturer accepted and traded in Europe for sugar, the sugar was traded for pig iron and finally the pig iron for U.S. dollars.

This somewhat complicated but effective transaction has become more common. In fact, an international marketing middleman, sometimes called an *intermerchant,* has evolved as a result of these switch or triangular trades involving several principals from different countries. In some countries where no exchange permits are issued, an increasing amount of trade is conducted on a barter basis. This is especially true with Eastern European countries, China, and the USSR where nearly 40 percent of trade is conducted with some form of countertrade.[7] Since exchange procedures can be very complicated, the exporter should seek the advice of a banker or other informed source when questions of foreign exchange arise.

Quotas.   Countries may also impose limitations on the quantity of certain goods imported during a specific period. These quotas may be applied to imports from specific countries or from all foreign sources in general. The United States, for example, has specific quotas for importing sugar, wheat, cotton, tobacco, and rice; in the case of some of these items, there are limitations on the amount imported from specific countries as well.

Quotas are set for a variety of reasons; the most important reason is to protect domestic industry and to conserve foreign exchange. Some importing countries also set quotas to insure an equitable distribution of a major market among friendly countries.

Import licenses.   As a means of regulating the flow of exchange and the quantity of a particular imported commodity, countries often require

---

[7] "Countertrade Gains Popularity as International Trade Tool," *Business America,* July 14, 1980, p. 15.

import licenses. The requirement of licenses for importing goods may be a means of maintaining control in administering exchange controls and tariffs, or it may be used similar to quotas in limiting the quantity of goods imported into the country. The fundamental difference between quotas and import licenses used to control the quantity of a commodity imported is the greater flexibility of the import license. Quotas are generally set for an extended period of time, but licensing can limit quantities on an individual basis from day to day.

Other restrictions. Many other restrictions may also be imposed on imports; such as regulations affecting the importation of harmful products, drugs and medicine, and amoral products and literature. Products must also comply with government standards set for health, sanitation, packaging, and labeling. For example, in the Netherlands, all imported hens' and ducks' eggs must be marked in indelible ink with the country of origin; in Spain, imported condensed milk must be labeled to show fat content if it is less than 8 percent fat; and in Mexico, all animals imported from the United States must be accompanied by a sanitary certificate issued by an approved veterinary inspector and a visa secured from a Mexican consulate. In addi-

---

BOX 20–2: A few examples of nontariff barriers

France—prohibits all whiskey advertising and levies huge taxes on grain-based spirits; forbids walnut imports before September 25 in order to exclude Italy's early crop; uses customs slowdowns to stop refrigerators at the border; burdens foreign automobiles with special insurance rates; has a state monopoly on phosphates; excludes Dutch cheese by prohibiting ingredients typically used in the Netherlands; charges a special transportation fee on foreign wine.

Italy—has slowed Volkswagen imports by a special tax; raises the cost of Bavarian milk by requiring Italian inspection at the time of production; has a state monopoly on matches and alcoholic beverages; covertly seeks bids on government projects only from national firms.

Germany—requires the use of Germany architects on all construction by German firms; prohibits the import of high-lead gasoline needed by French- and Italian-made cars; has strict packaging requirements that keep out most foreign foodstuffs; prohibits the use of preservatives and artificial flavorings in imported food; limits coal-derived fuel consumption to the northern part of the country.

Britain—gives loyalty rebate to steel users who have not purchased imported steel in six months; requires a costly "air worthiness" certificate for all imported aircraft; bans coal imports.

Japan—refuses to accept U.S. certification that American pharmaceutical exports are safe; insists on different-from-U.S. standards for electrical appliances and pressurized containers; requires that importer-distributors of foreign autos submit each car shipped to painstaking emissions-testing rather than, say, 1 out of every 10. The list is endless, and every country is involved.

Source: Author's compilation.

tion, an endless list of other nontariff barriers exists involving every country. France, for example, prohibits all whiskey advertising, Germany prohibits the use of preservatives and artificial flavorings in imported food, and Britain requires a costly "air worthiness" certificate for all imported aircraft.

Failure to comply with these regulations and other nontariff barriers can bring severe fines and penalties. Since requirements vary for each country, and change frequently, regulations for all countries must be consulted individually and on a current basis. *Overseas Business Reports,* issued periodically by the Department of Commerce, provides the foreign marketer with the most recent foreign trade regulations of each country as well as U.S. regulations regarding each country.

FOREIGN-TRADE ZONES[8]

To facilitate international trade and lessen the complexities of various import restrictions, some countries have established foreign or free-trade zones (FTZ) or ports. There are more than 200 of these facilities in operation throughout the world. A free port or foreign-trade zone receives shipments of goods, destined for importation, for storage or further processing without paying the required import duties unless and until they enter the country from the foreign-trade zone area. Thus, exporters can ship products for storage or processing in large quantities to free ports like Hong Kong, Beirut, or Barcelona and then supply other areas with smaller quantities as demand arises. A foreign-trade zone is in essence an enclave and not considered part of the country to which it is contiguous as far as import regulations are concerned. When an item leaves a foreign-trade zone for distribution and is imported into the country where the FTZ is located, all duties and regulations are imposed.

In recent years, U.S. FTZs have extended their services to over 1,000 firms engaged in a spectrum of international trade-related activities ranging from distribution to assembly and manufacturing.[9] More than 50 foreign-trade zones are located throughout the United States, including New York, New Orleans, San Francisco, Seattle, Toledo, Honolulu, Mayaques (Puerto Rico), Kansas City, Little Rock, and Sault St. Marie.[10] Goods subject to U.S. custom duties can be landed in these zones for storage or such processing as repackaging, cleaning, and grading before being brought into the United States or re-exported to another country. In situations where goods are imported into the United States to be combined with American-made goods and re-exported, the importer or exporter can avoid payment of U.S. import duties on the foreign portion and eliminate the complications of applying

---

[8] Foreign Trade Zones and Free Trade Zones have the same meaning.

[9] "U.S. Foreign Trade Zones: A Look Back, a Glance Ahead," *American Import/Export Bulletin,* March 1980.

[10] "U.S. Foreign Trade Zones: Grow in Scope and Number," *Business America,* June 2, 1980, pp. 13–15.

for a "drawback," that is, a request for a refund from the government of 99 percent of the duties paid on imports which are later re-exported. Other benefits for companies utilizing foreign-trade zones include: (1) lower insurance costs due to the greater security required in FTZs; (2) more working capital since duties are deferred until goods leave the zone; (3) the opportunity to stockpile products when quotas are filled or while waiting for ideal market conditions; (4) significant savings on goods or materials rejected, damaged, or scrapped for which no duties are assessed; and (5) exemption from paying duties on labor and overhead costs which when incurred in an FTZ are excluded in determining the value of the goods.[11]

A more elaborate variation of a foreign-trade zone exists on the Mexican-U.S. border. In 1971, the Mexican and U.S. governments established an "in-bond" program[12] which creates a favorable opportunity for U.S. companies to utilize abundant, low-cost Mexican labor.

The Mexican government allows U.S. processing, packaging, assembling and/or repair plants located in the In-Bond area to import parts and processed materials without import taxes provided the finished products are re-exported to the U.S. or to another foreign country. In turn, the U.S. government permits the reimportation of the packaged, processed, assembled, or repaired goods with a reasonably *low* import tariff applied only to the value added while in Mexico. More than 400 U.S. companies in electronics, health care, automotive, furniture, clothing, and toy manufacturing participate in the in-bond program.

Information about foreign-trade zones, free ports, and similar customs-privileged facilities abroad may be obtained from the Foreign Trade Zones Board, U.S. Department of Commerce.

EXPORT DOCUMENTS

Various documents are necessary for each export shipment to satisfy government regulations controlling exportation as well as to meet requirements for international commercial payment transactions. The most frequently required documents are export declarations, consular invoices or certificates of origin, bills of lading, commercial invoices, and insurance certificates. In addition, documents such as import licenses, export licenses, packing lists, and inspection certificates for agricultural products are often necessary.

The paperwork involved in successfully completing a transaction is considered by many to be the greatest of all nontariff trade barriers. There are 125 different types of documents in regular or special use in more than

---

[11] "Foreign-Trade Zones: What's in it for the Shipper?" *Distribution,* March 1980, pp. 44–47.

[12] Sometimes referred to as *twin-plant operations.* For discussion of this program, see "American Boom in Mexico," *Duns Review,* October 1978, pp. 119–27 and "Mexican In-Bond Assembly Gains," *Business America,* July 15, 1981, p. 223.

1,000 different forms. A single shipment may require more than 50 documents and can involve as many as 28 different parties and government agencies or require as few as five. Generally, preparation of documents can be handled routinely but their importance should not be minimized; incomplete or improperly prepared documents lead to delays in shipment. In some countries, penalties, fines, or even confiscation of goods can result from errors in some of these documents. Export documents are the result of requirements imposed by the exporting government, of requirements set by commercial procedures established in foreign trade, and, in some cases, of the supporting import documents required by the foreign government. Principal export documents are as follows.

Export declaration. In order to maintain a statistical measure of the quantity of goods shipped abroad and to provide a means of determining whether regulations are being met, most countries require shipments abroad to be accompanied by an export declaration. Usually such a declaration, presented at the port of exit, includes the names and addresses of the principals involved, the destination of the goods, a full description of the goods, and their declared value. When manufacturers are exporting from the United States, Customs and the Department of Commerce require an export declaration for all shipments. If specific licenses are required to ship a particular commodity, the export license must be presented with the export declaration for proper certification. It thus serves as the principal means of control for regulatory agencies of the U.S. government.

Consular invoice or certificate of origin. Not all countries require consular invoices, but those that do are typically very exacting about the manner in which the invoices are prepared. Proper forms must be obtained from the country's consulate and returned with two to eight copies in the language of the country along with copies of other required documents (e.g., import license, commercial invoice, and/or bill of lading) before certification is granted. The consular invoice probably produces the most red tape and is the most exacting to complete. Preparation of the document should be handled with extreme care because fines are levied for any errors uncovered. In most countries, the fine is shared with whomever detects it so few errors go undetected.

Bill of lading. The bill of lading is the most important document required to establish legal ownership and facilitate financial transactions. It serves the following purposes: (1) as a contract for shipment between the carrier and shipper, (2) as a receipt from the carrier for shipment, and (3) as a certificate of ownership, or title to the goods. Bills of lading are issued in the form of straight bills, which are nonnegotiable and are delivered directly to a consignee, or order bills, which are negotiable instruments. Bills of lading frequently are referred to as being either *clean* or *foul.* A clean bill of lading means the items presented to the carrier for shipment were properly packaged and clear of apparent damage when received; a foul bill of lading means the shipment was received in damaged condition, and the damage is noted on the bill of lading.

Commercial invoice.   Every international transaction requires a commercial invoice, i.e., a bill or statement for the goods sold. This document often serves several purposes in that some countries require a copy for customs clearance, plus it is one of the financial documents required in international commercial payments.

Insurance policy or certificate.   The risks of shipment due to political or economic unrest in some countries, and the possibility of damage from sea and weather, make it absolutely necessary to have adequate insurance covering loss due to damage, war, or riots. Typically the method of payment or terms of sale require insurance on the goods so few export shipments are uninsured. The insurance policy or certificate of insurance is considered a key document in export trade.

Licenses.   Export or import licenses are additional documents frequently required in export trade. In those cases where import licenses are required by the country of entry, a copy of the license or license number is usually required to obtain a consular invoice. Whenever a commodity requires an export license, it must be obtained before an export declaration will be properly certified.

Others.   Sanitary and health inspection certificates attesting to the absence of disease and pests may be required for certain agricultural products before a country will allow goods to enter its borders. Packing lists with correct weights are also required in some cases.

PACKING AND MARKING

Special packing and marking requirements must be considered for those shipments destined to be transported over water, subject to excessive handling, or destined for parts of the world with extreme climate. Packing adequate for domestic shipments often falls short for goods subject to the conditions mentioned. Protection against rough handling, moisture, temperature extremes, and pilferage may require heavy crating which increases total packing costs as well as freight rates because of increased weight and size. Since some countries determine import duties on gross weight, packing can add a significant amount to import fees. To avoid the extremes of too much or too little packing, the marketer should consult export brokers, export freight forwarders, or other specialists.

All countries have some import regulations for marking goods and containers; noncompliance can result in severe penalties. The exporter should be particularly careful that all marking on the container conforms exactly to the data on the export documents because discrepancies are often interpreted by custom officials as an attempt to defraud. A basic source of information for American exporters is the Department of Commerce series of pamphlets entitled *Preparing Shipment to (Country)* detailing the necessary export documents and outlining pertinent U.S. and foreign government regulations regarding such matters as labeling, marking, packing, and customs procedures.

THE FOREIGN FREIGHT FORWARDER

An indispensable agent for an exporting firm that cannot afford an in-house specialist to handle paperwork and other export trade mechanics is the *Foreign Freight Forwarder*. Even in large companies with active export departments capable of handling documentation, a forwarder is useful as a shipment coordinator at the port or at the destination.[13] Besides arranging for complete shipping documentation, the full-service foreign freight for-warder provides information and advice on routing and scheduling, rates and related charges, consular and licensing requirements, labeling require-ments, and export restrictions. Further, the agent offers shipping insurance, warehouse storage, packing and containerization, and ocean cargo or air freight space. Both large and small shippers find the freight forwarders' wide range of services useful and well worth the fees normally charged.

FOREIGN COMMERCIAL PAYMENTS

The sale of goods in other countries is further complicated by additional risks encountered when dealing with foreign customers. There are risks from inadequate credit reports on customers; problems of currency ex-change controls, distance, and different legal systems; and the cost and difficulty of collecting delinquent accounts which require a different empha-sis on payment systems utilized. In U.S. domestic trade, the typical payment procedure for established customers is an open account—the goods are delivered and the customer is billed on an end-of-the-month basis. The most frequently used term of payment in foreign commercial transactions for both export and import sales is letter of credit, followed closely in importance by commercial dollar drafts or bills of exchange drawn by the seller on the buyer. Internationally, open accounts are reserved for well-established customers, and cash in advance is required of only the poorest credit risks or when the character of the merchandise is such that incompletion of the contract may result in heavy loss. Because of the time required for shipment of goods from one country to another, advance payment of cash is an unusu-ally costly burden for a potential customer and places the seller at a definite disadvantage competitively.

Terms of sale are typically arranged between the buyer and seller at the time of the sale. Type of merchandise, the amount of money involved, business custom, the credit rating of the buyer, the country of the buyer, whether the buyer is a new or old customer, are items to be considered in establishing the terms of sale. The four basic payment arrangements—(1) letters of credit, (2) bills of exchange, (3) cash in advance, and (4) open accounts—are discussed in this section.

---

[13] "Freight Forwarders: The Export Experts," *Distribution,* March 1980, pp. 37–40.

Letters of credit

Most American exports are handled by export letters of credit opened in favor of the seller by the buyer. Letters of credit shift the buyer's credit risk to the bank issuing the letter of credit. When a letter of credit is employed, the seller ordinarily can draw a draft against the bank issuing the credit and receive dollars by presenting proper shipping documents. Except for cash in advance, letters of credit afford the greatest degree of protection for the seller.

The procedure for a letter of credit begins with completion of the contract when the buyer goes to a local bank and arranges for the issuance of a letter of credit; the buyer's bank then notifies its correspondent bank in the seller's country that the letter has been issued. After meeting the requirements set forth in the letter of credit, the seller can draw a draft against the credit (in effect, the bank issuing the letter) for payment of the goods. The precise conditions of the letter of credit are detailed in it and usually also require presentation of certain documents with the draft before the correspondent bank will honor it. The documents usually required are: (1) commercial invoice, (2) consular invoice (when requested), (3) clean bill of lading, and (4) insurance policy or certificate.

Since all letters of credit, by their nature, must be very exact in terms and considerations, it is important for the exporter to check the terms of the letter carefully to be certain all necessary documents have been acquired and properly completed. Some of the more frequent discrepancies found in documents causing delay in honoring drafts or letters of credit include:

Insurance defects such as inadequate coverage, no endorsement or countersignature, and a dating later than the bill of lading.

Bill-of-lading defects include the bill lacking an "on board" endorsement, or signature of carrier, missing an endorsement or failing to specify prepaid freight.

Letter-of-credit defects arise if it has expired or is exceeded by the invoice figure or when including unauthorized charges or disproportionate charges.

Invoice defects relate to missing signatures, failure to designate terms of shipment (C&F, CIF, FAS, etc.) as stipulated in letter of credit.

Other problems occur with documents that are missing, stale-dated or inaccurate.

To avoid one source of discrepancies in documentation, the exporter should become familiar with the common export trade terms detailed in Exhibit 20–1.

Bills of exchange

Another important international commercial payment form is sight or time drafts (bills of exchange) drawn by sellers on foreign buyers. In letters of

EXHIBIT 20–1:   Common export trade terms and what they include

Quotation	Cost of goods at factory	Transpor-tation to dock	Loading onto vessel	Ocean or air freight charges	Shipping in-surance	Unload-ing at foreign port
				Includes		
Ex factory	X					
Free alongside (FAS)	X	X				
Free on Board: Name of home port (FOB)	X	X	X			
Cost and freight: Name of foreign port (C & F)	X	X	X	X		
Cost, insurance, freight, name of overseas port (CIF)	X	X	X	X	X	
Ex dock	X	X	X	X	X	X

credit, the credit of one or more banks is involved, but, in the use of bills of exchange (or dollar drafts), the seller assumes all risk until the actual dollars are received. The typical procedure is for the seller to draw a draft on the buyer and present it with the necessary documents to the seller's bank for collection. The documents required are principally the same as those for letters of credit. On receipt of the draft, the U.S. bank forwards it with the necessary documents to a correspondent bank in the buyer's country; then the buyer is presented with the draft for acceptance and immediate or later payment. With acceptance of the draft, the buyer receives the properly endorsed bill of lading which is used to acquire the goods from the carrier.

Bills of exchange or dollar drafts have one of three time periods—at sight, arrival, or time. A sight draft requires acceptance and payment on presentation of the draft and often before arrival of the goods. An arrival draft requires payment be made on arrival of the goods. Unlike the other two, a date draft has an exact date for payment and in no way is affected by the movement of the goods. There may be time designations placed on sight and arrival drafts stipulating a fixed number of days after acceptance when the obligation must be paid. Usually this period is 30 to 120 days, thus providing a means of extending credit to the foreign buyer.

Dollar drafts have advantages for the seller because an accepted draft frequently can be discounted at a bank for immediate payment. Banks, however, usually discount drafts only with recourse, i.e., if the draft is not honored by the buyer, the bank returns it to the seller for payment. An accepted draft is also firmer evidence in case of default and necessary litigation than an open account would be.

BOX 20–3:   You can't sell to Cuba even if you ship from another country

U.S. export privileges of a Spanish firm located in Barcelona, Spain were suspended by the United States. The Department of Commerce is investigating charges that the Spanish company violated a 1962 U.S. ban on the sale of American goods to Cuba by purchasing equipment from American companies and then shipping it to Cuba. Under the suspension order, U.S. companies are prohibited from dealing with the Spanish company or any of its related companies without specific Commerce Department approval.

Source: From "U.S. Export Privileges of Spanish Firm Halted," *The Wall Street Journal*, March 10, 1982, p. 26.

Cash in advance

The volume of business handled on a cash-in-advance basis is not large. Cash places unpopular burdens on the customer and typically is used when credit is doubtful, when exchange restrictions within the country of destination are such that the return of funds from abroad may be delayed for an unreasonable period, or when the American exporter for any reason is unwilling to sell on credit terms.

Although payment in advance is infrequently employed, partial payment (from 25 to 50 percent) in advance is not unusual when the character of the merchandise is such that an incomplete contract can result in heavy loss. For example, complicated machinery or equipment manufactured to specification or special design would necessitate advance payment which would be, in fact, a nonrefundable deposit.

Open accounts

Sales on open accounts are not generally made in foreign trade except to customers of long standing with excellent credit reputations or to a subsidiary or branch of the exporter. Open accounts obviously leave sellers in a position where most of the problems of international commercial finance work to their disadvantage. It is generally recommended that sales on open account not be made when it is the practice of the trade to use some other method, when special merchandise is ordered, when shipping is hazardous, when the country of the importer imposes difficult exchange restrictions, or when political unrest requires additional caution.[14]

EXPORT SHIPPING

Whenever and however title to goods is transferred, those goods must be transported. Shipping goods to another country presents some important

---

[14] It is suggested that the reader refer to Chapter 21 for a discussion of credit guarantees available to the foreign marketer.

differences from shipping to a domestic location. The goods can be out
of the shipper's control for longer periods of time than in domestic distribution; more shipping and collections documents are required; packing must
be suitable; and shipping insurance coverage is necessarily more extensive.
The task is to match each order of goods to the shipping modes best suited
for swift, safe, and economical delivery. Ocean shipping, air freight, air
express, and parcel post are all possibilities; however, ocean shipping is

EXHIBIT 20–2: Examples of distribution costs from Paris to Denver via New York (U.S. dollars per metric ton)

	Conventional cargo handling	
	Commodity A: per metric ton	Commodity B: per metric ton
Domestic carrier	0.95	0.95
Inland warehouse, 1 month including handling and delivery	12.14	12.14
Transport to port	12.78	12.78
Ship's agent	1.89	5.18
Port forwarder	0.97	2.66
Port warehouse (average 4 days) including handling	2.92	2.92
Stevedore	3.93	5.70
Sea carrier	21.67	80.70
Stevedore + port warehouse	6.32	6.32
Ship's agent	0.94	2.59
Port forwarder	0.79	0.79
Inland transport	46.64	46.64
Unloading	11.50	11.50
Totals	123.44	190.87

	Containerized cargo handling	
	Commodity A: per metric ton	Commodity B: per metric ton
Domestic carrier	0.95	0.95
Inland warehouse, 1 month including handling and delivery	12.14	12.14
Transport to port	5.97	5.97
Ship's agent	1.69	4.65
Port forwarder	0.87	2.39
Stevedore	1.60	1.60
Sea carrier	23.07	78.35
Stevedore + port warehouse	6.32	6.32
Ship's agent	0.85	2.32
Forwarder	0.79	0.79
Inland transport	33.45	35.49
Unloading	11.50	11.50
Totals	99.20	162.47

Note: A = Industrial cooking oil in 10-gallon containers (low-tariff cargo).
      B = Industrial chemicals, harmless (high-tariff cargo).

usually the least-expensive method and the most frequently used for heavy bulk shipments while air freight can be the most economical and certainly the speediest for certain categories of goods.

Shipping costs are an important factor in a product's price in export marketing, and the selection of a transportation mode must be viewed in terms of the total impact on cost. In ocean shipping, one of the important innovations in reducing or controlling the high cost of transportation is the use of containerization. Containerizing of shipments, in place of the traditional bulk handling of full loads or break-bulk operations, has resulted in inter-modal transport between inland points, reduced cost, and simplified handling of international shipments.[15]

With the increased usage of containerization, rail container service has developed in many countries to provide the international shipper with door-to-door movement of goods under seal originating and terminating inland. This eliminates several loadings, unloadings, and changes of carriers and reduces costs substantially as illustrated in Exhibit 20–2.

The exhibit illustrates the savings for the commodities listed; such savings are not always possible for all types of cargo. Containerized cargo handling also reduces damage and pilferage in transit.

For many commodities of high unit value and low weight and volume, international air freight has become an important method of shipping. Air freight has shown the fastest growth rate for freight transportation even though it accounts for only a fraction of total international shipments. Depending on the point of origin and the destination, the commodity and size of shipment, air freight can cost two to five times surface charges for general cargo. Some cost reduction is realized through reduced packing requirements, paperwork, insurance, and the cost of money tied up in inventory but usually not enough to offset the higher rates charged for air freight. The key to air freight is time saving; if the commodity has high unit value or high inventory costs, or there is concern with delivery time, air freight can be a justifiable alternative. Many products moving in foreign markets meet the requirements. The top 10 commodities shipped by air are:

1. Newspapers, magazines, periodicals, books, and catalogs.
2. Industrial and agricultural machinery.
3. Personal effects.
4. Electrical equipment and appliances.
5. Surface vehicles and parts.
6. Printed matter.
7. Chemicals, drugs, and pharmaceuticals.
8. Clothing.
9. Cloth and textiles.
10. Baby poultry.

---

[15] Lisa H. Harrington, Senior Editor, "How We Do Business with the World," *Traffic Management,* October 1981, pp. 41–48.

Because it is a feasible choice for many products, preliminary figures indicate air freight will show a tenfold increase in volume between 1965 and 1985. Despite the high cost, air freight's speed and flexibility make it a viable alternative in many export shipping decisions.

While the selection of transportation mode has an important bearing on the cost of export shipping, it is not the only cost involved in the physical movement of goods from point of origin to ultimate market. Indeed, the selection of mode, the location of inventory, warehouses, and so forth, all figure in the cost of the physical movement of goods. A narrow solution to physical movement of goods is the selection of transportation; a broader application is the concept of logistics management or physical distribution.

LOGISTICS

When a company is primarily an exporter from a single country to a single market, the typical approach to the physical movement of goods is the selection of a dependable mode of transportation which will ensure safe arrival of the goods within a reasonable time for a reasonable carrier cost. However, as a company moves into the ranks of multinational companies, such a solution to the movement of products could prove costly and highly inefficient for seller and buyer.[16] There is a point in the growth and expansion of an international firm when costs other than transportation are such that an optimal cost solution to the physical movement of goods cannot be achieved without thinking of the physical distribution process as an integrated system. When a foreign marketer begins producing and selling in more than one country it is time to consider the concept of logistics management, i.e., a total systems approach to management of the distribution process including all those activities involved in physically moving raw material, in-process inventory, and finished-goods inventory from point of origin to point of use or consumption.

Interdependence of physical distribution activities

Distribution viewed as a system involves more than physical movement. At least five major activities are involved plus the ever-important considerations of customer service and contractual obligation.

1. *Facility locations:* Where should plant, warehouses, and depots be located?
2. *Inventory allocation:* Where should inventory be located and in what quantities?
3. *Transportation:* What mode or modes of transport should be used? Lease or buy?

---

[16] For a comprehensive coverage of logistics see Gary Davies',ed., *International Logistics* (West Yorkshire, Eng.: MCB Publications Ltd., 1981), 106 pp.

4. *Communications:* A distribution system must work in both directions—material flowing one way and information the other.
5. *Unitization:* How should the products be packaged and wrapped so that economies of movement and storage may be achieved?[17]

The physical distribution concept recognizes the costs of each activity are interdependent and a decision involving one affects the cost and efficiency of one or all others. In fact, because of their interdependence, there are an infinite number of "total costs" for the sum of each of the different activity costs. (*Total cost* of the system is defined as the sum of the costs of all these activities.) The idea of interdependence can be illustrated by the classic example of air freight. Exhibit 20–3 is a hypothetical illustration of a shipment of spare parts from Europe to the U.S. using two different modes of transportation—ocean freight and the more expensive air freight. When total costs are calculated, air freight is just slightly more costly than ocean freight. However, when the 26 days in time savings are considered, air freight could prove considerably less costly. One cost not included in the illustration is the potential cost of U.S. storage and warehousing that would be necessary with ocean freight to provide the same level of customer service by both systems. When total costs are calculated, air freight may be less costly because it is possible to reduce inventory investment, use less protective packaging, make one local destination delivery instead of two, and eliminate a warehouse. These overall savings more than offset the higher freight rate for air shipment.

EXHIBIT 20–3: Cost comparison between air freight and ocean shipping of spare parts—Europe to the United States

	Air	Ocean
Packing	19.57	37.99
Transportation to port of departure, handling	23.79	21.87
Freight	233.72	120.50
Transportation from port of destination, handling	52.19	45.67
Import duties	227.19	230.26
Insurance	2.69	6.52
Total cost of transportation	559.15	462.81
Number of days in transit	4 Days	30 Days
Cost of capital tied up in transit	2.30	12.66
Total cost transportation	561.45	475.47
Cost of goods	1,474.06	1,474.06
Total cost	2,035.51	1,949.53
Cost difference	$ 85.98	
Time savings	26 Days	

Adapted from: Felix Wentworth, Martin Christopher, Gordon Wills, and Bernard J. La Londe, *Managing International Distribution,* (New York: AMA-COM, American Management Association, 1979), p. 262.

[17] Martin Christopher, "Logistics in its Marketing Context," *European Journal of Marketing,* vol. 6, no. 2, 1972, p. 118.

Another example involves a large multinational firm with facilities and customers the world over. This firm shipped parts from its U.S. Midwest plant to the nearest East Coast port, then by water route around the Cape of Good Hope (Africa) and finally to its plants in the Orient, taking 14 weeks. Substantial inventory was maintained in the Orient as a safeguard against uncertain water-borne deliveries. The transportation carrier costs were the least expensive available; however, delivery delays and unreliable service caused the firm to make emergency air shipments to keep production lines going in the Orient. Air shipment costs rose to 70 percent of the total transport bill. An analysis of the problem in terms of physical distribution system showed that costs could be lowered by using higher cost motor carriers to truck the parts to West Coast ports, then ship them by sea. Transit time was reduced, delivery reliability improved, inventory quantities in the Orient lowered, and emergency air shipments eliminated. The new distribution system produced an annual savings of $60,000.[18] Obviously, a cost difference will not always be the case, but the examples serve to illustrate the interdependence of the various activities in the physical distribution mix and the total cost. A change of transportation mode affected a change in packaging and handling, inventory costs, warehousing time and cost, and delivery charges.

The concept of physical distribution is the achievement of optimum (lowest) system cost consistent with customer service objectives of the firm. If the activities in the physical distribution system are viewed separately without consideration of their interdependence, the final cost of distribution and quality of service rendered may be suboptimized. Distribution problems confronting the international marketer are compounded by additional variables and costs which are also interdependent and must be included in the total physical distribution decision. As the international firm broadens the scope of its operations, the additional variables and costs become more crucial in their effect on the efficiency of the distribution system.

Effect of environment on physical distribution costs

One of the most consistent variables to be dealt with is the physical environment or geography. Environmental differences encountered in foreign marketing place an extra burden on the process of physical distribution. The environmental differences that confront a company with one U.S. manufacturing plant selling in two geographical regions in the United States are substantially different from those of a company with a manufacturing plant in one country selling in two different countries. The company operating on an international front must deal with several currencies, several sets of laws, sometimes indefinable taxes, varied local transportation costs, and

---

[18] Dr. Lynn E. Gill, "Beware of Booby Traps in Multinational Distribution," *Handling and Shipping,* March 1976, p. 45.

different warehousing systems. In the Netherlands, Belgium, and Italy there is no limit on the time goods can be left in a bonded warehouse without paying import taxes, but in Germany and France there is a limit. In the United States, transportation tariffs are set by the ICC and all tariffs are on file resulting in uniform tariffs to all. This is not so in Europe where transportation rates are negotiated in open competition and prices may vary from day to day. To further confuse the situation, door-to-door delivery and ship unloading costs can vary substantially from port to port in Europe.

BOX 20–4: Mistakes in exporting

The biggest mistakes U.S. companies make in answering export inquiries:

1. Vague form letter, often with cavalier overtones. Typical are three identical letters turned in by the U.S. consulate in Trinidad and Tobago involving an export firm in California. "Please acknowledge our contact immediately and include all additional specifications," the California firm had replied to companies in Port of Spain. It added, "If the trade request notice is no longer desired or has been filled, please notify by cable so we don't waste time and will be inclined to serve your needs in the future."

2. Failure to specify freight charges. The U.S. consulate in Salzburg, Austria, recently relayed a letter from an Innsbruck firm regretting that an otherwise-attractive offer from an American exporter was turned down because it quoted FOB New York rather than the requested CIF (cost, insurance, and freight) rate.

Wrote the Austrian company, "You are certainly aware that CIF quotations are usual in Europe. This gives the European customer the guarantee that he does not have to be concerned about constantly changing freight rates, insurance, and so forth. We deem it to be a basic requirement that American firms offer their products CIF European port."

The consulate made its own survey as to how many U.S. companies had actually done so. It found that 40 trade opportunities dug up in March and April, 1975, had prompted 187 replies from U.S. firms. Of those, six specified CIF quotes, 40 mentioned FOB, and 14 "said nothing regarding method of quoting prices." That, observed the consulate, "is a nontariff trade barrier that U.S. firms themselves erect."

3. Delay in responding. From a U.S. consulate in South Africa: "Last year a South African import agency inquired through the TOP program about some products needed as a matter of urgency. Replies from other country suppliers were received with a minimum of delay, but a significant time lag occurred where U.S. companies were concerned. The enquirer says he is still receiving U.S. responses a full eight months after having placed his order with a third-country supplier at a price higher than those quoted by the Americans."

4. Wrong product. "I'm amazed by the number of times that a U.S. company quotes prices for products that have nothing to do with the inquiry," says Rice. Adds a consulate report from Sydney, Australia: "The offer by U.S. companies of products nothing like those requested is the most annoying response of all."

Source: "The Importance of Being Earnest," *Sales and Marketing Management,* May 10, 1976, pp. 17–18.

The flexibility and cost of the physical distribution activity also is affected by increasing pressure brought about by local governments as policies are expanded to encompass greater economic development. An individual logistics orientation could help minimize the adverse effects of government policy changes on worldwide distribution systems. Further, planning and location of production facilities are drawn into consideration of physical distribution systems. Some governments offer lucrative inducements for plant location in their country, but a company must look at the effect of that specific plant location on their marketwide physical distribution cost both with the inducement and without; a country that gives tariff protection, tax privileges, government financing, and favorable exchange rates can also take away those advantages after capital investments have been made. Evaluating the alternatives in a logistics system context could reveal impending problems with potential restrictions on inventory levels, taxes, and controls on imports, quotas, and tariffs. Certainly the "typical" pattern is for governments to change their policies toward foreign companies as it suits their natural internal policy development goals. All these factors must be accounted for in physical distribution because they are all interdependent and affect the total cost of distribution. A physical distribution system can aid in minimizing that total cost.[19]

Benefits of physical distribution systems

There are other benefits to a physical distribution system besides cost advantages. An effective physical distribution system can result in optimal inventory levels and, in multiplant operations, optimal production capacity, both of which result in better use of working capital. In making plant location decisions, a company with a physical distribution system can readily assess operating costs of alternative plant locations to serve various markets. For example, suppose a company is assessing the advantage of building a plant in Italy to supply markets there that are presently being sourced from Great Britain or West Germany.

> At the headquarters in New York, the logistics planning group is asked to examine this proposal. The logistics group takes five-year sales forecasts for all national markets and, using a linear programming model, calculates estimates of the minimum total variable cost of producing and shipping products from all plants to all markets. Two calculations are made, one assuming the new Italian plant is already "on stream," and the other assuming the British and West German plants are used to serve the Italian market. The study includes, of course, an estimate of the added investment to equip the proposed Italian plant, hire and train new workers, and put it on stream.[20]

---

[19] Felix Wentworth, Martin Christopher, Gordon Wills, and Bernard J. La Londe, *Managing International Distribution*, (New York: AMA-COM, American Management Assoc., 1979), p. 262.

[20] Robert E. McGarrah, "Logistics for the International Manufacturer," *Harvard Business Review*, March/April 1966, p. 165.

With this information it can now examine the decision in terms of its effect on operating costs of the entire distribution system.

A physical distribution system may also result in better (more dependable) delivery service to the market and, when products are produced at different locations, they are able to quickly determine the most economical source for a particular customer. As companies expand into multinational markets and source these markets from multinational production facilities, they are increasingly confronted with cost variables that make it imperative to employ a total systems approach to the management of the distribution process in order to achieve efficient operation. Finally, a physical distribution system can render the natural obstructions created by geography less economically critical for the multinational marketer.[21]

SUMMARY

An awareness of the mechanics of export trade is indispensable to the marketer who engages in exporting goods from one country to another; these mechanics, however, should not be considered the essence of foreign marketing since they are only one aspect to be incorporated in a total marketing plan. Although most marketing techniques are open to interpretation and creative application, the mechanics of exporting are very exact; there is little room for interpretation or improvisation with the requirements of export licenses, quotas, tariffs, export documents, packing, marking, and the various uses of commercial payments.

The very nature of the regulations and restrictions surrounding importing and exporting lead to frequent and rapid change. In handling the mechanics of export trade successfully, the manufacturer must keep abreast of all foreign and domestic changes in requirements and regulations pertaining to the product involved.

For firms unable to maintain their own export staff, foreign freight forwarders can handle many details for a nominal fee.

With paperwork completed, the physical movement of goods must be considered. Transportation mode affects total product cost because of the varying requirements of packing, inventory levels, time requirements, perishability, unit cost, damage and pilfering losses, and customer service. Transportation for each product must be assessed in view of the interdependent nature of all these factors. To assure optimum distribution at minimal cost, a physical distribution system can determine everything from plant location to final customer delivery in terms of the most efficient use of capital investment, resources, production, inventory, packing, and transportation.

---

[21] Joan Feldman, "Coping With Global Distribution," *Handling and Shipping Management,* July 1981, pp. 49–52.

QUESTIONS

1. Define and show the significance to international marketing of the following terms:

   Commodity control list   f.a.s.
   General license   Foul bill of lading
   Commodity classifications   Letter of credit
   Validated license   Clean bill of lading
   Exchange permits   Logistics
   Duty   Physical distribution
   Ad valorem duty   systems

2. Explain the reasoning behind the various regulations and restrictions imposed on the exportation and importation of goods.

3. Define the two types of licenses required for exporting goods from the United States.

4. What determines the type of license needed for exportation? Discuss.

5. Discuss the most frequently encountered trade restrictions.

6. What is the purpose of an import license? Discuss.

7. Explain free-trade zones and illustrate how they may be used by an exporter. By an importer. How do free-zones differ from bonded warehouses?

8. How do "in bond" areas differ from foreign trade zones? How would an international marketer use an in bond area?

9. Explain each of the following export documents:
   a. Bill of lading
   b. Counselor invoice or certificate of origin
   c. Commercial invoice
   d. Insurance certificate

10. What are the differences between straight bill of lading and order bill of lading? What are the differences between clean bill of lading and foul bill of lading?

11. Discuss the basic types of payment arrangements. Under what conditions would each be likely to be used?

12. Illustrate the typical procedure followed when using a letter of credit.

13. Why would an exporter use the services of a foreign freight forwarder? Discuss.

14. Besides cost advantages, what are the other benefits of a physical distribution system?

Case V-1

Consulting for Bebe Cola in Latino

Bebe Cola, one of the top three cola soft drink companies in the United States, has contacted you as a consultant with a problem they are experiencing in Latino (a Latin American country). Cola International, a subsidiary of Bebe Cola, Inc., has had operations in Latino since before World War II. Bebe Cola's organization consists of Bebe Cola, Inc., which is the parent company for Bebe Cola USA, the corporation for U.S. sales, and Bebe Cola International for their investments abroad. Bebe Cola International has as a partially owned subsidiary in Latino, Bebe Cola Latina. B.C. International owns 49 percent of Bebe Cola Latino, and Latino nationals own 51 percent. As is the case in the United States, B.C. Latino manufactures cola concentrate, which it sells to independently owned bottlers throughout Latino. B.C. Latino owns no bottling plants in Latino. The profit that B.C. Latino makes is solely from the sale of concentrate to bottlers. It is, therefore, extremely important to B.C. Latino, as well as to B.C., Inc., that the bottlers be profitable over the long run. If they do not grow with the market and make proper investments over time, and if market share is lost, B.C. Latino will suffer substantial profit reductions. This relationship is precisely the one that caused B.C. International concern. In an annual review of long-range projections of B.C. Latino, the President of B.C. International became concerned over a study that indicated most of the B.C. bottlers in Latino were operating at near production capacity and that their plans for the next five years did not include sufficient investment in production facilities. After visits with many of the B.C. bottlers, B.C., Inc., found that most were reluctant to make additional investments because of the continuing profit squeeze facing them.

In Latino, nonalcoholic beverages are classified as food and all food is under price control. Soft drinks have had virtually the same price for the past 12 years, but the bottler's costs, with the exception of sugar, the only other ingredient under price control, have increased. The net result is that over the last 11 years a very profitable gross margin has dwindled to the point that the more efficient bottlers can realize only a 5 cent to 10 cent

667

U.S. per case profit. This relatively slim profit margin is the major reason given by B.C. bottlers for not planning for future capital investments. Present retail price control for a 12-ounce bottle of B.C. cola (and this price applies to all of the colas) is 12 pesos or approximately 12 cents U.S. Wholesale prices are approximately: 7.20 pesos for a 6½-ounce bottle, 9.20 pesos for a 12-ounce bottle, and 15.20 pesos for a 26-ounce bottle.[1]

This preliminary investigation on the part of B.C., Inc., management was cause for alarm. Even though B.C. shares the cola market equally with Super Cola, the other major cola manufacturer (each has about 48 percent), B.C. management felt that, with the market growing, bottlers had to increase their investments in production facilities or they would subsequently lose share of market and suffer reduced profits. B.C., Inc., management could appreciate the reluctance of the Latino bottlers to increase their investments because the production equipment is all produced in the United States and is very expensive. Furthermore, the equipment carries an import tax of about 50 percent ad valorem. The heavy duty trucks used to deliver the product are also imported from the United States and have a 100-percent ad valorem tax applied to them. Consequently, an investment in production and delivery facilities in Latino costs about twice as much as it does in the United States.

The immediate response to this problem by B.C.'s management was to look for ways it could assist the Latino bottlers to increase their efficiency. A recent study of production facility utilization among Latino bottlers had been done by the production division and showed that they were perhaps the most efficient bottlers in the whole international company. They were operating, on the average, more than two eight-hour shifts per day, many running very close to 100 percent capacity. The only means to increase production efficiency would be the replacement of present production equipment with high-speed bottling machinery. That alternative would have required a heavy investment which they weren't willing to make with present profit margins. B.C. management looked elsewhere and considered the possibility of lobbying to have the minimum price for a soft drink raised. This avenue was rapidly discarded since no government official or politician would raise the price of a product so widely used as cola beverages. For example, the per capita consumption of cola-based drinks in Latino is close to 1,000 eight-ounce bottles per person per year. This compares to about 550 eight-ounce bottles per person per year in the U.S. Obviously, cola consumption is extremely popular in this country and any politician or government official advocating an increase in the price would incur the wrath of the population. That approach was immediately dropped.

Looking elsewhere for potential solutions, the management decided that distribution patterns utilized by the bottlers might be an avenue for improvement of efficiency. An extensive study of the distribution of soft drinks was

---

[1] Convert pesos to U.S. money at a rate of 96 pesos to $1 U.S.

conducted. B.C. cola has now employed you to analyze the data and provide them with suggestions and recommendations. A summary of the highlights of the study follows.

The cola market in Latino.   The market for soft drinks in Latino is an exceptionally large one. Latinians drink, on the average, about 1,000 to 1,100 eight-ounce equivalent bottles per year per person. Of this amount, about 50 percent are cola based, the other 50 percent are fruit-flavored drinks. The cola beverage market is about equally divided (approximately 48 percent each) between B.C. Cola and Super Cola. The remaining 4 percent is distributed among four or five other brands including Bubble Cola, Rex Cola, and Latinacola (the only wholly-owned Latino Cola company). The following comments will provide you with some general idea of the characteristics of the market. Where appropriate, U.S. comparisons will be made.

1.   Over 90 percent of all sales of bottled soft drinks in the Latino market are made as *cold bottle* in small quantities—one or two bottles at a time. They are either consumed at the point of sale or taken home for immediate use. One of the important characteristics of this market is the high per capita consumption of soft drinks as a refreshment between meals and with meals, both during lunch and dinner. In the United States, about 60 percent of bottled soft drinks are bought in supermarkets in packs of six or eight for consumption in the home. On-premise cold bottle consumption in the United States is only about 15 percent of the market.

Beer is sold in cans, but it does not come under price controls and thus the price can reflect the higher cost of cans. Glass is produced in Latino for bottles by a monopoly or cartel that controls the price of glass which is kept relatively high. While there are an increasing number of supermarkets involved in the distribution of food in Latino, they are still not significant in the distribution of soft drinks. In a major supermarket with floor space of 80,000–90,000 square feet, the beverage section generally contains, of all brands, no more than about 30 or 40 cases. In comparison, a supermarket of equal size in the U.S. stocks from 300 to 400 cases of soft drinks. Soft drinks are just not bought in packs of six or eight in Latino supermarkets.

2.   A large portion of the market does not have adequate refrigeration in the home and depends upon small neighborhood stores to provide them with a supply of chilled product. Off-premise consumption in the home follows a pattern similar to the following: A maid or young child is sent before the noon meal to buy one or two bottles to bring home for immediate consumption with the meal. This pattern probably holds true for most of Latino.

3.   There is some income distinction in brand preference among consumers. In Latino four income classes are generally recognized. Class A, with monthly incomes of $1,200 (U.S. equivalent) or more, and class B, with incomes between $700 and $1,200 account for about 8 percent of the population. About 30 percent of the population are in class C, earning

from $300 to $600 per month. The remaining 62 percent are in class D and have incomes below $300.

Super Cola has the status image preferred by class A and B, while B.C.'s image is strongest among classes C and D. Super Cola has had some success trading down to classes C and D while maintaining its upper class image. B.C. has attempted to trade up to class A and B and follows this strategy in much of its advertising.

4.   The predominant method of retail distribution is through small neighborhood stores. (In the United States the major method of retail distribution is through supermarkets.) Over 90 percent of soft drink sales are made in stores operated by one person, having about 150–200 square feet of selling space, and stocking soft drinks, bread, and a few canned goods. They are found in almost every block, and in some blocks there are two or three. They may be in the middle of the block or on a corner. They play a very important role in the economy and in the distribution of soft drinks. These stores are on a cash basis and rely on daily or three-times-a-week delivery. There is a problem of keeping them supplied with product. Frequently, even on a daily delivery basis, stores run out of product before the next delivery. Their lack of cash and small storage capacity prevents them from maintaining adequate inventory.

5.   House-to-house selling is employed as a means of distribution in large cities to customers in class A. Because of their high per capita consumption these households make large purchases, and deliveries are generally made on a once-a-week basis with one-to-two case drop. There is some question as to the profitability of house-to-house delivery. When franchises use this method of distribution it is generally considered to be more important as a promotional tool than as a profitable distribution method. Many feel that when they have good house-to-house delivery they also have greater total market penetration.

6.   A very small percentage of sales are made through vending machines. In most instances, the bottlers own the vending machines. They are placed in high traffic areas, such as factories, service stations, and schools. Vendors are activated by slugs which must be purchased from an attendant. The vendors are generally filled more than once a day.

Presently in Latino there are two sizes of vendor in general use: one, an upright vendor, has a capacity of about 110 bottles and costs 200,000 pesos; the other, a bar type with a top opening, has a capacity of about 200 bottles and costs 140,000 pesos. Vendors account for an extremely small part of the total sales.

7.   The large number of small accounts means that routes may have as many as 250 accounts to service with a typical case drop of one to two and a half cases serviced daily or three times weekly. In the U.S. a route has about 150 accounts with an average case drop of 30 to 50 cases, serviced weekly.

8.   Distribution to retail outlets is made by trucks with a driver/salesman

and one to three helpers. The driver/salesman has generally had experience as a helper, and is responsible for inventory on the truck and collections. The driver/salesmen are compensated by one of three methods: (1) straight commission, (2) salary plus commission, or (3) commission as an independent agent (an average income is $248 U.S. per month). The predominant method of compensation among the plants visited was salary plus commission. Some bottlers sold the driver/salesmen their trucks and dealt with them on an agency basis. The amount of compensation for driver/salesmen varied from franchise to franchise, but in most instances the driver/salesmen earned about twice as much as the helpers, who averaged $200 U.S. per month.

The responsibilities of the helpers included sales work. In fact, it appeared in some cases that personal contact with the retailer was most frequently made by helpers. In other words, the lowest-paid person in the sales/delivery team was responsible for the sales function. One franchise recognized this problem and had a system which required that the driver/salesmen visit each customer on the route at least once a week.

Supervisors are used by all franchises, and the number of routes supervised varied from as few as two to as many as five routes per supervisor. The supervisor's responsibility is primarily one of sales and customer contact. They are generally expected to call on accounts to help maintain rate of growth. They are also responsible for allocating promotional monies among the routes, and in some franchises are responsible for promotions with carnival trucks and similar affairs. There seemed to be no pattern as to former employment of supervisors. Some had been salesmen, others had been hired specifically for the position of supervisor.

9. Besides the normal promotion via newspaper, radio, and television, the local bottler spends a great deal of money on in-store displays, painting the stores with Bebe Cola signs, and conducting special events. Most bottlers maintain a supply of tables, chairs, and other equipment which they will lend to organizations as a public relations gesture.

10. B.C. is sold in 6½-, 12-, 16-, and 26-ounce sizes. The 12- and 16-ounce are the most predominant sizes, although there is some growth in the 26-ounce. The 6½-ounce bottle is sold mostly to bars, restaurants, and on special occasions. In the United States, the leading sizes are 16, 22, and 48 ounce. A 12-ounce bottle of B.C. sells at retail for 6 pesos, and the deposit on the bottle is 8 pesos. A very important part of the merchandising of B.C. in Latino is the cost of the glass. The bottler receives very high trippage (20–30 trips) on each of the returnable bottles, but the cost of each bottle is quite high.[2] In the United States, 10 trips per bottle is considered excellent. Thus, in Latino, while the price of glass is high, the high frequency of trips brings the cost per fill down. The general procedure is to charge each retail outlet for the glass as well as the liquid. Any replacement

---

[2] The number of trips means the number of times a bottle is refilled before it is lost or somehow destroyed.

of glass must be paid for by the retailer. Because the glass price is so high, it is frequently used as a promotional device: in some instances, both glass and liquid are given free, and in others the glass is sold but the liquid is given away. Many bottlers believe that Super Cola gives a large amount of glass away and is extremely competitive at this level. Glass is considered among the bottlers to be one of their most important problems— that is, how to overcome the high cost of glass and to compete with Super Cola which gives glass away. Many feel that their policy of charging for glass is necessary in their operation.

11.   Social Security payments provide for medical aid plus disability benefits. Total salary is paid while a person is disabled. Any difference between what Social Security pays and actual salary is made up by the company. The Social Security program in Latino is similar to that of the United States, but it also provides medical care and disability insurance. Retirement payments are quite low.

12.   Many bottlers don't plan for the growth of demand in their area, hence lack facilities for increased production. All of a sudden, demand far outstrips production. It takes approximately 12 months to increase production and in that time a tremendous vacuum can be created.

13.   There are 11 chains bottling B.C. Four of them have six plants each, one chain has three plants, two have three plants each, and one has four plants. There are approximately 50 B.C. plants in Latino, 37 of which are in chains (a chain is owned by one company).

14.   Super Cola has a larger number of small plants in all of Latino than B.C. has. For example, Super Cola has five plants in the largest cities in Latino versus only two for B.C. Since a larger plant is almost always more efficient than a smaller one, B.C. is probably more efficient in production than Super Cola.

15.   In general, the level of sophistication of managerial techniques used in the operation of franchises is low. There is, however, a very high interest in many plants to experiment with and use modern management methods. Some are beginning to employ new methods. On the average, however, the techniques employed are not fully tested or extremely sophisticated.

Controls such as forecasting, budgeting, market analysis, personnel evaluation, supervision, and motivation are not employed by all. There is growing awareness of the need for some of these more sophisticated management techniques, and, as mentioned above, many plants are experimenting with them.

Several of the bottlers visited had recently experienced a situation in which demand far exceeded supply, and for which their managerial efficiency was inadequate. When they passed from a seller's market to a buyer's market, or when Super Cola increased its competition, they immediately found that they could not cope as effectively as they would have liked to.

16.   In planning a program for B.C. bottlers, several major characteristics should be considered:

a. Domination of distribution by very small outlets and small sales (1–2½ cases) per account visited.

b. A very high per capita consumption of soft drinks, the majority of which are sold *cold*.

c. Competition from Super Cola.

d. Price control.

e. All sales on a cash basis.

f. High turnover in ownership of small stores.

g. Lack of depth and breadth in managerial talent.

h. Lack of experience in the use of many basic management tools.

17. A medium-sized plant in Latino manufactures and sells 4 million cases of product per year, a small plant about 2 million cases, and the largest in Latino over 25 million cases per year. In the United States, a small plant is one with a capacity of less than 1 million cases a year, while any plant having a capacity of more than 6 million would be considered very large.

18. The cost of transporting on large flatbed trucks from a production facility to a warehouse averages about a tenth of a centavo per kilometer per case.

19. One of the problems faced by most of the bottlers was a constant out-of-stock situation in the small stores. Even when the market preferred B.C., they would take Super Cola if B.C. wasn't available. The main cause of out-of-stock was that delivery could not be made frequently enough to keep small stores supplied. Most did not have enough money to carry more than 1–1½ cases at a time. They were also lacking in storage space. Some bottlers tried two deliveries per day, but found the cost too high to continue.

20. The small stores which predominate in the Latino market operate on a cash basis. Very little if any credit is extended by the bottler. One reason given was the high failure rate and high turnover in ownership.

21. The distribution process used in Latino is identical with that in the United States. There is a central bottling plant with warehousing. Trucks are dispatched daily from the plant to the market to call on the various outlets. At the end of the day, or when the route is serviced, they return empty, either for additional product or to be loaded for the following day.

QUESTIONS

1. As a consultant to B.C. Cola International, analyze this case carefully and suggest areas in which distribution efficiencies might be developed.

2. Based on the facts presented in the case, can you suggest a different means of distribution from what they are presently utilizing?

3. Can you suggest improvements in activities other than distribution? Discuss.

Case V–2

Marketing flying discs in Mexico*

A growing recreational activity in the United States is the sport of throwing flying discs. Flying discs, more commonly known by the registered brand name "Frisbee" owned by the Whamm-O Corp., are used in games ranging from backyard tossing from one person to another to organized flying disc tournaments on prescribed courses. The most well-known tournaments are sponsored by various regional groups of the National Frisbee Association. Flying discs appeal to all age groups and can be enjoyed with minimum training (if you can throw a paper airplane, you can toss a flying disc) to the most highly trained acrobatic free-style flying disc athletes, such as those that participate in regional and national tournaments. In the United States it is estimated that there are over 5 million flying discs in use. The majority are Frisbees, considered the best and only professional flying disc made.

Because of the widespread appeal of flying discs in the United States, three business associates—Roger Blake, owner of a recreational sports store and director of a regional Frisbee association; Jose Gutierez, a bank vice president employed in the United States but a citizen of Mexico; and Eloise Dunn, a marketing consultant—are considering the possibility of seeking a franchise to manufacture and market flying discs internationally. Preliminary research indicated some marketing of flying discs in several European countries, Great Britain, and Mexico. The success has been spotty in some cases, outstanding in others with sales resulting in a growing demand; in still others, initial sales acceptance but no sustained growth.

Roger Blake and Jose Gutierez approached Eloise Dunn with the idea of organizing a company to market flying discs internationally. At the initial meeting, Blake and Gutierez presented a brief outline of their idea and plans up to that time to Dunn. Briefly, Blake, involved with flying discs since his youth and completely involved as a business person, was certain that the appeal of the flying disc would be as great elsewhere as it has been in the United States if properly marketed. Gutierez indicated that in Mexico active sports participation of all types was widespread, and his own experience with flying dics led him to believe it would appeal to others. Both felt that the flying disc had not been more successful outside the United States because of inadequate marketing rather than lack of interest. They felt that such was the case in those situations with which they were familiar, primarily Germany and Mexico. While the flying disc is quickly learned,

---

* This case is developed on an actual situation but all dates, names, countries, and incidences have been altered to protect the identity of the actual participants.

to gain widespread acceptance it requires an introduction with a great deal of promotion activity to acquaint people with the new sport. Further, for sustained acceptance of the sport a continuous marketing program is necessary with adequate publicity, promotion, and distribution. Because of their convictions that proper marketing, both at the introduction and during the growth period, is necessary to successfully introduce the flying disc to a country, they went to Dunn for marketing expertise.

Roger Blake was experienced with the marketing of flying dics in the United States; besides being regional director of the Frisbee Association and sponsoring and developing several Frisbee tournaments, Blake also had produced and directed a 20-minute film on disc flying. The film was well received by many groups and Blake felt it was an effective promotional device for selling discs to new users. The film dealt with free-style flying disc competitions and was also an excellent illustration of the versatility and general appeal of flying disc games. Since Jose Gutierez was experienced in banking in Mexico and was "well connected" there, he was primarily interested in exploring the potential for the flying discs in Mexico. Initial investigation revealed that discs had been introduced to Mexico a number of years ago but presently were not being sold there. In fact, the few discs in Mexico were generally found in tourist areas such as Acapulco and Mazatlan and probably were brought down by U.S. citizens on vacation. Jose indicated that during a recent two-week vacation in Mazatlan he observed flying discs being used there by Mexican citizens which gave him some assurance that Mexicans would buy flying discs if they were properly marketed. Eloise Dunn agreed to participate in exploring the feasibility of marketing flying discs internationally. Since one of the three was experienced in Mexico, they decided to explore the possibility of acquiring a franchise in Mexico. Ms. Dunn agreed to call Ex-O Corp., a major U.S. flying disc manufacturer, to discuss the possibilities of acquiring a franchise for Mexico.

A call to the international franchisor for flying discs produced the following information: Ex-O Corp. had franchised the manufacture of their flying discs in Mexico about six years ago to Alejandro Garcia; the franchisee had not marketed any under the agreement but had purchased four molds and had the exclusive right to market the flying discs in Mexico. Since Garcia had not produced any flying discs within the time limit set by the franchise agreement, the international franchisor considered the contract void. Dunn inquired about the requirements for a current franchise to produce flying discs in Mexico. The international director indicated that the terms of the contract could be negotiated, but would include some initial payment for the right to an exclusive franchise in Mexico, royalty on all items produced, as well as the costs of molds sold exclusively by Ex-O Corp. However, because of their previous experience he would be reluctant to grant a franchise without a strong commitment by the new franchisee to market the discs effectively. He indicated he would like to see a tentative marketing plan of any potential franchise for Mexico before giving more details. He also suggested that since the former franchisee owned four molds he should be contacted about selling the molds and also about his current situation. The director gave the last-known address and telephone number of Garcia to Dunn.

In a second meeting of the three business associates, Dunn relayed the information acquired from the Ex-O Corp. They agreed to continue the preliminary investigation. Jose Gutierez was returning to Mexico on business and agreed to contact Alejandro Garcia for information on the existing molds. Dunn indicated that if information from Garcia and additional preliminary information on Mexico warranted they should draft a preliminary marketing plan to present to the Ex-O Corp.

Upon Gutierez's return to the United States he presented the following facts: Garcia had purchased four molds for the standard promotional flying disc. Garcia's primary business is plastic injection molding; he acquired the flying disc franchise after seeing a promotional flying disc in the United States because he felt that it was something he could sell primarily as a promotional piece. The idea was for a company to buy flying discs with a logo printed on them for free distribution as a sales promotion device. His first contact after acquiring the franchise was a major U.S. snack food company. In a contract with this snack food company he produced 50,000 with the company's logo. However, the project never materialized because in Mexico all promotions where merchandise is given away free must be approved by the government. Garcia had bought the molds, produced 50,000 flying discs, but the snack food company could not get a permit to distribute the flying discs. At this juncture, Mr. Garcia gave up the flying disc business. He indicated he tried to market a few, not spending any promotional dollars, but felt he did not know how to market the flying disc and further, could not find anybody who could demonstrate its use. Mr. Garcia said that as far as he knew no one else in Mexico was producing flying discs, that he had not produced any since his contact with the snack food company, that he had no continued interest in producing the flying disc, and that he was willing to sell the molds for $1,000 (U.S.) apiece for a total of $4,000 (he stated that the original cost was $3,000 apiece).

Gutierez also reported that Mr. Garcia produced the flying disc at about 30 cents (U.S.). Gutierez brought along a model of one of Garcia's discs and Blake indicated that it was a Regular model, the lowest quality of the line of four. The molds that Garcia has produce a Regular model. Ex-O Corp.'s discs are manufactured in four models: Regular, All-American, Pro, and Super Pro. The basic differences between the models were weight and balance, the Regular the lightest and the Super Pro the heaviest and best balanced. Ex-O Corp. has also recently introduced a new line they call the "World Class" Disc which is differentiated primarily by weight. World Class Discs are gaining in popularity in the United States as flying disc competition increases in importance. Blake believes that as flying disc competition increases in importance and the market becomes more sophisticated, the World Class will become the biggest seller in the United States. He said that the Super Pro and all of the World Class were well balanced and designed in such a way that maximum flexibility in flying styles could be accommodated. For amateur disc flyers, the Regular would be adequate, but as a person develops style and skill, the better-engineered and designed models have greater appeal. Although still popular in the U.S. market, the Regular or promotional discs are not much in demand by experienced disc throwers.

Gutierez also checked pricing in Mexico and found that similar items (toys and other sports items) on the market were priced between 200 and 400 pesos apiece (about $2.25 and $4.50 U.S. at an exchange rate of 92 pesos per dollar). He felt that the Pro model or Super Pro model could be sold in Mexico for 600 pesos ($6.50 U.S.). Jose contacted representatives of two major chain stores in Mexico to explain the product and their intentions to introduce it to Mexico to explain the product and their intentions to introduce it to Mexico through such stores. All indicated they would like a presentation of the product, thought it probably would sell, that they would place small initial orders, and, if the product sold well, they would include it as a regular product line in their stores. They did note that there would have to be some sustained demand for them to continue to stock and sell the item. The stores he visited were Comercial Mexicana, similar to Woolco or Target chains, with 26 stores throughout Mexico, and Tiendas Aurerra, comparable to K-Mart, with 45 stores mainly in the central part of Mexico. He also talked to Puerto de Liverpool, which is similar to the May Co. stores and has four stores in Mexico City. Jose also determined that the flying discs could be imported into Mexico with a 75-percent ad valorem tax; the importation permit would fall under the recreational plastic toys code number 9703A002.

The three associates were optimistic about Gutierez's findings in Mexico and felt that prospects were good for marketing the flying discs there; they also decided that if they proceeded they would definitely have to purchase Garcia's molds in order to prevent possible pirating should they become successful. Further discussion about a marketing plan raised the following questions: What model or models should they sell in Mexico? Roger Blake, because of his experience at the Pro level felt they should not bother with the Regular line but introduce the World Class Disc, Jose Gutierez countered that while the World Class is becoming increasingly successful in the United States (an established market), the Mexican market is new so they should start with the most inexpensive model, gain widespread distribution, then develop the more sophisticated items.

They agreed they would have to buy the molds from Garcia, but should they invest in new molds and manufacture the product in Mexico, an approach which would require substantial investment? (Jose assured them he knew someone in the plastics business who could produce from a standard mold in quantities close to 30 cents U.S.). Or should they import the flying discs to determine if there was an initial market? Jose Gutierez suggested it might be wise to import flying discs into Mexico and conduct a preliminary test market to get an idea about price, potential demand, and so forth.

Should they go with the Ex-O Corp. or some other manufacturer of flying discs? All agreed that if they were going to the expense of introducing the product, they should go with the most recognized brand name which is Ex-O. Also, they reasoned that should they successfully develop a product which was not an Ex-O product, the Ex-O Corp. could come in and sweep the market based on demand that the three associates had generated. Dunn proposed that they put their ideas down in terms of a tentative program, the basis of which they would develop as a presentation to the Ex-O Corp. She reminded them that the Ex-O Corp, did not want to discuss the situation without seeing a proposal of the program for Mexico. The meeting ended with the agreement that Dunn would put together a tentative program for marketing the flying discs in Mexico along with a proposed budget that would exclude the cost of molds purchased from Garcia and the franchise payment to Ex-O. She would formulate the proposal primarily on the information they had already gathered and perhaps some basic information on market characteristics in Mexico.

Consider that you are Ms. Eloise Dunn and prepare a tentative marketing plan for the introduction and marketing of flying discs in Mexico. In your plan, answer the following questions: (1) Should they buy the molds? (2) Should they buy Ex-O rights to their discs?, and (3) Should the introduction only be in Mexico City or throughout Mexico? Below are media prices to help you put together a budget.

There are five national TV channels in Mexico; their ad prices average for:

AAA time (19:30 p.m. to 24:00 p.m.) . . .30 seconds—$632   60 seconds—$1,264 (U.S.)
AA time (17:30 p.m. to 19:30 p.m.) . . .30 seconds—$437   60 seconds—$ 874 (U.S.)
A time (24:00 p.m. to 17:30 p.m.) . . .30 seconds—$300   60 seconds—$ 600 (U.S.)

The newspaper ads run on the average for:

1 Page . . . . .$1,441 (U.S.) one day
½ Page . . . . .$ 852 (U.S.) one day
¼ Page . . . . .$ 417 (U.S.) one day

The newspapers are "Novedades," "Excelsior," "Universal," "El Heraldo," "El Sol de Mexico." All these are national newspapers with an average daily circulation of 250,000 papers.

There is one national newspaper, "Esto," which publishes only sports and its rates are:

1 Page . . . . .$565 (U.S.) one day
½ Page . . . . .$282 (U.S.) one day
¼ Page . . . . .$141 (U.S.) one day

The TV stations and the newspapers have staff to design ads.

CASE V-3

Hypermarkets*

Many marketing ideas have first been developed in the United States and then have been adopted by companies in other countries. The hypermarket, however, is an exception. It originated in France in 1963, spread throughout Europe, and has slowly moved to the United States. It essentially is a shopping center under one roof with both wholesaling and retailing combined in the same area.

The hypermarket usually consists of a one-story building with a warehouse-type appearance (exposed beams and bare walls) with 200,000 plus square feet of selling space. There are over 40,000 permanent items for sale and

* Case written by Gregory M. Gazda and Mary J. Molenaar, San Diego State University.

forty or more checkout counters, usually all in a row. The goods are preticketed and coded and are stacked in tall aisles, sometimes as high as 18 feet or higher. Often they utilize very modular display containers made of metal, cardboard, or plastic. The goods are usually moved onto the display floor in pallets by forklifts.

Volume selling and low prices are stressed, which in Europe results in savings of up to 25 percent over conventional stores. The assortment of goods is extensive, ranging from food and drug items to bicycles, appliances, clothing, cameras, and so on. Each product line is short, utilizing a merchandising assortment technique called *cherry picking*. This technique essentially limits the choice to top-demand items. Another distinguishing characteristic of hypermarkets is the attempt to create a circus or fun-type atmosphere. Swinging mobiles are evident as well as loud speaker announcements of special deals. Sometimes baby-sitting services are available for mothers while they shop, and a band may provide entertainment. The hypermarket is a one-stop shopping store, but is impractical when shopping for just a few replacement items.

Assignment

1.   Choose a store in your city or a nearby city which most resembles a hypermarket.
2.   Travel to that store and spend at least 20 minutes analyzing it in terms of size, merchandise assortment, aesthetics, and so on.
3.   How does the store you are analyzing differ from a hypermarket?
4.   What do you like about the store? Dislike?
5.   What factors do you think will aid or hinder the spread of hypermarkets in the United States?
6.   What factors have made hypermarkets so successful in Europe?

CASE V-4

A Case study of production orientation: Malayan canned pineapple[1]

Malaya is the third largest producer of canned pineapple in the world. Its canned pineapple is sold in more than 80 countries, of which four, namely the United Kingdom, United States, West Germany, and Canada, account for about 80 percent of the total exports. About 40 percent of the canned pineapple imports into the United Kingdom come from Malaya, thus giving it the largest share of the market. In 1938 Malaya had an almost complete monopoly of the United Kingdom market for canned pineapple, but in 1968 its share was reduced to about 50 percent and finally, in 1980 this was further reduced to 38 percent. This phenomenon can be attributed to two factors: (1) the general decline in the share of the canned pineapple in the canned fruit market and (2) the lack of aggressive sales policy by Malaya.

A new marketing organization called the Pineapple Industry Marketing Corporation (PIMC) was established by the MPIB in 1975, to promote, manage, and market Malayan canned pineapple overseas. The existence of the PIMC has somewhat strengthened the position of the industry in the face of stiff international competition, but it has not been able to function smoothly. This is due in large measure to its lack of effective enforcement to maintain fixed minimum prices. The latter is particularly true with regard to the sales of canned pineapple to the United Kingdom where the many agents were found to indulge in price undercutting.[2] This rather disorganized marketing situation in the United Kingdom led to the establishment of a private limited company in 1978 called Consolidated Pineapple Sales Limited (CPS). All former functions of the PIMC were taken over by this company; and, in addition, it was also to act as the principal for all agents in the United Kingdom and undertake the necessary trading functions of accepting orders and processing them. The PIMC still caters for the other international markets.

---

[1] From "A Case Study of Production Orientation: Malayan Canned Pineapple," *European Journal of Marketing*, 6, no. 3.

[2] There are 20 agents to handle Malayan canned pineapple in the United Kingdom compared with other large supplying countries like South Africa, Philippines, the United States, and Australia which are known to have between one to three distributors each.

Distribution of canned pineapple and leading brand by country of origin

Country	Leading brand	Shops carrying the brand		Shops carrying country's canned pineapple	
		Number	Percent of total	Number	Percent of total
Malaya	Princess	45	22.5	151	75.5
South Africa	Libby's	95	47.5	118	59.0
Philippines	Del Monte	84	42.0	84	42.0
U.S.A. (Hawaii)	Del Monte	41	20.5	72	36.0
Australia	Golden Circle	52	26.0	56	28.0
Kenya	KC	18	9.0	21	10.5
Taiwan	Typhone	13	6.5	19	9.5
Other countries	Three Feathers	15	7.5	83	41.5

Source: Data based on a survey made by the Malayan Pineapple Industry Board of 200 retail outlets in the Brighton, Birmingham, and London areas.

Distribution.   The consumption of canned pineapple by social class and region does not show marked variation.[3] Canned pineapple is also purchased frequently by a fairly large proportion of the population (26 percent). These market characteristics would undoubtedly call for adoption of a policy of intensive distribution which can only be implemented successfully if retailers can be persuaded to stock. Faced with the problem of the multiplicity of brands, retailers would naturally choose brands or types of canned pineapple which they consider to have popular appeal and high turnover. Del Monte will definitely be featured in most supermarkets and other grocery shops because of its reputed high quality, followed by Libby's, Golden Circle, and any one of the Malayan brands. Malayan canned pineapple is featured in most, if not all, retail outlets, but it is impossible for any particular brand to have great advantage because of the lack of popular appeal. The main reason why Malayan canned pineapple is stocked by retailers is because Malaya is the only country supplying pineapple cubes and spiral slices which are popular among some consumers. The table shows that although Malaya's canned pineapple is widely distributed in the United Kingdom, representing about 76 percent of all shops surveyed, her leading brand, Princess, accounts for only 22.5 percent, as compared with Del Monte, Libby's, and Golden Circle. Malaya's unique position as the only supplier of the special cuts cannot be guaranteed indefinitely, as other low-

---

[3] Proportions of housewives reputed buying by social class and region*:

Social Class	Percent	Region	Percent
AB	30	South/South West	29
C1	35	London	35
C2	31	West Midlands/Wales	30
DE	30	North	32
		Scotland	31

* Source: Libby Food Ltd.

cost producing countries may try to produce them in the future. She must, therefore, try to strengthen her position in the market by creating consumer awareness and relating these cuts to a particular brand.

The structural changes taking place in the distribution trade, with the counter service share of the grocery trade declining through the years, make it necessary for canners to modify their merchandising strategies to suit the changing situation: *inter alia,* changes in the channels of distribution; and changes in approach towards branding, packaging, designing of packs; and changes in advertising and promotional strategies.[4] With the exception of sales to the Wholesale Cooperative Society, all Malayan canned pineapple is channeled through agents to the retailers, caterers, and manufacturers in the United Kingdom. For private labeling, the large retailers, other than cooperatives, have to order through the United Kingdom agents rather than direct to the canners. In view of the increase in the share of the grocery trade accounted for by the self-service shops, Malaya's continuing policy of avoiding direct sales to the large retailers will probably do more harm than good. This alone may be a reason for part of the decline in Malaya's share of the canned pineapple market.

The canned fruit market is very competitive and requires a dynamic marketing approach. At the moment, the Malayan canners interfere with the market only by offering special promotional allowances to the agents, through the Malayan Pineapple Industry Board's office in London, for certain slow-moving packs. But the promotional allowances are relatively small and periodic in nature, and therefore do not have much impact on the trade and consumers. A more aggressive sales policy would be to include in the marketing plans and strategies, effective advertising and promotions, supply of promotional materials, a sales and merchandising task force, continuous collection and gathering of market information on competition, trends and consumer research. The present organization is unlikely to be suited to the desired policy objective of increasing sales, and its retention will be a contributing factor to the decline in sales.

An office is urgently required in the United Kingdom to streamline and coordinate all marketing efforts here. It is rather surprising to find that, though Britain accounts for the largest share of the total overseas sales of Malayan canned pineapple, there is no office in the U.K. to manage and control the market. The Malayan Pineapple Industry Board's office in London is only carrying out regulatory and supervisory work. Ironically, one of the canneries maintains a sales office in the U.S.A. where Malaya's exports account for less than those to the United Kingdom.

---

[4] The share of the grocery trade accounted for by the counter service shops declined from 41.8 percent in February 1976 to 33.2 percent at the end of 1978. *Source:* Nielsen Retail Report.

QUESTION

Should Malayan pineapple actively pursue a marketing program for Malayan pineapple to effectively compete with Del Monte, Libby, and others? Develop a marketing plan to increase market share in the United Kingdom.

Case V-5

Masudaya Saitoh Boeki K.K.*

History and organization. The Masudaya Saitoh Boeki K.K. (hereinafter referred to as Masudaya) has been associated with the making of toys for over two hundred years. Although the company incorporated only 60 years ago, the official founding year of the company is listed as 1724. At that time Masudaya was a maker of dolls, a cottage industry in the Asakusa district of present-day Tokyo. During the Russo-Japanese war (1904–05), the firm began to make toy swords for the local market, and gradually expanded its manufacturing of toys. Today it ranks among the top three toy companies of Japan, with a capitalization of 100 million yen and yearly sales of 4,500 million yen. Reportedly, its financial structure is sounder than that of its leading competitors, and in that sense it is considered the top toy company in Japan.

The company is engaged in the business of manufacturing and distributing toys and dolls to domestic and foreign markets as well as importing toys and other products. It specializes in mechanical, metallic, plastic toys and dolls, and over 600 distinct items are offered in its product line. Manufacturing is accomplished through exclusive and nonexclusive makers. In order to facilitate sales, two other companies are included in the organization: Masudaya K.K. deals with domestic sales to department stores in the Tokyo-Yokohama area, and Masutoku Toy K.K. is concerned with direct exports worldwide, the United States being the principal buyer. For four consecutive years, 1964 to 1967, Masutoku Toy K.K. received an award from the Japanese Ministry of International Trade and Industry for its contribution to Japanese exports.

---

* This case was prepared by Terrence C. Kennedy, Sophia University, Tokyo, as a basis for class discussion. Copyright in Japan by Sophia University Socio-Economic Institute.

In order to maintain and expand international markets, promotion has been increased to this area. Products are introduced at the Japan International Toy Fair held every year at the Tokyo Industrial Hall. A New York liaison office and showroom serves customers from Canada and the United States. Two showrooms at the main office in Tokyo display complete lines of toys and dolls. In addition, Playwell, a retail store, was opened in 1974 in the shopping arcade of the Imperial Hotel, Tokyo, for the convenience of buyers visiting Japan. It is hoped that Playwell will be the forerunner of a chain of international Playwells in the United States and Europe that will retail Masudaya and other manufacturers' toys.

Foreign sales. Masudaya's principal foreign customer is the United States, which absorbs nearly 70 percent of all export sales. Since sales are not permitted by American law, a liaison office with a staff of three was established in New York City; its main function is to negotiate with prospective buyers, investigate credit standings, and report on market conditions.

Foreign sales are broken down into direct and indirect sales. The latter, through eight principal wholesalers, account for nearly 55 percent of foreign sales. Direct sales are handled by the Masutoku Toy K.K. It was established because it is cheaper to import into the United States through an intermediary company.

For toys, foreign procurement shows a general pattern. Buyers come to Japan for exclusive procurement. Toys are designed and manufactured according to a buyer's specifications or a modified basic model. At the same time, original products are displayed. Competition is keen. A buyer usually visits all possible toy manufacturers, gathers samples, and then makes a selection.

Masudaya aims at a medium-price line of toys, items that sell in the United States at about $10. Although Masudaya has no control over the retail selling price in the United States, it has been found that an $8 item is one that would retail for half or less in Japan. High-priced, quality goods such as radio-controlled vehicles are also marketed. The export toy market is primarily seasonal, Christmas being the prime season. Under a long-term contract, Masudaya has provided toys for other trademarks; the toys are shipped blank and the trademark is added at the point of destination.

Because a major marketing problem is space and freight, Masudaya limits itself to small- and medium-size products. Forty square feet equal one freight ton. It costs $32 per freight ton to ship to San Francisco, $40 to New York. Freight costs for Masudaya's famous line of trains average one dollar a dozen. Ocean freight, landing, and import charges, and inland freight all add up—the total amount largely determined by the size of the toy.

Profit is about the same in both domestic and foreign sales. However, the latter allow the company to sell its products in a cash-earning market.

Let us now turn to what is for Masudaya a most meaningful investment decision: the opening in March 1980 of a retail outlet called Playwell.

The number of foreign visitors coming to Japan has increased steadily year after year, and so has their average length of stay. They buy not only cameras, pearls, and so on, but also toys; Japan has become a famous toy maker, and toys are convenient to carry home as presents. Toys furthermore do not require a sizable expenditure on the part of purchasers. The Japanese Hotel Association decided for these reasons that toy stores should be located in hotel arcades among other stores that cater to foreign tourists. Since these arcades are a limited, specialized market, the hotels prefer approaching manufacturers rather than retail outlets that generally are not able to put up the required capital investment.

Playwell—Tokyo.   Playwell is located in the new Imperial Hotel arcade in Tokyo. This came about through personal contacts. Mr. Okubo, owner of Okubo Kyodai Shokai and personal friend of Mr. Saitoh, had a jewelry shop in the old Imperial Hotel and planned to move into the new arcade after the rebuilding of the hotel. Mr. Okubo convinced his friend that he should open an arcade toy shop, and approached the hotel management in Mr. Saitoh's favor. The hotel people then formally approached Masudaya Saitoh Boeki K.K., reportedly stating that the plan of a toy shop in the arcade would be given up if it was not Masudaya's. Such a shop would have to be a first-class store, one that would enhance the image of the Imperial Hotel. It was therefore essential that only a strong company with good financial backing should run the store; of all the leading toy makers of Japan, Masudaya was the only one to fulfill these requirements. Mr. Saitoh accepted the invitation and, without bank help, put up an initial investment of 70 million yen.

Reactions from the trade were favorable, for two main reasons. One reason was that the Imperial Hotel arcade must be entered from the hotel lobby, and Playwell's clientele would consist mainly of hotel guests and others who for various reasons would be visiting the hotel. Tokyoites are not considered part of the clientele, because it is felt that few people would enter the hotel to buy toys, and, further, because of a slight markup in price, local customers would shop elsewhere. The other reason was that only 20 percent of Playwell's stock was to be composed of Masudaya products, the remainder being competitor brands. Foreign buyers visiting Playwell would be able to inspect and compare a wide range of products. This convenience for foreign buyers has been stressed by Masudaya in its dealings with the trade. Further domestic expansion will not be opposed by wholesalers, so long as it is limited to hotel and airport arcades.

At Playwell, served by a staff of nine, sales were brisk from the start. It was estimated that 80 percent of the customers were foreign, mostly American. Masudaya feels that in addition to being another source of sales and profit, Playwell has contributed to its image, since the Imperial Hotel has a worldwide reputation. Mr. Saitoh is quite satisfied with the performance, and would like to establish a Playwell chain stretching from Hawaii through the United States to Europe.

The Playwell Chain. A current objective is to establish a chain of retail stores called Playwell. First, thought was given to domestic expansion. The inclination was to investigate possibilities of establishing Playwell stores in Tokyo and other cities in Japan.

Two immediate problems were encountered. Wholesalers are completely independent. The standard relationship between a wholesaler and manufacturer in the toy trade, as described earlier, is rather in the form of a gentleman's agreement concerning sales. If a particular product becomes a best seller, the ties between the manufacturer and wholesaler deepen. Masudaya has received awards for some of its products and generally has found that its product line is well received in Japan. Therefore, if a Playwell chain were established in Japan, all items, including Masudaya's, would have to be distributed through the existing wholesale network, Even if this were acceptable to Masudaya and the wholesalers, an attempt to open a Playwell store in, say, the Ginza area, would probably bring pressure from the Ginza Retail Stores Association on the wholesalers to oppose such an expansion. In all probability, any sales location in Japan that would be profitable for Masudaya would also draw protest from the Toy Retailers Association, unless domestic expansion were restricted to hotels and airports. Masudaya investigated the possibilities of entering the new Narita International Airport arcade, opened after considerable delays in 1978, but, at the time of this writing, had made no decision. If an arcade of the Imperial Hotel class were found, the company would not hesitate to invest in another toy shop.

For all practical purposes, the establishment of a retail chain in Japan appears impossible. Desiring to diversify into the retail business, Masudaya is now looking at overseas markets, where toy stores are good business. A Playwell chain could enhance the image of Masutoku K.K. and, at the same time, provide the means of diversification that Mr. Saitoh is seeking. The entry into foreign markets will be slow and gradual, and the company is the first to admit that its knowledge and experience in retailing is extremely limited. Mr. Saitoh has personally checked possible locations in Hawaii and has purchased market information from a well-known market research company. Arrangements are being made to finance the operation through Japanese banks. As a long-range plan, Masudaya is considering upgrading its New York liaison office to a New York branch, which, in turn, would be able to approach American banks for funds. At the beginning, Playwell management in foreign countries would be Japanese; it is hoped that it would soon be taken over by local nationals. It has been found that even in the United States Playwell may meet opposition from wholesaler groups if some type of understanding is not obtained. While a Playwell entry into the United States is still at the formative stage, Masudaya is eager to enter and is confident that its new endeavor will be successful.

APPENDIX

Masudaya's domestic and foreign sales (as percent of total)

	Domestic	Foreign
1980	60.0%	40.0%
1979	52.0	48.0
1970	55.0	45.0
1977	49.5	50.5
1976	45.0	55.0

Playwell's sales in 1980 (by month)

Month	Days	Sales	Sales per day	Cumulated sales
March 1980	22	2,853,677	129,700	2,853,677
April	30	4,433,465	137,800	7,287,142
May	31	4,828,410	155,700	12,115,552
June	30	4,758,326	158,600	16,873,878
July	31	5,498,065	177,000	22,350,403
August	31	6,390,658	306,000	28,741,062
September	30	6,280,425	209,333	34,921,487
October	31	6,338,784	210,000	43,026,831
November	30	5,700,000	190,000	47,020,000

Playwell's monthly expense statement (August 1980)

Building (rental)	¥ 452,100
Salaries	600,000
Bank interest	400,000
Building (utilities)	37,670
Trade association fee	50,200
Electricity	15,000
Telephone	10,000
Packaging costs	70,000
Lunch (employees)	22,500
Transportation (employees)	13,000
Miscellaneous	40,000
Total	¥1,710,470

Playwell's break-even points

A. Break-even points
    per month ¥4,750,000
    per day 158,000
B. Other costs
    Depreciation 590,000
    Fixed running cost 1,710,000

PART SIX

CORPORATE CONTEXT OF MARKETING

CHAPTERS:

CASES:

Chapter 21

Financial requirements for international marketing

Marketing and finance are inextricably intertwined with overall corporate planning, goals, and objectives; policies and decisions in each have a profound effect on the others. Without proper financial support, marketing activities cannot attain their ultimate potential; and, in turn, without adequate cash flows and profits generated by marketing activities, corporate ability to achieve full growth and development potential is limited. It is generally thought that financial considerations are the primary domain of the finance officer, but as any international marketer can attest, the financier's concerns are also those of the marketer.

Marketers have an intense interest in financial functions because money is the basic tool for facilitating marketing activities. Effective financial arrangements significantly strengthen competitive marketing positions. With adequate monetary resources at their disposal, marketing managers can effect greater profits by lowering costs or by increasing sales volume. Adequate inventories can be maintained if funds are available—a critical variable in international business where restocking can take months. The business with plentiful purchasing power usually can buy merchandise more cheaply by buying directly or in quantity, or have access to an array of sources by being able to pay cash. Plentiful money can permit a marketer to build the marketing channels which will be most effective for the firm—regardless of cost. Furthermore, advertising can be treated as a capital expenditure if adequate funds are available. Ability to finance customer purchases is another business-building, competitive activity often denied to underfinanced companies.

In addition to being concerned with the purely marketing aspects of financing, the marketer must also be aware of the company's financial objectives, the levels of profit required from operations, the expected balance between long- and short-term profits, and whether corporate policy calls for money to be repatriated or further invested in the customers' countries. Marketing decisions are directly affected by decisions regarding availability of funds for marketing, choice of profit center, cost of money, required rates of return, profit shifting, and opportunity cost factors.

As a company moves more deeply into the international arena, the interdependence of marketing and financial activities increases and places greater

691

financial demands on the company. Two areas of impact are: (1) the increased need for working capital, and (2) the enhanced financial risk resulting from fluctuating foreign exchange. This chapter emphasizes the financial
requirements of international marketing; it considers the causes for increased
need of funds and the sources of those funds, and the causes for increased
financial risk and methods of minimizing the risks. The entire treatment is
concerned less with the mechanics of international finance than with the
strategic marketing implications related to finance.

CAPITAL NEEDS FOR INTERNATIONAL MARKETING

Distance, time lags, tariffs, taxes, financial-participation requirements, exchange restrictions, fluctuating monetary values, and inadequate local financial strength are all elements differentiating the problems of financing international marketing activities from those related to domestic marketing. Effective
management of the financial functions of marketing can be a strategic factor
not only affecting profits but having great impact on the company's ability
to develop marketing channels.

Time lags caused by distance and crossing international borders add
cost elements to international marketing that make cash flow planning especially important. Even in a relatively simple transaction, money may be tied
up for months while goods are being shipped from one part of the world
to another; customs clearance may add days, weeks, or months; payment
may be held up while the international payment documents are being transferred from one nation to another; and breakage, commercial disputes, or
governmental restrictions can add further delay. When the cost of money
was 8 percent as in the early 1970s, this was less of a problem than today
when money costs are approaching 20 percent or more.

Slower cash flow from the international operation demands significant
injections to maintain cash position. In domestic markets, incremental payments may be received for a product in the process of custom development
or for which there is a long production process. While such terms may be
available in international contracts, typically, the manufacturer or developer
of such goods for foreign customers must wait until the products are actually
produced and delivered before receiving even partial payment. Nearly every international transaction encounters some kind of time lag during which
the marketing financing must be provided. Financial time lags exist even
when a company is dealing with its own subsidiaries or branches in overseas
operations.

Besides greater demands for working capital, the international marketer
may have to make long-term capital investments as well. In some instances
markets will be closed to a foreign business unless all or some portion of
the product is manufactured locally.

If a market is of sufficient size, it may be necessary to make additional
investment in production capacity and to incur added financial burdens

to gain access. Extra capital would be required if production could be accomplished in existing facilities had the host country not imposed restrictions of local manufacture. Thus, international marketing activities frequently require supplemental financing for (1) working capital and (2) capital investment.

Working capital requirements

Because of time lags, shipping costs, duties, higher start-up costs, inventory cost, market penetration costs, and increased financial needs for trade and channel credit, foreign operations typically require larger amounts of working capital than domestic activities operating at the same volume levels. Travel costs alone can consume working capital funds; in one instance, a U.S. firm discovered it was spending more on travel in a foreign market than on salaries. Even though costs can be kept under control through careful and creative management, there is a need for additional funds to cover the added costs of financing international operations.

Start-up costs. Larger amounts of working capital are frequently required to cover the start-up cost of a company entering new international markets. Such costs can come as a surprise to the firm accustomed to operating in a familiar domestic market. A firm may find it must pay for information usually assumed or acquired without cost in the home country. Start-up costs also include the legal and incorporational costs, establishing an office, purchase of licenses, and so on. Although illegal, start-up costs sometimes include payments to governments or government officials for the opportunity to do business in their country. Marketing research can become a major expense, particularly if a company has to research three or four countries before embarking on a business enterprise in any one of them. Even if the business is not started or does not succeed, start-up costs generally are not recoverable.

Inventory. The marketer's effectiveness in managing inventories can have considerable effect on the financial requirements of this function. Adequate servicing of overseas markets may require goods to be inventoried in several locations; one company which uses two factory warehouses for the entire United States needed six foreign distribution points which together handled less merchandise than either U.S. outlet. Slow transportation means maintenance of relatively larger inventories and even political factors can influence inventory levels. Some countries impose such severe currency controls that it is almost impossible to maintain adequate inventory levels or reasonable supplies of spare parts. In another instance, a pesticide manufacturer laid in a two-year inventory of one of its products because the Mexican government had notified it that the border would be closed to the product after three months' notice. Several years elapsed with no notice; but, to stay in the market as long as possible, the company was compelled to invest several hundred thousand dollars in surplus inventory.

Slower transportation and longer distances when shipping over water mean inventory turnover can be lengthened considerably over the customary time for domestic operations. Add loading and unloading time and the time in transit for an overseas shipment from a Midwest manufacturer in the United States to Europe and transit time can take as much as two months or longer. If your product is entering a congested port such as La Guaira in Venezuela, there may be a month delay just to get unloaded. The additional time required for delivery increases the capital requirements needed to finance inventories.

An entirely new type of inventory financing requirement is sometimes foisted on the marketer when he is forced to accept countertrade goods to close a transaction with a currency-short country or is forced to buy back goods as part of a financing package for capital equipment. Unless the goods are readily disposable, the company may find itself carrying them for significant periods of time before markets are found.

Imagine the problems of a West German company if they had accepted Mongolia's offer of a 150 million-year-old skeleton of a dinosaur as payment in a countertrade deal (the company declined). Obviously not all countertrades result in such unique products being offered. However, most goods offered in countertrade do not have a readily available market or there would be no need to offer them in countertrade in the first place. As a consequence, marketers either must hold the goods, incur the expense of marketing them, or discount them to get them out of inventory. In any one of the three situations, inventory costs are increased as a result of countertrading.[1]

Market penetration costs.   It is difficult to classify market penetration costs since they can be thought of as capital investments or as current expenditures. In accounting terms, most marketing penetration investment is considered current expenditure; from a planning standpoint, investments in promotion, building channels, and personnel actually represent a long-term investment of a sunk cost nature. Companies which do not maintain production or inventory facilities overseas may still have a very large investment in attempting market penetration.

The costs associated with promotion and advertising are obvious and basically parallel the kind of expenditures necessary to open new markets in the United States except they may be greater in foreign markets relative to anticipated sales. Markets are smaller, media usually more expensive, and multiple media generally required; these and other similar factors push investment up.

It is never inexpensive to establish a channel of distribution, but again, the complications of international distribution can require extra-large channel investments. Foreign middlemen are seldom adequately financed and may

---

[1] Schuster, Falko, "Barter Arrangements With Money: The Modern Form of Compensation Trading," *Columbia Journal of World Business,* Fall 1980, p. 61.

require extensive long-term credit if they are to carry adequate inventories and offer their customers adequate credit. The American firm's competitive position may be weaker in the world markets than in domestic markets because of the number of competitors vying for customers in certain product lines. One U.S. company which marketed insecticides in Spain through seven local distributors found that within a period of less than three years, six of those distributors had been purchased, or partially purchased, by competitive firms, thus blocking the initial supplier's distribution. The company found similar situations in Latin America, South Africa, Australia, and southern Europe. To retain a competitive position, the company in question was virtually forced to make major investments in buying distributors throughout the world. While many of these ventures are profitable, it requires huge infusions of funds to maintain market position. In the home market, such investments would probably have been unnecessary.

One company operating in Nicaragua was squeezed out of the market entirely within a two-year period because competitive firms had purchased all of the outlets. In that instance, the company cooperated with other noncompetitive suppliers and organized a distribution company which was foreign owned but financed largely by the supplier companies. The company invested only $50,000 and has realized approximately $40,000 per-year net return on investment. Companies buying partial control cannot always expect to dominate the channel; some have purchased 10, 15, or 20 percent equity in a distribution company and still found it to be handling competing products.

Manufacturers of durable goods have found they often must provide funds for service facilities before their products will be accepted. Japanese automakers met with little success in the United States until they provided funds for adequate service facilities and expanded inventories.

In some instances, companies have contributed directly to the cost of road facilities and distribution centers, invested in radio and television stations to be assured of high-quality coverage, and made other such investments designed to upgrade the very basic marketing infrastructure of the countries in which they were doing business. As foreign distribution systems grow, the financing of a nation's marketing infrastructure is less likely to fall on individual companies.

Trade and channel credit. Credit and payment terms have become major weapons of international competition in the global marketplace. Historically, U.S. business has been reluctant to offer advantageous credit terms to foreign markets. Strong product preferences internationally have permitted U.S. businesses to thrive despite this lack of credit. Such conditions no longer prevail since extended credit terms have become an important factor in selling. Moderate-size foreign exchange reserves and the willingness of West German, British, and Japanese competitors to offer favorable credit terms have increasingly put U.S. businesses at a disadvantage in international markets unless comparable credit terms are made available.

Credit is becoming as important to export sales as the price of a product. The fact that U.S. businesses are changing their attitudes toward issuing credit is supported by the evidence that most firms' export accounts receivable have shown substantial increases in the past few years. Many firms are extending open accounts rather than cash payment as the basic means of extending credit.

Channel credit requirements have surprised many American firms. Most of the world's middlemen are dreadfully underfinanced, and if they are to buy goods in economical quantities, interim credit must be provided by the producers. The international finance director of a machinery and equipment company says he expects increasing foreign sales volume to require additional working capital to "support from 50 percent to 75 percent of the sales increase."

Accounts receivable financing imposes great strains on international working capital. Both middlemen and industrial customers have learned they are in a position to pressure manufacturers into continuously longer and longer credit extensions because credit terms are such an important marketing weapon in the battle for competitive position in international markets. Marketing and product advantages are being offset by more advantageous financial terms from competing foreign suppliers. To get goods into the channel of distribution, marketers may have to compensate for the middlemen's lack of capital by providing consignment merchandise, floor-plan financing, or long-term credit. Without such financial assistance, most foreign middlemen cannot handle adequate inventories.

BOX 21–1: Long Korean channels—Rx credit

Ideally, the company would prefer to channel 90 percent of its sales directly to retailers and the remaining 10 percent to high-volume end-users. The large number and generally low turnover of retailers, however, makes this impossible. In addition to the physical impossibility of selling directly to 8,000 or 9,000 retailers—many of them family-run "mom and pop" stores with low profit margins and minimal turnover—the company is concerned about the risks involved in extending credit to such operations. It thus tends to deal directly with large urban retailers, leaving the smaller urban retailers and most of the nonurban outlets to wholesalers.

Besides the added costs involved, using wholesalers is neither an ideal nor a simple solution. The company finds reputable wholesalers are difficult to locate. It uses 130 of the country's 400, and is not entirely happy with some of these. A recurring difficulty is that wholesalers—and occasionally some retailers—take advantage of the highly competitive market (there are about 300 pharmaceutical makers in Korea) to demand large discounts.

Receivables create further problems. The company finds that many wholesalers collect quickly from retailers, but put payment to the manufacturer on a deferred basis. In the interim, they invest money in ventures offering high short-term returns. Some get involved in black market lending, where interest rates run as high as 3 percent per month.

Source: "Distributing Goods to Korean Consumers." Reprinted from page 149 of the May 13, 1977 issue of *Business Asia,* with permission of the publisher, Business International Corp. (New York).

The size of industrial credits, particularly for plant, equipment, and major agricultural transactions, is so immense as to be nearly incomprehensible. Capital equipment purchases often run in the $1-to-$10 million range. Turnkey industrial plants may cost tens to hundreds of millions of dollars. Some examples of recent transactions: Davy Powergas sold the Soviet Union two methanol plants at a cost of over $300 million. The Italian company, Pirelli, built a $400 million tire plant in Algeria, but the contract was contingent on finding $160 million in export credits. Fiat negotiated with Algerian officials on a $2.5 *billion* automobile plant. Credit was the key factor when Eastern Airlines purchased $800 million worth of airplanes from Airbus Industries, a French, German, and Spanish production consortium, for delivery through the entire decade of the 1980s. Agricultural purchases often run in the tens of millions but are less likely to require the 30-to-50 percent financing often associated with plant purchases.

Successful consummation of the tremendous marketing effort involved in such transactions usually hinges on the nature and availability of financing. Negotiations not only include marketing, finance personnel, and company chief executives, but because of the size of trade credits involved and the effect on national economies, often include foreign ministers, international bankers, even national presidents, premiers and prime ministers. Financing such huge transactions is incredibly complex and for individual companies a $1 million or $5 million sale can be taxing. Often the marketer is responsible for arranging financing, especially when longer trade terms are demanded or needed. Eastern European and developing countries tend to be in chronically overspent national positions. In some instances, permanent lending agencies will help out in others, commercial banks. Sometimes commercial paper can be discounted in various kinds of commercial institutions. In the Eastern Airlines transactions, Airbus considered public common stock and bond sales to procure funds to finance the purchase.

Buy-back agreements may provide for the flow of funds to maintain an industrial plant but they do not solve the initial financing problem and neither do the lease arrangements now being experimented with in Eastern European countries; countries which chronically overextend their international debt position. The particular ingenuity of this arrangement is that lease payments are made not with money but with products produced on the leased equipment. Again, this lease buy-back arrangement does not provide the initial financing.

An evaluation of numerous recent major plant purchases indicates that in situation after situation the price, delivery, and quality are subordinated to the type of financing available.

A decade or two ago international marketers had little concern about credit. Terms tended to be cash in advance or some sort of bank-guaranteed paper. Many small agricultural marketers or exporters continue to rely on these terms; but, in today's intensely competitive world marketplace, no major marketer can afford a cash-only posture. Consumers in developed markets or in wealthier sectors of developing markets have adopted the

American attitude that credit is a right rather than a privilege. Middlemen may require both extensive and intensive credit availability to develop the type of distribution systems requisite to large-scale marketing. A major arena of credit competition demands provision of long-term credit for major capital goods purchases. All three types—consumer, trade, and industrial markets, may make extreme credit demands on company resources.

Capital investment

Some markets are closed to foreign businesses unless they produce goods locally. The French government, for example, gave notice to Ford that if it expected to keep its large volume of sales in France, it had to be producing there; Ford prudently agreed to build its next European plant in France. In such cases, the production facility itself is a crucial element to market entry and may be considered part of the marketing system since market requirements alone dictated the expenditure. In addition, there are capital investment requirements for such marketing facilities as warehouses, shipping docks, retail stores, and sales offices; all of which require significant capital investment in physical facilities. In considering financial implications, the cost of the production facility as well as costs of marketing facilities may logically be related to marketing as a cost of market entry.

An important financial issue facing the international marketer is the availability and source of capital to finance the additional working capital needed. Besides a company's own resources, there are a variety of private and public funds available.

SOURCES OF FUNDS FOR INTERNATIONAL MARKETING OPERATIONS

Working capital for international marketing operations is usually derived from the assets of the company engaging in international trade or exporting. However, private external sources may be used for financing inventory, accounts receivable, construction of physical facilities, and other financing needs. Public sources of funds are likely to play a more important role in financing marketing operations internationally than they do domestically. A number of supranational agencies are engaged in financing international development and marketing activities, plus the foreign marketer may turn to foreign, national, state, and local governments for various kinds of financial assistance. This section will review briefly the major private and public sources of financing international business operations.

Even companies with the ability to finance their entire international operation need to be concerned with foreign money sources. For political reasons, more local capital may be required by foreign and domestic government regulations than the international company really wants. Specifically, numerous countries in recent years have placed strict controls on the amount of capital that can be invested overseas and local financial participation laws may require at least part of the ownership of foreign operations be national. Companies can find themselves in the position of helping local participants find capital sources in foreign markets. Importers, middlemen, and franchises often rely on vendor companies for assistance in securing financing.

United States multinational corporations in recent years have financed some 40 percent of overseas operations from cash flow generated from abroad, over one third from external sources abroad (and this is growing), and about one fourth through capital transfers.

Private sources

In international business, companies often cooperate both to share the risk and to provide a greater capital and credit base. Sometimes, as exemplified by international oil consortia, the cooperation is between companies in the same country joining in joint ventures to operate in other countries. In other instances, companies from different countries join forces to do business in one of the countries in question. The Iraq Petroleum Company, for example, is jointly owned by British Petroleum, Royal Dutch/Shell, Compagnie Française des Petroles, Jersey Standard, and Socony Mobil. Joint or single ventures doing exporting or operating overseas may be financed directly from existing company sources or by utilizing the company's credit in the financial marketplace. In recent years, the development of foreign capital markets has been significant even in lesser developed countries. There are many sources in the private sector of the world economy which may be tapped by international business.

Equity holders. With the development of organized capital markets in increasing numbers of countries, private funding is becoming an important factor in international business. Marketers still cannot look to widespread public equity sources in most countries; but, as nations become more affluent, increasing amounts of surplus capital are making their way into American business firms operating abroad. Despite these sources, the dominant source of private financing undoubtedly will continue to be association with individual local partners to provide equity financing for specific projects. Debt financing has also become an important factor.

Banks. Three types of banks are significant to the international marketer: commercial banks, Edge Act banks, and overseas development banks. Commercial banking has become a major factor in international marketing as banks throughout the world develop subsidiaries in other parts of the globe. They provide a major source of both secured and unsecured short-term financing, make loans against outstanding letters of credit, discount bills of exchange and time drafts, and perform other normal banking services. Proliferation of commercial banks during the 10 years preceding 1980 was so intense that the period could well be characterized as the decade when world banking came of age.

Edge Act banks are institutions operating under special charter of the United States government. Most are subsidiaries of large U.S. banks and have as their special domain middle- and long-term financing in cooperation with other financial partners. Overseas development banks have essentially the same long-range orientation. They often secure their funds from national or international governmental bodies that operate on a private basis and emphasize local development activities in emerging nations.

Even the People's Republic of China is permitting international banks to provide loan capital for purchases. A recent $50 million credit agreement between a group of international banks and the Italian government provided a loan which enabled an Italian firm to sell to a Chinese petrochemical company. This was one of the first syndicated commercial credit arrangements through international banks permitted by the Chinese.[2]

Investment companies and trusts.   Nearly every nation has its own investment companies which were formed to exploit business opportunities through financial participation in both their own and foreign countries. One outstanding example in the United States is the IBEC (International Basic Economy Corporation). A Rockefeller family investment, IBEC has assets of $700 million (U.S.) invested in a wide variety of projects and subsidiary operations. A cooperative international investment group called ADELA Investment Company was formed in 1964 with the object of combining economic development and profit-seeking motives. Financed by blue-chip companies from the United States and some major European companies, ADELA focuses its attentions on joint ventures in Latin America. Private Investment Company for Asia (PICA), with authorized capital of $40 million, is sponsored by Japanese, North American, European, and Australian investors. In general, investment companies' motives range from outright altruism to hard-nosed profit seeking and follow equally diverse organizational patterns.

Commercial finance and factoring companies.   Most major industrial countries have fairly well-developed finance companies which operate outside the commercial bank system. Such companies factor receivables, installment contracts, or accept other kinds of security. They also directly handle overseas installment credit through international offices located throughout the world. Examples of companies operating in this field are the Commercial Credit Company and the Beneficial Finance Company, both of which have branch offices in various countries.

Government sources

The great majority of sources of public funds for international business are oriented to industrial development activities. Some agencies, however, interpret industial development quite broadly and make funds available for a wide range of business activities. Public funds for private businesses

---

[2] "Peking Petrochemical Company Signs Credit Accord for $50 Million," *Asian Wall Street Journal,* August 10, 1981, p. 12.

are obtained from four different government levels—international government, national government, state governments, and local governments. The national, state, and local governments often finance business activities of any sort likely to bring greater prosperity within their bailiwick.

International government sources. Many international agencies exist that have little direct interest for the marketer except when they provide funds likely to be expended for equipment and supplies utilized in development programs. Of greater interest are those providing funds for private business activities such as the World Bank, the International Finance Corporation, International Development Associations, the Inter-American Development Bank, and the European Investment Bank. Nearly all of these groups make loans to private business firms in the areas which their charters include.

National government funds. As part of its mutual security program, the United States has set up several organizations designed to speed the development of certain countries. In addition, nearly every country has its own national organization to facilitate development within the country. For example, France has its Caisse Nationale Des Marches De l'Etat to finance firms working on government contract. The National Financiera of Mexico is a government development bank that finances private enterprise which contributes to the development of the nation. Spain provided a $1 billion loan to Indonesia for a petroleum construction project with the understanding that the money is to be used to buy supplies and equipment from Spanish companies.[3]

Export-Import Bank. Eximbank is the primary U.S. government agency in the business of providing funds for international trade and investment. Besides its many private financing functions, Eximbank also plays a key role in the U.S. export credit insurance program. This agency makes medium- and long-term loans to foreign countries, the proceeds of which must be expended on goods purchased in the United States. It also provides medium-term export credit for U.S. exporters.[4]

Eximbank is also the primary administrator for the foreign currencies generated abroad by the sale of U.S. surplus farm commodities. *Cooley funds,* as they are called, are available to American businesses operating abroad.

Agency for International Development (AID). An activity of the Department of State, AID has a major commitment to economic development through private enterprise. Like Eximbank, AID operates in Cooley funds, but it also has its own appropriation. It is supplemented by the Inter-American Social Progress Trust Fund, a source of capital for private and government borrowers in the Americas.

---

[3] "Spain to Lend Indonesia $1 Billion for Refinery," *Asian Wall Street Journal,* July 27, 1981, p. 19.

[4] For a complete discussion of the activities of this important financing agency see, *The Export-Import Bank: Financing of American Exports—Support for American Jobs,* The Exim Bank of the United States, Washington, D.C., 1980, p. 46.

Overseas Private Investment Corporation (OPIC). While best known as a United States agency whose major job is to provide insurance against loss due to specific noncommercial international operating risks, OPIC does engage in direct loans for development projects. These loans are to be spent for U.S. projects in LDCs and for goods purchased, from the United States.[5]

State and local funds. In many countries funds are available from governments on levels comparable to our states or municipalities. In Germany the *laender* (states) may provide direct capital, free land, or plant facilities. Massey-Ferguson GMBH, for example, was induced to build a plant in Eschwege on the promise of cheap credits from the state. A subsidiary of the U.S.'s Clevite Corporation received assistance from the city of Freiburg in the form of funds with which to build a plant.

Eurodollar market

The Eurodollar Market is one the more important sources of debt capital available to the MNC. The term *Eurodollar* refers to a deposit liability banked outside the United States, that is, dollars banked in Germany or any other country other than the U.S. While the Eurodollar market refers to dollars, the Eurodollar Market includes other national currencies banked outside their country of origin. Because the Eurodollar Market includes other than U.S. currencies, it is sometimes referred to as the Eurocurrency Market even though the predominate currency is the U.S. dollar. These currencies serve as a ready source of cash that holding banks can use as an asset on which a dollar-denominated loan can be made to someone else. This is an important source of funds for financing world trade. In 1980 it was estimated that the gross size of the Eurocurrency was $1,270 billion dollars.[6] Similar markets exist in Asia and the Caribbean and consist of national currencies deposited in banks outside the country of origin.

FINANCIAL RISKS

Several types of financial risk are encountered in international marketing; the major problems include commercial, political, and foreign exchange risk. Some risks are similar to domestic risks although usually intensified, while others are uniquely international. Every business should deal with the fact of risk through a structured risk-management program. Such a pro-

---

[5] For a complete discussion of OPIC activities as well as other government sources of funds, see "II—Cross-Border Financing, North American Government Sources," *Financing Foreign Operations* (New York: Business International Corp., August 1980), pp. 1–18.

[6] "II-Cross-Border Financing, Eurodollars," *Financing Foreign Operations* (New York: Business International Corp. December 1980), p. 1.

gram may call for assuming risks, engaging in some type of risk avoidance, or initiating risk-shifting behavior.[7]

Commercial risk

Commercial risks are handled essentially as normal credit risks encountered in day-to-day business. They include solvency, default, or refusal to pay bills. The major risk, however, is competition which can only be dealt with through consistently effective management and marketing. One unique risk encountered by the international marketer involves financial adjustments. Such risk is encountered when a controversy arises about the quality of goods delivered (but not accepted), a dispute over contract terms, or any other disagreement over which payment is withheld. One company, for example, shipped several hundred tons of dehydrated potatoes to a distributor in Germany. The distributor tested the shipment and declared it to be below acceptable taste and texture standards (not explicitly established). The alternatives for the exporter were reducing the price, reselling the potatoes, or shipping them home again, each involving considerable cost. Although there is less risk of substantial loss in the adjustment situation, it is possible for the selling company to have large sums of money tied up for relatively long periods of time until the client accepts the controversial goods if ever. In some cases, goods must be returned or remanufactured, and in other instances, contracts may be modified to alleviate the controversies. All such problems are uninsurable and costly.

Political risk

Political risk relates to the problems of war or revolution, currency inconvertibility, expropriation or expulsion, and restriction or cancellation of import licenses. Political risk is an environmental concern for all businesses and is treated at length in Chapter 6. Management information systems and effective decision-making processes are the best defenses against political risk. As many companies have discovered, sometimes there is no way to avoid political risk, so marketers must be prepared to assume them or give up doing business in a particular market. Some types of political risk are insured by the agencies mentioned in the risk management section that follows.

Foreign exchange risk

Exchange-rate fluctuations inevitably cause problems, but for many years, most firms could take protective action to minimize their unfavorable effects.

---

[7] S. L. Srinivasulu, "Strategic Response to Foreign Exchange Risks," *Columbia Journal of World Business,* Spring 1981, pp. 13–23.

Floating exchange rates of the world's major currencies have forced all marketers to be especially aware of exchange-rate fluctuations and the need to compensate for them in their financial planning. International Business Machines Corporation, for example, reported that exchange losses resulted in a dramatic 21.6 percent drop in their earnings in the third quarter of 1981.[8] Before rates were permitted to float, devaluations of major currencies were infrequent and usually could be anticipated, but exchange-rate fluctuations in the float system are daily affairs.

Until 1973 and the demise of the Bretton Woods Agreement, the international monetary system operated in an environment of quasi-fixed exchange rates pegged to a gold exchange standard.[9] During the time of the Bretton Woods Agreement, the exchange rate for the most industrialized countries' currencies were relatively stable and fluctuations were infrequent and relatively small. Thus, a firm's transactions in foreign currencies were fairly secure in terms of exchange rates to other currencies. Since 1973, a system of floating exchange rates has evolved, producing a heightened volatility in the prices of currencies. With world inflation, the swings of currencies have intensified since the late 70s. Exhibit 21–1 shows the variations which occurred against the dollar from 1979 to 1981. It is not hard to imagine the foreign exchange risk problems of MNCs that had large amounts in accounts receivable in yen, German marks, British pounds, or Swiss francs during this period. Depending on the specific time span, a firm could stand to lose substantial sums of money from too much exposure to fluctuating currencies. The variations in currencies have put severe strains on multinational company income streams and have resulted in major concern over the extent of *transaction exposure.*[10]

Transaction exposure occurs at any time a company has assets denominated in some currency other than that of its home country and expects to convert the foreign currency to its home currency to realize a profit.[11] When a U.S. company sells in a foreign country, it sometimes must accept payment in the buyer's currency in order to be competitive. The seller will then have to exchange the currency received for dollars. Between the time price is agreed on and payment actually received and converted to dollars, the company's transaction is exposed to exchange rate fluctuations, that is, the company experiences transaction exposure. As an example, suppose that on February 6, 1982, a U.S. company contracts to sell 100 gross

---

[8] "IBM Blames Exchange Losses for 21.6% Plunge in Earnings," *Associated Press,* October 14, 1981.

[9] Laurent L. Jacque, "Management of Foreign Exchange Risk: A Review Article," *Journal of International Business Studies,* Spring/Summer 1981, pp. 81–101.

[10] P. H. A. Kenyon, "Currency Exposure Management," *Long Range Planning,* June 1980, pp. 21–29.

[11] Robert R. Dince and Peter N. Umoh, "Foreign Exchange Risk and the Portfolio Approach: An Example From West Africa," *Columbia Journal of World Business,* Spring 1981, pp. 24–29.

EXHIBIT 21–1: Values of world's currencies 1979–1981 (percentage change)

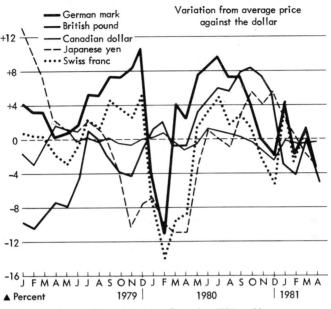

Source: *Survey of Current Business,* December 1981, p. 33.

of western shirts to a Japanese buyer for a total price of 20 million yen. The sale price is based on an exchange rate of $0.004944 U.S. per yen and the U.S. seller expects to realize $98,880 (20 million ¥ × 0.004944 U.S. = $98,880) in payment. The Japanese buyer has demanded the sale be quoted in yen. When the company enters the contract for the sale, it has incurred transaction exposure, that is, until it closes the sale and converts the yen to dollars, it is running the risk of a loss (if the exchange rate of dollar per yen is lower when the company exchanges the yen for dollars). During the time of the exposure,—between February 6, 1982 and July 6, 1982 when payment is received—the exchange rate of the U.S. dollar changed from $0.004944/yen to $0.004379/yen. Based on the exchange rate existing at the time the company receives the 20 million yen and converts the yen to dollars, the company would receive only $87,580 U.S. (20 million ¥ × $0.004379 = $87,580) in exchange, thereby losing $11,300 over the anticipated sales value of $98,880.[12]

---

[12] The company could receive a windfall profit if the dollar exchange rate were higher at the time of the final exchange. Had the rate gone to $0.005110 U.S. per yen, then the company would have made a windfall gain of $3,320. Since most companies are not interested in speculation but in the protection of their expected profits, the fear of a loss is much greater than the expectation of a gain and thus they may prefer to protect themselves against a loss at the expense of potential windfall gain.

In long-term transactions (even those of two or three years) exchange rate fluctuations can have extreme effects and at times can far exceed the profitability of a given transaction. Consider the following example of the cost of money in a strongly fluctuating money market.

August 19, 1980	U.S. firm borrows 10,000,000 Swiss francs (SwF) Interest rate 7 percent Exchange rate: 1 SwF = $0.3910 U.S. Company secures $3,910,000
August 19, 1981	U.S. firm owes 10,700,000 SwF Exchange rate: 1 SwF = $0.5128 U.S. Company requires $5,486,960
Transaction Cost	$1,576,960 to use $3,910,000 for 1 year 40.33 percent effective cost of money for 1 year.

Because of exchange rate exposure, a loan that was expected to cost 7 percent increased to a rate of 40.33 percent, certainly a substantial increase in the cost of doing business.

Transaction exposure occurs when a company:

1. Has assets in one currency which they expect to convert to another to realize a profit.
2. Has assets denominated in one currency which must be converted into another at some expected value.
3. Borrows money in one currency which, when repaid, must be exchanged to make repayment.
4. Purchases goods for resale in one currency, sells them in another, and needs to convert the proceeds into a third currency to realize planned profits.

A large MNC might encounter several or all of these situations in the course of normal business activity. Should the extent of risk be large, most firms try to minimize it. The most obvious way is to demand payment in the home-country currency, but competitively, that is not always possible. It must be remembered that when a company demands payment in home-country currency, the exchange risk is shifted to the buyer who is then similarly exposed. In a fluctuating exchange market such as the one that has existed since the early 1970s, there is a tendency for each party in a transaction to attempt to shift the exchange risk to the other. Thus, demand for payment in the seller's currency may not always be competitively possible. More formal methods of risk avoidance will be discussed in the following section on financial risk management.

FINANCIAL RISK MANAGEMENT

When financial risks become too high, companies either stop doing business in high-risk situations or seek ways to manage the risk to minimize potential loss. There are a variety of tools available although none provides perfect protection.

Commercial and political risks are insurable through a variety of U.S. government agencies. The principal agencies are: (1) Overseas Private Investment Corporation (OPIC); (2) The Foreign Credit Insurance Association (FCIA); and (3) The Export-Import Bank (Eximbank). OPIC and the Eximbank provide insurance against noncommercial losses arising from political activities such as expropriation, war, revolution, inconvertibility of currency, and insurrection. OPIC's emphasis is on developing countries while Eximbank provides assistance for most all nations considered friendly to the United States. In addition, Eximbank participates with the FCIA to provide insurance against failure to receive payment and other commercial losses.

Protection against risks resulting from exchange rate fluctuations is not available from any government agency. It comes only from effective financial risk management. Some companies avoid risks by refusing to enter transactions not denominated in home-country currency, others accept the consequences "of currency oscillations as a 'condition of doing business' ",[13] and an increasingly larger number shift the risk to a third party. An effective way to shift risk is by hedging.

Hedging in money is essentially no different from any other kind of hedging in the marketplace. Basically it consists of forward sale for dollars of a currency in danger of devaluation.

Referring back to the illustration of the U.S. company which sold 100 gross of western shirts to a Japanese buyer and lost $11,300 as a result of an adverse change in the value of the yen, there are several steps which might have been taken to avoid or minimize such a loss. Had the Japanese not insisted on paying in yen, the seller could have received payment in dollars and not suffered any loss or the seller could have included a clause in the contract stipulating an adjustment if the currency value changed more than a stipulated amount. Another possibility would have been to increase the selling price by some percentage in anticipation of a potential loss. None of these steps are generally possible in a highly competitive market. One other alternative is to hedge the risk even though hedging does not necessarily insure complete protection. Since trading in foreign exchange futures was begun by the International Monetary Market (IMM) in Chicago in 1972, there has been a viable opportunity to buy futures contracts in most of the world's major currencies either directly in the money market or through the international trade division of a major bank.

The same techniques used to buy futures in wheat, soybeans, and cattle can be used to reduce risks associated with fluctuations in the values of currencies. The process consists of offsetting risk incurred in the actual sale with buying a futures contract in that currency. Continuing the above exam-

---

[13] Financial Foreign Operations—Protecting Foreign Assets, (New York: Business International Corp., 1980), p. 6.

ple, had the company engaged in a hedge either through its bank or with a direct purchase of a contract on the IMM, it could have covered all or most of its risk.

Suppose that on February 6 when the company sold the shirts for 20 million yen with delivery for May and payment on July 6, the company decided to hedge the risk using Japanese yen futures. To do this, it would be necessary to make two transactions in the futures market. On February 6, an August 5[14] futures contract for 20 million yen is sold at a price of $0.004995 U.S. per yen. In other words, the company promises to deliver 20 million yen to the market on August 5. The value of this contract in U.S. dollars is 20 million times the futures price of $0.004995 U.S. for a total of $99,900, that is, for the 20 million yen they agreed to sell August 5 they expect to receive $99,900 U.S. At this point the company is said to be short in the futures market since there has been a sale of yen which will not be received until later.

On July 6, 1982, when the company receives the 20 million yen from the buyer of the western shirts, another contract to buy 20 million yen on the futures market is made to offset the earlier futures contract which comes due August 5. On this transaction, the buyers pay $0.004429 U.S./yen for a total cost of $88,580 dollars to be delivered on August 5. At this point the gain or loss on the actual sale should be offset with a gain or loss on the two futures contracts. Exhibit 21–2 summarizes the transactions and shows that the yen's value decreased during the 5 months of exposure and the company lost $11,300 when the yen received from the actual sale of shirts were exchanged for dollars. However, on the futures contracts the company realized a $11,320 gain which can be used to balance the $11,300 loss and pay commissions for the transactions, thereby protecting the original sales price of $98,880.

Had the value of the yen increased during the time of exposure, the original contract would have generated a windfall profit and the futures contract would have generated a loss. In such circumstances, the windfall gains would have been used to offset the loss in the futures contracts. The reason a company hedges is that increases or decreases in the value of currency cannot be predicted and, since companies are typically not in the business of speculation, they forego potential windfall profits for protection of their normal business profits.

It must not be inferred from the illustrations presented that hedging affords complete protection against price changes or that it is always as simple as indicated. It sometimes happens that factors operate which prevent a hedge from offering complete protection or providing the small profit as was illustrated. The primary reason for there being no perfect hedge (i.e., where the spot and future yields would be the same) is that the spread between

---

[14] An August 5 futures was purchased to insure some degree of safety since there was no guarantee that the payment would be received exactly on July 6. The futures contract could have been made for July 6 had the company wanted to.

EXHIBIT 21-2: A short hedge—U.S. company selling to a Japanese firm

	Spot market transactions		Future market transactions	

Spot market transactions

Feb. 6, 1982 U.S. company agrees to sell 100 gross of western shirts to a Japanese retailer for 20 million yen for delivery in May, 1982 with payment due July 6, 1982.
Current spot market for yen is
$0.004944 U.S./yen $98,880

July 6, 1982 U.S. company receives 20 million yen and exchanges the yen for dollars at the current price of $0.004379 U.S./yen to receive $87,580

The company realized a *loss* due to decreasing value of the yen during the time of exposure.
$98,880 − 87,580 = ... $(11,300)

Future market transactions

To hedge the risk of a falling price for yen, the company sells August 5, yen contracts for $0.004995 U.S./yen and receives a credit (20 million ¥ times $0.004995 =) for $99,900

The U.S. company completes the hedge by buying August 5 yen contracts for $0.004429 U.S./yen (20 million ¥ times $0.004429 =) $88,580

The company realized a gain in the futures market with which to offset the loss in the spot market. $99,900 − 88,580 = ... $11,320

Note: The $11,320 gain in the futures market less the $11,300 loss in the spot-market transactions left the company with a slight gain of $20. After commissions are paid, there will be a slight loss on this transaction.

the spot and futures markets does not always move at the same rate. The two prices may move in the same direction but at different degrees and different rates of speed. Thus, a company which hedges can receive an unexpected profit or incur an unexpected loss. However, in situations where exchange rates are fluctuating, the profits or losses are comparatively smaller than they would have been without a hedge.[15]

PAYOUT PLANNING AND STRATEGY

International marketing executives are plagued with a problem that does not concern their domestic counterparts; they must not only sell the goods but must find ways to repatriate payment for the goods and profits from operations to the parent country. In so doing, they are concerned with handling the profit, managing payout, and accomplishing repatriation of funds.

The multinational marketer has the option of allocating the profit from the activities to a variety of locations. Profit may be taken in a country in which the goods are sold, in a country in which they are produced, in the headquarters country, or, perhaps, in yet another country. Profits may be allocated to provide maximum profit for the subsidiary or for the corporation as a whole. By taking profits in a country with low tax rates, for example, the net profit after taxes can be optimized. The marketer may want to take the profits in countries with sound currencies, or where the funds are needed to finance further operations.

Profit can be allocated through manipulation of prices charged for goods exchanged internationally or through allocation of expenses; the marketing manager's salary, for example, may be charged off to the operation expenses of any of the countries involved in the production or distribution chain. To bring profits to the home company, the parent may charge its subsidiary licensing fees, franchise fees, or may allocate increasing portions of home-office expenses to the subunit. Such decisions generally are made at the corporate level.

Payout of profits is not only a question of location but must also be considered from the standpoint of time. Sometimes it is sensible to postpone profits from one tax-paying year to another or to stockpile profits to provide the basis for further expansion. Such activities are especially important in these days of widespread investment control.

[15a.] For a complete discussion of hedging and financial risk management see, Rita M. Rodriguez and E. Eugene Carter, *International Financial Management,* 2d ed. (Englewood Cliffs, N.J.: Prentice-Hall, 1979), p. 666.

[b.] For a complete discussion of the International Monetary Market, see *Understanding Futures in Foreign Exchange* (Chicago: International Monetary Market Division of Chicago Mercantile Exchange, 1979), p. 40.

[c.] Carl Schweser and Tom Peterson, "Risk Management for the Small Importer-Exporter," *American Journal of Small Business,* Summer 1980, pp. 13–21.

Both capital repatriation and repatriation from the sale of goods are important to marketers. If goods can be sold but funds cannot be returned, the marketer will soon be in a position of having no more goods to sell. Solutions include bartering, third-country (three-way) trading without the use of financial exchange, and switch trading. One English company sold $5 million worth of airplanes to Brazil and was paid entirely in coffee. Often, part of the selling price of goods can be repatriated directly with the balance being bartered. Vendors may find themselves in businesses they do not particularly enjoy, however, they can find help in specialized barter brokers. In switch trading, three or more parties are generally involved, one from each of the countries that have bilateral payment agreements with one or more of the other countries involved. When funds are blocked, the money may be repatriated through the export of goods from the foreign country to the parent country. Many countries maintain a list of goods on a deblockage list, and if these goods are exported, the funds need not be repatriated.

BOX 21–2: Financial management or laundry business

If they are willing to move into gray areas, multinational companies have certain techniques at their disposal simply as a result of their organizational structure. A U.S. parent company, for example, may consistently charge an ultra-high rate of interest—say 2 percent above the market—on loans to subsidiaries in blocked-account countries and get a steady trickle of money out. Or it may charge those subsidiaries exorbitant management fees or extravagant amounts for supplies and components, or overbill them on any other intracompany transaction. These are all legal business expenses; even when repatriation of profits is blocked, companies are allowed to pay their debts.

One strictly illegal—though used—device for a multinational is to find a friendly supplier in, say, Switzerland, that will agree to consistently overcharge for goods it sells to the company's subsidiary in a particularly blocked-account country. The Swiss company, to illustrate, may charge double the normal price, then put half the proceeds in a Swiss bank in the name of the multinational. There is a caveat here, however: the arrangement obviously will work only when there is complete trust between the corporate collaborators.

Source: "The Mysterious Market in Blocked Accounts." Reprinted with special permission of *Dun's Review*, October 1976. Copyright, 1976, Dun & Bradstreet Publications Corporation.

One such project that began as an effort to spend blocked currencies was the production of the movie "The Ninth Configuration" in Hungary. Pepsico, Inc., which has a compensation agreement with the Hungarians to provide syrup for Pepsi, made plans to pay for the film's production costs as a way to spend blocked currencies. The Hungarian government accepted the spending of funds for the movie's production. Pepsico owns half the movie rights and will receive royalties in the United States from box office receipts.[16]

---

[16] "Countertrade Gains Popularity as International Trade Tool," *Business America*, July 14, 1980, p. 15.

Obviously there are other financial alternatives to repatriation. The company having trouble repatriating funds may choose to reinvest them in other local enterprises or expand operations in the country. Sometimes if a company has stockholders in the foreign country it simply pays out dividends directly from the foreign subsidary rather than from the parent company. For this reason, some large multinational companies are encouraging the sale of their securities in foreign markets in which they operate. Such an action taken when foreign capital may still be sent to the parent country could lessen foreign exchange problems at a later date.

SUMMARY

Although it is not their formal domain, marketing executives should be acquainted with the requirements, sources, problems, and opportunities associated with the financing of international marketing operations. The financial needs of international marketing differ considerably from those of the domestic market. Most specifically, the international marketer must be prepared to invest larger-than-normal amounts of working capital in inventories, receivables, channel financing, and consumer credit. It is possible that market entry may require capital financing of production facilities for purely marketing reasons. International marketers need to be willing to undertake additional financial burdens if they are to operate successfully in foreign countries. Indeed, adequate financing may spell the difference between success and failure in foreign operations. The willingness of marketers to carry adequate inventories in strategic locations or to provide consumer or channel credit which they would not be likely to furnish in their home country may be key elements in market development.

Financial risks associated with international marketing are greater than those encountered domestically, but such risk taking is necessary for effective operations. Many companies have been so conservative in their credit and payment terms they have succeeded in alienating foreign customers. Consumer credit may be particularly perilous, but often no one but the marketer is willing to provide such credit; so if the consumer is dependent on credit for purchases, the marketer must take this risk. Larger inventories threaten possible financial loss through obsolescence or deterioration, and the totally larger financial involvement of international marketing may significantly alter the risk-return relationship. Nonetheless, these risks, as well as those of exchange availability or fluctuation and the various political risks, can be accommodated in an effective marketing plan.

The high cost of credit in foreign countries and the relative lack of capital available for financing operations may mean that the American marketer is in an especially good position to capitalize on opportunities because of superior capital position. The marketer needs to be well acquainted with the financial side of marketing to capitalize on these opportunities.

QUESTIONS

1. Define:
   Transaction exposure   Eurodollars
   Eximbank   AID
   OPIC

2. Explain why marketers should be concerned with the financial considerations associated with international business.

3. Identify the financial requirements for marketing internationally which are most likely to concern the domestic marketer.

4. Discuss the differences between financial requirements for export marketers and for overseas marketing operations.

5. What are the extra working capital requirements of the international marketer?

6. Review some of the ways by which financial requirements can be reduced by variations in marketing policies or strategies.

7. "Whenever possible, manufacturers should probably avoid consumer credit extensions as part of their basic merchandising program." Discuss.

8. What significance do government sources of funds have for marketers?

9. Discuss the importance of Eximbank and its services which facilitate international marketing activities.

10. "The principles of international credit are basically no different from those of domestic credit." Elaborate.

11. Compare the advantages and disadvantages of bills of exchange and letters of credit.

12. Review the types of financial risk involved in international operations and discuss how each may be reduced.

13. Using exchange data in *The Wall Street Journal* on the date assigned by the instructer, calculate the foreign exchange gain or loss on this transaction: a U.S. firm borrows five million Swiss francs one year before the assigned date, converts those to U.S. dollars, pays 6 percent interest per annum. How many dollars will be required to repay the loan and interest?

14. Define and give an example of a company that has a transaction exposure.

15. In what four situations does transaction rate exposure occur? Give an example of each.

16. Discuss the ways a company can reduce exchange risk.

17. Discuss the ways a company can reduce the risk of exchange rate fluctuations? Give examples of each.

18. In what way are marketing financial requirements of exporters different from those of full-scale international marketers?

19. Explain the forces behind the importance of long-term industrial credits.

Chapter 22

Coordinating and controlling world marketing operations

The complexity of a multinational marketer's strategies has been stressed in the preceding chapters. These complexities are a result of multinational, multicultural, and frequently, multimanaged operations. In spite of the diversity required to meet such varied demands, long and short-range plans and objectives must be met if the operation is to be successful. The key to meeting objectives is coordination and control. Through carefully planned coordination and well-designed lines of control, marketing efforts can be tailored to fit specific market needs and all or parts of plans, strategies, and marketing programs can possibly be standardized to cover worldwide markets.

Few business firms control all domestic functions or actvities as completely as they should; still fewer firms have adequate control of their international activities. While there are many reasons for not exercising total control, continuous coordination and effective managerial control are prime requisites for successful marketing operations. Time lags, cultural lags, communication lags, and varying country-market objectives contribute to the difficulty of establishing and managing an effective system of control for international marketing operations.

To perform consistently at an optimum profit level, all forms of international organization, centralized or decentralized, require a functioning coordination and control system for every area. Pricing policies, personnel utilization, channel and physical distribution arrangement, advertising, market evaluation, selling arrangements, and even the products themselves benefit from well-implemented coordination and control systems.

Establishment of a comprehensive system is not an easy task; a system which adequately controls the operations of one company may over-control the activities of a second or under-control those of yet another. Furthermore, within a given company a variety of control systems may be necessary if the company operates in divergent market situations. This chapter relates coordination and control to organizational structures and identifies specific areas of marketing control.

CONTROL AS A MANAGEMENT TOOL

Control means to direct, regulate, or manage. Controlling is the very essence of management and implies a means of measuring accomplished events against set standards. Control also implies that corrective action can and will be taken to realign operations on a schedule that will allow a firm to achieve stated objectives. Before there can be any meaningful control, however, plans and organizational structure must be clear, complete, and integrated.[1]

The interdependence and interaction of the many marketing functions as well as the full business spectrum, require all segments to attain individual goals in order to accomplish overall objectives. Control is the system used to effectively monitor business activities, measure deviations from standards, and signal those in command to adjust wayward operations to bring them back on course. A business can operate without formal control systems; indeed, a small business with few levels of management where all operations are concentrated, easily seen, and monitored, can frequently function without a formal system. But as the complexity of a business's operation builds, the ability to function efficiently without formal control lessens.

Reflecting on material covered in earlier chapters, the problems and futility of attempting to manage an international company without adequate control procedures can be appreciated. Ironically, even today, international business activities frequently receive inadequate coordination or control from top management. Such neglect results from the markedly different orientation to these functions in domestic and foreign operations, and because a company has no real interest in permanent foreign-market development; goods are exported with little thought or follow-up. Many times overseas business is turned over to an export manager who runs an almost autonomous operation with no coordinating or controlling strings attached. In such cases, the parent companies appear to be content with less-than-optimal overseas profits because they are not sufficiently committed to international operations to exert effective control. Inadequate control also results from inadequately designed systems; but, ultimately, inadequate control results from a lack of commitment. As companies remain in international programs and as these programs become more profitable, they realize that efficiently managed operations require a formal control system. This realization can come as profits from the international division are affected, or, more frequently, by the surfacing of a whole host of inefficiencies and intracompany conflicts that arise from inadequate controls. Inefficiencies result from corporate divisions in different countries being in competition with one another and from poorly managed customer services. Exhibit 22–1 lists some of the recurring problems that surface because of inadequate controls. In each situation,

---

[1] For an interesting discussion on management, organization, and control, see Rodman L. Drake and Lee M. Caudill, "Management of the Large Multinational: Trends and Future Challenges," *Business Horizons*, May/June 1981, pp. 83–91.

EXHIBIT 22–1: Control problems

Indicators	Characteristics
Conflicts among divisions or subsidiaries over territories or customers in the field.	Most common when a company is expanding into new geographic areas. Also caused by the introduction of new products abroad and acquisitions or mergers.
Failure of foreign operations to grow in accordance with plans and expectations.	May only apply to overall sales in a particular area, or to a particular product line. Obviously more acute if one's share of the market is falling even when sales are increasing.
Lack of financial control over operations abroad.	Related to the company's philosophy of centralization versus decentralization and the degree to which authority is delegated to managers overseas. Further complicated by foreign tax laws and accounting conventions.
Duplication of administrative personnel and services.	Most common when product lines go abroad as extensions of independent domestic divisions, or when major acquisitions are made.
Underutilization of manufacturing or distribution facilities abroad.	Often occurs when various product lines extend operations abroad independent of each other, or when consolidation does not take place after a merger.
Duplication of sales offices and specialized field salesmen.	Common within corporations selling technical products such as specialty chemicals or electronic equipment.
A proliferation of relatively small legal entities and/or operating units within a country or geographical area.	Often results from establishing a new subsidiary each time a domestic division enters a new foreign country, until five, six, or even more function side by side.
A proliferation of distributors.	Overlapping coverage and conflicting interests.
An increase in complaints relating to customer service abroad.	Often a symptom that field marketing personnel do not have a coordinated approach to handling a common customer

Source: J. W. Widing, Jr. "Reorganizing Your Worldwide Business," *Harvard Business Review*, vol. 51, no. 3, p. 155.

the problem arises because some phase of the business was not functioning as planned or expected. A system of controls attempts to monitor functions and measure deviations, allowing management to take necessary corrective action before overall objectives are impaired.

The process of developing a control system for a firm operating in several countries is further complicated by multinational and multicultural involvement. All involvements produce special factors which affect the design of the control system and a manager's ability to cope with them.

BOX 22-1: How Nestlé plans for control

Nestlé begins the annual marketing planning process with each subsidiary preparing a general fact book giving home country details and a product fact book for each of the major products the subsidiary sells. The general fact book provides a format for gathering information on factors that may affect the subsidiary's marketing activities such as population composition and trends, economic climate, industry outlook, competition, and marketing legislation. The product fact book contains—again in standardized format—specific information about each product such as total market size and segments, market shares and trends, consumers' habits and attitudes.

Using the fact book as a starting point, subsidiary managers then propose both one-year and six-year marketing plans in an internationally uniform format. In addition to detailed figure work, the annual plan has a qualitative part that is essential. It not only interprets the figure work but also discusses and justifies actions planned for the coming year, identifies critical success factors, spells out responsibilities and deadlines for implementation, and establishes yardsticks for performance measurement.

Source: Ralph Z. Sorenson and Ulrich E. Wiechmann, "How Multinationals View Marketing Standardization," *Harvard Business Review*, May/June 1975, Copyright © 1975 by the President and Fellows of Harvard College; all rights reserved, p. 166.

DEVELOPING AN INTERNATIONAL CONTROL SYSTEM

International marketing plans are among the most complex to adapt to a control system. This complexity can be attributed to the differences arising from the multinational, multicultural, and multimanaged nature of international business. In addition to typical control development problems found in domestic business, the design of an effective international control system is plagued by rapidly shifting political, cultural, and economic factors.

Unique factors in international control

One of the most crucial aspects affecting control processes is the *diversity* inherent to international markets. Market size, labor costs, currency value differences, legal structures, political structures, social features, and cultural factors all lend complication to the task of developing effective marketing programs and to controlling them.[2] Because of diversity, each division seeks specific plans reflecting local situations for each major product and major market. Divisions feel the need to function autonomously with plans, priorities, products, etc., reflecting their unique cultural demands; yet from a global strategy perspective, these units are highly interdependent. In developing global marketing strategy, all activities of foreign subsidiaries must be blended to achieve a single corporate goal. The final worldwide strategy is an agglomeration of programs of each functioning unit toward a single objective. These continuing conflicts between the country/cultural needs

---

[2] See, for example, John D. Whitt, "Financial Planning and Control in Latin American Affiliates of Multinational Firms," *Managerial Planning*, November/December 1977, pp. 27–29.

of each operating unit and the overall corporate objectives need to be reflected in a control system.

Physical distance separating countries and management is another important consideration in the design of a control system. As companies grow and as physical distances separating headquarters management and the worldwide operations increase, the time, expense, and potential error in communications affect the flexibility and speed with which changes in worldwide plans can be implemented and problems detected.

Control implies an ability to take corrective action if operations need adjustments, but foreign operations are frequently faced with *uncontrollable factors*. These influence the outcome of an operation, but local and/or international headquarters have little or no control over them. Outside stockholders with objectives different from those of the company, government regulations, host-country goals, and even codetermination are all uncontrollable factors which can affect the ultimate success of a program but cannot be influenced by management.[3]

A fourth factor to consider is the *inadequacy of data*. The inaccuracy and lack of completeness of economic and industrial data as discussed in Chapter 9 affect control. Goals and plans developed in many markets cannot reflect true potential because the information used to set the goals was inaccurate. Thus, controls established to monitor plans formulated on the basis of inaccurate data will not be workable. Further, because of economic planning by host countries and the instability of political and economic goals, it is difficult to make economic forecasts on which to base marketing plans. Government economic plans that change rapidly can affect the results of even the most carefully drawn marketing programs. A control process, therefore, must be sufficiently flexible to compensate for the inaccuracy and instability of the data on which plans are based.

A company's management philosophy and organization, whether *centralized* or *decentralized*, has a major affect on the development of a control system. Both those who argue in favor of centralized management and decentralized management use the factors discussed above as the bases for their positions. For example, centralized management advocates defend their position on the grounds that diversity, distance, inadequate data, etc, create such control problems that effective control can be assured only if handled centrally. Those in favor of decentralization support their position on the same basis suggesting that the problems outlined make centralized decision making unworkable because it lacks sufficient flexibility to permit immediate reaction to local problems. Conversely, those who argue for centralized control suggest that the conditions discussed have the potential for wasteful duplication of efforts and that the attainment of efficiency and ultimate maximization of worldwide profits can only be achieved through tight central

---

[3] Robert J. Kuhne, "Codetermination: A Statutory Re-structuring of the Organization," *Columbia Journal of World Business*, Summer 1976, p. 17.

decision making. Advocates of decentralization claim strong central management frequently means constant delays in reaching decisions; that instead of the central bureaucracy reacting to meaningful differences at the local level they ultimately react only to capital budgets and profitability, the tools primarily used for control. Critics contend that as centralized management becomes more highly structured, knowledge of the local situation is lost. This, of course, can produce errors which give rise to the question: "Why didn't someone ask a local?"

Regardless of the philosophy employed, the control system must be designed in a way that will minimize problems with either management philosophy. For a highly centralized management, the control system must function to permit effective communications between headquarters and the local decision maker so local input and contribution is not adversely affected; in a decentralized organization, the control system should assure local autonomy does not reach the point where global corporate efforts are jeopardized because of a lack of a common objective. The optimal balance between centralization and decentralization is difficult to achieve because the two forces are driving the multinational simultaneously in both directions.[4]

Regardless of the steps taken to compensate for some of the unique factors confronting attempts for effective control, there seems to exist a continual conflict between those in the home office and those in the field. The dichotomy that exists between headquarters and subsidiary managers is not too dissimilar to that which traditionally exists in any organization between staff and line personnel, that is, neither believes the other understands his or her own problems and, as a consequence, cooperation and communication sometimes suffer. This problem is exacerbated by the distance, culture, language, and differences in nationality that occur in international marketing.

This conflict was highlighted in a study which questioned headquarters and subsidiary personnel on what each considered to be the most pressing problems they faced.[5] Interestingly enough, some of the worst problems had to do with internal subsidiary headquarters relations rather than external environmental conditions. Central office managers' principal concerns fell into three categories. (1) A shortage of qualified persons to staff the international operations; the issue here was the expressed difficulty in finding qualified local managers for subsidiaries. (2) Subsidiary managers who had deficiencies in planning and marketing know-how; a major concern here were subsidiary managers too preoccupied with operational problems and who did not have a long-range, worldwide perspective. As a consequence, the company lacked marketing competence at the subsidiary level. (3) Shortcom-

---

[4] Henri Bodinat, "Multinational Decentralization: Doomed if You Do, Doomed if You Don't," printed in *International Business 1975: A Selection of Current Readings*, ed., Donald S. Henly (East Lansing: Michigan State University International Business and Economic Studies, 1975), p. 280.

[5] Ulrich E. Wiechmann and Louis G. Pringle, "Problems That Plague Multinational Marketers," *Harvard Business Review*, July/August 1979, pp. 118–24.

ings in the communications and control processes of the multinational operation.

In contrast, subsidiary personnel's major concerns dealt with:

1.   Too many constraints imposed by headquarters. They felt they had too little autonomy and were required to produce excessive paperwork to satisfy headquarters control and information requirements that were never effectively used by headquarters.

2.   Too little attention was given by headquarters to local differences. Many felt that headquarters had a domestic bias and as a consequence were insensitive to foreign market requirements. There was also a feeling that a heavy emphasis on standardization of marketing programs led to a disregard for subsidiary personnel's input in planning or marketing programs.

3.   Inadequate information from headquarters. In this situation, they felt that while they were required to provide information to headquarters, very little useful information flowed back from headquarters that would be beneficial in their decision-making processes. They felt central headquarters spent a great deal of time and effort collecting information but paid little attention to the dissemination of information.

These conflicts are in many respects inevitable. It is natural for subsidiaries to want less control, more authority, and fewer reports, and more local differentiation in operations. At the same time, it is equally natural to expect those who attempt to manage extended worldwide operations to require greater reporting to facilitate control and more centralized standardization. These conflicting needs can lead to misunderstanding if *proper control methods* are not utilized.

The key to effective management is the ability to guide the company toward achievement of worldwide objectives without stifling the initiative of local operations. To reach these goals, effective international control systems must contend with all the problems found in domestic business plus additional obstacles unique to international business. In developing an international control system, the unique factors discussed affect specifically each step of the control sequence.

Control sequence

There are two prerequisites to a control system: (1) plans and (2) organizational structure. The process of control begins with expected objectives; therefore, specific plans must precede development of the control system. Further, controls require that someone have the responsibility to implement action when operations are "out of control" and need to be corrected. Before adequate control can be established, lines of authority and responsibility must be developed within the organization. Assuming plans are established and responsibility assigned, a control system follows a logical sequence of steps beginning with objectives reflecting marketing plans and

EXHIBIT 22–2: The control sequence

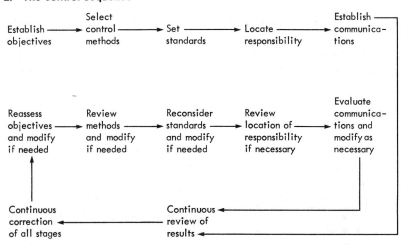

ending with responsibility for someone to initiate corrective action when needed. Exhibit 22–2 shows the relationship and dynamic nature of the seven steps of a control sequence. Whether controlling international marketing operations or domestic operations, a control system begins with (1) establishing objectives, then (2) selecting the control methods, (3) setting standards, (4) determining location of responsibility, (5) establishing a communications system, (6) devising a method for evaluating and reviewing results, and (7) establishing a method to initiate effective action where and when needed. Each step can be influenced by the unique factors outlined in the section above.

Establish objectives. Newcomers in international marketing are liable to have unformed ideas about their precise objectives in entering international competition. Lack of a sharply defined objective is not totally unacceptable, but it can prove to be a hazard if substituted for realistic goals and objectives which might be accomplished through adequate planning and a comprehensive control system. Management must outline explicitly in advance not only general objectives but also specific short- and long-term objectives for the international operation. Unless these are determined at the outset, management cannot know what resources are required or what gains are expected. Without knowing objectives, company standards cannot be established and planned control is impossible.

Companies with a variety of far-flung subordinate organizations often fail to communicate adequately about firm objectives and the goals for specific operating units. Unless statements of objectives are conveyed explicitly they have little relevance to subordinates. Objective statements should identify overall company goals so everyone concerned knows where the company is going, and they should provide specific details of operational objectives to the persons in charge. Statements may include specific, explicit goals such as the attainment of a given market share or specific dollar level of sales or profit or may spell out less-tangible goals such as increasing product visibility, developing channel structure, or improving product and company image. It is advantageous to be as concrete as possible in communicating objectives, but inclusion of abstract objectives lends perspective. After the general and operational objectives are established, management should select the basic method or methods of coordination and control most likely to be effective in a given circumstance.

Select control method.   Direct or indirect controls are the basic alternatives relevant to overseas marketing operations. Methods of direct control include contractual arrangements and ownership participation. Indirect control may rely on communications or competition. The extent and degree of control can very widely, regardless of the control methods utilized.

Formal contractual arrangements may provide a positive and direct mechanism for controlling overseas operations but do not automatically provide the control; specific contract provisions must be provided for effective control. Two of the more common control arrangements utilize quotas and license requirements. Both may require specific performance, but it should be noted that contractual provisions cannot always be enforced. Contractual provisions can rely on elaborate formal administrative mechanisms or depend solely on voluntary compliance, but the parent company may need to turn to alternative marketing arrangements if contractual requirements are not met.

When a company is able to participate in the administration (or at least policy setting) of its international representatives, a large degree of control is assured. Ownership, even a minority interest, will often offer a substantial opportunity for control through ownership participation in management.

Set standards.   Before a control mechanism can work effectively, an objective-based set of standards must be adopted to measure progress. Standards should be expressed as explicitly as possible, and need not be limited to financial or cost matters. Standards of achievement for the marketing task can be set concerning profits, sales volume, establishment of channels of distribution, achieving entry into a given foreign market, or some other relevant measure.

Revenue and the expense budgets should be included in the company's standards for overseas operations. Companies unfamiliar with overseas operations should immediately establish expense budgets to help appraise costs and make realistic plans. Expense budgets typically are understated while revenue plans have a tendency to work the other way. Companies frequently find from projecting domestic figures they have understated expenses and overstated anticipated revenues. Continuing research and analysis of budget and accomplishment standards should be undertaken early to permit realistic standard setting. Standards must be established at all levels of operation and must be reviewed sequentially by each higher level to determine if they are realistic and consonant with the company's world goals.

Locate responsibility. The complexities of international organization make it difficult to locate the *ultimate* responsibility for overseas operation, and assignment of responsibility sometimes involves much coordination. Different departments or functional areas of the parent company must be aware of what is going on in other functional areas. Companies organized by product line need greater coordination of efforts in international than in domestic markets. Firms organized for international operations on a national basis need to establish liaison and coordination links among the various nations in which they have trading activities. Whenever possible, primary responsibility should be located with one person who can coordinate the efforts of others to permit centralized action and control. In no case should someone be given responsibility which is not in line with the authority delegated to that person.

Establish communication system. A reporting and control system is a company's central nervous system necessary for accumulating data and disseminating messages calling for action. Informal communication systems can be adequate in domestic marketing, but in international business it is imperative that an organized and systematic information system be developed to provide for a continuous flow of data for central office analysis and decision.

Information collection and dispersion can be costly activities, so the communication system must be carefully geared to just the right level of reporting. Too much information wastes executive time, too little fails to give an adequate basis for control. Analyzing data from the reporting system must not consume so much of a manager's time that there is no time left for actual management of the operation. Because of improving communications technology, the tendency seems to be to ask for too much information, much of which has no apparent or real purpose. Besides being time consuming for those in the field, it runs the risk of denigrating the value of reporting. One country manager warned, "You must have good reasons for asking for greater amounts of data. Otherwise you run the danger of various forms of noncompliance, *including misinformation.*"[6]

Language and communication breakdowns occur not only between companies and customers but also between managers. Both outgoing and incoming communications must be thoroughly comprehensible to the recipient to be effective. Since the conceptual framework of various managers differs, there may be a loss of communication even with words that seem understandable. Such conceptual problems are most likely to occur when dealing with abstractions, such as "good customer relations," or "prompt delivery." Communications should be kept in concrete terms.

A key element of the communications system is an apparatus for collecting information. Rather than just one method for collecting information, a company should collect information from a variety of sources using periodic

---

[6] Controlling an MNC—II: Decentralizing Tendencies Among European Firms," *Business International*, March 27, 1981, p. 101.

inquiry, automatic collection, company records, and field audits. Regardless of the makeup of a foreign operation, a company should gather data from field personnel, foreign agents, local marketing researchers, and customers. A company may also rely on a variety of automatic reporting systems including such devices as customer guarantee cards and routine reports by field sales personnel or middlemen. All these routine reporting systems should be evaluated periodically to determine whether they are economical, flexible, accurate, and, most important, provide the necessary information for the control process. Field audits by headquarters personnel can add insights into a company's foreign problems and opportunities. Such visits can be determined by the number and kind of problems encountered, the value and profit potential in the area, the cost of such visits, and the capability of the local managers or representatives. Trips abroad, frequently looked on by local managers as being more of a burden than a benefit, should be handled by experienced personnel who know what to look for and who have developed a capacity to listen to local problems.[7]

BOX 22–2:   Help doesn't count when it's too late

Foreign subsidiary managers of American companies seem to feel that home-office comments were "incisive" and "useful"; nonetheless, they complained that "they (home-office staff) spend too much time circling budget variances and asking why." One European derided home-office personnel as "those super-specialized specialists who only see one tree in the forest. As a result, all they do is give us trouble." Timeliness of response was another criticism—the fact that home-office comments are often elaborate but too late to be useful. One manager commented, "We get this beautiful computer printout showing us where we stand and what to do, but the February results arrive on May 1. By this time we've already corrected our mistakes or we're in big trouble."

Source: William K. Brandt and James M. Hulbert, "Communications and Control in the Multinational Enterprise," *Multinational Product Management* (Proceedings of the American Management Association and the Management Science Institute Research Workshop, August 1976), pp. xiv–6.

Physical facilities for handling international communications are becoming more sophisticated each year. International communications systems incorporating leased circuits, radio, and teleprinters, and satellite communications systems permitting instantaneous transmission have all facilitated communications over long distances. Information inputs also provide direct access to computers from any place in the world and permit real-time systems of management allowing home-office personnel to participate in or observe operations as they occur. As impressive as these technological advancements in communications are, they are meaningless unless there are parallel conceptual break-throughs that facilitate meaningful use of the masses of information being transmitted internationally.

---

[7] For a humorous account of one person's review of headquarters' visitors see "Beware the 'Visiting Fireman,'" *International Management,* March 1981, pp. 31–33.

Evaluate results and make corrections. Evaluation of results and initiation of corrective action to modify defective programs are the final steps of the control sequence. Information gathered from the field must be compared with established operational standards and objectives. If the results do not meet expectations, corrective action can be taken, or the standards and objectives can be modified. In international marketing there is a special likelihood of a significant lag between the time corrective action is initiated and the time it is completed. While such a time lag is understandable in view of the distance, cultural variations, and organizational problems involved, it is particularly important that evaluation and correction be continuing activities. A company should establish, whenever possible, contingency plans in advance and prestructure action patterns which could be employed on short notice to meet unanticipated market conditions.

The control sequence as discussed has no ending, but is an ongoing cycle of establishing, evaluating, reestablishing, and reevaluating.[8]

Analytical problems of control

Whether dealing with branch, subsidiary, joint venture, or franchise organizational arrangements, the individual responsible for establishing coordination and control systems finds numerous problems requiring analysis and harmonization with company objectives. Each of the alternatives has a variety of solutions, none generally superior, but each offering specific advantages in unique circumstances. The system must be designed within the framework of the organizational structure, goals, level of maturity, and working relationship which has been established. The success of an operation can depend as much on the evaluation system and the control system selected as on the realities of the situation.

The basis of measurement is critical in measuring profit as well as in measuring sales volume. Even the approach to measuring a simple thing like volume must be given careful analysis.[9] If volume goals are set in terms of dollars, then inflation, monetary fluctuation, and price modification beyond the control of the manager can each affect results. Measurement in terms of number of units, tonnage, or some other physical measure is not necessarily correlated with the end goal of profit. Transfer pricing policies, inventory procedures (LIFO versus FIFO), and the way in which exchange rate fluctuations are handled also greatly affect operating results.

Profits can be distorted significantly depending on where the parent com-

---

[8] For an interesting study of the issues discussed in this section, see William K. Brandt and James M. Hulbert, "Communications and Control in the Multinational Enterprise," *Multinational Product Management* (Proceedings of the American Management Association and the Management Science Institute Research Workshop, August 1976), pp. xiv–1 to xiv–40.

[9] See, for example, "How Firms Measure Marketing Success," *Business International,* June 25, 1976, p. 204.

BOX 22–3: How do you control counterfeiting?

Brand-product piracy continues to plague the international marketer. Controlling it is almost impossible, yet poor quality imitations can damage a product's image. What would you do in these two situations?

An Associated Press story reported that LaChemise LaCoste sport shirts, Cartier jewelry, Christofle silver, and other fancy names fill stores in Mexico City's high-class hotels and shops. The names are there but the goods are fakes and the original French and Italian companies have lawsuits pending against the Mexican copies. Unfortunately, even if the companies are successful with their lawsuits, the damage to the product's image is done. Another AP story reported that 4,000 Cartier watches worth $1 million were destroyed by U.S. Customs officials. The watches were seized at the U.S./Mexican border in route to Mexico. Actual value of the watches was $10 to $15 each but would have sold in Mexico for about $500 each. A real Cartier sells for $650.

Sources: "Cartier, Gucci Luxury Items Inspire Mexican Imitations," *Associated Press*, September 9, 1980 and "Time Runs Out on $1 Million in Ersatz Watches," *Associated Press*, October 14, 1981.

---

pany wishes to allocate earnings for tax or other purposes. Profits can be located in any facet of the multinational company and can be variously allocated to subfunctions; for example, in a vertically integrated oil company, profit could be located at the production phase, the refining phase, or the distribution phase, or could be allocated in some mix predetermined by the corporation headquarters. Another profit question pertains to short- versus long-term profits; a manager might maximize short-term profits and receive bonuses and praise while jeopardizing long-term profits.

All of these questions relate directly to the level and extent of authority, responsibility, and control. The location and identification of profit centers should be subjected to careful analysis as should the appropriate level of control and the amount of reporting demanded from any level of the marketing system. Typically, no single system will be adequate for a large company with different types of organizational relationships and market situations; therefore, the coordination and control system requires continuous reanalysis to be sure that it is functioning in the manner for which it was designed.

AREAS OF CONTROL

Since international marketing costs have a tendency to get out of line, they require special emphasis; markets are small, transportation and communication are difficult, and auditing procedures often inadequate. Even the costs of operating the international division at the home office can easily escalate. The areas of international marketing control are similar to the domestic, but control systems and objectives can be quite different. To facilitate analysis, the international marketing manager may evaluate control activities from the viewpoint of volume, product, channel of distribution, promotion, personnel, and profit control mechanisms.[10]

Volume control

Measurement of sales volume is one of the most convenient control mechanisms available. The ease of securing aggregate weekly, monthly, or quarterly sales figures makes comparison with forecasts simple and provides management with a periodic check of subsidiary progress and sales by product line. Sales volume depends on the intensity of the marketing efforts, so the individual responsible can determine whether promotional expenditures and sales effort are appropriate to potential returns. That person should also be able to control profit levels through judicious care in other areas of marketing.

Detailed sales reports provide information on sales market by market, product by product, and by gross margin category. They give sales breakdowns to subsidiaries or other related companies and may identify government or other large-volume purchases.

Market share information should also be gathered on a regular basis so that management can have both absolute and relative bases of control.

Price control

Price cutting and excessively high prices jeopardize a company's market position. Management should receive regular reports of prices actually being collected and should be alert to the possibility of subsidiaries or middlemen competing against each other on a price basis. Such price competition can be beneficial to the winning member, but it is detrimental to the company as a whole. Also, multinational customers frequently are aware of prices in different countries and demand the lowest international price.[11]

Despite tariffs, transportation, and local market conditions which modify actual prices, central management should always retain basic control over prices. To provide competitive flexibility, management may establish price ranges for foreign markets and require transactions negotiated at different prices to be reported immediately. Such reporting lessens the number of such sales and permits decentralization of the pricing function without full loss of control. Regardless of the level of operation or the type of middlemen involved, price information is needed for effective home-office control.

---

[10] For one company's solution to control of nonfinancial fields, see "How International Paper Measures Performance in Nonfinancial Fields," *Business International,* September 17, 1976, p. 299.

[11] D. R. Cates and C. D. Fogg, "Some Practical and Conceptual Issues in International Marketing," *Multinational Product Management* (Proceedings of the American Management Association and the Management Science Institute Research Workshop, August 1976), pp. xiii–5.

Product control

Domestic marketing managers must be certain that a product is suitable for the market and delivered to customers in good condition. A product or brand image is directly dependent on a customer's experiences with the product and the firm. Foreign customers are more likely than domestic customers to indict all products of a particular firm if they have a bad encounter with one; products of the foreign producer are, so to speak, "on trial" at all times—in such cases, indeed, in all cases, product quality control is crucial.

Often, product image is more important than the product itself, and good quality alone is not enough to overcome a poor image. A single company cannot by itself overcome a poor industrywide or nationwide product image. The Japanese government helped its industries overcome the reputation for shoddy, imitative products by enforcing rigid government standards and inspection of export goods. No company should expect less of its products.

Domestic marketers cannot always foresee whether their products will be suitable for a foreign country, but effective communication and control systems can provide information about product and product-line decisions. Without an adequate feedback mechanism a manager may not be able to identify the cause of purchaser dissatisfaction. Other product hazards which must be controlled are excess damage which can be spotted through a well-organized control system, and pre- and post-sale servicing not measuring up to the standards necessary. Quality risk when a product is produced by a foreign subsidiary, a licensee, or franchisee can be minimized through adequate control systems. Only close control can assure management that the product's brand image will be preserved.

Promotional control

Advertising and personal selling should be subject to the same broad range of control systems and mechanisms applied in domestic markets. Personal selling cannot be directed from the home office, but it certainly can and should be managed. The advertising function may also be organized and developed centrally or decentrally, and, as discussed in Chapter 15, campaigns may be standardized for all markets or locally developed; whether standardized or not, all advertising needs control. In fact, the success of an advertising program may depend more on how well the campaign is being controlled than on whether or not it is standardized.[12] The home office particularly needs to know it is communicating effectively in all markets and corporate-wide objectives are being met throughout the world.

---

[12] Dean M. Peebles, John K. Ryans, Jr., and Ivan R. Vernon, "Coordinating International Advertising," *Journal of Marketing,* January 1978, pp. 28–34.

Channel control

The primary measure of a middleman's effectiveness will be the volume of purchases from the company, but such information does not provide adequate detail on whether the distributor is maintaining reasonable prices or is functioning effectively in the areas of sales and service. Because middlemen will not or cannot provide objective information about themselves, continuing customer research is the only method of gaining adequate feedback on the level of sales representation, speed of filling orders, quality of post-sale service, and other distributor functions. If volume and marketing-share goals are not being met, the entire distribution setup should be reviewed to determine if it is causing the market problems.

BOX 22–4: Out of control—or necessary?

It would certainly make it easier if there could be only one brand name for a product throughout the world. For some companies like Coca-Cola and Pepsi-Cola it is possible but others have to adapt to local customs. Gillette, the razor blade company, has found it necessary to have different brand names in different countries.

Atra, Gillette's swivel-head razor, is called *Contour* in most of Europe and Latin America. The same product is sold as *Actas* in Japan. Although it has no meaning, the word was chosen because of "the cultural effectiveness of a snappy first syllable and an 'a' at the end of the word."

The use of different names violates the old Gillette gospel of "one sight, one sound, one sell." That dictum fell when it was found that sales of Right Guard deodorant were flagging in Italy because the name was practically unpronounceable in Italian.

Gillette itself goes under different names in different countries, selling *Nacet* blades in the Middle East and *Minora* products in Africa and Latin American. In Eastern Europe, the company's products carry trademarks of *Mem* while in Indonesia they are *Rubie* and *Goal*.

Source: News report by *Associated Press*, August 1980.

Supervision and control of distribution channels require standards that differ from those in domestic trade. A company may have little decision latitude in foreign distribution-channel policy with less opportunity to manage and control these channels. For example, restricting the number of outlets for merchandise can cause problems because middlemen structures may not permit exclusive or restricted distribution. A company accustomed to a small number of middlemen may find itself confronted with an entirely different control system in order to supervise a large number of dissimilar outlets. And the caliber of middlemen is hard to control because in many cases there are no middlemen who meet normal predetermined standards.

Since sales volumes are often too low to permit extensive control mechanisms, many manufacturers are content with less control in overseas markets, but such laxity can destroy the effectiveness of a distribution system. For example, it was discovered quite by accident that a British franchisee of packaging machinery was making nearly one third of its quota through sales in another franchisee's territory on the Continent. This discovery highlighted both inadequate territorial control and an inadequate sales quota system.

Marketing personnel control

Personnel is a vital ingredient for the success of a marketing program. Home-office management must always be concerned with top-level marketing management in each country, but, increasingly, companies are taking greater interest in all marketing personnel, including hiring, management development, and compensation. Performance reports are accumulated on a regular basis, and records of managers in different parts of the world are routinely compared as a method of spotting managerial deficiencies. Companies using tight control in marketing personnel have encountered considerable resistance from field managers but maintain the practice because it has proven successful.

BOX 22–5: Government control

Socialist governments have found that one of their chief problems is maintaining control over the businesses they direct. Problems are sometimes aggravated in a mixed economy such as that of Egypt, where private business and socialized firms exist side by side.

The success of the flourishing general merchandise business of one *Mohamed X* in Cairo agitated government planners, so they established a subsidized store directly across the street from his place of business. The subsidized store purchased all it wanted of goods at reduced government prices, which imposed a distinct threat to the entrepreneur across the street. The private store owner, however, was a student of human nature and quickly made a bargain with the operator of the one-man government store. The former would purchase all of the merchandise from the latter, who could then fulfill his sales quotas and get his sales commission and not be troubled with the problems of keeping the store. Each morning when the government truck delivered the supplies, the government-store manager diverted them across the street, collected the day's receipts, and spent his day in leisure.

Officials from the Ministry of Supplies were delighted that the new store had become so successful so quickly. Eventually supervisors made a field investigation and discovered what was happening. Rather than report the situation to their superiors and show their own possible negligence, they approved the arrangement so everyone could continue doing business as usual.

Source: Related by Mohamed Khalil to the author.

Profit control

The goal of a corporation is generally to maximize worldwide *net* profits. Profit reports can communicate to management the overall health of subsidiary operations and current market conditions. They may also function effectively as trend reports to provide overall management guidance. Since profit is the ultimate goal of all marketing activity, the ultimate measure of success is in terms of profit. And while profit measures managerial effectiveness, success in building volume, maintaining margins, and controlling costs, success in all does not guarantee profit. Indeed, profit as a simple, concrete idea does not easily fit in an international business framework.

Some companies reinvest all profits and count their operations most successful. Obviously, any corporation must establish its own methodology for measuring and controlling profits. One of the critical decisions in profit management is determination of where the profits will be taken, so ultimate profit control must be at the home-office level. Another home-office decision is whether profits are to be maximized in the short or long term. Control is a much broader concept than accounting and applies to all areas of the marketing operation. Control in most areas of marketing is more difficult and expensive in world markets than in domestic markets, and each of the control areas mentioned above is closely related to *all* the others; effective control systems in one area will add little benefit unless all others are effective also. The requirements of close control and its resulting difficulties pose an ever-present dilemma for international marketers.

HOME-OFFICE RESPONSIBILITY

Although responsibility for international operations may be delegated to a chief international officer, the ultimate responsibility for the success or failure of an international enterprise falls on the chief operating officer of the company. Because of this primary responsibility, home-office management needs to exercise just the right degree of control over affiliated international organizations. Control functions must be carefully assigned at a level where they will be most appropriately implemented. At a minimum, the home office must make basic policy decisions, major fund allocations, and executive selection.

BOX 22–6: When is it overcontrol or how about the 25 cents spent for parking?

In the past, corporate headquarters often permitted overseas subsidiaries to be run as independent fiefdoms. Today, subsidiary managers must have strong relationships to corporate staff. An extreme example of this is the new CEO who required that the major product-line controllers within each operating division travel monthly to corporate headquarters for a formal presentation to the CEO and his corporate financial staff.

One executive of the firm interviewed by BI said that all work in his department effectively ceases for three full days each month while staff members prepare and rehearse this presentation. He also expressed the irony of the fact that, at one of these sessions, he was questioned in depth about an $11,000 item—part of a several-million-dollar report—by the CEO, who is responsible for running a multibillion-dollar MNC.

Source: "Corporate Staffs Are Playing Greater Role in Control of the MNC." Reprinted from *Business International*, April 3, 1981, pp. 106–7 with the permission of the publisher, Business International Corporation (New York).

The trend in international management thinking is shifting from decentralized control toward some balance between complete decentralization and complete centralization. Full decentralization has not proved consistently reliable, and communications and information-handling technology have developed to a point where home-office control is more feasible. Yet, full centralization has its detractors also. The major criticism of centralized decision making is the lack of responsiveness to local conditions. A reasonable reply to this issue is for a decision to be made centrally if control and standardization are critical factors or locally if local market conditions are of major importance.[13] Whatever the argument, corporate staffs are assuming greater responsibility in the control process.[14]

SUMMARY

In organizations, as in individuals, self-control is at least partly a function of maturity. Many companies new to international operations reason that the need for flexibility, the complexity of international organization, and the differences in operations from country to country justify neglect of coordination and control systems. However, companies that have been most successful in international operations have learned that control systems can be developed to handle most situations. Controlling marketing operations is always difficult, but it is especially so in international operations. All marketing areas can be coordinated and controlled through a basic control sequence. The planning stage of the control sequence includes establishing objectives, selecting control methods, setting up standards, and locating responsibility. Ideally, all four of these activities should be undertaken before a firm ever ventures into international marketing operations. Such control can be accomplished, however, through analysis of the firm's specific organizational structure as it affects control mechanism and determination of the exact areas in which control is desired. Coupling this information with a basic knowledge of the control sequence should result in an effective program of coordination and control.

The profitability of an international operation depends directly on the relationship between sales volume, the cost of producing the goods, and the cost of marketing or distribution. All four items—profit, volume, production cost, and marketing cost—are subject to control. Any effective program for coordinating and controlling world marketing operations requires special attention to the functions of price, promotion, product, and distribution channels. Information retrieval systems help to maintain communications, then

---

[13] For an interesting study of what influences the location of decision-making, see Jacques Picard, "Determinants of Centralization of Marketing Decision-Making in Multinational Corporations," *Marketing in the 80s,* 1980 Educator's Conference Proceedings, No. 46, August 1980, pp. 259–61.

[14] "Corporate Staffs are Playing Greater Role in Control of the MNC," *Business International,* April 3, 1981, pp. 105–07.

a continual review of results, with subsequent corrections and modifications, are required. These are the concepts relevant to coordination and control of international marketing operations.

QUESTIONS

1. Define:
   Volume control   Field audit
   Feedback   Cybernetic

2. What barriers make controlling an international operation more difficult than controlling domestic marketing activities?

3. How do company objectives relate to control systems?

4. "To minimize losses, management must be especially control conscious when it is engaging in the overseas business for some reason other than direct short-run profit." Explain.

5. Discuss the basic requisites of an effective control system.

6. Review the relative advantages of centralized and decentralized systems for controlling international marketing operations.

7. Develop a control system for a marketing program using autonomous foreign franchises to market a domestic product.

8. Review the control sequence.

9. Explain the importance of "timing" standards and controls.

10. Visit a firm with international sales or marketing activity. Compare their control system with one which you develop for them. Explain the differences.

11. Discuss the difficulties associated with field audits.

12. How can a company be certain its control system fits into organization and objectives?

13. Controlling is the very essence of management. Explain.

14. Discuss how the unique factors in international control affect the control process. Give examples.

Case VI-1

Dynamics International—writing a policy on bribery

Concerned about recent revelations of bribery, kickback payoffs, laundered money, and slush funds that companies have been involved in both domestically and internationally, Dynamics International's Board of Directors was surprised to learn they had no policy other than a few general "public relations" statements on the subject. Although they had not had problems in the United States or abroad, at least none they were aware of, they felt that without a specific set of guidelines they were setting policy by omission. They realized that some types of "unethical" or "questionable" behavior might be avoided if a person faced with a difficult decision specific guidelines. Their primary concern was with the international situation which they knew would be more difficult to deal with because of widely variable cultures in which businesses operate.

The Board of Directors felt this would be a good time to write a policy regarding bribery since it appeared the new Business Practices and Records Act (formerly the Foreign Corrupt Practices Act) which dealt with bribery was being established as the government's position on the subject. The Foreign Corrupt Practices Act (FCPA), passed in 1977, had created a great deal of confusion.

The FCPA made it illegal for companies to bribe foreign officials, candidates, or political parties. Further, the law provided for stiff penalties to be assessed against executives found guilty of having "a reason to know" that a company's independent agents were paying bribes. Immediately after the law was passed, many international companies were uncertain of the interpretation. Did it mean that any payment, even that given to a border guard to have papers processed rapidly, was illegal? Or would the small "lubrication" type payments every executive knew was being paid by most foreign agents expose an international executive that "had reason to know" to U.S. government action? Initially there was a great deal of confusion about the FCPA, but after a few months, the government issued several interpretations that seemed to clarify the issues. The major point of clarification had to do with "grease" type payments that seemed to be acceptable.

However, it was not until 1982 that Congress passed a new law which softened the original FCPA somewhat. The new law, now called the Business Practices and Records Act, specifies that illegal foreign bribery means only willful bribery. Thus, the reason-to-know provision of the FCPA no longer applies. Now executives will have to have "knowingly" authorized bribes before they can be held liable. In addition, payments made to facilitate a sale, if lawful in the country involved, do not constitute a bribe. But as long as there is room for interpretation, the Board feels the company cannot continue without a definite policy statement.

Dynamics International's foreign business accounts for about 40 percent of their total sales and produces an equal amount of their profits. They have wholly-owned subsidiaries in some countries, and, in other countries, they work through a series of agents and middlemen. The countries where they employ agents are notorious for bribery (primarily the Mideast and Latin America) and they are suspicious their agents may be involved. They are also concerned that some of their wholly-owned subsidiaries might be involved in paying bribes although not openly. The first principle to be established is, "What is unethical or unacceptable behavior?" This question is especially important because bribery can range from the relatively innocuous payment of a few cents to a minor official so that he does not take four hours to get papers processed, to the extreme of paying millions of dollars to a head of state to insure preferential treatment for a company. Obviously, a workable policy must effectively deal with all contingencies. Bribery must first be defined and there appear to be limitless variations. The difference between bribery and extortion also should be established. Voluntarily offered payments by someone seeking an unlawful advantage is bribery; payments extracted under duress by someone in authority from a person seeking only what they are lawfully entitled to is extortion. An example of extortion would be a finance minister of a country demanding heavy payments under the threat that millions of dollars of investment would be confiscated. Another variation of bribery that should be defined is the difference between *lubrication* and *subornation*.[1] *Lubrication* involves a relatively small sum of cash, gift, or service made to a low-ranking official in countries where such offerings are not prohibited by law; the purpose being simply to facilitate or expedite the normal, lawful performance of a duty by that official (a practice common in many countries of the world). Subornation, on the other hand, generally involves large sums of money, frequently not properly accounted for, which are designed to entice an official to commit an illegal act of magnitude on behalf of the one paying the bribe. Lubrication payments are requests for a person to do a job more

---

[1] Hans Schollhammer, "Ethics in an International Business Context," *MSU Business Topics,* Spring 1977, pp. 53–63.

rapidly or more efficiently, whereas subornation is a request for the official to turn his head, not do his job, or to break the law.

A third variation which may appear to be a bribe but may not be, is an agent's fee. A business person uncertain of the rules and regulations may hire an agent to represent the company in a particular country. This would be similar to hiring an agent in the United States, an attorney for example, to file and appeal for a variance in a building code on the basis that the attorney will do a more efficient and thorough job than someone unfamiliar with such procedures. Similar services may be requested of an agent in a foreign country when problems occur. However, a part of the agent's fees may be used to pay bribes, and sometimes it is impossible to determine if the intermediary's fees are being used unlawfully. There are many middlemen, attorneys, agents, distributors, and so forth who may function simply as conduits for illegal payments. The process is further complicated by legal codes which vary from country to country; what is illegal in one country is "winked at" in another and legal in a third.

It is obvious from this discussion that the issue of bribery is not absolute and the process of writing a policy on bribery will be intricate. Below are two different codes of ethics from two well-known U.S. companies. Each company considers its codes to be the final word on policy.

Company A
Some Thoughts to Consider for Ethical Conduct

1. A good name can't be bought; it must be earned . . . from the public, our customers, the government, even our competitors. Without their acceptance of us as an above-board corporation, we wouldn't be in business for long.

2. We care about business success, to be sure, but we also care how we achieve that success. At *Company A,* "anything goes *doesn't* go.

3. From board room to boiler room, it doesn't require a law degree to know you are doing something that's just plain wrong. If you're genuinely in doubt, ask a company lawyer.

4. Honesty isn't merely the best policy; it's the only policy. Dishonest, immoral, illegal, or unethical conduct is unacceptable in *Company A's* way of doing business.

5. Just as a reminder, illegal conduct includes price-fixing, giving or taking bribes or kickbacks, reciprocity, allocating markets, giving improper political contributions, pilferage, and misuse of company funds. It also includes revealing confidential information or accepting confidential information you should not have.

6. Simply ask yourself, Could I do business in complete trust with someone like myself? Make certain that the honest answer is an *unqualified* yes!

Company B
Ethical Business Conduct
Summary of Company Policies

In all instances, it is the policy of the Company that its business be conducted in a lawful and ethical manner. The policies which are summarized below need to be understood and followed by every employee who acts on behalf of the Company anywhere in the world. They are designed to protect and enhance the Company's integrity as an outstanding corporate citizen in every part of the world where it does business. The Company does not wish to obtain business which compromises its standards in any way.

Violation of the policies can expose the Company and the individuals involved to criminal actions, fines, injunctions, and lawsuits for damages or restitution. Individuals who violate these policies are subject to discharge or other disciplinary action.

It is against Company policy for any employee to authorize payment of or to use any funds (either Company or personal) for a "bribe," "kickback," or any other similar payment, whether lawful or unlawful, designed to secure favored treatment for the Company. It is equally against Company policy to use an intermediary to make any such payment or to disguise any such payment as a commission, refund, or in any other manner. Should you find yourself in any situation where a request is made for a bribe, kickback, or any other payment whose propriety you question, or where you have any knowledge of payments being made to an agent which are in excess of reasonable fees for services rendered, it is your responsibility to report the situation immediately to your manager and to Company counsel.

In all countries of the world, it is the policy of all affiliated companies that they do not make political contributions unless they (1) comply with both public policy and law of the country involved, (2) are recommended by the Board of Directors of the affiliate, (3) are reasonable in amount, (4) are made in approximately equal amounts to the major parties, and (5) are disclosed in advance to Company counsel and the Company Auditor.

Company A's and Company B's statements are dissimilar in that one is relatively general, the other more specific. Your task is to evaluate the two statements in terms of their adequacy in covering the kinds of ethical issues which arise internationally and then attempt to write a statement or a policy on bribery for Dynamics International which Dynamics will use as its official policy. Keep in mind that Dynamics International is interested in pursuing ethical corporate behavior anywhere in the world, but does not want a policy so rigid it would jeopardize the normal, ethical, and acceptable business practices with which their operating personnel would be confronted throughout the world.

Case VI–2

Freshtaste, Inc.—marketing milk sterilizers in Japan

Freshtaste, Inc.[1], a subsidiary of a U.S. manufacturing firm located in the Pacific Northwest, holds the patents for, and a working model of, a machine that sterilizes milk. A major advantage of sterilized milk over pasteurized is that once sterilized and properly packaged, the milk can be stored at room temperature for up to three months. There are several processes on the market for sterilizing milk, but the "Freshtaste" process is distinctively different from all others because it produces a sterilized milk with a taste that cannot be distinguished from fresh milk. In fact, the brand name Freshtaste was selected because it highlights the distinctive advantage this process for sterilizing milk has over all others. Other processes produce sterile milk products with a taste that is best described as cooked or slightly burned and which produces a cloying thickness that lingers after the milk is swallowed. A large number of milk drinkers object to that taste sensation. Scientists and food engineers claim the peculiar flavor or after-taste is caused when milk touches a hot surface as it is being sterilized. Milk is sterilized by raising the temperature of the milk to between 135° and 150°C (275° to 302°F) to eliminate all bacteria. When the sterilized milk is vacuum-packed in a manner which shuts out all light and air, the milk can last six weeks to three months at room temperature. Once opened and refrigerated, the milk has twice the shelf life of pasteurized milk.

The Freshtaste process sterilizes the milk as it falls in film-like sheets through a vat. Unlike other sterilizing processes where the milk is boiled and touches hot surfaces, the Freshtaste process prevents the milk from touching any surface hotter than itself. The milk is sterilized by an ultra-high temperature steam virtually while it is in mid-air. This eliminates the cooked taste that many people find objectionable. Several scientifically run blind taste tests have indicated that consumers cannot taste the difference between Freshtaste sterilized milk and regular milk.

A blind taste test in 1980 at the Dairy Marketing Forum at a midwestern university showed that 62 percent of the milk tasters incorrectly identified sterile milk as regular, homogenized whole milk and that 54 percent of the evaluators identified regular, homogenized whole milk as a sterile whole milk. On a scale of one (disliked extremely) to nine (liked extremely), the Freshtaste sterile milk had an overall acceptance rating of seven. This rating

---

[1] A fictitious company name.

was the highest acceptance score for any product tested at the Forum in the last several years. The process also can be used for juices and beer or any other liquid. Canned juices currently have a cooked flavor, but we are accustomed to it so we find no objection.

Freshtaste, Inc., has had an operating model for the last three years, but has not been successful in selling the idea to U.S. dairies. Because other sterilizing processes have produced milk with unacceptable flavors and textures, U.S. dairy companies have been reluctant to invest in yet another new process. This reluctance has been reinforced by the technical requirements for the container. The container must be completely airtight for the sterilized milk to have maximum shelf life. To date, the only true airtight containers are sealed cans or glass containers. While the cost of cans for juices has been accepted by consumers over the years, the dairy industry has always opted for the least-expensive containers, first using reusable bottles and now disposable cartons. They have used less-expensive containers to offset the higher cost of refrigeration required to keep the unsterilized milk from spoiling. The use of glass or can containers for sterilized milk would make the product too costly to effectively compete with regular milk even though there are some major cost advantages of sterilized milk. For example, warehousing and delivery costs of fresh milk are the greatest single costs in the industry; the product must be refrigerated from the plant until the customer actually consumes the product. Freshtaste executives say the transportation and energy savings realized from not having to refrigerate during the marketing and distribution of sterilized milk could reduce the total cost of milk in the long run. Since most states require milk to be sold within a few days after it is processed, additional cost savings would result from reduction of spoilage and returns. Pennsylvania, for example, requires milk to be sold within nine days after processing and New York allows only four days; all out-of-date milk (a substantial amount) must be destroyed.

The packaging is a major obstacle. With glass or cans too expensive, the only potentially usable package is a six-layered container constructed of paper, polyethylene, and aluminum foil sold under the name Seal-Pak.[2] This container permits a vacuum-packed process and it is assumed to be completely germ proof. It has several disadvantages, however: it requires scissors to open, has a nonresealable pouring spout which could create problems for the consumer, and it is about 50 percent more costly than the traditional paper milk containers now in use for fresh milk.

Because of the reasons outlined, Freshtaste, Inc., feels they must wait until an acceptable container is developed to sell their equipment in the United States. The use of sterilized milk in the United States may be minimal because of the nationwide network of refrigeration already available for fresh milk handling; thus, the company wants to look elsewhere for potential markets. They feel that markets where the per capita consumption of fresh

---

[2] A fictitious brand name.

milk is lower than in the United States but is growing might be effective markets for the introduction of the sterilized milk process. Eventually, the Freshtaste executives feel there will be a market for their equipment in the United States but the time needed for development of that market would be longer than they are willing to invest in at this stage. They are considering marketing the milk machinery in countries with expanding milk consumption.

Initially both Europe and Japan were considered as possible markets for the Freshtaste sterilizer, but it was decided to bypass Europe even though sterilized milk had been introduced in Sweden in 1961 and had spread rapidly to Europe during the mid-1960s. Today, sterilized milk accounts for about 16 percent of total milk consumption in Europe, but the degree of distribution varies considerably according to country. In Italy and West Germany, for example, where the consumption of sterilized milk is fairly high, the production of regular milk is low and most sterilized milk is packaged in paper containers and is available in stores and supermarkets. In other European countries where there are low consumption rates of sterilized milk, such as Britain and Norway, regular fresh milk production is high and is usually bottled and sold on a home-delivery basis. The sterilized milk currently being sold in Europe does not use the Freshtaste process and thus has the distinctive flavor problem that Freshtaste would not have. In Europe, fresh milk is produced in abundance, is reasonably priced, and most of the advantages associated with sterilized milk do not seem to be important. Thus, the decision was made not to enter Europe at this time.

In Japan, however, the situation is different. Consumption rates are increasing rapidly, and production of fresh milk is somewhat limited. It appears that there may be some significant advantages in sterilized milk for this market. Exhibit 1 presents some historical data on milk consumption in Japan and Europe.

Japanese market.   Prior to World War II, Japan had one of the world's lowest per capita consumption rates of milk. Since World War II, Japanese consumption of milk has increased considerably even though it does not

---

EXHIBIT 1:   Milk consumption—Japan and Europe (kg per head per year)

	Japan	Europe
1968	22.5	80.3
1970	24.4	82.0
1971	25.4	91.4
1973	26.4	102.0
1974	28.0	99.0
1977	35.8	102.0
1980	50.0	108.0

Source: *Eurostat: Basic Statistics of the Community* (Luxembourg: Statistical Office of the European Communities), eds. 9, 11–14 and *Focus Japan*, "Japanese Dietary Habits," May 1981.

have an extensive dairy industry. On the surface, it seems that Japan offers several opportunities for the successful marketing of Freshtaste sterilizers. For one, there are companies already in Japan with sterilizing equipment that have achieved some degree of acceptance even with the taste problems. Freshtaste executives feel their process is so superior in taste to all others that there would be no real competition. Sterilized milk has been produced in Japan for some years for use on ocean-going ships and on isolated islands. In 1973, Nestlé, Japan, first introduced sterilized milk but its share in total milk sales has never been significant (see Exhibits 2 and 3).

One reason for the poor acceptance may be due to the lack of effective educational advertising. Japanese consumers have shied away from sterilized milk bearing a production date a few weeks old. In addition, milk processors and supermarkets have remained cautious because of the Health and Welfare Administration's regulations affecting all types of milk. Distributors and outlets are required to keep all types of milk, including sterilized milk, at temperatures of 10°C or below.

EXHIBIT 2: Diffusion of sterilized milk in Europe and Japan (1980)

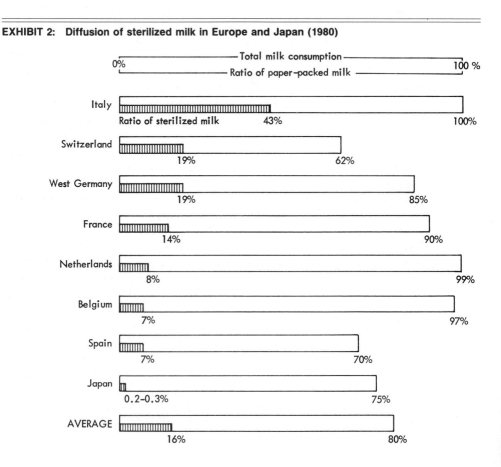

EXHIBIT 3: How Japanese consumers buy milk

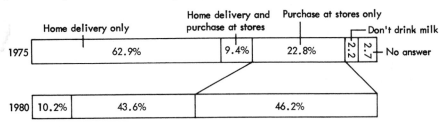

Even though the diffusion rate for sterilized milk had not been extremely rapid since its introduction in 1973, rates of consumption and potential demand for milk appeared so high that Freshtaste, Inc., made a financial commitment in early 1980 to enter the Japanese market. Freshtaste knew that Kagawa Consumers Cooperative, Japan's largest dairy farming co-op, and Daigaku, Inc., the nation's largest supermarket chain, were to introduce sterilized milk in 1980. They felt that if this introduction was successful it would stimulate demand for sterilized milk. Further, since the Freshtaste sterilizer was so superior to any on the market, the demand created for Freshtaste sterilizers would increase as a result of the Kagawa/Daigaku introduction. Additional market planning was underway by Freshtaste, Inc. when a heated controversy over sterilized milk developed in August 1980, with questions ranging from consumer safety to the possible impact on Japan's dairy farming. The Kagawa Consumers Cooperative and Daigaku, Inc. triggered the debate when they started full-scale marketing of sterilized milk in August, 1980, in a joint venture with Kimura Milk Industry Company and Seibu Milk Products Company, two of the three largest dairy product companies.

The Consumer's Union of Japan had planned to endorse the sale and consumption of sterilized milk but abruptly changed their minds and came out against the product because of their concern about sterilized milk's safety. The Union points out that sterilized milk cannot be considered as "fresh milk any longer, but rather is a factory product and high temperatures may alter the nutritional quality." Moreover, they are worried that ethylene-polymer may be released into the milk from the polyethylene lining used in the container.

Consumer attitudes were mixed: on one hand, many housewives do not see the need for sterilized milk in Japan because almost everyone shops everyday; on the other hand, many housewives expressed the opinion that "sterilized milk is richer than regular milk and is much more convenient because it can be stocked in the Pcks on the kitchen shelves and opened whenever wanted." The price of sterilized milk is about 10 percent more than regular milk, but it may still be considered more economical because of the lower spoilage rate.

The Consumer Science Association, a federation of 35 consumer organizations, mostly in Tokyo, supported sterilized milk as a means to boost per
capita milk consumption which is still only one fifth that of Britain. The Association had filed a request with the Health and Welfare Administry for removal
of the present ordinance requiring all milk to be refrigerated throughout
distribution routes and in retail stores so that redundant refrigeration costs
can be eliminated.

Dairy farmers were also split over the issue of sterilized milk; those in
areas neighboring big cities are dead-set against the distribution of sterilized
milk. They claimed that since sterilized milk can be shipped long distances
without refrigeration, small-scale dairy farming near large urban areas would
be all but destroyed by a massive inflow of milk from Hokkaido, the principal
dairy farming area of Japan.

The Consumer's Union also claimed that diffusion of sterilized milk from
Hokkaido could destroy small dairy farms in other regions, eventually opening the doors to low-priced milk from abroad. Hokkaido has a very sparse
population and about 87 percent of all milk produced there is currently
sold for processing into butter, cheese, and other milk products which bring
lower prices than milk sold for drinking. Thus, if dairy farmers in Hokkaido
sterilized their milk they could sell more milk at higher prices to populated
areas of Japan, if the market for sterilized milk were to grow.

The opposition to sterilized milk by dairy farmer's cooperatives resulted
in one co-op in Kyushu actually cutting shipments 30 percent to Seibu
Milk Products Company's local factory in protest against sterilized milk production. The ban was lifted when Seibu Milk Company promised not to
increase the quantity of sterilized milk presently being produced. Two other
major milk products companies made the same promise to the Central Dairy
Council of Agricultural Cooperatives Association.

As the controversy heated up, regional representatives of the Japanese
Cooperative Consumer Union, a nationwide federation of 620 consumer
cooperatives, met on Stptember 16, 1980, to establish an official policy.
The Union decided that it would not permit member cooperatives to sell
sterilized milk except in special cases. They criticized sterilized milk supporters for neglecting the importance of local, small-scale dairy farming which
supplies organic substances indispensable to agriculture. This point will
become increasingly more critical as the growing awareness of the alleged
harm of overdependence on chemical fertilizers spreads. Moreover, the
Union said that since the construction of processing plants for sterilized
milk required large-scale investment, the distribution of sterilized milk could
lead to a big-business monopoly of the dairy industry and hurt consumer
interest in the long run.

The Kagawa Milk Cooperative is one of the few co-ops that maintains
regular home delivery of fresh milk. One reason they began producing
sterilized milk was to relieve employees of early morning deliveries and
to lower distribution costs. They expected initially to have to deliver the

sterilized milk only once a week and eventually once a month, compared to every other day delivery for regular milk at the present time.

Milk specialty stores, whose main business is to make daily home deliveries of bottled milk and some paper-packaged milk, also spoke out against sterilized milk. They claimed the convenience of the present fresh-milk package and the home delivery system had helped spread the milk-drinking habit among the Japanese. Some worried that switching to once-a-week deliveries of sterilized milk would cut down on milk consumption. The fact is that the milk specialty stores have been losing market share ever since supermarkets started selling milk in cartons at lower prices. The distribution of sterilized milk could very well mean the end of milk specialty stores, and they are well aware of this possibility.

To further complicate the issue, the major advantage of sterilized milk, its long shelf life, is wasted because of the ordinance requiring all milk to be refrigerated. The supermarket industry believes, however, that it is only a matter of time before the requirement to refrigerate sterilized milk will be lifted. But, the Health and Welfare Administration and the Administration of Agriculture and Forestry have indicated they would wait and see how well sterilized milk is accepted by consumers before taking any action. As a result of the uproar caused by the different groups, sterilized milk's share of total factory output for milk was expected to reach only 2 percent by the end of 1980. Forecasts before the resistance predicted a 6-to-8 percent share by 1980.

When the controversy developed over sterilized milk, Freshtaste was about ready to approach a Japanese firm to begin discussing the possibility of a joint venture to introduce the sterilizers into Japan. The company was quite surprised by the reaction of the Japanese. They had not studied the market very thoroughly before getting involved so they decided to terminate all negotiations and to pull back to reexamine their initial decision. You have been asked to reevaluate the situation in Japan and to make a recommendation to the president of Freshtaste, Inc.

The President wants to see a preliminary report on the seriousness of the recent market reaction. Further, in light of the recent developments, he is interested in determining what additional information and research is necessary to complete a thorough feasibility study. The report should include (1) all the major resistances to the acceptance of sterilized milk and the relative importance of each; (2) some general idea of the strategies necessary to overcome the resistances in Item 1 and to develop a successful marketing program; (3) a rough idea of the time it will take to penetrate the market; and (4) based on your preliminary analysis and the data in Items 1, 2, and 3, a recommendation on whether or not the company should even attempt a marketing effort in Japan. Whether your response is to market or not, you should be prepared to defend your position.

Case VI–3

Market research reveals need to coordinate worldwide prices*

For some months retail and consumer audits had indicated a lower market share for Pandora Specialty Products in the U.K. than Charles Smith, the marketing director in Britain, was willing to believe.

Pandora's ex-factory sales were some 20 percent over the retail sales figures indicated by research. Meanwhile, the international company's young U.S. subsidiary, Pandora Inc., which had some 12 months earlier opened a plant in upper New York State, was having a rough time. Sales had declined sharply a month ago and showed no sign of recovery.

Jack Haldane, managing director of the U.K. company and a director of the international board, did not connect the two circumstances. The U.K. was doing well, so clearly the market research initiated by Smith was wrong.

Smith was concerned by the U.K. situation, although he would not admit it to Haldane. There had to be a reason for the difference between factory output in the U.K. and what was sold after passing through the independent wholesalers.

Smith now ran parallel samples and conducted further research in the U.K. all the figures tended to bear out the audit data.

A close examination of individual accounts revealed that much of the discrepancy could be traced to several large and medium-sized wholesalers. Visits to these companies revealed nothing untoward, however; their levels of stock had not appreciably increased.

A month or two later, Haldane received a confidential memo from the president of the U.S. company. It stated that, quite by accident, some U.K.-manufactured Pandora products had been found in a U.S. wholesaler. The man had been reticent about their source.

Haldane immediately called Smith into his office. Without comment he passed across the memo.

Smith grimmaced. "I had my suspicions," he said, handing the memo back. "After all, the sales volume unaccounted for in the U.K. almost exactly matches the sales lost in the U.S."

"So what has been going on?" Haldane demanded

"I have examined the price structure in the U.S. in detail," Smith replied, "and I have found that even allowing for freight and duty it would be

---

possible for an efficient single distributor to undercut our U.S. company's distributors by some 15 percent or even 20 percent."

Haldane frowned. "So the evidence points strongly to heavy unofficial exports to the United States," he said.

Smith nodded.

"Which no doubt has been made possible," Haldane continued, "by the fact that the U.S. company's pricing strategy placed their leading brand at the top end of the market."

"As you will recall," Smith said drily, "I voiced my objections to that policy at the time. I thought the product was overpriced. But in the end the accountants and the agency convinced me that, with the heavy cost of distribution and advertising, it was the only hope of a quick return on the plant."

"Well, it seems to have backfired," Haldane observed.

He got up from behind his desk and started pacing his office. "As managing director of the U.K. company I'm more than happy to see our plant here running to capacity," he said. "But as a member of the international board I'm also acutely aware of the growing problems of Pandora Inc. So what do we do? Any ideas?"

"Well, one thing is certain," Smith replied. "I don't see how we can stop our independent wholesalers exporting to the United States if they want to. And you can't really blame any wholesaler taking advantage of the exchange rates."

"That may be true but it is not much help to our U.S. company," Haldane said.

Smith felt like saying: "It's all very well saying that, but you ought to have sorted out the whole pricing strategy, at international board level, long ago."

Instead, he gave Haldane another unpalatable truth. "If the U.S. company alters its pricing strategy now," he said, "it's going to make nonsense of a very expensive advertising and promotion campaign. But if they don't do anything, can *we* do anything to tighten things up at this end?"

QUESTIONS

1. Evaluate each of the following choices as a solution to the price problem.
    a. Close the U.S. operations and export from the U.K. to the United States.
    b. Raise the U.S. price and supply from United States.
    c. Lower U.S. price and aggressively market the item in the United States.
2. Suggest and defend another solution.
3. Point out how better organization and control could have helped to avoid the problem in the beginning.

Case VI–4

W. H. Schwartz and Sons, Ltd.*

Introduction

Recently, Mr. R. A. Bureau, Vice President of Marketing and Sales of W. H. Schwartz and Sons Ltd., visited Australia to assess the possibility of Schwartz entering the Australian spice market. Mr. Bureau had to consider not only the volume potential of the Australian market, but also the strategy the company would use to enter the market, should the situation justify this.

Company history

W. H. Schwartz and Sons Ltd. is the oldest established spice house in North America, having been founded in the port city of Halifax, Nova Scotia, in 1841. In the early days of the company, the son of the founder was the only salesman, traveling around Nova Scotia by stagecoach in summer and by horse and sleigh in winter. Later, he imported the first bicycle with pneumatic tires from England and traveled throughout Nova Scotia selling his products.

Formed as a family firm, the company is still privately owned and family run. The company was the first in Canada to sell pure spices. Formerly only compound spices, such as ginger mixed with flour and cornmeal, were available. Even though pure spices were more costly than compound spices, Schwartz was able to convince the public that pure spices offered better value than compound spices which lacked strength and flavour. This emphasis on quality has continued throughout the company's history and remains the basis of its worldwide reputation today.

Sales of spices were modest and confined to Nova Scotia until after the First World War. Beginning in the 1920s the company expanded both its sales and product line. As the company grew, it acquired in 1930 Canada Spice and Specialty Mills in Saint John, New Brunswick. After this acquisition, the company's product line was extended to include peanut butter, flavouring extracts, and packaged dates and raisins. Later, in 1949, Schwartz purchased the second oldest Canadian spice company, S. W. Ewing Ltd. Within 10 years this Montreal plant was replaced by a new facility which served all of Quebec, Ontario and the Western Provinces.

---

* This case was prepared by Professor Philip Rosson and Janet Forrest of Dalhousie University, Halifax N.S., Canada as a basis for class discussion rather than to illustrate either effective or ineffective handling of an administrative situation.

Over the years the company has demonstrated its ability to adapt to changing market conditions. Although coffee had constituted the bulk of their sales, the line was dropped when it was found that instant coffee was posing a serious challenge. The company adapted to the supermarket "revolution" by introducing specially designed racks for the display of their spices, and were a forerunner in pack design, being the first to introduce the apothecary-type glass spice jar. A new merchandising technique was also pioneered by the company. This involved using full-time female staff to service display racks, so reducing costs and improving retail servicing. So successful was this method that Schwartz's competitors very quickly emulated the pioneering company.

In recent years, Schwartz has further expanded their manufacturing facilities and continue to expand its markets at home and abroad. In 1957, Schwartz entered the British spice market, where their high-quality pure spice was immediately recognized by the housewife. Initial losses were turned around and by 1976 Schwartz had become brand leader. This involved unseating its arch rival, the large American McCormick organization, from the top spot.

The company now sells in some 50 overseas markets, has gross sales of $27 million, and employs 300 people worldwide. Schwartz is optimistic about its future position in the spice market which accounts for 44 percent of its sales revenues. As one of their managers, commented ". . . we have the best quality in the world, the most attractive jar in the world, and the best method of merchandising in the world. How can we fail?"

The spice industry

A great deal of the production of the world's spices takes place in the countries of the developing world, where, for example, chilli peppers, ginger, nutmeg, sesame, cloves, and black and white peppers are grown. Spice production in more developed, nontropical countries consists mostly of herbs like rosemary, thyme, basil, tarragon and sage.

The developed nations of the western world are the most important markets for spices. In most countries the spice trade is concentrated in the hands of a few importers and spice packers, and processing usually takes place in the importing country. The main users of spices are households and the food industry. In the household sector, only a few spices such as pepper, nutmeg, and paprika are important and the bulk of household consumption is accounted for by these spices. Most consumers are unfamiliar with spices such as turmeric, coriander, mace, and cardamom and the food industry provides the major market for these spices. In recent years, however, increased travel and greater numbers of foreign restaurants have led many households to experiment with the more exotic spices. There are, in fact, many spices and the principal companies may sell a hundred or more different varieties.

One principal problem of the spice industry is the frequent and wide fluctuations in the prices of most major spices, notably pepper, ginger, and cloves in recent years. These fluctuations are caused by a number of factors including supply irregularities and speculative trading.

The packaging of spices is an important element in the marketing policy of the major packers. Traditional packs involved the use of a cardboard tube system with metal or plastic top, and the plastic drum or sachet. Schwartz and McCormick pack the majority of their spices in American-style glass jars. Both companies utilize racks in self-service stores, using their own merchandisers to keep the display stocked. Advertising of spices is minimal, but various promotions such as spice rack offers and recipe suggestions are frequently used by the major companies.

Trip to Australia

A variety of information was collected by Mr. Bureau on his visit to the Australian market. In overall terms the vice president felt that Schwartz should

---

EXHIBIT 1: Indicators of the market size for spices: Canada and Australia (Canadian dollars)

Indicator	Canada	Australia
Total population	21,089,000	12,881,064
Annual rate of population increase	1.7 percent	1.9 percent
Net migration gain	127,000	123,000
Percent population between 20–40 years of age	33.1 percent	28.3 percent
Percent population 40 years and over	32.0 percent	34.3 percent
Population growth (compared to 8 major developed Western economies)	Fastest	Second fastest
Urbanization	22 percent population live in Metro Toronto and Montreal	40 percent Population live in Sydney and Melbourne
Gross National Product	$84.5 billion	$52.9 billion
National product per capita	$4,005	$4,107
Per capita disposable income	$2,541	$2,477
Total retail sales—all food products	$7.5 billion	$5.0 billion
Per capita retail food sales	$354	$385
Market size spices at retail	$18.0 million	$10.2 million
Per capita sales spices at retail	$.85	$.78

contemplate entering the Australian market but had to sell the board of directors on the concept. As well as an entry decision, Mr. Bureau had also to think in terms of a marketing strategy which showed the best potential for success in this market. For as his investigations had shown him, the market was "anticipated to grow approximately 20 percent per year in coming years" (see Exhibit 3), but some industry sources felt that "there was some indication that the spice market was proliferating with too many brands" (see Exhibit 4).

With a board meeting one week away, Mr. Bureau began to closely evaluate the data he had collected on the Australian market, which is shown in Exhibits 1 through 7.

EXHIBIT 2: Grocery product sales and population

	Grocery prod-uct sales	Percent	Population	Percent
Australia:	$2,008,575,000	100.0	12,957,000	100.0
States:				
New South Wales and Australian				
Capital Territory	750,500,000	37.3	4,847,000	37.4
Victoria	578,675,000	28.8	3,564,000	27.5
Queensland	280,450,000	13.9	1,890,000	14.6
South Australia	161,950,000	8.1	1,205,000	9.3
West Australia	173,800,000	8.7	1,063,000	8.2
Tasmania	63,200,000	3.2	388,000	3.0
Urban centers:				
Sydney	462,000,000	23.0	2,717,000	21.3
Melbourne	392,000,000	19.5	2,389,000	18.7
Brisbane	n.a.	n.a.	817,000	6.4
Adelaide	n.a.	n.a.	809,000	6.3
Perth	n.a.	n.a.	640,000	5.0

EXHIBIT 3: Competitive data (extracted from the trade journal, *Food Week,* Fast Facts, no. 12)

Fast Facts Herbs and Spices: McCormick Foods describes the market, what it did to it, how the company merchandises its products, and the cooperation it receives from retailers.

Spice consumption rising 20 percent a year without any fall in margins. *In seven years, McCormick Foods has risen from a zero share of the Australian spice market and now claims to be volume market leader.* The company estimates that in 1966, the year it launched in Australia, the market was worth about $2 million, with the average supermarket offering the housewife a range of about 30 spice products. Today the market is worth between $7 million and $8 million and the average supermarket offers a range of over 120 items. *Ted McLendon,* managing director of McCormicks in Australia, said: "As world leaders in spices, we introduced the expertise necessary to develop the market and stepped into the quality void that existed. In 1966, our products were distributed by *Socomin,* the *Petersville* company. We opened our own manufacturing plant here and now handle our own sales in Sydney, Melbourne, and Brisbane, with Socomin looking after the other states. In 1976–77 we grew rapidly and now have in excess of 20 percent of the total spice volume sales: our share of the supermarket trade

---

EXHIBIT 3 (*continued*)

---

alone would be in excess of 50 percent. We're beginning to concentrate on the smaller food stores and I'm confident that the next two years will see us doubling our sales.

"*The market is one of the fastest-growing food sectors, with consumption growing annually at about 20 percent.* Rivals in growth over the last five years would be frozen foods and soft drinks. And the potential of spices is excellent. On a per-capita basis, Australians consume probably less than half the spice intake of Americans. In Australia we're presently marketing 180 products and sizes in three basic ranges—gourmet, regular, and the one-shot aluminum foil pouch range of gravies, sauces, and spice blends. The foil pouch range is our fastest-growing section. It has been available on a limited scale in Australia since 1966 but it is only during the last year that it has really taken off. *One of the major trends* has been the move away from the cardboard tube container to glass or tin. Cardboard is a very poor spice container; in a relatively short period of time it absorbs the essential oils of the spice, leaving the housewife with a flavour-depleted cellulose. That's the major reason we have never used it as a container. Another trend is toward spice blends as distinct from traditional spices."

Ted McLendon continued: "In Australia, spices sell according to areas and there's a lot more to servicing supermarkets than people realise. We normally start in a supermarket by installing a standard range of products. Over a period of time we study movement and then stock accordingly, planning the right mix for the right area. While we're introducing new products all the time we rarely drop any of the old. Australians are becoming more spice conscious and we haven't yet reached the plateau where we have too many products. From the retailer's point of view, spices are a profit spinner. They don't lend themselves to specialising and we make sure he enjoys a handsome margin and emphasize this point to him. Now we find that more and more the retailer is beginning to appreciate the value of his spice section. Spices are impulse items and we do a lot of in-store demonstration work, which is quite expensive, to encourage the housewife to purchase."

Fast Facts Herbs and Spices: Master Foods and Somerset Cottage policies.

Van delivery service and merchandising reps help reduce out-of-stocks. *Master Foods has 46 varieties of herbs and spices* and claims the biggest share of the dollar market. Master Foods started a retail van delivery service for herbs and spices and raised sales of some of its products by over 50 percent in a year. One reason why it started this service was caused by many out-of-stocks which retailers suffered with stocking over 100 items. Master Foods says most major chains now stock the company's range. Some use the van delivery service and some the company's merchandising service (company reps bring stock from the store's back room and restock the shelves themselves). Retailers usually carry either a two-shelf spice rack of 18–24 varieties, or a four-shelf rack of 46 varieties. *Master Foods estimates the market to be worth about $6 million at retail prices,* including all herbs, spices, flavoured sugar, seasoned salt, curry and mustard powder, pepper, and miscellaneous items such as meat tenderiser and monosodium glutamate. White pepper is the biggest commodity in the market. Parsley flakes, garlic salt, and garnishes are also volume-sellers.

The market is in three segments: (1) health food sales, which comprise mainly herbs and spices packed by the health food stores in cellophane packs; *(2) cannister and packet sales* of traditional herbs and spices such as peppers, cinnamon, and nutmeg, and *(3) the shaker-pack ranges* produced by Master Foods, McCormicks, and Somerset Cottage. Master Foods says the first two segments provide high sales but low margins. The shaker packs sell fewer units but have the highest dollar sales because of high unit price, and also have the highest margins and highest quality image. The market has good potential for expanding its distribution through butchers, health shops, and delicatessens, apart from grocery outlets. As people become more conscious of herbs and spices, cookbook sales, the art of cooking, newspaper and women's magazine coverage of the subject re all rapidly increasing. Master Foods says the market is rising at 15–20 percent a year, and should increase its growth rate in the future years. The

EXHIBIT 3 (*concluded*)

company is using such promotional materials as a wall chart for the kitchen listing the herbs and spices to use for certain dishes. The increasing number of Continental restaurants in capital cities and major towns is making people more conscious of herbs and spices.

John Hemphill, managing director of Hemphill Herbs and Spices, of Dural, N.S.W., says his *Somerset Cottage* range has maintained a steady growth rate in the 15 years he has been in business. There are now also more volume-selling lines. Many people use a jar of chives, onion flakes, garlic powder, or parsley flakes in a week or a fortnight. "We have had a demand for larger sizes in these lines and did introduce them. But they weren't popular with the supermarkets who felt they were too bulky," said Mr. Hemphill. Items such as nutmeg, ground ginger, and cinnamon continued to be bought at rare intervals because they last so long. Dried herbs have been the fastest-growing segment of the market. "Spices have always been around, but the herbs such as oregano, sage, and marjoram are just beginning to be noticed and are really jumping ahead. Certain spices sell better in some areas than others. "For instance, in the higher-income suburbs, herbs sell better, and in the poorer areas, items like garlic salt and onion salt sell well."

Other minor brands of spices available in Australia include Lawry's seasoning, Hoyts, Tasty, John Ball, McKenzie's, and Harper's.

EXHIBIT 4: Discussions with buyers in the grocery trade

Meeting 1

McCormicks has approximately 50–60 listings and without doubt had good control of the sections. The stores can adjust listings by deleting items which are listed at the head office. They also have a form which can request new products. These are then sent to head office and if the head office receives several requests, they usually list the product. He summarized the effectiveness of McCormicks by the following points:

1. Thorough approach to the market.
2. Good service.
3. Good lines.
4. Good stands and organization of the category for the first time.

Spice Island apparently tried to come into the market a couple of years ago, but were not thorough enough and failed.

The buyer indicated that frankly at this stage, he would not add another range because of the money tied up in relation to the return. This may be a point that would have to be clearly defined. He estimates a return of 6–7 times a year. He also pointed out that McCormicks did good stock rotation and gross profit return was satisfactory at approximately 25–30 percent. He was by no means suggesting that it would be easy or that his store group would even accept another line. He indicated that Master Foods' spices were only being stocked in three of his stores and that they had them for six months and nothing much had come of it. Apparently, Master Foods has been aggressive with its new line only for a couple of years. He did indicate that service and supply might be a bit of a problem with McCormicks and left the door open on the basis that with a proper programme, they might well be interested as long as the price was right.

Meeting 2

The buyer indicated that his group is extremely happy with McCormicks. The market was developing satisfactorily and the gross margins were in the region of 30–35 percent. He indicated that specialist stores might be interested in another line of spices.

EXHIBIT 4 (*concluded*)

Apparently, his group tend to be somewhat diffident with suppliers and he was not at all keen to see me, so I was limited to a discussion on the telephone. After discussion with him, he somewhat backed off and suggested that the market might be accessible, but he was not at all optimistic.

Meeting 3

This buyer indicated that the spice section, in his judgment, was becoming proliferated with too many brands. He agreed that there are essentially four elements: the bag; another section which we call the "tube section"; a third section, the regular McCormick-type product; and a fourth section, McCormick's gourmet which is also like Master Foods' product. It was apparent that this buyer intended to thin out the spice section and probably remove one of the major items, but it will not be McCormicks for whom he has a lot of respect as a result of their selling in the past few years.

He indicated that white pepper is a very big item by far and the tube product sells extremely well. There is a low margin on this line of between 16–18 percent. On the other items, there is a 25–30 percent markup. In his opinion, the market is overpriced and really, McCormicks should be selling between 20–25 percent markup.

He indicated that to do in-store demonstrations, which is quite good to move products in the spice section, costs $100 a store for demonstrator space. In addition to that, one has to pay for the demonstrators and the material.

It was obvious this buyer knew his business and was very willing to talk. He indicated by direct question that getting into the spice market may be difficult, but he believed that with the right pricing and promotion that it would not be impossible. However, this is in relation to the fact that the present spice market is probably already overserviced by a number of spice companies.

EXHIBIT 5: Visits to grocery stores

Store 1

Spice section is 9 feet—6 feet of McCormicks and 3 feet of Master Foods—4 shelves of each of them.

Store 2

Six feet of shelving—3 of Master Foods and 3 of McCormicks. The gourmet 1½ ounce McCormicks was 55 cents. Cinnamon sticks gourmet were 99 cents.

Store 3

Spice section 6 feet, 3 shelves—1 shelf gourmet and the rest regular McCormicks. Regular peppercorns, 35 cents and gourmet 53 cents. Regular size is 1¼ ounce and gourmet size is 1⅞ ounce.

Store 4

Spice section has only 1 shelf of gourmet and 2 shelves of regular—6-foot section. The 4-shelf unit has 37 varieties only.

Store 5

Store was approximately 10,000–15,000 square feet in size.

Two brands were represented, primarily Master Foods and McCormicks. The Master Foods shelves were 80 percent empty. A third brand was Somerset Cottage. The shelves were made of metal with shelf dividers. Division of shelves was as follows:

Master Foods: 4 shelves
Somerset Cottage: 3 shelves
McCormicks: 3 shelves

The length of the shelves were approximately 3 feet each.

EXHIBIT 5: (*continued*)

Shelf prices were as follows:

Master Foods:	Ground cinnamon	35 cents
	Sage	28 cents
	White pepper wh.	40 cents
McCormicks:	Garlic salt	33 cents
	Garlic powder	55 cents

The McCormicks products were regular line not the gourmet line.

Store 6

McCormicks had a 2-foot section; Master Foods a 3-foot section; and Somerset Cottage, a 3-foot section. Again, Master Foods was very poorly serviced, but McCormicks and Somerset Cottage were in better condition. In the case of Master Foods and Somerset Cottage, there were 4 shelves for each and McCormicks had 7 shelves. Prices were as follows:

McCormicks:	Garlic powder	49 cents
	Garlic salt	29 cents
Somerset Cottage:	Garlic powder	55 cents
	Garlic salt	38 cents

Store 7

This was a basement operation, similar to a North American department store gourmet section. This was in downtown Sydney, part of a complex called "Centre Point" which is a very up-scale shopping centre on several levels with stores all around. The food section in the store was quite messy, but may have been due to delivery that day. It had all the makings of a typical downtown store, so did not check prices on spices which might well have been different than the norm.

The spice section was round a pillar and included McCormicks' gourmet jars, regular tins and bottles, as well as Master Foods. It looked to me as if organization of the total spice section would not have been amiss in this store.

The Master Foods' and the McCormicks' stands were a little more modeled on the English-type stand about 3 feet each with 7 shelves made of tin, though the McCormicks was a gravity-fed metal affair looking like wood. Underneath each stand were two cupboards similar to the U.K. stands that we use. The McCormicks' 3-foot stand for the regular McCormicks product was a metal stand of white chrome. The single-shelf McCormicks' spice racks containing probably 6 or 7 bottles were also available in this store—priced at $8.95 each.

Store 8

8,000 square feet. Six feet of McCormicks—3 feet regular, 3 feet gourmet. 5 shelves double stacked of the regular and also about 6 feet of baskets of tub products.

Store 9

Five checkouts; this store has about 2,000—3,000 square feet. This store has Master Foods' and McCormick's gourmet, as well as regular—total of about 9 feet.

Store 10

It has 8 checkouts and is approximately 7,000 square feet. It is a clean store, much more like the regular American supermarket.

Nine feet of spices, 8 shelves high—including McCormick's gourmet, 2 shelves on the top; Master Foods, 3 shelves; and then baskets, 2 shelves below with the salt underneath. McCormick's gourmet is gravity fed.

Store 11

A little store about 4,000 or 5,000 feet. A small Master Foods spice section—3 feet; only 4 shelves. Also a McCormick's section.

Store 12

About 10,000 square feet. Spice section is about 6 feet, very poorly serviced. McCormick's gourmet and regular.

EXHIBIT 5: (*concluded*)

Store 13

A department store with a food section. The section runs about 500–600 square feet. Small spice section, very empty—just the regular McCormicks; 3 foot, 2 shelves, only.

Store 14

There is a 3-foot McCormicks stand with 3 shelves gravity fed of the gourmet and 4 shelves doubled up with the regular underneath.

Store 15

There was a complete gondola, with spices all the way around with gravity fed McCormick's gourmet bottles. Below that were McCormick's regular items.

EXHIBIT 6: **The spice market at the retail level (Australian dollars)**

	Bags/tubes	Regular	Gourmet	Total $s
Dollars	3,000,000	2,000,000	1,500,000	6,500,000
Percent	46 percent	31 percent	23 percent	100 percent
Average unit price	19 percent	29 percent	49 percent	—
Trade margin percent	12–16 percent	22 percent	30 percent	20 percent
Volume dozens	1,300,000	575,000	255,000	2,130,000
Percent volume	61 percent	27 percent	12 percent	100 percent
Profit to trade dollars	420,000	440,000	450,000	1,310,000
Profit percent	32 percent	34 percent	34 percent	100 percent

EXHIBIT 7: Cost price comparisons—Schwartz and McCormick (Australian dollars)

| | Schwartz regular | | | McCormick | | | | | | | |
| | | | | Regular | | | | Gourmet | | | |
Spice	Ounce	Wholesale price*	Retail price at 32 percent trade margin	Ounce	Wholesale price	Retail price	Trade markup (percent)	Ounce	Wholesale price	Retail price	Trade markup (percent)
Black pepper ground	1¼	3.18	0.39	1	2.24	0.25	24	1½	4.56	0.55	30.9
Cinnamon ground	1⅛	5.63	0.69	1¼	4.40	0.49	24	1¾	8.20	0.99	31.0
Curry powder mild	1⁹⁄₁₆	2.37	0.29	1⅛	3.16	0.35	26	2	3.72	0.45	31.0
Paprika	1⅜	3.67	0.45	1⅛	3.52	0.39	26	1¾	4.72	0.57	31.0
Bay leaves whole	³⁄₁₆	7.26	0.89	³⁄₁₆	3.52	0.39	26	¼	9.68	1.17	31.0
Nutmeg whole	1⅛	4.00	0.49		n. a.			1½	5.56	0.65	28.7
Garlic salt	2¹³⁄₁₆	4.00	0.49	2	2.96	0.33	24	3	4.56	0.55	30.9
Onion salt	2½	4.00	0.49	1¾	2.96	0.33	24	2¾	4.56	0.55	30.9
Black pepper whole	1¼	2.86	0.35	1¼	3.16	0.35	26	1⅞	4.40	0.53	30.8
Parsley	³⁄₁₆	3.18	0.39	⅛	2.96	0.33	24	¼	4.40	0.53	30.8
Oregano	¼	2.37	0.29		n. a.			⁷⁄₁₆	3.72	0.46	31.0
Red pepper	1⅛	2.69	0.33	1	3.52	0.39	26	1⅞	4.40	0.53	30.8
Allspice	1⁵⁄₁₆	5.63	0.69	1½	5.32	0.59	25	1¾	7.36	0.89	31.0

* Price per dozen.

Case VI–5

Al Yousef Plastics*

The Al Yousef Group of Companies is typical of business organizations in Saudi Arabia. It operates much like a small conglomerate of businesses bound together by family ownership and management. Their development was spawned by the cultural and traditional Saudi Arab values in combination with the rapid expansion and development of the economy due to oil exportation and the increase in oil prices.

All mineral resources in the Kingdom are owned by the government, therefore, economic expansion is caused mainly by government-sponsored projects. The great influx of petrodollars into a relatively small country[1] has created intensive demand for all industrial and consumer products. Government policy encourages private business to satisfy this demand through government interest-free loans for construction, land provided in industrial parks, controlled business licenses when suppliers in the market reach a saturation point, special dispensation allowing local suppliers to bid 10 percent higher on government projects, and government-sponsored encouragement to buy from local industry even when products are of lower quality. In addition, foreign companies must share ownership through joint ventures or other more favorable arrangements.

Saudi businessmen fortunate enough to find an unsatisfied demand they can meet are, at least partially, protected from competition by government policies. Some of the most successful of these operations have been the family businesses which combine a group of companies—each satisfying a high-demand segment of the market and each managed by a male family member. Together, the family is likely to be powerful, influential, and highly capitalized. The families are close, identifying with a particular area of the country, and marriage of first cousins within the family is common. Within the family, the male members informally operate much like a board of directors, but at this point, any similarity to Western business ends.

Costs of doing business are unusually high. As with the Al Yousef Group of Companies, all top management is Saudi and related to the Al Yousefs either directly or by marriage. All labor and specialized management are expatriate. In order to set up and equip a manufacturing plant, machinery must be purchased from outside the Kingdom and, besides installation and

---

* Case written by William K. Cunningham, University of Petroleum and Minerals, Dhahran, Saudi Arabia.

[1] Population estimates of Saudis range from 5½ to 7 million, largely skewed downward in age.

technical training, the contract usually includes housing, recreation facilities, utilities, and transportation for labor. Without a permanent work force, it is common to find factories operating well below their potential capacity, producing products of lower quality and higher price than those which could be imported.

Although the Al Yousef Group of Companies is one of the older and more experienced of the Saudi business organizations, they have never attempted to engage in export activities. All export products from Saudi Arabia are raw materials, namely oil, or products related to oil production, such as LPG, and urea (fertilizer produced from natural gas). It is an important feature of Saudi business that few have experience beyond the partially protected competitive environment of Saudi Arabia. Al Yousef has been concerned primarily with construction of related products which are sold within the Kingdom to take advantage of the demand created by government development plans.

In 1977, Al Yousef approached a major American manufacturer of air-conditioning equipment and negotiated a deal to manufacture under license a limited line of wall and window air conditioners. "Manufacturing" in this sense was fabrication of air-conditioning units from parts and modules imported from the United States. As with most manufacturing agreements, technical representatives and specialized management were to come from the American manufacturer to train labor, set up the factory, and control production. Since the market demand for air conditioners far exceeded production capacity, the arrangement between Al Yousef and the U.S. company proved to be highly successful for both. However, Al Yousef eventually intended to phase out all foreign representation and manufacture the units under their own name.

In mid-1980, Al Yousef was offered the opportunity to purchase the As Sharq Plastic Ware Factory at a fraction of its cost. Established in 1977 by two Saudi financial backers and an expatriate manager, the factory produced a line of plastic proprietary items, such as cups, saucers, bowls, and so forth. Stiff competition from higher quality, lower-priced imports created continuing losses. Al Yousef considered the factory a worthwhile addition to its "Group"; they felt with their strong capitalization and management, they would be able to achieve a favorable return on investment.

Renamed the "Al Yousef Plastics Factory," but continuing under the same manager, new lines were developed and introduced into the domestic market. These new lines related more to local demand and included jerry cans, pipe spacers and plugs, PVC gaskets, small cans for hospitals, plastic bag handles, and ice cream containers.

Al Yousef investigated applications of the plastic factory's production to some of their other companies' production processes. The most promising application appeared to be in the air-conditioning factory. The majority of air conditioners produced by this plant were small wall units used by small suqs (stores) and apartments. The front covers, or frames, were plastic and purchased completely finished from the licensor in the United States. Further study of the possibility of using the Al Yousef Plastics Factory to produce these frames proved it was feasible both in plant capacity and on a cost basis. Producing their own frames was also enhanced by the fact that they would be moving from a "fabricator" of air conditioners to total manufacturing.

Once this decision was made, the next step was to have molds made to produce the frames. Mold making, a highly specialized craft, was unavailable within the Kingdom. The search for a qualified mold maker was narrowed to two—one in the Netherlands, and the other in Italy. The Italian mold maker, Ponti and Sons, enjoyed a widespread reputation for precision and high quality workmanship. After a meeting between Mr. Ghassan, the manager of Al Yousef Plastics Factory, and Mr. Robinson, chief engineer for Al Yousef Air Conditioning Factory, Mr. Ghassan requested the specifications and measurements of the plastic frame in order to contract for molds from Ponti and Sons. Mr. Robinson provided a complete set of samples for the frame; but since he did not have sectional drawings, these were ordered sent from the company in the United States.

In August, 1980, Mr. Ghassan, with the set of samples, went to Italy to meet with Ponti and Sons and work out the contractual details for producing and delivering molds. Mr. Danieli, manager for Ponti and Sons, agreed that 12 molds which would produce framed parts "similar"[2] to the samples provided would be delivered to Al Yousef Plastics Factory by February, 1981. As part of the agreement, a letter of credit was lodged with the local bank to insure payment upon satisfactory compliance with the terms of the contract. Cost for the completed molds was set at 700,000 Saudi Riyals (1 US $ = 3.4 SR); 10 percent of this amount was advanced to bind the contract.

Three months later, the production engineer for Al Yousef Plastics Factory flew to Milan to check the molds in the process of being made. His intention was to make minor modifications in the molds so that they would conform to the requirements of the manufacturing machinery. Minor modifications of this type were part of the contractual arrangement and were expected. He made no comments concerning the technical specifications of the molds since he considered this to be beyond his area of specialization. However, he did remark to Mr. Danieli that on his return to Saudi Arabia he would talk with Mr. Robinson and recommend he inspect the molds in Milan. Neither the production engineer nor Mr. Ghassan had had experience manufacturing precision products.

On receiving sectional drawings of the plastic frames from the home company in the United States, Mr. Robinson visited Ponti and Sons to measure the molds which were in the final stages of preparation. Returning to Saudi Arabia, Mr. Robinson called a meeting with the concerned operational managers of both Al Yousef Plastics and Al Yousef Air Conditioning Facto-

_____

[2] In Arabic, the same word is used to mean *similar* and *identical*.

ries. His presentation revealed serious discrepancies between the measurements he had taken of the molds and the measurements given in the sectional drawings. A hurried order was sent to Ponti and Sons for alterations to conform to the sectional drawings. Mr. Danieli immediately objected since some of the changes were impossible without recasting the molds. His contention was that he had complied with the contract which read "the molds should be *similar* to the samples" and did not specify conforming to sectional drawings. The variation between the samples and the sectional drawings was due to a 5 percent shrinkage factor in plastic after being molded. In the proprietary items normally manufactured by Al Yousef Plastics Factory, this shrinkage factor was not significant; but, in the case of the air-conditioner frames, it rendered them useless. The mold manufacturer should have allowed for this shrinkage factor since they were experienced in the field— or so argued Mr. Ghassan. Mr. Ghassan also stated that the request for alterations was not beyond the contractual arrangement since he had intended for Ponti and Sons to manufacture molds producing frames of the exact size of the samples given to them.

While this controversy continued without agreement, it became apparent to Al Yousef that their financial situation was deteriorating. The letter of credit expired, but was extended for three months with the condition that no payments be made to Ponti and Sons until the molds were checked and accepted by Al Yousef Plastics Factory. This was unlikely since Mr. Danieli refused to send the molds under those conditions and he refused to recast any more molds. Al Yousef management must consider the following:

1. Al Yousef Plastics purchased and installed new machinery at a cost of 1.2 million SR to manufacture the frames using the molds. This machinery has been sitting idle for 10 months.

2. Because of the time involved in acquiring foreign labor, Al Yousef Plastics hired, transported, housed, and trained sufficient additional labor from Pakistan to manufacture the air-conditioning frames. This labor can be absorbed into other operations of the group of companies through normal attribution, but they will lose some of this investment.

3. Daily production of air conditioners is 480 units. Frames purchased from the United States cost 35 SR delivered at the factory in Saudi Arabia. Direct costs of manufacturing their own frames is approximately 22 SR (excluding machinery and mold expense). The factory operates 26 days a month.

QUESTIONS

1. Analyze some of the cost consequences of this conflict.

2. Should Al Yousef submit this controversy to arbitration? litigation? Who is at fault?

3. Suggest alternatives which might be satisfactory to both Al Yousef Plastics and Ponti and Sons.

4. Would it be worthwhile for Al Yousef Plastics to find another mold maker and negotiate a new contract? What would be the likely consequence of such an action?

CASE VI–6

The American Beer Company—going international

The American Beer Company,* one of the leading U.S. beer companies, is considering the possibility of expanding market coverage to other countries. They are considering Germany and Japan. Their major brand of beer—America Beer—currently is exported to these countries in very small quantities.

The company

In 1980, the American Beer Company brewed, packaged (under eight different brand names), and sold 50.2 million barrels of beer. The company widened its lead over its nearest competitor by an estimated 12.9 million barrels.

In 1980, industry sales increased 3.1 percent while American Beer Company achieved record gross sales of $3.8 billion, a 17.1 percent increase over 1979 gross sales of $3.3 billion. Net sales for the company were a record $3.3 billion, an increase of 18.7 percent over 1979 net sales of $2.8 billion. During the last three years, net sales have increased 18.7 percent, 22.8 percent, and 22.9 percent, respectively.

In 1980, industry sales increased 3.1 percent while the company's sales increased by 8.5 percent. Capital investment plans for new facilities and expansion of existing ones are underway to increase U.S. beer production to 70 million barrels by 1984.

---

* American Beer Company, Smith Brewing Company, German Beer, and Japan Beers are fictitious company names.

EXHIBIT 1: America Beer sales growth—1964–1980 (in millions of barrels)

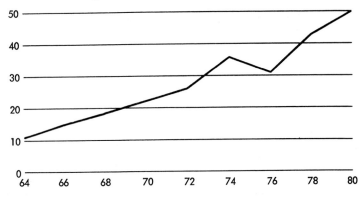

In 1980, the company launched its first international venture by licensing a Canadian brewer to manufacture America beer for sale in Canada. Although the company is the world's largest brewer, less than 1 percent of its total output is sold overseas.

In 1981 the company entered a distribution arrangement with Britain's second largest brewer to provide them with America Beer. American Beer gained access to the U.K. brewer's retail distribution network and chain of nearly 3,000 wholly-owned or associated pubs. Because of the growth in demand for lager beer in England, the U.K. brewer wants to sell more lager beer; the arrangement with American Beer provides them with help in the growing take-home market where lager beer is expected to experience rapid growth.

Two major trends exist in the English beer market: a move away from ale to lager beers and the growth of the take-home market. Twenty years ago almost all the beer sold in Great Britain was the traditional brown ale. In 1959, lager accounted for only 3 percent of the market. Today, 1981, lager accounts for nearly one third of sales, and its market share has been increasing by 25 percent a year for the last several years, making it the fastest-growing part of the market.

More than 90 percent of all beer sold in the U.K. is consumed in pubs and private clubs compared with 30 to 35 percent in the United States. But off-license sales in Britain are growing rapidly and now account for 24 percent of all lager sales. Take-home sales are expected to open up a potentially huge new market for sales to women. Women consume less than 10 percent of the beer in Britain because British women still do not frequent pubs.

Statement of objectives for international marketing

The company has made a definite decision to explore international markets. As a consequence, it formed American Beer International, Inc. to explore opportunities for export and license production of American Beer Company's beers in international markets.

The world beer market is four times the size of the U.S. market, representing a significant opportunity for long-term growth. Initially, American Beer International will approach this new market through export of U.S. brewed beers and licensed local production. Where the high delivered price of exports limits volume potential, local production (as in Canada) will allow American Beer, Inc.'s brands to compete with local beers.

New export and license production agreements will be selectively pursued during the 1980s. Selecting desirable partners and establishing a marketing franchise for American Beer, Inc.'s beers in foreign countries will be carefully developed with an emphasis on long-term success.

Reasons for going international. Growth in beer consumption is leveling off in the United States, while costs are climbing. The strong penetration of the U.S. market by Smith Brewing Co. since it was bought by a major cigarette manufacturer is, of course, a well-known story. American Beer is still the leading brewer with 26 percent of the market but Smith is a close second with 20 percent and Smith has indicated its interest in becoming number one. Continued expansion means taking market share away from someone else. For the last few years, the market in the U.S. has been relatively flat (see Exhibit 1) and many believe that future expansion of the market will not be great without excessive and unprofitable expenditures. For example, in 1978, American Beer and Smith collectively raised their sales by 12 million barrels, while total American beer consumption increased only 5 million barrels. (See Exhibit 2.) This trend continued into 1979. Taking consumers from other brands becomes more costly as companies spend more money to protect their market share.

Tentative plans

At the moment, the American Beer Company is considering the possibility of entering negotiations with brewers or distributors in Germany and Japan.

In Germany, American Beer is considering an agreement with German Beer, one of the largest German brewers. In this proposed arrangement, German Beer will get a premium beer to help them compete against the Danish, super-premium priced Tuborg. In return, American Beer will get the rights to distribute German Beer's beer in the United States. The same

---

EXHIBIT 2: U.S. beer and soft drink consumption, 1978–1981 (gallons per capita per year)

	1978	1979	1980	1981 (estimate)
Beer	23.6	24.3	24.8	24.8
Soft drinks	37.8	38.9	39.6	40.8

Source: *Beverage Industry*, May 22, 1981, p. 19.

containers that will be used to ship American's beer to Germany will be used to return German Beer's beer to the United States.

In Japan, plans are underway to sell directly to Japan Beers. Japan Beers is a subsidiary of Japan's largest distiller although its beer has only 7 percent of the Japanese beer market. Japan Beer (the fourth largest brewer in Japan) feels that by associating with respected foreign beers, which American Beer is, they will be able to enhance their reputation for their domestically produced beers. Japan Beers has been importing American Beer through indirect channels for the last few years and it has sold well in Japan. Japan Beers will import American Beer directly from the company and is considering entering an agreement to brew the beer in Japan under license.

Industry reactions

Reactions by marketing experts are not very favorable. One big risk is whether or not Germans and Japanese will buy American beer. American beer is very different than most foreign brews. It is fizzier and blander and is meant to be drunk very chilled, something almost unknown to foreign tastes. One German newspaper recently described foreign lagers as "imitation continental beer drunk only by refined ladies, people with digestive ailments, tourists and other weaklings." However, this may be true chauvinism at its best.

Problem

While the company is not necessarily having second thoughts about its tentative moves to enter these two markets, it has not yet spent very much money in market development. However, if it is to establish significant positions in Germany and Japan, a substantial amount of capital will have to be spent in both markets to effectively promote the product. Before they make a decision to increase their marketing expenditures from less than $1 million to over $5 million, they want to examine their position intensely. As a consultant, you have been asked for an outside opinion. With the data presented below and other information you can gather, give the company an opinion on their tentative decisions. Make specific recommendations for action.

INDUSTRY STATISTICS

World beer production and market growth

A recent study in Europe indicated the European Market will grow 16 percent during the 1980s. (See Exhibit 4.) The Netherlands is projected to grow 56 percent; the Italian market, 50 percent; Great Britain, Europe's number-two beer consumer, 18 percent; and Germany only 4 percent. One third of all beer purchased in Europe is consumed at home, the study says the home market will be the scene of a major clash for market share during the 1980s (see Exhibits 5 and 6). World beer production increased in 1979. Total volume was up 4.2 percent over 1978 (see Exhibit 3).

EXHIBIT 3:   World beer production—1975-1979

	Percent share of total 1975	Percent share of total 1979	Percent growth rate 1978–79	Percent growth rate 1975–79
Europe	52.4	49.6	3.2	6.8
Americas	33.7	35.1	4.0	17.4
Asia	7.2	8.7	10.3	35.4
Africa	3.7	3.9	9.5	19.6
Australasia	3.0	2.7	−1.6	negligable
Total	100.0	100.0	4.2	12.7

EXHIBIT 4:   Europe beer production by container—1980 (1,000 hl)

	Barrels/tanks	Percent of total production	Bottles/cans	Percent of total production
Belgium	5,942	43.0%	7,877	57.00
Denmark	711	8.3	7,823	91.67
Germany	27,752	29.4	66,595	70.59
France	4,473	19.6	18,298	80.36
Ireland	5,138	90.8	524	9.25
Italy	292	4.0	7,008	96.00
Luxembourg	285	41.0	410	58.99
Netherlands	3,854	27.6	10,116	72.41
United Kingdom	51,015	78.2	14,222	21.80
Total	99,462	42.8	132,873	57.19

EXHIBIT 5:   Top ten beer-producing countries (1975–1979)

	Percent share of world output 1975	Percent share of world output 1979
United States	22.1	22.0
W. Germany	11.9	10.3
USSR	7.6	7.9
U.K.	8.2	7.6
Japan	5.0	5.0
Brazil	2.2	3.2
Mexico	2.5	2.8
Czechoslovakia	2.8	2.7
East Germany	2.6	2.6
Canada	2.7	2.3
Total top ten	67.6	66.4

EXHIBIT 6:   Estimated European beer market growth: 1975–1990 (million hl)

Country	1975	1976	1977	1980	1985	1990
Germany	93	96	94	93	95	97
U.K.	65	66	65	72	80	85
France	22	24	23	24	26	28
Netherlands	12	14	14	16	20	25
UEBL	15	15	15	15	15	16
Denmark	9	9	9	9	10	11
Italy	6	7	7	8	10	12
Ireland	6	6	6	6	6	7
Totals	228	237	233	243	262	281

MARKET DATA—GERMANY AND JAPAN

Germany

Germans consume 145.6 liters per capita which amounts to about 38 gallons compared to 23 gallons in the United States. (See Exhibit 7.) U.S. and German consumption patterns are similar. U.S. consumers drink beer in clubs 35 percent of the time and at home 65 percent of the time and so do Germans.

In Germany 1,400 breweries produce 1.6 million gallons of beer each under 5,000 different brands. The market consists of many small breweries; the 10 largest beer groups share only 22 percent of the beer market. The market is fragmented with strong local and regional loyalty. The best known beer brands in Germany are Beck's, Bitburger Pils, Fuerstenberger Pils, and Lowenbrau. The two best known imports are Pilsener Urquell (Czecho-slovakia) and Turborg. In 1980, imports accounted for only 1 percent of the total German beer market. Important market factors include the following.

1. *Market characteristics.*   Presently, dark beers account for a larger percentage of beer sales than light. However, there is a growing consumer interest in lighter beers due to the current emphasis on better health and fewer calories. Light beer in Germany is the same as regular beer in the United States.

Although Germans consume 146 liters (310 pints) of beer per person per year, the market has been stagnating since the mid-1970s. Beer consumption has actually decreased slightly, and the actual number of beer-

EXHIBIT 7:   German per capita beverage consumption

Beer	145.6 litres
Wine	24.4
Spirits	2.5
Gaseous drinks	22.1
Mineral water	47.6
Fruit juice	2.0

EXHIBIT 8:   Beer sales by retail store group

Hypermarkets/discounters	28 percent
Chains/co-ops	25
Independents	30
Small shops	17

drinking Germans is declining. The smaller brewers are feeling this change. The number of brewers dropped from 1,800 in 1970 to 1,400 in 1977.

In 1976, bottled beer represented 70.6 percent of total domestic beer sales, as compared to 33.8 percent in 1960. Beer accounts for 11 percent of consumer sales of food and beverages. (See Exhibit 8.)

German beer is usually higher in alcohol content and much heavier bodied than U.S. beer. Germans tend to prefer the type beer known as *Pilsner beer* which is a premium type of beer. Pilsner beers now make up 56 percent of the total beer market whereas 10 years ago they accounted for only 25 percent.

2. *Legal problems.* West German law requires that beer be made only from barley, malt, yeast, hops, and water; this also applies to imported beer as well. Most U.S. beer includes rice.

Japan

1. *Market characteristics.* Imports have doubled in the past two years (1976–1978) while domestic beer sales have risen only 5 percent. In 1979 alone, imports increased by 23.3 percent.

Average consumption per adult was 83.2 bottles of beer in 1975 and in 1980, average per capita consumption reached 106.67 bottles per year. Per capita expenditure for alcoholic beverages is 1 percent of annual income. Per capita consumption in 1978 was 36.5 liters.

Men account for most of the beer consumption. As yet, women are not big beer drinkers, but they choose it as a gift to give during the summer months. Eighty to 90 percent of the housewives in Japan feel it is almost an obligation to send "mid-summer gifts" to acquaintances. Beer, especially imported brands, is among the items chosen for this purpose.

Beer can be obtained in both supermarkets and department stores. The latter is by far the more important of the two, with imported beers being displayed in the gourmet foods section. Vending machines, which in 1978 accounted for $10 billion in sales, sell beer and sake along with the traditional items such as coffee and soft drinks. Alcoholic beverages are widely available by vending machine.

Along with imported beers, several well-established domestic breweries exist. The largest, Kirin, commands an unprecedented 63 percent market share. Kirin is so large they have had to restrict their growth for fear of government antimonopoly action. Kirin has 12 modern breweries with a total capacity of 20.4 million bbls. Only 9.4 million bbls. were sold in 1977. The next largest is Sapporo Breweries, whose market share totals almost 20 percent, followed in size by Asahi and Suntory breweries.

Several imports are presently being marketed in Japan. The leading beer exporters to Japan were the United States with a 38.5 percent share, West Germany with 17.9 percent, and Singapore with 15.5 percent. At the end of 1979, 40 brands of foreign beer were available to the Japanese.

Japanese beer enjoys an international reputation for quality. But beer makers in Japan say they've detected a change in tastes that's spurring the growth of imports. (See Exhibits 9 and 11.) Many Japanese want to recapture the taste of some foreign beer they have tried while traveling overseas.

Imported beers cost about 30 percent more than local brews; and nearly everyone in Japan agrees they don't taste as good as Japanese beer. However, that isn't stopping status-conscious Japanese drinkers, especially young people, from drinking imports in growing quantities. Part of the Japanese attitude is that anything foreign has "class."

EXHIBIT 9: Top ten brands of foreign beer in the Japanese market, 1979 (000 cases imported)

Heineken	180
Budweiser	85
Tuborg	80
Guinness	74.7
Lowenbrau	70
Henninger	55
Holsten Bier	51
Schlitz	40
Primo	38
Carlsberg	35

EXHIBIT 10: Japans top beer producers (000 kiloliters)

	Production	Market share
Kirin Brewery	2,767,000 kiloliters	62.1 percent
Sapporo	873,000	19.6
Asahi	517,000	11.6
Suntory	299,000	6.7

EXHIBIT 11: Major exporters of beer to Japan in 1979

United States	38.5 percent
West Germany	17.9
Singapore	15.5

In 1979, 4,480,000 kiloliters of beer was produced by domestic brewers. Japan's imports amounted to 10,000 kiloliters which is equal to about .002 percent of the market.

2. *Domestic competition.*   There are currently four major domestic breweries in Japan. Kirin Brewery is the leader with a 62.1 percent share of market (see Exhibit 10).

APPENDIX

INTERNATIONAL MARKETING INFORMATION SOURCES

Here are some information sources to help you with your research for term projects, cases, and other assignments. Some, if not all, of these sources will be in your library.

Abstracts, bibliographies, and indexes

Business International. *Master Key Index.* New York: Business International. Quarterly; covers Business International publications.

Business Periodical Index. New York: H. W. Wilson, 1958– . Monthly with quarterly and annual cumulations. Arranged alphabetically by subject.

Business Index. Menlo Park, Calif.: Information Access Corporation, 1979– Monthly cumulation on a 16 mm computer-output-microfilm. Indexes articles, reviews, news, and other related material of interest to the business community.

Encyclopedia of Geographic Information Sources. Companion volume to *Encyclopedia of Business Information Sources.* Detroit: Gale Research, 1978. Listings by foreign country cover basic sources for statistics, directories, guides for doing business, and so on.

F & S Index International and F & S Europe. Cleveland: Predicasts. Monthly with quarterly and annual cumulations. Indexes foreign companies, product, and industry information with emphasis on sources giving data or statistics.

New York Times Index. New York: 1851– . Biweekly with annual cumulations. Indexes the late city edition. Alphabetically arranged by subject.

The International Executive. 64 Ferndale Drive, Hastings-on-Hudson, N.Y. 10706. Quarterly annotated bibliography. Reviews over 195 publications. All articles are on international business topics.

Sources of European Economic Information. 3d ed. Compiled by Cambridge Information and Research Services Ltd., Cambridge, U.K.; Gower Publishing Co. Ltd., 1980. Alphabetical by country with a separate index listing sources by subject and country.

Statistics Europe: Sources for Social, Economic, and Market Research. 4th ed. Beckenham, Kent, U.K.: CBD Research Ltd./Gale Research, 1981. Arranged by country.

Wall Street Journal Index. Princeton, N.J.: Dow Jones, 1956– . Monthly with annual cumulations. Compiled from the final eastern edition. Divided into two sections: Corporate News and General News by broad subject headings.

Wasserman, Paul, ed. *Statistics Sources.* 6th ed. Detroit: Gale Research, 1980. Subject guide to data on industrial, business, social, educational, financial, and other topics for the United States and other countries.

Sources of marketing statistics

Business International. *Bi-Data Printout Summary.* New York. Annual: economic, demographic, trade, and other statistics. Name recently changed to: *Worldwide Economic Indicators.*

Consumer Europe. London: Euromonitor Publications. Annual; marketing indicators and trends for various markets.

European Marketing Data and Statistics. London: Euromonitor Publications. Annual. Supplement, *Europe in 1980; Trends and Forecasts in Basic Marketing Data Through to the Year 1980.* Euromonitor Pub.

International Labour Office. *Yearbook of Labour Statistics.* Geneva. Annual; current statistics in its *Bulletin of Labour Statistics.*

International Marketing Data and Statistics. London: Euromonitor Publications, Ltd. Annual; covers the Americas, Asia, Africa, and Australasia. Includes data on retail and wholesale sales, living standards, and general consumer marketing data.

International Monetary Fund. *International Financial Statistics.* Monthly; statistics on exchange rate, international liquidity, money and bank statistics, interest, prices, production, and so on.

Retail Trade International, vol. 2: Europe. London: Euromonitor Publications, 1980. Data on consumer purchase patterns by product, retail store type. Some prices, middleman markups, and other data.

Statistical Yearbook for Latin America. United Nations: Economic Commission for Latin America. Updated by *Statistical Bulletin for Latin America.*

BIBLIOGRAPHY

General

Aonuma, Yoshimatsu. "A Japanese Explains Japan's Business Style." *Across the Board,* February 1981, p. 41.

Bair, Frank E. *International Marketing Handbook: Detailed Marketing Profiles for 138 Nations,* vols. I and II. Detroit, Mich.: Gale Research Company, 1981.

Ball, Robert. "Europe Outgrows Management American Style." *Fortune,* October 20, 1980, pp. 147–48.

Barnet, Richard J., and Muller, Ronald. *Global Reach: The Power of the Multinational Corporation.* New York: Simon & Schuster, 1974.

Bartels, Robert. *Global Development and Marketing.* Columbus, Ohio: Grid, 1981.

Daniels, John D., Ogram, Ernest W., Jr.; and Lee H. Radebaugh. *International Business: Environments and Operations*. Reading, Mass.: Addison-Wesley Publishing, 1976.

Drucker, Peter. "Japan Gets Ready for Tougher Times." *Fortune,* November 3, 1980, pp. 108-15.

Farley, John U., and Wind, Yorum. "International Marketing: The Neglect Continues." *Journal of Marketing,* Summer 1980, pp. 5–6.

Fayerweather, John, ed. *International Business Management and Administration.* Cambridge: Ballinger Publishing Co., 1978.

Jaffe, Eugene. "Are Domestic and International Marketing Dissimilar." *Management International Review* 20, no. 3, (1980), p. 83.

Jain, Subbash C., and Tucker, Lewis R. Jr. *International Marketing: Managerial Perspectives.* Boston, Mass.: CBI Publishing Co., 1979.

Keegan, Warren J. *Multinational Marketing Management,* 2d ed. Englewood Cliffs, N.J.: Prentice-Hall, 1980.

McCann, Thomas. *An American Company: The Tragedy of United Fruit.* New York: Crown Publishers, 1976.

Madsen, Axel. *Private Power: Multinational Corporations for the Survival of Our Planet.* New York: W. Morrow, 1980.

Mason, R. Hal; Miller, Robert R.; and Dale R. Weigel. *International Business.* New York: John Wiley & Sons, 1981.

Moore, Russell M., and Cunningham, Isabella C. M. "Urban Markets in Industrializing Countries: The São Paulo Experience." *Journal of Marketing,* April 1974, pp. 2–12.

Ricks, David. *Big Business Blunders: Mistakes In Multinational Marketing.* Homewood, Ill.: Richard D. Irwin, 1983.

Robinson, Richard D. *International Business Management.* New York: Holt, Rinehart, & Winston, 1973.

Robock, Stefan H., and Simmonds, Kenneth. *International Business and Multinational Enterprises.* Homewood, Ill.: Richard D. Irwin, 1973.

Rogers, Everett M., and Shoemaker, F. Floyd. *Communication of Innovations,* 2d ed. New York: Free Press, 1971.

Sasaki, Naoto. *Management and Industrial Structure In Japan.* New York: Pergamon Press, 1981.

Terpstra, Vern. *International Marketing.* Hinsdale, Ill.: Dryden Press, 1978.

Thorelli, Hans B., and Becker, Helmut, eds. *International Marketing Strategy.* New York: Pergamon Press, 1980.

Tsurumi, Yoshi. *Multinational Management: Texts, Readings and Cases.* Cambridge, Mass.: Ballinger Publishing Co., 1976.

Turner, Louis. *Multinational Companies and the Third World.* New York: Hill and Wang, 1973.

Vernon, Raymond, and Wells, Louis T. Jr. *Economic Environment of International Business,* 3d ed. Englewood Cliffs, N.J.: Prentice-Hall, 1981.

Vernon, Raymond, and Wells, Louis T. Jr. *Manager in the International Economy,* 4th ed. Englewood Cliffs, N.J.: Prentice-Hall, 1981.

"Management of the Large Multinational: Trends and Future Challenges." *Business Horizons,* May/June 1981, pp. 83–91.

"Once A Frenchman Always A Frenchman." *International Management,* June 1980.

The Cultural Environment of International Business. Cincinnati: South-Western Publishing, 1978.

Part 1

Agmon, Tamir, and Kindleberger, Charles P. *Multinational From Small Countries.* Cambridge: MIT Press, 1977.

Cannon, T. "Managing International and Export Marketing." *European Journal of Marketing* 14, no. 1, (1980), pp. 34–49.

Cavusgil, S. Tamer, and Nevin, John R. "Internal Determinants of Export Marketing Behavior: An Empirical Investigation." *Journal of Marketing Research,* February 1981.

Green, Robert T., and Lutz, J. M. "U.S. High Technology Import/Export Performance in Three Industries." *Journal of International Business,* Fall 1980, pp. 112–17.

Kelly, Marie W. *Foreign Investment Evaluation Practices of U.S. Multinational Corporations.* Ann Arbor, Mich.: UMI Research Press, 1981.

Klaus, Freidrich. *International Economics.* New York: McGraw-Hill, 1977.

La Polombara, Joseph, and Blank, Stephen. *Multinational Corporation in Comparative Perspective.* New York: The Conference Board, Inc., Report no. 725, 1977.

Negandhi, Anant R. *Functioning of the Multinational Corporation.* New York: Pergamon Press, 1980.

Reid, Stan, and Mayer, C. "Exporting Behavior and Decision-Making Characteristics: An Empirical Investigation." *Marketing 1980: Towards Excellence in the Eighties,* V. Jones, ed., Administrative Sciences Association of Canada, 1980.

Root, Franklin R. *International Trade and Investment,* 3d ed. Cincinnati: South-Western Publishing, 1973.

Wattenberg, Ben J. *The Wealth Weapon: U.S. Foreign Policy and Multinational Corporations.* New Brunswich, N.J.: Transaction Books, 1980.

"Japan's Strategy for the '80s Special Issue." *Business Week,* December 14, 1981, pp. 39–120.

"Protection Against Protection." *Financial World,* September 1, 1980, pp. 24–25.

Part 2

Almaney, Adinan. "The Behavioral Effects of the Arabic Language." *University of Michigan Business Review,* July 1979, pp. 13–17.

Briggs, Jean A. "The Inscrutable West." *Forbes,* June 23, 1980, p. 39.

Chance, S. K. "Codes of Conduct For Multinational Corporations." *Business Lawyer,* April 1978, p. 1799.

Estey, John S., and Marston, David W. "Pitfalls (and Loopholes) in the Foreign Bribery Law." *Fortune,* October 1978, p. 182.

Ghymn, Kyung-Il. "An Empirical Study of U.S. Import Managers' Purchasing Behavior." *Marketing in the 80s*, 1980 Educators' Conference Proceeding Series No. 46. American Marketing Association, 1980, pp. 262–64.

Hall, Edward T. *The Silent Language*. New York: Doubleday & Co., Inc., 1959.

Hall, Edward. *Beyond Culture*. Garden City, N.Y.: Anchor Press/Doubleday, 1976.

Harris, Philip R. "Cultural Awareness Training for Human Resource Development." *Training and Development Journal*, March 1979, p. 64.

Harris, Philip R., and Moran, Robert T. *Managing Cultural Differences*. Houston, Tex.: Gulf Publishing, 1979.

Izraeli, Dafna N. et al. "Women Executives in MNC Subsidiaries." *California Management Review*, Fall 1980, p. 53.

Kelley, Lane, and Worthley, Reginald. "The Role of Culture in Comparative Management." *Academy of Management Journal*, March 1981, p. 164.

Kolde, Endel. *Environment of International Business*, Boston, Mass.: Kent Publishing Co., 1982.

Luqmani, Musthaq; Quraeshi, Zahir A.; and Linda Delene. "Marketing in Islamic Countries: A Viewpoint." *MSU Business Topics*, Summer 1980, pp. 17–25.

McClelland, David C. *The Achieving Society*, New York: Van Nostrand Reinhold, 1961.

Martens, J. A., "Patenting in Communist Countries." *Journal of the Patent Office Society*, April 1978.

Nielsen, Richard P. "Cultural-Economic Nationalism and International Trade Policy." *Academy of Management Review*, July 1979, pp. 449–52.

Richardson, Bradley M., and Ueda, Taizo, *Business and Society in Japan*, New York: Praeger Publishers, 1981.

Segall, Marshall H. *Cross-Cultural Psychology: Human Behavior in Global Perspectives*, Monterey, Calif.: Brooks/Coie Publishing, 1979.

Servan-Schreiber, J. J. *The American Challenge*, New York: Atheneum Publishers, 1968.

Terpstra, Vern. *The Cultural Environment of International Business*. Cincinnati: South-Western Publishing, 1978.

Thorelli, H. B. "The Information Seekers: Multinational Strategy Target." *California Management Review*, 1980–1981.

Turner, Louis. *Multinational Companies and the Third World*. New York: Hill and Wang, 1973.

Zaltman, Gerald; and Duncan, Robert. *Strategies for Planned Change*. New York: John Wiley & Sons, 1977.

Part 3

Davis, Harry L.; Douglas, Susan P.; and Alvin J. Silk. "Measure Unreliability: A Hidden Threat to Cross-National Marketing Research?" *Journal of Marketing*, Spring 1981, pp. 98–109.

Ferber, Robert. *Consumption and Income Distribution in Latin America.* Washington, D.C.: Organization of American States, 1980.

Greer, Thomas V. *Marketing in the Soviet Union.* New York: Praeger Publishers, 1973.

Heenan, David A.; and Keegan, Warren J. "The Rise of Third World Multinationals." *Harvard Business Review,* January/February 1978, p. 101.

Helleiner, Gerald K. *International Economic Disorder: Essays in North-South Relations.* Toronto: University of Toronto Press, 1981.

Jaffe, E. "Multinational Marketing Intelligence." *Management International Review,* vol. 19, issue no. 2, 1979, pp. 53–60.

Kaynak, Erdener. "Difficulties of Undertaking Marketing Research in the Developing Countries." *European Research,* November 1978, pp. 251–59.

McGuier, E. Patrick. "Consumer Protection: Implications for International Trade." *New York: The Conference Board,* 1980.

McMiller, Carl H. "The Rise of the Eastern Bloc Multinationals." *International Management,* December 1980, p. 19.

Mayer, C. S. "Multinational Marketing Research: Methodological Problems." European Research, March 1978, pp. 77–83.

Myers, Massy, and Greyser. *Marketing Research and Knowledge Development: An Assessment for Marketing Management.* Englewood Cliffs, N.J.: Prentice-Hall, 1980.

Pass, C. L., and Sparkes, J. R. "Competition Policy in the E.E.C." *Journal of General Management,* Summer 1980, p. 54.

Permut, S. E. "The European View of Marketing Research." *Columbia Journal of World Business,* Fall 1977, pp. 94–104.

Thorelli, Hans B., and Engledow, Jack L. "Information Seekers and Information Systems: A Policy Perspective." *Journal of Marketing,* Spring 1980, pp. 9–24.

Walters, Kenneth D., and Monsen, R. Joseph. "State-Owned Business Abroad." *Harvard Business Review,* March/April 1979, p. 160.

Van Dam, Andre. "Marketing in the New International Economic Order." *Journal of Marketing,* January 1977, pp. 19–23.

Yavas, Ugur, and Kaynak, Erdener. "Current Status of Marketing Research in Developing Countries: Problems and Opportunities." *Journal of International Marketing and Marketing Research,* 1980, pp. 79–89.

"The Third World Grows Its Own Multinationals." (An interview with Louis Wells, Jr.) *International Management,* January 1982, pp. 39–40.

Part 4

Ayal, Igal, and Zif, Jehiel. "Market Expansion Strategies in Multinational Marketing." *Journal of Marketing,* Spring 1979, pp. 84–87.

Badawy, M. K. "Styles of Mideastern Managers." *California Management Review,* Spring 1980, pp. 50–59.

Boddewyn, J. J. "The Global Spread of Advertising Regulation." *MSU Business Topics,* Spring 1981, pp. 5–11.

Colvin, Michael; Heeler, Roger; and Jim Thorpe. "Developing International Advertising Strategy." *Journal of Marketing,* Fall 1980, pp. 73–79.

Davis, Stanley M. *Managing and Organizing Multinational Corporations.* New York: Perganion Press, 1979.

de la Torre, Jose. "Product Life Cycle as a Determinant of Global Marketing Strategies." *Atlanta Economic Review,* September/October 1975, pp. 29–34.

Doz, Y. L. "Strategic Management in Multinational Companies." *Sloan Management Review,* Winter 1980, pp. 27–46.

Dunn, S. Watson, and Lorimer, E. S. *International Advertising and Marketing.* Columbus, Ohio: Grid, 1979.

Harari, Ehud, and Zeira, Yoram. "Training Expatriates for Managerial Assignments in Japan." *California Management Review,* Summer 1978, p. 56.

Harrell, Gilbert D., and Kiefer, Richard O. "Multinational Strategic Marketing Portfolios." *MSU Business Topics,* Winter 1981, p. 10.

Heenan, David A., and Perlmutter, Howard V. *Multinational Organization Development.* Reading, Mass.: Addison-Wesley Publishing, 1979.

Hollensheed, N. H., and Conway, M. R. *International Products Liability,* November 1980.

Hulbert, J. M., Brandt, W. K.; and R. Richers. "Marketing Planning in the Multinational Subsidiary: Practices and Problems." *Journal of Marketing,* Summer 1980, pp. 7–15.

Illman, Paul E. *Developing Overseas Managers and Managers Overseas.* New York: American Management Association, 1980.

Janger, Allen R. "Organization of International Joint Ventures," New York: The Conference Board, 1980.

Kohls, Robert L. *Survival Kit for Overseas Living.* Chicago: Intercultural Press, Inc., 1979.

Lichota, Edith. "Consumerism and the E.E.C. Directive." *Risk Management,* March 1980, p. 12.

McGuinnes, Norman W., and Little, Blair. "The Influence of Product Characteristics on the Export Performance of New Industrial Products." *Journal of Marketing,* Spring 1981, pp. 110–22.

Metwally, M. M. "Sales Response to Advertising of Eight Australian Products." *Journal of Advertising Research,* October 1980, p. 34.

Miller, Edwin L., and Cheng, Joseph L. C. "A Closer Look at the Decision to Accept an Overseas Position." *Management International Review,* 1978, p. 25.

Misa, K. F., and Fabricatore, J. M. "Return on Investment of Overseas Personnel." *Financial Executive,* Spring 1979, p. 42.

Neelankavil, James P. *Advertising Self-Regulation: A Global Perspective.* New York: Hastings House, 1980.

Peebles, Dean M.; Ryans, John K., Jr.; and Ivan R. Vernon. "Coordinating International Advertising." *Journal of Marketing,* January 1978, pp. 39–45.

Picard, Jacques. "Determinants of Centralization of Marketing Decision-Making in Multinational Corporations." *Marketing in the 80's: Changes and Challenges.* Chicago: American Marketing Association, pp. 259–61.

Plummer, J. T. "Consumer Focus in Cross-National Research." *Journal of Advertising,* 1977, pp. 5–15.

Samli, A. Coskum. *Marketing and Distribution Systems in Eastern Europe.* New York: Praeger Publishers, 1978.

Shanflin, William L., and Ryans, John K., Jr. "Is the International Cash Cow Really a Prize Heifer?" *Business Horizons,* March/April 1981, pp. 10–16.

Vernon, Raymond. "Gone are the Cash Cows of Yesteryear." *Harvard Business Review,* November/December 1980, p. 150.

Weigand, Robert E. "Barter and Buy-Backs—Problems for the Marketing Channel." *Marketing in the 80's.* American Marketing Association, 1980, pp. 256–58.

White, Phillip D. "Attitudes of U.S. Purchasing Managers Toward Industrial Products Manufactured in Selected Western European Nations." *Journal of International Business Studies,* Spring/Summer 1979, p. 81.

Zeira, Yoram. "Ethnocentrism in Host-Country Organizations." *Business Horizons,* June 1979, pp. 66–75.

"Comparative Management." *The Columbia Journal of World Business,* Summer 1978, p. 2.

"Countertrade Gains Popularity as International Trade Tool." *Business America,* July 14, 1980, pp. 12–16.

Part 5

Baker, James C., and Ryans, John K., Jr. *Multinational Marketing: Dimensions in Strategy.* Columbus, Ohio: Grid, 1975.

Cao, N. D. "Non-tariff Barriers to U.S. Manufactured Exports." *Columbia Journal of World Business,* Summer 1980, pp. 93–101.

Davies, Gary. *International Logistics.* Bradford, West Yorkshire, England: MCB Publications, Ltd, 1981.

Du Jonchay, Ivan. *The Handbook of World Transport.* New York: Facts on File, Inc., 1980.

Dunn, Don T., Jr. "Agents and Distributors in the Middle East." *Business Horizons,* October 1979, pp. 69–78.

Farley, John U.; Hulbert, James M., and David Weinstein. "Price Setting and Volume Planning by Two European Industrial Companies: A Study and Comparison of Decision Processes." *Journal of Marketing,* Winter 1980, pp. 46–54.

Hollander, S. C. *Multinational Retailing.* East Lansing: Michigan State University Press, 1970.

Jones, H. Ralph. "Clearing the Way for Exporters." *Business Horizons,* October 1980, pp. 26–32.

Quirt, John. "Wickes Corporation's Retailing Triumph in Europe." *Fortune,* August 13, 1979, p. 178.

Shimaguchi, Mitsuaki, and Rosenberg, Larry J. "Demystifying Japanese Distribution." *Columbia Journal of World Business,* Spring 1979, p. 32.

Shimaguchi, Mitsuaki, and Lazer, William. "Japanese Distribution Channels: Invisible Barriers to Market Entry." *MSU Business Topics,* Winter 1979, pp. 49–62.

Shimaguchi, Mitsuaki. *Marketing Channels in Japan.* University of Michigan Research Press, 1977.

Thorelli, H. B., and Becker, Helmut, eds. *International Marketing Strategy.* New York: Pergamon Press, 1980.

Wentworth, Felix; Christopher, Martin; Wills, Gordon; and Bernard J. La Londe. *Managing International Distribution.* New York: American Management Association, 1979.

European Marketing Data & Statistics Euromonitor. London: Euromonitor Publications, Ltd., 1981.

Financing of Exports and Imports. New York: Morgan Guaranty Trust Co., May 1977.

International Marketing Data and Statistics. London: Euromonitor Publications, Ltd., 1981.

Retail Trade International Europe. London: Euromonitor Publications, Ltd., 1980.

"Structure and Prospects of the In-Bound Industry." *Review of the Economic Situation of Mexico.* Banco Nacional de Mexico, July 1979, p. 244.

Part 6

Brandt, William K., and Hulbert, James M. "Communications and Control in the Multinational Enterprise." *Multinational Product Management,* Proceedings of the American Management Association and the Management Science Institute Research Workshop, August 1976.

Davis, Stanely M. *Managing and Organizing Multinational Corporations.* New York: Pergamon Press.

Donaldson, J. A. "Managing Currency Exposures After the End of Exchange Controls." *The Banker,* August 1980, pp. 77–85.

Drake, Rodman L., and Caudill, Lee M. "Management of the Large Multinational: Trends and Future Challenges." *Business Horizons,* May/June 1981, pp. 3–7.

Drucker, Peter F. *Management.* New York: Harper & Row, 1974.

Eiteivan, David K., and Stonehill, Arthur I. *Multinational Business Finance.* Reading, Mass.: Addison-Wesley Publishing, 1982.

Jacque, Laurent L. "Management of Foreign Exchange Risk." *Journal of International Business Studies,* Spring/Summer 1981, pp. 81–101.

Kenyon, P. H. A. "Currency Exposure Management." *Long Range Planning,* June 1980, pp. 21–29.

Kettell, Brian. *The Finance of International Business.* Westport, Conn. Greenwood Press, 1981.

Picard, Jacques. "How European Companies Control Marketing Decisions Abroad." *Columbia Journal of World Business,* Summer 1977, pp. 113–21.

Srinivasulu, S. L. "Strategic Response to Foreign Exchange Risks." *Columbia Journal of World Business,* Spring 1981, pp. 13–21.

Venkatesh, Alladi, and Wilenion. "American and European Product Managers: A Comparison." *Columbia Journal of World Business,* Fall 1980, pp. 67–74.

Understanding Foreign Exchange. Chicago: International Monetary Market, 1977.

NAME INDEX

SUBJECT INDEX

*This book has been set CAP, in 10 and 9 point
Stymie Light, leaded 2 points. Part numbers and
titles and chapter numbers and titles are 18 point
Stymie Light. The size of the type page is 31
by 47½ picas.*